Anonymous

A practical grammar of the Sanskrit language:

Arranged with reference to the classical languages of Europe, for the use of English students

Anonymous

A practical grammar of the Sanskrit language:
Arranged with reference to the classical languages of Europe, for the use of English students

ISBN/EAN: 9783337809836

Printed in Europe, USA, Canada, Australia, Japan

Cover: Foto ©ninafisch / pixelio.de

More available books at **www.hansebooks.com**

A PRACTICAL GRAMMAR OF THE SANSKṚIT LANGUAGE,

ARRANGED WITH REFERENCE TO

THE CLASSICAL LANGUAGES OF EUROPE,

FOR THE USE OF

ENGLISH STUDENTS.

BY

MONIER WILLIAMS, M.A., D.C.L.,

Hon. Doctor in Law of the University of Calcutta;
Hon. Member of the Bombay Asiatic Society;
Member of the Royal Asiatic Society of Great Britain and Ireland, and of the Oriental Society of Germany;
Boden Professor of Sanskṛit in the University of Oxford.

FOURTH EDITION.

ENLARGED AND IMPROVED.

Oxford:

AT THE CLARENDON PRESS.

M.DCCC.LXXVII.

PREFACE

TO THE FOURTH EDITION.

NOW that this Grammar has reached a fourth edition it may, perhaps, without presumption, be allowed to rest on its own merits. I have, therefore, dispensed with much of the prefatory matter which introduced the previous editions.

Any one who compares the present Grammar with its predecessor will see at once the difference between the two, not indeed in its structure and arrangement, nor even in the numbering of the rules, but in the fuller and more complete explanation of points of detail.

It may be well, however, to draw attention to some of the most noteworthy alterations and improvements.

A table shewing the interchange of letters in the three sister languages, Sanskṛit, Greek, and Latin, has been given at pages 18–20.

The list of suffixes at pages 57–75 has been considerably enlarged, and arranged in alphabetical order under each declension.

The subject of declension has been elucidated by a clearer method of synopsis.

A more complete account of Sanskṛit accentuation has been given at the end of the volume.

The Reading Exercises have been slightly curtailed. The publication by the Delegates of the Clarendon Press of such a Class-book as the *Nala*, and quite recently of the *Śakuntalá*, sufficiently supplies what is likely to be needed for the prosecution of the study of Sanskṛit after the elements of Grammar have been acquired.

Four indices instead of two have been appended.

In order to bring the present edition into harmony with the Greek and Latin grammars now in use, some of the grammatical terms have been altered, e.g. *suffix* has been substituted for *affix*; *stem* for *base*; *special* and *general* tenses for *conjugational* and *non-conjugational* tenses respectively.

Some errors which, notwithstanding all my efforts, crept into the last edition have been corrected, and a few other improvements effected. But I dare not even now hope to have attained the standard of perfection. Sanskṛit is far too vast and intricate a subject to admit of such pretensions. I can, however, with truth affirm, that I have done what I could to bring the present work up to the level of the scholarship of the day; and my acknowledgments are due to Mr. E. L. Hogarth, M.A., of Brasenose College, for his aid in conducting the sheets through the Press.

In conclusion I may, perhaps, be permitted to express a hope that my second visit to India will add to my powers of improving any future edition that may be required, as it certainly will increase my ability to promote a more general knowledge of the Sanskṛit language and literature among my own fellow-countrymen, to whose rule a vast Eastern Empire has been committed, and who cannot hope, except through Sanskṛit, to gain a proper acquaintance with its spoken dialects, or to understand the mind, read the thoughts, and reach the very heart and soul of its vast populations.

M. W.

OXFORD, October 1876.

CONTENTS.

	PAGE
CHAP. I.—LETTERS	1
Pronunciation	9
Classification	14
Interchange of letters in Sanskṛit, Greek, and Latin	18
Method of writing	20
CHAP. II.—SANDHI OR EUPHONIC COMBINATION OF LETTERS	23
Sect. I. Changes of vowels	24
Sect. II. Changes of consonants	32
CHAP. III.—ROOTS, AND THE FORMATION OF NOMINAL STEMS	51
Formation of the stems of nouns by suffixes	57
CHAP. IV.—DECLENSION OF NOUNS. GENERAL OBSERVATIONS	76
Sect. I. Inflexion of nouns whose stems end in vowels	83
Sect. II. Inflexion of nouns whose stems end in consonants	95
Sect. III. Adjectives	113
Sect. IV. Numerals	118
CHAP. V.—PRONOUNS	123
CHAP. VI.—VERBS. GENERAL OBSERVATIONS	133
Terminations	136
Summary of the ten conjugational classes	144
The augment	146
Reduplication	147
Formation of the stem in the four Special tenses:	
Of group I. or verbs of the first, fourth, sixth, and tenth classes	150
Of groups II. and III.—Preliminary observations	155
The new rules of Sandhi required for group II.	157
Of group II. or verbs of the second, third, and seventh classes	160
Of group III. or verbs of the fifth, eighth, and ninth classes	166
Formation of the stem in the six General tenses:	
Perfect	168
First and Second Future	178
Rules for inserting or rejecting the vowel *i*	180
Aorist	186
Precative or Benedictive	193
Conditional	196
Infinitive	196
Passive verbs	197
Causal verbs	203
Desiderative verbs	209
Frequentative or Intensive verbs	213
Nominal verbs	217

PAGE

Participles 219
Participial nouns of agency 234
Examples of verbs inflected at full:
Table of verbs of the ten conjugational classes inflected at full 235
Table of passive verbs inflected at full 244
Auxiliary verbs conjugated 249
Group I. Verbs of the first class conjugated 250
Verbs of the fourth class conjugated 266
Verbs of the sixth class conjugated 271
Verbs of the tenth class conjugated 276
Group II. Verbs of the second class conjugated 279
Verbs of the third class conjugated 287
Verbs of the seventh class conjugated 291
Group III. Verbs of the fifth class conjugated 296
Verbs of the eighth class conjugated 301
Verbs of the ninth class conjugated 304
Passive verbs conjugated 309
Causal verbs conjugated 311
Desiderative verbs conjugated 312
Frequentative or Intensive verbs conjugated 314

CHAP. VII.—INDECLINABLE WORDS.
Adverbs 317
Conjunctions 321
Prepositions 322
Adverbs in government with nouns 323
Interjections 324

CHAP. VIII.—COMPOUND WORDS.
Sect. I. Compound nouns 325
Tat-purusha or dependent compounds 327
Dvandva or copulative (aggregative) compounds . . . 330
Karma-dháraya or descriptive (determinative) compounds . 333
Dvigu or numeral (collective) compounds 334
Avyayí-bháva or adverbial (indeclinable) compounds . . 335
Bahu-vríhi or relative compounds 336
Complex compounds 341
Changes of certain words in certain compounds . . . 344
Sect. II. Compound verbs 347
Sect. III. Compound adverbs 353

CHAP. IX.—SYNTAX 354
CHAP. X.—EXERCISES IN TRANSLATION AND PARSING . . . 387
SCHEME OF THE MORE COMMON SANSKṚIT METRES 392
ACCENTUATION 397
INDICES 401
LIST OF COMPOUND OR CONJUNCT CONSONANTS 415

CHAPTER I.

LETTERS.

1. The Deva-nágarí or Nágarí character (or its modifications *), in which the Sanskṛit language is usually written, is adapted to the expression of nearly every gradation of sound; and almost every letter has a fixed and invariable pronunciation (see, however, 16).

There are fourteen vowels (or without *lṛí* thirteen, see 3. *d*) and thirty-three simple consonants. To these may be added a nasal sign, standing for either true or substitute *Anusvára* (see 6), and a sign for a hard breathing, called *Visarga* (see 8). They are here first exhibited *in the order followed in dictionaries.* All the vowels, excepting *a*, have two forms; the first is the initial, the second the medial or non-initial.

VOWELS.

अ *a*, आ ा *á*, इ ि *i*, ई ी *í*, उ ु *u*, ऊ ू *ú*, ऋ ृ *ṛi*, ॠ ॄ *ṛí*, ऌ ॢ *lṛi*, ॡ ॣ *lṛí*, ए े *e*, ऐ ै *ai*, ओ ो *o*, औ ौ *au*.

Nasal sign called true or proper *Anusvára*, ं *ṉ*. Substitute *Anusvára*, ं *ṃ*.

Sign for a hard breathing, called *Visarga*, ः *ḥ*.

CONSONANTS.

Gutturals,	क *k*	ख *kh*	ग *g*	घ *gh*	ङ *ṅ*
Palatals,	च *ć*	छ *ćh*	ज *j*	झ *jh*	ञ *ñ*
Cerebrals,	ट *ṭ*	ठ *ṭh*	ड *ḍ*	ढ *ḍh*	ण *ṇ*
Dentals,	त *t*	थ *th*	द *d*	ध *dh*	न *n*
Labials,	प *p*	फ *ph*	ब *b*	भ *bh*	म *m*
Semivowels,	य *y*	र *r*	ल *l*	व *v*	
Sibilants,	श *ś*	ष *sh*	स *s*		
Aspirate,	ह *h*				

Two characters, ळ *ḷ*, ळ्ह *ḷh* (often = ड *ḍ*, ढ *ḍh*), are used in the Veda.

---

* Such as the Bengálí, Gujarátí, &c. In the South of India Sanskṛit is generally written, not in the Deva-nágarí, but in the Telugu, Kanarese, and Malayálam

B

The characters are written from left to right, like the Roman.

The compound or conjunct consonants (see 5) may be multiplied to the extent of four or five hundred. The most common are given here. A more complete list will be found at the end of the volume.

THE MORE COMMON CONJUNCT CONSONANTS.

क्क *kk*, क्त *kt*, क्र or क्र *kr*, क्ल *kl*, क्व *kv*, क्ष *ksh*, ख्य *khy*, ग्न *gn*, ग्र *gr*, ग्ल *gl*, घ्र *ghr*, ङ्क *ṅk*, ङ्ग *ṅg*, च्च *ćć*, च्छ *ććh*, च्य *ćy*, ज्ज *jj*, ज्ञ *jñ*, ज्व *jv*, ञ्च *ñć*, ञ्छ *ñćh*, ञ्ज *ñj*, ट्ट *ṭṭ*, ट्य *ṭy*, ड्ग *ḍg*, ड्य *ḍy*, ण्ट *ṇṭ*, ण्ठ *ṇṭh*, ण्ड *ṇḍ*, ण्ण *ṇṇ*, ण्य *ṇy*, त्त *tt*, त्थ *tth*, त्न *tn*, त्म *tm*, त्य *ty*, त्र or त्र *tr*, त्व *tv*, त्स *ts*, थ्य *thy*, द्ग *dg*, द्ध *ddh*, द्भ *dbh*, द्म *dm*, द्य *dy*, द्र *dr*, द्व *dv*, ध्य *dhy*, ध्व *dhv*, न्त *nt*, न्द *nd*, न्न *nn*, न्य *ny*, प्त *pt*, प्य *py*, प्र *pr*, प्ल *pl*, ब्ज *bj*, ब्द *bd*, ब्य *by*, ब्र *br*, भ्य *bhy*, भ्र *bhr*, म्भ *mbh*, म्म *mm*, म्य *my*, म्ल *ml*, य्य *yy*, र्क *rk*, र्म *rm*, ल्प *lp*, ल्ल *ll*, व्य *vy*, व्र *vr*, श्च *ść*, श्य *śy*, श्र *śr*, श्ल *śl*, श्व *śv*, ष्ट *shṭ*, ष्ठ *shṭh*, ष्ण *shṇ*, ष्य *shy*, स्क *sk*, स्ख *skh*, स्त *st*, स्थ *sth*, स्न *sn*, स्म *sm*, स्य *sy*, स्र *sr*, स्व *sv*, स्स *ss*, ह्म *hm*, ह्य *hy*, ह्ल *hl*, क्त्य *kty*, क्त्र *ktr*, क्त्व *ktv*, क्ष्ण *kshṇ*, क्ष्म *kshm*, क्ष्य *kshy*, ग्न्य *gny*, ग्भ्य *gbhy*, ग्र्य *gry*, ङ्क्त *ṅkt*, ङ्क्य *ṅky*, च्छ्य *ććhy*, च्छ्र *ććhr*, ण्ड्य *ṇḍy*, त्स्न *tsn*, त्म्य *tmy*, त्र्य *try*, त्स्य *tsy*, त्त्र *ttr*, त्त्व *ttv*, द्द्य *ddy*, द्ध्य *ddhy*, द्भ्य *dbhy*, द्र्य *dry*, न्त्य *nty*, म्ब्य *mby*, र्द्र *rdr*, र्य्य *ryy*, र्व्व *rvv*, ष्ट्र *shṭr*, स्थ्न *sthn*, स्त्य *sty*, स्त्र *str*, त्स्न्य *tsny*, न्त्र्य *ntry*, र्त्स्य *rtsy*, र्त्स्न्य *rtsny*.

---

characters, as well as in the Grantha (or Grantham), which is a name for the character used for Sanskṛit in the Tamil country, the Tamil alphabet being too defective to represent all the necessary sounds. In the second edition of this Grammar I gave a comparative table of old Inscription characters from Mr. Edward Thomas' edition of *Prinsep's Indian Antiquities*, which shows that the present form of Deva-nágarí character is traceable to the inscriptions of Aśoka, who is called Piyadasi for Priyadarśin—a well-known Buddhist king, grandson of Ćandra-gupta =Sandrakottos—and who must have reigned over nearly the whole of India, his capital being Páṭali-putra (=Páli-bothra, the modern Patna). These inscriptions are found on rocks at Giri-nagara (Girnár) in Gujarát on the Western coast, and at Dhaulí in Kuttack on the Eastern coast (in the province of Orissa); and again at a place called Kapurdigiri, quite N. of the Pañjáb, a little to the E. of Purusha-pura (Peshávar). It is from the Girnár rock-inscriptions that the present Deva-nágarí is most evidently derived, and these are not yet clearly traceable to a Phenician origin, those of Kapurdigiri being more so.

Observe—In reading the following pages for the first time, the attention should be confined to the large type.

Observe also—When reference is made to other parts of the Grammar, the numbers will denote the paragraphs, not the pages.

The letters (except *r*, called *Repha*, and except the nasal sign called *Anusvára* and the sign for the hard breathing called *Visarga*) have no names (like the names in the Greek alphabet), but the consonants are enunciated with the vowel *a*. Native grammarians, in designating any letter, add the word कार *kára;* thus, अकार *a-kára*, 'the letter *a;*' ककार *ka-kára*, 'the letter *ka*.'

NUMERICAL FIGURES.

१	२	३	४	५	६	७	८	९	१०	११	१२	३४५
1	2	3	4	5	6	7	8	9	10	11	12	345

THE VOWELS AND THE METHOD OF WRITING THEM.

2. The short vowel अ *a* is never written unless it begin a word, because it is supposed to be inherent in every consonant. Thus, *ak* is written अक्, but *ka* is written क; so that in such words as कनक *kanaka*, नगर *nagara*, &c., no vowel has to be written. The mark ् under the *k* of अक्, called *Viráma* (see 9), indicates a consonantal stop, that is, the absence of any vowel, inherent or otherwise, after a final consonant. It is omitted in the first tables that the letters may be kept unencumbered by additional marks.

a. The other vowels, if written after a consonant, take the place of the inherent *a*. They assume two forms, according as they are initial or not initial. Thus, आक् *ák*, का *ká;* इक् *ik*, कि *ki*.

b. Observe here, that the *short* vowel ि *i*, when *initial*, is written in its right place, but when *not initial*, is always written *before* the letter *after* which it is pronounced. Hence, in order to write such a word as *iti*, the letters would have to be arranged thus, *iit* इति.

c. Perhaps the true explanation of this peculiarity is that in the earliest alphabets the two *i*'s were written over the consonant to which they belonged, short *i* inclining to the left, and long *í* to the right, a perpendicular stroke having been afterwards added.

3. The long vowels ा *á* and ी *í*, not initial, take their proper place after a consonant. Also the non-initial *o* and *au* (which are formed by placing े and ै over ा *á*), like ा *á*, take their proper place after

their consonants; thus, को *ko*, कौ *kau*. The vowels *u*, *ú*, *ṛi*, *ṛí*, *lṛi*, not initial, are written *under* the consonants after which they are pronounced; as, कु *ku*, कू *kú*, कृ *kṛi*, कॄ *kṛí*, कॢ *klṛi*.

a. Except when *u* or *ú* follows र् *r*, in which case the method of writing is peculiar; thus, रु *ru*, रू *rú*.

b. When, however, the vowel ऋ *ṛi* follows र् *r* the vowel is written in its initial form and *r* in the crescent shape placed over it (see 5. *a*); thus, निर्ऋति *nirṛiti*, 'the goddess of destruction.'

c. The vowels *ṛi*, *ṛí*, *lṛi* and *lṛí* are peculiar to Sanskrit (see 11. *c*). ऌ *lṛi* only occurs in the root क्लृप् *klṛip*, 'to make,' and its derivatives.

d. The long ॡ *lṛí* is only used in technical grammatical explanations; strictly it has no existence, and is useless except as contributing to the completeness of the alphabetical system.

e. The vowels *e* and *ai*, not initial, are written *above* the consonants after which they are pronounced; thus, के *ke*, कै *kai*.

f. In a few words initial vowels follow other vowels; e.g. अऋणिन् *a-ṛiṇin*, 'without debt;' गोअग्र *go-agra*, 'a number of cows;' प्रउग *pra-üga*, 'the pole of a chariot;' तितउ *titaü*, 'a sieve.'

METHOD OF WRITING THE SIMPLE CONSONANTS.

4. The consonants have only one form, whether initial or not initial. And here note that in every consonant, and in the initial vowels, there is a perpendicular stroke or the commencement of one, and that all have a horizontal line at the top; but in two of the letters, ध् *dh* and भ् *bh*, this horizontal line is broken. In writing rapidly, the student will do well to form the perpendicular stroke first, then the distinctive parts of the letter, and lastly the horizontal line. The natives, however, sometimes form the horizontal line first.

METHOD OF WRITING THE CONJUNCT CONSONANTS.

5. The necessity for conjunct consonants is caused by the fact that every consonant is supposed to have the vowel अ *a* inherent in it, so that it is never necessary to write this vowel, excepting at the beginning of a word or, in a few cases, of a syllable (see 3. *f*). Hence when any simple consonants stand alone in any word, the short vowel अ *a* must always be pronounced after them; but when they appear in conjunction with any other vowel, this other vowel of course takes the place of short अ *a*. Thus such a word as

कलानतया would be pronounced *kalánatayá*, where long आ *á* being written after *l* and *y* takes the place of the inherent vowel. But supposing that, instead of *kalánatayá*, the word had to be pronounced *klántyá*, how are we to know that *kl* and *nty* have to be uttered without the intervention of any vowel? This occasions the necessity for conjunct or compound consonants. *Kl* and *nty* must then be combined together thus, क्ल्, न्त्य्, and the word is written क्लान्त्या. And here we have illustrated the two methods of compounding consonants; viz. 1st, by writing them one above the other; 2ndly, by placing them side by side, omitting in all, except the last, the perpendicular line which lies to the right.

a. Some letters, however, change their form entirely when combined with other consonants. Thus र् *r*, when it is the *first* letter of a conjunct consonant, is written above in the form of a crescent, as in कूर्म *kúrma*, कार्त्स्न्य *kártsnya*; and when the *last*, is written below in the form of a small stroke, as in the word क्रमेण *kramena*.

b. So again in क्ष * *ksha* and ज्ञ † *jña* the simple elements क् ष् and ज् ञ् are scarcely traceable.

c. In some conjunct consonants the simple letters slightly change their form; as, श *śa* becomes श्‍ in श्च *śća*; द् *d* with य *ya* becomes द्य *dya*; द् *d* with ध *dha* becomes द्ध *ddha*; द् *d* with भ *bha* becomes द्भ *dbha*; त् *t* with र *ra* becomes त्र *tra* or त्र *tra*; क् *k* with त *ta* becomes क्त *kta*.

d. Observe, that when *r* comes in the middle of a conjunct consonant, it takes the same form as at the end; thus, ग्र्य *grya*, ग्र *gra*. When conjunct consonants commencing with ॅ are followed by the vowels *i*, *í*, *e*, *ai*, *o*, *au*, or by a nasal symbol (see 6), then ॅ is for the convenience of typography written on the right of all; thus, र्णि *rṇi*, र्णी *rṇí*, र्के *rke*, र्कौ *rkau*, र्कं *rkaṃ*.

ANUSVÁRA AND ANUNÁSIKA.

6. *Anusvára* (ं *ṃ*), i. e. 'after-sound,' is a nasal sound which always belongs to a preceding vowel, and can never be used like a nasal consonant to begin a syllable (though like a consonant it imparts, in conjunction with a following consonant, prosodial length to the preceding short vowel). It is denoted by a simple dot,

---

* Sometimes formed thus क्ष, and pronounced *kya* in Bengálí.

† This compound is sometimes pronounced *gya* or *nya*, though it will be more convenient to represent it by its proper equivalent *jña*.

which ought to come either immediately over the vowel after which the nasalization is sounded, or on the right of the vowel-mark; thus, कं *kaṃ*, कुं *kuṃ*, किं *kiṃ*, कीं *kíṃ*.

This dot serves two purposes. It marks, 1. the Anusvára proper or *True Anusvára*; 2. a short substitute for the five nasal consonants; in which latter case it may be called *Substitute Anusvára*.

a. True Anusvára denotes the nasalization of the vowel which precedes it before श् *ś*, ष् *sh*, स् *s*, and ह् *h*, in the body of words. It is then pronounced with the nose only (like *n* in the French *mon*, &c.), and will in this Grammar be represented in the Indo-Romanic type by *ṇ̱*, as in अंश *aṇ̱śa*, अंहति *aṇ̱hati*.

But since the true Anusvára must take the place of a final म् *m* when the three sibilants श् *ś*, ष् *sh*, स् *s*, and the aspirate ह् *h* (but see 7. *c*) follow; and also generally when र् *r* follows at the beginning of a word (see *e*. next page); it is then in this Grammar expressed by *ṃ*; thus, तम् शत्रुम् is written तं शत्रुम् *taṃ śatrum*; तम् राजानम् becomes तं राजानम् *taṃ rájánam*; and सम् with root हृ is written संहृ *saṃhṛi*.

b. Substitute Anusvára is sometimes used, for shortness, as a *substitute* for any of the five nasal consonants ङ् *ṅ*, ञ् *ñ*, ण् *ṇ*, न् *n*, म् *m*, which belong to the five classes of letters (see 15), when no vowel intervenes between these and a following consonant *in the middle of the same word* (thus the syllables इङ्क् *iṅk*, इञ्च् *iñć*, अण्ड् *aṇḍ*, इन्त् *int*, इम्प् *imp* may for shortness be written इंक्, इंच्, अंड्, इंत्, इंप्). In these cases Anusvára must be pronounced like the nasal consonant for which it has been substituted, and in this Grammar it will always be represented in Indo-Romanic type by these nasal consonants.

But Anusvára is more usually substituted for these nasals *when final* and resulting from the euphonic adaptation of the final *m* of accus. cases sing., nom. cases neut., some adverbs and persons of the verb to a following word (see 60). It will then in this Grammar be represented in the Indo-Romanic type by *ṃ*, as in the cases mentioned in 6. *a*.

c. Anusvára is even used in some printed books, though less correctly, for the final म् *m* of the words specified in the last paragraph when they stand in a pause (i. e. at the end of a sentence or clause, or when not followed by another word). In such cases, too, it should be represented by *ṃ*.

d. But Anusvára is never admitted as a substitute for the original final न् *n* of a *pada* or inflected word (as in accus. cases plur., loc. cases of pronominals, the 3rd pers. plur. and pres. part. of verbs, &c., see 54), unless the next word begin with *ć*, *ṭ*, *t*, or their aspirates, when, by 53, a sibilant is interposed before the initial letter.

e. And in the case of *roots* ending in न् *n* or म् *m*, these final nasals, if not dropped, pass into Anusvára before terminations or suffixes beginning with a sibilant or *h*, but are *not changed* before semivowels; thus मन् + स्यते = मंस्यते *maṇsyate*, 'he will think;' मन् + ये = मन्ये *manye*, 'I think' (617); यम् + स्यति = यंस्यति *yaṇsyati*, 'he will restrain;' गम् + य = गम्य *gamya*, 'accessible' (602); नम् + र = नम्र *namra*, 'bent.' सम् followed by राज् is सम्राज् *samráj*, 'a sovereign.'

f. Hence it appears that the nasal sign Anusvára is peculiarly the nasal of the three sibilants श् *ś*, ष् *sh*, स् *s*, and the aspirate ह् *h;* and that the true Anusvára always occurs before these letters. It is also to a certain degree the nasal of the semivowel र् *r;* so that these five consonants having a nasal sign of their own have no relationship to the corresponding nasal consonant of their respective classes.

7. That Anusvára is less peculiarly the nasal of the semivowels is evident from *e.* above. Hence म् *m* final in a word (not a root) may, before य् *y*, ल् *l*, व् *v*, either pass into Anusvára or be represented by यँ, लँ, वँ, or assimilate itself to these letters; thus सम् + यम = संयम or सय्ँयम, यम् + लोकम् = यं लोकम् or यल्ँलोकम्.

In the latter case the nasal character of य् *y* and ल् *l* is denoted by a nasal symbol called *Anunásika* (i. e. 'through the nose,' sometimes called *Ćandra-vindu*, 'the dot in the crescent'), which is also applied to mark the nasality of a final ल् *l* deduced from a final न् *n* when followed by initial ल *l*, see 56. Of course the word सम्यञ्च् *samyańć*, 'going conformably' (formed from समि + अञ्च्), retains the *m*.

a. And this *Anunásika* ँ is not only the sign of the nasality of य् *y*, ल् *l*, and व् *v*, in the preceding cases, but also marks the nasality of vowels, though in a less degree than Anusvára, see 11. *f.*

b. In the Veda Anunásika is written for a final न् *n* after a long vowel before another vowel; as, यस्याँ इन्द्रासि for यस्मान् इन्द्रासि Ṛig-veda VIII. 1, 6.

c. Observe—A final म् *m* before ह्म *hm*, ह्न *hn*, ह्य *hy*, ह्ल *hl*, ह्व *hv*, may either be changed to Anusvára or undergo assimilation with the second letter; thus किं ह्मलयति or किम् ह्मलयति, किं ह्नुते or किन् ह्नुते, किं ह्यः or कियँ ह्यः, &c. (see 7).

VISARGA, JIHVÁMÚLÍYA, AND UPADHMÁNÍYA.

8. The sign *Visarga*, 'emission of breath,' (sometimes said to derive its name from symbolizing the rejection of a letter in pronunciation,) usually written thus :, but more properly in the form of two small circles ⸰, is used to represent a distinctly audible and harder aspiration than the letter ह् *h*. It is reckoned under the *váhya-prayatna*, and is said, like the hard consonants, to be *a-ghosha*, without the soft articulation. This sign is never the representative of ह् *h*. Although conveniently represented by *ḥ*, it should be borne in mind that Visarga (*ḥ*) is a harder aspirate than ह् *h*, and is in fact a kind of sibilant, being often a substitute for *s* and *r* preceded by vowels whenever the usual consonantal sound of these letters passes into an aspiration at the end of a sentence or through the influence of a *k*, *kh*, *p*, *ph*, or a sibilant commencing the next word.

And since, according to native grammarians, स् *s* ought not to be allowed at the end of a complete word, all those inflections of nouns and verbs which end in *s* and stand separate from other words are, in native Grammars, made to end in Visarga.

But in this Grammar such inflections are allowed to retain their final स् *s*. We have only to bear in mind that this *s* is liable at the end of a sentence, or when followed by certain consonants, to pass into an audible breathing more distinct than *s* in the French *les* or the English *isle*, *viscount*, when it is represented by *ḥ* (:).

In some parts of India Visarga has a slightly reverberating sound very difficult of imitation; thus रामः *rámaḥ* is almost like रामह *rámaha*, अग्निः *agniḥ* like अग्निहि *agnihi*, शिवैः *śivaiḥ* like शिवैहि *śivaihi*.

a. An *Ardha-visarga*, 'half-visarga,' or modification of the symbol Visarga, in the form of two semicircles ᳲ, is sometimes employed before *k*, *kh*, and *p*, *ph*. Before the two former letters this symbol is properly called *Jihvámúlíya*, and the organ of its enunciation said to be the root of the tongue (*jihvá-múla*). Before *p* and *ph* its proper name is *Upadhmáníya*, 'to be breathed upon,' and its organ of utterance is then the lips (*oshṭha*).

The Jihvámúlíya and Upadhmáníya are therefore to be regarded as the sibilants of the guttural and labial classes respectively. (See Páṇ. I. I, 9.)

b. The sign Ardha-visarga is now rarely seen in printed Sanskṛit texts. In the

Vedas the Upadhmáníya occurs, but only after an Anusvára or Anunásika; thus, नॄं ᳶ पाहि or नॄँ ᳶ पाहि, and in this case also the symbol Visarga may be used for it.

VIRÁMA, AVAGRAHA, &C.

9. The *Viráma*, 'pause' or 'stop,' placed under a consonant (thus क् *k*), indicates the absence of the inherent अ *a*, by help of which the consonant is pronounced.

Observe—Viráma properly means the *pause of the voice at the end of a sentence.* In some MSS. it is employed like a mark of punctuation at the close of a sentence ending with a consonant, while the mark । is the proper means of denoting the close of a sentence ending in a vowel, all the preceding words being written without separation, because supposed to be pronounced without pause.

10. The mark ऽ (*Avagraha*, sometimes called *Ardhákára*, half the letter *a*), placed between two words, denotes the elision (*lopa*) or suppression (*abhinidhána*) of an initial अ *a* after ए *e* or ओ *o* final preceding. It corresponds to our apostrophe in some analogous cases. Thus, तेऽपि *te'pi* for ते अपि *te api.*

a. In books printed in Calcutta the mark ऽ is sometimes used to resolve a long *á* resulting from the blending of a final *á* with an initial *a* or *á;* thus तथाऽपश्यं for तथा अपश्यं, usually written तथापश्यं. Sometimes a double mark ऽऽ denotes an initial long आ. The mark ऽ is also used in the Veda as the sign of a hiatus between vowels, and in the *pada* text to separate the component parts of a compound or of other grammatical forms.

b. The half pause । is a stop or mark of punctuation, usually placed at the end of the first line of a couplet or stanza.

c. The whole pause ॥ is placed at the end of a couplet, or is used like a full stop.

d. The mark of repetition ° indicates that a word or sentence has to be repeated. It is also used to abbreviate a word, just as in English we use a full point; thus प° stands for पर्व, as *chap.* for *chapter;* so °भ for शुभ.

PRONUNCIATION OF SANSKṚIT VOWELS.

11. The vowels in Sanskṛit are pronounced for the most part as in Italian or French, though occasional words in English may exemplify their sound; but every vowel is supposed to be *alpa-práṇa,* 'pronounced with a slight breathing' (see 14. *a*).

a. Since अ *a* is inherent in every consonant, the student should be careful to acquire the correct pronunciation of this letter. There are many words in English which afford examples of its sound, such as *vocal, cedar, zebra, organ*. But in English the vowel *u* in such words as *fun, bun, sun*, more frequently represents this obscure sound of *a;* and even the other vowels may occasionally be pronounced with this sound, as in *her, sir, son*.

b. The long vowel आ *á* is pronounced as *a* in the English *father, far, cart;* इ *i* as the *i* in *pin, lily;* ई *í* as the *i* in *marine, police;* उ *u* as the *u* in *push;* ऊ *ú* as the *u* in *rude*.

c. The vowel ऋ *ṛi*, peculiar to Sanskṛit, is pronounced as the *ri* in *merrily*, where the *i* of *ri* is less perceptible than in the syllable *ri*, composed of the consonant *r* and the vowel *i**. ॠ *ṛí* is pronounced nearly as the *ri* in *chagrin*, being hardly distinguishable from the syllable री; but in the case of the vowels *ṛi* and *ṛí* there is a mere vibration of the tongue in the direction of the upper gums, whereas in pronouncing the consonant *r*, the tongue should actually touch them (see 19, 20): ए *e* as the *e* in *prey, there;* ओ *o* as in *so;* ऐ *ai* as *ai* in *aisle;* औ *au* as *au* in the German *Haus* or as *ou* in the English *house* †. ऌ *lṛi* and ॡ *lṛí* differ little in sound from the letter ल् *l* with the vowels *ṛi* and *ṛí* annexed.

d. Hence it appears that every simple vowel in Sanskṛit has a short and a long form, and that each vowel has one invariable sound; so that the beginner can never, as in other languages, be in doubt as to pronunciation or prosody.

e. Note, however, that Sanskṛit possesses no short *ĕ* and *ŏ* in opposition to the long diphthongal sounds of *e* and *o*.

f. Although for all practical purposes it is sufficient to regard vowels as either short or long, it should be borne in mind that native grammarians give eighteen different modifications of each of the vowels *a, i, u, ṛi*, and twelve of *lṛi*, which are thus explained:—Each of the first four vowels is supposed to have three prosodial lengths or measures (*mátrá*), viz. a short (*hrasva*), a long (*dírgha*), and a prolated

* That there is not, practically, much difference between the pronunciation of the vowel *ṛi* and the syllable रि *ri* may be gathered from the fact that some words beginning with ऋ are also found written with रि, and *vice versa;* thus, रिष्टि and ऋष्टि, रिपि and ऋपि, रिश्य and ऋश्य. Still the distinction between the definition of a vowel and consonant at 19 and 20 should be borne in mind. There is no doubt that in English the sound of *ri* in the words *merrily* and *rich* is different, and that the former approaches nearer to the sound of a vowel.

† Colloquially in India *ai* is often pronounced rather like *e* and *au* like *o*.

(*pluta*); the long being equal to two, and the prolated to three short vowels. Each of these three modifications may be uttered with a high tone, or a low tone, or a tone between high and low; or in other words, may have the acute, or the grave, or the circumflex accent. This gives nine modifications to *a, i, u, ṛi;* and each of these again may be regarded either as nasal or non-nasal, according as it is pronounced with the nose and mouth, or with the mouth alone. Hence result eighteen varieties of every vowel, excepting *ḷṛi, e, ai, o, au,* which have only twelve, because the first does not possess the long and the last four have not the short prosodial time. A prolated vowel is marked with three lines underneath or with ३ on one side, thus आ (with ≡ underneath) or आ३ (see Páṇ. 1. 2, 27).

PRONUNCIATION OF SANSKṚIT CONSONANTS.

12. क् *k*, ज् *j*, प् *p*, ब् *b* are pronounced as in English.

a. ग् *g* has always the sound of *g* in *gun, give,* never of *g* in *gin.*

b. च् *ć* is pronounced like *ch* in *church,* or as *c* in Italian. Observe that च् *ć* is a simple consonantal sound, although represented in English words by *ch.* It is a modification or softening of *k,* just as *j* is of *g,* the organ of utterance being in the palate, a little in advance of the throat. Hence, in Sanskṛit and its cognate languages, the palatals *ć* and *j* are often exchanged with the gutturals *k* and *g.* See 25.

c. त् *t*, द् *d* are more dental than in English, *t* being something like *t* in *stick,* and *d* like *th* in th*is;* thus *veda* ought to be pronounced rather like *vetha.* But in real fact we have no sound exactly equivalent to the Indian dentals *t* and *d.* The sound of *th* in th*in,* th*is,* is really dental, but, so to speak, *over-dentalized,* the tongue being forced *through* the teeth instead of *against* them. Few Englishmen acquire the correct pronunciation of the Indian dentals. They are said to be best pronounced by resting the end of the tongue against the inside of the front teeth and then suddenly removing it.

13. ट् *ṭ*, ड् *ḍ*. The sound of these cerebral letters is in practice hardly to be distinguished from the sound of our English *t* and *d.* Properly, however, the Sanskṛit cerebrals should be uttered with a duller and deeper intonation, produced by keeping the tongue as far back in the head (*cerebrum*) as possible, and slightly turning it upwards. A Hindú, however, would always write any English word or name containing *t* and *d* with the cerebral letters. Thus such words as *trip, drip, London* would be written ट्रिप्, ड्रिप्, लण्डन्.

In Bengal the cerebral ड् *ḍ* and ढ् *ḍh* have nearly the sound of a dull *r;* so that *viḍála,* 'a cat,' is pronounced like *virála.*

In some words both ट् *ṭ* and ड् *ḍ* seem interchangeable with र् *r* and ल् *l;* so that खोट् *khoṭ,* 'to be lame,' may be also written खोड्, खोर्, खोल्. In Prákṛit cerebral letters often stand for the Sanskṛit dentals. Cerebrals rarely begin words in Sanskṛit.

14. ख् *kh,* घ् *gh,* छ् *ćh,* झ् *jh,* ठ् *ṭh,* ढ् *ḍh,* थ् *th,* ध् *dh,* फ् *ph,* भ् *bh.* These are merely aspirated forms of simple consonants. They are not double or compound letters; *h* is only added to denote a distinct aspiration. Thus ख् is pronounced like *kh* in *ink*h*orn,* not like the Greek χ; थ् as *th* in *an*th*ill,* not as in th*ink;* फ् as *ph* in *u*ph*ill,* not as in ph*ysic,* but colloquially *ph* is often pronounced like *f* (as *phala* is pronounced *fala*); भ् *bh* as in *cab*h*orse.* Care must be taken not to interpolate a vowel before the aspirate. Indeed it is most important to acquire the habit of pronouncing the aspirated consonants distinctly. *Dá* and *dhá, pṛishṭa* and *pṛishṭha, stamba* and *stambha, kara* and *khara* have very different meanings, and are pronounced very differently. Few Englishmen pay sufficient attention to this, although the correct sound is easily attainable. The simple rule is to breathe hard while uttering the aspirated consonant, and then an aspirated sound will come out with the consonant before the succeeding vowel.

a. With regard to aspiration we may note that according to Páṇ. I. 1, 9, the letters are all either slightly aspirated (*alpa-práṇa*) or more strongly aspirated (*mahá-práṇa*). To the former belong vowels, semivowels, nasals, and *k, g, ć, j, ṭ, ḍ, t, d, p, b,* which are supposed to require a slight breathing in uttering them when they are initial. The *mahá-práṇa* letters are *kh, gh, ćh, jh, ṭh, ḍh, th, dh, ph, bh, ś, sh, s, h,* Anusvára, Visarga, Jihvámúlíya, and Upadhmáníya.

15. ङ् *ñ,* ञ् *ṅ,* ण् *ṇ,* न् *n,* म् *m.* Each of the five classes of consonants in Sanskṛit has its own nasal sound, represented by a separate nasal letter. In English and most other languages the same fivefold division of nasal sounds might be made, though we have only one nasal letter to express the guttural, palatal, cerebral, and dental nasal sounds. The truth is, that in all languages the nasal letters take their sound from the organ employed in uttering the consonant that follows them. Thus in English it will be found that guttural, palatal, cerebral, dental, and labial nasals are followed by consonants of the same classes, as in *ink, sing, inch, under, plinth,*

imp. If such words existed in Sanskṛit, the distinction of nasal sounds would be represented by distinct letters; thus, इङ्क्, सिङ्ग्, इञ्च्, अण्डर्, प्रिन्ट्, इम्प्. Compare 6.

a. It should be observed, however, that the guttural nasal ङ *ṅ*, which is rarely found by itself at the end of a word in Sanskṛit, never at the beginning, probably has, when standing alone, the sound of *ng* in *sing*, where the sound of *g* is almost imperceptible. So that the English *sing* might be written सिङ्. The palatal ञ् *ñ* is only found in conjunction with palatal consonants, as in ञ्च *ñć*, ञ्ज *ñj*, च्ञ *ćñ*, and ज्ञ् *jñ*. This last may be pronounced like *ny*, or like *gn* in the French *campagne*. In Bengal, however, it always has the sound of *gy*: thus राज्ञा is pronounced *rágyá*. The cerebral nasal ण् *ṇ* is generally the result of a preceding cerebral letter, as explained at 58. It is found in conjunction with cerebral consonants, but is not found at the beginning of pure Sanskṛit words (except when used artificially as a substitute for roots beginning with न् *n*). It is pronounced, as the other cerebrals, by turning the tip of the tongue rather upwards. The dental and labial nasals न् *n* and म् *m* are pronounced with the same organs as the class of letters to which they belong. See 21.

16. य् *y*, र् *r*, ल् *l*, व् *v* are pronounced as in English. Their relationship to and interchangeableness with (*samprasáraṇa*) the vowels *i*, *ṛi*, *lṛi*, *u*, respectively, should never be forgotten. See 22. *a*.

When व् *v* is the last member of a conjunct consonant it is pronounced like *w*, as द्वार is pronounced *dwára;* but not after *r*, as सर्व *sarva*. To prevent confusion, however, व् will *in all cases* be represented by *v*, thus द्वार *dvára*. See Preface to Sanskṛit-English Dictionary, p. xix.

a. The character ळ् *ḷ* is peculiar to the Veda. It appears to be a mixture of ल् *l* and र् *r*, representing a liquid sound formed like the cerebrals by turning the tip of the tongue upwards; and it is often in the Veda a substitute for the cerebral ड् *ḍ* when between two vowels, as ळ्ह् *ḷh* is for ढ् *ḍh*.

b. The semivowels *r* and *l* are frequently interchanged, *r* being an old form of *l*. Cf. roots *rabh*, *rip*, with the later forms *labh*, *lip*. (See examples at 25.)

17. श् *ś*, ष् *sh*, स् *s*, ह् *h*. Of these, श् *ś* is a palatal sibilant, and is pronounced like *sh* or like *s* in *sure;* (compounded with *r* it is sounded more like *s* in *sun*, but the pronunciation of *ś* varies in different provinces and different words.) ष् *sh* is a cerebral, rather softer than our *sh*. That its pronunciation is hardly to be distinguished from that of the palatal is proved by the number of words written indiscriminately with श or ष; as, कोश or कोष. This ष्

is often corrupted into ख् in conversation, and क्ष् *ksh* is often pronounced like छ् *ćh*. The dental स् *s* is pronounced as the common English *s*. Different sibilants, of course, exist in English, though represented by one character, as in the words *sure*, *session*, *pressure*, *stick*, *sun*.

ह *h* is pronounced as in English, and is gùttural.

CLASSIFICATION OF LETTERS.

18. In the arrangement of the alphabet at page 1, all the consonants, excepting the semivowels, sibilants, and *h*, were distributed under the five heads of gutturals (*kaṇṭhya*), palatals (*tálavya*), cerebrals (*múrdhanya*), dentals (*dantya*), and labials (*oshṭhya*). We are now to show that *all the forty-seven* letters, vowels, semivowels, and consonants, may be referred to one or other of these five grand classes, according to the organ principally concerned in their pronunciation, whether the throat, the palate, the upper part of the palate, the teeth, or the lips *.

a. We have also to show that all the letters may be regarded according to another principle of division, and may be all arranged under the head of either HARD or SOFT, according as the effort of utterance is attended with expansion (*vivára*), or contraction (*saṃvára*), of the throat.

---

* *a.* According to some native grammars the classes (*varga*) of consonants are distinguished thus: *ka-varga* the class of guttural letters beginning with *k*, including the nasal, *ća-varga* the palatals, *ṭa-varga* the cerebrals, *ta-varga* the dentals, *pa-varga* the labials, *ya-varga* the semivowels, *śa-varga* the sibilants and the aspirate *h*.

b. In the Śiva-sútras of Páṇini the letters are arranged in fourteen groups: thus, *a i u ṇ—ṛi lṛi k—e o n—ai au ć—h y v r ṭ—l ṇ—ṅ m n ṇ n m—jh bh ṅ—gh ḍh dh sh—j b g ḍ d ś—kh ph ćh ṭh th ć ṭ t v—k p y—ś sh s r—h l*. By taking the first letter of any series and joining it to the last of any other series various classes of letters are designated; thus *al* is the technical name for the whole alphabet; *hal* for all the consonants; *ać* the vowels; *ak* all the simple vowels; *aṇ* the vowels *a*, *i*, *u*, short or long; *eć* the diphthongs; *yaṇ* the semivowels; *jaś* the soft consonants *g*, *j*, *ḍ*, *d*, *b*; *jhaś* the same with their aspirates; *jhash* the soft aspirates alone; *yar* all the consonants except *h*; *jhal* all the consonants except the nasals and semivowels; *jhar* all the consonants except the aspirate, nasals, and semivowels.

b. The following tables exhibit this twofold classification, the comprehension of which is of the utmost importance to the study of Sanskṛit grammar.

Gutturals	अ *a* आ *á*	क *ka* ख *kha*	ग *ga* घ *gha*	ङ *ṅa*	ह *ha*	
Palatals	इ *i* ई *í* ए *e* ऐ *ai*	च *ća* छ *ćha*	ज *ja* झ *jha*	ञ *ña*	य *ya*	श *śa*
Cerebrals	ऋ *ṛi* ॠ *ṛí*	ट *ṭa* ठ *ṭha*	ड *ḍa* ढ *ḍha*	ण *ṇa*	र *ra*	ष *sha*
Dentals	ऌ *lṛi* ॡ *lṛí*	त *ta* थ *tha*	द *da* ध *dha*	न *na*	ल *la*	स *sa*
Labials	उ *u* ऊ *ú* ओ *o* औ *au*	प *pa* फ *pha*	ब *ba* भ *bha*	म *ma*	व *va*	

The first two consonants in each of the above five classes and the sibilants, including Visarga, are hard; all the other letters, including Anusvára, are soft, as in the following table:

HARD OR SURD LETTERS.		SOFT OR SONANT LETTERS.			
क *ka** ख *kha**		अ *a* आ *á*	ग *ga** घ *gha**	ङ *ṅa*	ह *ha*
च *ća** छ *ćha**	श *śa*	इ *i* ई *í* ए *e* ऐ *ai*	ज *ja** झ *jha**	ञ *ña*	य *ya*
ट *ṭa** ठ *ṭha**	ष *sha*	ऋ *ṛi* ॠ *ṛí*	ड *ḍa** ढ *ḍha**	ण *ṇa*	र *ra*
त *ta** थ *tha**	स *sa*	ऌ *lṛi* ॡ *lṛí*	द *da** ध *dha**	न *na*	ल *la*
प *pa** फ *pha**		उ *u* ऊ *ú* ओ *o* औ *au*	ब *ba** भ *bha**	म *ma*	व *va*

Note—Hindú grammarians begin with the letters pronounced by the organ furthest from the mouth, and so take the other organs in order, ending with the lips. This as a technical arrangement is perhaps the best, but the order of creation would be that of the Hebrew alphabet; 1st, the labials; 2nd, the gutturals; 3rd, the dentals.

c. Observe, that although ए *e*, ऐ *ai*, are more conveniently connected with the palatal class, and ओ *o*, औ *au*, with the labial, these letters are really diphthongal, being made up of *a* + *i*, *á* + *i*, *a* + *u*, *á* + *u*, respectively. Their first element is therefore guttural. (In the Prátiśákhyas the diphthongs *e*, *ai*, *o*, *au* are called *Sandhy-akshara.*)

d. Note also, that it is most important to observe which hard letters have kindred soft letters, and *vice versa.* The kindred hard and soft are those in the same line marked with a star in the above table; thus *g*, *gh*, are the corresponding soft letters to *k*, *kh*; *j*, *jh*, to *ć*, *ćh*, and so with the others.

In order that the foregoing classification may be clearly understood, it is necessary to note the proper meaning of the term vowel and consonant, and to define the relationship which the nasals, semivowels, and sibilants, bear to the other letters.

19. A vowel is defined to be a sound (*svara*) or vocal emission of breath from the lungs, modified or modulated by the play of one or other of five organs, viz. the throat, the palate, the tongue, the teeth, or the lips, but not interrupted or stopped by the actual *contact* of any of these organs.

a. Hence अ *a*, इ *i*, उ *u*, ऋ *ṛi*, ऌ *ḷṛi*, with their respective long forms, are simple vowels, belonging to the guttural, palatal, labial, cerebral, and dental classes respectively, according to the organ principally concerned in their modulation. But ए *e* and ऐ *ai* are half guttural, half palatal; ओ *o* and औ *au* half guttural, half labial. See 18. *c.*

b. The vowels are, of course, held to be soft letters.

20. A consonant is not the modulation, but the actual stoppage, of the vocal stream of breath by *the contact* of one or other of the five organs, and cannot be enunciated without a vowel. Hence the consonants from *k* to *m* in the table on p. 1 are often designated by the term *sparśa* or *spṛishṭa*, 'resulting from contact;' while the semivowels *y*, *r*, *l*, *v* are called *íshat-spṛishṭa*, 'resulting from slight contact.' By native grammarians they are sometimes said to be *avidyamána-vat*, 'as if they did not exist,' because they have no *svara* (sound or accent). Another name for consonant is *vyañjana*, probably so called as 'distinguishing' sound.

a. All the consonants, therefore, are arranged under the five heads of gutturals, palatals, cerebrals, dentals, and labials, according to the organ concerned in *stopping* the vocal sound.

b. Again, the first two consonants in each of the five classes, and the sibilants, are called *hard* or *surd*, i. e. non-sonant (*a-ghosha*), because the vocal stream is abruptly and completely interrupted, and no *ghosha* or sound allowed to escape; while all the other letters are called *soft* or *sonant* (*ghosha-vat*, 'having sound'), because the vocal sound is less suddenly and completely arrested, and they are articulated with a soft sound or low murmur (*ghosha*).

c. Observe, that the palatal stop is only a modification of the guttural, the point of contact being moved more forward from the throat towards the palate *.

In the same way the cerebral (*múrdhanya*) stop is a modification of the dental. See 13.

d. The cerebral letters have probably been introduced into Sanskṛit through pre-existing dialects, such as the Drávidian, with which it came in contact (see 24). As these letters are pronounced chiefly with the help of the tongue, they are sometimes appropriately called *linguals.*

21. A nasal or narisonant letter is a soft letter, in the utterance of which the vocal stream of breath incompletely arrested, as in all soft letters, is forced through the nose instead of the lips. As the soft letters are of five kinds, according to the organ which interrupts the vocal breathing, so the nasal letters are five, viz. guttural, palatal, cerebral, dental, and labial. See 15.

22. The semivowels *y, r, l, v* (called अन्तःस्थ *antuḥstha* or *antaḥsthá* because they *stand between* the other consonants and the sibilants) are formed by a vocal breathing, which is only half interrupted, the several organs being only slightly touched (*íshat-spṛishṭa*) by the tongue. They are, therefore, soft or sonant consonants, approaching nearly to the character of vowels—in fact, half vowels, half consonants. See 16.

a. Each class of soft letters (excepting the guttural) has its own kindred semivowel to which it is nearly related. Thus the palatal soft letters इ *i*, ई *í*, ए *e*, ऐ *ai*, ज् *j*, have य् *y* for their kindred semivowel. Similarly र् *r* is the kindred semivowel of the cerebral soft letters ऋ *ṛi*, ॠ *ṛí*, and ड् *ḍ;* so also ल् *l* of the dentals ऌ *lṛi*, ॡ *lṛí*, and द् *d* †; and व् *v* of उ *u*, ऊ *ú*, ओ *o*, औ *au*, and ब् *b*.

b. The guttural soft letters have no kindred semivowel in Sanskṛit, unless the aspirate ह् *h* be so regarded.

* The relationship of the palatal to the guttural letters is proved by their frequent interchangeableness in Sanskṛit and in other languages. See 24, 25, and 176, and compare *church* with *kirk*, Sanskṛit *ćatvár* with Latin *quatuor*, Sanskṛit *ća* with Latin *que* and Greek καί, Sanskṛit *jánu* with English *knee*, Greek γόνυ, Latin *genu*. Some German scholars represent the palatals च् and ज् by *k'* and *g'*.

† That ल् *l* is a dental, and kindred to द् *d*, is proved by its interchangeableness with *d* in cognate languages. Thus *lacrima*, δάκρυμα. Compare also दीप् with λαμπ.

23. The sibilants or hissing sounds (called ऊष्मन् *úshman* by native grammarians) are hard letters, which, nevertheless, strictly speaking, have in some measure the character of vowels. The organs of speech in uttering them, although not closed, are more contracted and less opened (*íshad-vivṛita*) than in vowels, and the vocal stream of breath in passing through the teeth experiences a friction which causes sibilation.

a. The aspirate ह् *h*, although a soft letter, is also called an *úshman*.

b. The palatal, cerebral, and dental classes of letters have each their own sibilant (viz. श्, ष्, स्, respectively, see 17). The Ardha-visarga, called *Jihvámúlíya* (ᳵ = χ), was once the guttural sibilation, and that called *Upadhmáníya* (ᳶ = φ) the labial sibilation (see 8. *a*); but these two latter, though called *úshman*, have now gone out of use. Visarga (:) is also sometimes, though less correctly, called an *úshman*. The exact labial sibilation denoted by *f*, and the soft sibilation *z* are unknown in Sanskṛit.

24. That some of the consonants did not exist in the original Sanskṛit alphabet, but have been added at later periods, will be made clear by a reference to the examples below, exhibiting the interchange of letters in Sanskṛit, Greek, and Latin. The palatals *ć, ćh, j, jh, ñ* were probably developed out of the corresponding gutturals; the cerebrals *ṭ, ṭh, ḍ, ḍh, ṇ* are thought to be of Drávidian origin; the guttural nasal *n* is evidently for an original *n* or *m* before a guttural letter; *l* is supposed to be a more modern form of *r*; *ś* belongs to the palatal class, and is generally for an original *k*; *sh* is for an original *s*, cf. root *ush*, 'to burn,' with Lat. *us-tu-s*, from *ur-o*; *h* is for an original *gh*, sometimes for *dh*, and occasionally for *bh* (e. g. root *grah*, 'to seize,' for the Vedic *grabh*).

Of the vowels probably only *a, i, u* were original; *ṛi* is not original, and seems to have been a weakened pronunciation of the syllable *ar*, and at a later period *lṛi* of *al*. In Prákṛit *ṛi* is represented by either *i* or *u*. The diphthongs are of course formed by the union of simple vowels (see 29).

INTERCHANGE OF LETTERS IN SANSKṚIT, GREEK, AND LATIN.

25. The following is a list of examples exhibiting some of the commonest interchanges of letters in Sanskṛit, Greek, and Latin.

Sanskṛit *a* = Greek *α, ε, ο,* = Latin *a, e, o, i, u*; e. g. Sk. *ajra-s*, 'a plain,' Gr. ἀγρό-ς, L. *ager*; Sk. *jan-as*, 'race,' Gr. γέν-ος, L. *gen-us*; Sk. *janas-as*, gen. c., Gr. γένε(σ)-ος, γένους, L. *gener-is*; Sk. *nava-s*, 'new,' Gr. νέο-ς, L. *novu-s*; Sk. *apas-as*, 'of work,' L. *oper-is*.

Sanskṛit *á* = Gr. *α, η, ω,* = L. *á, é, ó*; e. g. Sk. *má-tṛi* (stem *mátar-*), 'a mother,' Gr. μήτηρ (stem μήτερ-), Dor. μάτηρ, Lat. *máter*; Sk. *jñá-ta-s*, 'known,' Gr. γνω-τό-ς, L. (*g*)*nó-tu-s*; Sk. *sámi-*, 'half,' Gr. ἡμι-, L. *sémi-*.

Sanskṛit *i* = Gr. *ι,* = L. *i, e*; e. g. Sk. *sámi-*, 'half,' Gr. ἡμι-, L. *semi-*.

Sanskṛit *í* = Gr. *ι,* = L. *í*; e. g. Sk. *jív-a-s*, 'living,' Gr. βίο-ς, L. *vív-u-s*.

Sanskṛit *u* = Gr. *υ,* = L. *u, o*; e. g. Sk. *uru-s*, 'broad,' Gr. εὐρύ-ς; Sk. *jánu*, 'knee,' Gr. γόνυ, L. *genu*.

Sanskṛit *ú* = Gr. *υ*, = L. *u*; e. g. Sk. *músh*, *músh-a-s*, &c., 'a mouse,' Gr. μῦς, L. *mus*.

Sanskṛit *ṛi*, i. e. *ar* = Gr. *ρ* with a short vowel, = L. *r* with a short vowel; e. g. Sk. *mṛi-ta-s*, 'dead,' Gr. βρο-τό-ς (for μρο-τό-ς or μορ-τό-ς), L. *mor-tuu-s*; Sk. *mátṛibhyas*, 'from mothers,' L. *matribus*; Sk. *mátṛishu*, 'in mothers,' Gr. μητράσι.

Sanskṛit *ṛí* = Gr. *ρ* with a vowel, = L. *r* with a vowel; e. g. Sk. *dátṛín*, acc. pl. of *dátṛi*, 'a giver,' Gr. δο-τῆρ-ας, L. *da-tor-es*; Sk. *mátṛís*, L. *matres*.

Sanskṛit *e* = Gr. αι, ει, οι, = L. *ai*, *é*, *oi*, *æ*, *œ*, *i*, *ú*; e. g. Sk. *veś-a-s*, 'an abode,' Gr. (Ϝ)οἶκο-ς, L. *vicu-s*; Sk. e-*mi*, 'I go,' Gr. εἶ-μι; Sk. *eva-s*, 'going,' 'a course,' Gr. αἰ-ών, L. *ævu-m*.

Sanskṛit *ai* = Gr. ᾳ, ῃ, ῳ, = L. *æ* in certain inflexions; e. g. Sk. *devyai*, 'to a goddess,' Gr. θεᾷ, L. *deæ*.

Sanskṛit *o* = Gr. αυ, ευ, ου, = L. *au*, *o*, *u*; e. g. Sk. *gola-s*, 'a ball,' Gr. γαυλό-ς; Sk. *ojas*, 'power,' L. *augeo*.

Sanskṛit *au* = Gr. αυ, ηυ, = L. *au*; e. g. Sk. *nau-s*, 'a ship,' Gr. ναῦς, νηῦς, L. *navis*, *nauta*, 'a sailor.'

Sanskṛit *k*, *kh*, *ć*, *ś*, = Gr. κ, = L. *c*, *q*; e. g. Sk. *kravis*, *kravya-m*, 'raw flesh,' Gr. κρέας, κρεῖον, L. *cru-or*, *caro*; Sk. kh*ala-s*, 'a granary,' *śálá*, 'a hall,' Gr. καλιά, L. *cella*; Sk. *ća*, 'and,' Gr. καί, L. -*que*.

Sanskṛit *g*, *j*, = Gr. γ (β), = L. *g* (*b*); e. g. Sk. *yug-a-m*, 'a yoke,' Gr. ζυγ-ό-ν, L. *jug-u-m*; Sk. *jánu*, 'knee,' Gr. γόνυ, L. *genu*; Sk. *ajra-s*, 'a plain,' Gr. ἀγρό-ς, L. *ager*; Sk. *gau-s*, 'a cow,' Gr. βοῦ-ς, L. *bos*; Sk. *guru-s*, 'heavy,' Gr. βαρύ-ς, L. *grav-i-s*.

Sanskṛit *gh* = Gr. χ, = L. *g*; e. g. Sk. rt. *stigh*, 'to ascend,' Gr στείχ-ω, στίχο-ς, L. *ve-stig-ium*; Sk. *laghu-s*, 'light,' Gr. ἐλαχύ-ς.

Sanskṛit *ćh* = Gr. σκ, = L. *sc*; e. g. Sk. *ćháyá*, 'shade,' Gr. σκιά; Sk. rt. *ćhid*, 'to cleave,' Gr. σχίζ-ω, σχίδ-η, L. *scind-o*.

Sanskṛit *t* (*th*) = Gr. τ, = L. *t*; e. g. Sk. *trayas*, 'three,' Gr. τρεῖς, L. *tres*.

Sanskṛit *d* = Gr. δ, = L. *d*; e. g. Sk. *dam-a-s*, 'a house,' Gr. δόμο-ς, L. *domu-s*.

Sanskṛit *dh* = Gr. θ, = L. initial *f*, non-initial *d*, *b*; e. g. Sk. *da-dhá-mi*, 'I place, Gr. τί-θη-μι; Sk. dh*ú-ma-s*, 'smoke,' Gr. θυ-μό-ς, L. *fu-mu-s*; Sk. *údh-ar*, 'udder,' Gr. οὖθαρ, L. *uber*; Sk. *andh-as*, 'food,' &c., Gr. ἄνθ-ος, L. *ad-or*.

Sanskṛit *p* (*ph*) = Gr. π (φ), = L. *p* (*f*); e. g. Sk. *pitṛi*, Gr. πατήρ, L. *pater*; Sk. ph*ulla-m*, 'a flower,' Gr. φύλλο-ν, L. *foliu-m*.

Sanskṛit *b* = Gr. β (π), = L. *b* (*f*); e. g. Sk. rt. *lamb*, 'to hang down,' L. *lab-i*; Sk. b*udh-na-s*, 'ground,' Gr. πυθ-μήν, L. *fundu-s*; Sk. b*udh*, 'to know,' Gr. πυνθάνομαι (πυθ-).

Sanskṛit *bh* = Gr. φ, = L. initial *f*, non-initial *b*; e. g. Sk. rt. bh*ṛi*, bh*ar-á-mi*, 'I bear,' Gr. φέρ-ω, L. *fer-o*; Sk. *nabh-as*, 'vapour,' 'a cloud,' Gr. νέφ-ος, L. *nub-e-s*.

Sanskṛit *n*, *ṅ*, = Gr. γ before gutturals, = L. *n*; e. g. Sk. *aṅ-ka-s*, 'a hook,' Gr. ἀγκ-ών, ὄγκ-ο-ς, L. *anc-u-s*, *unc-u-s*; Sk. *pańćan*, 'five,' Gr. πέντε, L. *quinque*.

Sanskṛit ṇ, n, = Gr. ν, = L. n; e.g. Sk. *nava-s*, 'new,' Gr. νέο-ς, L. *novu-s*.

Sanskṛit m = Gr. μ, = L. m; e.g. Sk. *má-tṛi*, 'a mother,' Gr. μή-τηρ, L. *ma-ter*.

Sanskṛit y = Gr. ', ζ, = L. j; e.g. Sk. *yakṛit*, 'liver,' Gr. ἧπαρ, L. *jecur*; Sk. *yug-a-m*, Gr. ζυγ-ό-ν, L. *jug-u-m*.

Sanskṛit r = Gr. ρ, λ, = L. r, l; e.g. Sk. *rájan*, 'king,' L. *rex* (stem *reg-*); Sk. *sara-s*, 'whey,' Gr. ὀρό-ς, L. *seru-m*; Sk. *rudh-i-ra-s*, 'blood-red,' Gr. ἐρυθ-ρός, L. *ruber*, *rufus*; Sk. rt. *śru*, *śravas*, *śru-ta-s*, Gr. κλέ-ος, κλυ-τό-ς, L. *in-cly-tu-s*.

Sanskṛit l = Gr. λ, = L. l; e.g. Sk. rt. *lú*, *lu-ná-mi*, 'I cut,' Gr. λύ-ω, L. *re-lu-o*, *so-lv-o* (for *se-lu-o*); Sk. *lih* (= *rih*), 'to lick,' Gr. λείχ-ω, λίχ-νο-ς, L. *ling-o*, *lig-uri-o*.

Sanskṛit v = Gr. ϝ (υ), or disappears, = L. v (u); e.g. Sk. *nava-s*, 'new,' Gr. νέϝο-ς, i.e. νέο-ς, L. *novu-s*; Sk. *vish-a-s*, 'poison,' Gr. ἰ-ό-ς, L. *vírus*; Sk. *dvi*, 'two,' Gr. δύο, L. *duo*.

Sanskṛit ś (for an original k) = Gr. κ, = L. c, q; e.g. Sk. *daśan*, 'ten,' Gr. δέκα, L. *decem*; Sk. *aśva-s*, 'a horse,' Gr. ἵππο-ς, ἴκκο-ς, L. *equu-s*; Sk. *śvá*, 'a dog,' Gr. κύ-ων, L. *can-is*.

Sanskṛit s, sh, = Gr. σ, ', disappears between two vowels, = L. s, changes to r between two vowels; e.g. Sk. *asti*, 'he is,' Gr. ἐστί, L. *est*; Sk. *janas-as*, 'of a race,' Gr. γένε(σ)-ος, γένους, L. *gener-is*; Sk. *vish-as*, 'poison,' Gr. ἰ-ός, L. *vir-us*; Sk. *shaṭ*, 'six,' Gr. ἕξ, L. *sex*.

Sanskṛit h (for an original gh, sometimes for dh, and occasionally for bh) = Gr. χ, κ (sometimes θ), = L. h, c, q; e.g. Sk. *hi-ma-s*, 'winter,' Gr. χι-ών, L. *hiems*; Sk. *hṛid-aya-m*, 'the heart,' Gr. καρδ-ία, L. cor (stem *cord-*); Sk. *han* for *ghan* and *dhan* (in *ja-ghán-a*, 'he killed;' *ni-dhan-a*, 'death'), Gr. θάν-ατος; Sk. *hita* for *dhita*, 'placed' (fr. *dhá*, Gr. θη), Gr. θετός.

THE INDIAN METHOD OF WRITING.

26. According to Hindú grammarians every syllable ought to end in a vowel*, except at the end of a clause or sentence, and every final consonant ought to be attracted to the beginning of the next syllable; so that where a word ends in a consonant, that consonant ought to be pronounced with the initial letter of the next word. Hence in some Sanskṛit MSS. all the syllables are separated by slight spaces, and in others all the words are joined together without any separation. Thus the two words आसीद् राजा *ásíd rájá* would in some books be written आ सी द्रा जा and in others आसीद्राजा. There seems little reason for considering the mere spaces left between the words of a sentence to be incompatible with the

---

* Unless it end in Anusvára or Visarga *ḥ*, which in theory are the only consonantal sounds allowed to close a syllable until the end of a sentence.

operation of euphonic laws. Therefore in some Sanskṛit books printed in Roman type every uncompounded word capable of separation is separated, e. g. *pitur dhanam ádatte;* which is even printed in Deva-nágarí letters (by those scholars who allow an extension of the use of the mark called Viráma) thus, पितुर् धनम् आदत्ते, for पितुर्धनमादत्ते.

The following words and passages in the Sanskṛit and English character, are given that the Student, before proceeding further in the Grammar, may exercise himself in reading the letters and in transliteration.

To be turned into English letters.

अक, अज, अश, आस, आप, इल, इष, ईड, ईर, उख, उच, ऊह, ऋण, ऋज, एध, ओख, कण, कित, कुमार, क्षम, क्षिप, क्षुध, क्षै, क्लृप, खन, खिद, गाह, गुज, गृध, गॄ, घृण, घुष, चकास, चक्ष, चित, छिद, छो, जीवा, झष, टीका, ठः, डीनं, ढौक, णिद, तापः, तडागः, दया, दमकः, दशरथः, दुरालापः, देव, धूपिका, धृतः, नटः, नील, नेम, परिदानम्, पुरुषस्, पौरः, पौरुषेयी, पुरोडाशः, बहुः, बालकस्, भोगः, भोजनम्, मुखम्, मृगः, मेदस्, मेदिनी, यकृत्, योगः, रेणु, रेचक, रै, रैवत, रुजा, रूपम्, रुरुदिषु, लोह, वामः, वैरम्, शक्, शौरः, षट्, साधुः, हेमकूटः, हेमन्.

To be turned into Sanskṛit letters.

Ada, asa, ali, ádi, ákhu, ágas, iti, íśaḥ, íhá, udára, upanishad, uparodha, úru, úsha, ṛishi, eka, kakud, kaṭu, koshaḥ, gaura, ghaṭa, ćaitya, ćet, ćhalam, jetṛi, jhirí, ṭagara, ḍamara, ḍhála, ṇama, tatas, tathá, tṛiṇa, tushára, deha, daitya, dhavala, nanu, nayanam, nidánam, pitṛi, bhauma, bheshajam, marus, mahat, yuga, rush, rúḍhis, lauha, vivekas, śatam, shoḍaśan, sukhin, hṛidaya, tatra, adya, buddhi, arka, kratu, aṇsa, aṅka, aṅga, añćala, añjana, kaṇṭha, aṇḍa, anta, manda, sampúrṇa.

The following story has the Sanskṛit and English letters interlined.

अस्ति हस्तिनापुरे विलासो नाम रजकः। तस्य गर्द-
asti hastinápure viláso náma rajakaḥ tasya garda-

भोऽतिभारवाहनाद् दुर्बलो मुमूर्षुर् अभवत्। ततस् तेन
bho 'tibháraváhanád durbalo mumúrshur abhavat tatas tena

रजकेनासौ व्याघ्रचर्मणा प्रच्छाद्यारण्यसमीपे शस्यक्षेत्रे
rajakenásau vyághraćarmaṇá praććhádyáraṇyasamípe śasyakshetre

मोचितः। ततो दूराद् अवलोक्य व्याघ्रबुद्ध्या क्षेत्रप-
moćitaḥ tato dúrád avalokya vyághrabuddhyá kshetrapa-

तयः सत्वरं पलायन्ते। अथ केनापि शस्यरक्षकेण धूसर-
tayaḥ satvaraṃ paláyante atha kenápi śasyarakshakeṇa dhúsara-

कम्बलकृततनुत्राणेन धनुःकाण्डं सज्जीकृत्यावनतकायेन
kambalakṛitatanutráṇena dhanuḥkáṇḍaṃ sajjíkṛityávanatakáyena

एकान्ते स्थितम्। ततस् तं च दूरे दृष्ट्वा गर्दभः पुष्टाङ्गो
ekánte sthitam tatas taṃ ća dúre dṛishṭvá gardabhaḥ pushṭáṅgo

गर्दभीयमिति मत्वा शब्दं कुर्वाणस् तदभिमुखं धावितः।
gardabhíyamiti matvá śabdaṃ kurváṇas tadabhimukhaṃ dhávitaḥ

ततस् तेन शस्यरक्षकेण गर्दभोऽयमिति ज्ञात्वा लीलयैव
tatas tena śasyarakshakeṇa gardabho 'yamiti jṅátvá lílayaiva

व्यापादितः॥
vyápáditaḥ.

The following story is to be turned into Sanskṛit letters.

Asti śríparvatamadhye brahmapurákhyaṃ nagaram. Tatra śaila-śikhare ghaṇṭákarṇo náma rákshasaḥ prativasatíti janapravádaḥ śrú-yate. Ekadá ghaṇṭám ádáya paláyamánaḥ kaśćić ćauro vyághreṇa vyápáditaḥ. Tatpáṇipatitá ghaṇṭá vánaraiḥ práptá. Te vánarás táṃ ghaṇṭám anukshaṇaṃ vádayanti. Tato nagarajanair manushyaḥ khá-dito dṛishṭaḥ pratikshaṇaṃ ghaṇṭárávásća śrúyate. Anantaraṃ ghaṇṭákarṇaḥ kupito manushyán khádati ghaṇṭáṃ ća vádayatítyu-

ktvá janáḥ sarve nagarát paláyitáḥ. Tataḥ karálayá náma kuṭṭinyá vimṛiśya markaṭá ghaṇṭáṃ vádayanti svayaṃ vijñáya rájá vijñápitaḥ. Deva yadi kiyaddhanopakshayaḥ kriyate tadáham enaṃ ghaṇṭákarṇaṃ sádhayámi. Tato rájñá tushṭena tasyai dhanaṃ dattam. Kuṭṭinyá ća maṇḍalaṃ kṛitvá tatra gaṇeśádigauravaṃ darśayitvá svayaṃ vánarapriyaphalányádáya vanam praviśya phalányákírṇáni. Tato ghaṇṭám parityajya vánaráḥ phalásaktá babhúvuḥ. Kuṭṭiní ća ghaṇṭáṃ gṛihítvá nagaram ágatá sakalalokapújyábhavat.

CHAPTER II.

SANDHI OR EUPHONIC COMBINATION OF LETTERS.

WE are accustomed in Greek and Latin to certain euphonic changes of letters. Thus for the perfect passive participle of *reg-o* (stem *reg-*) we have (not *reg-tu-s* but) *rec-tu-s*, the soft *g* being changed to the hard *c* before the hard *t* (cf. *rex* for *reg-s*). In many words a final consonant assimilates with an initial; thus *συν* with *γνώμη* becomes *συγγνώμη*; *ἐν* with *λάμπω*, *ἐλλάμπω*. *Suppressus* is written for *subpressus*; *appellatus* for *adpellatus*; *immensus* for *inmensus*; *affinitas* for *adfinitas*; *offero* for *obfero*, but in perfect *obtuli*; *colloquium* for *conloquium*; *irrogo* for *inrogo*. In English, assimilations of the same kind take place in pronunciation, though they are not always recognized in writing; thus *cupboard* is pronounced as if written *cub-board*, and *blackguard* as if written *blag-guard*. These laws for the euphonic junction of letters are applied throughout the whole range of Sanskṛit grammar; and that, too, not only in the interior of words when a stem is united with its terminations and suffixes, but in combining words in the same sentence. Thus, if the sentence '*Rara avis in terris*' were Sanskṛit, it would require, by the laws of Sandhi or combination, to be written *Raráviriṇsterriḥ*. The learner is recommended, after learning the most common rules of combination, printed in large type, to pass at once to the declension of nouns and conjugation of verbs.

There are two classes of rules of Sandhi, viz. 1. Those affecting the junction of final and initial letters of *completely formed* words in sentences as well as of the stems of words in compounds; 2. Those which take effect in the *process of forming* words by the junction of roots and of stems, whether nominal or verbal, with suffixes and terminations (see 74. *a*). As the rules which apply to one class are generally applicable to the other, it will be convenient to consider them together; but some of the rules which come into operation in the formation of *verbs*, are reserved till they are wanted (see 294).

Sect. I.—EUPHONIC PERMUTATION AND COMBINATION OF VOWELS.

27. The changes of vowels called Guṇa and Vṛiddhi should at once be impressed on the memory. When the vowels इ *i* and ई *í* become ए *e*, this is called a Guṇa change, or *qualification* (*guṇa* meaning 'quality'). When *i* and *í* become ऐ *ai*, this is called a Vṛiddhi change, or *increase*. Similarly, उ *u* and ऊ *ú* are often changed to their Guṇa ओ *o*, and Vṛiddhi औ *au;* ऋ *ṛi* and ॠ *ṛí* to their Guṇa अर् *ar*, and Vṛiddhi आर् *ár;* and अ *a*, though it can have no corresponding Guṇa change, has a Vṛiddhi substitute in आ *á*.

a. Native grammarians consider that *a* is already a Guṇa letter, and on that account can have no Guṇa substitute. Indeed they regard *a*, *e*, *o* as the only Guṇa sounds, and *á*, *ai*, *au* as the only Vṛiddhi; *a* and *á* being the real Guṇa and Vṛiddhi representatives of the vowels ऋ and ऌ. It is required, however, that *r* should always be connected with *a* and *á* when these vowels are substituted for *ṛi;* and *l*, when they are substituted for *lṛi*.

b. Observe—It will be convenient in describing the change of a vowel to its Guṇa or Vṛiddhi substitute, to speak of that vowel as *gunated* or *vriddhied*.

28. In the formation of stems, whether nominal or verbal, the vowels of roots cannot be gunated or vriddhied, if they are followed by double consonants, i.e. if they are long by position; nor can a vowel long by nature be so changed, *unless it be final.* The vowel अ *a* is, as we have seen, already a Guṇa letter. See 27. *a*.

a. But in secondary derivatives long vowels are sometimes vriddhied: स्थौल *sthaula*, 'robust,' from स्थूल *sthúla;* ग्रैव *graiva*, 'belonging to the neck,' from ग्रीवा *grívá;* मौल *maula*, 'radical,' from मूल *múla* (see 80. B).

29. The Guṇa sounds ए *e*, ओ *o* are diphthongal, that is, composed of two simple vowel sounds. Thus, ए *e* is made up of *a* and *i;* ओ *o* of *a* and *u;* so that a final अ *a* will naturally coalesce with an

initial इ *i* into *e;* with an initial उ *u* into *o.* (Compare 18. *c.*) Again, अर् *ar* may be regarded as made up of *a* and *ṛi;* so that a final अ *a* will blend with an initial ऋ *ṛi* into *ar.*

a. Similarly, the Vṛiddhi diphthong ऐ *ai* is made up of *a* and *e*, or (which is the same) *á* and *i;* and औ *au* of *a* and *o*, or (which is the same) *á* and *u.* Hence, a final *a* will naturally blend with an initial ए *e* into *ai;* and with an initial ओ *o* into *au.* (Compare 18. *c;* and see note to table in next page.) The simple vowels in their diphthongal unions are not very closely combined, so that *e, o, ai, au* are liable to be resolved into their constituent simple elements.

b. If *ai* is composed of *á* and *i*, it may be asked, How is it that long *á* as well as short *a* blends with *i* into *e* (see 32), and not into *ai?* In answer to this some scholars have maintained that a long vowel at the end of a word naturally shortens itself before an initial vowel (see 38. *i*), and that the very meaning of Guṇa is the prefixing of short *a*, and the very meaning of Vṛiddhi, the prefixing of long *á*, to a simple vowel. Hence the Guṇa of *i* is originally *a i*, though the two simple vowels blend afterwards into *e.* Similarly, the original Guṇa of *u* is *a u*, blending afterwards into *o;* the original Guṇa of *ṛi* is *a ṛi*, blending into *ar.*

c. The practice of gunating vowels is not peculiar to Sanskṛit. The Sanskṛit *a* answers to the Greek ε or ο (see 25), and Sanskṛit एमि *emi*, 'I go,' which in the 1st pers. plural becomes इमस् *imas*, 'we go,' is originally *a i mi*, corresponding to the Greek εἶμι and ἴμεν. Similarly in Greek, the root φυγ (ἔ-φυγ-ον) is in the present φεύγ-ω. Compare also the Sanskṛit *veda* (*vaida*), 'he knows,' with Greek οἶδα; and compare λέ-λοιπ-α, perfect of λιπ, with the Sanskṛit perfect.

30. Again, let it be borne in mind that य् *y* is the kindred semivowel of *i, í, e,* and *ai;* व् *v* of *u, ú, o,* and *au;* र् *r* of *ṛi* and *ṛí;* and ऌ् *l* of *lṛi* and *lṛí.* So that *i, í, e, ai*, at the end of words, when the next begins with a vowel, may often pass into *y, y, ay, áy*, respectively; *u, ú, o, au*, into *v, v, av, áv;* and *ṛi, ṛí*, into *r.* [Observe—*lṛi* is not found as a final.]

The interchange of vowels with their own semivowels is called by Sanskṛit grammarians *samprasáraṇa.*

In English we recognize the same interchangeableness, though not in the same way; thus we write *holy, holier; easy, easily;* and we use *ow* for *ou* in *now, cow*, &c.

In order to impress the above rules on the mind, the substance of them is embodied in the following table:

Simple vowels,	*a* or *á*	*i* or *í*	*u* or *ú*	*ṛi* or *ṛí*	*lṛi* or *lṛí*
Guṇa substitute,		*e*	*o*	*ar*	*al*
Vṛiddhi substitute,	*á*	*ai*	*au*	*ár*	*ál*
Simple vowels,		*i* or *í*	*u* or *ú*	*ṛi* or *ṛí*	*lṛi* or *lṛí*
Corresponding semivowel,		*y*	*v*	*r*	*l*
Guṇa,		*e*	*o*		
Guṇa resolved,		*a* + *i*	*a* + *u*		
With semivowel substitute,		*ay*	*av*		
Vṛiddhi,		*ai*	*au*		
Vṛiddhi resolved,		*a* + *e*	*a* + *o*		
		a + *a* + *i*	*a* + *a* + *u*		
		**á* + *i*	**á* + *u*		
With semivowel substitute,		*áy*	*áv*		

The following rules will now be easily understood. They apply generally to the junction (1) of separate words in sentences and compounds; (2) of roots and stems with suffixes and terminations. To distinguish the second class of combinations the sign + will be used in the examples given. The object of most of the rules is to prevent a hiatus between vowels †.

31. If any *simple* vowel (short or long) is followed by a similar simple vowel (short or long), the two vowels blend into one long similar vowel (Páṇ. VI. 1, 101); e.g.

न अस्ति इह *na asti iha* becomes नास्तीह *nástíha*, 'he is not here.'

राजा अस्तु उत्तमः *rájá astu uttamaḥ* becomes राजास्तूत्तमः *rájástúttamaḥ*, 'let the king be supreme.'

जीवा अन्त *jívá anta* becomes जीवान्त *jívánta*, 'end of life.'

अधि ईश्वर *adhi íśvara* becomes अधीश्वर *adhíśvara*, 'supreme lord.'

ऋतु उत्सव *ṛitu utsava* becomes ऋतूत्सव *ṛitútsava*, 'festival of the season.'

पितृ ऋद्धि *pitṛi ṛiddhi* becomes पितॄद्धि *pitṛíddhi*, 'a father's prosperity.'

* Since *e*=*a*+*i* and *o*=*a*+*u*, therefore *a*+*e* will equal *a*+*a*+*i* or *á*+*i*; and *a*+*o* will equal *a*+*a*+*u* or *á*+*u*.

† In the Vedic hymns hiatus between vowels is not uncommon; cf. note to 66.

32. अ *a* or आ *á*, followed by the dissimilar vowels इ *i*, उ *u*, ऋ *ṛi* (short or long), blends with *i* or *í* into the Guṇa ए *e;* with *u* or *ú* into the Guṇa ओ *o**; with *ṛi* or *ṛí* into the Guṇa अर् *ar* (Páṇ. VI. 1, 87); e.g.

परम ईश्वर *parama íśvara* becomes परमेश्वर *parameśvara*, 'mighty lord.'
हित उपदेश *hita upadeśa* becomes हितोपदेश *hitopadeśa*, 'friendly instruction.'
गङ्गा उदक *gangá udaka* becomes गङ्गोदक *gangodaka*, 'Ganges-water.'
तव ऋद्धि *tava ṛiddhi* becomes तवर्द्धि *tavarddhi*, 'thy growth.'
महा ऋषि *mahá ṛishi* becomes महर्षि *maharshi*, 'a great sage.'
Similarly, तव ऌकार *tava ḷṛikára* becomes तवल्कार *tavalkára*, 'thy letter *ḷṛi*.'

33. अ *a* or आ *á*, followed by the diphthongs ए *e*, ओ *o*, ऐ *ai*, or औ *au*, blends with *e* into the Vṛiddhi *ai;* with *ai* also into *ai;* with *o* into the Vṛiddhi *au;* with *au* also into *au* (Páṇ. VI. 1, 88); e.g.

पर एधित *para edhita* becomes परैधित *paraidhita*, 'nourished by another.'
विद्या एव *vidyá eva* becomes विद्यैव *vidyaiva*, 'knowledge indeed.'
देव ऐश्वर्य *deva aiśvarya* becomes देवैश्वर्य *devaiśvarya*, 'majesty of deity.'
अल्प ओजस् *alpa ojas* becomes अल्पौजस् *alpaujas*, 'little energy.'
गङ्गा ओघ *gangá ogha* becomes गङ्गौघ *gangaugha*, 'Ganges-current.'
ज्वर औषध *jvara aushadha* becomes ज्वरौषध *jvaraushadha*, 'fever-medicine.'

34. इ *i*, उ *u*, ऋ *ṛi* (short or long), followed by any dissimilar vowel or diphthong, pass into their kindred semivowels; viz. *i* or *í* into *y;* *u* or *ú* into *v*†; *ṛi* or *ṛí* into *r* (Páṇ. VI. 1, 77); e.g.

अग्नि अस्त्र *agni astra* becomes अग्न्यस्त्र *agny-astra*, 'fire-arms.'
प्रति उवाच *prati uváča* becomes प्रत्युवाच *praty-uváča*, 'he spoke in reply.'
तु इदानीम् *tu idáním* becomes त्विदानीम् *tv idáním*, 'but now.'
मातृ आनन्द *mátṛi ánanda* becomes मात्रानन्द *mátr-ánanda*, 'a mother's joy.'
मातृ औत्सुक्य *mátṛi autsukya* becomes मात्रौत्सुक्य *mátr-autsukya*, 'a mother's anxiety.'

35. Final ए *e* and ओ *o*, followed by an initial अ *a*, if it *begin another word*, remain unchanged, and the initial अ *a* is cut off (Páṇ. VI. 1. 109); e.g.

ते अपि *te api* becomes तेऽपि *te 'pi*, 'they indeed' (see 10).
सो अपि *so api* becomes सोऽपि *so 'pi*, 'he indeed.'

---

* The blending of *a* and *i* into the sound *e* is recognized in English in such words as *sail*, *nail*, &c.; and the blending of *a* and *u* into the sound o is exemplified by the French *faute*, *baume*, &c.

† Illustrated by some English words; thus we pronounce a word like *million* as if written *millyon;* and we write *evangelist* (not *euangelist*), *saying*, *playing*, &c.

a. In compounds the elision of initial *a* after a stem like *go* appears to be optional, e.g. *go-'śváḥ* or *go-aśváḥ*, 'oxen and horses' (Páṇ. VI. 1, 122). See 38. *e.*

b. But *go* may become *gava* in certain compounds, as *go agram* may become *gavágram*, see 38. *e;* so *go indra* becomes *gavendra*, 'lord of kine,' or *gav-indra* by 36.

36. But followed by *á, i, í, u, ú, ṛi, ṛí, e, o, ai, au*, if any one of these *begin another word*, final ए *e* and ओ *o* are changed to *ay* and *av* respectively; and the *y* of *ay*, and more rarely the *v* of *av*, may be dropped, leaving the *a* uninfluenced by the following vowel (Páṇ. VI. 1, 78); e.g.

ते आगताः *te ágatáḥ* becomes तयागताः *tay ágatáḥ*, and then त आगताः *ta ágatáḥ*, 'they have come.'

Similarly, विष्णो इह *vishṇo iha* becomes विष्णविह *vishṇav iha*, and then विष्ण इह *vishṇa iha*, 'O Vishṇu, here!'

Observe—When *go*, 'a cow,' becomes *gav* in compounds, *v* is retained; e.g.

गो ईश्वर *go íśvara* becomes गवीश्वर *gav-íśvara*, 'owner of kine.'

गो ओकस् *go okas* becomes गवोकस् *gav-okas*, 'abode of cattle.'

a. And in the case of ए *e* and ओ *o* followed by any vowel or diphthong *in the same word*, even though the following vowel or diphthong be *a* or *e* or *o*, then *e* must still be changed to *ay*, and *o* to *av*, but both *y* and *v* must be retained; e.g.

जे + अ *je+a* becomes जय *jaya*, the present stem of *ji*, 'to conquer' (see 263).

अग्ने + ए *agne+e* becomes अग्नये *agnaye*, 'to fire' (dative case).

भो + अ *bho+a* becomes भव *bhava*, the present stem of *bhú* (see 263).

37. ऐ *ai* and औ *au*, followed by any vowel or diphthong, similar or dissimilar, are changed to *áy* and *áv* respectively (Páṇ. VI. 1, 78); e.g.

कस्मै अपि *kasmai api* becomes कस्मायपि *kasmáy api*, 'to any one whatever.'

रै + अस् *rai+as* becomes रायस् *ráyas*, 'riches' (nom. plur.).

ददौ अन्नम् *dadau annam* becomes ददावन्नम् *dadáv annam*, 'he gave food.'

नौ + औ *nau+au* becomes नावौ *návau*, 'two ships' (nom. du.).

a. If both the words be complete words, the *y* and *v* are occasionally dropped, but not so usually as in the case of *e* at 36; thus कस्मा अपि *kasmá api* for कस्मायपि *kasmáy api*, and ददा अन्नम् *dadá annam* for ददावन्नम् *dadáv annam*.

PRAGṚIHYA EXCEPTIONS.

38. There are some exceptions (usually called *pragṛihya*, 'to be taken or pronounced separately') caused by vowels which must, under all circumstances, remain unchanged. The most noticeable are the terminations of duals (whether of nouns, pronouns, or verbs)

in *í*, *ú*, or *e* (Páṇ. I. I, II). These are not acted on by following vowels; e.g.

कवी एतौ *kaví etau*, 'these two poets;' बन्धू इमौ *bandhú imau*, 'these two relations;' अमू आसाते 'these two sit down;' पचेते इमौ 'these two cook;' शेवहे आवाम् 'we two lie down.'

Observe—The same applies to अमी *amí*, nom. pl. masc. of the pronoun अदस्.

a. The Vedic *asme* and *yushme* are also *pragṛihya* according to Páṇ. I. I, 13.

b. Prolated vowels (II. *f*) remain unchanged, as आगच्छ कृष्ण ३ अत्र 'Come, Kṛishṇa, here,' &c. (Páṇ. VI. I, 125; VIII. 2, 82).

c. A vocative case in *o*, when followed by the particle *iti*, may remain unchanged, as विष्णो इति *vishṇo iti*, or may follow 36.

d. Particles, when simple vowels, and ओ *o*, as the final of an interjection, remain unchanged, as इ इन्द्र *i indra*, 'O, Indra!' उ उमेश *u umeśa*, 'O, lord of Umá!' अहो इन्द्र *aho indra*, 'Ho, Indra!' (Páṇ. I. I, 14, 15.)

Observe—This applies also to the exclamation आ *á* (but not to the *á* which native grammarians call आङ् *áṅ*, and which is used as a preposition before verbs and before nouns with the meanings 'to,' 'up to,' 'as far as,' 'until,' 'a little'); e.g. आ एवम् *á evam*, 'Ah, indeed!' (but *á udakát* becomes *odakát*, 'as far as water;' *á ushṇa* becomes *oshṇa*, 'slightly warm').

e. Before initial अ *a* the ओ *o* of गो *go*, 'a cow,' remains unchanged and optionally cuts off the *a*; e.g. गोअग्रम् *go-agram*, or गोऽग्रम् *go-'gram*, 'a multitude of cows' (cf. 35. *a*. *b*, 36. Obs.).

Other Exceptions.

f. The final *a* or *á* of a preposition blends with the initial ऋ *ṛi* of a root into *ár* (not into *ar*); e.g. प्र ऋछ् = प्रार्छ् 'to go on;' उप ऋछ् = उपार्छ् 'to approach;' प्र ऋष् = प्रार्ष् 'to flow forth;' आ ऋछ् = आर्छ् 'to obtain' (Páṇ. VI. I, 91). Compare ~~260. a.~~ 251 a

g. The final *a* of a preposition is generally cut off before verbs beginning with ए *e* or ओ *o*; see 783. *k*. Obs. and 783. *p*. Obs. (Páṇ. VI. I, 89, 94).

Observe—The particle एव when it denotes uncertainty is said to have the same effect on a preceding final *a*.

h. The ऊ *ú* which takes the place of the वा of वाह् in the acc. pl. of such words as प्रष्ठवाह्, 'a steer training for the plough,' requires Vṛiddhi after *a*, as प्रष्ठौहस्.

i. The उ *u* of किमु may remain or be changed to व् *v* before a vowel, as किमु उक्तम् or किंवुक्तम् 'whether said.'

j. According to Śákalya, *a*, *i*, *u*, *ṛi* (short or long), final in a word, may optionally either remain unchanged (but, if long, must be shortened) before a word beginning with ऋ or follow the usual rule, thus ब्रह्म ऋषिः (or even ब्रह्मा ऋषिः 'a Brahman who is a Ṛishi') may be either ब्रह्म ऋषिः or ब्रह्मर्षिः, but in no case can ब्रह्मा ऋषिः be allowed to remain unchanged. Similarly, यथा ऋषि may be either यथर्षि or यथऋषि 'according to the Ṛishi.'

So in the case of *í* or *ú* or *ṛí*, final in a word, followed by dissimilar vowels, thus

चक्री अत्र is either चक्र्यत्र or चक्रि अत्र 'the discus armed here.' But compounded words follow the usual rule, as नदी उदक = नद्युदक 'river-water.' Except before words beginning with *ṛi*, as in the example कुमारीऋश्यः or कुमारिऋश्यः (Benfey's larger Gram. p. 52), and in असिऋद्धित 'made prosperous by (the power of) the sword,' Mahá-bh. XVIII. 105.

k. The words ओतु 'a cat' and ओष्ठ 'the lip,' when used in compounds, may optionally cut off a preceding final *a;* e.g. स्थूल ओतु is स्थूलोतु or स्थूलौतु; अधर ओष्ठ is अधरोष्ठ or अधरौष्ठ 'the lower lip;' (see Páṇ. VI. 1, 94. Várt.); and दिव ओकस् may be either दिवोकस् or दिवौकस् 'a deity.'

l. So also the sacred syllable ओम् and the preposition आ *á* may cut off a final *a;* e.g. शिवाय ओं नमः = शिवायों नमः 'Om! reverence to S'iva;' शिव एहि (i.e. आ with इहि) = शिवेहि 'O S'iva, come!'

m. The following words illustrate the same irregularity: शक अन्धु becomes शकन्धु; कर्क अन्धु becomes कर्कन्धु 'jujube;' लाङ्गल ईषा becomes लाङ्गलीषा 'plough-handle;' (see Gaṇa S'akandhv-ádi to Páṇ. VI. 1, 94.)

n. The following compounds are also irregular (see Páṇ. VI. 1, 89. Várt.):

अक्षौहिणी *akshauhiṇí*, 'a complete army' (from *aksha úhiní* for *váhiní*).

प्रौढ *prauḍha*, 'grown up' (from *pra úḍha*).

प्रौह *prauha*, 'reflection' (from *pra úha*).

स्वैर *svaira*, स्वैरिन् *svairin*, 'self-willed' (from *sva íra*).

सुखार्त *sukhárta*, 'affected by joy' (from *sukha ṛita*).

प्रार्ण *prárṇa*, 'principal debt' (from *pra ṛiṇa*).

कम्बलार्ण *kambalárṇa*, 'debt of a blanket' (from *kambala ṛiṇa*).

वसनार्ण *vasanárṇa*, 'debt of a cloth' (from *vasana ṛiṇa*).

ऋणार्ण *ṛiṇárṇa*, 'debt of a debt' (from *ṛiṇa ṛiṇa*).

प्रैष *praisha*, 'an invitation;' प्रैष्य *praishya*, 'a servant' (from *pra esha*).

The annexed table exhibits the combinations of vowels at one view. Supposing a word to end in *ú*, and the next word to begin with *au*, the student must carry his eye down the first column (headed 'final vowels') till he comes to *ú*, and then along the top horizontal line of 'initial vowels,' till he comes to *au*. At the junction of the perpendicular column under *au* and the horizontal line beginning *ú*, will be the required combination, viz. *v au*.

INITIAL VOWELS.	1 *a*	2 *á*	3 *i*	4 *í*	5 *u*	6 *ú*	7 *ṛi*	8 *ṛí*	9 *e*	10 *ai*	11 *o*	12 *au*
FINAL VOWELS.												
a or *á*	*á* 31	*á* 31	*e* 32	*e* 32	*o* 32	*o* 32	*ar* 32	*ar* 32	*ai* 33	*ai* 33	*au* 33	*au* 33
i or *í*	*y a* 34	*y á* 34	*í* 31	*í* 31	*y u* 34	*y ú* 34	*y ṛi* 34	*y ṛí* 34	*y e* 34	*y ai* 34	*y o* 34	*y au* 34
u or *ú*	*v a* 34	*v á* 34	*v i* 34	*v í* 34	*ú* 31	*ú* 31	*v ṛi* 34	*v ṛí* 34	*v e* 34	*v ai* 34	*v o* 34	*v au* 34
ṛi or *ṛí*	*r a* 34	*r á* 34	*r i* 34	*r í* 34	*r u* 34	*r ú* 34	*ṛí* 31	*ṛí* 31	*r e* 34	*r ai* 34	*r o* 34	*r au* 34
e 35, 36	*e* ’	*a á*	*a i*	*a í*	*a u*	*a ú*	*a ṛi*	*a ṛí*	*a e*	*a ai*	*a o*	*a au*
36. *a.*	*ay a*	*ay á*	*ay i*	*ay í*	*ay u*	*ay ú*	*ay ṛi*	*ay ṛí*	*ay e*	*ay ai*	*ay o*	*ay au*
ai 37	*áy*† *a*	*áy á*	*áy i*	*áy í*	*áy. u*	*áy ú*	*áy ṛi*	*áy ṛí*	*áy e*	*áy ai*	*áy o*	*áy au*
o 35, 36	*o** ’	*av*† *á*	*av i*	*av í*	*av u*	*av ú*	*av ṛi*	*av ṛí*	*av e*	*av ai*	*av o*	*av au*
au 37	*áv*† *a*	*áv á*	*áv i*	*áv í*	*áv u*	*áv ú*	*áv ṛi*	*áv ṛí*	*áv e*	*áv ai*	*áv o*	*áv au*

Observe, that in the above table, as in the examples, the final letter, in its changed state, has been printed, for greater clearness, separate from the initial; except in those cases where the blending of the two vowels made this impossible.

* If the initial *a* belong to a termination, suffix, &c., and not to a complete word, then *a* is not cut off, and *o* becomes *av* before it. See 36. *a.*

† If both the words are complete words, the *y* and *v* may be dropped throughout, but not so usually as in the case of *e*.

Sect. II.—EUPHONIC COMBINATION OF CONSONANTS.

39. Before proceeding to the combination of consonants, let the letters be again regarded as divided into two grand classes of Hard and Soft, as explained at 20. *b*.

HARD OR SURD.				SOFT OR SONANT.									
k	*kh*			*g*	*gh*	*ṅ*	*h*	*a*	*á*			
ć	*ćh*	*ś*		*j*	*jh*	*ñ*	*y*	*i*	*í*	*e*	*ai*	*ṉ*
ṭ	*ṭh*	*sh*	*ḥ*	*ḍ*	*ḍh*	*ṇ*	*r*	*ṛi*	*ṛí*			or
t	*th*	*s*		*d*	*dh*	*n*	*l*	*lṛi*	*lṛí*			*ṃ*
p	*ph*			*b*	*bh*	*m*	*v*	*u*	*ú*	*o*	*au*	

40. The stems of nouns and the roots of verbs may end in almost any letter, and these final letters (whether single or conjunct) are allowed to remain when the crude words stand alone; but *complete words*, when they stand alone or at the end of a sentence, can only, according to the native system, end in one of nine consonants (or, including Visarga and the Anusvára substituted for final *m*, eleven), viz. क् *k*, ट् *ṭ*, त् *t*, प् *p*, ङ् *ṅ*, ण् *ṇ*, न् *n*, म् *m*, ल् *l*, Visarga (ः), and Anusvára (*ṃ*); and even stems of words not ending in one of the above eleven letters are liable to undergo changes which shall make them so end, before the process of their euphonic union with other suffixes and other words in sentences is commenced.

Páṇini (VIII. 4, 56), however, seems to allow a word ending in one of the soft consonants *g*, *ḍ*, *d*, and *b*, optionally to stand at the end of a sentence or before a pause; e.g. वाक् or वाग्, &c.

41. In this Grammar the soft letters *g*, *ḍ*, *d*, *b*, the sibilant स् *s*, and the semivowel र् *r* will be admitted as possible finals of complete words standing alone, as well as of stems preparing for euphonic combinations; but the following five preliminary laws must be enforced under any circumstances, without reference to the initial letters of succeeding words.

FIVE PRELIMINARY LAWS.

I. A conjunct quiescent consonant (i. e. a conjunct consonant having no vowel after it) is not generally allowed to remain at the end of a word, but must be reduced to a simple one. As a general rule this is done by dropping every consonant except the first; thus *ćarants* becomes *ćaran*, *avets* becomes *avet*, *ćikírsh* becomes *ćikír* (see 166. *a*).

Observe, however, that क् *k*, ट् *ṭ*, त् *t*, प् *p*, when preceded by र् *r*, remain conjunct if both elements of these conjunct letters are either radical or substitutes for radical letters, e.g. *úrk*, nom. of *úrj*, 'strength' (176. *h*); *amárṭ*, 3rd sing. Impf. of rt. *mṛij* (Páṇ. VIII. 2, 24). But in *abibhar* for *abibhart*, *t* is rejected as not being radical (see the table at 583; cf. ἔτυπτον for ἔτυπτοντ).

II. An aspirated quiescent consonant is not allowed to remain final, but is changed to its corresponding *unaspirated* letter; e. g. चित्रलिख् *ćitralikh* becomes *ćitralik* (see 43); छ् *ćh*, however, usually becomes ट् *ṭ* (see under IV. below).

III. The aspirate ह् *h* is not allowed to remain final, but is usually changed to ट् *ṭ* (thus *lih* becomes *liṭ*); sometimes to क् *k* or त् *t** (see 182, 305, 306).

IV. Final palatals, as being of the nature of gutturals, are generally changed to gutturals; thus च् *ć* is usually changed to क् *k*, e.g. *váć* becomes *vák* (see 176); but छ् *ćh* becomes ट् *ṭ* (see 176); ज् *j* is changed to ग् *g* (or क् *k*) and sometimes to ड् *ḍ* (or ट् *ṭ*), (see 176) †. [Technical grammatical expressions are excepted; cf. 50. *b*.]

V. The sibilants श् *ś*, ष् *sh*, if final, are generally changed into ट् *ṭ*; sometimes, however, श् *ś* becomes क् *k*; and ष् *sh* either क् *k* or Visarga (see 181) ‡.

a. The above changes must hold good before all suffixes and terminations of nouns and verbs beginning with strong consonants (i.e. all consonants except nasals and semivowels), and before Taddhita suffixes beginning with nasals.

b. But before terminations of nouns and verbs beginning with vowels, and generally before weak consonants (i.e. nasals and semivowels), the finals of roots and stems remain unchanged (see *váć*, 176; *vać*, 650), even in opposition to the general rule which requires the softening of a hard letter when a soft letter follows.

GENERAL RULES FOR COMBINATION OF CONSONANTS.

42. If two hard or two soft unaspirated letters come in contact, there is generally no change; thus

विद्युत् प्रकाश *vidyut prakáśa* remains विद्युत्प्रकाश *vidyut-prakáśa*, 'the brilliance of lightning.'

---

* So in Arabic ة *h* becomes ت *t*.

† So in cognate languages *ch* is often pronounced as *k* or passes into *k*. Compare *archbishop*, *archangel*, *church*, *kirk*, &c. Again, *nature* is pronounced *nachure*, and *g* in English is often pronounced as *j*.

‡ Compare *parochial* with *parish*, and *nation* pronounced *nashun*.

कुमुद् विकास *kumud vikása* remains कुमुद्विकास *kumud-vikása*, 'the blossoming of the lotus.'

दृशद् अधोगति *driśad adhogati* remains दृशदधोगति *driśad-adhogati*, 'the descent of the rock.'

विद्युत् + सु *vidyut+su* remains विद्युत्सु *vidyutsu*, 'in lightnings' (loc. case plur.).

43. If any hard letter (except a sibilant, see 64–66) ends a word when any soft initial letter follows, the hard (unless affected by some special rule) is changed to its own soft, which must always be in the unaspirated form by 41. II. (but see *d.* below); thus

सरित् रय *sarit raya* becomes सरिद्रय *sarid-raya*, 'the current of a river.'

चित्रलिक् लिखित *ćitralik* (for *ćitralikh*, 41. II.) *likhita* becomes चित्रलिग्लिखित *ćitralig-likhita*, 'painted by a painter.'

वाक् देवी *vák* (for *váć*, 41. IV.) *deví* becomes वाग्देवी *vág-deví*, 'the goddess of eloquence;' similarly, वाक् ईश *vák íśa* becomes वागीश *vág-íśa*, 'the lord of speech.'

विट् भव *viṭ* (for *vish*, 41. V.) *bhava* becomes विड्भव *viḍ-bhava*, 'generated by filth.'

a. An option is allowed before nasals, as follows: When two words come together, the initial of the second word being a nasal, then the final of the first word is usually (though not necessarily) changed to the nasal of its own class (see Páṇ. VIII. 4, 45); thus

तत् नेत्रम् *tat netram* becomes तन्नेत्रम् *tan netram* (or *tad netram*), 'that eye.'

अप् मूलम् *ap múlam* becomes अम्मूलम् *am múlam* (or *ab múlam*), 'water and roots.'

सरित् मुख *sarit mukha* becomes सरिन्मुख *sarin-mukha* (or सरिद्मुख *sarid-mukha*), 'the source of a stream.'

b. Before *maya* and *mátra*, the nasalization is not optional but compulsory; thus

चित् मय *ćit maya* becomes चिन्मय *ćin-maya*, 'formed of intellect.'

वाक् मय *vák* (for *váć*, 41. IV.) *maya* becomes वाङ्मय *váṅ-maya*, 'full of words.'

विट् मय *viṭ* (for *vish*, 41. V.) *maya* becomes विण्मय *viṇ-maya*, 'full of filth.'

तत् मात्रम् *tat mátram* becomes तन्मात्रम् *tan-mátram*, 'merely that,' 'an element.'

c. In the case of roots followed by Krit suffixes there is not usually any change; e. g. छद् + मन् *ćhad+man* becomes छद्मन् *ćhadman*, 'disguise.'

d. It will be seen from 41. V. *a. b.* that the general rule 43 applies to case-endings of nouns beginning with consonants, but not to case-endings beginning with vowels. In the latter case, the final consonant attracts the initial vowel, so as to form with it a separate syllable; thus *vák* + *bhis* becomes *vág-bhis*, 'by words;' but in *vác* + *á*, *c* attracts *á*, thus *vá-cá*, 'by a speech' (not *váj-á*): *sarit* + *bhis* = *sarid-bhis*, 'by rivers;' but in *sarit* + *á*, *t* attracts *á*, thus *sari-tá*, 'by a river' (not *sarid-á*). So also *samidh* + *á* becomes *sami-dhá*, 'by fuel' (not *samid-á*).

e. Similarly, in the case of *verbal* terminations beginning with vowels or with *m*, *v*, *y*, attached to roots ending in hard letters (see *pat*, 597. *c*; *kship*, 635; *vac*, 650), rule 43 does not apply.

f. षष् 'six' (becoming षड् by 41. V.), when followed by the augment *n* before the case-ending आम् *ám*, becomes षण्णाम् *shaṇ-ṇ-ám*, because the final ड् becomes ण् and cerebralizes also the inserted *n* coming in contact with it. Similarly, षड् नवति becomes षण्णवति *shaṇ-ṇavati*, 'ninety-six,' and षड् नगर्यः becomes षण्णगर्यः *shaṇ ṇagaryaḥ*, 'six cities.' Compare 58. *b*.

44. If a soft letter ends a word or stem, when any hard initial letter follows, the soft is changed to its own hard, which must always be in the unaspirated form by 41. II; thus

कुमुद् + सु *kumud*+*su* becomes कुमुत्सु *kumutsu*, loc. pl. of *kumud*, 'a lotus.'
समिद् + सु *samid* (for *samidh*, 41. II.)+*su* becomes समित्सु *samitsu*, loc. pl. of *samidh*, 'fuel.'

Note—Similarly in Latin, a soft guttural or labial passes into a hard before *s* and *t*; thus *reg*+*si* becomes (*reksi*) *rexi*, *scrib*+*si*=*scripsi*, *reg*+*tum*=(*rektum*) *rectum*, &c.

a. With regard to palatals see 41. IV.

b. Soft letters, which have no corresponding hard, such as the nasals, semivowels, and ह् *h*, are changed by special rules.

c. If the final be an aspirated soft letter, and belong to a stem whose initial is ग् *g* or ड् *ḍ*, द् *d* or ब् *b*, then the aspiration, which is suppressed in the final, is transferred back to the initial letter of the stem; as बुध् + सु *budh*+*su* becomes भुत्सु *bhutsu*, loc. pl. of *budh*, 'one who knows' (177; cf. also *duh*, 182). Similarly दध् + तस् *dadh*+*tas* becomes धत्तस् *dhattas*, 'they two place;' and see 306. *a*, 299. *a*. *b*, 664.

Note—Greek recognizes a similar principle in τρέχω, θρέξομαι; τρυφ, θρύπτω: cf. also θρίξ, i. e. θρικ-ς from the stem τριχ-.

CLASSIFICATION OF SPECIAL RULES.

It is stated at 40, 41, that complete words as well as stems preparing for combination can only end in certain consonants. Of these the most usually occurring final consonants are त् *t* and द् *d*, the nasals न् *n* and म् *m*, the dental sibilant स् *s* (changed to Visarga by native grammarians), and the semivowel र् *r* (also by them changed to Visarga). It will be sufficient, therefore, for all practical purposes to give special rules under four heads:

1st, Changes of final त् and द्.

2nd, Changes of the nasals, especially न् and म्.

3rd, Changes of final स्.

4th, Changes of final र्.

CHANGES OF FINAL त् *t* AND द् *d*.

45. By the general rule (43), final त् *t* becomes द् *d* before soft consonants, and before vowels; as मरुत् वाति *marut váti* becomes मरुद्वाति *marud váti*, 'the wind blows.'

a. Certain exceptions are provided for by 41. V. *b*, 43. *d*. Hence also stems ending in *t* followed by the suffixes *vat, mat, vin, vala* do not necessarily change; e.g. *vidyut-vat*, 'possessed of lightning;' *garut-mat*, 'possessed of wings.'

46. And, by 44, final द् *d* generally becomes त् *t* before hard consonants; as दृशद् पतन becomes दृशत्पतन *dṛiśat-patana*, 'the fall of a stone.'

47. And, by 43. *a*, final त् *t* or द् *d* may become न् *n* before *n* or *m*.

Assimilation of final त् t *or* द् d.

48. If त् *t* or द् *d* ends a word, when an initial च् *ć*, ज् *j*, or ल् *l* follows, then त् *t* or द् *d* assimilates with these letters; thus

भयात् लोभात् च *bhayát lobhát ća* becomes भयाल्लोभाच्च *bhayál lobháć ća*, 'from fear and avarice.'

तद् जीवनम् *tad jívanam* becomes तज्जीवनम् *taj jívanam*, 'that life.'

a. A final त् *t* or द् *d* also assimilates with a following छ् *ćh* or झ् *jh*, but by 41. II. the result will then be *ć ćh; j jh;* thus तत् छिनत्ति becomes तच्छिनत्ति 'he cuts that;' तद् झषः = तज्झषः 'the fish of him.'

b. Final त् *t* or द् *d* assimilates in the same way with ट् *ṭ*, ड् *ḍ*, and their aspirates; thus तत् टीका becomes तट्टीका; तद् डीनम्, तड्डीनम्; तत् ठक्कुरः, तट्ठक्कुरः.

Observe—The converse does not take place in the contact of complete words; thus षट् ते (not षट्टे) 'those six:' but ईड् + ते = ईट्टे 'he praises,' see 325.

Final त् *t* or द् *d* may also assimilate with initial ङ् *ṅ* and ण् *ṇ*.

49. If त् *t* or द् *d* ends a word and the next begins with श् *ś* immediately followed by a vowel, semivowel, or nasal, then *t* or *d* is changed to च् *ć*, and the initial श् *ś* is usually changed to छ् *ćh;* e.g.

तत् श्रुत्वा *tat śrutvá* becomes तच्छ्रुत्वा *tać ćhrutvá*, 'having heard that;' but तच्श्रुत्वा *tać śrutvá* is allowable.

a. Similarly, the change of initial श् *ś* to छ् *ćh* is optional after a final क्; thus वाक्शत may either remain so or be written वाक्छत 'a hundred speeches.' Again, after a final ट् *ṭ* and प् *p* this rule is said to be optional; but examples are not likely to occur: though in Ṛig-veda III. 33, 1, we have विपाट्छुतुद्री for विपाट् शुतुद्री, the two rivers Vipáś and S'utudrí in the Pañjáb.

50. If त् *t* ends a word, when initial ह् *h* follows, the final त् *t* is changed to द् *d* (by 43), and the initial ह् *h* optionally to ध् *dh;* thus तत् हरति *tat harati* becomes तद्धरति *tad dharati*, 'he seizes that;' but तद् हरति *tad harati* is allowable.

a. By a similar rule, and on the same principle, any consonant (except a nasal, semivowel, or sibilant) followed by ह्, must be softened if hard, and its soft aspirate optionally substituted for the initial ह्; thus वाक् हरति *vák harati* becomes वाग्घरति *vág gharati*, 'speech captivates.'

b. Similarly, अच् ह्रस्वः *ać hrasvaḥ* becomes अज्झ्रस्वः *aj jhrasvaḥ*, 'a short vowel.'

Insertion of त् t *changeable to* च् *ć*.

51. When छ् *ćh* is between two vowels (long or short) in the body of a simple word, त् *t* changeable by 48. *a*. to च् *ć* must be inserted before छ् *ćh;* thus root प्रछ् *praćh* followed by a vowel must be written प्रच्छ *praććha* (as in पप्रच्छ *papraććha*, पृच्छामि, &c. at 631); so also चि * + छेद becomes चिच्छेद 'he has cut;' अ * + छिनत् = अच्छिनत् 'he was cutting' (see Páṇ. VI. 1, 73, 75).

Observe—In the case of root *murćh* there is no insertion of *ć* in *múrćhana*, &c., because *ćh* is not between two vowels.

a. This insertion of *ć* is obligatory when छ् *ćh* is initial, and when a previous syllable of any word, either separate or compounded, ends in a *short* vowel; as, शैलस्य च्छाया or शैलच्छाया 'the shadow of a rock.'

b. The same is obligatory after the preposition आ *á* and the particle मा *má;* as आ छन्न becomes आच्छन्न 'covered;' so मा छिदत् becomes मा च्छिदत् *má ććhidat*, 'let him not cut' (Páṇ. VI. 1, 74).

c. In all other cases after *long* vowels the insertion of च् *ć* is optional; as, बदरीछाया or बदरीच्छाया 'the shade of a jujube tree;' सा छिनत्ति or सा च्छिनत्ति 'she cuts' (Páṇ. VI. 1, 76).

d. An augment त् *t* may optionally be inserted after final ट् *ṭ* before initial स् *s;* as, षट्सन्तः or षट्त्सन्तः 'being six' (Páṇ. VIII. 4, 42; 3, 39).

---

* चि *ći* is the syllable of reduplication to form the perfect of छिद् *ćhid* (252), and अ *a* the augment to form the imperfect of all verbs (251).

CHANGES OF THE NASALS, ESPECIALLY न् *n*.

52. If the letter न् *n*, preceded by a *short* vowel, ends a word, when the next begins with any vowel, the *n* is doubled; thus

आसन् अत्र *ásan atra* becomes आसन्नत्र *ásann atra*, 'they were here.'

तस्मिन् उद्याने *tasmin udyáne* becomes तस्मिन्नुद्याने *tasminn udyáne*, 'in that garden.'

a. This applies equally to final ङ् *ṅ* and ण् *ṇ*; as प्रत्यङ् एति becomes प्रत्यङ्ङेति 'he goes towards the west;' सुगण् अस्ति = सुगण्णस्ति 'he is a good calculator' (see Páṇ. VIII. 3, 32); but these, especially the last, rarely occur as finals.

b. Technical terms in grammar, such as Uṇ-ádi (i. e. 'a list of suffixes beginning with *uṇ*'), are said to be exceptions to this rule.

53. If न् *n* ends a word, when an initial च् *ć* or त् *t* or ट् *ṭ* (or their aspirates) follows, a sibilant is inserted between the final and initial letter, according to the class of the initial letter; and the न् *n* then passes into the true Anusvára, see 6. *d*; e. g.

कस्मिन् + चित् *kasmin*+*ćit* becomes कस्मिंश्चित् *kasmiṇśćit*, 'in a certain person.'

अस्मिन् तडागे *asmin taḍáge* becomes अस्मिंस्तडागे *asmiṇs taḍáge*, 'in this pool.'

महान् टङ्कः *mahán ṭaṅkaḥ* becomes महांष्टङ्कः *maháṇsh ṭaṅkaḥ*, 'a large axe.'

a. The same holds good before छ् *ćh* (as, तांश्छादयति 'he covers them'), and before थ् *th*, ठ् *ṭh*; but the two latter are not likely to occur.

b. If *s* immediately follows *t* in a conjunct consonant, as in the word त्सरु 'a sword-hilt,' there is no change; thus सन् त्सरुः remains सन्त्सरुः.

c. A similar euphonic *s* is inserted between the prepositions *sam*, *ava*, *pari*, *prati*, and certain words which begin with *k*, as संस्कार *saṇs-kára*, संस्कृत *saṇs-kṛita*, परिष्कार *parish-kára*, प्रतिष्कार *pratish-kára*, &c. (see 70); just as in Latin, between the preposition *ab* and *c*, &c., e. g. *ab-s-condo*. Also, between पुम् 'a male,' and a word beginning with a hard consonant, as कोकिल 'a cuckoo,' thus पुंस्कोकिलः; also when कान् is repeated, e. g. कांस्कान् or काँस्कान् 'whom?' 'whom?' 'which of them?' (Páṇ. VIII. 3, 12, but cf. Vopa-deva II. 35.)

d. न् *n* at the end of a root does not require an inserted *s* before terminations beginning with *t*; thus हन् + ति *han* + *ti* is हन्ति *hanti*, 'he kills' (but see 57, 57. *a. b*).

e. Except, also, प्रशान् *praśán* (nom. of *praśám*, 179. *a*); as, प्रशान्तनोति 'the peaceful man spreads;' प्रशान्चिनोति 'the peaceful man collects' (Páṇ. VIII. 3, 7).

54. The only cases in which न् *n*, when originally the final of a word, can pass into Anusvára are given above at 53, 53. *a*; thus in classical Sanskṛit combinations like तान् करोति or तान् ददाति must not be written तां करोति, तां ददाति.

55. If न् *n* ends a word, when the next begins with श् *ś*, then न् *n* and श् *ś* may be combined in either of the two following ways:

1st, the final न् *n* may be changed to palatal ञ् *ñ*; thus महान् शूरः *mahán śúraḥ* may be written महाञ्शूरः 'a great hero.'

2ndly, the initial श् *ś* may be changed to छ् *ćh*; thus महाञ्छूरः.

a. According to native authorities an augment *t*, changeable to *ć* (51), may be inserted in both cases, thus महाञ्छूरः or महाञ्छ्छूरः, but this is rarely done; and in practice, both न् and श् are sometimes erroneously left unchanged against the rule (thus, महान् शूरः).

b. Final ङ् *ṅ* may optionally insert an augment क् *k* when any sibilant begins the next word or syllable. Hence प्राङ् शत may be either प्राङ्क्शत (or प्राङ्क्छत by 49. *a*) or may remain unchanged.

c. Similarly, final ण् *ṇ* may insert ट् *ṭ*, and final न् *n* may insert त् *t* before स् *s*; e.g. सुगण्, 'a good reckoner,' is in loc. pl. सुगणसु or सुगण्ट्सु; and सन् सः, 'he being,' may be सन्त्सः; and some say the inserted letters may optionally be aspirated. The insertion of त् between a final न् and initial स् is common in the Veda; but in later Sanskṛit these insertions are not usual.

56. If न् *n* ends a word, when the next begins with ल् *l*, the *n* assimilates with the *l*, and the Ćandra-vindu mark ँ is placed over the *l*, substituted for *n*, to denote its nasality; thus पक्षान् लुनाति becomes पक्षाँल्लुनाति or पक्षाल्ँ लुनाति 'he clips the wings;' see 7. Similarly, ἐν + λάμπω = ἐλλάμπω; *con*+*ligo*=*colligo*.

a. Final न् *n*, before ज् *j* or झ् *jh*, and ञ् *ñ*, is properly written in the palatal form ञ्, but in practice is often allowed to remain unchanged against the rule.

b. Final न् *n*, before ड् *ḍ*, ढ् *ḍh*, and ण् *ṇ*, should be written in the cerebral form ण्.

c. But final न् *n*, before gutturals, labials, semivowels (except य् *y*), and the sibilants स् *s*, ष् *sh*, remains unchanged; as, तान् षट् 'those six.'

57. न् *n* as the final of nominal stems is rejected before terminations and suffixes beginning with consonants; thus धनिन् + भिस् *dhanin* + *bhis* becomes धनिभिस् *dhanibhis*, 'by rich people;' युवन् + त्व *yuvan* + *tva* becomes युवत्व *yuva-tva*, 'youth.' Similarly *svámin* + *vat* becomes *svámi-vat*, 'like a master.' But राजन्वत् *rájan-vat* is excepted in the sense of 'having a good king.' (Raghu-v. VI. 22; Páṇ. VIII. 2, 14; cf. also उदन्वत् *udan-vat*, 'the ocean,' Raghu-v. X. 6.)

a. न् *n* as the final of a root is rejected before those terminations beginning with consonants (excepting nasals and semivowels) which have no indicatory P (see 307 and 323); thus हन्+*ti*P is हन्ति, but हन्+*tas* is हतस्, see 654.

b. Also, when a word ending in न् *n* is the first (or any but the last) member of a compound word, even though the next member of the compound begins with a vowel; e.g. राजन् पुरुष *rájan purusha* becomes राजपुरुष *rája-purusha*, 'the king's servant;' राजन् इन्द्र *rájan indra* becomes राजेन्द्र *rájendra*, 'chief of kings;' स्वामिन् अर्थम् *svámin artham* becomes स्वाम्यर्थम् *svámy-artham*, 'on the master's account.'

c. न् *n* not final, immediately preceded by a palatal, is changed to the palatal form; e.g. याच् + ना = याच्ञा 'prayer,' यज् + न = यज्ञ 'a sacrifice;' similarly, राज्ञी 'a queen,' fem. of राजन् 'a king.'

Change of न् n (*not final*) *to* ण् ṇ.

58. If न् *n* (*not final*, and having immediately after it any vowel, or one of the consonants न् *n*, म् *m*, य् *y*, व् *v*) follows any one of the

three cerebral letters ऋ *ṛi* (short or long), र् *r*, ष् *sh*, *in the same word* (*samána-pade*), then न् *n* must be changed to the cerebral ण् *ṇ*, even though any vowel or any of the guttural or labial consonants at page 15 (viz. *k*, *kh*, *g*, *gh*, *ṅ*, *h*, and *p*, *ph*, *b*, *bh*, *m*, *v*), or *y* or *Anusvára*, either singly or combined together or with any vowel, intervene; as in the following examples formed with suffixes or terminations: क्षिपाणि (635); कर्मणा (152); मृगेण (107); बृंहण 'causing to grow fat;' शृङ्गिण 'horned;' ब्रह्मण्य 'devout.' आचार्यानी *ááryání*, 'the wife of an Áćárya,' is an exception (Páṇ. IV. 1, 49. Várt.)*.

Obs. 1. न् *n* final (i. e. followed by Viráma) in a word is not so changed; e. g. दातॄन्, not दातॄण् (see 127).

Obs. 2. In a word like कुर्वन्ति, 'they do,' *t* immediately after *n* prevents the change. Similarly, रुन्ध्वस् (671).

Obs. 3. This change of a dental to a cerebral letter is called *nati* in the Práti-śákhyas.

a. The intervention of any of the palatal, cerebral, or dental consonants at p. 15, except *y* (viz. *ć*, *ćh*, *j*, *jh*, *ñ*, *ś*, *ṭ*, *ṭh*, *ḍ*, *ḍh*, *ṇ*, *t*, *th*, *d*, *dh*, *l*, *s*), prevents the operation of this rule, as in अर्चना 'worship;' सर्जन 'abandoning;' क्रीडन 'playing;' वर्त्मानि 'roads' (nom. pl. of वर्त्मन्); शृगालेन 'by a jackal' (149).

The intervention of a labial, *conjunct* with न् *n*, precludes any change in the conjugational forms of the verb तृप् 'to satisfy,' cl. 5. (तृप्नोति &c., 618), and in those of क्षुभ् 'to shake,' cl. 9. (क्षुभ्नाति &c., 694); see Páṇ. VIII. 4, 39. In the Veda, however, तृप्णोति is found. But the intervention of nasals, semivowels, or *h*, though conjunct with the न्, do not prevent cerebralization, as in अर्यम्णा (157); अराव्णा inst. c. of अरावन् 'hostile;' ग्राव्णा of ग्रावन् 'a stone.'

Observe—According to Páṇ. VI. 1, 16, the past pass. part. of *vraść*, 'to cut,' and *ruj*, 'to break,' should be वृक्ण, रुग्ण.

b. If two conjunct न् *n*s follow the letters causing the cerebralization, they each become ण्, as in विषण्ण *vishaṇṇa* † (540).

c. Even in compound words where ऋ, ॠ, ष्, र् are in the first member of the compound, and न् occurs in the second member, the change to ण may sometimes take place (especially when the separate ideas inherent in each word are lost sight of in a single object denoted), and sometimes is optional. When, however, the

---

* The whole rule 58 is thus expressed in the first two Sútras of Páṇini VIII. 4, रषाभ्यां णो नः समानपदे । अट्कुप्वाङ्नुम्व्यवायेऽपि. The vowel *ṛi* is supposed to be included in र. अट् stands for the vowels, diphthongs, *y*, *r*, *v*, and *h*; कु for the guttural class of consonants; पु for the labial; आङ् for the preposition आ; नुम् for Anusvára.

† Except a word like प्राणिणत् redup. aorist of अन् 'to breathe,' with प्र.

words do not, so to speak, merge their individuality in a single object, no change is generally allowed, but even in these cases it is impossible to lay down a precise rule. The following are a few examples: ग्रामणी 'a village-chief,' अग्रणी 'foremost,' रामायण 'the Rámáyaṇa,' वार्ध्रीणस 'a Rhinoceros' ('leather-snouted animal'), खरणस 'having a sharp nose,' but चर्मनासिका 'a whip,' and सर्वनामन् 'a pronoun,' स्वर्नदी or स्वर्णदी 'the river of heaven,' वृषनाशन 'a plant' (where वृषणाशन might be expected), गिरिनदी or गिरिणदी 'a mountain-stream,' आम्रवण 'a mango-grove,' ब्रह्महणम् (acc. of ब्रह्महन्) 'the killer of a Bráhman.' Similarly, वृत्रहणम् acc. c. of वृत्रहन् 'the slayer of Vṛitra,' but वृत्रघ्न (where *han* becomes *ghna*); सर्वाह्न 'the whole day;' and in other similar compounds when the first member ends in short *a*, but पराह्ण 'afternoon' (if from परा अहन्). See Páṇ. VIII. 4, 3, &c.

d. In a compound, न् *n* is not generally changed to ण् *ṇ*, if the first member ends in ष् *sh*, and the next word is formed with a Kṛit suffix containing न् *n*, as निष्पान, दुष्पान, यजुष्पावन (Páṇ. VIII. 4, 35).

e. If the second member of a compound contain a guttural or be monosyllabic, the change of न् *n* to ण् *ṇ* is necessary, as in स्वर्गकामिणौ, हरिकामेण (Páṇ. VIII. 4, 13), क्षीरपेण (Páṇ. VIII. 4, 12); but not in compounds with *agni*, as शराग्नि.

59. The prepositions अन्तर्, निर् (for निस्), परा, परि, प्र, and दुर् (for दुस्) require the change of न् *n* to ण् *ṇ* in most roots beginning with न् (which in the Dhátu-páṭha are therefore written with cerebral ण्); e.g. प्रणमति 'he bows,' अन्तर्णयति 'he leads inside,' निर्णुदति 'he drives out,' पराणुदति 'he drives away,' प्रणय 'guidance,' प्रणायक 'a guide,' परिणाह 'circumference.'

a. But in the following roots the न् is never changed, and these roots are therefore written in the Dhátu-páṭha with dental न् *n*: नृत् 'to dance,' नन्द् 'to rejoice,' नर्द् 'to roar,' नक्क् 'to kill,' नट् 'to dance*,' नाथ् 'to ask,' नाध् 'to ask,' नॄ 'to lead.'

b. In the case of नश् 'to destroy,' the change of न् into ण् only takes place, when श् is not changed to ष्, as प्रणश्यति, परिणश्यति, but प्रनष्ट, परिनष्ट (Páṇ. VIII. 4, 36).

c. In the case of हन् 'to kill,' the change of न् to ण् takes place except when ह् is changed to घ्, as in प्रहण्यते, प्रहणन, but प्रघ्नन्ति (Páṇ. VIII. 4, 24). An option is allowed when न् is followed by म् or व्, as in प्रहन्मि or प्रहण्मि, &c. (Páṇ. VIII. 4, 23).

d. When the preposition नि intervenes between the above-mentioned prepositions and the root, the change of न् into ण् takes place in the following verbs, गद्, नद्, पत्, पद्, मा, मे, सो, हन्, या, वा, द्रा, प्सा, वप्, वह्, शम्, चि, दिह्. In most other verbs the change is optional, as प्रनिभिनत्ति or प्रणिभिनत्ति (Páṇ. VIII. 4, 17, 18).

e. After prepositions containing an *r*, the *n* of certain suffixes like *ana* is liable to be cerebralized, but in the case of causal stems, and in some other cases, the

* According to some the resistance of this root to cerebralization is only when it belongs to class 10, and means 'to drop or fall.'

change is optional (see Páṇ. VIII. 4, 29-31); e.g. प्रकोपन or प्रकोपण, प्रयापन or प्रयापण. In प्रवेपन, प्रभञ्जन, प्रकम्पन, प्रगमन, प्रभान, &c., no change to ṇ is allowed (Páṇ. VIII. 4, 32, 34). In the case of root अन् 'to breathe,' the final becomes ण् in प्राण् and पराण्, making प्राणिति 'he breathes,' and पराणिति (Páṇ. VIII. 4, 19). The causal aorist allows two cerebral nasals, e.g. प्राणिणत्; as does also the desid. of पराण्, e.g. पराणिणिषति. In this way final न् may be changed to ण् at the end of a word, as in प्राण्, पराण्, formed from rt. an. But this is only true of rt. अन्. In no other case can final न् become ण्. When r is separated from the n of an by more than one letter, no change is allowed, as in पर्यनिति.

Changes of final म् m.

60. If म् *m* ends a word, when any one of the consonants *k*, *kh*, *g*, *gh*; *ć*, *ćh*, *j*, *jh*; *ṭ*, *ṭh*, *ḍ*, *ḍh*; *t*, *th*, *d*, *dh*, *n*; *p*, *ph*, *b*, *bh*, *m* follows, then म् *m* may pass into Anusvára, or may, before any one of those consonants, be changed to its own nasal; thus गृहम् जगाम *gṛiham jagáma* is written either गृहं जगाम or गृहञ्जगाम 'he has gone home;' and *nagaram prati* either नगरं प्रति or नगरम्प्रति 'towards the city;' but in these cases Anusvára is generally used. So also डीन preceded by prep. *sam* becomes either संडीन or सण्डीन 'flight;' सम् चय either संचय or सञ्चय 'collection;' सम् न्यास either संन्यास or सन्न्यास 'abandonment;' but in these cases Anusvára is not so usual.

a. The final म् *m* of a root is changed to न् *n* or ण् *ṇ* before suffixes beginning with any consonant except *y*, *r*, *l*, *s*; thus जङ्गम् + मि = जङ्गन्मि (see 709). So also चक्षम् + वहे = चक्षण्वहे (see 58; and Páṇ. VIII. 2, 65).

b. Before श्, ष्, स्, ह्, a final म् is represented by Anusvára; also generally before the semivowels, but see 6. *e*. *f*, 7.

c. With regard to final म् before ह् when followed by *m*, *n*, *y*, *l*, *v*, see 7. *c*.

d. When the next word begins with a vowel, then म् *m* must always be written; thus गृहम् आयाति becomes गृहमायाति 'he comes home' (not गृहं आयाति).

e. Observe—When न् *n* or म् *m* not final is preceded by छ् *ćh*, the latter becomes श् *ś*, as प्रछ् + न = प्रश्न 'a question;' विछ् + न = विश्न 'lustre' (Páṇ. VI. 4, 19); पाप्रछ् + मि = पाप्रश्मि 'I ask frequently.'

CHANGES OF FINAL स् *s*.

61. Many cases of nouns and many inflections of verbs end in स् *s*, which is changeable to श् *ś* and ष् *sh*, and is liable to be represented by Visarga (:, i.e. the sign for a hard breathing, see 8), or to pass into र् *r* (regarded as the corresponding soft letter of the

hard sibilants and Visarga). *As these changes will constantly meet the student's eye*, the following five rules must be carefully studied.

Observe—In other grammars these rules are designated 'rules for the changes of Visarga,' a sibilant not being allowed at the end of a complete word standing alone (see 40).

In the following pages, however, *s* is preserved as a final, both in declension and conjugation, for two reasons: 1st, because it is more easily pronounced than a mere breathing; 2ndly, because it keeps in view the resemblance between Sanskṛit and Greek and Latin terminations.

62. First Rule. *When does the final sibilant remain unrejected?*—Before त् *t*, च् *ć*, and ट् *ṭ*, and their aspirates, respectively; thus, final स् *s* before *t*, *th*, remains unchanged; before *ć*, *ćh*, passes into the palatal sibilant श् *ś*; and similarly, before *ṭ*, *ṭh*, passes into the cerebral sibilant ष् *sh*.

a. Final स् *s* is also allowed to remain unchanged before initial स् *s*, and to assimilate with initial श् *ś* and ष् *sh* *. More commonly, however, it is in these cases represented by Visarga; see 63.

b. So also, the final स् *s* of a root must always remain unchanged before the terminations *si*, *se*; thus शास् + से = शास्से; वस् + से = वस्से; see 304.

c. When an initial त् *t* is compounded with a sibilant, a preceding final *s*, instead of remaining unchanged, may become Visarga as if before a sibilant; e.g. हरिः त्सरुं गृह्णाति 'Hari grasps the sword-belt.'

d. For exceptions in *as*, *is*, *us*, see 69.

63. Second Rule. *When does final* स् s *pass into Visarga* (:)?—Before क् *k*, प् *p*, and their aspirates, and generally (but see 62. *a*) before the three sibilants स् *s*, श् *ś*, and ष् *sh* †.

a. Before a pause, i.e. at the end of a sentence.

b. When an initial sibilant is compounded with another hard consonant, the preceding final *s* is often dropped in MSS.; e.g. हरि स्कन्दति or हरिः स्कन्दति 'Hari goes.'

c. Nouns ending in *is* or *us* followed by verbs beginning with *k*, *p*, or their aspirates, and grammatically connected with these verbs, may optionally substitute *sh* for Visarga; e.g. सर्पिष्करोति or सर्पिः करोति 'he makes ghee' (Páṇ. viii. 3, 44).

64. Third Rule. *When does final* अस् as *become* o?—Before all *soft* consonants.

a. Similarly, before short अ *a*, which *a* is then cut off.

This rule is more properly, but less simply, stated thus. When does final स् *s*

* The assimilation of स् with an initial ष् is rare; but तयष्षष्ठ is an example.

† Examples before initial ष्, like तयःषष्ठ, are rare.

blend with a preceding *a* into the vowel *o*? Before all *soft* consonants final स् *s* is treated as if liquefied into *u* *.

b. The names of the worlds (*bhuvas, mahas, janas, tapas*, &c.) change *s* to *r* before soft consonants; e.g. *bhuvar-loka, mahar-loka*, &c.

65. Fourth Rule. *When does final* स् s *become* र् r?—When preceded by any other vowel but अ *a* or आ *á*, and before all *soft* letters, consonants or vowels.

a. Unless र् *r* itself be the soft letter following, in which case, to avoid the conjunction of two *r*'s, final स् *s* is dropped, and the vowel preceding it (if short) is lengthened.

The interchangeableness of *s, r*, and *Visarga* is illustrated in some Greek and Latin words; e.g. *flos, floris; genus, generis; labor* for *labos; sex* = ἕξ; *suavis* = ἡδύς, &c.

66. Fifth Rule. *When is final* स् s *rejected?*—When preceded by short अ *a*, before any other vowel except short अ *a* †. NB. The अ *a*, which then becomes final, opens on the initial vowel without coalition ‡.

a. When preceded by long आ *á*, before any soft letter, consonant or vowel. NB. If the initial letter be a vowel, the आ *á*, which then becomes final, opens on it without coalition.

b. When preceded by any other vowel but अ *a* or आ *á*, before the letter *r*, as noticed at 65. *a*.

c. Native grammarians say that final *s* passes into Visarga, which is then changed to *y*; which *y* is rejected in accordance with 36, 37.

The above five rules are illustrated in the following table, in which the nominative cases नरस् *naras*, 'a man;' नरास् *narás*, 'men;' हरिस् *haris*, 'the god Vishṇu;' रिपुस् *ripus*, 'an enemy;' and नौस् *naus*, 'a ship'—are joined with verbs.

---

* That is, it is first changed to *r*, as at 65, and *r* is then liquefied into a vowel; just as *l* is often changed to *u* in French. The plural of *animal* is *animaux*.

† That is, it blends with *a* into *o*, as in 64; and *o* becoming *av* before any vowel but *a*, the *v* is rejected by 36. Indian grammarians hold that final *s* or Visarga here becomes *y*, which would also be rejected by 36.

‡ This is one of the three cases in which a hiatus of two vowels is admissible in Sanskrit. The three cases are, 1. when final *s* is rejected from *as* or *ás* (66); 2. when a complete word, ending in *e*, is followed by any other vowel but *a* (see 36); 3. when certain dual terminations, ई *í*, ऊ *ú*, ए *e*, are followed by vowels (see 38). In the middle of a word a hiatus is very rare (see 5. *b*).

First Rule. Final sibilant remains unrejected.	**Second Rule.** Final स् *s* passes into Visarga.	**Third Rule.** Final अस् *as* becomes ओ *o*.	**Fourth Rule.** Final स् *s* becomes र् *r*.	**Fifth Rule.** Final स् *s* is rejected.
नरस् तरति *naras tarati* नरास् तरन्ति *narás taranti* हरिस् तरति *haris tarati* नौस् तरति *naus tarati* नरश् चरति *naraś ćarati* नराश् चरन्ति *naráś ćaranti* हरिश् चरति *hariś ćarati* नौश् चरति *nauś ćarati* Final *s* rarely remains unchanged before स *s*, and assimilates with श *ś*; thus, नरस् सरति *naras sarati* नरास् सरन्ति *narás saranti* हरिस् सरति *haris sarati* नरश् शोचति *naraś śoćati* नराश् शोचन्ति *naráś śoćanti* हरिश् शोचति *hariś śoćati*	नरः करोति *naraḥ karoti* नराः कुर्वन्ति *naráḥ kurvanti* हरिः करोति *hariḥ karoti* नरः खनति *naraḥ khanati* नराः खनन्ति *naráḥ khananti* हरिः खनति *hariḥ khanati* नरः पचति *naraḥ paćati* नराः पचन्ति *naráḥ paćanti* हरिः पचति *hariḥ paćati* नरः सरति *naraḥ sarati* नराः सरन्ति *naráḥ saranti* हरिः सरति *hariḥ sarati* नरः शोचति *naraḥ śoćati* नराः शोचन्ति *naráḥ śoćanti* हरिः शोचति *hariḥ śoćati* Before a pause, करोति नरः *karoti naraḥ*	नरो गच्छति *naro gaććhati* नरो जयति *naro jayati* नरो याति *naro yáti* नरो रक्षति *naro rakshati* Similarly, before all other soft consonants. Also before अ *a*, which अ *a* is then cut off; thus, नरोऽत्ति *naro 'tti* for *naro atti*	हरिर् अत्ति *harir atti* रिपुर् अत्ति *ripur atti* नौर् आयाति *naur áyáti* हरिर् एति *harir eti* रिपुर् एति *ripur eti* नौर् एति *naur eti* हरिर् गच्छति *harir gaććhati* रिपुर् गच्छति *ripur gaććhati* नौर् गच्छति *naur gaććhati* हरिर् याति *harir yáti* रिपुर् याति *ripur yáti* नौर् याति *naur yáti* Similarly, final *s* preceded by any vowel but *a* or *á*, before all soft letters except *r*. Before *r* final *s* also becoming *r* is rejected, and the preceding vowel lengthened; e.g. हरी रक्षति *harí rakshati* रिपू रक्षति *ripú rakshati*	नर आयाति *nara áyáti* नरा अदन्ति *nará adanti* नर ईक्षते *nara íkshate* नरा ईक्षन्ते *nará íkshante* नर एधते *nara edhate* नरा एधन्ते *nará edhante* नरा गच्छन्ति *nará gaććhanti* नरा यान्ति *nará yánti* नरा रक्षन्ति *nará rakshanti* Similarly, final अस् *as* before all other vowels except अ *a* (see third rule); and similarly, final आस् *ás* before all other soft letters, consonants or vowels.

67. There is one common exception to 62, 63, 64: सस् *sas*, 'he,' and एषस् *eshas*, 'this,' the nominative case masc. of the pronouns तद् *tad* and एतद् *etad* (220, 223), drop the final *s* before any *consonant*, hard or soft; as, स करोति *sa karoti*, 'he does;' स गच्छति *sa gaććhati*, 'he goes;' एष पचति *esha paćati*, 'this (man) cooks.' But rules 64. *a*, 66, and 63. *a*, are observed; thus, सोऽपि *so 'pi*, 'he also;' स एषः *sa eshaḥ*, 'he himself.' Sometimes (but only पादपूरणे to fill up a verse or suit the metre) *sa* may blend with a following vowel, as सैषः for स एषः.

In poetry *syas*, 'he,' nom. masc. of *tyad*, may optionally follow the same rule (Páṇ. VI. 1, 133).

Compare Greek ὁ for ὅς. Compare also Latin *qui* for *quis*, and *ille*, *iste*, *ipse*, for *illus*, *istus*, *ipsus*. The reason why *sa* dispenses with the termination *s* may be that this termination is itself derived from the pronoun *sa*.

68. The preceding rules are most frequently applicable to स् *s*, as the final of the cases of nouns and inflexions of verbs; but they come equally into operation in substantives or adjectives, whose stem ends in अस् *as*, इस् *is*, and उस् *us*; thus, by 65, चक्षुस् ईक्षते *ćakshus íkshate* becomes चक्षुरीक्षते *ćakshur íkshate*, 'the eye sees;' and चक्षुस् + भिस् *ćakshus* + *bhis* = चक्षुर्भिस् *ćakshurbhis*, 'by eyes.' Similarly, by 64, मनस् जानाति *manas jánáti* becomes मनो जानाति *mano jánáti*, 'the mind knows;' and मनस् + भिस् *manas* + *bhis* = मनोभिस् *manobhis*, 'by minds.'

Exceptions in अस् as, इस् is, उस् us.

69. अस् *as* at the end of the first member of a compound word retains its *s* before derivatives of the roots कृ and कम्, and before कंस, कुम्भ, पात्र, कुशा, कर्णी (see Páṇ. VIII. 3, 46); e.g. तेजस्कर 'causing light,' अयस्कार 'a blacksmith,' नमस्कार 'adoration,' तिरस्कार 'disrespect *,' पयस्काम 'a lover of milk.' The *s* is also retained in some other compounds, generally when the second member begins with क्, प्; as, दिवस्पति 'lord of day,' वाचस्पति 'lord of speech;' similarly also, भास्कर 'the sun.' Also before the Taddhita suffixes वत् *vat*, विन् *vin*, and वल *vala*; e.g. तेजस्वत्, तेजस्विन् 'possessing light.'

a. Words ending in इस् *is*, उस् *us*, such as हविस्, सर्पिस्, धनुस्, &c., and the prefixes निस्, बहिस्, आविस्, दुस्, प्रादुस्, when compounded with words beginning with क्, ख्, प्, फ्, change their final स् into ष् (Páṇ. VIII. 3, 41, 45); e.g. हविष्कृत् 'performing a sacrifice,' सर्पिष्पान 'drinking ghee,' धनुष्कर 'a bow-maker,' निष्कृत

---

* In forms of तिरस्कृ the retention of स् *s* is considered optional (Páṇ. VIII. 3, 42); e.g. तिरस्कर्तृ or तिरःकर्तृ.

'removed,' निष्फल 'fruitless,' बहिष्कृत 'excluded,' आविष्कृत 'made evident,' दुष्पान 'difficult to be drunk,' प्रादुष्कृत 'made manifest.'

b. Nouns ending in इस् *is*, उस् *us*, before the Taddhita suffixes मत् *mat*, वत् *vat*, विन् *vin*, वल *vala*, change the final स् *s* to ष् *sh* according to 70; e.g. अर्चिष्मत्, ज्योतिष्मत् 'possessing splendour,' धनुष्मत् 'armed with a bow.'

c. Similarly before Taddhita suffixes beginning with त् *t*, as *tva*, *tama*, *tara*, *taya*, &c. (see 80), final *s* of *is* and *us* is changed to *sh*, but the initial *t* is then cerebralized; thus ज्योतिस् + त्व becomes ज्योतिष्ट्व *jyotish-ṭva*, 'brightness.' So ज्योतिष्टम *jyotish-ṭama*, 'most brilliant.'

d. Similarly स्, liable to be changed to ष् according to 70, is retained before the suffixes क, कल्प, पाश, and when compounded with the nominal verb काम्यति; as, तेजस्क 'splendid,' यशस्क 'glorious,' पयस्कल्प 'a little milk,' सर्पिष्कल्प 'a little ghee,' यजुष्काम्यति 'he desires sacrifice' (Páṇ. VIII. 3, 39).

70. स् *s*, *not final*, if followed by a vowel or by *t*, *th*, *n*, *m*, *y*, *v*, or by certain Taddhita suffixes, such as *ka*, *kalpa*, &c. (see 69. *d*), passes into ष् *sh* when preceded by any other vowel but अ *a* or आ *á*, and when preceded by क् *k*, or र् *r*, or ल् *l*; thus अग्नि + सु *agni* + *su* becomes अग्निषु *agnishu*, 'in fires;' करो + सि *karo* + *si* = करोषि *karoshi*, 'thou doest;' वाक् + सु *vák* + *su* = वाक्षु *vákshu*, 'in words;' बिभर् + सि *bibhar* + *si* = बिभर्षि *bibharshi*, 'thou bearest.' See 69 and 69. *a*.

a. An intervening Anusvára or Visarga or sibilant does not prevent this rule; e.g. हवींषि, चक्षूंषि, हविःषु (or हविष्षु), चक्षुःषु.

b. In accordance with this rule, certain roots and their derivatives beginning with स् change their initials to ष् after the prepositions अभि, अधि, वि, नि, परि, प्रति, अति, अनु, अपि; thus, अभिष्टु from अभि and स्तु, परिषिच् from परि and सिच्, निष्णा from नि and स्ना; and the change may even be preserved though the augment अ *a* intervenes, as in न्यषिञ्चत् from सिच् with नि, अध्यष्ठात् from स्था with अधि; and though the reduplicated syllable of the perfect tense intervene, as अधितष्ठौ (but not always in either case, as अन्वस्थात्, अनुतस्थौ).

c. Hence roots beginning with *s* and followed by a vowel or a dental consonant are written in the Dhátu-páṭha as if beginning with *sh*; e.g. षिध् (for सिध्), ष्टु (for स्तु), ष्ठा (for स्था), ष्णा (for स्ना); and this applies also to the roots स्मि, स्विद्, स्वद्, स्वञ्ज्, स्वप्, &c.

d. Certain roots beginning with *s* resist all change to *sh* and are therefore always written with *s*; e.g. सृप्, सृज्, स्तृ, स्तॄ, स्त्यै, सेक्, सृ, स्पूर्ज्. In certain roots the change is optional, as in स्यन्द्, स्कन्द्, &c.

e. The root स्तम्भ् changes its initial to ष after अव, as अवष्टभ्नाति.

f. In a few roots the change is optional, as परिस्कन्दति or परिष्कन्दति, विस्फुरति or विष्फुरति; and there are cases where *s* is retained quite exceptionally, e.g. परिसेधति, अभिसेसिच्यते, परिसोढुम्.

g. The root अस् *as*, 'to be,' when it drops initial *a*, leaves the *s* liable to be changed to *sh* if it be followed by *y* or a vowel; e. g. अभिष्यात्, अभिषन्ति, निषन्ति, प्रादुःष्यात्, प्रादुःषन्ति (Páṇ. VIII. 3, 87).

Even in compounds the initial *s* of the second member of the compound may be affected by rule 70, especially if a single object is denoted, as in the names हरिषेण *hari-sheṇa* for *hari-sena*, युधिष्ठिर *yudhi-shṭhira* for *yudhi-sthira*; and in अग्निष्ठ *agni-shṭha* for *agni-stha*, 'a frying-pan.' So also in अग्निष्टोम, पितृष्वसृ, दुःषम, &c.

h. In compounds formed with साह् (rt. सह्), the initial becomes ष् where ह् is changed to a cerebral (ट्, ड्, or ढ्). See 182. *e*.

i. The स् of the suffix सात् is not changed, as अग्निसात्कृ 'to consume by fire.'

j. Observe—The preposition *nis* followed by the root *tap* does not become *nish* if repeated action is denoted; e. g. निस्तप् 'to melt (gold &c.) repeatedly' (Páṇ. VIII. 3, 102); otherwise निष्टप्.

CHANGES OF FINAL र् *r*.

71. For purposes of Sandhi nearly all words ending in र् *r* may be regarded as ending in स् *s*. Most of the cases in which the changes of final र् *r* differ from those of final स् *s* will be found below in large type.

a. Thus, by 63, प्रातर् काल *prátar kála* becomes प्रातःकाल *prátaḥ-kála*, 'the time of morning;' अन्तर् पुर *antar pura* becomes अन्तःपुर *antaḥ-pura*, 'the female apartments;' and *prátar snána* becomes प्रातःस्नान *prátaḥ-snána*, 'morning ablution.'

b. But *r* as the final of a stem, or as a radical letter, remains unchanged before a sibilant; thus वार् + सु = वार्षु (70); पिपर् + सि = पिपर्षि; चतुर् + सु = चतुर्षु (see 203, cf. 62. *b*); and sometimes before the hard letter प् *p* in compounds; as, गीर्पति *gír-pati*, 'lord of speech' (also written गीःपति, गीष्पति); स्वर्पति *svar-pati*, 'lord of heaven' (also written स्वःपति).

c. After the analogy of 62, प्रातर् तु *prátar tu* becomes प्रातस्तु *prátas tu*; and प्रातर् च *prátar ća* becomes प्रातश्च *prátaś ća*.

The transition of *r* into *s* before *t* is exemplified in Latin by *gestum* from *gero*, *ustum* from *uro*, &c. On the other hand, *r* in the middle of words is preserved before *t* in Sanskṛit, as in *kartum*, &c.

d. But in opposition to 64 and 66, final अर् *ar*, unlike अस् *as*, remains unchanged before any soft letter (consonant or vowel); thus प्रातर् आश *prátar áśa* remains प्रातराश *prátar-áśa*, 'morning meal;' पुनर् याति *punar yáti* remains पुनर्याति *punar yáti*, 'again he goes;' पुनर् उक्त *punar ukta* remains पुनरुक्त *punar-ukta*, 'repeated' (cf. *nir-ukta*, 'described,' for *nis-ukta*, by 65).

e. After the analogy of 65. *a*, final *ar* before initial *r* drops its own *r*, and lengthens the preceding *a*; as पुनर् रक्षति *punar rakshati* becomes पुना रक्षति *puná rakshati*, 'again he preserves.' Analogously, गीरथ *gí-ratha* (i.e. गिर् रथ *gir ratha*), 'epithet of Bṛihaspati.'

f. Analogously to 69. *c*, चतुर्+तय *ćatur*+*taya* becomes चतुष्टय *ćatush-ṭaya*, 'the aggregate of four.'

72. Prefixes such as *nir* and *dur* must be treated as originally ending in *s;* see *nis, dus*, 69. *a*.

73. र् *r* preceded by a vowel may optionally double a consonant immediately following; thus निर् दय *nir daya* may be written either निर्दय *nirdaya* or निर्द्दय *nirddaya*, 'merciless;' except ह् *h* and a sibilant followed by a vowel, as in चर्पुं 71. *b;* but *karshyate* may be written *karshshyate*. In doubling an aspirated letter, the aspiration of the first is rejected, as अर्द्धं (for अर्धं). ह् *h* is said to have the same effect in doubling a consonant immediately following; thus *brahman* may be written *brahmman;* but for the sake of simplicity it is better to avoid doubling in both cases, and write always *nirdaya* and *brahman*.

a. The doubling of consonants, when they come in contact with others, is constantly allowable in Sanskṛit, though not usual in practice. Thus, in any conjunction of two (or even more) consonants preceded by any vowel, especially if a semivowel be the last letter in the compound, the first letter, provided it be not र् or ह्, may be doubled (Páṇ. VIII. 4, 47); thus पुत्त्र may be written for पुत्र, मद्धत्र for मध्वत्र, इत्त्याकर्ण्यं for इत्याकर्ण्यं, but the more simple form is preferable.

b. Again, any one of the first four consonants of any class may be doubled before the nasal of its own class, and if this takes place the middle consonant is called the *yama* of the preceding; thus in *kkniti* (Páṇ. I. 1, 5) the second *k* is the *yama* or twin letter.

c. It should be noted that by Páṇ. VIII. 4, 65, there is an optional rejection of one of two homogeneous consonants after any consonant, so that कीर्त्ति may be written कीर्ति.

The following table exhibits the more common combinations of consonants at one view. In the top line of initial letters the aspirated consonants have been omitted, because it is a universal rule, that whatever change takes place before any consonant, the same holds good before its aspirate.

INITIAL VOWELS AND CONSONANTS.	1 अ *a*	2 आ, इ, *á, i,* &c.	3 क् *k*	4 ग् *g*	5 च् *ć*	6 ज् *j*	7 त् *t*	8 द् *d*	9 न् *n*	10 प् *p*	11 ब् *b*	12 म् *m*	13 य् *y*	14 र् *r*	15 ल् *l*	16 व् *v*	17 श् *ś*	18 स् *s*	19 ह् *h*
FINAL CONSONANTS.																			
क् *k* or ग् *g*	*g a*	*g á* *g i*	*k k*	*g g*	*k ć*	*g j*	*k t*	*g d*	*n n* *g n* 43.*a.b.*	*k p*	*g b*	*n m* *g m* 43.*a.*	*g y*	*g r*	*g l*	*g v*	*k ś*	*k s*	*g gh* 50.*a.*
त् *t* or द् *d*	*d a*	*d á* *d i*	*t k*	*d g*	*ć ć* 48	*j j* 48	*t t*	*d d*	*n n* *d n* 43.*a.*	*t p*	*d b*	*n m* *d m* 43.*a.*	*d y*	*d r*	*l l* 48	*d v*	*ć ćh* 49	*t s*	*d dh* 50
न् *n*	*nn* a* 52	*nn* á* *nn i*	*n k*	*n g*	*ṃś ć* 53	*ṅ† j*	*ṃs t* 53	*n d*	*n n*	*n p*	*n b*	*n m*	*n y*	*n r*	*l l*	*n v*	*ṅ† ś* or *ṅ† ćh* 55	*n s*	*n h*
अस् *as*	*o '* 64.*a.*	*a á* *a i* 66	*aḥ k* 63	*o g* 64	*aś ć* 62	*o j*	*as t* 62	*o d*	*o n*	*aḥ p* 63	*o b*	*o m*	*o y*	*o r*	*o l*	*o v*	*aḥ ś* 63	*aḥ s* 63	*o h*
आस् *ás*	*á a* 66.*a.*	*á á* *á i* 66.*a.*	*áḥ k* 63	*á g* 66.*a.*	*áś ć* 62	*á j* 66.*a.*	*ás t* 62	*á d*	*á n*	*áḥ p* 63	*á b*	*á m*	*á y*	*á r*	*á l*	*á v*	*áḥ ś* 63	*áḥ s* 63	*á h*
इस् *is*, ईस् *ís* उस् *us*, ऊस् *ús* एस् *es*, ऐस् *ais* ओस् *os*, औस् *aus*	*ir a* 65 *ur a* &c.	*ir á* 65 *ur á* &c.	*iḥ k* 63 *uḥ k* &c.	*ir g* 65 *ur g* &c.	*iś ć* 62 *uś ć* &c.	*ir j* 65 *ur j* &c.	*is t* 62 *us t* &c.	*ir d* *ur d* &c.	*ir n* *ur n* &c.	*iḥ p* 63 *uḥ p* &c.	*ir b* *ur b* &c.	*ir m* *ur m* &c.	*ir y* *ur y* &c.	*í r* 65.*a.* *ú r* &c.	*ir l* *ur l* &c.	*ir v* *ur v* &c.	*iḥ ś* 63 *uḥ ś* &c.	*iḥ s* 63 *uḥ s* &c.	*ir h* *ur h* &c.
र् *r*, preceded by *any* vowel.	*r a* 71	*r á* &c.	*ḥ k* 71	*r g* 71	*ś ć* 71	*r j*	*s t*	*r d*	*r n*	*ḥ p*	*r b*	*r m*	*r y*	*· r*	*r l*	*r v*	*ḥ ś*	*ḥ s*	*r h*

* *n* is only doubled if preceded by a short vowel.

† A final *n* before *ś* and *j* is often allowed to remain unchanged.

CHAPTER III.

ON SANSKṚIT ROOTS AND THE FORMATION OF NOMINAL STEMS.

Before treating of the declension of Sanskṛit nouns (*náman* or *sañjñá*), it is necessary to point out the peculiar method of forming the stem from the root.

74. Every Sanskṛit noun (including substantives, adjectives, pronouns, and numerals) has at least two distinct states prior to the formation of the nominative case; viz. 1st, a root (*dhátu*); 2ndly, a stem (*prátipadika* or *anga**) formed directly from the root or from a modification of the root, generally by the addition of a suffix (*pratyaya*); which stem becomes a complete word (*pada*) by the addition of a case-ending (*vibhakti*)†.

a. The root is of such importance in Sanskṛit that it should be clearly defined before another step is taken.

A root (*dhátu*) is to language what the primitive elements are to chemistry; it is that primitive part of a word which, being incapable of grammatical decomposition, is supposed to contain the primary meaning antecedent to any addition or modification. When a root has been developed in any way by the addition of letters or syllables or by internal change it becomes a stem, which again is subject to further development by the addition of letters or syllables called case-endings or inflexions (*vibhakti*), whether nominal or verbal. Thus *dána* and *dadá* are stems (the former nominal, the latter verbal) developed out of the root *dá*, but *dána* and *dadá* are not fully

---

* According to Páṇ. I. 4, 13, the term *anga* is used for the stem when speaking of some suffix (*pratyaya*) or termination which is required to be added to it, whereas *prátipadika* is a general term for a stem without reference to its suffix.

† The process of forming a complete word (*pada*), in the case of nouns, may be shewn, as it were algebraically, thus: Root (*dhátu*) + Suffix (*pratyaya*) = Stem (*prátipadika*); again, Stem (*prátipadika*) + Case-ending (*vibhakti*) = a complete word (*pada*); e.g. in the word *jan-a-s*, 'a person,' *jan* is the root, *a* is the suffix, and *s* is the masculine termination for the nominative case.

developed until they have received terminations or inflexions, when they become complete words (*pada*); thus *dána-m*, 'a gift;' *dadá-ti*, 'he gives' (cf. Lat. *do-nu-m*, Gr. *δί-δω-σι*).

b. There are in Sanskṛit about 2000 roots, and every one of these conveys some simple idea, conveniently expressed in English by the sign of the infinitive 'to,' as in *ad*, 'to eat,' though it must be noted that the simple root *ad* only denotes the *idea* of 'eating,' which appears under different modifications in its derivatives (see 76. *a*). The following are a few of the commonest roots, with the leading idea conveyed by each (omitting 'to'):

अद् *ad*, 'eat.'
अर्च् *arć*, 'honour.'
अस् *as*, 'be.'
आप् *áp*, 'obtain.'
इ *i*, 'go.'
इष् *ish*, 'wish.'
कम् *kam*, 'love.'
कृ *kṛi*, 'do.'
कृष् *kṛish*, 'draw.'
क्रम् *kram*, 'go.'
क्री *krí*, 'buy.'
क्रुध् *krudh*, 'be angry.'
क्षि *kshi*, 'waste away.'
क्षिप् *kship*, 'throw.'
ख्या *khyá*, 'relate.'
गम् *gam*, 'go.'
ग्रह् *grah*, 'seize.'
घ्रा *ghrá*, 'smell.'
चर् *ćar*, 'go.'
चि *ći*, 'collect.'
चिन्त् *ćint*, 'think.'
छद् *ćhad*, 'cover.'
जन् *jan*, 'produce.'
जि *ji*, 'conquer.'
जीव् *jív*, 'live.'
ज्ञा *jñá*, 'know.'
तन् *tan*, 'stretch.'
तप् *tap*, 'warm.'
तुद् *tud*, 'strike.'
त्यज् *tyaj*, 'quit.'
दह् *dah*, 'burn.'
दा *dá*, 'give.'
दिव् *div*, 'shine.'
दिश् *diś*, 'point out.'
दीप् *díp*, 'shine.'
दृश् *dṛiś*, 'see.'
द्युत् *dyut*, 'shine.'
द्रु *dru*, 'run.'
द्विष् *dvish*, 'hate.'
धा *dhá*, 'place.'
नन्द् *nand*, 'rejoice.'
नश् *naś*, 'perish.'
निन्द् *nind*, 'blame.'
नी *ní*, 'lead.'
पच् *pać*, 'cook.'
पत् *pat*, 'fall.'
पद् *pad*, 'go.'
पा *pá*, 'drink.'
पा *pá*, 'protect.'
पू *pú*, 'purify.'
प्रछ् *prаćh*, 'ask.'
बन्ध् *bandh*, 'bind.'
बुध् *budh*, 'know.'
ब्रू *brú*, 'speak.'
भक्ष् *bhaksh*, 'eat.'
भा *bhá*, 'shine.'
भिद् *bhid*, 'split.'
भी *bhí*, 'fear.'
भुज् *bhuj*, 'enjoy.'
भू *bhú*, 'become.'
भृ *bhṛi*, 'bear.'
मद् *mad*, 'rejoice.'
मन् *man*, 'think.'
मा *má*, 'measure.'
मुच् *muć*, 'liberate.'
मुह् *muh*, 'be foolish.'
मृ *mṛi*, 'die.'
यज् *yaj*, 'sacrifice.'
यत् *yat*, 'strive.'
यम् *yam*, 'restrain.'
या *yá*, 'go.'
यु *yu*, 'join.'
युज् *yuj*, 'join.'
युध् *yudh*, 'fight.'
रह् *rah*, 'quit.'
रुह् *ruh*, 'grow.'
लभ् *labh*, 'obtain.'
वच् *vać*, 'speak.'
वद् *vad*, 'speak.'
वस् *vas*, 'dwell.'
वह् *vah*, 'bear.'

विद् *vid*, 'know.'
विश् *viś*, 'enter.'
वृत् *vṛit*, 'be.'
शंस् *śaṇs*, 'praise.'
शक् *śak*, 'be able.'
शी *śí*, 'lie down.'
शुच् *śuć*, 'grieve.'
शुभ् *śubh*, 'shine.'
श्रु *śru*, 'hear.'
सह् *sah*, 'bear.'
साध् *sádh*, 'complete.'
सृ *sṛi*, 'go.'
सृज् *sṛij*, 'create.'
सृप् *sṛip*, 'creep.'
स्कन्द् *skand*, 'go.'
स्तु *stu*, 'praise.'
स्था *sthá*, 'stand.'
स्ना *sná*, 'bathe.'
स्पृश् *spṛiś*, 'touch.'
स्मि *smi*, 'smile.'
स्मृ *smṛi*, 'remember.'
स्वप् *svap*, 'sleep.'
स्वृ *svṛi*, 'sound.'
हन् *han*, 'kill.'
हस् *has*, 'laugh.'
हा *há*, 'quit.'
हृ *hṛi*, 'seize.'
हृष् *hṛish*, 'be glad.'
ह्लाद् *hlád*, 'be glad.'
ह्वे *hve*, 'call.'

75. A cursory glance at the above list of common roots will serve to shew that they are all monosyllabic. In other respects they differ. Some consist of a single vowel only; some begin with one or two consonants, and end in a vowel, but none end in either अ *a* or औ *au;* some begin with a vowel, and end in one or two consonants; and some begin and end with one or two consonants, inclosing a medial vowel; so that a root may sometimes consist of only one letter, as इ *i*, 'to go;' and sometimes of four or more, as स्कन्द् *skand*, 'to move.' Roots consisting of simple letters, such as कृ, भू, इ, जि, इष्, &c., are probably primitive; and those which have compound consonants, such as स्कन्द् &c., are in all likelihood developed out of more primitive forms*. Those with cerebral letters, such as लुट् 'to roll,' have some of them been formed by adopting sounds from aboriginal dialects.

a. The few polysyllabic words recognized as roots have probably resulted from a constant habit of joining some particular preposition with some particular monosyllabic root till it has at length come to be regarded as part of the root; e.g. in सङ्ग्राम् *sangrám*, 'to fight,' अवधीर् *avadhír*, 'to despise,' the prepositions सम् *sam* and अव *ava* have combined thus with the root. A few other polysyllabic roots are the result of the constant habit of reduplication; (as, दरिद्रा *daridrá*, to be poor;' जागृ *jágṛi*, 'to be awake;' चकास् *ćakás*, 'to shine;' वेवी *veví*, 'to go,' 'pervade;') and a few are derived from nouns; as, कुमार् 'to play,' from कुमार *kumára*, a boy.' Most of the latter are of the 10th class, and may be regarded as nominal verbs (see 288. *b*).

* Thus श्च्युत् *śćyut* (also written *śćut*), 'to drop,' beginning with three consonants, was probably merely developed out of rts. *ćyu*, *ćyut*, a sibilant and dental having been added (cf. 51, 53, 84. III).

b. न् *n* and स् *s* at the beginning of a root are liable, according to 58 and 70, to be changed to ण् *ṇ* and ष् *sh*. Hence these roots are generally represented in Native Grammars as beginning with ण् and ष्, because the Indian system exhibits that form which may occur under any circumstances (see 70. *c. d*). But in this Grammar, the real initials न् *n* and स् *s* will be retained.

c. According to Indian grammarians, roots are either *udátta* or *anudátta* (see explanation of accentuation at end of Grammar). *Udátta* roots take the inserted इ *i* in certain tenses (see 391), *anudátta* roots reject this inserted vowel (Páṇ. VII. 2, 10). Native grammarians attach to roots (either at the beginning or end) certain symbolical letters or syllables indicative of peculiarities of conjugation, called *anubandhas*, 'appendages' (or technically इत् *it*), which have the *udátta* accent on the vowel used as an anubandha, to shew that the verb takes the Parasmai (243) terminations only (such verbs being then called *udáttetaḥ*); or the *anudátta*, to shew that it takes the Átmane only (such verbs being *anudáttetaḥ*); or the *svarita*, to shew that it takes both (such verbs being *svaritetaḥ*). See Páṇini I. 3, 12. 72. 78.

The following is a list of Páṇini's *anubandhas* (with one or two added by Vopadeva):

आ indicates that the past participle suffixes (530, 553, called *nishṭhá* in native grammars) do not take the inserted *i*, VII. 2, 16. इ that a nasal is inserted before the last letter of the root in all the tenses; thus *nid-i* shews that the present is *nindámi* &c., VII. 1, 58. इर् that the Aorist (or 3rd Pret.) is formed in two ways, either with form I (418) or form II (435); thus *ghush-ir* shews that the Aor. is either *aghoshisham* &c. or *aghusham* &c., and *dṛiś-ir* that the Aor. is either *adrákshaṃ* or *adarśam*. ई that the past participle (530, 553) is formed without *i*, VII. 2, 14. उ that the indeclinable participle (555) may optionally reject *i*, while the past part. always rejects it, VII. 2, 56, 15. ऊ that *i* may optionally be inserted in the general tenses, VII. 2, 15. ऋ that in the Caus. Aor. the radical long vowel must not be shortened, VII. 4, 2. ॠ that the vowel may be either lengthened or shortened in the Caus. Aor. ऌ that the Aor. takes form II (435) in the Par., III. 1, 55. ए that Vṛiddhi is not admitted in the Aor. Par., VII. 2, 5. ओ that the past pass. part. is formed with *na* instead of *ta*, VIII. 2, 45. औ that a root is *anudátta*, i.e. that it rejects the inserted *i*. ङ् that a root is inflected in the Átm., I. 3, 12. ञ् that a root is inflected in the Par. and Átm., I. 3, 72. ञि that the past part. has a present signification, III. 2, 187. टु that a noun with the suffix *athu* may be formed from the root; thus *ṭu-kshu* indicates that *kshavathu* may be formed from *kshu*, III. 3, 89. डु that a noun with the suffix *trima* may be formed from the root; thus *ḍu-kṛi* shews that *kṛitrima* may be formed from *kṛi*, III. 3, 88. म् that the vowel *a* must not be lengthened in forming the Causal, that in the 3rd sing. Aor, pass. (technically called *ćiṇ*, 475) and indec. part. of repetition (567, technically named *ṇamul*) the vowel can be optionally lengthened or shortened, and that nouns of agency in *a* (580) can be formed from Causal stems having short radical vowels, VI. 4, 92. 93.

94. अ that a noun may be formed from the root by adding the suffix *á* (80. I), III. 3, 104.

76. Since every word in Sanskṛit, whether substantive, adjective, verb, or adverb, stands in close filial relationship to its root, the learner is recommended to commit to memory the commonest roots, as given at 74. *b.* He will thus become master of a large family of words, which are easily remembered when attention is directed to the leading radical idea running through them all.

a. For example: let him take one of the foregoing roots, *budh*, 'to know;' out of it are developed, 1st, a set of simple substantives; 2ndly, of simple adjectives; 3rdly, of simple verbs: e. g. *bodha* or *bodhana*, 'knowledge;' *buddhi*, 'intellect;' *bodhaka*, 'an informer;' *bauddha*, 'a Buddhist;' *budha*, 'wise;' *buddhimat*, 'intellectual;' and the following verbs, *bodhati*, 'he knows;' *budhyate*, 'it is known;' *bodhayati*, 'he informs;' *bubhutsate* or *bubodhishati*, 'he wishes to know;' *bobudhyate*, 'he knows well.' And the simple idea contained in the root may be endlessly extended by the prefixing of prepositions; as, *prabodha*, 'vigilance;' *prabudhyate*, 'he awakes,' &c.

b. Similarly, from the root *man*, 'to think,' a vast number of derivatives are developed, throughout all of which the leading radical idea is traceable; e. g. *ma-ta* (i. e. *man+ta*), 'thought,' 'an opinion;' *ma-ti* (i. e. *man+ti*), 'mind;' *mati-mat*, 'mind-possessing;' *man-ana*, 'thoughtful;' *man-as*, 'mind;' *manas-vin*, 'intelligent;' *maná*, 'devotion;' *maná-yu*, 'zealous;' *man-íshá*, 'reflection;' *maní-shita*, 'desired;' *manishin*, 'wise;' *man-u*, 'man;' *man-tu*, 'an adviser;' *man-tṛi*, 'a thinker;' *man-tra*, 'a sacred text;' *mantrin*, 'a counsellor;' *mantri-tva*, 'office of a minister;' *man-maṇ*, 'desire;' *manyu*, 'courage;' *mána*, 'pride;' *mánana*, 'honouring;' *mánava*, 'belonging to man,' &c.; *mánasa*, 'mental;' *mánita*, 'honoured;' *mánin*, 'proud;' *mánusha*, 'human;' *mímáṃsá* (from the Desid. stem), 'investigation;' *mímáṃsya*, 'to be investigated.'

Similarly, after prefixing prepositions (such as *anu*, *abhi*, *ava*, *ni*, *prati*, *vi*, *sam*, &c.) to the root, the meaning may be extended and a large number of derivatives formed; e. g. from *anu-man*, 'to assent:'—*anu-mata*, 'agreed to;' *anu-mati*, 'assent;' *anu-manana*, 'assenting.' From *ava-man*, 'to despise;'—*ava-mata*, 'despised;' *ava-mati*, 'disrespect;' *ava-mána* and *ava-mánana*, 'dishonour;' *ava-mánin*, 'holding in contempt;' *avamáni-tá*, 'disrespectfulness.'

77. It has been shewn at 74 that a stem (*prátipadika*) is an intermediate state between the root and nominative case—the crude form of the noun, which serves as a kind of stock out of which its eight cases, beginning with the nominative, are made, as it were, to grow. In a Greek or Latin dictionary we look for the noun under the nominative case; but in Sanskṛit we look for it under its stem. Thus, *bodha*, *bodhana*, *tat*, *pañćan*, *bhavat* are the stems under

which the nominative cases *bodhas, bodhanam, sas, pańća, bhaván* are to be sought.

The stem is, in truth, no mere useless grammatical invention. It is that form of the noun which, with occasional modifications, is used in the formation of compound words, and in this respect may be regarded as the most general of cases. And since every Sanskṛit sentence contains more compound words than simple, it may even be said, that the stem is the form under which the noun most usually appears.

Similarly, Greek and Latin grammarians might have supposed a root λεγ, from which was drawn out the nouns λέξις, λεξικός, λεκτός, καταλογή, ἔλλογος, and the verbs λέγω, καταλέγω, ἐλλογέω: so also, a root *scrib*, from which was derived the nouns *scriptio, scriptum, scriptor, scriptura;* and the verbs *scribo, perscribo, ascribo:* or a root *nau*, from which would come *nauta, navis, nauticus, navalis, navigo*, &c. And a stem λεξι and λεξικο of λέξι-ς and λεξικό-ς, and *navi* of *navi-s;* which stem is, in fact, the form used in the formation of compound words, as in λεξικο-γράφο-ς and *navi-ger*.

78. It will now be perceived that the consideration of Sanskṛit nouns must divide itself into two heads: 1st, the formation of the stem; 2ndly, the inflexion or declension of the stem; that is, the adaptation of the stem to a common scheme of case-terminations.

a. In fact, the same system applies both to nouns and verbs. As in verbs (see 248) the formation of a verbal stem from a root precedes the subject of verbal inflexion or conjugation, so in nouns the method of forming the stem from the root precedes declension.

b. Moreover, nouns, substantive and adjective, are classified into separate declensions, according to the finals of their *stems*, not according to the finals of their nominative cases. In Greek and Latin grammars a similar system of classification is now adopted.

c. The final syllable of nominal stems may end in almost any letter of the alphabet except ङ् *n*, ञ् *ñ*, and य् *y*.

Those stems that end in vowels may be conveniently separated under four classes, each class containing masc., fem., and neuter nouns; the 1st ending in अ *a*, आ *á*, and ई *í;* the 2nd in इ *i;* the 3rd in उ *u;* and the 4th in ऋ *ṛi*.

Those that end in consonants may also be arranged under four classes; the 1st, 2nd, and 3rd, ending in त् *t* and द् *d*, न् *n*, and स् *s*, respectively (compare 44); and the 4th comprising all other final consonants.

Primary and Secondary Derivatives.

79. Nominal stems (*prátipadika*), formed by means of suffixes (*pratyaya*), are of two kinds: 1. Primary derivatives formed immediately from a root, or from a modified form of it, by addition of a *Kṛit*-suffix (hence called *Kṛid-anta*, 'ending in a *Kṛit*-suffix,' the word *Kṛit* being an example of a primary derivative); under which head are included some participles formed with *aníya*, *tavya*, *ya* (which with *elima* are sometimes called *Kṛitya* suffixes); as also words formed with *Uṇádi* * suffixes. 2. Secondary derivatives, formed from the stems of primary derivatives by means of Taddhita suffixes, and therefore called secondary (for examples see 80. A. B).

Observe—It is not intended that the student should commit the following lists of suffixes to memory, but he is recommended to note carefully the final letters of the stem under each of the eight classes.

FORMATION OF THE STEMS OF NOUNS.

80. First Class.—*Stems ending in* अ a (m. n.); *in* आ á *and* ई í (f.)

A. Primary Derivatives, formed from Roots by adding the following *Kṛit* suffixes—

Observe—A list of adverbial suffixes will be found at 718–725, and the participial suffixes will be more fully explained 524–582. Feminine suffixes must be looked for under their corresponding masculine forms. In the examples which follow, the meaning of roots will not be given when they coincide with that of their derivatives. Thus when *bheda*, 'division,' is said to come from *bhid*, it is implied that the root *bhid* means 'to divide.' In a few cases the meanings of roots are omitted when doubtful. *From* is written fr.; *Root*, rt.

I. अ *-a*, forming, 1st, abstract nouns, generally masculine, after Vṛiddhi of a medial radical *a* and Guṇa (with some exceptions) of a vowel capable of gunation; a final palatal *ć* or *j* being changed to its corresponding guttural *k* or *g*† (cf. 20. c, 24, 25); e.g. *bheda*, m. 'division,' fr. *bhid*; *veda*, m. 'knowledge,' fr. *vid*;

* A list of suffixes 'beginning with the suffix *uṇ*' (i.e. *u*, with the indicatory letter *ṇ*), so called from the words *káru*, *váyu*, &c. in the first Sútra being formed with this suffix. The sense of Uṇádi derivatives frequently does not agree with the meaning of the root, and even when it does, usually receives a special signification; e.g. *káru*, though it involves the general idea of *doing*, means especially 'an artizan.'

† Forms like *paća*, *varja*, &c. (from *pać*, *vṛij*), generally found at the end of a compound, retain the palatal; e.g. *kim-paća*, *rasa-varja*, &c.

bhava, *bháva*, m. 'existence,' fr. *bhú*; *bhara*, *bhára*, m. 'a load,' fr. *bhṛi*, 'to bear;' *bodha*, m. 'knowledge,' fr. *budh*; *jaya*, m. 'conquest,' fr. *ji*; *páka*, m. 'cooking,' fr. *pać*; *yoga*, m. 'joining' &c., *yuga*, n. 'a yoke,' fr. *yuj*; *yága*, m. 'a sacrifice,' fr. *yaj*.

Forming, 2ndly, other nouns, substantive and adjective, especially nouns of agency (fem. *á*, sometimes *í*); e.g. *plava*, 'what swims,' fr. *plu*; *sarpa*, 'what creeps,' fr. *sṛip*; *deva*, 'a god,' fr. *div*, 'to shine;' *ćara* (fem. *í*), 'one who goes,' fr. *ćar*; *jana*, 'a man,' fr. *jan*, 'to produce;' *śubha*, 'beautiful,' fr. *śubh*; *kara*, 'doing,' fr. *kṛi*; *jaya*, 'conquering,' fr. *ji*; *dama*, 'subduing,' fr. *dam*. Cf. Gr. forms in *ο* = Sk. *a*; e.g. λύκο-ς, λόγο-ς, φόρο-ς, φορό-ς, ζυγό-ν, ἔργο-ν, &c.: Lat. *sonu-s*, *deu-s*, *vivu-s*, &c. Words like *kara*, *ćara*, *jaya*, *plava* often occur at the end of such compounds; as, *bhayan-kara* or *bhaya-kara* (fem. *í*), 'fear-causing' (see 580); *arin-dama*, 'foe-taming;' (cf. ἱππό-δαμος, *veri-dicus*, *grandi-loquus*, *omni-vorus*, &c.) When *su*, 'well,' and *dus*, 'ill,' are prefixed to such words, they take a Passive sense, as in Greek (576. *a*); e.g. *su-kara* (fem. generally *í*), 'easy to be done;' *dush-kara* (fem. generally *í*), 'difficult to be done,' &c. Cf. εὔ-φορος, δύς-φορος, δύς-τομος, &c.

आ -*á*, frequently without change of the radical vowel, forming feminine substantives (Páṇ. III. 3, 103–105); e.g. *bhidá*, 'splitting,' fr. *bhid*; *kshudhá*, 'hunger,' fr. *kshudh*; *mudá*, 'joy,' fr. *mud*, 'to rejoice;' *spṛihá*, 'desire,' fr. *spṛih*; *lekhá*, 'writing,' fr. *likh*; *jará*, 'old age,' fr. *jṛí*, 'to grow old:' often added to the desiderative stem (Páṇ. III. 3, 102); e.g. *pipásá*, 'thirst,' fr. Desid. of *pá*, 'to drink:' sometimes to the intensive stem; e.g. *lolúyá*, 'determination to cut,' fr. Intens. of *lú*, 'to cut.' Cf. Gr. forms in α, η; e.g. φορ-ά, φυγ-ή, τομ-ή, σπουδ-ή: Lat. *tog-a*, *mol-a*.

ई -*í*, forming a large class of feminine nouns, generally corresponding to masculines in *a* (see 123); e.g. *gopí*, 'a herdsman's wife' (see Páṇ. IV. 1, 48); *deví*, 'a goddess;' *nadí*, 'a river;' *vṛikí* (nom. *ís*), 'a she-wolf;' *siṇhí*, 'a lioness;' *putrí*, 'a daughter.' Many of such feminines in *á* and *í* are not strictly formed with Kṛit suffixes, being rather derived from masculines, or formed with Taddhita suffixes: some words like *Indra*, 'the god Indra,' have a fem. form for the goddess; e.g. *Indráṇí*, 'the wife of Indra.'

II. अक -*aka* (having six technical names, वुन्, वुन्, ष्वुन्, वुञ्, णवुल्, वुष्), forming adjectives (fem. *aká* or *iká*) and nouns of agency (see 582. *b*), after Vṛiddhi of a final vowel and generally of medial *a*, and Guṇa of any other vowel; e.g. *táp-aka*, 'inflammatory,' fr. *tap*, 'to burn;' *kár-aka*, 'a doer,' fr. *kṛi*; *náy-aka*, 'a leader,' fr. *ní*; *nart-aka*, 'a dancer,' fr. *nṛit*; *sádh-aka* (fem. *aká* or *iká*), 'effective,' fr. *sádh*; *khan-aka*, 'a digger,' fr. *khan*.

Observe—The feminine of the agents is usually formed with *iká*; e.g. *káriká*, *náyiká*.

III. अत्र -*a-tra*. See -*tra*.

IV. अन -*ana* (having nine technical names, क्यु, क्युन्, युच्, युन्, ल्यु, ल्युन्, ल्युट्, ख्युट्, ख्युन्), forming, 1st, a large class of chiefly neuter substantives after

Guṇa of the root; e. g. *nay-ana*, n. 'the eye,' fr. *ní*, 'to guide;' *dána*, n. 'a gift,' fr. *dá; sthána*, n. 'place,' fr. *sthá*, 'to stand;' *darp-aṇa*, 'a mirror,' fr. *dṛip*, 'to make proud;' *ćay-ana*, n. 'collection,' fr. *ći; vad-ana*, 'the mouth,' fr. *vad*, 'to speak;' *śay-ana*, 'a couch,' fr. *śí*, 'to lie down.'

Forming, 2ndly, nouns of agency (see 582. *c*) and adjectives (fem. *aná* or *aní*); as, *nart-ana*, 'a dancer,' fr. *nṛit; śobh-ana*, 'bright,' fr. *śubh*.

Observe—The feminine of the agents is in *aní*. Cf. ὄργανο-ν, δρέπανο-ν, ἱκανό-ς, πιθανό-ς, &c.

V. अनीय -*aníya*, forming future passive participles (see 570) after Guṇa of a radical vowel liable to gunation; e. g. *ćay-aníya*, 'to be collected,' fr. *ći*, 'to collect.' According to Schleicher -*aníya* is for -*ana*+*ya*.

VI. आ -*á*. See page 58.

VII. आक -*áka* (fem. *ákí*), forming a few adjectives and nouns of agency; e. g. *jalp-áka*, 'chattering,' fr. *jalp; bhiksh-áka*, m., *bhiksh-ákí*, f. 'a beggar,' fr. *bhiksh*.

VIII. आन -*ána* (शानच्, चानश्, शानन्, चानच्), forming, 1st, present participles Átm. (see 526; cf. -*mána*, XXVII); e. g. *lih-ána*, 'licking,' fr. *lih; śay-ána*, 'lying down,' fr. *śí; ćinv-ána*, 'collecting,' fr. *ći-nu*, present stem of *ći*.

Forming, 2ndly, perfect participles Átm. (see 554. *d*); e. g. *bubhuj-ána*, 'one who has bent,' fr. *bu-bhuj*, perfect stem of *bhuj*, 'to bend;' *dadṛiś-ána*, 'one who has seen,' fr. *da-dṛiś*, perfect stem of *dṛiś*.

IX. इत -*i-ta*, इतव्य -*i-tavya*. See -*ta*, -*tavya*.

X. इर -*ira*, इल -*ila*. See -*ra*, -*la*.

XI. ई -*í*. See page 58.

XII. उक -*uka* (कुकन्, उकन्, उकञ्, लुकञ्, षुकन्), forming a few adjectives after Guṇa or Vṛiddhi of a radical vowel; e. g. *varsh-uka*, 'rainy,' fr. *vṛish; kám-uka*, 'amorous,' fr. *kam*.

XIII. ऊक -*úka*, forming adjectives and nouns of agency from intensive stems; e. g. *vávad-úka*, 'talkative,' fr. Intens. of *vad*, 'to speak;' *yáyaj-úka*, 'constantly sacrificing,' fr. Intens. of *yaj*, 'to sacrifice.'

XIV. एन्य -*enya*, forming a kind of future passive participle after either gunation or weakening of the root; e. g. *var-eṇya*, 'desirable,' fr. *vṛi*, 'to choose;' *uś-enya*, 'to be wished,' fr. *vaś*, 'to wish.'

XV. एर -*era*, forming a few adjectives and substantives; e. g. *pat-era*, 'flying,' 'a bird,' fr. *pat*, 'to fly;' *muh-era*, 'a fool,' fr. *muh*.

XVI. क -*ka*, forming a few words; e. g. *śush-ka*, 'dried up,' fr. *śush* (see 548); *dhá-ka*, m. 'a receptacle,' fr. *dhá*, 'to hold.' Cf. Gr. θή-κη: Lat. *lo-cu-s*, *pau-cu-s*. For the Taddhita suffix -*ka*, see LVI.

XVII. त -*ta*, -*i-ta*, forming past passive participles (see 530 &c.); sometimes without change of the root; sometimes with weakening of the root; sometimes with rejection of the final nasal of a root; frequently with insertion of *i* (which takes the place of *aya* in Causals and verbs of the 10th class); e. g. *śru-ta*, 'heard,' fr. *śru; jñá-ta*, 'known,' fr. *jñá; kṛi-ta*, 'done,' fr. *kṛi; sthi-ta*, 'stood,' fr. *sthá; ga-ta*, 'gone,' fr. *gam; ta-ta*, 'stretched,' fr. *tan; pat-i-ta*, 'fallen,' fr. *pat; gṛih-í-ta*, 'seized,' fr. *grah* (inserted *i* lengthened); *ved-i-ta*, 'made known,' fr. Caus. of *vid*. Cf. Gr. κλυ-τό-ς, γνω-τό-ς, στα-τό-ς: Lat. *da-tu-s, sta-tu-s, (g)no-tu-s*, &c.

XVIII. तव्य *-tavya, -i-tavya*, forming future passive participles from the stem of the first future (see 569); e.g. *kar-tavya*, 'to be done,' fr. *kṛi; dá-tavya*, 'to be given,' fr. *dá; sto-tavya*, 'to be praised,' fr. *stu; ćhet-tavya* (for *ćhed-tavya*), 'to be cut,' fr. *ćhid; yok-tavya*, 'to be joined,' fr. *yuj; pak-tavya*, 'to be cooked,' fr. *pać; bhav-i-tavya*, 'to be become,' fr. *bhú; bodhay-i-tavya*, 'to be made known,' fr. Caus. of *bhú; grah-í-tavya*, 'to be seized,' fr. *grah*. Cf. Gr. participials in -τέο-ς (for τεϝ-yo-ς), as δο-τέο-ς, θε-τέο-ς.

XIX. त्य *-tya*, forming future passive participles after roots ending in short vowels (see 572); e.g. *kṛi-tya*, 'to be done,' fr. *kṛi; i-tya*, 'to be gone,' fr. *i; stu-tya*, 'to be praised,' 'laudable,' fr. *stu; bhṛi-tya*, 'to be borne,' fr. *bhṛi*. These are occasionally used as substantives; e.g. *bhṛityá*, f. 'maintenance.'

XX. त्र *-tra* (*-trá*), *-a-tra, -i-tra* (for the adverbial suffix *tra* see 720), forming (after Guṇa of a root capable of gunation) nouns denoting some instrument or organ, generally neuter; e.g. *śro-tra*, n. 'organ of hearing,' 'ear,' fr. *śru; pá-tra*, n. 'a drinking-vessel,' fr. *pá; vas-tra*, n. 'a garment,' fr. *vas*, 'to wear;' *ćhat-tra*, n. 'an umbrella,' fr. *ćhad*, 'to cover;' *gá-tra*, n. 'a limb,' fr. *gá*, 'to go;' *vak-tra*, n. 'the mouth,' fr. *vać*, 'to speak;' *ne-tra*, n. 'an eye,' fr. *ní*, 'to lead.'

A few are masculine and feminine; e.g. *daṇsh-ṭra*, m. or *daṇsh-ṭrá*, f. 'instrument of biting,' 'a tooth,' fr. *daṇś; man-tra*, m. 'a holy text,' 'prayer,' fr. *man*, 'to reflect;' *yá-trá*, 'provisions (for a journey),' fr. *yá*, 'to go;' *vara-trá*, f. 'instrument of surrounding,' 'a strap,' fr. *vṛi*.

Sometimes *i* is inserted between the root and suffix; e.g. *khan-i-tra*, n. 'a spade,' fr. *khan*, 'to dig;' *ćar-i-tra*, n. 'proceedings,' fr. *ćar*, 'to go:' and sometimes the present stem is used; e.g. *kṛinta-tra*, n. 'a plough,' fr. *kṛit*, 'to cleave;' *pata-tra*, n. 'a wing,' fr. *pat*, 'to fly;' *vadha-tra*, n. 'a weapon,' fr. *vadh*, 'to kill.' Cf. similar Gr. forms in -τρο-ν, -θρο-ν, &c.; e.g. νίπ-τρο-ν, ἄρο-τρο-ν, βάκ-τρο-ν, βά-θρο-ν, ῥή-τρα, φρά-τρα, κοιμή-θρα: Lat. *ras-tru-m, ros-tru-m, ara-tru-m, plec-tru-m, fulge-tra*, &c.

XXI. त्व *-tva* (for secondary suffix *-tva* see LXVIII), forming a kind of future passive participle (probably an abbreviated form of *-tvya, -tavya*) after Guṇa of a radical vowel capable of gunation; e.g. *kar-tva*, 'to be done,' fr. *kṛi; je-tva*, 'to be conquered,' fr. *ji; vak-tva*, 'to be spoken,' fr. *vać; sná-tva*, 'fit for ablutions,' fr. *sná*.

-tvá, forming indeclinable past-participles (see 555), appears to be a kind of instrumental case of a suffix *tva* (see 555. *a*), and is either added to the root or to the same weakened form of the root as the *-ta* of the past passive participle (see XVII); e.g. *kṛi-tvá*, 'having done,' fr. *kṛi; sthi-tvá*, 'having stood,' fr. *sthá; uk-tvá*, 'having spoken,' fr. *vać*, 'to speak:' sometimes an *i* is inserted; e.g.

vid-i-tvá, 'having known,' fr. *vid*; *likh-i-tvá* or *lekh-i-tvá*, 'having written,' fr. *likh*; *ćorayi-tvá*, 'having stolen,' fr. *ćur*, 'to steal.'

-tví, a Vedic form of *-tvá* (e.g. *kṛi-tví*, 'having done'), appears to be for *tvyá* (which is thought to be for *tvayá*).

XXII. त्व -*tvya*, a Vedic abbreviated form of *-tavya* (see XVIII); e.g. *kṛi-tvya*, 'able to perform,' 'effectual,' fr. *kṛi*.

XXIII. थ -*tha* or -*a-tha*, forming some nouns of either gender; e.g. *yú-tha*, n. 'a herd,' 'flock,' &c., fr. *yu*, 'to unite;' *uk-tha*, n. 'praise,' fr. *uć*, a form of *vać*, 'to speak;' *tír-tha*, m. n. 'a sacred bathing-place,' fr. *tṛí*, 'to cross over;' *ní-tha*, m. n. 'guiding,' fr. *ní*; *gam-a-tha*, m. 'a traveller,' fr. *gam*, 'to go;' also *uć-atha*, *rav-atha*, *śap-atha*, *śvas-atha*.

XXIV. न -*na*, forming (in place of -*ta*, q.v.) many past passive participles (see 530–540); e.g. *bhin-na*, 'broken,' fr. *bhid*; *bhag-na*, 'broken,' fr. *bhañj*; *an-na*, 'eaten,' fr. *ad*; *stír-ṇa*, 'spread,' fr. *stṛi*.

Forming also a few nouns, generally masculine; as, *yaj-ña* (57. c), m. 'sacrifice,' fr. *yaj*; *yat-na*, m. 'effort,' fr. *yat*; *svap-na*, m. 'sleep,' fr. *svap*; *ush-ṇa*, m. n. 'heat,' fr. *ush*, 'to burn.'

Forming also a few feminine nouns in -*ná*; e.g. *ush-ṇá*, 'heat;' *tṛish-ṇá*, 'thirst,' fr. *tṛish*; *yáć-ñá* (57. c), 'a request,' fr. *yáć*. Cf. Gr. ὕπ-νο-ς, στυγ-νό-ς, δει-νό-ς, στέρ-νο-ν: Lat. *som-nu-s*, *mag-nu-s*, *ple-nu-s*, *reg-nu-m*.

XXV. म -*ma* (मक्, मन्), forming adjectives and a few masculine and neuter substantives, generally without change of the radical vowel; e.g. *bhí-ma*, 'terrible,' fr. *bhí*, 'to fear;' *tig-ma*, 'sharp,' fr. *tij* (cf. 80. I); *idh-ma*, m. 'fuel,' fr. *indh*, 'to burn;' *ghar-ma*, m. 'heat,' fr. *ghṛi* (after Guṇa); *dhú-ma*, m. 'smoke,' fr. *dhú*; *yug-ma*, n. 'a pair,' fr. *yuj*, 'to join.' Cf. Gr. θερ-μό-ς, θυ-μό-ς, ἄν-ε-μο-ς: Lat. *fu-mu-s*, *an-i-mu-s*.

XXVI. मर -*mara* (क्मरच्), forming a few adjectives and substantives; e.g. *ghas-mara*, 'voracious,' fr. *ghas*, 'to devour;' *ad-mara*, 'gluttonous,' fr. *ad*, 'to eat.'

XXVII. मान -*mána* (liable to become *máṇa*), added to the stem of the present tense of the first, fourth, sixth, and tenth classes of verbs Primitive, and of verbs Causal and Passive (see 526–528) to form present participles Átm., and to the stem of the second future tense to form future participles Átm. (see 578); e.g. *bhara-máṇa*, 'bearing,' fr. *bhṛi*; *kṛiya-máṇa*, 'being made,' fr. Pass. of *kṛi*; *bodhaya-mána*, 'informing,' fr. Caus. of *budh*; *dásya-mána*, 'about to give,' fr. the stem of the second future of *dá*. In the Veda *mána* is also added (instead of *ána*) to the stem of the perfect, to form perfect participles Átm.; e.g. *sasṛi-máṇa* (for *sasráṇa*), fr. *sṛi*, 'to go;' *ija-mána*, fr. *yaj*, 'to sacrifice;' cf. suffix -*ána*. Cf. Gr. φερό-μενο-ς, διδό-μενο-ς, δωσό-μενο-ς: Lat. *alu-mnu-s* (for *alo-meno-s*), *Vertu-mnu-s* (for *verto-meno-s*).

XXVIII. य -*ya* (क्यप्, यक्, यत्, य, ण्यत्), forming future passive participles (see 571–576), adjectives, and substantives, generally after Guṇa or Vṛiddhi, and sometimes other changes of the root (see 571); e.g. *će-ya*, 'to be gathered,' fr. *ći*; *stav-ya* or *stáv-ya*, 'to be praised,' fr. *stu*; *yog-ya* and *yoj-ya*, 'to be joined,' fr. *yuj*; *guh-ya* and *goh-ya*, 'to be concealed,' fr. *guh*.

Forming also many neuter abstract substantives; e.g. *vák-ya*, n. 'speech,' fr. *vać*; *bhog-ya*, n. 'wealth,' 'corn,' *bhoj-ya*, n. 'food,' both fr. *bhuj*, 'to enjoy.'

Forming also feminine substantives in *yá*; e.g. *vid-yá*, f. 'knowledge,' fr. *vid*; *vraj-yá*, f. 'wandering about,' fr. *vraj*; *śay-yá*, f. 'a couch' (for *śe-yá*), fr. *śí*, 'to lie down;' cf. *já-yá* (i.e. *jan-yá*), 'a wife;' *ćhá-yá* (i.e. *ćhad-yá*), 'shade;' *má-yá* (i.e. *man-yá*), 'illusion.' Cf. Gr. ἅγ-ιο-ς (= *yáj-ya-s*), στύγ-ιο-ς: Lat. *gen-iu-s*, *in-gen-iu-m*, *con-jug-iu-m*.

For the indeclinable participial suffix *ya* (ल्यप्) see 555.

XXIX. र *-ra* (क्रन्, रक्, र, रन्, इरच्), *-a-ra*, *-i-ra* (किरच्), *-u-ra*, forming adjectives, nouns of agency, &c.; e.g. *díp-ra*, 'shining,' fr. *díp*; *kship-ra*, 'swift,' fr. *kship*, 'to throw;' *vand-ra*, 'worshipping,' fr. *vand*; *ćhid-ra*, 'pierced,' 'a hole' (neut.), fr. *ćhid*, 'to cut;' *aj-ra*, m. 'a plain,' *aj-i-ra*, 'active,' 'an area' (neut.), fr. *aj*; *pat-a-ra*, 'flying,' fr. *pat*: also with *i* or *u* inserted; e.g. *ćhid-i-ra*, m. 'an axe,' *ćhid-u-ra*, 'cutting,' fr. *ćhid*, 'to cut;' *rudh-i-ra*, 'red;' *bhid-u-ra*, 'splitting,' 'fragile,' 'a thunderbolt' (neut.); *bhás-ura*, 'shining' (= *bhás-vara*), fr. *bhás*. Cf. Gr. λαμπ-ρό-ς, ἐρυθ-ρό-ς, ἀγ-ρό-ς, φαν-ε-ρός: Lat. *rub-er* (stem *ru-bro*), *rubra*, *ag-er*, *gna-ru-s*, *pu-ru-s*.

XXX. ल *-la* (क्ल, लच्), *-a-la*, *-i-la*, *-u-la*, forming adjectives, &c. = *-ra*, &c. above; e.g. *śuk-la* (= *śuk-ra*), 'white,' fr. *śuć*, 'to shine;' *tar-a-la*, 'tremulous,' fr. *tṛí*; *an-i-la*, 'wind,' fr. *an*, 'to blow;' *harsh-u-la*, 'delighted,' fr. *hṛish*. Cf. Gr. μεγ-άλο-ς, δει-λό-ς, τροχ-αλό-ς, φῦ-λο-ν: Lat. *sel-la* (for *sed-la*), *trem-ulu-s*, &c.

XXXI. व *-va* (क्वन्, वन्, व), forming participles, adjectives, and substantives; e.g. *pak-va*, 'cooked,' fr. *pać* (regarded as a past passive participle, see 548); *aś-va*, 'a horse,' fr. an assumed rt. *aś*, 'to be quick;' *e-va*, 'going,' fr. *i*; *pad-va*, 'a road,' fr. *pad*, 'to go.' Cf. Gr. ἵπ-πο-ς (for ἰκ-Ϝο-ς): Lat. *eq-uu-s*, *ard-uu-s* (= *úrdh-va*), *ar-vu-m*, *æ-vu-m*.

XXXII. वर *-vara* (क्वरप्, वरच्, वरट्, &c.), forming adjectives, nouns of agency, &c. (fem. generally *í*); *naś-vara* (fem. *í*), 'perishing,' fr. *naś*, 'to perish;' *íś-vara*, 'a ruler,' fr. *íś*; *sthá-vara*, 'stationary,' fr. *sthá*, 'to stand.' After roots ending in short vowels or a nasal, *t* is sometimes inserted; as, *i-t-vara*, 'going' (fem. *í*), fr. *i*; *ji-t-vara*, 'conquering,' fr. *ji*; *ga-t-vara*, 'going,' fr. *gam*.

XXXIII. स्न *-sna* (क्स्न), forming a few adjectives; e.g. *tík-shṇa*, 'sharp,' fr. *tij*; *ślak-shṇa*, 'smooth' (said to be fr. *ślish*).

XXXIV. Other uncommon suffixes (mostly Uṇádi, see 79. note) forming primary derivatives of this class are, *-anga*, e.g. *tar-anga* (according to some rather *taran-ga*), *pat-anga*; *-aṇḍa*, e.g. *kar-aṇḍa*, *tar-aṇḍa*; *-ata*, e.g. *darś-ata*, *pać-ata*, *yaj-ata*; *-anta*, e.g. *jay-anta*, *tar-anta*, *vas-anta*; *-anya*, e.g. *tur-aṇya*, *nabh-anya*, *parj-anya*; *-apa*, e.g. *ul-apa*, *ush-apa*, *maṇḍ-apa*; *-abha*, e.g. *ṛish-abha*, *gard-abha*, *vṛish-abha, śar-abha; -ama*, e. g. *kal-ama, ruś-ama, sar-amá; -amba*, e. g. *kar-amba; -asa*, e. g. *ćam-asa, div-asa, man-asa, vać-asa; -asána*, 'being,' pres. part. of *as*, 'to be,' e. g. *mand-asána, vṛidh-asána; -áṇaka*, e. g. *dhav-áṇaka, lav-áṇaka; -ánaka*, e. g. *bhay-ánaka, śay-ánaka; -áyya*, e. g. *pan-áyya, panay-áyya, mah-áyya; -ára*, e. g. *ang-ára, tush-ára; -ála*, e. g. *kap-ála, kar-ála, ćash-ála; -ika*, e. g. *kṛish-ika, vṛiś-ć-ika; -isha* (i. e. *-isa*), e. g. *ám-isha, tav-isha, aryath-isha; -íka*, e. g. *an-íka, dṛiś-íka, ćarćar-íka; -íṭa*, e. g. *kṛip-íṭa; íra*, e. g. *gabh-íra, śar-íra, hiṇs-íra; -ísha*, e. g. *ṛij-ísha, pur-ísha, man-íshá; -utra*, e. g. *tar-utra, var-utra; -una*, e. g. *ar-uṇa, arj-una, yam-uná, var-uṇa; -usha*, e. g. *nah-usha, pur-usha, man-usha; -úkha*, e. g. *may-úkha; -útha*, e. g. *jar-úṭha, var-útha; -úra*, e. g. *may-úra; -úla*, e. g. *láṇg-úla; -elima*, e. g. *pać-elima, bhid-elima* (576. *b*); *-ora*, e. g. *kaṭh-ora, sah-ora; -kara*, e. g. *push-kara, tas-kara; -trima*, e. g. *kṛi-trima, pak-trima* (Páṇ. III. 3, 88); *-thaka*, e. g. *gá-thaka* (perhaps for *gátha-ka*); *-sa*, e. g. *drap-sa, vṛik-sha, ghraṇ-sa*.

B. Secondary Derivatives, formed from the Nominal Stems of primary derivatives.

Preliminary Observations.

a. The final vowels of the nominal stems of primary derivatives are liable to certain changes before Taddhita suffixes beginning with vowels or *y;* thus (1) *a, á, i, í* are rejected; e. g. *śući*, 'pure;' *śauća*, 'purity:' (2) *u, ú* are gunated into *o*, which then becomes *av;* e. g. fr. *Manu* comes *Mánav-a*, 'a descendant of Manu:' (3) *o* and *au* become *av* and *áv* according to the general rules of Sandhi; e. g. from *go*, 'a cow,' comes *gavya*, 'relating to cows;' from *nau*, 'a ship,' comes *návika* and *návya*, 'belonging to a ship.'

b. A final *n* is generally rejected before Taddhita suffixes beginning with consonants; and both *n* and its preceding vowel are sometimes rejected before vowels and *y;* e. g. *yuvan*, 'young,' *yuva-tá* or *yuva-tva*, 'youth;' *átman*, 'self,' *átmya* and *atmíya*, 'own,' 'personal.' There are, however, many exceptions to the latter part of this rule; e. g. *yauvana*, 'youth,' fr. *yuvan; rájanya*, 'regal,' fr. *rájan; átmanína* fr. *átman*.

c. It will be found that Taddhita or secondary suffixes often require Vṛiddhi of the first syllable of the words to which they are added, as in *maula*, 'radical,' fr. *múla*, 'a root;' *śauća*, 'purity,' fr. *śući*, 'pure.' Similarly, in the case of derivatives formed from compound words; e. g. *sauhṛida*, 'friendship,' fr. *su-hṛid*, 'a friend:' sometimes a double Vṛiddhi takes place, as in *sauhárda*, 'friendship,' fr. *su-hṛid; saubhágya*, 'good fortune,' fr. *su-bhaga*, 'fortunate.'

d. When the initial consonant of a word is compounded with *y* or *v* followed by *a* or *á*, as VY*ághra*, 'a tiger,' SV*ara*, 'sound,' the *y* and *v* are generally resolved into *iy* and *uv*, thus VIY*ághra* and SUV*ara*, and then vriddhied, e. g. *vaiyághra*, 'relating to a tiger,' *sauvara*, 'relating to sound;' so also *sva*, 'self,' makes *sauva*, 'relating to self;' *śvan*, 'a dog,' *śauvana*, 'canine.' Similarly, *svasti* makes *sauvastika; nyáya, naiyáyika; sv-aśva, sauvaśvi*, &c.

XXXV. अ *-a* (fem. *í*), after Vṛiddhi of the first syllable, forming abstract nouns, collectives, patronymics, and adjectives expressing some relationship to the primitive noun; e. g. *śauća*, n. 'purity,' fr. *śući*, 'pure;' *sauhṛida*, n. or *sauhárda*, n. 'friendship,' fr. *su-hṛid* (see Preliminary Obs. *c*); *paurusha*, n. 'manliness,' fr. *purusha*, 'a man;' *śaiśava*, n. 'childhood,' fr. *śiśu*, 'a child;' *kshaitra*, n. 'a collection of fields,' fr. *kshetra*, 'a field;' *Vásishṭha*, 'a descendant of Vasishṭha;' *Mánava*, 'a descendant of Manu,' fr. *Manu; Vaishṇava*, 'a worshipper of Vishṇu,' fr. *Vishṇu; paurusha*, 'manly,' fr. *purusha*, 'a man;' *saikata*, 'sandy,' fr. *sikatá; dárava*, 'wooden,' fr. *dáru*, 'wood' (see Preliminary Obs. *a*); *vaiyákaraṇa*, 'grammatical,' fr. *vyákaraṇa*, 'grammar' (see Preliminary Obs. *d*).

XXXVI. अक *-aka* (वुञ्, वुक्, वुन्, इवुन्, वुम्), generally after Vṛiddhi of the first syllable, forming adjectives (fem. generally *í*) and substantives (cf. *-ika, -ka*); e. g. *aumaka*, 'flaxen,' fr. *umá*, 'flax;' *Áṅgaka*, 'coming from An·ga;' *aushṭraka*, 'coming from camels,' 'a quantity of camels' (neut.), fr. *ushṭra*, 'a camel;' *vátsaka*, n. 'a number of calves,' fr. *vatsa*, 'a calf.' The fem. of this suffix is sometimes *iká*, which, however, may be regarded as the fem. of *ika*.

XXXVII. आट *-áṭa*, as *váćáṭa*, 'talkative,' fr. *váć*, 'speech;' similarly, *śṛiṅgáṭa* fr. *śṛiṅga*.

XXXVIII. आनी *-ání*, forming feminines from masculine nouns like *Indra*, see *Indráṇí* under *-í*, page 58. (Observe—*Agni*, 'fire,' has a fem. form *Agnáyí*, 'the goddess of fire.')

XXXIX. आयन *-áyana* (ष्फ, ष्फञ्, फक्, ष्फक्, फञ्), forming patronymics, &c., after Vṛiddhi of the first syllable; e. g. *Náráyaṇa*, 'a name of Vishṇu,' fr. *nara*.

XL. आल *-ála*, as *váćála*, 'talkative,' fr. *váć*, 'speech.'

XLI. इक *-ika* (fem. *ikí*), forming adjectives and a few collective nouns after Vṛiddhi of the first syllable; e. g. *dhármika*, 'religious,' fr. *dharma*, 'religion;' *vaiṇavika*, 'a flute-player,' fr. *veṇu; Vaidika*, 'Vedic,' fr. *Veda; áhnika*, 'daily,' fr. *ahan*, 'a day;' *naiyáyika*, 'knowing the Nyáya philosophy,' fr. *nyáya; dauvárika*, 'a porter,' fr. *dvára; kaidárika*, n. 'a quantity of meadows,' fr. *kedára*. Cf. Gr. πολεμ-ικό-ς, βασιλ-ικό-ς: Lat. *bell-icu-s, naut-icu-s*, &c.

XLII. इत *-ita*, as *phalita*, 'having fruit,' fr. *phala* (the past passive part. of *phal* being *phulla*, 547. *b*); *rathita*, 'furnished with a chariot,' fr. *ratha*. Observe—This may be regarded as a past passive participle suffix added to the stems of nominal verbs, cf. *-ina* below.

XLIII. इन *-ina* (इनच्), as *phalina*, 'fruitful,' fr. *phala; malina*, 'dirty,' fr. *mala; śṛiṅgiṇa*, 'horned,' fr. *śṛiṅga; rathina*, 'having a carriage,' fr. *ratha*.

XLIV. इनेय *-ineya*, forming a few patronymics after Vṛiddhi of the first syllable; e. g. *saubhágineya*, 'the son of an honoured mother,' fr. *su-bhagá*.

XLV. इय *-iya* (fem. *á*), as *agriya*, 'foremost,' 'the best part' (neut.), fr. *agra*.

XLVI. इर *-ira* (fem. *á*), as *medhira*, 'intelligent,' fr. *medhá*, 'intelligence;' *rathira*, 'going in a carriage,' fr. *ratha* (cf. *-ra*, LXXVIII).

XLVII. इल *-ila* (fem. *á*), as *phenila*, 'foamy,' fr. *phena*, 'foam' (cf. *-la*, LXXX).

XLVIII. इष्ठ *-ishṭha* (fem. *á*), forming superlatives, as *alpishṭha*, 'least,' fr. *alpa*, 'little,' which also uses *kanishṭha* fr. rt. *kan* (see 192–194). Observe—Perhaps this suffix is in most cases rather primary than secondary, being generally added to the root or modified root, as *uru*, 'wide,' forms *varishṭha* fr. *vṛi* (see *-íyas*, 86. V). Cf. Gr. μέγ-ιστο-ς, ἥδ-ιστο-ς: Lat. *juxta* for *jug-(i)sta*, lit. 'most joined.'

XLIX. ईन *-ína* (ख, खञ्), forming adjectives and substantives, as *grámíṇa*, 'rustic,' fr. *gráma*, 'a village;' *kulína*, 'of good family,' fr. *kula; navína*, 'new,' fr. *nava; adhvanína*, 'a traveller,' fr. *adhvan*, 'a road;' *anupadíná*, f. 'a boot,' fr. *anupada; áśvína*, 'being a day's journey for a horse,' fr. *aśva*.

L. ईय *-íya*, forming adjectives, sometimes after Vṛiddhi of the first syllable of the stem; e.g. *svásríya*, 'a sister's son,' fr. *svasṛi*, 'a sister;' *bhrátríya*, 'fraternal,' fr. *bhrátṛi; párvatíya* or *parvatíya*, 'mountainous,' fr. *parvata; aśvíya*, 'relating to horses,' 'a number of horses' (neut.), fr. *aśva; parakíya* (fem. *á*), 'belonging to another,' fr. *para* (in this the final of the stem apparently remains and *k* is inserted); *saukhíya*, 'pleasurable,' fr. *sukha*.

Forming also possessive pronouns, as *madíya, tvadíya*, &c. (see 231).

LI. ईर *-íra, -íla*, only lengthened forms of *ira, ila*, qq.vv.

LII. उर *-ura*, as *dantura*, 'having long teeth,' fr. *danta*.

LIII. उल *-ula*, as *mátula*, 'a maternal uncle,' fr. *mátṛi*.

LIV. ऊल *-úla*, as *dantúla*, 'having teeth,' fr. *danta; vátúla*, 'rheumatic,' 'a whirlwind' (masc.), fr. *váta*.

LV. एय *-eya* (fem. *í*), forming adjectives and substantives after Vṛiddhi of the first syllable; e.g. *paurusheya*, 'manly,' fr. *purusha; ágneya*, 'fiery,' fr. *agni; dáseya*, 'born of a slave-girl,' fr. *dásí; maheya*, 'earthen,' fr. *mahí; jñáteya*, n. 'relationship,' fr. *jñáti*. Cf. Gr. λεόντειο-ς, λεόντεο-ς: Lat. *igneu-s*, &c.

LVI. क *-ka*, forming adjectives, collective nouns, and nouns expressing diminution or depreciation; e.g. *Sindhuka*, 'belonging to Sindh,' fr. *Sindhu; madhuka*, 'sweet,' fr. *madhu; rájaka*, n. 'a number of kings' or 'a petty king' (m.), fr. *rájan; aśvaka*, 'a hack,' fr. *aśva*, 'a horse.' Sometimes almost redundant, as *madhyamaka* (fem. *iká*), 'middlemost,' fr. *madhyama; bhíru-ka*, 'timid,' fr. *bhíru; putraka*, 'a son;' *bálaka* (fem. *iká*), 'young.' For the Kṛit suffix *-ka*, see 80. XVI.

Observe—Some of these may equally be regarded as formed with the suffix *-aka*, q.v. Cf. also *-ika*.

LVII. कल्प *kalpa* (कल्पप्), regarded by native grammarians as a secondary suffix (see Páṇ. v. 3, 67. 68, &c.), denoting 'similitude with inferiority,' or in the sense of 'nearly,' 'about;' as, *kavi-kalpa*, 'a sort of poet;' *mṛita-kalpa*, 'nearly dead;' *paćati-kalpam*, 'he cooks fairly well.' See Dict. *kalpa*.

LVIII. तन *-tana* (fem. *í*), forming adjectives from adverbs of time; e.g. *śvas-tana*, 'future,' fr. *śvas*, 'to-morrow;' *hyas-tana*, 'of yesterday,' fr. *hyas; prátas-tana*, 'belonging to the early morning,' 'early morning' (neut.), fr. *prátar*, 'at day-break;' *prák-tana*, 'former,' fr. *prák*, 'previously;' other examples are *práhṇe-tana, pratana, nútana, ćirantana*. Cf. Gr. ἐπ-ηε-τανό-ς: Lat. *crus-tinu-s, diu-tinu-s*.

LIX. तम -*tama* (तमप्), (-*tamám*), forming, 1st, the superlative degree, &c. (see 191, 195–197); e.g. *puṇya-tama*, 'most holy' (see 191); *uććais-tama*, 'very lofty,' fr. *uććais*. Sometimes added to pronominal stems (see 236). Cf. -*tara*, -*ma*: Lat. *op-timu-s, ul-timu-s*, &c.

Forming, 2ndly, ordinals (तमट्); e.g. *viṅśati-tama* (fem. *í*), 'twentieth,' fr. *viṅśati*, 'twenty' (see 211–213).

Tamám, derived from the first, is added adverbially; e.g. *uććais-tamám*, 'exceedingly high;' *vadati-tamám*, 'he talks incessantly.'

LX. तय -*taya*, forming adjectives (fem. *í*) and neuter substantives from numerals; e.g. *tri-taya*, 'consisting of three,' 'a collection of three' (neut.); *ćatush-ṭaya*, 'four-fold,' 'a collection of four,' &c. (neut.), fr. *ćatur*, 'four' (see 214).

LXI. तर -*tara* (तरप्), forming the comparative degree (see 191, 195–197, 236); e.g. *puṇya-tara*, 'more holy;' *uććais-tara*, 'higher,' fr. *uććais*, 'aloft.' Sometimes added to pronominal stems (see 236). Cf. -*tama*: Gr. γλυκύ-τερο-ς, μελάν-τερο-ς.

Tarám, derived from -*tara*, is added adverbially; e.g. *uććais-tarám*, 'in a higher degree' (cf. *bahu-tarám*); *vadati-tarám*, 'he speaks more (than he ought).'

LXII. ता -*tá* (= -*tva* below), forming feminine abstract substantives from stems of nouns or adjectives; e.g. *bahu-tá*, 'multitude,' fr. *bahu*, 'many;' *pṛithu-tá*, 'breadth,' fr. *pṛithu*, 'broad;' *yuva-tá*, 'youthfulness,' 'youth,' fr. *yuvan*, 'young;' *purusha-tá*, 'manliness,' fr. *purusha*, 'a man;' *deva-tá*, 'a divinity.' Cf. Lat. *juven-ta, senec-ta, vindic-ta*.

LXIII. तिथ -*titha* (fem. *í*), forming ordinal adjectives, &c.; e.g. *bahu-titha*, 'manifold,' fr. *bahu*; *távatitha*, 'the so-manieth,' fr. *távat*.

LXIV. तीय -*tíya* (fem. *á*), forming ordinals; e.g. *dvi-tíya*, 'second;' *tṛi-tíya*, 'third' (see 208).

LXV. त्न -*tna*, forming adjectives; e.g. *ćira-tna*, 'old,' 'ancient,' fr. *ćira*, 'long;' other examples are *nútna, pratna*. Cf. -*tana* above.

LXVI. त्य -*tya* (त्यप्, त्यक्), forming a few adjectives; e.g. *tatra-tya*, 'being there,' fr. *tatra*; *iha-tya*, 'being here,' fr. *iha*. Sometimes with Vṛiddhi of first syllable; e.g. *páśćát-tya*, 'subsequent,' fr. *paśćát*, 'behind.' Similarly, *dákshiṇá-tya* fr. *dakshiṇá*; *pauras-tya* fr. *puras*.

LXVII. त्रा -*trá*, forming a few feminine collective nouns; e.g. *go-trá*, 'a herd of cattle,' fr. *go*. For the adverbial suffixes -*tra*, -*trá*, see 720.

LXVIII. त्व -*tva* (= -*tá* above, q.v.), forming neuter abstract nouns; e.g. *bahu-tva, yuva-tva, pṛithu-tva, deva-tva*, &c.

LXIX. त्वन -*tvana* (= -*tva*), Vedic, forming neuter abstract nouns; e.g. *mahi-tvana*, 'greatness,' fr. *mahi* or *mahin*, 'great' (Vedic); *sakhi-tvana*, 'friendship,' fr. *sakhi*, 'a friend;' *vasu-tvana*, 'wealth,' fr. *vasu*, 'rich.'

LXX. दघ्न *daghna* (दघ्नच्), regarded (like *dvayasa* and *mátra*) as a secondary suffix (Páṇ. v. 2, 37), denoting 'height,' 'measure,' &c.; e. g. *úru-daghna* (fem. *í*), 'reaching to the thighs.'

LXXI. **देशीय** *deśíya* (**देशीयर्**), regarded (like *kalpa*, q. v.) as a secondary suffix (Páṇ. v. 3, 67), denoting 'about,' 'nearly;' e. g. *paṭu-deśíya*, 'tolerably clever.'

LXXII. **द्वयस** *dvayasa* (**द्वयसच्**), denoting 'height,' 'measure,' &c. (see *daghna* above); e. g. *úru-dvayasa* (fem. *í*), 'reaching to the thighs.'

LXXIII. **न** *-na* (**न, नञ्**), forming adjectives and substantives, sometimes after Vṛiddhi of the first syllable; e. g. *purá-ṇa* (fem. *á* or *í*), 'old,' fr. *purá*, 'formerly;' *pra-ṇa*, 'old,' fr. *pra*; *pauṉsna* (fem. *í*), 'virile,' 'manhood' (neut.), fr. *puṉs*, 'a man;' *straiṇa* (fem. *í*), 'womanly,' 'womanhood' (neut.), fr. *strí*.

LXXIV. **म** *-ma* (probably an old superlative suffix, cf. *-tama*, *-ra*), forming ordinals and other adjectives; e. g. *pańća-ma*, 'fifth;' *sapta-ma*, 'seventh' (see 209); *madhya-ma*, 'middlemost,' fr. *madhya*, 'middle;' *ava-ma*, 'undermost,' fr. *ava*, 'away;' *para-ma*, 'furthest,' fr. *para*, 'beyond.' Cf. Gr. ἕβδο-μο-ς: Lat. *septi-mu-s*, *pri-mu-s*, *infi-mu-s*, *sum-mu-s*, &c.

LXXV. **मय** *-maya* (**मयट्**), forming adjectives (fem. *í*) denoting 'made of,' 'consisting of;' e. g. *loha-maya*, 'made of metal,' 'iron,' fr. *loha*, 'metal;' *tejo-maya*, 'full of light,' fr. *tejas*, 'lustre;' *buddhi-maya*, 'intellectual.'

LXXVI. **मात्र** *mátra* (**मात्रच्**), added to words to denote 'measure,' 'height,' &c. (cf. *daghna*, *dvayasa*); e. g. *yava-mátra* (fem. *í*), 'of the size of a barleycorn;' *úru-mátra*, 'up to the thighs.' See *mátra* in Sanskṛit-English Dictionary.

LXXVII. **य** *-ya* (**यप्, य, ड्य, यस्, ष्यङ्, ख्य, ञ्यण्, ढ्यण्, यक्, यत्, ञ्यत्, ण्यत्, यल्, यन्, ण्य**), forming adjectives, patronymics, and neuter abstract substantives, generally after changes similar to those required by secondary suffixes beginning with vowels (see Prelim. Obs. *a*. *b*. at 80. B); e. g. *dhanya*, 'wealthy,' fr. *dhana*, 'wealth;' *rahasya* (fem. *á*), 'secret,' 'a secret' (neut.), fr. *rahas*, 'secrecy;' *pitrya*, 'fatherly,' fr. *pitṛi*; *ṛitavya*, 'seasonable,' fr. *ṛitu*; frequently after Vṛiddhi of the first syllable, e. g. *saumya* (fem. *á* or *mí*), 'lunar,' fr. *soma*, 'the moon;' *mádhurya*, n. 'sweetness,' fr. *madhura*, 'sweet;' *ćaur-ya*, n. 'theft,' fr. *ćora*, 'a thief;' *sauhṛid-ya*, n. 'friendship,' fr. *su-hṛid*, 'a friend;' *saubhág-ya*, n. 'good fortune,' fr. *su-bhaga* (see Prelim. Obs. *c*); *svám-ya*, 'lordship,' fr. *svámin*; *vaiyághrya*, n. 'the state of a tiger,' fr. *vyághra*. Sometimes the nasal and preceding vowel are not rejected; e. g. *brahmaṇ-ya* (fem. *á*), 'relating to Brahman;' *rájan-ya*, 'regal,' fr. *rájan* (see Prelim. Obs. *b*. *d*). Cf. Gr. πάτρ-ιο-ς, πατρ-ία, σωτήρ-ιο-ς, σωτηρ-ία: Lat. *patr-iu-s*, *patr-ia*, *nefar-iu-s*, &c. (cf. the primary suffix *-ya*, 80. XXVIII).

LXXVIII. **र** *-ra* (probably an old comparative suffix, cf. *-tara*, *-ma*), forming a few adjectives (fem. *á*); e. g. *madhu-ra*, 'sweet,' fr. *madhu*; *aśma-ra*, 'stony,' fr. *aśman*; *ava-ra*, 'inferior,' fr. *ava*, 'down;' *apa-ra*, 'posterior,' fr. *apa*, 'away.' Cf. Lat. *sup-eru-s*, *sup-er*; *inf-eru-s*, *inf-er*.

LXXIX. **रूप** *rúpa* (**रूपप्**), regarded as a secondary suffix giving the sense 'composed of,' 'consisting of,' 'full of,' &c., and sometimes almost redundant; e. g. *satya-rúpaṃ vákyam*, 'a speech full of truth,' or simply 'a true speech;' *árya-*

rúpa, 'respectable.' Sometimes giving the sense 'good,' 'well,' and even used with verbs adverbially; e.g. *paṭu-rúpa*, 'very clever;' *vaiyákaraṇa-rúpa*, 'a good grammarian;' *paćati-rúpam*, 'he cooks well' (Páṇ. v. 3, 66).

LXXX. ल *-la* (fem. *á*), forming a few adjectives (cf. *-i-la*); e.g. *śrí-la*, 'fortunate,' fr. *śrí; páṇśu-la*, 'dusty,' fr. *paṇśu; phena-la*, 'foamy,' fr. *phena*.

LXXXI. व *-va* (probably for *-vat*, 84. VII), as *keśa-va*, 'hairy,' fr. *keśa*.

LXXXII. वल *-vala* (वलच्, इलच्), forming a few adjectives (fem. *á*) and substantives; e.g. *úrjas-vala*, 'strong,' fr. *úrjas; śikhá-vala*, 'crested,' 'a peacock' (masc.), fr. *śikhá*, 'a crest;' *dantá-vala*, m. 'an elephant,' fr. *danta*, 'a tooth.'

LXXXIII. व्य *-vya* (व्यत्, व्यन्), as *pitṛi-vya*, 'a paternal uncle,' fr. *pitṛi*, 'a father.' Cf. Gr. πατρ-υιό-ς: Lat. *patr-uu-s*.

LXXXIV. श *-śa*, forming a few adjectives (fem. *á*) and substantives; e.g. *loma-śa*, 'hairy,' 'a sheep' (masc.), 'a fox' (*á*, fem.), fr. *loman*, 'hair.'

LXXXV. स *-sa*, forming a few adjectives, sometimes with Vṛiddhi; e.g. *tṛiṇa-sa*, 'grassy,' fr. *tṛiṇa; trápusha*, 'made of tin,' fr. *trapu*, 'tin.'

81. Second Class.—*Stems ending in* इ i (m. f. n.)

A. Primary Derivatives, formed from Roots by adding the following *Kṛit* suffixes—

I. इ *-i*, forming abstract nouns, nouns of agency of all genders, and adjectives (with occasional Guṇa or Vṛiddhi of the radical vowel); e.g. *kavi*, m. 'a poet,' fr. *ku; ahi*, m. 'a snake' (ἔχις, *anguis*), fr. *aṇh; dhvani*, m. 'sound,' fr. *dhvan; yaj-i*, m. 'a worshipper,' fr. *yaj; pesh-i*, m. 'a thunderbolt,' fr. *pish*, 'to crush;' *tvish-i*, f. 'splendour,' fr. *tvish*, 'to shine;' *sać-i*, f. 'friendship,' fr. *sać; kṛish-i*, f. 'ploughing,' fr. *kṛish; lip-i*, f. 'a writing,' fr. *lip*, 'to smear;' *ćhid-i*, f. 'an axe,' fr. *ćhid*, 'to cut;' *vár-i*, n. 'water,' fr. *vṛi*, 'to surround;' *aksh-i*, n. 'an eye,' fr. *aksh; śuć-i*, 'pure,' fr. *śuć*, 'to be pure;' *bodh-i*, 'knowing,' fr. *budh*. Sometimes with reduplication; e.g. *jagm-i*, 'quick,' fr. *gam*, 'to go;' *jaghn-i*, 'slaying,' fr. *han*. Cf. Gr. πόλι-ς, δύναμι-ς, στάσι-ς, ὄψι-ς, &c.: Lat. *ovi-s*, *trudi-s*, &c.

Often added to *dhá*, 'to hold,' after various prepositions and prefixes, to form masculine nouns, the final of the root being dropped; e.g. *ni-dhi*, m., *vi-dhi*, m., *san-dhi*, m.; one or two are exceptionally fem. (e.g. *oshadhi*).

II. ति *-ti* (cf. *-ni*), forming feminine abstract nouns and a few masculines, and closely related to the *-ta* of the past pass. part. at 80. XVII, being added with similar changes (except that *i* is rarely inserted); e.g. *śru-ti*, f. 'hearing,' fr. *śru; bhú-ti*, f. 'existence,' fr. *bhú; sthi-ti*, f. 'state,' fr. *sthá; mati*, f. 'mind,' fr. *man; uk-ti*, f. 'speech,' fr. *vać*, 'to speak;' *púr-ti*, 'fulness,' fr. *pṛí*, 'to fill;' *dat-ti*, f. 'a gift,' fr. *dá; bhit-ti*, f. 'a fragment,' fr. *bhid*, 'to split' (but past part. *bhin-na*); *ćhit-ti*, f. 'splitting,' fr. *ćhid* (but past part. *ćhin-na*); *vṛid-dhi* (i.e. *vṛidh* + *ti*), f. 'increase,' fr. *vṛidh; yati*, m. 'a sage,' fr. *yam*, 'to restrain;' *jńáti*, m. 'a relation,' fr. *jñá;* *pati*, m. 'a husband' (for *páti*), fr. *pá*, 'to protect.' Cf. Gr. μῆ-τι-ς, φά-τι-ς, φά-σι-ς, μάν-τι-ς, πό-σι-ς: Lat. *ves-ti-s*, *mes-si-s* (for *met-ti-s*), *mor-s* (stem *mor-ti*), *po-ti-s*, *com-pos* (stem *com-po-ti*).

III. नि -*ni*, forming feminine abstract nouns (in many respects analogous to those formed with -*ti*, so that when the past passive participle ends in -*na*, q.v., a noun may generally be formed with -*ni*), also a few masculines and adjectives; as, *glá-ni*, f. 'weariness,' fr. *glai*, 'to be languid;' *lú-ni*, f. 'cutting,' fr. *lú;* *jír-ṇi*, f. 'old age,' fr. *jṛí*, 'to grow old;' *há-ni*, f. 'loss,' fr. *há* (but past part. *hína*); *agni*, m. 'fire,' fr. *ang* or *añj;* *vah-ni*, m. 'fire,' fr. *vah*, 'to bear;' *vṛish-ṇi*, 'raining,' 'a ram' (m.), fr. *vṛish*. Cf. Gr. μῆ-νι-ς, σπά-νι-ς: Lat. *ig-ni-s* (=Sk. *ag-ni-s*), *pa-ni-s*.

IV. मि -*mi*, as *bhú-mi*, f. 'the earth,' fr. *bhú*, 'to be;' *dal-mi*, m. 'Indra's thunderbolt,' fr. *dal;* *úr-mi*, m. f. 'a wave' (perhaps fr. *vṛi*); *raś-mi*, m. 'a ray' (perhaps fr. *raś* for *las*). Cf. Gr. φῆ-μι-ς: Lat. *ver-mi-s*.

V. रि -*ri*, as in *aṅh-ri*, *angh-ri*, *aś-ri*, *vank-ri*, *vadh-ri*. Cf. Gr. ἴδ-ρι-ς.

VI. वि -*vi*, as in *ghṛish-vi*, *jír-vi*, *śír-vi*, *jágṛi-vi*, *dádhṛi-vi*.

VII. सि -*si*, as in *dhá-si*, *pluk-shi*, *śuk-shi*.

B. Secondary Derivatives, formed from the Nominal Stems of primary derivatives by adding the following *Taddhita* suffixes.
(See Prelim. Obs. at 80. B.)

VIII. अकि -*aki*, forming a few patronymics after Vṛiddhi of the first syllable; e.g. *Vaiyásaki*, 'a descendant of Vyása.'

IX. आयनि -*áyani*, forming patronymics; e.g. *vásináyani* fr. *vásin* (Páṇ. VI. 4, 174).

X. इ -*i*, forming patronymics after Vṛiddhi of the first syllable; e.g. *Daushyanti*, 'the son of Dushyanta;' so *Dáśarathi*, 'a descendant of Daśa-ratha;' *Sauvaśvi* fr. *Sv-aśva*.

XI. तादि -*táti* (= -*tá*), forming Vedic abstract substantives; e.g. *deva-táti*, f. 'divinity,' fr. *deva;* *vasu-táti*, f. 'wealth,' fr. *vasu;* *sarva-táti*, f. 'entirety,' fr. *sarva*, 'all.' Cf. Gr. φιλό-της (i.e. φιλό-τητ-ς), κακό-της (κακό-τητ-ος): Lat. *civi-tas* (stem *civi-tát-* or *civi-táti-*), *celeri-tas* (stem *celeri-táti-*), *vetus-tas*, &c.

XII. ति -*ti*, as in *yuva-ti*, 'a young woman,' fem. of *yuvan* (Páṇ. IV. 1, 77).

82. Third Class.—*Stems ending in* उ u (m. f. n.)

A. Primary Derivatives, formed from Roots by adding the following *Kṛit* suffixes—

I. अथु -*athu* (अथुच्), after Guṇa of a radical vowel; e.g. *kshay-athu*, m. 'consumption,' fr. *kshi*, 'to waste away;' *śvay-athu*, m. 'swelling,' fr. *śvi;* also *vep-athu*, *vam-athu*.

II. आतु -*átu*, as *jív-átu*, m. f. n. 'life,' &c., fr. *jív*, 'to live.'

III. आरु -*áru*, as *śar-áru*, 'hurtful,' fr. *śṛí*, 'to injure;' *vand-áru*, 'polite,' fr. *vand*, 'to praise.'

IV. आलु -*álu* (= -*áru* above), as *śáy-álu*, 'sleepy,' fr. *śí*, 'to lie down;' *spṛihay-álu*, 'desirous,' fr. *spṛih* (10th class), 'to desire.'

V. इत्नु -*itnu*, forming adjectives &c. from verbal stems of the 10th class; e. g. *gaday-itnu*, 'talkative,' fr. *gad*, 'to speak;' *stanay-itnu*, m. 'thunder,' fr. *stan*, 'to sound.'

VI. इष्णु -*ishṇu* (i. e. *i-snu*) = *snu*, as *ksay-ishṇu*, 'perishing,' fr. *kshi*; *bhav-ishṇu* = *bhú-shṇu*, 'becoming,' fr. *bhú*.

VII. उ -*u* (कु, डु, उ, डुन्, उण्, भुण्), forming adjectives (fem. *us* or *ví*) and a few nouns, the radical vowel generally undergoing change; e. g. *pṛith-u*, 'broad,' fr. *prath*, 'to extend;' *mṛid-u*, 'mild,' fr. *mṛid*, 'to crush;' *svád-u*, 'sweet,' fr. *svad* or *svád*; *lagh-u*, 'light,' fr. *langh*, 'to spring;' *tan-u*, 'thin,' fr. *tan*, 'to stretch;' *áś-u*, 'swift;' *bandh-u*, m. 'a kinsman,' fr. *bandh*, 'to bind;' *bhid-u*, m. 'a thunderbolt,' fr. *bhid*, 'to cleave;' *kár-u*, m. 'an artisan,' fr. *kṛi*, 'to make;' *tan-u*, f. 'the body,' fr. *tan*; *dár-u*, n. 'timber,' fr. *dṛí*, 'to split;' *madh-u*, n. 'honey.' Cf. Gr. ὠκ-ύ-ς, ἡδ-ύ-ς, πλατ-ύ-ς: Lat. *ac-u-s*, *id-u-s*, *suáv-i-s* (for *suádu-i-s*).

Forming also desiderative adjectives (sometimes governing an accusative, see 824) from desiderative stems; e. g. *jigamish-u*, 'desirous of going,' fr. *jigamisha*, desiderative stem of *gam*, 'to go:' similarly, *didṛikshu*, 'anxious to see;' *jigíshu*, 'striving to conquer.'

VIII. तु -*tu* (तु, तुन्), forming nouns of agency &c., generally masculine; e. g. *gan-tu*, m. 'a wayfarer,' fr. *gam*, 'to go;' *yá-tu*, 'a goer,' &c., 'time,' fr. *yá*, 'to go;' *bhá-tu*, m. 'the sun,' fr. *bhá*, 'to shine' (cf. *bhá-nu*); *jan-tu*, m. 'a creature,' fr. *jan*; *ṛi-tu*, m. 'a season,' fr. *ṛi*, 'to go;' *vas-tu*, n. 'an object,' also *vás-tu*, m. n. 'building-ground,' fr. *vas*, 'to dwell.' Cf. Gr. βοη-τύ-ς, ἐδη-τύ-ς, ἄσ-τυ (for Ϝασ-τυ): Lat. *sta-tu-s*, *vic-tu-s*, *cur-su-s* (for *cur-tu-s*).

Observe—The accusative of this suffix is used to form the infinitive; e.g. *yátum*, 'to go:' and in the Ṛig-veda other cases, as the dative, genitive, are used as infinitives; e. g. *yátave*, *yátavai*, *yátos* (see 458, 459).

IX. नु -*nu* (क्नु, नु), as *gṛidh-nu*, 'eager,' 'greedy,' fr. *gṛidh*, 'to covet;' *tras-nu*, 'timid,' fr. *tras*, 'to tremble;' *sú-nu*, m. 'a son,' *sú-nu* or *sú-nú*, f. 'a daughter,' fr. *su*, 'to bring forth;' *bhá-nu*, m. 'the sun,' fr. *bhá*; *dhe-nu*, f. 'a milk-cow,' fr. *dhe*, 'to suck.' Cf. Gr. θρῆ-νυ-ς, λιγ-νύ-ς.

X. यु -*yu*, as *śundh-yu*, 'bright,' 'fire' (m.), fr. *śundh*, 'to purify;' *jan-yu*, 'a creature,' fr. *jan*; *man-yu*, 'wrath,' fr. *man*, 'to think;' also *bhuj-yu*, *das-yu*, *mṛi-t-yu*.

XI. रु -*ru*, as *bhí-ru* (nom. fem. *rus* or *rús*), 'timid,' fr. *bhí*, 'to fear;' *aś-ru*, 'a tear' (said to be fr. *aś*).

XII. स्नु -*snu* (cf. -*ishṇu*), as *sthá-snu*, 'firm,' fr. *sthá*, 'to stand;' *ji-shṇu*, 'victorious,' fr. *ji*, 'to conquer;' *bhú-shṇu*, 'being,' fr. *bhú*.

B. SECONDARY DERIVATIVES, formed from the NOMINAL STEMS of primary derivatives by adding the following *Taddhita* suffixes—

XIII. यु *-yu*, forming adjectives, frequently in the sense of 'wishing for,' and a few nouns; e. g. *úrṇá-yu*, 'woollen,' fr. *úrṇá*; *svar-yu*, 'desiring heaven,' fr. *svar*, 'heaven;' also *śubhaṃ-yu*, *kaṃ-yu*, *ahaṃ-yu*, *asma-yu*.

XIV. लु *-lu*, as *kṛipá-lu*, *dayá-lu*, 'compassionate,' fr. *kṛipá*, *dayá*.

Stems ending in ई í *and* ऊ ú (see 123).

XV. ई *-í*, forming numerous feminine nouns, which will be found under their corresponding masculine suffixes, see 80. I. &c., 123–126. Others, mostly monosyllabic, and often formed by taking a naked root to serve as a noun, are, *bhí*, f. 'fear;' *dhí*, f. 'understanding;' *śrí*, f. 'prosperity;' *strí*, f. 'a woman;' *Lakshmí*, f. 'the goddess Lakshmí;' *ní*, m. f. 'a leader' (whence *sená-ní*, m. 'a general;' *gráma-ṇí*, m. f. 'the chief of a village').

XVI. ऊ *-ú*, forming feminine nouns, which will be found under their corresponding masculine forms, as *sú-nú*, *bhí-rú*, 82. IX. XI. (see also 125, 126). Others, sometimes monosyllabic, and formed by taking a naked root to serve as a noun, are, *lú*, m. f. 'a reaper;' *bhú*, f. 'the earth;' *Svayam-bhú*, m. 'the Self-existent;' *vadhú*, f. 'a wife.'

83. FOURTH CLASS.—*Stems ending in* ऋ ṛi (m. f. n.)

PRIMARY DERIVATIVES, formed from ROOTS by adding the *Kṛit* suffix—

तृ *-tṛi*, forming, 1st, nouns of agency of three genders, and a kind of future participle, the same change of the root being required which takes place in the first future, and the same euphonic changes of *t* (see 386 and 581); thus *kshep-tṛi*, 'a thrower,' fr. *kship*; *dá-tṛi*, 'a giver,' fr. *dá*; *bhar-tṛi*, 'a protector,' fr. *bhṛi*, 'to bear;' *boddhṛi*, 'a knower,' fr. *budh*; *soḍhṛi*, 'patient,' fr. *sah*, 'to bear;' *bhav-i-tṛi*, 'about to become' (=*fu-turu-s*), fr. *bhú*, 'to become' (Raghu-v. VI. 52).

2ndly, nouns of relationship, masculine and feminine; in these the vowel of the root is frequently modified; as, *pi-tṛi*, 'a father,' fr. *pá*, 'to protect;' *má-tṛi*, 'a mother,' fr. *má*, 'to form,' 'produce;' *bhrá-tṛi*, 'a brother,' fr. *bhṛi*, 'to support.' Cf. Gr. δο-τήρ, πα-τήρ, μη-τήρ: Lat. *da-tor*, *da-turu-s*, *pa-ter*, *ma-ter*, *fra-ter*.

84. FIFTH CLASS.—*Stems ending in* त् t *and* द् d (m. f. n.)

A. PRIMARY DERIVATIVES, formed from ROOTS by adding the following *Kṛit* suffixes—

I. अत् *-at*, forming present and future participles Par. from the stems of the present and the second future tenses respectively (see 524, 525, 578); e. g. *ad-at*, 'eating,' fr. *ad*; *ćinv-at*, 'collecting,' fr. *ći*; *karishy-at*, 'about to do,' fr. *kṛi*;

dadh-at, 'placing,' fr. *dhá*. Cf. Gr. φέρ-ων (stem φερ-οντ-), διδ-ού-ς (stem διδοντ-), τιθ-εί-ς (stem τιθ-εντ-): Lat. *veh-ens* (stem *veh-ent-*), *i-ens* (stem *e-unt-*).

II. इत् *-it*, forming a few nouns and adjectives; e.g. *sar-it*, 'a river,' fr. *sṛi*, 'to flow;' *har-it*, 'green.'

III. त् *-t*, frequently added to roots ending in a short vowel, to form nouns of agency, substantives, and adjectives (often used at the end of compounds); e.g. *ji-t*, 'conquering,' in *sarva-jit*, 'all-conquering,' fr. *ji*; *kṛi-t*, 'a doer,' in *karma-kṛit*, 'a doer of work,' fr. *kṛi*.

Sometimes *t* is substituted for a final *m* of a root, generally at the end of a compound; as, *ga-t* in *adhva-gat*, m. 'a traveller,' fr. *gam*, 'to go.'

IV. This class, besides comprehending a few nouns already ending in *d*, as *śarad*, f. 'autumn;' *dṛiśad*, f. 'a stone;' *kumud*, n. 'a lotus,' includes a number of monosyllabic nouns formed by taking roots ending in *t* or *d*, and using them in their unchanged state as substantives and nouns of agency, the technical suffix *kvip* (leaving *v*) being theoretically added, for which a blank is substituted (see 87); e.g. *ćit*, f. 'the mind;' *mud*, f. 'joy;' *vid*, 'a knower' (in *dharma-vid*); *ad*, 'an eater' (in *kravyád*, 'a flesh-eater'); *dyut*, f. 'splendour;' *pad*, m. 'a step.'

Some nouns falling under this class are formed by prefixing prepositions to roots ending in *t* or *d*, or in a short vowel; e.g. *sam-pad*, f. 'success;' *saṃ-vid*, f. 'an agreement;' *vi-dyut*, f. 'lightning;' *upa-ni-shad*, 'a philosophical treatise;' *sam-i-t*, 'conflict' (fr. *sam-i*, 'to go together').

The practice of using roots at the end of compounds prevails also in Greek and Latin; as in χέρ-νιψ (-νιβ-), βου-πλήξ (-πληγ-), &c., *arti-fex* (*-fic-*), *carni-fex* (*-fic-*), *præ-ses* (*-sid-*), &c. And there is a very remarkable agreement between Sanskṛit and Latin in the practice of adding *t* to roots ending in short vowels; thus, *com-it-* (*comes*), 'a goer with;' *equ-it-* (*eques*), 'a goer on horseback;' *al-it-* (*ales*), 'a goer with wings;' *super-stit-* (*superstes*), 'a stander by,' &c. Greek adds a similar *t* to roots with a long final vowel; as, ἀ-γνωτ- (ἀγνώς), ἀ-πτωτ- (ἀπτώς), &c.

B. Secondary Derivatives, formed from the Nominal Stems of primary derivatives by adding the following *Taddhita* suffixes—

V. तात् *-tát*, a Vedic suffix (= *-táti*, 81. XI); e.g. *deva-tát*, f. 'worship;' *satya-tát*, 'truth.'

VI. मत् *-mat* (मतुप्, ड्मतुप्), forming adjectives (fem. *atí*) signifying 'possessed of,' 'full of,' &c. = *-vat* below; usually added to stems ending in *i*, *í*, or *u*; e.g. *agni-mat*, 'having fire;' *śrí-mat*, 'prosperous;' *dhí-mat*, 'wise;' *aṇśu-mat*, 'radiant;' *yava-mat*, 'abounding in barley;' *madhu-mat*, 'full of honey;' *vidyun-mat* = *vidyut-vat*, 'possessing lightning,' fr. *vidyut*; *jyotish-mat*, 'brilliant,' fr. *jyotis*, 'light;' *dhanush-mat*, 'armed with a bow' (see 69); *arćish-mat*, 'brilliant' (69. *b*).

VII. वत् *-vat* (वतुप्, वति), forming, 1st, adjectives (fem. *atí*) signifying 'possessed of,' &c.; usually added to stems ending in *a*, *á*, or *m*, and in some other consonants; e.g. *dhana-vat*, 'possessed of wealth;' *aśva-vat*, 'having horses;' *víra-vat*, 'abounding in heroes;' *śikhá-vat*, 'crested,' fr. *śikhá*; *vidyá-vat*, 'learned,' fr. *vidyá*, 'knowledge;' *rája-vat* or *rájan-vat* (see 57), 'having a king,' fr. *rájan; agni-vat=agni-mat*, 'having fire;' *kiṃ-vat*, 'possessed of what;' *pad-vat*, 'having feet,' fr. *pad*, 'a foot;' *vidyut-vat*, 'possessing lightning,' fr. *vidyut* (see under *-mat*); *tejas-vat*, 'brilliant,' fr. *tejas*, 'splendour;' *bhás-vat*, 'shining,' 'the sun' (m.), fr. *bhás*, 'light;' *srug-vat*, 'having a ladle,' fr. *sruć*. Cf. Gr. forms in -Ϝεις (i.e. for Ϝεντ-ς), -Ϝεσσα (i.e. Ϝετya = *vatí* for *vatyá*), -Ϝεν (for Ϝεντ); as, χαρί-εις (stem χαρι-Ϝεντ-), δακρυό-εις (stem δακρυο-Ϝεντ-).

Forming, 2ndly, past active participles (see 553); e.g. *kṛita-vat*, 'one who has done;' *bhagna-vat*, 'one who has broken.'

For the suffix *-vat*, in *tá-vat*, 'so many,' *yá-vat*, &c., see 234; and for the adverbial suffix *-vat*, expressing 'similitude,' see 724.

85. Sixth Class.—*Stems ending in* अन् an *and* इन् in (m. f. n.)

A. Primary Derivatives, formed from Roots by adding the following *Kṛit* suffixes—

I. अन् *-an*, forming several nouns, chiefly masculine; e.g. *rájan*, m. 'a king' (fem. *rájñí*, 'a queen,' 57. c), fr. *ráj*, 'to govern;' *taksh-an*, m. 'a carpenter,' fr. *taksh*, 'to form by cutting;' *sneh-an*, m. 'a friend,' fr. *snih*, 'to love;' *uksh-an*, m. 'a bull,' fr. *uksh*, 'to impregnate;' *aś-an*, m. 'a stone,' fr. *aś; ud-an*, n. 'water,' fr. *ud* or *und*, 'to wet.' Cf. Gr. κλύδ-ων, τέκτ-ων (stem τεκτ-ον-), εἴκ-ων (stem εἰκ-ον-): Lat. *hom-o* (stem *hom-in-*), *asperg-o* (stem *asperg-in-*), *pect-en* (*pec-tin-*).

II. इन् *-in*, forming numerous substantives, adjectives, and nouns of agency (fem. *iní*); e.g. *math-in*, m. 'a churning-stick,' fr. *math*, 'to shake;' *path-in*, m. 'a path,' fr. *path*, 'to go' (see 162); *kár-in*, m. 'an agent,' fr. *kṛi*, 'to do;' *dvesh-in*, m. 'an enemy,' fr. *dvish*, 'to hate.' Cf. the secondary suffix *-in* at VI.

III. त्वन् *-tvan* (fem. *tvarí*), see under *-van* below.

IV. मन् *-man* (मनिन्, मनि, मनिण्), *-iman*, forming neuter and a few masculine abstract substantives, and rarely adjectives, often after Guṇa of the radical vowel (those in *iman* being generally masc.); e.g. *kar-man*, n. 'a deed,' fr. *kṛi*, 'to do;' *jan-man* or *jan-iman*, n. 'birth,' fr. *jan*, 'to beget;' *veś-man*, n. 'a house,' fr. *viś*, 'to enter;' *ná-man*, n. (for *jñá-man*), 'a name,' fr. *jñá*, 'to know;' *śar-man*, n. 'happiness,' probably fr. *śri; pre-man*, m. n. 'affection,' fr. *prí*, 'to please;' *ush-man*, m. 'heat,' fr. *ush*, 'to burn:' also *sí-man*, f. 'a boundary;' *aś-man*, m. 'a stone;' *śush-man*, m. 'fire,' 'strength' (neut.); *páp-man*, m. 'sin.'

Sometimes with insertion of *i* (and Vedic *í*), in which case the gender is generally masculine (cf. the secondary suffix *-iman*); e.g. *sar-iman* or Ved. *sar-íman*, m. 'going,' fr. *sṛi*, 'to go;' *star-iman* or Ved. *star-íman*, m. 'a couch,' fr. *stṛí*, 'to spread;' *dhar-iman*, m. 'form,' fr. *dhṛi*, 'to hold;' *har-iman*, m. 'time,' fr. *hṛi*, 'to seize.' Cf. Gr. ἄκ-μων (stem ἄκ-μον-), γνώ-μων (stem γνω-μον-), πυθ-μήν (stem πυθ-μέν-): Lat. *no-men* (stem *no-min-*), *stra-men* (stem *stra-min-*), *ag-men*, *teg-men*, *teg-i-men*.

V. वन् *-van* (क्वनिप्, वनिप्), forming substantives, adjectives, and nouns of agency (fem. generally *varí;* cf. suffix *-vara*, with which *-van* appears to be connected); e.g. *pad-van*, m. 'a way,' fr. *pad*, 'to go;' *mad-van* (fem. *varí*), 'intoxicating,' fr. *mad*, 'to gladden;' *ṛik-van* (fem. *varí*), 'praising,' fr. *aré* (or *ṛić*); *dṛiś-van*, 'one who has seen' (generally at the end of a comp.), fr. *dṛiś; yaj-van* (fem. *varí*), 'sacrificing,' fr. *yaj*.

When a root ends in a short vowel, *t* is inserted; e.g. *kṛi-t-van* (fem. *varí*), 'effecting,' fr. *kṛi; ji-t-van*, 'conquering,' fr. *ji; i-t-van*, 'going,' fr. *i*.

B. Secondary Derivatives, formed from the Nominal Stems of primary derivatives by adding the following *Taddhita* suffixes—

VI. इन् *-in*, forming numerous adjectives of possession, &c.; e.g. *dhan-in*, 'wealthy,' fr. *dhana*, 'wealth;' *bal-in*, 'strong,' fr. *bala*, 'strength;' *mál-in*, 'wearing a garland,' fr. *málá*, 'a garland;' *vríh-in*, 'having rice,' fr. *vríhi*, 'rice;' *keś-in*, 'having hair,' fr. *keśa*, 'hair;' *padm-in*, 'abounding in lotuses' (*padminí*, f. 'a quantity of lotuses'), fr. *padma*, 'a lotus.'

VII. इमन् *-iman* (इमनिच्, इमनित्), forming masculine abstract substantives, mostly from adjectival stems, the finals being generally rejected, and the same changes being frequently required as before the comparative and superlative suffixes *-íyas, -ishṭha* (cf. the Kṛit suffix *-man*, 85. IV); e.g. *kál-iman*, 'blackness,' fr. *kála*, 'black;' *lagh-iman*, 'lightness,' fr. *laghu*, 'nimble;' *mah-iman*, 'greatness,' fr. *mahat;* also *gar-iman, drágh-iman, prath-iman*, &c. (cf. comparisons, 194).

VIII. मिन् *-min*, forming adjectives of possession (cf. the suffixes *-in, -vin, -mat, -vat*); e.g. *vág-min*, 'eloquent,' fr. *váć*, 'speech;' *go-min*, 'possessing herds,' fr. *go*, 'a cow;' *svá-min*, 'an owner,' fr. *sva*, 'self.'

IX. विन् *-vin*, forming adjectives, generally from stems ending in *á* or *as;* e.g. *medhá-vin*, 'intellectual;' *tejas-vin*, 'splendid' (69); *srag-vin*, 'wearing a garland,' fr. *sraj*.

86. Seventh Class.—*Stems ending in* अस् as, इस् is, उस् us (m.f.n.)

A. Primary Derivatives, formed from Roots by adding the following *Kṛit* suffixes—

I. अस् *-as*, forming numerous nouns, mostly neuter, and a few adjectives, generally after Guṇa of the root; e.g. *man-as*, n. 'the mind,' fr. *man*, 'to think;' similarly formed are *nam-as*, n. 'adoration;' *tap-as*, n. 'penance;' *tam-as*, n. 'darkness;' *jan-as*, 'a race;' *sar-as*, n. 'water,' fr. *sṛi*, 'to go;' *ćet-as*, n. 'mind,' fr. *ćit; srot-as*, n. 'stream,' fr. *sru*, 'to flow' (in this case *t* is inserted); *ush-as*, f. (nom. *ás*), 'dawn,' fr. *ush* (=*vas*), 'to shine;' *jar-as*, f. 'old age,' fr. *jṛí*, 'to grow old' (171); *vedh-as* (nom. m. f. n. *ás, ás, as*), 'creating,' 'name of Brahman' (m.) Cf. Gr. γέν-ος, μέν-ος, εὐ-γεν-ής (stem εὐ-γεν-ες-), εὐ-μεν-ής (=*su-manas*): Lat. *gen-us* (stem *gen-es-* or *gen-er-*), *scel-us*.

II. इस् *-is* (= *-as* above), as *hav-is*, n. 'ghee,' fr. *hu*, 'to offer;' also *arć-is, jyot-is, dyot-is, roć-is, śoć-is*, n. 'light,' 'lustre,' fr. *arć, jyut, dyut, ruć, śuć*, 'to shine.'

III. उस् *-us* (= *-as*, 86. I), as *ćaksh-us*, n. 'an eye,' fr. *ćaksh*, 'to see;' also *vap-us*, n. 'body;' *tanus*, n. 'body;' *dhan-us*, n. (m.) 'a bow;' *jan-us*, n. 'birth;' *man-us*, m. 'man.'

IV. वस् *-vas*, *-ivas* (nom. m. f. n. *ván*, *ushí*, *vat*), forming perfect participles from the stem of the reduplicated perfect (see 554); e. g. *vivid-vas*, 'one who has known,' fr. *vivid* (cf. *vidvas*, 168. *e*); similarly, *ten-ivas*, *jagm-ivas*, &c. (see 168).

B. Secondary Derivatives, formed from the Nominal Stems of primary derivatives by adding the following *Taddhita* suffixes—

V. ईयस् *-íyas*, forming the comparative degree (see 167, 193, 194); e. g. *bal-íyas*, 'stronger,' fr. *bala* for *balin* or *bala-vat*. Observe—Perhaps this suffix is in most cases rather primary than secondary, being generally added to the root or modified root; as, *uru*, 'wide,' forms *varíyas* fr. *vṛi* (cf. *-ishṭha*, 80. XLVIII).

VI. यस् *-yas* (= *-íyas* above), as *bhú-yas*, 'more,' comparative of *bahu* (see 194): also *jyá-yas* (194); *nav-yas*, Ved. (comparative of *nava*, 'recent').

87. Eighth Class.—*Stems ending in* any Consonant, except त् t *and* द् d, न् n, स् s (m. f. n.)

Almost any root may be used alone in its naked unchanged state as a nominal stem, no suffix of any kind being apparently added, but as it is a rule of native grammarians that no word can be formed without a suffix, they suppose a suffix technically called *kvip* (leaving *v*), for which a blank is then substituted. Most naked roots so used, form nouns of agency, especially at the end of compounds.

Those roots which end in *t* or *d*, or in a short vowel, having *t* affixed, have been already noticed as falling under the fifth class, see 84. III. IV. This eighth class is intended to comprise all other roots, ending in *any consonant*; e.g. *bhuj* (nom. *bhuk*), 'an eater;' so, *budh* (nom. *bhut*), 'a knower' (see 44. c); *spṛiś* (nom. *spṛik*), 'one who touches;' *viś* (nom. *viṭ*), 'one who enters,' 'a Vaiśya' (m.), 'a house' (f.); *lih* (nom. *liṭ*), 'one who licks;' *duh* (nom. *dhuk*), 'one who milks.'

a. Some require modifications; as, *práćh* (nom. *práṭ*), 'an asker,' fr. *praćh*. A desiderative stem is sometimes used alone in the same way; e. g. *pipaksh* (nom. *pipak*), 'one who wishes to cook.'

b. Many roots are taken in this way to form substantives; e. g. *yudh*, f. (nom. *yut*), 'battle;' *kshudh*, f. (nom. *kshut*), 'hunger:' some requiring modifications of the radical vowel; e. g. *váć*, f. (nom. *vák*), 'speech,' fr. *vać*, 'to speak;' *pur*, f. (nom. *púr*), 'a city,' probably fr. *pṛí*; *gir*, f. (nom. *gír*), 'praise,' fr. *gṛí*.

c. Many roots ending in nasals, when used in this way, especially at the end of compounds, either reject the nasal, or exchange it for *t* (see *-t*, 84. III): *gam*, 'to go,' has *ga* or *gat*; *jan* has *ja*; *han* has *ha* or *ghna*.

d. There are also a few dissyllabic nouns formed from roots which must be made to fall under this eighth class; as, *tṛishṇaj* (nom. *tṛishṇak*), 'thirsty;' *asṛij*, n. (nom. *asṛik*), 'blood:' also a few substantives formed by prefixing prepositions to roots; as, *sam-idh* (nom. *samit*), 'fuel.'

CHAPTER IV.

DECLENSION; OR INFLEXION OF THE STEMS OF NOUNS, SUBSTANTIVE AND ADJECTIVE.

GENERAL OBSERVATIONS.

88. Having explained how the stem of a noun is formed, we have now to shew how it is inflected.

In the last chapter, nouns, Substantive and Adjective, were arranged under eight classes, according to the final of their stems (the first four classes comprising those ending in vowels, the last four those ending in consonants). In the present chapter their declension or inflexion will be exhibited under the same eight classes. Moreover, as every class comprises Adjectives as well as Substantives, so the example of masculine, feminine, and neuter Substantives given under each class will serve as a model for the declension of masculine, feminine, and neuter Adjectives coming under the same class.

Gender of Nouns.

89. The noun has three genders, and its gender is, in many cases, determinable from the termination of its stem. Thus, nearly all stems in *á*, *í*, and those formed with the suffix *ti* (81. II), are feminine: most abstract nouns and those denoting an act or instrument, formed with the suffixes *ana*, *tva* (80. LXVIII), *ya*, *tra* (see under 80), *as*, *is*, *us* (86), and *man* (85. IV), are neuter; those formed with the suffixes *na* (80. XXIV) and *iman* (85. VII) are generally masculine; but those in *a*, *i*, *u*, and *ṛi* are not reducible to rule. The Nominative case is, however, in the first of these instances a guide to the gender; as, *deva-s*, 'a deity,' is masculine; but *phala-m*, 'fruit,' neuter. And in other cases the meaning of the word; as, *pitṛi*, 'a father,' is masculine; and *mátṛi*, 'a mother,' feminine.

It may be noted also that words denoting gods, mountains, seas, divisions of time, are generally masculine; words denoting rivers, the earth, and night, are usually feminine; while adjectives and participles, used as abstract nouns, the names of woods, flowers, fruits, towns, and water, are generally neuter.

Cases of Nouns.

90. In Sanskṛit, nearly all the relations between words in a sentence are expressed by inflexions (*vibhakti*, Páṇ. I. 4, 104). Many prepositions exist, but in Post-Vedic Sanskṛit they are not often used alone in government with cases, their chief use being as prefixes to verbs and nouns. Hence the necessity for eight cases. These, as it were, grow out of the stem, and are called, 1. Nominative (*prathamá*, scil. *vibhakti*, 'the first case'); 2. Accusative (*dvitíyá*, 'the second'); 3. Instrumental (*tṛitíyá*, 'the third'); 4. Dative (*ćaturthí*, 'the fourth'); 5. Ablative (*pańćamí*, 'the fifth'); 6. Genitive (*shashṭhí*, 'the sixth'); 7. Locative (*saptamí*, 'the seventh'); 8. Vocative (see 92). 1. The Nominative is the *kartṛi* or 'agent,' but the agent is not always in the N. case *; thus in the sentences, 'he did that,' and 'that was done by me,' the agent in the last sentence is in the I. case. 2. The Accusative is the *karman* or 'that acted on,' but the *karman* is not always in the Ac. case; as in 'that was done by me,' where 'that' is the *karman*, and is in the N. case. 3. The Instrumental expresses *karaṇa*, 'instrumentality,' i.e. it denotes the instrument or agent by which or by whom a thing is done; as, *tena kṛitam*, 'done by him †.' 4. The Dative is used in the sense *sampradána*, 'giving,' 'delivering over,' &c. 5. The Ablative generally expresses *apádána*, 'taking away,' and is usually translateable by 'from,' and not as in Latin and Greek by 'with,' 'by,' 'in' (see 812). 6. The Genitive expresses *sambandha*, 'relationship,' 'connexion ‡.' 7. The Locative is used in the sense *adhikaraṇa*, 'location,' and generally expresses the place or time in which anything is done; as, *Ayodhyáyám*, 'in Ayodhyá;' *púrva-kále*, 'in former time;' *bhúmau*, 'on the ground †.' 8. The Vocative is used in the sense *sambuddhi* and *sambodhana*, 'addressing,' 'calling to.'

* These cases will sometimes be denoted by their initial letters. Thus N. will denote Nominative; I., Instrumental; Ac., Accusative; Ab., Ablative.

† The Instrumental and the Locative cases denote various other relations. See Syntax, 805, 817.

‡ The Genitive in Sanskṛit generally denotes 'possession,' but is of very extensive application. See Syntax, 815, 816.

91. According to the Indian system, each of these eight cases has three numbers, singular (*eka-vaćana*), dual (*dvi-vaćana*), and plural (*bahu-vaćana*); and to each belongs a termination which is peculiarly its own, serving alike for masculine (*puṃ-linga*), feminine (*strí-linga*), and neuter gender (*klíva* or *napuṇsaka-linga*).

Again, according to the native system, some terminations are technically combined with servile or indicatory letters to indicate some peculiarity, or to distinguish one from the other, or to enable Pratyáháras to be formed (see note below). Thus the proper termination of the Nominative singular is स् *s* (expressible by Visarga : before *k*, *kh*, *p*, *ph*, and before the sibilants, or at the end of a sentence, see 63); but the technical termination is *su*, the letter *u* being servile*. Similarly, the termination of the Nominative plural is really *as*, but technically *jas*, the *j* being servile. The two schemes of termination, with and without the servile letters, are here exhibited. The first, or merely technical scheme, is given in small type.

	Technical Terminations with the indicatory letters in capitals.			*Real Terminations without the indicatory letters.*		
	SING.	DUAL.	PLURAL.	SING.	DUAL.	PLURAL.
N.	सु *sU**	औ *au*	जस् *Jas*	*s*	*au*	*as*
Ac.	अम् *am*	औट् *auṬ**	शस् *S'as*	*am*	*au*	*as*
I.	टा *Ṭá*	भ्याम् *bhyám*	भिस् *bhis*	*á*	*bhyám*	*bhis*
D.	ङे *N·e*	— *bhyám*	भ्यस् *bhyas*	*e*	*bhyám*	*bhyas*
Ab.	ङसि *N·asI*	— *bhyám*	— *bhyas*	*as*	*bhyám*	*bhyas*
G.	ङस् *N·as*	ओस् *os*	आम् *ám*	*as*	*os*	*ám*
L.	ङि *N·i*	— *os*	सुप् *suP*	*i*	*os*	*su*

* The servile *u* may possibly indicate that final *s*, in certain positions, is liable to be liquefied into *u*. The object of the ट् of औट् in the Ac. du. is to enable a *pratyáhára* सुट् to be formed, denoting the first five inflexions, i. e. the Strong cases of masculine and feminine nouns (see 135). The terminations for the D. Ab. G. and L. sing. are called by Páṇini *nitaḥ*, 'having *n* as their *it*,' to indicate that they are applicable to the four cases, admitting occasional substitutions; cf. the inflexion of *mati*, *dhenu* at 112, *śrí*, &c. at 123. The *pratyáhára* सुप् *sup* is used to denote all the cases from the N. sing. to the L. pl. Pratyáháras are generally formed by combining the first member of a series with the final consonant of the last member, as above (cf. page 14, note *b*).

92. The Vocative is held to be a peculiar aspect of the Nominative, and coincides with the Nom. in the dual and plural. Hence it is not supposed to have a separate termination of its own. In the singular it is sometimes identical with the stem, sometimes with the Nominative. Sometimes, however, it differs from both *.

a. The terminations beginning with vowels will sometimes be called *vowel-terminations;* and those beginning with consonants, including the Nom. sing., *consonantal terminations.*

Again, those cases which take the vowel-terminations will sometimes be called *vowel-cases;* and those which take the consonantal, *consonantal cases.*

See also the division into Strong, Middle, and Weak cases at 135. *a.*

Observe—The terminations should be read horizontally, i.e. for each case in all three numbers; not perpendicularly, i.e. not for all the cases of the singular before passing to the dual. Hence the expression '*śas* and all the remaining cases' must be taken to mean the Ac. pl. and all the other cases sing. du. and pl., and the 'first five inflexions' must be taken to denote *s*, *au*, *as*, *am*, *au*, or N. sing. du. pl., Ac. sing. du.

93. Having propounded the above scheme as the general type of the several case-suffixes in the three numbers, Indian grammarians proceed to adapt them to every Substantive and Adjective in the language, as well as to Pronouns, Numerals, and Participles, whether masculine, feminine, or neuter.

In fact, their theory is, that there is but one declension in Sanskṛit, and that the stem of a noun being given, and the regular case-terminations being given, the stem is to be joined to those terminations according to the regular laws of euphonic combination, as in the following examples of the two stems, नौ *nau*, f. 'a ship' (*navi*, *vav*), and हरित् *harit*, m. f. 'green.'

---

* In the first or commonest class of nouns the masculine stem stands alone in the Vocative, just as the termination is dropped from the 2nd pers. sing. Imperative Parasmai in the first group of classes in conjugation, see 246.

94.

	SINGULAR.	DUAL.	PLURAL.
Nom. Voc.	नौस् *naus* *nau* + *s*	नावौ *návau* *nau* + *au*. See 37.	नावस् *návas* *nau* + *as*. 37.
Acc.	नावम् *návam* *nau* + *am*. 37.	— *návau*	— *návas*
Inst.	नावा *nává* *nau* + *á*. 37.	नौभ्याम् *naubhyám* *nau* + *bhyám*	नौभिस् *naubhis* *nau* + *bhis*
Dat.	नावे *náve* *nau* + *e*. 37.	— *naubhyám*	नौभ्यस् *naubhyas* *nau* + *bhyas*
Abl.	नावस् *návas* *nau* + *as*. 37.	— *naubhyám*	— *naubhyas*
Gen.	नावस् *návas* *nau* + *as*. 37.	नावोस् *návos* *nau* + *os*. 37.	नावाम् *návám* *nau* + *ám*. 37.
Loc.	नावि *návi* *nau* + *i*. 37.	— *návos*	नौषु *naushu* *nau* + *su*. 70.

95.

	SINGULAR.	DUAL.	PLURAL.
Nom. Voc.	हरित् *harit* *harit* + *s*. See 41. I.	हरितौ *haritau* *harit* + *au*. 43. *d*.	हरितस् *haritas* *harit* + *as*. 43. *d*.
Acc.	हरितम् *haritam* *harit* + *am*. 43. *d*.	— *haritau*	— *haritas*
Inst.	हरिता *haritá* *harit* + *á*. 43. *d*.	हरिद्भ्याम् *haridbhyám* *harit* + *bhyám*. 43.	हरिद्भिस् *haridbhis* *harit* + *bhis*. 43.
Dat.	हरिते *harite* *harit* + *e*. 43. *d*.	— *haridbhyám*	हरिद्भ्यस् *haridbhyas* *harit* + *bhyas*. 43.
Abl.	हरितस् *haritas* *harit* + *as*. 43. *d*.	— *haridbhyám*	— *haridbhyas*
Gen.	— *haritas*	हरितोस् *haritos* *harit* + *os*. 43. *d*.	हरिताम् *haritám* *harit* + *ám*. 43. *d*.
Loc.	हरिति *hariti* *harit* + *i*. 43. *d*.	— *haritos*	हरित्सु *haritsu* *harit* + *su*. 42.

96. Unfortunately, however, नौ *nau*, 'a ship,' is nearly the only noun, ending in a vowel, that joins its stem thus regularly with case-endings; and although nouns ending in consonants are numerous, and nearly as regular as *harit*, they are far less common than nouns in *a*, *á*, *i*, *í*, *u*, and *ṛi*, whose declension requires frequent changes in the finals, both of stem and terminations.

97. Thus in cl. 1 of stems ending in *a* (comprising almost as many nouns as the other seven classes together; compare 80 with 81–87), not only is the final *a* of the stem liable to be lengthened and changed to *e*, but also the termination *ina* is substituted for *á*, the proper termination of the Inst. sing. masc.; *ya* for *e* of the Dat.; *t* for *as* of the Ab.; *sya* for *as* of the Gen.; *n* for *as* of the Ac. pl.; *ais* for *bhis* of the Inst. pl. And in other nouns changes and substitutions are required, some of which are determined by the gender. (Compare the first group of verbal stems at 257. *a*.)

The annexed table repeats synoptically the terminations, with the most usual substitutions, throughout all the classes of nouns.

	SINGULAR.	DUAL.	PLURAL.
N.	स् (m.f.), म्* (n.)	औ (m.f.), ई (f.*n.)	अस् (m.f.), इ (n.)
Ac.	अम् (m.f.), म्* (m.f.n.)	औ (m.f.), ई (f.*n.)	अस्, स् (m.f.), न्* (m.), इ (n.)
I.	आ (m.f.n.), इन* (m.n.)	भ्याम् (m.f.n.)	भिस् (m.f.n.), ऐस्* (m.n.)
D.	ए (m.f.n.), य* (m.n.)	भ्याम् (m.f.n.)	भ्यस् (m.f.n.)
Ab.	अस् (m.f.n.), स् (m.f.), त्* (m.n.)	भ्याम् (m.f.n.)	भ्यस् (m.f.n.)
G.	अस् (m.f.n.), स् (m.f.), स्य* (m.n.)	ओस् (m.f.n.)	आम् (m.f.n.)
L.	इ (m.f.n.), आम् (f.), औ (m.f.)	ओस् (m.f.n.)	सु (m.f.n.)

Obs. 1. Those substitutions marked * are mostly restricted to nouns ending in *a*, and are therefore especially noticeable. Feminines in *á* are peculiar in taking the neut. substitution *í* in du. N. Ac. V.

Obs. 2. It will be perceived that the Accusative pl. of all masc. nouns in the first four declensions ends in *n*, whilst that of all fem. nouns ends in the regular termination *s*.

a. Comparing the above terminations with those of Latin and Greek, we may remark that *s* enters into the Nom. sing. masc., and *m* or *n* into the neuter, in all three languages. In regard to the Sk. dual *au*, the original termination was *á*, as found in the Vedas; and *á* equals the Greek *α*, *ω*, and *ε*. In Nom. pl. masc. the *s* appears in many Lat. and Gr. words. In Ac. sing., Sk. agrees with Lat., and even with Gr., final *μ* in Gr. being changed into *ν*. *S* appears in all three languages in Ac. pl.; and when the Sanskṛit ends in *n*, as in the first class of nouns, this *n* is probably for *ns*, since a preceding *a* is lengthened to compensate for the rejection of *s*. Cf. some Vedic Ac. plurals; cf. also ἵππους Ac. pl. in the Cretic dialect; and Gothic forms, such as *balgins, sununs;* cf. likewise the *r* added in the Veda after the Ac. pl., e. g. ऋतूँरनु *ṛitū̃r anu* (Ṛig-v. I. 49, 3). In Inst. pl. *bhis* is preserved in the Lat. *nobis, vobis,* and Gr. φι(ν) for φις (ναῦ-φιν = *naubhis*). The *ais* which belongs to Sk. nouns in *a* is probably a contraction of *ábhis*, since in the Vedas *ebhis* for *ábhis* is found for *ais*, as *vṛikebhis* for *vṛikais*, &c. &c. This *ais* probably answers to the Latin Dat. and Abl. plural in *is*, just as *bhis* and *bhyas* answer to the Latin *bus*. In the Gen. sing. all three languages have preserved the *s* (नावस्, *nav-is*, νη-ός for ναϝος); and in the Gen. pl. *ám*=Gr. ων and Lat. *um* (पदाम् = ποδῶν, *pedum*). In Loc. sing. Sanskṛit *i* is preserved in Lat. and Gr. in such words as οἴκοι, 'at home,' Ἰσθμοῖ, 'on the Isthmus;' *humi, domi,* &c.; and in the Dative (निशि = νυκτί, नावि = *navi*). In Loc. pl. *su* = Gr. σι; e.g. θύρασι(ν), 'at the door;' ὥρασι(ν), 'at the right time' (नौषु = ναυσί). Sanskṛit stems in *a* prefix *i* to *su;* so that *vṛikaishu* (29. *b*) = λυκοῖσι. The Voc. sing. in Gr. is frequently identical with the stem, and the Voc. du. and pl. with the Nom., as in Sanskṛit; e.g. πολίτη-ς, stem and Voc. πολιτα; ῥήτωρ, stem and Voc. ῥητορ; εὐγενής, stem and Voc. εὐγενες.

98. In the following pages no attempt will be made to explain how or why particular nouns deviate from the general scheme of terminations. A division of nouns into eight classes, four ending in vowels, and four ending in consonants, will be made; and under every one of the eight classes a model noun for the masculine, feminine, and neuter, serving for adjectives as well as substantives, will be declined in full.

99. But the student must understand, that this division into eight classes is entirely arbitrary. It does not imply that there are eight separate declensions in Sanskṛit. All that is meant is, that the final letters of the stems of nouns may be conveniently arranged under four general heads for vowels, and four for consonants. Indeed, according to native grammarians, there is only one declension in Sanskṛit, all nouns, whatever may be the final of their stems, being forced to adapt themselves to one common scheme of nearly similar case-terminations.

100. It is most important to remember, that the formation of every case in a Sanskṛit noun supposes the application of a rule of *Sandhi* or 'junction;' and that *declension* in Sanskṛit is strictly 'junction,' i.e. not a divergence from an upright line (*rectus*), but a *joining together* of a stem with its terminations.

101. Sometimes, however, before this *joining together* takes place, the original final of the stem has to be changed to its Guṇa or Vṛiddhi equivalent (see 27), or even to some other letter (see 41. II–V), so that it will often be necessary to point out in what manner the *inflective* stem (*anga*, see 135. *c*) varies from the original stem (*prátipadika*); and sometimes the original termination of the scheme will have to be changed, as indicated at 97; thus, at 103, under the Gen. du. *śivayos*, *śive + os* denotes, that before the stem *śiva* is joined to the termination *os*, the final letter *a* is to be changed to *e*; and the reference 36. *a.* indicates the rule of Sandhi (explained at 36. *a*) which must come into operation in joining *śive* and *os* together. Similarly, when the original termination has to be modified, the termination will be exhibited in its altered form; thus, at 103, under the Ac. sing., *śiva + m* denotes, that the stem is to be joined with *m*, substituted for the original termination *am*. See the table at 97.

102. In declining the first model noun *śiva*, the stem with the sign +, and after it the termination will be exhibited under each inflexion, and a reference will be given to the number of the rule of Sandhi which must come into operation.

In the other nouns the process of Sandhi will be explained when necessary, along with the changes of the stem, immediately before the paradigms of declension, and in the paradigms a transliteration in Italic type will be generally given immediately under the Sanskṛit type.

Section I.—FIRST FOUR CLASSES OF NOUNS.

Inflexion of Nouns, Substantive and Adjective, whose stems end in vowels.

First Class in अ *a*, आ *á*, and ई *í*.

This large class corresponds to a common class of Latin and Greek words in *us* and *ος*, *um* and *ον*, *a* and *α*, e.g. *lupu-s*, λύκο-ς (=Sk. *vṛika-s*, Nom. of *vṛika*); *donu-m*, δῶρο-ν; *terra*, χώρα (=*dhará*); and to adjectives like *bonus*, ἀγαθός, e.g. Sk. *nava-s*, *navá*, *nava-m*, 'new,'=Lat. *novu-s*, *nova*, *novu-m*; Gr. νέο-ς (for νεϝο-ς), νέα, νέο-ν.

103. Masculine stems in *a*, like शिव *śiva*, m. 'the god Śiva,' or as an adjective, 'prosperous.'

The final of the stem is lengthened in D. Ab. sing., I. D. Ab. du., Ac. G. pl.; and changed to *e* in G. L. du., D. Ab. L. pl.: *n* is euphonically affixed to the final in G. pl. Hence the four inflective stems *śiva, śivá, śive, śiván*.

	SINGULAR.	DUAL.	PLURAL.
N.	शिवस् *śivas* *śiva+s*	शिवौ *śivau* *śiva+au*. See 33.	शिवास् *śivás* *śiva+as*. See 31.
Ac.	शिवम् *śivam* *śiva+m*	— *śivau*	शिवान् *śiván* *śivá+n*
I.	शिवेन *śivena* *śiva+ina*. 32.	शिवाभ्याम् *śivábhyám* *śivá+bhyám*	शिवैस् *śivais* *śiva+ais*. 33.
D.	शिवाय *śiváya* *śivá+ya*	— *śivábhyám*	शिवेभ्यस् *śivebhyas* *śive+bhyas*
Ab.	शिवात् *śivát* *śivá+t*	— *śivábhyám*	— *śivebhyas*
G.	शिवस्य *śivasya* *śiva+sya*	शिवयोस् *śivayos* *śive+os*. 36. *a*.	शिवानाम् *śivánám* *śiván+ám*
L.	शिवे *śive* *śiva+i*. 32.	— *śivayos*	शिवेषु *śiveshu* *śive+su*. 70.
V.	शिव *śiva* *śiva* (*s* dropped). 92.	शिवौ *śivau* *śiva+au*. 33.	शिवास् *śivás* *śiva+as*. 31.

Obs.—The Vedic I. sing. may end in *á*, e.g. *śivá* for *śivena*; N. Ac. du. may end in *á*, e.g. *śivá* for *śivau*; N. pl. may end in *ásas*, e.g. *śivásas* for *śivás*; I. pl. may end in *ebhis*, e.g. *śivebhis* for *śivais*. Cf. *ebhis*, I. pl. of *idam*, 224.

104. Neuter stems in *a*, like शिव *śiva*, n. 'prosperity,' or as an adjective, 'prosperous.'

The final of the stem is lengthened and assumes *n* in N. Ac. V. pl.

N. Ac.	शिवम् *śivam* *śiva+m*. 97.	शिवे *śive* *śiva+í*. 32.	शिवानि *śiváni* *śivá+n+i*

The Vocative is शिव *śiva*, शिवे *śive*, शिवानि *śiváni*; all the other cases are like the masculine.

105. Feminine stems in *á* and *í*, like शिवा *śivá*, f. 'the wife of Śiva,' or as an adjective, 'prosperous,' and नदी *nadí*, f. 'a river.' Their declension is exhibited side by side that their analogy may be more easily perceived.

In *śivá* the final of the stem is changed to *e* in I. sing., G. L. du.; *yá* is inserted in D. Ab. G. L. sing.; and *n* in G. pl. Hence the inflective stems *śivá, śive*. In *nadí* the final is changed to *y* before the vowel-terminations by 34; *á* is inserted in D. Ab. G. L. sing.; and *n* in G. pl.; in V. sing. the final of the stem is shortened.

Junction of stem with termination: N. sing. *s* rejected; N. du. *śivá*+*í*=*śive* by 32; N. pl. *śivá*+*as*=*śivás* by 31; I. sing. *śive*+*á*=*śivayá* by 36. *a;* D. sing. *śivá*+*yá*+*e*=*śiváyai* by 33; G. L. du. *śive*+*os*=*śivayos* by 36. *a.* D. sing. *nadí* +*á*+*e*=*nadyai* by 34 and 33; L. pl. *nadí*+*su*=*nadíshu* by 70.

	SING.	DUAL.	PLURAL.	SING.	DUAL.	PLURAL.
N.	शिवा *śivá*	शिवे *śive*	शिवास् *śivás*	नदी *nadí*	नद्यौ *nadyau*	नद्यस् *nadyas*
Ac.	शिवाम् *śivám*	— *śive*	— *śivás*	नदीम् *nadím*	— *nadyau*	नदीस् *nadís*
I.	शिवया *śivayá*	शिवाभ्याम् *śivábhyám*	शिवाभिस् *śivábhis*	नद्या *nadyá*	नदीभ्याम् *nadíbhyám*	नदीभिस् *nadíbhis*
D.	शिवायै *śiváyai*	— *śivábhyám*	शिवाभ्यस् *śivábhyas*	नद्यै *nadyai*	— *nadíbhyám*	नदीभ्यस् *nadíbhyas*
Ab.	शिवायास् *śiváyás*	— *śivábhyám*	— *śivábhyas*	नद्यास् *nadyás*	— *nadíbhyám*	— *nadíbhyas*
G.	— *śiváyás*	शिवयोस् *śivayos*	शिवानाम् *śivánám*	— *nadyás*	नद्योस् *nadyos*	नदीनाम् *nadínám*
L.	शिवायाम् *śiváyám*	— *śivayos*	शिवासु *śivásu*	नद्याम् *nadyám*	— *nadyos*	नदीषु *nadíshu*
V.	शिवे *śive*	शिवे *śive*	शिवास् *śivás*	नदि *nadi*	नद्यौ *nadyau*	नद्यस् *nadyas*

Obs. 1. The Vedic I. sing. may be *śivá* for *śivayá;* D. sing. *śivai* for *śiváyai;* N. pl. *śivásas;* G. pl. *śivám.*

Obs. 2. The Vedic N. pl. of nouns in *í* may end in *ís*, e. g. *nadís* for *nadyas.*

106. Monosyllabic nouns in ई *í*, like श्री f. 'fortune,' भी f. 'fear,' &c., vary from *nadí* in the manner explained at 123.

107. In accordance with 58, such words as मृग *mṛiga*, m. 'a deer;' पुरुष *purusha*, m. 'a man;' भार्या *bháryá*, f. 'a wife;' कुमारी *kumárí*, f. 'a girl'—must be written, in the Inst. sing. m. and the Gen. pl. m. f., with the cerebral ण् *ṇ;* thus, मृगेण *mṛigeṇa*, पुरुषेण, मृगाणाम्, पुरुषाणाम्, भार्याणाम्, कुमारीणाम्. When *n* is final, as in the Ac. pl. m., it remains unchanged.

108. When a feminine noun ending in *á* forms the last member of a compound adjective, it is declined like *śiva* for the masc. and neut. Thus fr. *vidyá*, 'learning,' *alpa-vidyas* (m.), *alpa-vidyá* (f.), *alpa-vidyam* (n.), 'possessed of little learning.' Similarly, a masculine noun takes the fem. and neut. terminations; and a neut. noun, the masc. and fem.

a. When roots ending in *á*, such as *pá*, 'to drink' or 'to preserve,' form the last member of compound words, they assume the terminations at 91 regularly for their masculine and feminine, rejecting, however, the final of the stem in Ac. pl. and remaining Weak or vowel-cases; thus, सोमपा *soma-pá*, m. f. 'a drinker of Soma juice;' N. V. -पास्, -पौ, -पास्; Ac. -पाम्, -पौ, -पस्; I. -पा, -पाभ्याम्, &c.; D. -पे, &c. They form their neuter like that of *śiva*, e. g. neut. N. Ac. V. सोमपम्, -पे, -पानि, &c.

Similarly, विश्वपा 'protector of the universe,' and शङ्ख्मा 'a shell-blower.'

b. Analogously in Ṛig-veda IV. 9, 4, ग्ना 'a woman' is in N. sing. ग्नास्.

c. Masculine nouns in *á*, like हाहा *háhá*, m. 'a Gandharva,' not derived from verbal roots, assume the terminations with the regular euphonic changes, but the Ac. pl. ends in न्; thus, N. V. हाहास्, हाहौ, हाहास्; A. हाहाम्, हाहौ, हाहान्; I. हाहा, हाहाभ्याम्, हाहाभिस्, &c.; D. हाहै, &c.; Ab. हाहास्, &c.; G. हाहास्, हाहौस्, हाहाम्; L. हाहे, &c.

d. The Voc. cases of अम्बा *ambá*, अक्का *akká*, and अल्ला *allá*, all signifying 'mother,' are अम्ब, अक्क, अल्ल, 'O mother!'

e. दन्त m. 'a tooth,' मास m. 'a month,' पाद m. 'a foot,' यूष m. n. 'soup,' आस्य n. 'the face,' हृदय n. 'the heart,' उदक n. 'water,' शीर्ष n. 'the head,' मांस n. 'flesh,' निशा f. 'night,' नासिका f. 'the nose,' पृतना f. 'an army,' are declined regularly, but may substitute दत्, मास्, पद्, यूषन्, आसन्, हृद्, उदन्, शीर्षन्, मांस्, निश्, नस्, पृत् in the Ac. pl. and remaining cases (see 184). In the neut. nouns, the Nom. pl. does not admit the same substitute as Ac. pl. Thus, उदक will be Ac. pl. उदकानि or उदानि; I. sing. उदकेन or उद्ना. Again, नासिका in I. du. will be नासिकाभ्याम् or नोभ्याम्; and मांस, मांसाभ्याम् or मान्भ्याम्.

109. To understand the importance of studying the declension of this first class of nouns, the student has only to turn back to pp. 57–68, where the formation of the stems of nouns, substantive and adjective, which follow this declension, is explained. All masculine and neuter substantives in this list are declined like *śiva*, and all feminine either like *śivá* or *nadí*, all the adjectives following the same three examples for their three genders.

SECOND CLASS in इ *i*. THIRD CLASS in उ *u*.

The inflexion of the 2nd and 3rd classes of nouns (see 81, 82) is exhibited side by side, that their analogy may be more readily perceived.

The 2nd answers to Latin and Greek words like *igni-s*, *turri-s*, πόλι-ς, πίστι-ς, *mare*, μέλι; the 3rd, to words like *gradu-s*, *cornu*, βότρυ-ς, ἡδύ-ς, μέθυ.

110. Masculine stems in इ *i* and उ *u*, like अग्नि *agni*, m. (*ignis*), 'fire;' भानु *bhánu*, m. 'the sun.'

The final of the stem is gunated in D. Ab. G. V. sing., N. pl.; lengthened in N. Ac. V. du., Ac. G. pl.; dropped in L. sing., or, according to Páṇini, changed to *a*; *n* is inserted in I. sing., G. pl. Hence the inflective stems *agni, agní, agne, agn*; *bhánu, bhánú, bháno, bhán*; according to some the Locative of *bhánu* was originally *bhánavi* (such a form occurring in the Veda), and *i* being dropped, *bhánav* would become *bhánáv* (*bhánau*).

Junction of stem with termination: V. sing., N. Ac. V. du., case-termination rejected; N. pl. *agne+as=agnayas* by 36. *a*; D. sing. *agne+e=agnaye*, 36. *a*; G. L. du. *agni+os=agnyos*, 34; L. pl. *agni+su=agnishu*, 70. Similarly, N. pl. *bháno+as=bhánavas*, 36. *a*; D. sing. *bháno+e=bhánave*, 36. *a*; G. L. du. *bhánu+os=bhánvos*, 34; L. pl. *bhánu+su=bhánushu*, 70.

	SING.	DUAL.	PLURAL.	SING.	DUAL.	PLURAL.
N.	अग्निस् *agnis*	अग्नी *agní*	अग्नयस् *agnayas*	भानुस् *bhánus*	भानू *bhánú*	भानवस् *bhánavas*
Ac.	अग्निम् *agnim*	— *agní*	अग्नीन् *agnín*	भानुम् *bhánum*	— *bhánú*	भानून् *bhánún*
I.	अग्निना *agniná*	अग्निभ्याम् *agnibhyám*	अग्निभिस् *agnibhis*	भानुना *bhánuná*	भानुभ्याम् *bhánubhyám*	भानुभिस् *bhánubhis*
D.	अग्नये *agnaye*	— *agnibhyám*	अग्निभ्यस् *agnibhyas*	भानवे *bhánave*	— *bhánubhyám*	भानुभ्यस् *bhánubhyas*
Ab.	अग्नेस् *agnes*	— *agnibhyám*	— *agnibhyas*	भानोस् *bhános*	— *bhánubhyám*	— *bhánubhyas*
G.	— *agnes*	अग्न्योस् *agnyos*	अग्नीनाम् *agnínám*	— *bhános*	भान्वोस् *bhánvos*	भानूनाम् *bhánúnám*
L.	अग्नौ *agnau*	— *agnyos*	अग्निषु *agnishu*	भानौ *bhánau*	— *bhánvos*	भानुषु *bhánushu*
V.	अग्ने *agne*	अग्नी *agní*	अग्नयस् *agnayas*	भानो *bháno*	भानू *bhánú*	भानवस् *bhánavas*

111. The Vedic Gen. sing. may be *bhánvas*, which form may also serve for the Nom. and Ac. pl.

112. Feminine stems in इ *i* and उ *u*, like मति *mati*, f. 'the mind,' and धेनु *dhenu*, f. 'a milch cow.'

The final of the stem is gunated in D. Ab. G. V. sing., N. pl.; lengthened in N. Ac. V. du., Ac. G. pl.; dropped in L. sing. (unless the termination be आम्); *n* is inserted in G. pl. Hence the inflective stems *mati, matí, mate, mat*; *dhenu, dhenú, dheno, dhen*.

The junction of stem with termination is generally the same as in the masculines *agni* and *bhánu*. Inst. sing. *mati+á=matyá*, 34; D. *mate+e=mataye*, 36. *a*; *mati+á+e=matyai*, 33.

	SING.	DUAL.	PLURAL.	SING.	DUAL.	PLURAL.
N.	मतिस् *matis*	मती *matí*	मतयस् *matayas*	धेनुस् *dhenus*	धेनू *dhenú*	धेनवस् *dhenavas*
Ac.	मतिम् *matim*	— *matí*	मतीस् *matís*	धेनुम् *dhenum*	— *dhenú*	धेनूस् *dhenús*
I.	मत्या *matyá*	मतिभ्याम् *matibhyám*	मतिभिस् *matibhis*	धेन्वा *dhenvá*	धेनुभ्याम् *dhenubhyám*	धेनुभिस् *dhenubhis*
D.	मतये or मत्यै *mataye* or °*tyai*	— *matibhyám*	मतिभ्यस् *matibhyas*	धेनवे or धेन्वै *dhenave* or °*nvai*	— *dhenubhyám*	धेनुभ्यस् *dhenubhyas*
Ab.	मतेस् or मत्यास् *mates* or °*tyás*	— *matibhyám*	— *matibhyas*	धेनोस् or धेन्वास् *dhenos* or °*nvás*	— *dhenubhyám*	— *dhenubhyas*
G.	— *mates* or °*tyás*	मत्योस् *matyos*	मतीनाम् *matínám*	— *dhenos* or °*nvás*	धेन्वोस् *dhenvos*	धेनूनाम् *dhenúnám*
L.	मतौ or मत्याम् *matau* or °*tyám*	— *matyos*	मतिषु *matishu*. 70.	धेनौ or धेन्वाम् *dhenau* or °*nvám*	— *dhenvos*	धेनुषु *dhenushu*. 70.
V.	मते *mate*	मती *matí*	मतयस् *matayas*	धेनो *dheno*	धेनू *dhenú*	धेनवस् *dhenavas*

With the optional forms in D. Ab. G. L. sing., compare similar forms in the same cases of *nadí*.

113. The Vedic Nom. pl. may be *dhenvas*.

114. Neuter stems in इ *i* and उ *u*, like वारि *vári*, n. 'water,' and मधु *madhu*, n. 'honey' (μέθυ).

The stem inserts *n* before the vowel-terminations, and the final is lengthened in N. Ac. V. and G. pl. Hence the inflective stems *vári, varí; madhu, madhú.*

	SING.	DUAL.	PLURAL.	SING.	DUAL.	PLURAL.
N. Ac.	वारि *vári*	वारिणी *váriṇí*. 58.	वारीणि *váríṇi*	मधु *madhu*	मधुनी *madhuní*	मधूनि *madhúni*
I.	वारिणा *váriṇá*	वारिभ्याम् *váribhyám*	वारिभिस् *váribhis*	मधुना *madhuná*	मधुभ्याम् *madhubhyám*	मधुभिस् *madhubhis*
D.	वारिणे *váriṇe*	— *váribhyám*	वारिभ्यस् *váribhyas*	मधुने *madhune*	— *madhubhyám*	मधुभ्यस् *madhubhyas*
Ab.	वारिणस् *váriṇas*	— *váribhyám*	— *váribhyas*	मधुनस् *madhunas*	— *madhubhyám*	— *madhubhyas*
G.	— *váriṇas*	वारिणोस् *váriṇos*	वारीणाम् *váríṇám*. 58.	— *madhunas*	मधुनोस् *madhunos*	मधूनाम् *madhúnám*
L.	वारिणि *váriṇi*	— *váriṇos*	वारिषु *várishu*. 70.	मधुनि *madhuni*	— *madhunos*	मधुषु *madhushu*. 70.
V.	वारि or वारे *vári* or *váre*	वारिणी *váriṇí*	वारीणि *váríṇi*	मधु or मधो *madhu* or *madho*	मधुनी *madhuní*	मधूनि *madhúni*

115. The Vedic Ac. pl. may be *madhú*.

116. Neuter nouns in *i* and *u* follow the analogy of nouns in *in* at 159, except in G. plur. and V. sing.

a. सानु n. 'summit,' 'ridge,' optionally substitutes स्नु in all cases except the first five inflexions.

117. There are not many substantives declined like *agni* and *vári* (81), but nouns like *mati* are numerous (81. II). Moreover, adjectives like *śuči*, and compound adjectives in *i*, are declined like *agni* in masc., like *mati* in fem., and like *vári* in neut.

118. Again, there are few substantives declined like *dhenu* and *madhu*, yet many simple adjectives like *tanu* and *pipásu* (82), all compound adjectives in *u*, are declined like *bhánu* in the masc., like *dhenu* in the fem., and like *madhu* in the neut.

a. Many adjectives in *u*, however, either optionally or necessarily follow *nadí* in fem.; as, *tanu*, 'thin,' makes Nom. fem. either *tanus* or *tanví*; मृदु, 'tender,' makes Nom. f. मृद्वी *mridví*; and गुरु, 'heavy,' गुर्वी *gurví*: and some optionally lengthen *u* in the fem.; as, *bhíru*, 'timid,' makes fem. भीरु or भीरू, declinable like nouns in *ú*, 125.

119. When feminine nouns in *i* and *u* form the last member of a compound adjective, they must be declined like *agni* in masc., and *vári* in neut. Thus *alpa-mati*, 'narrow-minded,' in the Ac. plur. masc. would be *alpa-matín*; fem. *alpa-matís*; neut. *alpa-matíni*.

Similarly, a masc. or neut. noun, at the end of a comp., may take a fem. form.

a. Although adjectives in *i* and *u* are declined like *vári* and *madhu* for the neut., yet in the D. Ab. G. L. sing., and in the G. L. du., they may optionally follow the masculine form; thus *śuči* and *tanu* will be, in D. sing. neut., शुचिने or शुचये, तनुने or तनवे; and so with the other cases.

120. सखि *sakhi*, m. 'a friend,' has two stems, सखाय् for the Strong cases (see 135. *a*), and सखि for the others; thus, N. सखा, सखायौ, सखायस्; Ac. सखायम्, सखायौ, सखीन्; I. सख्या, सखिभ्याम्, सखिभिस्; D. सख्ये, सखिभ्याम्, सखिभ्यस्; Ab. सख्युस्, सखिभ्याम्, सखिभ्यस्; G. सख्युस्, सख्योस्, सखीनाम्; L. सख्यौ, सख्योस्, सखिषु; V. सखे, सखायौ, सखायस्. Hence it appears that *sakhi* in some cases assumes the terminations at 91 more regularly than *agni*. In the rest it follows *agni*.

Obs.—The feminine सखी, 'a female friend,' is declined like नदी.

121. पति m. 'a master,' 'lord' (πόσις), when not used in a compound word, follows *sakhi* at 120 in I. D. Ab. G. L. sing. (thus, I. पत्या, D. पत्ये, Ab. G. पत्युस्, L. पत्यौ); in the other cases, *agni*. But *pati* is more usually found at the end of compounds, and then follows *agni* throughout (thus, भूपतिना 'by the lord of the earth').

Obs.—The feminine of पति is पत्नी *patní*, declinable like नदी.

122. A few neuter nouns, अस्थि n. 'a bone' (ὀστέον), अक्षि n. 'an eye' (*oculus*, ὄκος), सक्थि n. 'a thigh,' दधि n. 'coagulated milk,' drop their final *i* in I. sing. and remaining weak or vowel-cases, and are declined in those cases as if derived from obsolete forms in *an*, such as अस्थन्, &c. (cf. *náman* at 152); thus,

अस्थि 'a bone:' N. V. Ac. अस्थि, अस्थिनी, अस्थीनि; I. अस्थ्ना, अस्थिभ्याम्, &c.; D. अस्थ्ने, अस्थिभ्याम्, &c.; Ab. अस्थ्नस्, &c.; G. अस्थ्नस्, अस्थ्नोस्, अस्थ्नाम्; L. अस्थ्नि or अस्थनि, अस्थ्नोस्, अस्थिषु.

Hence, अक्षि, 'an eye,' will be in I. sing. अक्ष्णा; in D. अक्ष्णे, &c. (see 58).

Nouns ending in ई í *and* ऊ ú.

123. Besides the feminines of adjectives and participles, &c., declined like *nadí* at 105 (cf. 80. XI), there are a few common monosyllabic words in long ई *í* (generally roots used as substantives) *primitively* feminine, i. e. not derived from masculine substantives (see 82. XV), whose declension must be noticed separately. They vary from the declension of नदी (105) by forming the Nom. with स्, and using the same form for the Voc., and by changing the final *í* to *iy* before the vowel-terminations; thus,

श्री f. 'prosperity:' N.V. श्रीस्, श्रियौ, श्रियस्; Ac. श्रियम्, श्रियौ, श्रियस्; I. श्रिया, श्रीभ्याम्, श्रीभिस्; D. श्रिये or श्रियै, श्रीभ्याम्, श्रीभ्यस्; Ab. श्रियस् or श्रियास्, श्रीभ्याम्, श्रीभ्यस्; G. श्रियस् or श्रियास्, श्रियोस्, श्रियाम् or श्रीणाम्; L. श्रियि or श्रियाम्, श्रियोस्, श्रीषु.

a. Similarly, भी f. 'fear,' ह्री f. 'shame,' and धी f. 'understanding;' thus, N. V. भीस्, भियौ, भियस्; Ac. भियम्, &c.; I. भिया, &c.; D. भिये or भियै, &c.

b. स्त्री f., 'a woman' (not being itself a root like the examples above), follows नदी in N. V. sing., and varies also in other respects; thus, N. स्त्री, स्त्रियौ, स्त्रियस्; V. स्त्रि, स्त्रियौ, स्त्रियस्; Ac. स्त्रीम् or स्त्रियम्, स्त्रियौ, स्त्रीस् or स्त्रियस्; I. स्त्रिया, स्त्रीभ्याम्, स्त्रीभिस्; D. स्त्रियै, स्त्रीभ्याम्, स्त्रीभ्यस्; Ab. स्त्रियास्, स्त्रीभ्याम्, स्त्रीभ्यस्; G. स्त्रियास्, स्त्रियोस्, स्त्रीणाम्; L. स्त्रियाम्, स्त्रियोस्, स्त्रीषु.

As the last member of a compound adjective, it shortens its final, and in some of its cases follows *agni* and *mati;* e. g.

अतिस्त्रि m. f. n. 'surpassing a woman:' N. masc. -स्त्रिस्, -स्त्रियौ, -स्त्रयस्; Ac. -स्त्रिम् or -स्त्रियम्, -स्त्रियौ, -स्त्रीन् or -स्त्रियस्; I. -स्त्रिणा, -स्त्रिभ्याम्, &c.; D. -स्त्रये, &c.; Ab. -स्त्रेस्, &c.; G. -स्त्रेस्, -स्त्रियोस्, -स्त्रीणाम्; L. -स्त्रौ, &c.; V. -स्त्रे, &c. The fem. form is like the masc., but Ac. pl. -स्त्रीस् or -स्त्रियस्; I. -स्त्रिया; D. -स्त्रियै or -स्त्रये; Ab. -स्त्रियास् or -स्त्रेस्, &c. For neut., see 126. *j.*

124. A few primitively feminine words *not* monosyllabic, such as लक्ष्मी 'the goddess of prosperity,' तन्त्री 'a lute-string,' तरी 'a boat,' like श्री, take *s* in the Nom. sing., but in other respects follow नदी; thus, N. लक्ष्मीस्, लक्ष्म्यौ, लक्ष्म्यस्; Ac. लक्ष्मीम्, &c.; V. लक्ष्मि.

Obs.—Analogously in the Veda वृकी 'a she-wolf' (Ṛig-v. I. 117, 18), and (according to some authorities) सिंही 'a lioness,' make N. sing. वृकीस्, सिंहीस्.

But गौरी f. 'the brilliant (goddess),' as a derivative fem. noun, is N. sing. गौरी.

125. Feminine nouns in long ऊ *ú*, not monosyllabic, are declined like primitively feminine nouns of more than one syllable in ई *í*, i.e. like लक्ष्मी, they follow the analogy of *nadí* except in N. sing., where *s* is retained. In the other cases ऊ *ú* becomes *v*, wherever ई *í* is changed to *y* (see 34); thus,

वधू 'a wife:' N. वधूस्, वध्वौ, वध्वस्; Ac. वधूम्, वध्वौ, वधूस्; I. वध्वा, वधूभ्याम्, वधूभिस्; D. वध्वै, वधूभ्याम्, वधूभ्यस्; Ab. वध्वास्, वधूभ्याम्, वधूभ्यस्; G. वध्वास्, वध्वोस्, वधूनाम्; L. वध्वाम्, वध्वोस्, वधूषु; V. वधु, वध्वौ, वध्वस्.

Similarly, चमू f. 'a host;' श्वश्रू f. 'a mother-in-law.'

a. Again, monosyllabic words in *ú* primitively feminine are declined analogously to श्री f. at 123; *ú* being changed to *uv*, wherever *í* is changed to *iy;* thus,

भू f. 'the earth:' N.V. भूस्, भुवौ, भुवस्; Ac. भुवम्, भुवौ, भुवस्; I. भुवा, भूभ्याम्, भूभिस्; D. भुवे or भुवै, भूभ्याम्, भूभ्यस्; Ab. भुवस् or भुवास्, भूभ्याम्, भूभ्यस्; G. भुवस् or भुवास्, भुवोस्, भुवाम् or भूनाम्; L. भुवि or भुवाम्, भुवोस्, भूषु.

Observe that the V. is like the N.

b. Similarly, भ्रू f. 'the eye-brow' (ὀφρύς): N.V. भ्रूस्, भ्रुवौ, भ्रुवस्, &c.

126. Roots of one syllable ending in *í* and *ú*, used as masc. or fem. nouns, follow the declension of monosyllabic words in *í* and *ú*, such as श्री at 123 and भू at 125.*a;* but in the D. Ab. G. L. sing., G. pl., take only the first inflexion; thus,

क्री m. f., 'one who buys,' makes D. क्रिये only for m. and f., and लू m. f., 'a reaper,' makes D. लुवे only for m. and f.

a. The same generally holds good if they have adjectives prefixed to them; thus, परमक्री m.f. 'the best buyer' (N.V. -क्रीस्, -क्रियौ, -क्रियस्; Ac. -क्रियम्, &c.)

b. And when they are compounded with another noun as a dependent term they generally change their final *í* and *ú* to *y* and *v*, before vowel-terminations, and not to *iy* and *uv* (unless *í* and *ú* are preceded by a double consonant, as in यवक्री 'a buyer of barley'), thus conforming more to the declension of polysyllables; e. g.

जलपी (for जलपा) m. f., 'a water-drinker,' makes N.V. जलपीस्, -प्यौ, -प्यस्; Ac. जलप्यम्, -प्यौ, -प्यस्; I. जलप्या, -पीभ्याम्, &c.; D. जलप्ये, &c.; Ab. जलप्यस्, &c.; G. जलप्यस्, -प्योस्, &c.; L. जलप्यि (in opposition to 31), &c.

So also, खलपू m. f. 'a sweeper:' N.V. खलपूस्, -प्वौ, -प्वस्; Ac. खलप्वम्, &c.; I. खलप्वा, &c.; L. खलप्वि, &c.: सुलू 'one who cuts well;' N.V. सुलूस्, -ल्वौ, -ल्वस्.

c. Similarly, वर्षाभू m. f. 'a frog,' दृन्भू m. 'a thunderbolt,' करभू m. 'a finger-nail,' पुनर्भू m. f. 'born again' (N.V. पुनर्भूस्; Ac. -र्भ्वम्, &c.; I. -र्भ्वा; D. -र्भ्वे; Ab. G. -र्भ्वस्, -र्भ्वि. But if the sense is limited to a distinct female object, as 'a virgin widow remarried,' the D. will be -र्भ्वै; Ab. G. -र्भ्वास्; L. -र्भ्वाम्, like वधू).

d. Similarly also, सेनानी m. 'a general,' ग्रामणी m. f. 'the chief of a village;' but these, like नदी, take *ám* for the termination of the L. sing. even in masc.; thus, N.V. सेनानीस्, -न्यौ, -न्यस्; Ac. -न्यम्, &c.; I. -न्या; L. सेनान्याम्, सेनान्योस्,

सेनानीषु, &c. This applies also to the simple noun नी m. f. 'a leader,' but the final becomes *iy* before vowel-terminations.

e. But स्वयम्भू and स्वभू m. 'self-existent,' as a name of Brahmá, follow भू at 125. *a*, taking only the first inflexions; thus, D. -भुवे; Ab. -भुवस्, &c.

f. Masculine non-compounds in *í* and *ú* of more than one syllable, like पपी m. 'who drinks' or 'cherishes,' 'the sun,' हूहू m. 'a Gandharva,' follow जलपी and खलपू at 126. *b*, except in Ac. sing. and pl.; thus, N. V. पपीस्, पप्यौ, पप्यस्; Ac. पपीम्, पप्यौ, पपीन्; and in L. sing. the final *í* combines with the *i* of the termination into *í* (31), not into *yi*; thus, L. sing. पपी (but हूह्वि from हूहू). Again, वातप्रमी m. 'an antelope' (surpassing the wind), as a compound, may follow जलपी; but Vopadeva makes Ac. sing. and pl. follow पपी. When such nouns have a feminine, the Ac. pl. ends in *s*; thus चारू m. f., 'tawny,' makes चारूस् for the Ac. pl. fem.

g. A word like प्रधी f. 'superior understanding' (formed from the compound verb प्रध्यै), when used as a fem. noun, is treated as a polysyllable, and follows जलपी, except in D. Ab., &c., where it takes the second inflexions (D. sing. प्रध्यै, &c.) But when used adjectively, in the sense 'having superior understanding,' it follows जलपी throughout, both for masc. and fem., but may optionally for the fem. be declined like the fem. substantive. The Voc. fem. may be प्रधीस् or प्रधि.

Two rare nouns, सुखी 'one who loves pleasure' and सुती 'one who wishes for a son,' also follow जलपी, but in Ab. G. sing. make सुख्युस्, सुत्युस्.

h. Monosyllabic nouns primitively feminine (like भी f., धी f., श्री f., at 123, भ्रू f. 'the eye-brow'), forming the last member of a compound adjective, still follow the declension of monosyllables, but use the first inflexions only in the D. Ab. G. L. cases and G. plur. for the masc., and may optionally use them for the fem.; thus, N. गतभीस् m. f., 'fearless,' is गतभिये only in D. sing. m., -भिये or -भियै in D. sing. f. So also, सुधी m. f. 'intelligent,' शुद्धधी m. f. 'having pure thoughts,' दुर्धी m. f. 'stupid,' सुश्री m. f. 'having good fortune,' सुभ्रू m. f. 'having beautiful brows;' thus, N. V. सुभ्रूस्, -भ्रुवौ, -भ्रुवस्; Ac. सुभ्रुवम्, &c. According to Vopadeva, the Voc. f. may be सुभ्रु, and this form occurs once in the Bhaṭṭi-kávya.

i. Words necessarily feminine (*nitya-strí-linga*), such as *kumárí*, 'a girl,' *Gaurí*, 'the goddess Gaurí,' &c. (not like ग्रामणी, which may be masc. and fem.), retain their *nadí* character (Páṇ. 1. 4, 3), even though they afterwards assume another sense which makes them masculine. This may happen in a compound, as in

बहुश्रेयसी m. 'a man of many excellences:' N. बहुश्रेयसी, -स्यौ, -स्यस्; V. -सि, &c.; Ac. -सीम्, -स्यौ, -सीन्; I. -स्या, -सीभ्याम्, &c.; D. -स्यै, &c.; Ab. G. -स्यास्, &c.; L. -स्याम्, &c.

Or in words not compounded, as in कुमारी 'a man who acts like a girl,' N. masc. कुमारी. But these differ in Ac. sing. and pl. (कुमार्यम्, कुमार्यस्). Cf. the name *Gopála-sarasvatí* in Sanskṛit-English Dictionary.

Also like *bahu-śreyasí* (but N. sing. will end in स्), अतिलक्ष्मी m. f. 'one who has surpassed Lakshmí,' आत्तलक्ष्मी m. f. 'deprived of fortune,' अतिचमू m. f. 'victorious over hosts' (N. अतिचमूस्, -म्वौ, -म्वस्; V. -मु; Ac. -मूम्, -म्वौ, -मून्, Ac. pl. f. -मूस्; I. -म्वा, -मूभ्याम्, &c.; D. -म्वै, &c.; Ab. -म्वास्, &c.); but these three may follow Vopadeva's declension of वातप्रमी at 126. *f*.

j. Adjectives ending in *í* and *ú* shorten the final vowel for the neuter, and follow *vári;* but in the I. D. Ab. G. and L. cases they may optionally take the masc. terminations; thus, N. V. sing. neut. गतभि; I. गतभिना or गतभ्या; D. गतभिने or गतभ्ये, &c. N. V. Ac. sing. जलपि; I. जलपिना or -प्वा, &c. N. V. Ac. खलपु; I. -पुना or -प्वा. N. V. Ac. बहुश्रेयसि; I. -श्रेयसिना or -श्रेयस्या; D. -श्रेयसिने or -श्रेयस्यै, &c. N. V. Ac. ग्रामणि; I. -णिना or -ण्या.

Fourth Class in ऋ *ṛi.*

This class answers to δοτήρ, πατήρ, *pater*, &c.; *ṛi* being equivalent to *ar:* and it is remarkable, that *dátáram*, *dátáras*, &c., bear the same relation to *pitaram*, *pitaras*, &c., that δοτῆρα, δοτῆρες, δοτῆρι, &c., bear to πατέρα, πατέρες, πατέρι, &c. Compare also the Latin *datoris* from *dator* with *patris* from *pater*.

127. Masculine stems in *ṛi*, like दातृ *dátṛi*, m. 'a giver,' and पितृ *pitṛi*, m. 'a father.' The former is the model of nouns of agency (83); the latter, of nouns of relationship.

In nouns of agency like *dátṛi* the final *ṛi* is vriddhied (28), and in nouns of relationship like *pitṛi* (except *naptṛi*, 'a grandson,' and *svasṛi*, 'a sister') gunated, in the Strong cases (see 135); but the *r* of *ár* and *ar* is dropped in N. sing., and to compensate in the last case *a* is lengthened. In both, the final *ṛi* is gunated in L. V. sing., and *ur* is substituted for final *ṛi* and the initial *a* of *as* in Ab. G. sing. In Ac. G. pl. final *ṛi* is lengthened, and assumes *n* in G. pl. Hence the inflective stems *dátṛi*, *dátár*, *dátar*, *dátṛí*, *dátur;* *pitṛi*, *pitar*, *pitṛí*, *pitur*.

Junction of stem with terminations: *s* is elided at the end of a conjunct consonant after *r;* hence in Ab. G. *dáturs* and *piturs* become *dátur* and *pitur*. See 41. I.

	SING.	DUAL.	PLURAL.	SING.	DUAL.	PLURAL.
N.	दाता *dátá*	दातारौ *dátárau*	दातारस् *dátáras*	पिता *pitá*	पितरौ *pitarau*	पितरस् *pitaras*
Ac.	दातारम् *dátáram*	— *dátárau*	दातॄन् *dátṛín*	पितरम् *pitaram*	— *pitarau*	पितॄन् *pitṛín*
I.	दात्रा *dátrá*	दातृभ्याम् *dátṛibhyám*	दातृभिस् *dátṛibhis*	पित्रा *pitrá*	पितृभ्याम् *pitṛibhyám*	पितृभिस् *pitṛibhis*
D.	दात्रे *dátre*	— *dátṛibhyám*	दातृभ्यस् *dátṛibhyas*	पित्रे *pitre*	— *pitṛibhyám*	पितृभ्यस् *pitṛibhyas*
Ab.	दातुर् *dátur*	— *dátṛibhyám*	— *dátṛibhyas*	पितुर् *pitur*	— *pitṛibhyám*	— *pitṛibhyas*
G.	— *dátur*	दात्रोस् *dátros*	दातॄणाम् *dátṛíṇám.* 58.	— *pitur*	पित्रोस् *pitros*	पितॄणाम् *pitṛíṇám.* 58.
L.	दातरि *dátari*	— *dátros*	दातृषु *dátṛishu.* 70.	पितरि *pitari*	— *pitros*	पितृषु *pitṛishu.* 70.
V.	दातर् *dátar*	दातारौ *dátárau*	दातारस् *dátáras*	पितर् *pitar*	पितरौ *pitarau*	पितरस् *pitaras*

128. *Pitṛi* seems to be a weakened form of *pátṛi*, 'a protector' (*pá*, 'to protect'). The cognate languages have preserved the root in πατήρ, *pater*, 'father,' &c. The Latin *Jupiter*, however, is literally *Dyu-pitar*, or rather *Dyaush-pitar*, 'father of heaven.' It is clear that stems like *dátṛi*, *pitṛi*, &c., originally ended in *ar*.

a. नप्तृ *naptṛi*, 'a grandson' (thought by some to be derived from *na*, 'not,' and *pátṛi*, 'a protector'), is declined like दातृ *dátṛi*.

b. There are a few nouns in *ṛi* expressing neither relationship nor agency.

नृ *nṛi*, m. 'a man,' is said to be declined like *pitṛi;* thus, N. ना *ná*, Ac. नरम्, I. न्रा, D. न्रे, Ab. G. नुर्, &c. But the forms न्रा, न्रे, नुर् are seldom, if ever, used. The following forms certainly occur: N. sing. ना, Ac. नरम्; N. Ac. du. नरौ, I. D. Ab. नृभ्याम्, G. L. नरोस्; N. pl. नरस्, Ac. नॄन्, D. Ab. नृभ्यस्, G. नृणाम् or नॄणाम्, L. नृषु. In the I. D. G. L. sing., the corresponding cases of नर are generally substituted.

c. क्रोष्टु m., 'a jackal,' *must* form its Strong cases (except V. sing.) and *may* form its Weak cases (135) from क्रोष्टृ. N. क्रोष्टा, -ष्टारौ, -ष्टारस्; Ac. -ष्टारम्, -ष्टारौ, -ष्टून् or -ष्टॄन्; I. -ष्ट्रा or -ष्टुना, -ष्टुभ्याम्, &c.; D. -ष्ट्रे or -ष्टवे, &c.; Ab. -ष्टुर् or -ष्टोस्, &c.; G. -ष्टुर् or -ष्टोस्, -ष्ट्रोस् or -ष्ट्वोस्, -ष्टॄणाम् or -ष्टूनाम्; L. -ष्टरि or -ष्टौ, &c.; V. -ष्टो.

As the last member of a compound adjective, in the neuter, क्रोष्टु alone is used.

d. Nouns like क्षत्तृ m. 'a charioteer,' त्वष्टृ m. 'a carpenter,' नेष्टृ m., होतृ m., पोतृ m. 'different kinds of priests,' योद्धृ m. 'a warrior,' of course, follow *dátṛi*. But सव्येष्टृ m., 'a charioteer,' follows *pitṛi*.

129. Feminine stems in ऋ *ṛi* belong to nouns of relationship, like *mátṛi*, 'a mother' (from *má*, 'to create,' 'the producer'); and only differ from *pitṛi* in Ac. pl., which ends in *s* instead of *n;* thus, मातॄस्. Compare μήτηρ, μητέρα, Voc. μῆτερ.

a. स्वसृ *svasṛi*, 'a sister,' exceptionally follows दातृ *dátṛi;* but the Ac. pl. is still स्वसॄस्. The lengthening of the penultimate in the Strong cases is probably caused by the loss of the *t* from *tṛi*, preserved in the English *sister*. So *soror* for *sostor*.

b. The feminine stem of nouns of agency is formed by adding ई *í* to the final ऋ *ṛi;* thus, दातृ + ई, दात्री *dátrí*, f. 'a giver;' and कर्तृ + ई, कर्त्री f. 'a doer.' Their inflexion follows *nadí* at 105.

130. The neuter stem is thus declined: N. Ac. दातृ, दातृणी, दातॄणि; V. दातर् or दातृ. The rest may conform to *vári* at 114, or resemble the masc.; thus, I. दात्रा or दातृणा, &c. But neuter stems in ऋ *ṛi* belong generally to nouns of agency or of relationship, when used at the end of compound adjectives, such as बहुदातृ *bahu-dátṛi*, 'giving much,' or दिव्यमातृ *divya-mátṛi*, agreeing with neuter words like कुलम्, i. e. 'a family having a divine mother,' or द्विमातृ 'having two mothers' (compare διμήτωρ). Their declension may resemble that of *vári* at 114, or conform to the masc. in all cases but the N. V. Ac.; thus, N. Ac. दातृ, दातृणी, दातॄणि; V. दातृ or दातर्, &c.; I. दातृणा or दात्रा, &c.; D. दातृणे or दात्रे, &c.; Ab. G. दातृणस् or दातुर्, &c.; L. दातृणि or दातरि, &c. N. Ac. -मातृ, -मातृणी, -मातॄणि; V. -मातृ or -मातर्, &c.; I. -मातृणा or -मात्रा, &c.

Nouns ending in ऐ ai, ओ o, औ au.

131. We may notice here a few monosyllabic nouns in ऐ, ओ, and औ, not sufficiently numerous to form separate classes.

132. रै *rai*, m. f. 'substance,' 'wealth' (Lat. *res*): N. V. रास्, रायौ, रायस्; Ac. रायम्, &c.; I. राया, राभ्याम्, राभिस् (*rebus*); D. राये, राभ्याम्, राभ्यस्; Ab. रायस्, &c.; G. रायस्, रायोस्, रायाम्; L. रायि, रायोस्, रासु.

133. गो *go*, m. f. 'a cow' or 'ox' (*bos*, βοῦς), 'the earth:' N. V. गौस्, गावौ, गावस्; Ac. गाम्, गावौ, गास्; I. गवा, गोभ्याम्, गोभिस्; D. गवे, &c.; Ab. गोस्, &c.; G. गोस्, गवोस्, गवाम्; L. गवि (*bovi*), गवोस्, गोषु. Compare गाम् with γῆν.

a. द्यो *dyo*, f. 'the sky,' follows गो; thus, N. V. द्यौस्, द्यावौ, द्यावस्; Ac. द्याम्, द्यावौ, द्यास्; I. द्यवा, द्योभ्याम्, द्योभिस्; D. द्यवे, &c. The Vedic N. du. is द्यावा.

134. नौ *nau*, f. 'a ship' (cf. *navis*, ναῦς), is declined at 94, taking the terminations with perfect regularity. With the N. pl. *návas*, compare *naves*, νᾶες (νῆες). The gen. νηός for νᾶος or ναϝος = *návas*.

Similarly may be declined ग्लौ m. 'the moon:' N. *glaus*, *glávau*, *glávas*, &c.

a. The above nouns sometimes occur at the end of compounds; as, बहुरै 'rich,' N. m. f. बहुरास्, &c.; बहुनौ 'having many ships,' N. m. f. बहुनौस्, &c. The neuter is बहुरि, बहुनु; of which the Inst. cases will be बहुरिणा, बहुनुना; and so with the other cases: the masc. forms being equally allowable in बहुरि throughout, except in N. Ac. V. sing. du. pl.; e.g. बहुरिणा or बहुराया.

b. In the case of *go*, 'a cow,' the compound seems always formed with *gu*; e.g. *dvi-gu, us, us, u*, 'worth two cows;' *pańća-gu*, 'bought with five cows;' *śata-gu*, 'possessing a hundred cows.'

Section II.—LAST FOUR CLASSES OF NOUNS.

Inflexion of Nouns, Substantive and Adjective, whose stems end in consonants.

135. The last four classes of nouns, though including substantives, consist chiefly of adjectives, participles, or roots at the end of adjective compounds. All masc. and fem. nouns under these remaining classes regularly take the terminations at 91. Neut. nouns take the substitutions at 97 in N. Ac. du. pl.

a. The case-terminations are here repeated with Bopp's division into Strong, Weaker, and Weakest, as applicable especially to nouns ending in consonants (though not to all of these even). The Strong cases will be here denoted by the letter **S**; the Weaker, sometimes called Middle, will be denoted by M; and the Weakest by w. In those nouns which distinguish between Strong and Weak cases only, the Weak will be marked by both M and w.

SINGULAR. M.F.	N.	DUAL. M.F.	N.	PLURAL. M.F.	N.
Nom. Voc. स् *s* (S),	(Neut. M)	औ *au* (S),	(Neut. w)	अस् *as* (S),	(Neut. S)
Acc. अम् *am* (S),	(Neut. M)	— *au* (S),	(Neut. w)	— *as* (w),	(Neut. S)
Inst. आ *á* (w)		भ्याम् *bhyám* (M)		भिस् *bhis* (M)	
Dat. ए *e* (w)		— *bhyám* (M)		भ्यस् *bhyas* (M)	
Abl. अस् *as* (w)		— *bhyám* (M)		— *bhyas* (M)	
Gen. — *as* (w)		ओस् *os* (w)		आम् *ám* (w)	
Loc. इ *i* (w)		— *os* (w)		सु *su* (M)	

The Vocative, though identical with the Nom. in the dual and plural, has sometimes a peculiar form of its own in the singular (see 92).

b. Páṇini always considers the Nom. sing. masc. as having the termination *s*, which is supposed to retain its effect, though it experiences *lopa* (cutting off); but in the N. Ac. Voc. sing. neut. there is *luk* of the terminations *s* and *am*, i. e. these terminations disappear altogether (Páṇ. VII. 1, 23).

c. The terms *aṅga*, *pada*, *bha* (the first two of which have also general meanings, see 74 with note) are applied in a restricted sense to different forms of the Prátipadika or stem as modified by the above terminations or by suffixes; thus, the stem is called *aṅga* before the terminations of the so-called Strong cases or Páṇini's *sarva-náma-sthána* (viz. the Nom. sing. du. pl., Ac. sing. and du. of masc. and fem. nouns, and the Nom. and Ac. pl. of neuter nouns, see the above table); *pada* * before the terminations of the Middle cases (viz. *bhyám*, *bhis*, *bhyas*, and *su*), as well as before Taddhita suffixes beginning with any consonant except *y* (Páṇ. I. 4, 17); *bha* before the terminations of the Weak cases beginning with vowels (except of course the *aṅga* terminations mentioned above), as well as before Taddhita suffixes beginning with vowels and *y* (see Páṇ. I. 4, 18).

d. A stem is made strong by lengthening the vowel of the last syllable, or by inserting a nasal, e. g. *yuvan*, *yuván*; *dhanavat*, *dhanavant*: and made weak by eliminating one or more letters, e. g. *yuvan*, *yún*; *pratyañć*, *pratíć*.

e. It should be noted that the Ac. pl., and in neuter nouns the

* Probably so called because the laws of Sandhi which come into operation at the junction of separate words (*pada*) in a sentence generally hold good before the terminations of the Middle cases.

Inst. sing., is generally the guide to the form assumed before the remaining vowel-terminations.

f. This division of cases has not been noticed before, because it is of no real importance for stems ending in vowels. That it applies to stems ending in *ṛi* is accounted for by the fact that these originally ended in *ar*.

Fifth Class in त् *t* and द् *d*.

This class answers to Latin words like *comes* (stem *comit-*), *eques* (stem *equit-*), *ferens* (stem *ferent-*); and to Greek words like χάρις (stem χαριτ-), κέρας (stem κερατ-), ἐλπίς (stem ἐλπιδ-), χαρίεις (stem χαριεντ-).

136. Masculine and feminine stems in त् *t* and द् *d*, like हरित् *harit*, m. f. 'green' (declined at 95), and सरित् *sarit*, f. 'a river,' and the compound धर्मविद् *dharma-vid*, m. f. 'knowing one's duty' (see 84. IV).

Observe—The Nom. sing. is properly *harits*, *dharma-vits*, but *s* is rejected by 41. I. The same applies to all nouns ending in consonants. So αἰδήμων for αἰδημονς. Latin and Greek, when the final of the stem refuses to combine with the *s* of the Nom., often prefer rejecting the final of the stem; thus, χάρις for χαριτς, *comes* for *comits*; and in these languages the final consonant frequently combines with the *s* of the Nom., as in *lex* (for *leks*), φλόξ (for φλοκς).

	SING.	DUAL.	PLURAL.	SING.	DUAL.	PLURAL.
N.V.	सरित् *sarit*	सरितौ *saritau*	सरितस् *saritas*	-वित् *-vit*	-विदौ *-vidau*	-विदस् *-vidas*
Ac.	सरितम् *saritam*	— *saritau*	— *saritas*	-विदम् *-vidam*	— *-vidau*	— *-vidas*
I.	सरिता *saritá*	सरिद्भ्याम् *saridbhyám*	सरिद्भिस् *saridbhis*	-विदा *-vidá*	-विद्भ्याम् *-vidbhyám*	-विद्भिस् *-vidbhis*
D.	सरिते *sarite*	— *saridbhyám*	सरिद्भ्यस् *saridbhyas*	-विदे *-vide*	— *-vidbhyám*	-विद्भ्यस् *-vidbhyas*
Ab.	सरितस् *saritas*	— *saridbhyám*	— *saridbhyas*	-विदस् *-vidas*	— *-vidbhyám*	— *-vidbhyas*
G.	— *saritas*	सरितोस् *saritos*	सरिताम् *saritám*	— *-vidas*	-विदोस् *-vidos*	-विदाम् *-vidám*
L.	सरिति *sariti*	— *saritos*	सरित्सु *saritsu*	-विदि *-vidi*	— *-vidos*	-वित्सु *-vitsu*

137. Neuter stems in त् *t* and द् *d*, like हरित् *harit*, n. 'green,' धर्मविद् *dharma-vid*, n. 'knowing one's duty,' and कुमुद् *kumud*, n. 'a lotus.'

These only differ from the masculine and feminine in the N. du. pl., Ac. sing. du. and pl., the usual neuter terminations ई *í*, इ *i* (see 97), being required, and *n* being inserted before the final of the stem in N. Ac. pl.; thus,

N. Ac. V. हरित् *harit*, हरिती *harití*, हरिन्ति *harinti*; I. हरिता *haritá*, हरिद्भ्याम् *haridbhyám*, &c., like masc. and fem.

N. Ac. V. धर्मवित्, धर्मविदी, धर्मविन्दि; I. धर्मविदा, &c.

Similarly, N. Ac. V. कुमुत्, कुमुदी, कुमुन्दि; I. कुमुदा, &c.

138. All nouns at 84. II–IV. follow हरित् and धर्मविद्.

139. हृद् *hṛid*, n. 'the heart,' is said to be defective in the first five inflexions, these cases being supplied from *hṛidaya* (see 108. *e*).

140. Possessive adjectives formed with the suffixes वत् *-vat* (84. VII) and मत् *-mat* (84. VI), like धनवत् *dhana-vat*, 'rich,' and धीमत् *dhí-mat*, 'wise,' are declined like *harit* for the masculine; but in the Strong cases (see 135. *a*) *n* is inserted before the final of the stem.

In N. sing. *dhanaván* for *dhanavants*, *ts* is rejected by 41. I, and the final vowel of the stem lengthened by way of compensation.

N.	धनवान् *dhanaván*	धनवन्तौ *dhanavantau*	धनवन्तस् *dhanavantas*
Ac.	धनवन्तम् *dhanavantam*	— *dhanavantau*	धनवतस् *dhanavatas*

I. धनवता *dhanavatá*, धनवद्भ्याम् *dhanavadbhyám*, &c., like *harit*.

V. धनवन् *dhanavan*, &c.

Similarly, धीमत् 'wise:' N. धीमान्, धीमन्तौ, धीमन्तस्; Ac. धीमन्तम्, धीमन्तौ, धीमतस्, &c.; V. धीमन्, &c.

a. Like *dhana-vat* are declined Past Active Participles, such as कृतवत् 'one who has done' (553); thus, N. masc. कृतवान्, कृतवन्तौ, कृतवन्तस्, &c.

b. The feminine stems of adjectives like धनवत् and धीमत्, and Participles like कृतवत्, are formed by adding ई *í* to the Weak form of the masc. stem; as, धनवती, धीमती, कृतवती, declined like नदी at 105; thus, N. धनवती, धनवत्यौ, धनवत्यस्, &c.

c. The neuter is like the neut. of *harit*: N. Ac. V. धनवत्, धनवती, धनवन्ति.

141. Present Participles (524) like पचत् *paćat*, 'cooking,' and Future Participles (578) like करिष्यत् *karishyat*, 'about to do,' are declined after *dhanavat* (140), excepting in the N. sing. masc., where *a* is not lengthened before *n*; thus,

N. V. sing. पचन् *paćan* (for *paćants*), and not पचान् *paćán*: N. du. pl. पचन्तौ, पचन्तस्; Ac. पचन्तम्, पचन्तौ, पचतस्; I. पचता, &c. Cf. Latin and Greek Participles like *ferens, ferent-is, ferent-em*, &c.; φέρων, φέροντ-ος, φέροντ-α, &c.

a. Observe, however, that all reduplicated verbs of the 3rd class and Frequentatives (but not Desideratives); a few verbs from polysyllabic roots (75. *a*), and some few other verbs—such as जक्ष् 'to eat,' शास् 'to rule'—which reject the nasal in the 3rd pl. Pres. of the Parasmai-pada, reject it also in the declension of the Pres. Participle. Hence the Pres. Participle of such verbs is declined like *harit*, the N. sing. being identical with the stem; thus, fr. *dá*, cl. 3, 'to give,' N. V. sing. du. pl. *dadat, dadatau, dadatas*; Ac. *dadatam*, &c.: fr. *bhṛi*, cl. 3, 'to bear,' N. V. sing. du. pl. *bibhrat, bibhratau, bibhratas*. So also, *jágrat*, 'watching' (fr. *jágṛi*), *śásat*, 'ruling' (fr. *śás*), *jakshat*, 'eating' (fr. *jaksh*). The rejection of the nasal is doubtless owing to the encumbrance of the syllable of reduplication.

Obs. 1. Quasi-reduplicated verbs of cl. 1 and Desideratives do not reject the nasal; e.g. *tishṭhat*, fr. *sthá*, 'to stand,' makes N. sing. du. pl. *tishṭhan, tishṭhantau, tishṭhantas*, &c. Similarly, *jighrat*, fr. *ghrá*, 'to smell;' *jighṛikshat*, Desid. of *grah*, 'to take.'

Obs. 2. The reduplicated verbs of cl. 3, &c., mentioned above, optionally reject the nasal from the N. V. Ac. pl. neut.; thus, *dadati* or *dadanti, jakshati* or *jakshanti*.

But *jagat*, n. 'the world,' is only *jaganti* in N. Ac. pl.

b. In Present Participles derived from verbs of cl. 1, 4, 10, a nasal is inserted for the feminine stem; thus, पचन्ती fr. पच्, cl. 1 (declined like *nadí* at 105); and this nasal is carried through all the inflexions, not merely, as in the masculine, through the first five. So दीव्यन्ती fr. *div*, cl. 4; and चोरयन्ती fr. *ćur*, cl. 10.

Similarly with quasi-reduplicated verbs of cl. 1 and Desideratives; e.g. *tishṭhantí*, fr. *sthá*; *jighrantí*, fr. *ghrá*; *jighṛikshantí*, fr. Desid. of *grah* (cf. Obs. 1. above).

The same conjugational classes also insert a nasal in the N. V. Ac. du. neut. as well as the pl.; thus, पचत्, पचन्ती, पचन्ति.

In all verbs of cl. 6, in verbs ending in *á* of the 2nd, and in all Participles of the 2nd Fut. Parasmai, the insertion of the nasal in the feminine is optional; thus, *tudatí* or *tudantí*, fr. *tud*, cl. 6; *yátí* or *yántí*, fr. *yá*, cl. 2; *karishyatí* or *karishyantí*, fr. *kṛi*. It is also optional in the N. V. Ac. du. neut., which will resemble the Nom. sing. fem.; thus, *tudantí* or *tudatí, yántí* or *yátí, karishyantí* or *karishyatí*.

c. Verbs of cl. 2, 3, 5, 7, 8, 9 follow 140. *b. c*, and insert no nasal for feminine nor for N. Ac. V. du. neut.; although all but cl. 3 assume a nasal in the first five inflexions in the masculine; thus, *adat* (fr. *ad*, cl. 2); N. V. masc. *adan, adantau, adantas*; fem. *adatí*: *juhvat* (fr. *hu*, cl. 3); N. V. masc. *juhvat, juhvatau, juhvatas*; fem. *juhvatí*: *rundhat* (fr. *rudh*, cl. 7); N. V. masc. *rundhan, rundhantau, rundhantas*; fem. *rundhatí*. The neut. will be N. Ac. V. *adat, adatí, adanti*; *juhvat*, du. *juhvatí*, but pl. *juhvanti* or *juhvati* (see 141. *a*).

142. The adjective महत्, 'great,' is properly a Pres. Part. fr. मह् *mah*, 'to increase;' but its masculine lengthens the *a* of *at* before *n* in the N. Ac. sing., N. V. Ac. du., N. V. pl., and neuter in N. V. Ac. pl.; thus, N. masc. महान्, महान्तौ, महान्तस्; Ac. महान्तम्, महान्तौ, महतस्; I. महता, &c.; V. महन्, महान्तौ, &c.: N. fem. महती, &c., see 140. *a. b*: N. V. Ac. neut. महत्, महती, महान्ति.

a. बृहत् m. f. n. 'great,' जगत् m. f. n. 'moving,' पृषत् m. f. 'a deer,' follow Pres. Participles; e.g. N. V. masc. बृहन्, बृहन्तौ, बृहन्तस्. Fem. बृहती. Neut. बृहत्, &c.

143. The honorific pronoun भवत् (said to be for भावत् *bhá-vat*) follows धनवत् (at 140), making the *a* of *at* long in the N. sing.; thus, भवान् 'your honour,' and not भवन्. The V. is भवन्. The fem. is भवती, see 233.

भवत् 'being,' Pres. Part. of भू 'to be,' follows of course पचत् at 141.

144. यकृत् n. 'the liver' (ἧπαρ, *jecur*), and शकृत् n. 'ordure,' may optionally be declined in Ac. pl. and remaining cases as if their stems were यकन् and शकन्; thus, N. V. यकृत्, यकृती, यकृन्ति; Ac. यकृत्, यकृती, यकृन्ति or यकानि; I. यकृता or यक्ना, यकृद्भ्याम् or यकभ्याम्, यकृद्भिस् or यकभिस्; D. यकृते or यक्ने, &c.

a. A defective noun दत् is optionally substituted for दन्त in Ac. pl. and remaining cases (see 183), and is often used at the end of compounds; e.g. *su-dat*, 'having good teeth,' making N. masc. fem. neut. *su-dan, su-datí, su-dat.*

145. पाद्, 'a foot,' at the end of compounds becomes पद् in Ac. pl. and remaining Weakest cases; thus, सुपाद्, 'having beautiful feet,' makes in masc. N. V. सुपाद्, सुपादौ, सुपादस्; Ac. सुपादम्, सुपादौ, सुपदस्; I. सुपदा, सुपाद्भ्याम्, सुपाद्भिस्, &c. The fem. is सुपदी, like *nadí* at 105. Neut. N. V. Ac. सुपाद्, सुपदी, सुपादि.

a. Similarly, द्विपाद्, but according to Páṇ. IV. 1, 9, the fem. is *dvi-padá*, if agreeing with *ṛik*, 'a verse;' *dvi-padí*, if agreeing with *strí*, 'a woman.' So also त्रिपाद्, &c.

Sixth Class in अन् *an* and इन् *in*.

This class answers to Lat. and Gr. words like *sermo* (stem *sermon-*), *homo* (stem *homin-*), δαίμων (stem δαιμον-). Latin agrees with Sanskṛit in suppressing the *n* in N. masc. and fem., but not in neut.; thus *homo* is N. of masc. stem *homin*, the stronger vowel *o* being substituted for *i*, just as *í* is substituted for *i* in Sanskṛit; but *nomen* is N. of the neut. stem *nomin*.

146. Masculine and feminine stems in अन् *an*, of two kinds, A and B.

A. If *an* be preceded by *m* or *v* at the end of a conjunct consonant, then the model is आत्मन् *átman*, m. 'soul,' 'self.'

B. But if *an* be preceded by *m* or *v* not conjunct, as in सीमन् *síman*, f. (sometimes m.) 'a border,' or by any other consonant, whether conjunct or not, than *m* or *v*, as in तक्षन् *takshan*, m. 'a carpenter,' राजन् *rájan*, m. 'a king,' then the *a* of *an* is dropped in the Ac. pl. and before all the other *vowel*-terminations, and the remaining *n* is compounded with the preceding consonant.

Obs.—In the Loc. sing. this dropping of *a* is optional.

All nouns ending in *an*, lengthen the *a* in the Strong cases (V. sing. excepted); and drop the *n* before all the consonantal terminations (see 57). The inflective stem will be *átman, átmán, átma; síman, símán, símn* (see above), *síma*.

Junction of stem with termination: N. sing. *n* final of stem, and *s* case-termination rejected by 57 and 41. I; V. sing. case-termination rejected.

	A.			B.		
	SING.	DUAL.	PLURAL.	SING.	DUAL.	PLURAL.
N.	आत्मा *átmá*	आत्मानौ *átmánau*	आत्मानस् *átmánas*	सीमा *símá*	सीमानौ *símánau*	सीमानस् *símánas*
Ac.	आत्मानम् *átmánam*	— *átmánau*	आत्मनस् *átmanas*	सीमानम् *símánam*	— *símánau*	सीम्नस् *símnas*
I.	आत्मना *átmaná*	आत्मभ्याम् *átmabhyám*	आत्मभिस् *átmabhis*	सीम्ना *símná*	सीमभ्याम् *símabhyám*	सीमभिस् *símabhis*

D.	आत्मने *átmane*	आत्मभ्याम् *átmabhyám*	आत्मभ्यस् *átmabhyas*	सीम्ने *símne*	सीमभ्याम् *símabhyám*	सीमभ्यस् *símabhyas*
Ab.	आत्मनस् *átmanas*	— *átmabhyám*	— *átmabhyas*	सीम्नस् *símnas*	— *símabhyám*	— *símabhyas*
G.	— *átmanas*	आत्मनोस् *átmanos*	आत्मनाम् *átmanám*	— *símnas*	सीम्नोस् *símnos*	सीम्नाम् *símnám*
L.	आत्मनि *átmani*	— *átmanos*	आत्मसु *átmasu*	सीम्नि or सीमनि *símni* or *símani*	— *símnos*	सीमसु *símasu*
V.	आत्मन् *átman*	आत्मानौ *átmánau*	आत्मानस् *átmánas*	सीमन् *síman*	सीमानौ *símánau*	सीमानस् *símánas*

147. Like आत्मन् are declined यज्वन् *yajvan*, m. 'a sacrificer' (e.g. N. यज्वा, यज्वानौ, यज्वानस्; Ac. यज्वानम्, यज्वानौ, यज्वनस्; I. यज्वना, &c.); पाप्मन् *pápman*, m. 'sin;' अश्मन् *aśman*, m. 'a stone;' ऊष्मन् *ushman*, m. 'the hot season;' शुष्मन् *śushman*, m. 'fire;' ब्रह्मन् *brahman*, m. 'the god Brahman;' अध्वन् *adhvan*, m. 'a road;' दृश्वन् *dṛiśvan*, m. 'a looker.'

Like सीमन् are declined मूर्धन् m. 'head' (I. मूर्ध्ना, &c.; L. मूर्ध्नि or मूर्धनि, &c.); पीवन् m. 'fat' (Ac. pl. पीव्नस्); वेमन् m. 'a loom;' लघिमन् m. 'lightness' (I. लघिम्ना, &c.)

148. Similarly, like सीमन्, are declined तक्षन् m. 'a carpenter' and राजन् m. 'a king.'

Obs.—In the inflexion of words like *takshan*, *rájan* (which follow the B form *síman* in combining *m* and *n*), the dental *n* of the stem being combined with a cerebral or palatal is changed to the cerebral or palatal nasal respectively. See 57. *c*, 58.

	SING.	DUAL.	PLURAL.	SING.	DUAL.	PLURAL.
N.	तक्षा *takshá*	तक्षाणौ *taksháṇau*	तक्षाणस् *taksháṇas*	राजा *rájá*	राजानौ *rájánau*	राजानस् *rájánas*
Ac.	तक्षाणम् *taksháṇam*	— *taksháṇau*	तक्ष्णस् *takshṇas*. 58.	राजानम् *rájánam*	— *rájánau*	राज्ञस् *rájñas*. 57. *c*.
I.	तक्ष्णा *takshṇá*. 58.	तक्षभ्याम् *takshabhyám*	तक्षभिस् *takshabhis*	राज्ञा *rájñá*. 57. *c*.	राजभ्याम् *rájabhyám*	राजभिस् *rájabhis*
D.	तक्ष्णे *takshṇe*	— *takshabhyám*	तक्षभ्यस् *takshabhyas*	राज्ञे *rájñe*	— *rájabhyám*	राजभ्यस् *rájabhyas*
Ab.	तक्ष्णस् *takshṇas*	— *takshabhyám*	— *takshabhyas*	राज्ञस् *rájñas*	— *rájabhyám*	— *rájabhyas*
G.	— *takshṇas*	तक्ष्णोस् *takshṇos*	तक्ष्णाम् *takshṇám*	— *rájñas*	राज्ञोस् *rájños*	राज्ञाम् *rájñám*
L.	तक्ष्णि * *takshṇi*	— *takshṇos*	तक्षसु *takshasu*	राज्ञि † *rájñi*	— *rájños*	राजसु *rájasu*
V.	तक्षन् *takshan*	तक्षाणौ *taksháṇau*	तक्षाणस् *taksháṇas*	राजन् *rájan*	राजानौ *rájánau*	राजानस् *rájánas*

* Or तक्षणि *takshaṇi*. † Or राजनि *rájani*.

149. Masculine stems in वन्, like पीवन्, दृश्वन्, यज्वन्, generally form their feminines in वरी (Páṇ. IV. 1, 7); e.g. पीवरी, दृश्वरी, यज्वरी, declined like *nadí* at 105.

150. When a feminine stem in ई *í* is formed from words like राजन्, it follows the rules at 146. A. B. for the rejection of the *a* of *an*; thus, राज्ञी *rájñí*, 'a queen.'

151. When *rájan* occurs at the end of a compound, it may be declined like *śiva* (103); as, N. sing. masc. *mahárájas*; Ac. *mahárájam*, &c. (cf. 778): but not necessarily, as *bahu-rájan*, m. f. n. 'having many kings.' The fem. stem of which may be *bahu-rájan* or *bahu-rájá* or *bahu-rájñí*.

152. Neuter stems in अन् *an*, like कर्मन् 'an action' and नामन् 'a name' (*nomen*, ὄνομα*).

Obs.—The retention or rejection of *a* in *an* before the Inst. sing. and remaining vowel-terminations, as well as optionally before the Nom. Acc. du., is determined by the same rule as in masculines and feminines (146. A. B). They only differ from masculine nouns in Nom. Voc. and Acc. sing. du. pl.

	SING.	DUAL.	PLURAL.	SING.	DUAL.	PLURAL.
N. Ac.	कर्म *karma*	कर्मणी *karmaṇí*	कर्माणि *karmáṇi*	नाम *náma*	नाम्नी or नामनी °*mní* or °*maní*	नामानि *námáni*
I.	कर्मणा *karmaṇá*	कर्मभ्याम् *karmabhyám*	कर्मभिस् *karmabhis*	नाम्ना *námná*	नामभ्याम् *námabhyám*	नामभिस् *námabhis*
D.	कर्मणे, &c. *karmaṇe*, &c.	like *átman*. 146.		नाम्ने, &c. *námne*, &c.	like *síman*. 146.	
V.	कर्म or कर्मन्, &c. *karma* or *karman*, &c.	like N. Ac.		नाम or नामन्, &c. *náma* or *náman*, &c.	like N. Ac.	

153. Like कर्मन् n. are declined जन्मन् 'birth,' वेश्मन् 'house,' वर्मन् 'armour,' ब्रह्मन् 'prayer,' 'the Supreme Spirit,' वर्त्मन् 'road,' चर्मन् 'leather,' छद्मन् 'pretext,' पर्वन् 'a joint.'

Like नामन् n. are declined दामन् 'string,' सामन् 'conciliation,' धामन् 'mansion,' व्योमन् 'sky,' रोमन् (for रोहन् *rohman*, from *ruh*), 'hair,' प्रेमन् (also m.) 'love.'

154. When nouns in *an*, *man*, and *van* form the last member of adjective compounds, the feminine may be declined like the masc., or its stem may end in *á*, and be declined like *śivá*; the neuter follows the declension of neuter nouns at 152. Those in *an*, if they follow the declension of *síman* and *rájan*, may also form their feminine in *í*, rejecting the *a* of *an*, and be declined like *nadí* (Páṇ. IV. 1, 28).

155. There are a few anomalous nouns in *an*, as follow:

a. श्वन् m. 'a dog' (*canis*, κύων): N. श्वा, श्वानौ, श्वानस्; Ac. श्वानम्, श्वानौ, शुनस्; I. शुना, श्वभ्याम्, श्वभिस्; D. शुने, &c.; Ab. शुनस्, &c.; G. शुनस् (κυνός), शुनोस्,

---

* Greek has a tendency to prefix vowels to words beginning with consonants in the cognate languages. Cf. also *nakha*, 'nail,' ὄνυξ; *laghu*, 'light,' ἐλαχύ-ς; भ्रू 'brow,' ὀφρύ-ς.

शुनाम्; L. शुनि, शुनोस्, श्वसु; V. श्वन्, श्वानौ, &c. See 135. *a*. Fem. शुनी, &c. (like *nadí* at 105).

b. युवन् m. 'a youth,' 'young:' N. युवा, युवानौ, युवानस्; Ac. युवानम्, युवानौ, यूनस्; I. यूना, युवभ्याम्, युवभिस्; D. यूने, &c.; Ab. यूनस्, &c.; G. यूनस्, यूनोस्, यूनाम्; L. यूनि, यूनोस्, युवसु; V. युवन्, युवानौ, &c. See 135. *a*. Fem. यूनी (like *nadí*) or युवति (like *mati*). Neut. युव, यूनी, युवानि, &c.

c. मघवन् m. 'a name of Indra:' N. मघवा, -वानौ, -वानस्; Ac. मघवानम्, -वानौ, मघोनस्; I. मघोना, मघवभ्याम्, -वभिस्; D. मघोने, मघवभ्याम्, &c.; Ab. मघोनस्, &c.; G. मघोनस्, मघोनोस्, मघोनाम्; L. मघोनि, मघोनोस्, मघवसु; V. मघवन्, &c. Fem. मघोनी or मघवती.

The last may also be declined like a noun in *vat:* N. मघवान्, -वन्तौ, &c. See 140.

156. अहन् n., 'a day,' forms its N. Ac. V. sing. fr. अहर् *ahar*, and the consonantal middle cases fr. अहस् *ahas;* in the other cases it is like *náman;* thus,

N. Ac. V. अहर् (41. I), अह्नी or अहनी, अहानि; I. अह्ना, अहोभ्याम्, अहोभिस्; D. अह्ने, अहोभ्याम्, अहोभ्यस्; Ab. अह्नस्, &c.; G. अह्नस्, अह्नोस्, अह्नाम्; L. अह्नि or अहनि, अह्नोस्, अहस्सु or अहःसु. At the beginning of compounds the form is generally अहर्, as in *ahar-niśam*, 'day and night.' At the end of compounds it may be declined as a masc.; thus, N. दीर्घाहास्, -हाणौ, -हाणस्; Ac. -हाणम्, &c.; V. -हस्, &c., or sometimes becomes अह or अह्न.

a. दिवन् m., 'a day,' lengthens the *i* in those cases where the *a* of *an* is rejected; thus, Ac. pl. दीव्नस्; I. दीव्ना, &c.

b. शीर्षन् n., 'the head,' is said to be defective in N. sing. du. and pl. and Ac. sing. du., these cases being supplied from शिरस् n., or शीर्ष 108. *e*.

c. यकन् n., 'the liver,' and शकन् 'ordure,' are said to be defective in the first five inflexions, these cases being supplied from *yakṛit* and *śakṛit* respectively, see 144.

157. अर्यमन् m., 'the sun,' does not lengthen *a* of *an* in N. du. pl., Ac. sing. du.; thus,

N. अर्यमा, अर्यमणौ, अर्यमणस्; Ac. अर्यमणम्, अर्यमणौ, अर्यम्णस्; I. अर्यम्णा, &c.

a. Similarly, पूषन् 'the sun:' N. पूषा, पूषणौ, &c.; Ac. पूषणम्, &c.; but the Ac. pl., and remaining Weakest cases, may be optionally formed from a stem पूष्; thus, Ac. pl. पूष्णस् or पूषस्.

b. Similarly, compounds having -हन् as the last member, such as ब्रह्महन् m. 'the slayer of a Bráhman:' N. ब्रह्महा, ब्रह्महणौ, &c.; but in Ac. pl. ब्रह्मघ्नस्; I. ब्रह्मघ्ना, ब्रह्महभ्याम्, &c. (*h* becoming *gh* where the *a* of *han* is dropped).

158. अर्वन् m. 'a horse,' or m. f. n. 'low,' 'vile,' is declined like nouns in *vat* at 140, excepting in N. sing.; thus, N. अर्वा, अर्वन्तौ, अर्वन्तस्; Ac. अर्वन्तम्, &c.; I. अर्वता, अर्वद्भ्याम्, अर्वद्भिस्; V. अर्वन्, &c. If the negative अन् precedes, अर्वन् is regular; thus, N. अनर्वा, अनर्वाणौ, &c.; Ac. अनर्वाणम्, &c.; I. pl. अनर्वभिस्.

159. Masculine stems in इन् *in*, like धनिन् *dhanin*, m. 'rich.'

In N. sing. *dhaní* for *dhanins*, *n* and *s* are rejected (by 57 and 41. I), and the vowel lengthened by way of compensation.

	SINGULAR.	DUAL.	PLURAL.
N.	धनी *dhaní*	धनिनौ *dhaninau*	धनिनस् *dhaninas*
Ac.	धनिनम् *dhaninam*	— *dhaninau*	— *dhaninas*
I.	धनिना *dhaniná*	धनिभ्याम् *dhanibhyám*. 57.	धनिभिस् *dhanibhis*. 57.
D.	धनिने *dhanine*	— *dhanibhyám*	धनिभ्यस् *dhanibhyas*. 57.
Ab.	धनिनस् *dhaninas*	— *dhanibhyám*	— *dhanibhyas*
G.	— *dhaninas*	धनिनोस् *dhaninos*	धनिनाम् *dhaninám*
L.	धनिनि *dhanini*	— *dhaninos*	धनिषु *dhanishu*. 70.
V.	धनिन् *dhanin*. 92.	धनिनौ *dhaninau*	धनिनस् *dhaninas*

Obs.—Many adjectives of the forms explained at 85. VI. VIII. IX. are declined in masc. like धनिन्; thus, मेधाविन् *medhávin*, 'intellectual;' N. मेधावी, -विनौ, -विनस्, &c. Also numerous nouns of agency, like कारिन् 'a doer,' at 85. II; thus, N. कारी, कारिणौ (58), कारिणस्, &c.

160. The feminine stem of such adjectives and nouns of agency is formed by adding ई *í* to the masc. stem; as, fr. धनिन्, धनिनी f.; fr. कारिन्, कारिणी f.; declined like *nadí* at 105; thus, N. धनिनी, -न्यौ, -न्यस्, &c.

161. The neuter is regular, and is like *vári* as far as the Gen. pl.; N. Ac. धनि, धनिनी, धनीनि. But the G. pl. धनिनाम्, not धनीनाम्; V. sing. धनि or धनिन्.

162. पथिन् m. 'a road,' मथिन् m. 'a churning-stick,' and ऋभुक्षिन् m. 'a name of Indra,' are remarkable as exhibiting both suffixes, *an* and *in*, in the same word. They form their N. V. sing. from the stems पन्थस्, मन्थस्, ऋभुक्षस्; their other Strong cases, from the stems पन्थन्, मन्थन्, ऋभुक्षन्; their Ac. pl., and remaining Weak cases, from the stems पथ्, मथ्, ऋभुक्ष्; in their Middle cases they follow *dhanin* regularly; thus,

N. V. पन्थास् (163), पन्थानौ, पन्थानस्; Ac. पन्थानम्, पन्थानौ, पथस्; I. पथा, पथिभ्याम्, पथिभिस्; D. पथे, &c. Similarly, N. V. मन्थास्, &c.; ऋभुक्षास्, &c.: I. मथा, &c.; ऋभुक्षा, &c. Observe—The V. is the same as the N.

a. The compound सुपथिन्, 'having a good road,' is similarly declined for the masc.; the N. fem. is सुपथी, -थ्यौ, -थ्यस्, like *nadí* at 105; the neut. is N. Ac. सुपथि, -पथी, -पन्थानि, &c.; V. सुपथिन् or सुपथि; the rest as the masc.

Seventh Class in अस् *as*, इस् *is*, and उस् *us*.

This class answers to Gr. and Lat. words like πάθος, μένος, *genus*, *scelus*, &c.

163. Masculine and feminine stems in अस् *as*, like चन्द्रमस् *ćandramas*, m. 'the moon.'

In N. sing. *as* is lengthened to compensate for rejection of the termination *s*;

ćandramas becomes *ćandramo* by 64 before the terminations *bhyám, bhis, bhyas;* in L. pl. *ćandramas+su* becomes *ćandramaḥsu* by 63, or *ćandramassu* by 62. *a*.

N.	चन्द्रमास् *ćandramás*	चन्द्रमसौ *ćandramasau*	चन्द्रमसस् *ćandramasas*
Ac.	चन्द्रमसम् *ćandramasam*	— *ćandramasau*	— *ćandramasas*
I.	चन्द्रमसा *ćandramasá*	चन्द्रमोभ्याम् *ćandramobhyám*	चन्द्रमोभिस् *ćandramobhis*
D.	चन्द्रमसे *ćandramase*	— *ćandramobhyám*	चन्द्रमोभ्यस् *ćandramobhyas*
Ab.	चन्द्रमसस् *ćandramasas*	— *ćandramobhyám*	— *ćandramobhyas*
G.	— *ćandramasas*	चन्द्रमसोस् *ćandramasos*	चन्द्रमसाम् *ćandramasám*
L.	चन्द्रमसि *ćandramasi*	— *ćandramasos*	चन्द्रमःसु *ćandramaḥsu* or -स्सु
V.	चन्द्रमस् *ćandramas*. 92.	चन्द्रमसौ *ćandramasau*	चन्द्रमसस् *ćandramasas*

a. Similarly, अप्सरस् *apsaras*, f. 'a nymph:' N. अप्सरास्, &c.

164. Neuter stems in अस् *as*, like मनस् *manas*, n. 'mind' (μένος, *mens*).

These differ from the masc. and fem. in the N. Ac. V. The *a* of *as* remains short in N. sing. after the rejection of the case-termination *s*, but is lengthened in N. Ac. V. pl. before inserted Anusvára.

N. Ac. V. मनस् *manas* मनसी *manasí* मनांसि *manáṇsi*

I. मनसा *manasá*, मनोभ्याम् *manobhyám*, &c., like the masc. and fem.

a. Obs.—Nearly all simple substantives in *as* are neuter like *manas;* but these neuters, when at the end of compound adjectives, are declinable also in masc. and fem. like *ćandramas*. Thus *mahá-manas*, 'magnanimous,' makes in N. (m. f. sing. du. pl.) *mahá-manás, mahá-manasau, mahá-manasas*. Similarly, *sumanas*, 'well-intentioned;' *durmanas*, 'evil-minded' (N. m. f. *sumanás, durmanás*, &c.): cf. εὐ-μενής, δυσ-μενής, m. f., but neut. and stem εὐ-μενές, δυσ-μενές, derived from μένος.

b. Where final *as* is part of a root and not a suffix, the declension will follow पिण्डग्रस् 'one who devours a mouthful;' thus, N. V. sing. m. f. पिण्डग्रस्; Ac. -ग्रसम्. N. V. Ac. du. -ग्रसौ, pl. -ग्रसस्; I. -ग्रसा, -ग्रोभ्याम्, &c. N. V. Ac. neut. -ग्रस्, -ग्रसी, -ग्रंसि. When a root ends in *ás*, *s* will be rejected before *bh* by 66. *a;* thus, चकास्, 'brilliant,' makes in I. du. चकाभ्याम्.

c. But स्रस् (fr. स्रंस्) and ध्वस् (fr. ध्वंस्), at the end of compounds, change final स् to त् before the consonantal terminations, making N. sing. स्रत् and ध्वत्; e.g. उखास्रत्, पर्णध्वत् (see Páṇ. III. 2, 76; VII. 1, 70; VIII. 2, 72).

165. Neuter stems in इस् *is* and उस् *us* are declined analogously to मनस् *manas* at 164, *i* and *u* being substituted for *a* throughout, *sh* for *s* (70), *ir* or *ur* for *o* (65); thus,

हविस् *havis*, n. 'ghee:' N. Ac. V. हविस्, हविषी, हवींषि; I. हविषा, हविर्भ्याम्, हविर्भिस्; D. हविषे, हविर्भ्याम्, हविर्भ्यस्; Ab. हविषस्, हविर्भ्याम्, हविर्भ्यस्; G. हविषस्, हविषोस्, हविषाम्; L. हविषि, हविषोस्, हविःषु or -ष्षु.

a. चक्षुस् *ćakshus*, n. 'the eye:' N. Ac. V. चक्षुस्, चक्षुषी, चक्षूंषि; I. चक्षुषा,

P

चक्षुर्भ्याम्, चक्षुर्भिस्; D. चक्षुषे, चक्षुर्भ्याम्, चक्षुर्भ्यस्; Ab. चक्षुषस्, चक्षुर्भ्याम्, चक्षुर्भ्यस्; G. चक्षुषस्, चक्षुषोस्, चक्षुषाम्; L. चक्षुषि, चक्षुषोस्, चक्षुःषु or -ष्षु.

166. Nouns formed with the suffixes *is* and *us* are generally neuter. In some nouns, however, the final sibilant is part of the root itself, and not of a suffix; such as आशिस् *áśis*, f. 'a blessing' (fr. rt. शास्), and सजुस् m. f. 'an associate' (fr. जुष्). These follow the analogy of masc. and fem. nouns in *as* (163) in the N. Ac. cases; and, moreover, before the consonantal terminations, where the final sibilant is changed to *r*, unlike nouns formed with *is* and *us*, lengthen the *i* and *u* (compare nouns in *r* at 180); thus,

N. आशीस्, -शिषौ, -शिषस्; Ac. -शिषम्, -शिषौ, -शिषस्; I. -शिषा, -शीर्भ्याम्, -शीर्भिस्, &c.; L. pl. -शीःषु or -शीष्षु.

N. सजूस्, -जुषौ, -जुषस्; Ac. -जुषम्, &c.; I. -जुषा, -जूर्भ्याम्, &c.

a. Nouns formed from Desiderative stems in *ish* (497), such as जिगदिस् (for *jigadish*), 'desirous of speaking,' are similarly declined; thus,

N. V. m. f. जिगदीस्, -दिषौ, &c.; I. du. -दीर्भ्याम्. The N. V. Ac. neut. pl. is जिगदिषि, the nasal being omitted (cf. 181. *d*).

So चिकीर्ष्, 'desirous of doing,' makes N. V. m. f. चिकीर्, -कीर्षौ, &c.

b. सुतुस् 'well-sounding,' where *us* is radical, makes N. V. sing. m. f. सुतूस्; Ac. सुतुसम्; N. V. Ac. du. सुतुसौ, pl. सुतुसस्; I. सुतुसा, सुतूर्भ्याम्, सुतूर्भिस्, &c. N. V. Ac. neut. सुतूस्, सुतुसी, सुतुंसि.

c. Obs.—When neuter nouns in *is* or *us* are taken for the last member of compound adjectives, analogy would require them to be declined in masc. and fem. according to *ćandramas* at 163; but, according to the best authorities, the N. sing. does not lengthen the vowel of the last syllable; thus, उत्पलचक्षुस् m. f. n. 'having lotus eyes,' N. masc. and fem. उत्पलचक्षुस्, -चक्षुषौ, &c.; and शुचिरोचिस् m. f. n. 'having brilliant rays,' N. masc. and fem. शुचिरोचिस्, शुचिरोचिषौ, &c.

d. दोस् *dos*, m. 'an arm,' follows the declension of nouns in *is* and *us*; but in Ac. pl., and remaining cases, optionally substitutes *doshan* for its stem (see 184); thus, N. V. दोस्, -षौ, -षस्; Ac. दोषम्, -षौ, -षस् or -ष्णस्; I. दोषा or दोष्णा, दोर्भ्याम् or दोषभ्याम्, &c. As a neuter noun it makes in N. Ac. V. दोस्, दोषी, दोंषि.

167. Comparatives formed with the suffix ईयस् *íyas* (192), lengthen the *a* of *as*, and insert *n*, changeable to Anusvára before *s*, in N. sing. du. pl., V. du. pl., Ac. sing. du. masc.; thus, बलीयस् m. f. n., 'more powerful,' makes N. masc. बलीयान् (for बलीयांस्, *s* rejected by 41. A), -यांसौ, -यांसस्; Ac. -यांसम्, -यांसौ, -यसस्; I. -यसा, -योभ्याम्, &c., like *ćandramas* at 163. The V. sing. is बलीयन्; du. and pl. like the Nom.

a. The fem. बलीयसी follows *nadí* at 105. The neut. बलीयस् is like *manas*.

168. Perfect Participles, formed with *vas* (see 554), are similarly declined in the Strong cases (135. *b*). But in Ac. pl., and remaining Weak cases, *vas* becomes *ush*, and in the Middle cases *vat*; so that there are three forms of the stem, viz. in *váṉs*, *ush*, and *vat* *; thus,

---

* *Vat* is evidently connected with the Greek οτ. Compare *tutupvat* (fr. rt. *tup*) with τετυφ-(ϝ)οτ, and *tutupvatsu* with τετυφ-ο(τ)σι.

विविद्वस् (Perf. Part., fr. विद् 'to know'): N. विविद्वान्, विविद्वांसौ, विविद्वांसस्; Ac. विविद्वांसम्, विविद्वांसौ, विविदुषस्; I. विविदुषा, विविद्वद्भ्याम्, विविद्वद्भिस्; D. विविदुषे, &c.; V. विविद्वन्, विविद्वांसौ, &c.

The neuter is N. Ac. विविद्वत्, -दुषी, -द्वांसि; for fem. see *d* below.

a. When this Participle is formed with *ivas* instead of *vas* (see 554), the vowel *i* is rejected in the cases where *vas* becomes *ush;* thus,

जग्मिवस् (fr. गम् 'to go'): N. masc. जग्मिवान्, &c.; Ac. जग्मिवांसम्, जग्मिवांसौ, जग्मुषस्, &c.; I. जग्मुषा, &c.; V. जग्मिवन्, जग्मिवांसौ, &c.

b. Similarly, तेनिवस् (fr. तन् 'to stretch'): N. तेनिवान्, तेनिवांसौ, &c.; Ac. तेनिवांसम्, तेनिवांसौ, तेनुषस्, &c.; V. तेनिवन्, -वांसौ, &c.

c. But not when the *i* is part of the root; thus, चिचिवस् (fr. चि), निनीवस् (fr. नी) make in the Ac. pl. चिच्युषस्, निन्युषस्. चकृवस् (fr. कृ) makes, of course, चक्रुषस्.

d. The N. fem. of these Participles is formed from *ush;* and the N. Ac. neut. sing. du. pl. from *vat*, *ush*, and *vas*, respectively; thus, N. fem. विविदुषी, &c., declined like *nadí* at 105. Similarly, from the root तुप् comes तुतुपुषी (cf. τετυφυῖα). Those formed with *ivas* do not retain *i* in the feminine; thus, *tenivas* makes N. sing. masc. fem. neut. *tenivân*, *tenushí**, *tenivat*.

e. The root विद्, 'to know,' has an irregular Pres. Part. विद्वस् *vidvas*, used commonly as an adjective ('learned'), and declined exactly like विविद्वस् above, leaving out the reduplicated *vi;* thus, N. masc. विद्वान्, विद्वांसौ, विद्वांसस्; V. विद्वन्, &c. With reference to 308. *a*, it may be observed, that as a contracted Perfect of *vid* is used as a Present tense, so a contracted Participle of the Perfect is used as a Present Participle. The fem. is विदुषी, and the neut. विद्वत्.

169. पुंस् m., 'a male,' forms its V. sing. from पुमंस्, and its other Strong cases (135. *b*) from पुमांस्; but Ac. pl., and remaining Weakest cases, from पुंस्; and I. du., and remaining Middle cases, from पुम्; thus,

N. पुमान्, पुमांसौ, पुमांसस्; Ac. पुमांसम्, पुमांसौ, पुंसस्; I. पुंसा, पुम्भ्याम्, पुम्भिस्; D. पुंसे, &c.; Ab. पुंसस्, &c.; G. पुंसस्, पुंसोस्, पुंसाम्; L. पुंसि, पुंसोस्, पुंसु; V. पुमन्, पुमांसौ, &c.

170. उशनस् m., 'a name of the regent of the planet S'ukra,' forms N. sing. उशना from a stem उशनन् (147). Similarly, पुरुदंशस् m. 'a name of Indra,' and अनेहस् m. 'time.' The other cases are regular; thus, N. du. उशनसौ. But उशनस् may be optionally in Voc. sing. उशनस् or उशन or उशनन्.

171. जरस् f., 'decay' (γῆρας), supplies its consonantal cases (viz. N. V. sing., I. D. Ab. du. pl., L. pl.) from जरा f. Its other cases may be either from जरस् or जरा; thus, N. sing. जरा; V. जरे; Ac. जरसम्† or जराम्; I. जरसा and जरया, जराभ्याम्, जराभिस्, &c.

---

* There seems, however, difference of opinion as to the rejection of *i;* and some grammarians make the feminine *tenyushí*.

† Since जरसम् certainly occurs, it may be inferred that the N. Ac. V. du. are जरसौ or जरे; N. Ac. V. pl. जरसस् or जरास्. These forms are given in the grammar of I'śvara-ćandra Vidyá-ságara, p. 51.

EIGHTH CLASS.—Stems ending in any consonant except त् *t*, द् *d*, न् *n*, स् *s*.

172. This class consists principally of roots used as nouns, either alone or at the end of compounds, or preceded by prepositions and adverbial prefixes. Stems ending in त् *t* or द् *d*, formed in this manner, are of common occurrence; but their declension falls under the fifth class at 136.

With regard to stems ending in other consonants which we place under the eighth class, the only difficulty in their declension arises from their euphonic combination with the consonantal terminations.

173. Whatever change of the final consonant takes place in Nom. sing. is preserved before all the consonantal terminations; provided only, that before such terminations the rules of Sandhi come into operation.

174. Before the vowel-terminations the final consonant of the stem, whatever it may be, is generally preserved. If in some nouns there is any peculiarity in the formation of the Ac. pl., the same peculiarity runs through the remaining Weakest or vowel cases.

The terminations themselves undergo no change, but the *s* of the Nom. sing. is of course cut off by 41. I (see, however, 135. *b*). There is generally but one form of declension for both masc. and fem.; the neuter follows the analogy of other nouns ending in consonants.

175. Stems ending in क् *k*, ख् *kh*, ग् *g*, घ् *g* declined.

शक् m. f. 'one who is able' (in *sarva-śak*, 'omnipotent').

N. V.	शक् *śak*	शकौ *śakau*	शकस् *śakas*
Ac.	शकम् *śakam*	— *śakau*	— *śakas*
I.	शका *śaká*	शग्भ्याम् *śagbhyám*	शग्भिस् *śagbhis*
D.	शके *śake*	— *śagbhyám*	शग्भ्यस् *śagbhyas*
Ab.	शकस् *śakas*	— *śagbhyám*	— *śagbhyas*
G.	— *śakas*	शकोस् *śakos*	शकाम् *śakám*
L.	शकि *śaki*	— *śakos*	शक्षु *śakshu*

The neuter is N. Ac. V. शक्, शकी, शङ्कि, &c.; the rest like the masc.

a. Similarly, लिख् 'one who paints' (in *ćitra-likh*, 'one who paints a picture'): N. V. लिक् (41. II, 41. I), लिखौ (174), लिखस्; Ac. लिखम्, &c.; I. लिखा, लिग्भ्याम्, लिग्भिस्, &c.; L. pl. लिक्षु.

The neuter is N. Ac. V. लिक्, लिखी, लिङ्खि, &c.; the rest like the masc.

b. In the same way final ग्, घ् are changed to क्, and when final घ्, ढ्, ध्, भ्, ह् lose their aspirate form, the aspirate must be transferred to the initial, if that initial be ग्, ड्, द्, or ब् (see 44. *c*).

c. सुवल्ग् m.f., 'jumping well,' makes N.V. सुवल् (41. I), सुवल्गौ, &c.; Ac. सुवल्गम्, &c.; I. सुवल्गा, सुवल्भ्याम्, &c.; D. सुवल्गे, &c.; Ab.G. सुवल्गस्, &c.; L. सुवल्गि, सुवल्गोस्, सुवल्षु (see 70). Neut. N. Ac. V. सुवल्, सुवल्गी, सुवल्ङ्गि or (see 176. *h*) सुवल्गि.

176. Stems ending in च् *ć*, छ् *ćh*, ज् *j*, झ् *jh* declined.

Final च् is changed to क् or ग्; final छ् is changed to श्, which becomes ट् or ड् before the consonantal terminations; final ज् to क् (ग्) or ट् (ड्); and final झ्, which is rare, to क् or ग्, before the consonantal terminations (41. IV, 92. *a*).

वाच् f. 'speech' (fr. rt. वच्): N. V. वाक् (for *vâks*, 41. I; *vox*, ὄψ), वाचौ (ὄπε), वाचस् (*voces*, ὄπες); Ac. वाचम् (*vocem*), वाचौ, वाचस् (ὄπας); I. वाचा, वाग्भ्याम्, वाग्भिस्; D. वाचे, वाग्भ्याम्, वाग्भ्यस्; Ab. वाचस्, वाग्भ्याम्, वाग्भ्यस्; G. वाचस्, वाचोस्, वाचाम्; L. वाचि (ὀπί), वाचोस्, वाक्षु. Compare Latin *vox*, and Greek ὄψ or ὀπ for *Fοπ* throughout.

Similarly, मुच् 'a liberator:' N. V. मुक्, मुचौ, मुचस्.

भुज् m. f. 'one who eats:' N. V. भुक्, भुजौ, भुजस्; Ac. भुजम्, &c.; I. भुजा, भुग्भ्याम्, भुग्भिस्, &c.

प्राछ् m. f. 'an asker' (fr. rt. प्रछ्): N. V. प्राट्, प्राशौ, प्राशस्; Ac. प्राशम्, &c.; I. प्राशा, प्राड्भ्याम्, &c.; L. pl. प्राट्सु.

The root भज् becomes भाज् (just as *vać* becomes *vâć*); e. g. N. V. भाक् m. f. n. 'a sharer.'

a. The neuters are thus formed: N. Ac. V. वाक्, वाची, वाञ्चि, &c. (as in सुवाच् 'speaking well'); भुक्, भुजी, भुञ्जि, &c.; प्राट्, प्राशी, प्राञ्शि, &c.

b. The root अञ्च् *anć*, 'to go,' preceded by certain prepositions and adverbial prefixes, forms a few irregular nouns (such as प्राञ्च् 'eastern'), and is found at the end of a few compounds after words ending in *a*; such as अधराञ्च् 'tending downwards,' &c. These all reject the nasal in the Ac. pl. and remaining cases masculine. In Nom. sing. the final च् *ć* being changed to क् *k*, causes the preceding nasal to take the guttural form, and the क् is rejected by 41. I. In the Ac. pl., and remaining Weakest cases, there is a further modification of the stem in the case of प्रत्यञ्च्, &c.

प्राञ्च् m. 'eastern,' 'going before:' N. V. प्राङ्, प्राञ्चौ, प्राञ्चस्; Ac. प्राञ्चम्, प्राञ्चौ, प्राचस्; I. प्राचा, प्राग्भ्याम्, प्राग्भिस्; D. प्राचे, &c.; L. pl. प्राक्षु. Similarly, अवाञ्च् m. 'southern.'

प्रत्यञ्च् m. 'western:' N. V. प्रत्यङ्, प्रत्यञ्चौ, प्रत्यञ्चस्; Ac. प्रत्यञ्चम्, प्रत्यञ्चौ, प्रतीचस्; I. प्रतीचा, प्रत्यग्भ्याम्, प्रत्यग्भिस्; D. प्रतीचे, &c. Similarly, सम्यञ्च् 'going with,' 'fit,' and even उदञ्च् 'northern,' which make in Ac. pl., and remaining Weakest cases, समीचस्, उदीचस्.

So also, विष्वञ्च्, 'going everywhere,' forms its Ac. pl., and remaining Weakest cases, fr. a stem विषूच्, making विषूचस्, &c.

Analogously, तिर्यच् 'going crookedly,' 'an animal,' forms its Weakest cases fr. a stem तिरश्च्, making Ac. pl. तिरश्चस्, &c.

The feminine form and the neut. du. of these nouns follow the analogy of the Ac. pl.; thus, N. fem. प्राची &c., अवाची &c., प्रतीची &c., उदीची &c., समीची &c., तिरश्ची &c., declined like नदी.

The neuter is N. Ac. V. प्राक्, प्राची, प्राञ्चि, &c.; प्रत्यक्, प्रतीची, प्रत्यञ्चि, &c.

c. प्राञ्च्, when it signifies 'worshipping,' retains the nasal, which has become guttural, throughout; but *ć*, which has become *k*, is rejected before the consonantal terminations; thus,

N. V. प्राङ्, प्राञ्चौ, &c.; Ac. प्राञ्चम्, &c.; I. प्राञ्चा, प्राङ्भ्याम्, &c.

Similarly, क्रुञ्च् 'a curlew:' N. V. क्रुङ्, क्रुञ्चौ, &c.; Ac. क्रुञ्चम्, &c.; I. क्रुञ्चा, क्रुङ्भ्याम्, &c.; L. pl. क्रुङ्क्षु or क्रुङ्षु (55. *b*).

d. असृज् n., 'blood,' is regular; thus, N. Ac. V. असृक्, असृजी, असृञ्जि, &c.; but it may optionally take its Ac. pl. and remaining inflexions from a defective stem, असन् *asan;* thus, N. V. pl. असृञ्जि; Ac. pl. असृञ्जि or असानि; I. असृजा or अस्ना, असृग्भ्याम् or असभ्याम्, &c.; L. असृजि or असनि or अस्नि, &c.

e. Nouns formed with the roots यज् 'to worship,' राज् 'to shine,' मृज् 'to rub,' भ्राज् 'to shine,' भ्रस्ज् 'to fry,' व्रज् 'to wander,' सृज् 'to create,' generally change the final ज् to ट् or ड् before the consonantal terminations; thus,

देवेज् m. 'a worshipper of the gods' (यज् becoming इज्): N. V. sing. देवेट्. Similarly, राज् m. 'a ruler:' N. sing. राट्; I. राजा, राड्भ्याम्, &c. So also, परिमृज् 'a cleanser:' N. sing. परिमृट्. So also, विभ्राज् m. f. 'splendid:' N. sing. विभ्राट्. Similarly, परिव्राज् m. 'a religious mendicant' (व्रज् becoming व्राज्): N. sing. परिव्राट्. So also, विश्वसृज् m. 'the creator of the world:' N. sing. विश्वसृट्.

But विश्व when it precedes राज्, as in विश्वराज् m. 'a universal ruler,' becomes विश्वा wherever ज् becomes ट् or ड्; thus, N. विश्वाराट्, विश्वराजौ, &c.

ऋत्विज् m., 'a priest' (ऋतु + इज् for यज्), is regular: N. V. ऋत्विक्.

f. अवयाज् m. 'a kind of priest,' 'part of a sacrifice,' forms the consonantal cases from an obsolete stem, अवयस्: N. V. sing. du. pl. अवयास्, -याजौ, -याजस्; Ac. -याजम्, &c.; I. -याजा, -योभ्याम्, &c.; L. pl. अवयस्सु or अवयःसु.

g. भ्रस्ज्, 'one who fries,' may take भृज्ज् for its stem, and make N. V. भृट्, भृज्जौ, भृज्जस्; Ac. भृज्जम्, &c. Similarly, व्रश्च्, 'one who cuts,' makes, according to some, वृट्, &c., and not व्रट्, &c.; but others allow *vraṭ*.

h. ऊर्ज् f., 'strength,' makes N.V. ऊर्क् (41. I. Obs.), &c.; Ac. ऊर्जम्, &c.; I. ऊर्जा, ऊर्ग्भ्याम्, &c. At the end of a comp. the neuter is N. Ac. V. *úrk, úrjí, únrji*. But in these cases where a word ends in a conjunct consonant, the first member of which is *r* or *l*, the nasal may be optionally omitted in the plural, so that *úrji* would be equally correct.

i. खञ्ज्, 'lame,' makes N. खन्, खञ्जौ, खञ्जस्; I. pl. खन्भिस्; L. pl. खन्सु.

177. Stems ending in थ् *th*, ध् *dh* declined.

The final aspirate is changed to its unaspirated form before the consonantal terminations (41. II, 43), but not before the vowel (43. *d*). कथ् m. f. 'one who tells:' N. V. कत्, कथौ, कथस्; Ac. कथम्, &c.; I. कथा, कद्भ्याम्, &c.

So also, युध् f. 'battle:' N.V. युत्, युधौ, युधस्; Ac. युधम्, &c.; I. युधा, युद्भ्याम्, &c.

In the case of बुध् m. f., 'one who knows,' the initial ब् *b* becomes भ् *bh* wherever the final ध् *dh* becomes *t* or *d*, by 175. *b.* and 44. *c;* thus, N. V. भुत्, बुधौ, बुधस्; Ac. बुधम्, &c.; I. बुधा, भुद्भ्याम्, &c.; L. pl. भुत्सु.

a. The neuter is N. Ac. V. कत्, कथी, कन्थि, &c.; बुत्, बुधी, बुन्धि, &c.

178. Stems ending in प् *p*, फ् *ph*, ब् *b*, भ् *bh* declined.

गुप् m. f. 'one who defends:' N. V. गुप्, गुपौ, गुपस्; Ac. गुपम्, &c.; I. गुपा, गुब्भ्याम्, गुब्भिस्, &c.

लभ् m. f. 'one who obtains:' N. V. लप्, लभौ, लभस्; Ac. लभम्, &c.; I. लभा, लब्भ्याम्, लब्भिस्, &c.; L. pl. लप्सु.

a. The neuter is N. Ac. V. गुप्, गुपी, गुम्पि, &c.; लप्, लभी, लम्भि, &c.

b. अप् f. 'water,' declined in the plural only, substitutes *t* (*d*) for its final before *bh;* thus, N. V. आपस्; Ac. अपस्; I. अद्भिस्; D. Ab. अद्भ्यस्; G. अपाम्; L. अप्सु. In the Veda it is sometimes singular.

179. Stems ending in म् *m* declined.

The final *m* becomes *n* before the consonantal terminations. शम् *śam*, m. f. 'one who pacifies:' N. V. शन्, शमौ, शमस्; Ac. शमम्, &c.; I. शमा, शन्भ्याम्, शन्भिस्, &c.; L. pl. शन्सु.

a. Similarly, प्रशाम् m. f., 'quiet,' makes N. V. प्रशान्, प्रशामौ, प्रशामस्; Ac. प्रशामम्, &c.; I. प्रशामा, प्रशान्भ्याम्, &c.; L. pl. प्रशान्सु or प्रशान्त्सु. Compare 53. *e*.

b. The neuter is N. Ac. V. शन्, शमी, शमि, &c.; प्रशान्, -शामी, -शामि, &c.

180. Stems ending in र् *r* and व् *v* declined.

If the vowel that precedes final *r* be *i* or *u*, it is lengthened before the consonantal terminations (compare 166); and final *r*, being a radical letter, does not become Visarga before the *s* of the Loc. pl. (71. *b*).

चर् m. f. 'one who goes:' N. V. चर्, चरौ, चरस्; Ac. चरम्, &c.; I. चरा, चर्भ्याम्, चर्भिस्, &c.; L. pl. चर्षु.

द्वार् f. 'a door:' N. V. द्वार्, द्वारौ, द्वारस्, &c.

गिर् f. 'speech:' N. V. गीर्, गिरौ, गिरस्; Ac. गिरम्, &c.; I. गिरा, गीर्भ्याम्, गीर्भिस्, &c.; L. pl. गीर्षु.

a. The neuter is N. Ac. V. चर्, चरी, चरि, &c.; गीर्, गिरी, गिरि, &c.

So also, वार् n. 'water:' N. Ac. वार्, वारी, वारि.

b. One irregular noun ending in व् *v*, viz. दिव् f. 'the sky,' forms its N. V. sing. from द्यो (133. *a*), and becomes द्यु in the other consonantal cases; thus,

N. V. द्यौस्, दिवौ, दिवस्; Ac. दिवम्, दिवौ, दिवस्; I. दिवा, द्युभ्याम्, &c.

Similarly, सुदिव् m. f. 'having a good sky,' but the neuter is N. Ac. V. सुद्यु, सुदिवी, सुदीवि.

181. Stems ending in श् *ś* and ष् *sh* declined.

The difficulty in these is to determine which stems change their finals to क् and which to ट् (see 41. V). In the roots दिश्, दृश्, मृश्, स्पृश्, and धृष् (the last forming

दधृष् 'impudent') the final becomes क्, and in नश् optionally क् or ट् (नक् or नट्). Otherwise both श् and ष् at the end of stems pass into ट्.

विश् m. f. 'one who enters,' or 'a man of the mercantile and agricultural class:' N. V. विट् (41. V), विशौ, विशस्; Ac. विशम्, &c.; I. विशा, विड्भ्याम्, &c. दिश् f. 'a quarter of the sky:' N. V. दिक् (41. V, 24), दिशौ, दिशस्; Ac. दिशम्, &c.; I. दिशा, दिग्भ्याम्, &c. द्विष् m. f. 'one who hates:' N. V. द्विट् (41. V), द्विषौ, द्विषस्; Ac. द्विषम्, &c.; I. द्विषा, द्विड्भ्याम्, &c. मृष् m. f. 'one who endures:' N. V. मृट् (41. V), मृषौ, मृषस्; Ac. मृषम्, &c.; I. मृषा, मृड्भ्याम्, &c. स्पृश् 'one who touches:' N. V. स्पृक्, स्पृशौ, स्पृशस्, &c.

The neuters are N. Ac. V. विट्, विशी, विंशि, &c.; दिक्, दिशी, दिंशि, &c.; द्विट्, द्विषी, द्विंषि, &c.; मृट्, मृषी, मृंषि, &c.

a. पुरोडाश् 'a priest,' in the Veda, makes N. V. sing. पुरोडास्, and forms its other consonantal cases from an obsolete stem, पुरोडस्. Compare 176. *f.*

b. सुहिंस् m. f., 'very injurious,' makes N. V. सुहिन्, सुहिंसौ, &c.; Ac. सुहिंसम्, &c.; I. सुहिंसा, सुहिन्भ्याम्, &c. But nouns ending in स्, preceded by vowels, fall under 163.

c. गोरक्ष्, 'a cow-keeper,' makes N. V. गोरक् or गोरट्, गोरक्षौ, &c.

d. Similarly, nouns from Desiderative stems, like पिपक्ष् 'desirous of cooking,' and विवक्ष् 'desirous of saying,' make N. V. पिपक्, पिपक्षौ, &c.; विवक्, विवक्षौ, &c. (see 166. *a*).

182. Stems ending in ह् *h* declined.

In stems beginning with द् *d*, the final aspirate generally becomes क् *k* (ग् *g*), in other stems ट् *ṭ* (ड् *ḍ*), before the consonantal terminations; and in stems whose initial is द् *d* or ग् *g*, the loss of the *h*, which disappears as a final, is compensated for by aspirating the initial, which becomes *dh* or *gh* wherever final *h* becomes *k* (*g*) or *ṭ* (*ḍ*). See 44. *c*, 175. *b*. लिह् m. f. 'one who licks:' N. V. लिट् (41. III), लिहौ, लिहस्; Ac. लिहम्, &c.; I. लिहा, लिड्भ्याम्, &c.; L. pl. लिट्सु or लिट्त्सु. दुह् m. f. 'one who milks:' N. V. धुक्, दुहौ, दुहस्; Ac. दुहम्, &c.; I. दुहा, धुग्भ्याम्, धुग्भिस्, &c.; L. pl. धुक्षु.

The neuter is N. Ac. V. लिट्, लिही, लिंहि, &c.; धुक्, दुही, दुंहि, &c.

a. But द्रुह् m. f., 'injuring,' makes N. ध्रुक् or ध्रुट् (44. *c*); I. द्रुहा, ध्रुग्भ्याम् or ध्रुड्भ्याम्, &c.; L. pl. ध्रुक्षु or ध्रुट्सु. Similarly, मुह् m. f. 'infatuating:' N. मुक् or मुट्. The same option is allowed in स्निह् 'one who loves' and स्नुह् 'one who vomits.'

b. उष्णिह् f., 'a kind of metre,' changes its final to *k* (*g*) before the consonantal terminations, like stems beginning with *d*: N. उष्णिक्, उष्णिहौ, &c.

c. वाह्, 'bearing' (fr. rt. वह् 'to bear'), changes वा to ऊ *ú* in Ac. pl. and remaining Weakest cases (and before the ई *í* of the fem.) if the word that precedes it in the compound ends in *a* or *á*; this *a* or *á* combining with *ú* into औ *au* (instead of ओ *o*, by 32); thus,

भारवाह् m. f. 'a burden-bearer:' N. V. masc. भारवाट् भारवाहौ, भारवाहस्; Ac. भारवाहम्, भारवाहौ, भारौहस्; I. भारौहा, भारवाड्भ्याम्, &c. N. fem. भारौही, &c. So प्रष्ठवाह् m. 'a steer' and विश्ववाह् 'all-sustaining.' Under other circumstances the change of *váh* to *úh* is optional; thus, शालिवाह्, 'bearing rice,' makes in Ac. pl. शाल्यूहस् or शालिवाहस्.

d. श्वेतवाह् m., 'Indra' ('borne by white horses'), may optionally retain वा in Ac. pl. &c.; and in consonantal cases is declined as if the stem were श्वेतवस्; thus, N. V. श्वेतवास्, श्वेतवाहौ, श्वेतवाहस्; Ac. श्वेतवाहम्, श्वेतवाहौ, श्वेतौहस् or श्वेतवाहस्; I. श्वेतौहा or श्वेतवाहा, श्वेतवोभ्याम्, श्वेतवोभिस्, &c.

e. In तुरासाह्, 'a name of Indra,' the स् is changed to ष् wherever ह् becomes ट् or ड्: N. तुराषाट्, तुरासाहौ, तुरासाहस्; Ac. तुरासाहम्, &c.; I. तुरासाहा, तुराषाड्भ्याम्, &c.

f. अनडुह् m., 'an ox' (for अनोवाह् fr. अनस् 'a cart' and वाह् 'bearing'), forms the N.V. sing. from अनड्वत्; the other Strong cases from अनड्वाह्, and the Middle cases from अनडुत्; thus, N. अनड्वान्, अनड्वाहौ, अनड्वाहस्; Ac. अनड्वाहम्, अनड्वाहौ, अनडुहस्; I. अनडुहा, अनडुद्भ्याम्, अनडुद्भिस्, &c.; L. pl. अनडुत्सु; V. अनड्वन्. There is a feminine form अनड्वाही, but at the end of compounds this word makes fem. N. sing. अनडुही; neut. N. V. अनडुत्, अनडुही, अनड्वांहि.

183. नह् 'binding,' 'tying,' at the end of compounds, changes the final to त् or द्, instead of ट् or ड्; thus, उपानह् f., 'a shoe,' makes N. V. उपानत्, उपानहौ, उपानहस्; Ac. उपानहम्, &c.; I. उपानहा, उपानद्भ्याम्, &c.; L. pl. उपानत्सु. See 306. *b*.

Defective Nouns.

184. The following nouns are said to be defective in the first five inflexions, in which cases they make use of other nouns (see Páṇ. VI. 1, 63): असन् n. (176. *d*); आसन् n. (108. *e*); उदन् n. (108. *e*); दत् m. (108. *e*); दोषन् n. m. (166. *d*); नस् f. (108. *e*); निश् f. (108. *e*); पद् m. (108. *e*); पृत् f. (108. *e*); मांस् n. (108. *e*); मास् m. (108. *e*); यकन् n. (144, 156. *c*); यूषन् m. (108. *e*); शकन् n. (144, 156. *c*); शीर्षन् n. (156. *b*); स्नु n. (116. *a*); हृद् n. (108. *e*).

185. Examples of nouns defective in other cases are अहन् n. (156); क्रोष्टु m. (128. *c*); जरस् f. (171).

SECTION III.—ADJECTIVES.

186. The declension of substantives includes that of adjectives; and, as already seen, the three examples of substantives, given under each class, serve as the model for the three genders of adjectives falling under the same class. Adjectives may be grouped under three heads, A, B, C, as follow:

A. Simple adjectives, coming immediately from roots, and not derived from substantives. These belong chiefly to the first, second, and third classes of nouns (see 80. A, 81. A, 82. A, 103–115).

B. Adjectives *formed from substantives* by secondary or *Taddhita* suffixes. They belong chiefly to the first, fifth, and sixth classes of nouns (see 80. B, 84. B, 85. B, 103, 140, 159).

C. Compound adjectives, formed by using roots and substantives at the end of compounds. These are common under every one of the eight classes.

187. A. *Examples of Simple Adjectives.*

शुभ *śubha*, 'beautiful,' 'good:' masc. and neut. stem शुभ *śubha;* fem. stem शुभा *śubhá.*

An example of an adjective of cl. 1 is here given in full, that the declension of the masc., fem., and neut. forms may be seen at once and compared with that of Latin adjectives in *us*, like *bonus*, 'good.' The fem. of some of these adjectives is in *í*, and then follows *nadí* at 105. In the succeeding examples only the Nom. cases sing. will be given.

SINGULAR.	MASC.	FEM.	NEUT.
N.	शुभस्	शुभा	शुभम्
Ac.	शुभम्	शुभाम्	—
I.	शुभेन	शुभया	शुभेन
D.	शुभाय	शुभायै	शुभाय
Ab.	शुभात्	शुभायास्	शुभात्
G.	शुभस्य	—	शुभस्य
L.	शुभे	शुभायाम्	शुभे
V.	शुभ	शुभे	शुभ

DUAL.	MASC.	FEM.	NEUT.
N. Ac. V.	शुभौ	शुभे	शुभे
I. D. Ab.	शुभाभ्याम्	शुभाभ्याम्	शुभाभ्याम्
G. L.	शुभयोस्	शुभयोस्	शुभयोस्
PLURAL.			
N. V.	शुभास्	शुभास्	शुभानि
Ac.	शुभान्	—	—
I.	शुभैस्	शुभाभिस्	शुभैस्
D. Ab.	शुभेभ्यस्	शुभाभ्यस्	शुभेभ्यस्
G.	शुभानाम्	शुभानाम्	शुभानाम्
L.	शुभेषु	शुभासु	शुभेषु

CLASS.	STEM.	NOM. MASC.	NOM. FEM.	NOM. NEUT.
1.	प्रिय 'dear'	प्रियस्	प्रिया	प्रियम्
	सुन्दर 'beautiful'	सुन्दरस्	सुन्दरा or सुन्दरी. 105.	सुन्दरम्
2.	शुचि 'pure'	शुचिस्	शुचिस्	शुचि
3.	पाण्डु 'pale'	पाण्डुस्	पाण्डुस्	पाण्डु
	साधु 'good'	साधुस्	साधुस् or साध्वी. 105.	साधु
	मृदु 'tender'	मृदुस्	मृद्वी	मृदु
	भीरु 'timid'	भीरुस्	भीरुस् or भीरूस्. 125.	भीरु

Obs.—The neuter of adjectives in *i* and *u* may in D. Ab. G. L. sing. and G. L. du. optionally follow the masculine form; thus, D. sing. *śućine* or *śućaye, mṛidune* or *mṛidave;* Ab. G. sing. *śućinas* or *śućes, mṛidunas* or *mṛidos;* L. sing. *śućini* or *śućau, mṛiduni* or *mṛidau;* G. L. du. *śućinos* or *śućyos, mṛidunos* or *mṛidvos.* See 119. *a.*

188. B. *Examples of Adjectives formed from Substantives.*

CLASS.	STEM.	NOM. MASC.	NOM. FEM.	NOM. NEUT.
1.	मानुष 'human'	मानुषस्	मानुषी	मानुषम्
	धार्मिक 'religious'	धार्मिकस्	धार्मिकी	धार्मिकम्
5.	बलवत् 'strong'	बलवान्	बलवती. 105.	बलवत्
	श्रीमत् 'prosperous'	श्रीमान्	श्रीमती. 105.	श्रीमत्
6.	सुखिन् 'happy'	सुखी	सुखिनी. 105.	सुखि

189. C. *Examples of Compound Adjectives.*

CLASS.	STEM.	NOM. MASC.	NOM. FEM.	NOM. NEUT.
1.	बहुविद्य 'very learned'	बहुविद्यस्	बहुविद्या	बहुविद्यम्
2.	दुर्बुद्धि 'foolish'	दुर्बुद्धिस्	दुर्बुद्धिस्	दुर्बुद्धि
3.	अल्पतनु 'small-bodied'	अल्पतनुस्	अल्पतनुस्	अल्पतनु
4.	बहुदातृ 'very liberal'	बहुदाता	बहुदात्री. 105.	बहुदातृ
5.	सर्वजित् 'all-conquering'	सर्वजित्	सर्वजित्	सर्वजित्
6.	सुजन्मन् 'well-born'	सुजन्मा	सुजन्मा	सुजन्म
7.	गतचेतस् 'deprived of sense'	गतचेतास्	गतचेतास्	गतचेतस्
8.	मर्मस्पृश् 'piercing the vitals'	मर्मस्पृक्	मर्मस्पृक्	मर्मस्पृक्

190. *Examples of some other Compound Adjectives.*

शङ्खध्मा 'a shell-blower' (108. *a*).	शङ्खध्मास्	शङ्खध्मास्	शङ्खध्मम्
नष्टश्री 'ruined' (126. *h*).	नष्टश्रीस्	नष्टश्रीस्	नष्टश्रि
खलपू 'a sweeper' (126. *b*).	खलपूस्	खलपूस्	खलपु
दिव्यमातृ 'having a divine mother' (130).	दिव्यमाता	दिव्यमाता	दिव्यमातृ
बहुरै 'rich' (134. *a*).	बहुरास्	बहुरास्	बहुरि
बहुनौ 'having many ships' (134. *a*).	बहुनौस्	बहुनौस्	बहुनु

DEGREES OF COMPARISON.

191. The degrees of comparison are formed in two ways:

1st, by adding to the stem तर *tara* (= Gr. -τερο-ς) for the comparative (see 80. LXI), and तम *tama* (= Lat. *-timu-s*, Gr. -τατο-ς) for the superlative (see 80. LIX), both of which suffixes are declined in m. f. n. like *śubha* at 187; thus,

पुण्य *puṇya*, 'holy,' पुण्यतर *puṇya-tara* (Nom. m. f. n. *as, á, am*), 'more holy,' पुण्यतम *puṇya-tama* (Nom. m. f. n. *as, á, am*), 'most holy.' Similarly, धनवत् *dha-*

navat, 'wealthy,' धनवत्तर *dhanavat-tara*, 'more wealthy,' धनवत्तम *dhanavat-tama*, 'most wealthy.'

a. A final *n* is rejected; as, धनिन् *dhanin*, 'rich,' धनितर *dhani-tara*, 'more rich,' धनितम *dhani-tama*, 'most rich.'

b. विद्वस्, 'wise,' makes विद्वत्तर, विद्वत्तम. Compare 168. *e.*

192. 2ndly, by adding ईयस् *íyas* (Nom. m. f. n. *-íyán*, *-íyasí*, *-íyas*, see declension below, cf. Gr. ἴων) for the comparative (see 86. V), and इष्ठ *ishṭha* (Nom. m. f. n. *-ishṭhas*, *-ishṭhá*, *-ishṭham*, declined like *śubha* at 187, cf. Gr. -ιστος) for the superlative (see 80. XLVIII).

Obs.—The difference in the use of *tara*, *tama*, and *íyas*, *ishṭha*, seems to be this—that *íyas* and *ishṭha*, being of the nature of primary suffixes, are generally added to roots or to modifications of roots (the root being sometimes weakened, sometimes gunated), while *tara* and *tama* are of more general application.

a. Note, that while the Sanskṛit comparative suffix ends in *n* and *s* (*íyans*) for the Strong cases, the Greek has adhered to the *n* throughout (N. *íyán* = ιων, Voc. *íyan* = ιον); and the Latin has taken the *s* for its neuter (*íyas* = *ius*, neuter of *ior*; *s* being changed to *r*, in the masc. and oblique cases). Cf. Sk. *garíyas* with Lat. *gravius*.

193. Before *íyas* and *ishṭha*, the stem generally disburdens itself of a final vowel, or of the more weighty suffixes *in*, *vin*, *vat*, *mat*, and *ṭri*; thus, बलिन् 'strong,' बलीयस् 'more strong,' बलिष्ठ 'strongest;' पापिन् 'wicked,' पापीयस् 'more wicked,' पापिष्ठ 'most wicked;' लघु 'light,' लघीयस् 'lighter,' लघिष्ठ 'lightest;' मेधाविन् 'intelligent,' मेधीयस् 'more intelligent,' मेधिष्ठ 'most intelligent.' Similarly, महत् 'great,' महीयस् 'greater,' महिष्ठ 'greatest.'

a. Compare स्वादीयान् (N. of *svádíyas*) from *svádu*, 'sweet,' with ἡδ-ίων from ἡδύς; and स्वादिष्ठस् with ἥδ-ιστος.

The declension of बलीयस् masc. is here given in full (see 167).

	SINGULAR.	DUAL.	PLURAL.
N.	बलीयान् *balíyán*	बलीयांसौ *balíyáṇsau*	बलीयांसस् *balíyáṇsas*
Ac.	बलीयांसम् *balíyáṇsam*	— *balíyáṇsau*	बलीयसस् *balíyasas*
I.	बलीयसा *balíyasá*	बलीयोभ्याम् *balíyobhyám*	बलीयोभिस् *balíyobhis*
D.	बलीयसे *balíyase*	— *balíyobhyám*	बलीयोभ्यस् *balíyobhyas*
Ab.	बलीयसस् *balíyasas*	— *balíyobhyám*	— *balíyobhyas*
G.	— *balíyasas*	बलीयसोस् *balíyasos*	बलीयसाम् *balíyasám*
L.	बलीयसि *balíyasi*	— *balíyasos*	बलीयःसु *balíyaḥsu*
V.	बलीयन् *balíyan*	बलीयांसौ *balíyáṇsau*	बलीयांसस् *balíyáṇsas*

बलीयसी fem. is like *nadí* (105), and बलीयस् neut. like *manas* (164).

194. Besides the rejection of the final, the stem often undergoes change, as in Greek (cf. ἐχθίων, ἔχθιστος, fr. ἐχθρός); and its place is sometimes supplied by a substitute (cf. βελτίων, βέλτιστος, fr. ἀγαθός).

The following is a list of the substitutes:

POSITIVE.	SUBSTITUTE.	COMPARATIVE.	SUPERLATIVE.
अन्तिक *antika*, 'near'	नेद *neda* (rt. निद्)	नेदीयस्	नेदिष्ठ
अल्प *alpa*, 'little' *	कन *kana* (rt. कन्)	कनीयस्	कनिष्ठ
उरु *uru*, 'large' (εὐρύς)	वर *vara* (rt. वृ)	वरीयस्	वरिष्ठ
ऋजु *ṛiju*, 'straight' *	ऋज *ṛija* (rt. ऋज्)	ऋजीयस्	ऋजिष्ठ
कृश *kṛiśa*, 'thin,' 'lean'	क्रश *kraśa* (rt. कृश्)	क्रशीयस्	क्रशिष्ठ
क्षिप्र *kshipra*, 'quick'	क्षेप *kshepa* (rt. क्षिप्)	क्षेपीयस्	क्षेपिष्ठ
क्षुद्र *kshudra*, 'small,' 'mean'	क्षोद *kshoda* (rt. क्षुद्)	क्षोदीयस्	क्षोदिष्ठ
गुरु *guru*, 'heavy' (βαρύς)	गर *gara* (rt. गॄ)	गरीयस्	गरिष्ठ
तृप्र *tṛipra*, 'satisfied'	त्रप *trapa* (rt. तृप्)	त्रपीयस्	त्रपिष्ठ
दीर्घ *dírgha*, 'long'	द्राघ *drágha* (rt. द्राघ्)	द्राघीयस्	द्राघिष्ठ
दूर *dúra*, 'distant'	दव *dava* (rt. दु)	दवीयस्	दविष्ठ
दृढ *dṛiḍha*, 'firm'	द्रढ *draḍha* (rt. दृंह्)	द्रढीयस्	द्रढिष्ठ
परिवृढ *parivṛiḍha*, 'eminent'	परिव्रढ *parivraḍha*	परिव्रढीयस्	परिव्रढिष्ठ
पृथु *pṛithu*, 'broad' (πλατύς)	प्रथ *pratha* (rt. प्रथ्)	प्रथीयस्	प्रथिष्ठ
प्रशस्य *praśasya*, 'good'	श्र† *śra* (rt. श्री)	श्रेयस्	श्रेष्ठ
	ज्या† *jyá* (rt. ज्या)	ज्यायस्	ज्येष्ठ
प्रिय *priya*, 'dear'	प्र† *pra* (rt. प्री)	प्रेयस्	प्रेष्ठ
बहु *bahu*, 'much,' 'frequent'	भू† *bhú* (rt. भू)	भूयस्	भूयिष्ठ
बहुल *bahula*, 'much'	बंह *baṇha* (rt. बंह्)	बंहीयस्	बंहिष्ठ
भृश *bhṛiśa*, 'excessive'	भ्रश *bhraśa* (rt. भृश्)	भ्रशीयस्	भ्रशिष्ठ
मृदु *mṛidu*, 'soft'	म्रद *mrada* (rt. म्रद्)	म्रदीयस्	म्रदिष्ठ
युवन् *yuvan*, 'young' (*juvenis*)	यव *yava* (rt. यु)	यवीयस्	यविष्ठ
वाढ *váḍha*, 'firm,' 'thick'	साध *sádha* (rt. साध्)	साधीयस्	साधिष्ठ
वृद्ध *vṛiddha*, 'old'	वर्ष *varsha* (rt. वृष्)	वर्षीयस्	वर्षिष्ठ
	ज्या† *jyá* (rt. ज्या)	ज्यायस्	ज्येष्ठ
वृन्दार *vṛindára*, 'excellent'	वृन्द *vṛinda*	वृन्दीयस्	वृन्दिष्ठ
स्थिर *sthira*, 'firm,' 'stable'	स्थ *stha* (rt. स्था)	स्थेयस्	स्थेष्ठ
स्थूल *sthúla*, 'gross,' 'bulky'	स्थव *sthava* (rt. स्थू)	स्थवीयस्	स्थविष्ठ
स्फिर *sphira*, 'turgid'	स्फ *spha* (rt. स्फाय्)	स्फेयस्	स्फेष्ठ
ह्रस्व *hrasva*, 'short'	ह्रस *hrasa* (rt. ह्रस्)	ह्रसीयस्	ह्रसिष्ठ

* अल्प may be also regularly अल्पीयस्, अल्पिष्ठ; and ऋजु may be रजीयस्, &c.

† In the case of श्र and प्र the final vowel is not rejected, but combines with *íyas* and *ishṭha* agreeably to Sandhi. In ज्या and भू, *yas* is affixed in place of *íyas*.

195. *Tara* and *tama* may be added to substantives; as, fr. राजन्, 'a king,' राजतर, &c.; fr. दुःख, 'pain,' दुःखतर, &c. If added to a word like सर्पिस्, 'clarified butter,' the usual euphonic changes must take place; thus, सर्पिष्टर, &c. (70).

These suffixes are also added to inseparable prepositions; as, उत् 'up,' उत्तर 'higher,' उत्तम 'highest' (cf. Lat. *ex-timus*, *in-timus*, &c.); also to pronominal stems (236); and *tama* is added to numerals (209, 211).

196. *Tará* and *tamá* may sometimes be added to feminine stems ending in *í* and *ú* (like स्त्री 'a woman,' सती 'a faithful wife,' विदुषी 'a wise woman'), which may optionally be retained or shortened; e.g. स्त्रीतरा, स्त्रीतमा, or स्त्रितरा, स्त्रितमा; सतीतरा, सतीतमा, or सतितरा, सतितमा; विदुषीतमा or विदुषितमा (Páṇ. VI. 3, 44. 45).

But if the feminine be the feminine of a masculine substantive, as ब्राह्मणी of ब्राह्मण, the shortening is compulsory, as ब्राह्मणितरा (Páṇ. VI. 3, 42).

197. *Tara* and *tama* may even be added, in conjunction with the syllable आम् *ám*, to the inflexions of verbs; as, जल्पतितराम् 'he talks more than he ought.' See 80. LIX, LXI.

a. Sometimes *íyas* and *tara*, *ishṭha* and *tama* are combined together in the same word (just as in English we say *lesser*); thus, श्रेयस्तर, श्रेष्ठतम; ज्येष्ठतम; नेदिष्ठतम, &c.: and *tara* may be even added to *ishṭha*; thus, ज्येष्ठतर.

SECTION IV.—NUMERALS.

CARDINALS.

198. The cardinals are, एक m. f. n. 1, १; द्वि m. f. n. 2, २; त्रि m. f. n. 3, ३; चतुर् m. f. n. 4, ४; पञ्चन् m. f. n. 5, ५; षष् m. f. n. 6, ६; सप्तन् m. f. n. 7, ७; अष्टन् m. f. n. 8, ८; नवन् 9, ९; दशन् 10, १०; एकादशन् 11, ११; द्वादशन् 12, १२; त्रयोदशन् 13, १३; चतुर्दशन् 14, १४; पञ्चदशन् 15, १५; षोडशन् 16, १६; सप्तदशन् 17, १७; अष्टादशन् 18, १८; नवदशन् or ऊनविंशति 19, १९; विंशति f. 20, २०; एकविंशति 21; द्वाविंशति 22; त्रयोविंशति 23; चतुर्विंशति 24; पञ्चविंशति 25; षड्विंशति 26; सप्तविंशति 27; अष्टाविंशति 28; नवविंशति or ऊनत्रिंशत् 29; त्रिंशत् f. 30; एकत्रिंशत् 31; द्वात्रिंशत् 32; त्रयस्त्रिंशत् 33; चतुस्त्रिंशत् 34; पञ्चत्रिंशत् 35; षट्त्रिंशत् 36; सप्तत्रिंशत् 37; अष्टात्रिंशत् 38; नवत्रिंशत् or ऊनचत्वारिंशत् 39; चत्वारिंशत् 40; एकचत्वारिंशत् 41; द्विचत्वारिंशत् or द्वाचत्वारिंशत् 42; त्रिचत्वारिंशत् or त्रयश्चत्वारिंशत् 43; चतुश्चत्वारिंशत् 44; पञ्चचत्वारिंशत् 45; षट्चत्वारिंशत् 46; सप्तचत्वारिंशत् 47; अष्टाचत्वारिंशत् or अष्टचत्वारिंशत् 48; नवचत्वारिंशत् or ऊनपञ्चाशत् 49; पञ्चाशत् 50; एकपञ्चाशत् 51; द्विपञ्चाशत् or द्वापञ्चाशत् 52; त्रिपञ्चाशत् or त्रयःपञ्चाशत् 53; चतुःपञ्चाशत् 54; पञ्चपञ्चाशत् 55; षट्पञ्चाशत् 56; सप्तपञ्चाशत् 57; अष्टपञ्चाशत् or अष्टापञ्चाशत् 58; नवपञ्चाशत् or ऊनषष्टि 59; षष्टि 60; एकषष्टि 61; द्विषष्टि or द्वाषष्टि 62; त्रिषष्टि or त्रयःषष्टि* 63; चतुःषष्टि* 64; पञ्चषष्टि 65; षट्षष्टि 66; सप्तषष्टि 67; अष्टषष्टि or अष्टाषष्टि

* These may also be written त्रयष्षष्टि, चतुष्षष्टि. See 62. *a.* and 63.

68; नवषष्टि or ऊनसप्तति 69; सप्तति 70; एकसप्तति 71; द्विसप्तति or द्वासप्तति 72; त्रिसप्तति or त्रयःसप्तति 73; चतुःसप्तति 74; पञ्चसप्तति 75; षट्सप्तति 76; सप्तसप्तति 77; अष्टसप्तति or अष्टासप्तति 78; नवसप्तति or ऊनाशीति 79; अशीति 80; एकाशीति 81; द्व्यशीति 82; त्र्यशीति 83; चतुरशीति 84; पञ्चाशीति 85; षडशीति 86; सप्ताशीति 87; अष्टाशीति 88; नवाशीति or ऊननवति 89; नवति 90; एकनवति 91; द्विनवति or द्वानवति 92; त्रिनवति or त्रयोनवति 93; चतुर्नवति 94; पञ्चनवति 95; षण्णवति 96 (43.*f*); सप्तनवति 97; अष्टनवति or अष्टानवति 98; नवनवति or ऊनशत n. (m.) 99; शत n. (also m.*) or एकं शतम् 100; एकशत n. 101; द्विशत n. 102; त्रिशत 103; चतुःशत 104; पञ्चशत 105; षट्शत 106; सप्तशत 107; अष्टशत 108; नवशत 109; दशशत 110; द्विशतम् (nom. sing. n.) or द्वे शते (nom. du. n.) or शते (nom. du. n.) 200; त्रिशतम् (nom. sing. n.) or त्रीणि शतानि (nom. pl. n.) 300; चतुःशतम् or चत्वारि शतानि (nom. pl. n.) 400; पञ्चशतम् or पञ्च शतानि 500; षट्शतम् or षट् शतानि 600; and so on up to सहस्र n. (also m.) 1000, which is also expressed by एकं सहस्रम् or by दश शतानि or by दशशती f.; द्वे सहस्रे 2000; त्रीणि सहस्राणि 3000; चत्वारि सहस्राणि 4000, &c.†

199. The intervening numbers between 100 and 1000, those between 1000 and 2000, and so on, may be expressed by compounding the adjective अधिक *adhika* (or occasionally उत्तर *uttara*), 'more,' 'plus,' with the cardinal numbers; thus 101 is एकशतम् (see above) or एकाधिकं शतम् (or occasionally एकोत्तरं शतम्), i. e. 'a hundred plus one,' or compounded thus, एकाधिकशतम्. Similarly, द्व्यधिकं शतम् or द्व्यधिकशतम् 102; त्र्यधिकं शतम् or त्र्यधिकशतम् 103; सप्ताधिकं शतम् or सप्तोत्तरं शतम् 107; त्रिंशदधिकशतम् 130; पञ्चाशदधिकशतम् 150 (also expressed by सार्धशतम् 'one hundred and a half'); षड्विंशत्यधिकद्विशतम् 226; त्र्यशीत्यधिकत्रिशतम् 383; पञ्चाशीत्यधिकचतुःशतम् 485; षण्णवत्यधिकपञ्चशतम् 596; षट्षष्ट्यधिकषट्शतम् 666; षष्ट्यधिकसहस्रम् or षष्ट्युत्तरसहस्रम् 1060; षोडशशतम् or षट्शताधिकसहस्रम् 1600; षट्षष्ट्यधिकषोडशशतम् 1666‡.

---

* I have found शतं शताः 'a hundred hundred' and सप्तशताः 'seven hundred' (agreeing with गाथाः) in the Mahá-bhárata.

† चतुःसहस्रम् is used in Ṛig-veda V. 30, 15 for 4000; and on the same principle त्रिसहस्रम् might stand for 3000, and द्विसहस्रम् for 2000, &c.; but it is a question whether these might not also stand for 1004, 1003, 1002 respectively.

‡ Similarly 2130 may be expressed by त्रिंशदधिकैकविंशतिशतम् or -शतानि or by using पर; thus, त्रिंशदधिकैकशतपरे द्वे सहस्रे. Other forms of expressing numerals are also found; e.g. 21,870 सहस्राण्येकविंशतिः शतान्यष्टौ भूयश्च सप्ततिः; 109,350 शतसहस्रं नव सहस्राणि पञ्चाशच्छतानि त्रीणि. According to Páṇ. vi. 3, 76, एकान्न may be prefixed to a number in the sense 'by one not,' 'less by one;' e.g. एकान्नविंशति 'by one not twenty,' 'one less than twenty,' i. e. 19.

In the same way the adjective ऊन 'less,' 'minus,' is often placed before a cardinal number, to denote one less than that number, एक 'one' being either expressed or understood; thus, ऊनविंशति or एकोनविंशति 'twenty minus one' or 'nineteen' (cf. Lat. *undeviginti*, i.e. *unus de viginti*). And other cardinals, besides एक 'one,' are sometimes prefixed to ऊन, to denote that they are to be subtracted from a following number; as, पञ्चोनं शतम् or पञ्चोनशतम् 'a hundred less five' or 'ninety-five.'

a. Again, the ordinals are sometimes joined to the cardinals to express 111 and upwards; thus, एकादशं शतम् or एकादशशतम् 111; पञ्चदशं शतम् 115; विंशं शतम् 120; त्रिंशं शतम् or त्रिंशशतम् 130; पञ्चाशं शतम् 150; चतुर्णवतं शतम् 194; पञ्चदशं द्विशतम् 215; विंशं सहस्रम् or विंशसहस्रम् 1020.

b. There are single words for the highest numbers; thus, अयुत n. (also m.) 'ten thousand;' लक्ष n. or लक्षा f. or नियुत n. (also m.) 'a lac,' 'one hundred thousand' (शतसहस्र); प्रयुत n. (also m.) 'one million;' कोटि f. 'a krore,' 'ten millions;' अर्बुद m. n. 'one hundred millions;' महार्बुद m. n. or पद्म n. or अब्ज n. 'one thousand millions;' खर्व n. 'ten thousand millions;' निखर्व n. 'one hundred thousand millions;' महापद्म n. 'a billion;' शङ्कु m. (or महाखर्व n.) 'ten billions;' शङ्ख m. n. or समुद्र m. 'a hundred billions;' महाशङ्ख m. n. or अन्त्य 'a thousand billions;' हाहा m. or मध्य 'ten thousand billions;' महाहाहा m. or परार्ध m. 'one hundred thousand billions;' धुन n. (धुल) 'one million billions;' महाधुन n. (महाधुल) 'ten million billions;' अक्षौहिणी f. 'one hundred million billions;' महाक्षौहिणी 'one thousand million billions.'

Note—Some variation occurs in some of the above names for high numbers, according to different authorities.

DECLENSION OF CARDINALS.

200. एक 1, द्वि 2 (*duo*, δύο), त्रि 3 (*tres*, τρεῖς, τρία), चतुर् 4 (*quatuor*), are declined in three genders.

एक *eka*, 'one' (no dual), follows the declension of the pronominals at 237: Nom. m. एकस् *ekas;* Dat. m. एकस्मै *ekasmai;* Nom. f. एका *ekā;* Dat. f. एकस्यै *ekasyai;* Nom. n. एकम् *ekam;* Nom. pl. m. एके *eke*, 'some.' It may take the suffixes *tara* and *tama;* thus, *eka-tara*, 'one of two;' *eka-tama*, 'one of many;' which also follow the declension of pronominals; see 236, 238.

201. द्वि *dvi*, 'two' (dual only), is declined as if the stem were द्व *dva*, like *śiva;* thus, N. Ac. V. m. द्वौ *dvau*, f. n. द्वे *dve;* I. D. Ab. m. f. n. द्वाभ्याम्; G. L. द्वयोस्.

202. त्रि *tri*, 'three' (pl. only), is declined in the masculine like

the plural of nouns whose stems end in इ *i* at 110, except in Gen.; thus, N. V. masc. त्रयस्; Ac. त्रीन्; I. त्रिभिस्; D. Ab. त्रिभ्यस्; G. त्रयाणाम् (Ved. त्रीणाम्); L. त्रिषु. The feminine forms its cases from a stem तिसृ; thus, N. Ac. V. fem. तिस्रस्; I. तिसृभिस्; D. Ab. तिसृभ्यस्; G. तिसृणाम्; L. तिसृषु. The N. Ac. V. neut. is त्रीणि; the rest like masc.

203. चतुर् *ćatur*, 'four' (plural only), is thus declined: N. V. masc. चत्वारस् (τέτταρες, τέσσαρες); Ac. चतुरस्; I. चतुर्भिस्; D. Ab. चतुर्भ्यस्; G. चतुर्णाम्; L. चतुर्षु. N. Ac. V. fem. चतस्रस्; I. चतसृभिस्; D. Ab. चतसृभ्यस्; G. चतसृणाम्; L. चतसृषु. N. Ac. V. neut. चत्वारि; the rest like the masculine.

a. In *ćatur*, *shash*, *pańćan*, &c., an augment *n* is inserted before *ám*, the termination of Gen., by Páṇ. VII. 1, 55.

204. पञ्चन् *pańćan*, 'five' (plural only), is the same for masc., fem., and neut. It is declined in I. D. Ab. L. like nouns in *an* (146). The Gen. lengthens the penultimate; thus, N. Ac. V. पञ्च (πέντε); I. पञ्चभिस्; D. Ab. पञ्चभ्यस्; G. पञ्चानाम्; L. पञ्चसु.

Like पञ्चन् are declined, सप्तन् 'seven' (*septem*, ἑπτά), नवन् 'nine' (*novem*), दशन् 'ten' (*decem*, δέκα), एकादशन् 'eleven' (*undecim*), द्वादशन् 'twelve' (*duodecim*), and all other numerals ending in *an*, excepting अष्टन् 'eight.'

205. षष् *shash*, 'six,' is the same for masc., fem., and neut., and is thus declined: N. Ac. V. षट्; I. षड्भिस्; D. Ab. षड्भ्यस्; G. षण्णाम् *shaṇṇám* (43. *f*); L. षट्सु.

a. Similarly without distinction of gender, अष्टन् *ashṭan*, 'eight:' N. Ac. V. अष्टौ or अष्ट (*octo*, ὀκτώ); I. अष्टाभिस् or अष्टभिस्; D. Ab. अष्टाभ्यस् or अष्टभ्यस्; G. अष्टानाम्; L. अष्टासु or अष्टसु.

b. The numerals from पञ्चन् 'five' to नवदशन् 'nineteen' have no distinction of gender, but agree in number and case with the nouns to which they are joined; thus, पञ्चभिर् नारीभिः 'by five women.'

206. All the remaining cardinal numbers, from ऊनविंशति 'nineteen' to शत 'a hundred,' सहस्र 'a thousand,' and upwards, may be declined in the *singular*, even when joined with masculine, feminine, or neuter nouns in the plural. Those ending in ति *ti* are feminine, and declined like मति *mati* at 112; and those in त् *t* are also feminine, and declined like सरित् *sarit* at 136; thus, विंशत्या पुरुषैः 'by twenty men;' विंशतिं नरान् acc. pl. 'twenty men;' त्रिंशता पुरुषैः 'by thirty men;' त्रिंशतं नरान् acc. pl. 'thirty men.' शत 'a hundred' and सहस्र 'a thousand' and all the higher numbers are declined according to their final

vowels, whether *a, á, i, í,* or *u;* thus, शतं पितरः 'a hundred ancestors;' शतात् पितृभ्यः 'from a hundred ancestors;' एकाधिकशतं पितरः 'a hundred and one ancestors;' सहस्रेण पितृभिः 'with a thousand ancestors;' प्रयुतं नराः 'a million men;' कोट्या पुरुषैः 'with ten million men,' &c.

207. Although these numerals, from ऊनविंशति 'nineteen,' when joined with plural nouns, may be declined in the singular, yet they may take a dual or plural when used alone and in particular constructions; as, विंशती 'two twenties;' त्रिंशतौ 'two thirties;' त्रिंशतस् 'many thirties;' शते 'two hundred;' शतानि 'hundreds;' सहस्राणि 'thousands;' 'sixty thousand sons,' षष्टिः पुत्रसहस्राणि.

The things numbered are often put in the genitive; thus, द्वे सहस्रे रथानाम् 'two thousand chariots;' सप्तशतानि नागानाम् 'seven hundred elephants;' एकविंशतिः शराणाम् 'twenty-one arrows.' See other examples in Syntax at 835.

ORDINALS.

208. The ordinals are, प्रथम 'first'* (cf. πρῶτος, *primus*); द्वितीय 'second' (δεύτερο-ς); तृतीय 'third' (*tertiu-s*); which three are all declined like *śiva* and *śubha* at 187; but the first may optionally follow *sarva* at 237 in N. V. pl. m. (प्रथमे or प्रथमास्); and the other two the pronominals at 237, 238 in D. Ab. L. sing. m. f. n.; thus, D. द्वितीयस्मै or द्वितीयाय m. n., द्वितीयस्यै or द्वितीयायै f. See also 239.

209. चतुर्थ 'fourth'† (τέταρτος); पञ्चम 'fifth;' षष्ठ 'sixth;' सप्तम 'seventh' (*septimus*); अष्टम 'eighth;' नवम 'ninth' (*nonus*); दशम 'tenth' (*decimus*); declined like *śiva* and *śubha* for masc. and neut., and like *nadí* at 105 for feminine; thus, Nom. m. चतुर्थस्, f. चतुर्थी. (In पञ्चम &c. the old superlative suffix *ma* may be noted.)

210. The ordinals from 'eleventh' to 'nineteenth' are formed from the cardinals by rejecting the final *n;* thus, from एकादशन् 'eleven,' एकादश 'eleventh' (Nom. m. f. n. एकादशस्, -शी, -शम्, 103, 105, 104).

211. 'Twentieth,' 'thirtieth,' 'fortieth,' and 'fiftieth' are formed either by adding the superlative suffix *tama* (195) to the cardinal, or by rejecting the final syllable or letter of the cardinal; as, from विंशति 'twenty,' विंशतितम or विंश 'twentieth' (Nom. m. f. n. -मस्, -मी, -मम्; -शस्, -शी, -शम्, 103, 105, 104). Similarly, त्रिंशत्तम or त्रिंश 'thirtieth,' पञ्चाशत्तम or पञ्चाश 'fiftieth,' &c. The intermediate ordinals are formed by prefixing the numeral, as in the cardinals; thus, एकविंशतितम or एकविंश 'twenty-first,' &c.

---

* Other adjectives may be used to express 'first;' as, आद्यस्, -द्या, -द्यम्; आदिमस्, -मा, -मम्; अग्रस्, -ग्रा, -ग्रम्; अग्रिमस्, -मा, -मम्.

† तुरीयस्, -या, -यम्; तुर्यस्, -र्या, -र्यम् are also used for 'fourth.'

212. The other ordinals, from 'sixtieth' to 'ninetieth,' are formed by adding *tama;* also by changing *ti* to *ta* in the case of another numeral preceding, but not otherwise; thus, from षष्टि 'sixty,' षष्टितम 'sixtieth;' but षष्ट for 'sixtieth' can only be used when another numeral precedes, as एकषष्ट or एकषष्टितम 'sixty-first,' त्रिषष्ट or त्रिषष्टितम 'sixty-third;' from नवति 'ninety,' नवतितम 'ninetieth;' but नवत for 'ninetieth' can only be used when another numeral precedes (see Páṇ. v. 2, 58).

213. 'Hundredth' and 'thousandth' are formed by adding *tama* to शत and सहस्र, declinable in three genders; thus, शततम 'hundredth' (Nom. m. f. n. शततमस्, -मी, -मम्). Similarly, सहस्रतमस्, -मी, -मम्, 'thousandth.'

214. The aggregation of two or more numbers is expressed by modifications of the ordinal numbers; thus, द्वयम् 'a duad,' त्रयम् 'a triad,' चतुष्टयम् 'the aggregate of four.'

215. There are a few adverbial numerals; as, सकृत् 'once,' द्विस् 'twice,' त्रिस् 'thrice,' चतुस् 'four times.' कृत्वस् may be added to cardinal numbers, with a similar signification; as, पञ्चकृत्वस् 'five times.' The neuter of the ordinals may be used adverbially; as, प्रथमम् 'in the first place.'

For a table of the numerical symbols see page 3.

CHAPTER V.

PRONOUNS.

216. Pronouns (*sarva-náman*) have no one stem equally applicable to all the cases. In the 1st personal pronoun, the stem of the sing. is practically अह् *ah* in Nom., and in the oblique cases म *ma*. In the 2nd, the stem of the sing. is practically त्व *tva* or तु *tu*, while that of the dual and plural is यु *yu*. The 3rd has स *sa* for the stem of the Nom. sing., and त *ta* for the other cases.

217. Nevertheless the form of the pronoun used in derivative and compound words is regarded by grammarians as expressive of its most general and comprehensive state, and this in the pronouns of the first and second persons, corresponds with the Ablative cases, singular and plural, and in the other pronouns, with the Nominative and Accusative cases singular neuter.

DECLENSION OF THE PERSONAL PRONOUNS.

Obs.—In Sanskṛit, as in other languages, the general and indefinite character of the first two personal pronouns is denoted by the fact that no distinction of gender is admitted. For the same reason, the termination of the Nom. case of some pronouns is made to resemble the neuter, as the most general state. This may also be the reason why the 3rd pronoun *sa* drops the *s* of the Nom. case before all consonants. There is no Vocative case.

218. मद् *mad*, sing. 'I,' अस्मद् *asmad*, pl. 'we.'

N.	अहम् *aham*, 'I'	आवाम् *ávám*, 'we two'	वयम् *vayam*, 'we'
Ac.	माम् *mám* or मा *má*, 'me'	— *ávám* or नौ *nau*, 'us two'	अस्मान् *asmán* or नस् *nas*, 'us'
I.	मया *mayá*	आवाभ्याम् *ávábhyám*	अस्माभिस् *asmábhis*
D.	मह्यम् *mahyam* or मे *me*	— *ávábhyám* or नौ *nau*	अस्मभ्यम् *asmabhyam* or नस् *nas*
Ab.	मत् *mat* *	— *ávábhyám*	अस्मत् *asmat*
G.	मम *mama* or मे *me*	आवयोस् *ávayos* or नौ *nau*	अस्माकम् *asmákam* or नस् *nas*
L.	मयि *mayi*	— *ávayos*	अस्मासु *asmásu*

219. त्वद् *tvad*, sing. 'thou,' युष्मद् *yushmad*, pl. 'you.'

N.	त्वम् *tvam*, 'thou'	युवाम् *yuvám*, 'you two'	यूयम् *yúyam*, 'you' or 'ye'
Ac.	त्वाम् *tvám* or त्वा *tvá*	— *yuvám* or वाम् *vám*	युष्मान् *yushmán* or वस् *vas*
I.	त्वया *tvayá*	युवाभ्याम् *yuvábhyám*	युष्माभिस् *yushmábhis*
D.	तुभ्यम् *tubhyam* or ते *te*	— *yuvábhyám* or वाम् *vám*	युष्मभ्यम् *yushmabhyam* or वस् *vas*
Ab.	त्वत् *tvat* *	— *yuvábhyám*	युष्मत् *yushmat*
G.	तव *tava* or ते *te*	युवयोस् *yuvayos* or वाम् *vám*	युष्माकम् *yushmákam* or वस् *vas*
L.	त्वयि *tvayi*	— *yuvayos*	युष्मासु *yushmásu*

Obs.—The alternative forms *má, me, nau,* &c., have no accent, and cannot be used at the beginning of sentences, nor before the particles *ća*, 'and;' *vá*, 'or;' *eva*, 'indeed,' &c.

220. तद् *tad*, 'he,' 'that.'

MASCULINE.

N.	सस् *sas* (usually स *sa*†), 'he'	तौ *tau*, 'they two'	ते *te*, 'they,' 'those'
Ac.	तम् *tam*	— *tau*	तान् *tán*
I.	तेन *tena*	ताभ्याम् *tábhyám*	तैस् *tais*

---

* As the stems *mad* and *tvad* are generally used in compounds, *mat-tas* and *tvat-tas* more commonly stand for the Ablative; see 719. Similarly, the Ablative plural may be *yushmat-tas, asmat-tas;* but these very rarely occur.

† By 67, स will be the usual form. सस् usually exists as सो, see 64. *a*.

D. तस्मै *tasmai*	ताभ्याम् *tábhyám*	तेभ्यस् *tebhyas*
Ab. तस्मात् *tasmát*	— *tábhyám*	— *tebhyas*
G. तस्य *tasya*	तयोस् *tayos*	तेषाम् *teshám*
L. तस्मिन् *tasmin*	— *tayos*	तेषु *teshu*

FEMININE.

N. सा *sá*, 'she'	ते *te*, 'they two' (fem.)	तास् *tás*, 'they' (fem.)
Ac. ताम् *tám*	— *te*	— *tás*
I. तया *tayá*	ताभ्याम् *tábhyám*	ताभिस् *tábhis*
D. तस्यै *tasyai*	— *tábhyám*	ताभ्यस् *tábhyas*
Ab. तस्यास् *tasyás*	— *tábhyám*	— *tábhyas*
G. — *tasyás*	तयोस् *tayos*	तासाम् *tásám*
L. तस्याम् *tasyám*	— *tayos*	तासु *tásu*

NEUTER.

N. Ac. तत् *tat*, ते *te*, तानि *táni*; the rest like the masculine.

a. Observe the resemblance of the Sanskṛit personal pronouns to those of the dead and living cognate languages. *Aham* or *ah* is the Greek ἐγώ (Æolic ἐγών), Latin *ego*, German *ich*, English 'I;' *mám* or *má* (the latter being the oldest form found in the Vedas) equals ἐμέ, *me; mahyam=mihi; mayi=mei;* the *mat* of the Abl. sing. and of *asmat*, *yushmat*, corresponds to the Latin *met* in *memet*, *nosmet*, &c.: *vayam* or *va* is the English 'we;' *asmán=us; nas=nos; tvam=tu*, 'thou;' *tvám* or *tvá=te*, 'thee;' *tubhyam=tibi; tvayi=tui; yúyam=*ὑμεῖς, English 'you;' *vas=vos*. The 3rd personal pronoun corresponds to the Greek article; thus, *tau* =τώ, *tam*=τόν; *tábhyám*=τοῖν, ταῖν, &c.

DEMONSTRATIVE PERSONAL PRONOUNS.

221. The third personal pronoun तद् *tad*, 'he,' declined above, is constantly used in a demonstrative sense, to signify 'that' or 'this.'

a. It is sometimes used *emphatically* with other pronouns, like *ille* and *ipse;* thus, सोऽहम् '*ille ego;*' ते वयम् '*illi nos;*' स त्वम् '*ille tu;*' सा त्वम् '*illa tu;*' ते यूयम् '*illi vos;*' स एषः '*ille ipse;*' तद् एतत् '*id ipsum.*'

222. It is also combined with the relative *ya* to form another demonstrative pronoun (rarely used except in the Veda), of which the stem is *tyad:* N. स्यस् (67), त्यौ, त्ये; Ac. त्यम्, &c. Fem. स्या, त्ये, त्यास्, &c. Neut. त्यत्, त्ये, त्यानि, &c.

223. By prefixing ए *e* to तद्, another common pronoun is formed, more proximately demonstrative; thus,

एतद् *etad*, 'this.'

MASCULINE.

N.	एषस् *eshas* (usu. एष *esha*). 70.	एतौ *etau*	एते *ete*
Ac.	एतम् *etam* or एनम् *enam*	— *etau* or एनौ *enau*	एतान् *etán* or एनान् *enán*
I.	एतेन *etena* or एनेन *enena*	एताभ्याम् *etábhyám*	एतैस् *etais*
D.	एतस्मै *etasmai*	— *etábhyám*	एतेभ्यस् *etebhyas*
Ab.	एतस्मात् *etasmát*	— *etábhyám*	— *etebhyas*
G.	एतस्य *etasya*	एतयोस् *etayos* or एनयोस् *enayos*	एतेषाम् *eteshám*
L.	एतस्मिन् *etasmin*	— *etayos* or — *enayos*	एतेषु *eteshu*

The feminine is N. एषा *eshá*, एते *ete*, एतास् *etás*; Ac. एताम् or एनाम्, एते or एने, एतास् or एनास्; I. एतया or एनया, एताभ्याम्, एताभिस्; D. एतस्यै, &c.

The neuter is N. एतत्, एते, एतानि; Ac. एतत् or एनत्, एते or एने, एतानि or एनानि, &c.

a. The alternative forms एनम्, एनेन, एनाम्, &c. are, like those of the 1st and 2nd person, enclitic, and ought not to be used at the beginning of a sentence. Moreover, they can only be used with reference to some one or something mentioned in a previous sentence (see Syntax 836).

With *etad* cf. Lat. *iste, ista, istud; etam = istum, etasya = istius, etat = istud.*

224. There is another common demonstrative pronoun, of which इदम् *idam*, 'this,' the N. neuter, is supposed to represent the most general state (cf. Lat. *is, ea, id*), though there are really two stems—the vowels अ *a* and इ *i* (cf. *a-tas, i-tas*, 719). The latter serves also as the stem of certain pronominals, such as इतर, ईदृश, इयत्. See 234, 234. *b*, and 236.

MASCULINE.

N.	अयम् *ayam*, 'this'	इमौ *imau*, 'these two'	इमे *ime*, 'these'
Ac.	इमम् *imam*	— *imau*	इमान् *imán*
I.	अनेन *anena*	आभ्याम् *ábhyám*	एभिस् *ebhis* *
D.	अस्मै *asmai*	— *ábhyám*	एभ्यस् *ebhyas*
Ab.	अस्मात् *asmát*	— *ábhyám*	— *ebhyas*
G.	अस्य *asya*	अनयोस् *anayos*	एषाम् *eshám*
L.	अस्मिन् *asmin*	— *anayos*	एषु *eshu*

* This is an example of the old form for the Inst. pl. of masculine nouns of the first class, common in the Vedas.

FEMININE.

N. इयम् *iyam*	इमे *ime*	इमास् *imás*
Ac. इमाम् *imám*	— *ime*	— *imás*
I. अनया *anayá*	आभ्याम् *ábhyám*	आभिस् *ábhis*
D. अस्यै *usyai*	— *ábhyám*	आभ्यस् *ábhyas*
Ab. अस्यास् *asyás*	— *ábhyám*	— *ábhyas*
G. — *asyás*	अनयोस् *anayos*	आसाम् *ásám*
L. अस्याम् *asyám*	— *anayos*	आसु *ásu*

NEUTER.

N. Ac. इदम् *idam*	इमे *ime*	इमानि *imáni*

225. There is another demonstrative pronoun (rarely used, excepting in Nom. sing.), of which अदस्, 'this' or 'that,' is supposed to represent the most general state, though the stem is अमु *amu*, and in N. sing. असु *asu*. It is thus declined: Masc. N. असौ, अमू, अमी; Ac. अमुम्, अमू, अमून्; I. अमुना, अमूभ्याम्, अमीभिस्; D. अमुष्मै, अमूभ्याम्, अमीभ्यस्; Ab. अमुष्मात्, अमूभ्याम्, अमीभ्यस्; G. अमुष्य, अमुयोस्, अमीषाम्; L. अमुष्मिन्, अमुयोस्, अमीषु. Fem. N. असौ, अमू, अमूस्; Ac. अमूम्, अमू, अमूस्; I. अमुया, अमूभ्याम्, अमूभिस्; D. अमुष्यै, अमूभ्याम्, अमूभ्यस्; Ab. अमुष्यास्, &c.; G. अमुष्यास्, अमुयोस्, अमूषाम्; L. अमुष्याम्, अमुयोस्, अमूषु. Neut. N. Ac. अदस्, अमू, अमूनि.

RELATIVE PRONOUN.

226. The relative is formed by substituting य् *y* for the initial letter of the pronoun *tad* at 220; thus,

यद् *yad*, 'who,' 'which.'

MASCULINE.

N. यस् *yas*	यौ *yau*	ये *ye*, 'who' or 'which'
Ac. यम् *yam*	— *yau*	यान् *yán*
I. येन *yena*	याभ्याम् *yábhyám*	यैस् *yais*
D. यस्मै *yasmai*	— *yábhyám*	येभ्यस् *yebhyas*
Ab. यस्मात् *yasmát*	— *yábhyám*	— *yebhyas*
G. यस्य *yasya*	ययोस् *yayos*	येषाम् *yeshám*
L. यस्मिन् *yasmin*	— *yayos*	येषु *yeshu*

The feminine and neuter follow the fem. and neut. of *tad* at 220. Fem. N. या *yá*, ये *ye*, यास् *yás*; Ac. याम् *yám*, &c. &c. Neut. N. Ac. यत् *yat*, ये *ye*, यानि *yáni*; the rest like the masculine.

With *yas*, *yá*, *yat*, &c., cf. Gr. ὅς, ἥ, ὅ, &c., Sk. *y* corresponding to *spiritus asper* in Gr. (see 25).

INTERROGATIVE PRONOUNS.

227. The interrogative differs from the relative in substituting *k* instead of *y* for the initial letter of the pronoun *tad* at 220; and in making the N. Ac. sing. neut. किम् instead of कत्*; thus, N. masc. कस् *kas*, कौ *kau*, के *ke*, 'who?' 'which?' 'what?' Ac. कम् *kam*, 'whom?' &c. N. fem. का *ká*, के *ke*, कास् *kás*, &c. The N. Ac. neut. are किम् *kim*, के *ke*, कानि *káni*. Although the real stem of this pronoun is *ka*, yet *kim* is taken to represent the most general state, and occurs in a few compounds; such as किमर्थम् 'on what account?' 'why?'

a. To the true stem *ka* may be affixed *ti*, to form कति *kati* (*quot*), 'how many?' The same suffix is added to *ta* and *ya*, the proper stems of the third personal and relative pronouns, to form *tati*, 'so many' (*tot*), and *yati*, 'as many.' These are thus declined in pl. only:

N. Ac. V. कति; I. कतिभिस्; Dat. Ab. कतिभ्यस्; G. कतीनाम्; L. कतिषु.

Note—The Latin *quot* and *tot*, which drop the final *i*, take it again in composition; as, *quotidie*, *totidem*, &c.

INDEFINITE PRONOUNS.

228. The indeclinable suffixes *ćid*, *api*, and *ćana* (718), affixed (in accordance with the rules of Sandhi) to the several cases of the interrogative pronouns, give them an indefinite signification; as, कश्चिद् *kaśćid*, 'somebody,' 'some one,' 'any one,' 'a certain one.'

MASCULINE.

N.	कश्चित् *kaśćit*. 62.	कौचित् *kaućit*	केचित् *kećit*, 'some persons'
Ac.	कंचित् *kańćit*. 59.	— *kaućit*	कांश्चित् *káṇśćit*. 53.
I.	केनचित् *kenaćit*	काभ्यांचित् *kábhyáńćit*	कैश्चित् *kaiśćit*. 62.
D.	कस्मैचित् *kasmaićit*	— *kábhyáńćit*	केभ्यश्चित् *kebhyaśćit*
Ab.	कस्माच्चित् *kasmáććit*. 48.	— *kábhyáńćit*	— *kebhyaśćit*
G.	कस्यचित् *kasyaćit*	कयोश्चित् *kayośćit*. 62.	केषांचित् *keshánćit*
L.	कस्मिंश्चित् *kasmiṇśćit*. 53.	— *kayośćit*	केषुचित् *keshućit*

Similarly, Fem. Nom. काचित्, केचित्, काश्चित्; Ac. कांचित्, &c.: and Neut. Nom. Ac. किंचित् 'something,' 'anything,' केचित्, कानिचित्, &c.

229. So also by affixing अपि; as, Nom. masc. कोऽपि (64. *a*) 'some one,' 'a certain one,' कावपि, केऽपि (37, 35); Ac. कमपि, &c.; I. केनापि, &c. (31); D. कस्मा-

* *Kat* (or *kad*), however (= Latin *quod*), was the old form, and is, like *kim*, found at the beginning of compounds; such as *kaććid*, 'perhaps;' *kad-artha*, 'useless' ('of what use?'); *kad-adhvan*, 'a bad road' ('what sort of a road?').

यपि, &c. (37); Ab. कस्मादपि, &c.; G. कस्यापि, &c.; L. कस्मिन्नपि, &c. (52). Nom. fem. कापि, &c.; Ac. कामपि, &c.; I. कयापि, &c. &c. Nom. neut. किमपि 'something,' 'anything,' &c. The suffix *ćana* is rarely found, except in Nom. masc. कश्चन 'some one,' 'any one;' and in Nom. neut. किञ्चन 'something.'

230. In the same way interrogative adverbs are made indefinite; thus, from *kati*, 'how many?' *katićid*, 'a few;' from *kadá*, 'when?' *kadáćid* or *kadáćana* or *kadápi*, 'at some time;' from *katham*, 'how?' *kathanćana*, 'some how;' from *kva*, 'where?' *kvaćid* or *kvápi*, 'somewhere.'

a. 'Whosoever,' 'whatsoever' are expressed by prefixing the relative to the indefinite; thus, यः कश्चित् or यः कोऽपि 'whosoever,' यत् किञ्चित् 'whatsoever:' or sometimes to the interrogative; as, येन केन उपायेन 'by any means whatsoever:' or sometimes by repeating the relative; as, यो यः, यद् यत्.

POSSESSIVE PRONOUNS.

231. Possessive pronouns (Páṇ. IV. 3, 1–3) are mostly formed by affixing *íya* (80. L) to those forms of the personal pronouns, ending in *d*, which are used as stems; thus, fr. मद् 'I,' मदीय *madíya*, 'mine;' fr. अस्मद् 'we,' अस्मदीय *asmadíya*, 'our;' fr. त्वद् 'thou,' त्वदीय *tvadíya*, 'thine;' fr. तद् 'he,' तदीय *tadíya*, 'his.' Similarly, भवदीय 'yours' (Páṇ. IV. 2, 115) is formed from *bhavad*, and not from the regular stem *bhavat* (see 233). They are declined like *śubha* at 187; e.g. Nom. m. मदीयस्, f. मदीया, n. मदीयम्.

a. Other possessive pronouns differently formed are *mámaka* (fem. *akí*, but generally *iká*) and *mámakína* (fem. *á*), 'mine;' *távaka* (fem. *akí*) and *távakína* (fem. *á*), 'thine;' *ásmáka* (fem. *ákí*) and *ásmákína* (fem. *á*), 'our;' *yaushmáka* (fem. *ákí*) and *yaushmákíṇa* (fem. *á*), 'your.' *Mámaka* and those formed with the suffix *ína* (80. XLIX) make their feminines in *á*, and are declined like *śubha* at 187; the others follow *śiva* or *śubha* for masc. and neut., and *nadí* (105) for fem.

Obs.—The genitive case of the personal pronouns is often used as a possessive; thus, तस्य पुत्रः 'his son;' मम पुत्री 'my daughter.'

REFLEXIVE PRONOUNS.

232. The oblique cases sing. of आत्मन् *átman*, 'soul,' 'self' (declined at 146), are used reflexively, in place of the three personal pronouns, like the Latin *ipse*.

Thus, *átmánam* (*me ipsum*) *anáhárena hanishyámi*, 'I shall kill myself by fasting;' *átmánam* (*te ipsum*) *mṛitavad darśaya*, 'show thyself as if dead;' *átmánaṃ* (*se ipsum*) *nindati*, 'he blames himself.' It is used in the singular, even when it refers to a plural; as, *átmánam punímahe*, 'we (will) purify ourselves;' *abudhair átmá paropakaraṇíkṛitaḥ*, 'foolish people make themselves the tools of others.'

a. The indeclinable pronoun स्वयम् *svayam* is sometimes joined, in the sense of 'self,' to the three personal pronouns; thus, अहं स्वयम् 'I myself,' &c.

b. स्व *sva* (*suus*) is used reflexively, with respect to all three persons, and may stand for 'my own' (*meus*), 'thy own' (*tuus*), 'his own,' 'our own,' &c. (cf. σφός, σφή, σφόν). It often occupies the first place in a compound, e. g. स्वगृहं गच्छति 'he goes to his own house.'

The Gen. case of आत्मन् *átman*, or often the simple stem, is used with the same signification; as, आत्मनो गृहं or आत्मगृहं गच्छति. It is used in the singular even when it refers to more than one*. In the most modern Sanskṛit, निज *nija* is often used in place of स्व and आत्मन्, and from it transferred to Bengálí.

स्व, in the sense of 'own,' is declined like *sarva* at 237; as a pronominal the Ab. L. sing. masc. neut. and N. pl. masc. may optionally follow *śubha* at 187; thus, N. pl. m. *sve* or *svás* in the sense of 'own;' but used substantively in the sense of 'kinsmen' or 'property,' *sva* can only follow *śiva* or *śubha* (N. pl. m. *svás*).

c. स्वीय (f. *á*), स्वकीय (f. *á*), and स्वक (f. *aká* or *iká*), declinable like *śubha*, sometimes take the place of स्व in the sense of 'own,' 'one's own.'

HONORIFIC OR RESPECTFUL PRONOUN.

233. भवत् *bhavat*, 'your Honour,' requiring the 3rd person of the verb, is declined like *dhanavat* at 140; thus, N. masc. भवान् *bhaván*, भवन्तौ *bhavantau*, भवन्तस् *bhavantas*; V. भवन्; N. fem. भवती *bhavatí*, भवत्यौ *bhavatyau*, भवत्यस् *bhavatyas*, &c.; V. भवति. It is constantly used to denote 'respect,' in place of the 2nd personal pronoun; thus, भवान् गृहं गच्छतु 'let your Honour go home' for 'go thou home.'

PRONOUNS OF QUANTITY AND SIMILITUDE.

234. Modifications of the demonstrative, relative, and interrogative pronouns may take the suffix वत् *vat* to express 'quantity,' and दृश *dṛiśa*, दृक्ष *dṛiksha* or दृश् *dṛiś* (Nom. masc. neut. *dṛik*, fem. *dṛiśí*) to express 'similitude,' frequently used as correlative pronouns; thus,

तावत् *távat*, एतावत् *etávat*, 'so many,' 'so much' (*tantus*); यावत् (*quantus*) 'as many,' 'as much' (declined like *dhanavat* at 140); तादृश *tádṛiśa* or तादृक्ष *tádṛiksha* or तादृश् *tádṛiś*, 'such like' (*talis*, τηλίκος); एतादृश *etádṛiśa* or एतादृश् *etádṛiś*, 'like this or that,' following *śubha* (187) for masc. and neut. of those ending in श *śa* and क्ष *ksha*; and *diś*, at 181, for masc. and neut. of those in श् *ś*; and *nadí*,

---

* Lassen cites an example (Rámáyaṇa II. 64, 28) in which *átman* refers to the dual: *Putram átmanaḥ spṛishṭvá nipetatuḥ*, 'they two fell down after touching their son.'

at 105, for the fem. of all three. Similarly, the correlatives यादृश or यादृक्ष or यादृश् 'as like,' 'how like' (*qualis*, ἡλίκος); ईदृश or ईदृक्ष or ईदृश् 'so like;' कीदृश or कीदृक्ष or कीदृश् 'how like?' (*qualis?*)

a. Note, that दृश is derived from the root *dṛiś*, 'to see,' 'appear,' and is in fact our English 'like,' *d* being interchangeable with *l*, and *ś* with *k*.

b. कियत् 'how much,' and इयत् 'so much,' are declined like धनवत् (140).

c. A few peculiar pronouns of quantity, some of which are of the nature of ordinals, are formed with the suffix *tha* (*itha*), thought by some to be an old superlative, or *titha* (80. LXIII); e.g. *yávatitha, as, í, am,* 'to whatever stage or degree advanced,' 'how-manieth,' 'as-manieth;' *katitha, as, í, am,* 'to whatever degree,' 'how-manieth;' *katitho divasaḥ,* 'what day of the month is it?' *katipaya-tha, as, í, am,* 'advanced to a certain degree.'

PRONOMINALS.

235. There are certain common adjectives, called *pronominals*, which partake of the nature of pronouns, and follow the declension of *tad* at 220; but may also take a vocative case.

236. These are, इतर 'other' (but in Veda the neut. may be *itaram* as well as *itarat*, Páṇ. VII. 1, 26, cf. Latin *iterum*); कतर 'which of the two?' (πότερος for κότερος); कतम 'which of many?' ततर 'that one of two;' ततम 'that one of many;' यतर 'who or which of two;' यतम 'who or which of many' (formed by adding the comparative and superlative suffixes to the various pronominal stems, 195); अन्य 'other,' 'another;' अन्यतर 'one of two;' and एकतम 'one of many.' They are declined like तद्, and make the N. V. Ac. neut. sing. in *at;* thus, *anyat, itarat, anyatarat, katarat, katamat,* &c.; but they have a vocative, viz. V. masc. *anya*, V. fem. *anye*, V. neut. *anyat*, &c.; the V. du. and plural is like the Nom.

a. With regard to *itara*, it loses its pronominal declension at the end of Dvandva compounds, but at the end of Dvandvas (748) it may optionally follow *tad* in the Nom. pl.; e.g. *varṇáśrametarás* (or *-re*), 'classes, orders, and others.'

237. There are other pronominals, which make *am* instead of *at* in the N. Ac. neuter. The model of these is सर्व *sarva*, 'all;' thus,

MASCULINE.

	SINGULAR.	DUAL.	PLURAL.
N.	सर्वस् *sarvas*	सर्वौ *sarvau*	सर्वे *sarve*
Ac.	सर्वम् *sarvam*	— *sarvau*	सर्वान् *sarván*
I.	सर्वेण *sarveṇa*	सर्वाभ्याम् *sarvábhyám*	सर्वैस् *sarvais*
D.	सर्वस्मै *sarvasmai*	— *sarvábhyám*	सर्वेभ्यस् *sarvebhyas*
Ab.	सर्वस्मात् *sarvasmát*	— *sarvábhyám*	— *sarvebhyas*
G.	सर्वस्य *sarvasya*	सर्वयोस् *sarvayos*	सर्वेषाम् *sarveshám*
L.	सर्वस्मिन् *sarvasmin*	— *sarvayos*	सर्वेषु *sarveshu*
V.	सर्व *sarva*	सर्वौ *sarvau*	सर्वे *sarve*

FEMININE.

	SINGULAR.	DUAL.	PLURAL.
N.	सर्वा *sarvá*	सर्वे *sarve*	सर्वास् *sarvás*
Ac.	सर्वाम् *sarvám*	— *sarve*	— *sarvás*
I.	सर्वया *sarvayá*	सर्वाभ्याम् *sarvábhyám*	सर्वाभिस् *sarvábhis*
D.	सर्वस्यै *sarvasyai*	— *sarvábhyám*	सर्वाभ्यस् *sarvábhyas*
Ab.	सर्वस्यास् *sarvasyás*	— *sarvábhyám*	— *sarvábhyas*
G.	— *sarvasyás*	सर्वयोस् *sarvayos*	सर्वासाम् *sarvásám*
L.	सर्वस्याम् *sarvasyám*	— *sarvayos*	सर्वासु *sarvásu*
V.	सर्वे *sarve*	सर्वे *sarve*	सर्वास् *sarvás*

NEUTER.

N. Ac.	सर्वम् *sarvam*	सर्वे *sarve*	सर्वाणि *sarváṇi*
V.	सर्व *sarva*	— *sarve*	— *sarváṇi*

The other cases like the masculine.

238. Like *sarva* are declined उभय 'both' (properly only found in sing. and pl., *ubha* being used in du.; the fem. of *ubhaya* is *ubhayí*, like *nadí*); विश्व 'all;' एकतर 'one of two' (ἑκάτερος); अन्यतम 'one of many;' सम meaning 'all,' but not when it signifies 'equal;' सिम 'the whole;' त्व 'other;' नेम 'half.' The N. Ac. sing. neuter of these will end in *am*, but त्व is optionally त्वत्. In N. V. pl. masc. नेम is नेमे or नेमास्.

Obs.—उभ, 'both' (*ambo*, ἄμφω), is declined like *sarva*, but only in du.; thus, N. Ac. V. masc. उभौ, fem. and neut. उभे; I. D. Ab. उभाभ्याम्; G. L. उभयोस्.

a. अधर 'inferior,' पर 'other,' अपर 'other,' अवर 'posterior,' 'west,' उत्तर 'superior,' 'north,' दक्षिण 'south,' 'right,' पूर्व 'east,' 'prior,' अन्तर meaning either 'outer' or 'inner' (as applied to a garment), स्व 'own' (232), follow *sarva*, and optionally *śubha*, at 187, in Abl. Loc. sing. masc. and neut., and Nom. Voc. pl. masc.; as, अधरस्मात् or अधरात्, &c. They can only be declined like pronominals when they denote relative position; hence *dakshiṇáḥ* (not *dakshiṇe*) *kavayaḥ*, 'clever poets.' Moreover, the pronominal inflexion is optional in certain compounds.

239. एक, 'one,' follows *sarva*, see 200; द्वितीय 'second,' तृतीय 'third,' follow *śubha* (187), and optionally *sarva* in certain cases, see 208; they make their fem. in *á*.

240. अल्प 'a few,' अर्ध or अर्द्ध 'half,' कतिपय (fem. *á* or *í*) 'several,' 'few,' 'some,' प्रथम 'first,' चरम 'last,' द्वय (fem. *í*), द्वितय (fem. *í*) 'twofold,' पञ्चतय (fem. *í*) 'five-fold,' and all in *-ya* and *-taya*, properly follow *śiva* at 103; but may make their Nom. V. pl. masc. in *e*; as, अल्पे or अल्पास् 'few,' &c. (see Páṇ. I. 1, 33).

a. अन्योन्य, इतरेतर, 'one another,' 'mutual,' make their Nom. Ac. sing. neut. in *am*, not *at*; and V. in *a*.

b. In some pronouns the syllable *ka* or *ak* is introduced, generally before the last vowel or syllable, to denote contempt, in the same way that *ka* is added to nominal stems; e.g. मयका for मया 'by me,' युष्मकाभिस् for युष्माभिस् 'by you.' Similarly, सर्वके, विश्वके, for सर्वे, विश्वे 'all' (see Páṇ. v. 3, 71).

CHAPTER VI.

VERBS.

GENERAL OBSERVATIONS.

241. ALTHOUGH the Sanskṛit verb (*ákhyáta, kriyá*) offers many striking and interesting analogies to the Greek, yet our explanations of its structure are not likely to fall in with the preconceived notions of the student of Greek grammar.

There are ten tenses and moods (*kála*). Seven of them are of common occurrence; viz. 1. the Present (technically called लट् *laṭ*, which, with the other technical names, is applicable also to the terminations of each tense respectively); 2. the Imperfect, sometimes called the First Preterite (लङ् *laṅ*); 3. the Potential or Optative (लिङ् *liṅ*); 4. the Imperative (लोट् *loṭ*); 5. the Perfect, sometimes called the Second Preterite (लिट् *liṭ*); 6. the First Future (लुट् *luṭ*); 7. the Second Future (लृट् *lṛiṭ*). Three are not so commonly used; viz. 8. the Aorist, sometimes called the Third Preterite (लुङ् *luṅ*); 9. the Precative, also called the Benedictive (आशिर् लिङ् *áśir liṅ*); 10. the Conditional (लृङ् *lṛiṅ*). There is also an Infinitive, and several Participles. Of these, the Present, the three Past tenses, and the two Futures belong to the Indicative mood. The Imperative, Potential, Precative, and Conditional (see 242) are moods susceptible of various times; but, as there is only one form for each, it can lead to no embarrassment to call them tenses, and to arrange them indiscriminately with the tenses of the Indicative.

The first four tenses, viz. the Present, Imperfect, Potential, and Imperative, are frequently called *Special tenses**, because in these each of the ten classes of roots has a special structure of its own (as will be explained at 248).

a. Obs.—The ancient Sanskṛit of the Veda is more rich in grammatical forms than the later or classical Sanskṛit. There is a Vedic Subjunctive mood, technically called लेट् *leṭ*, which comprises under it a Present, Imperfect, and Aorist; moreover, the Vedic Potential and Imperative are thought to have distinct forms for various tenses. The Vedic Infinitive, too, has ten or eleven different forms (see 459. *a*).

* In the previous editions of this Grammar these tenses were called 'Conjugational.' I have thought it better to bring the present edition into harmony with other Grammars by adopting Bopp's designation of 'Special.'

242. Although the three past tenses are used without much distinction, yet it should be observed, that they properly express different degrees of past time. The Imperfect (*anadyatana-bhúta*) corresponds in form to the Imperfect of Greek verbs, and properly has reference to an event done at some time recently past, but before the current day. It may denote action past and continuing, or it may be used like the Greek Aorist. The Perfect (*paroksha-bhúta*) is said to have reference to an event completely done before the present day at some remote period, unperceived by or out of sight of the narrator; it answers in form to the Greek Perfect, but may also be used like the Aorist. The Aorist refers to an event done and past at some indefinite period, whether before or during the current day; it corresponds in form and sense to the Greek 1st and 2nd Aorist, and sometimes to the Pluperfect *. Again, the two Futures properly express, the First, definite, the Second, indefinite futurity †: the Second, however, is the most used, and answers to the Greek Future. The Potential or Optative may generally be rendered in English by some one of the auxiliaries 'may,' 'can,' 'would,' 'should,' 'ought.' It is said to denote 'command,' 'direction,' 'expression of wish,' 'enquiry,' 'condition,' 'supposition' (*sambhávana*, Páṇ. III. 3, 161). See Syntax, 879. The Conditional (or Imperfect of the Future) is occasionally used after the conjunctions *yadi* and *ćed*, 'if:' it has an augment like the Imperfect and Aorist, and ought on that account to be classed with the tenses of the Indicative (see 891). The Precative or Benedictive is a tense sometimes used in praying and blessing (*áśishi*). It is a modification of the Potential. There is no tense exactly equivalent to the Pluperfect in Sanskṛit, although the form of some Aorists (in a few primitive verbs, and in verbs of Cl. 10 and Causals) resembles that of the Greek Pluperfect by taking both augment and reduplication: the sense of this tense, however, may often be expressed by the Past Indeclinable Participle or by the Past Passive Participle; as, *tasminn apakránte*, 'after he had departed.' See Syntax, 840, 899. *a*.

a. According to some, the form of the Imperfect and Aorist, which remains after rejecting the augment of these tenses in the Indicative, and which is especially used after the particles मा *má* and मा स्म *má sma* (see 884. Obs. and 889), ought to be called the Subjunctive Imperfect and Subjunctive Aorist.

b. The Infinitive generally has an Active, but is capable of a Passive signification (see Syntax, 867–872).

---

* The fact is, that the three past tenses are not very commonly used to represent the completeness of an action. This is generally done by employing the Past Passive Participle with an inst. case; or by adding *vat* to the Past Pass. Part., and combining it with the Present tense of *as*, 'to be;' as, *uktaván asmi*, 'I have said.' See Syntax, 897.

† The First Future (*luṭ*) is said to be *an-adyatane*, i. e. to be so far definite as to denote what will happen at a future period, not in the course of the current day; as, श्वो गन्तास्मि 'to-morrow I shall go' (Páṇ. III. 3, 15); whereas the Second Future may refer to immediate futurity; as, अद्य सायंकाले श्वो वा गमिष्यामि 'this very evening or to-morrow I shall be going.'

243. Every tense has three numbers, singular, dual, and plural.

To each tense belong two sets of Active terminations; one for the Active voice (properly so called), the other for a kind of Middle or Reflexive voice. The former of these voices is called by Indian grammarians *Parasmai-pada* ('word* directed to another'), because the action is supposed to be Transitive, or to pass *parasmai*, 'to another (object);' the latter is called *Átmane-pada* ('word* directed to one's self'), because the action is supposed to refer *átmane*, 'to one's self.' This distinction, however, is not always observed, and we often find both Parasmai and Átmane employed indifferently for Transitive verbs.

Some verbs, however, are conjugated only in the Átmane-pada, especially when they are Intransitive, or when the direct fruit of the action accrues to the agent (see the distinction of *Udáttetaḥ* and *Anudáttetaḥ* at 75.*c*), or when particular prepositions are used; thus,

Mud and *ruć* meaning 'to be pleased,' 'please one's self;' *bhuj* meaning 'to eat' (not 'to protect'); *dá*, 'to give,' with *á* prefixed, meaning 'to give to one's self,' 'to take,' are restricted to the Átmane-pada. Sometimes, when a verb takes both Padas, the Átmane, without altering the idea expressed by the root, may be used to direct the action in some way towards the agent; thus, *paćati* means 'he cooks,' but *paćate*, 'he cooks for himself:' *yajati*, 'he sacrifices;' *yajate*, 'he sacrifices for himself:' *namati*, 'he bends;' *namate*, 'he bends himself:' *darśayati* (Causal), 'he shews;' *darśayate*, 'he shews himself,' 'appears:' *kárayati*, 'he causes to make;' *kárayate*, 'he causes to be made for himself:' and *yáć*, 'to ask,' although employing both Padas, is more commonly used in the Átmane, because the act of asking generally tends to the advantage of the asker. (See this subject more fully explained at 786.)

a. Passive verbs are conjugated in the Átmane-pada. Indeed, in all the tenses, excepting the first four, the Passive is generally undistinguishable from the Átmane-pada of the primitive verb. But in the four Special tenses, viz. the Present, Imperfect, Potential, and Imperative (unlike the Greek, which exhibits an identity between the Middle and Passive voices in those tenses), the Sanskṛit Passive, although still employing the Átmane-pada terminations, has a special

* Pada is an inflected word as distinguished from an uninflected root (Páṇ. I. 4, 14). The term *pada* has here reference to the scheme of terminations only; so that in this sense there are only two voices in Sanskṛit, and they are often used indiscriminately. Although the Átmane-pada has occasionally a kind of Middle signification, yet it cannot be said to correspond entirely to the Greek Middle.

structure of its own, common to all verbs, and distinct from the conjugational form of the A'tmane-pada in all but the fourth class*.

Thus the Greek ἀκούω makes for both the Middle and Passive of those four tenses, 1st sing. ἀκούομαι, ἠκουόμην, ἀκουοίμην, ἀκούου (2nd sing.) But the Sanskṛit *śru*, 'to hear,' makes for the conjugational form of the A'tmane, शृण्वे, अशृण्वि, शृण्वीय, शृणवै; while for the Passive it is श्रूये, अश्रूये, श्रूयेय, श्रूयै.

244. As in nouns the formation of a nominal stem out of a root precedes declension, the root generally requiring some change or addition before the case-terminations can be affixed, so in verbs the formation of a verbal stem out of a root must precede conjugation. Again, as in nouns every case has its own proper termination, so in verbs each of the three persons, in the three numbers of every tense, has a termination (*vibhakti*), one for the Parasmai-pada, and one for the A'tmane-pada, which is peculiarly its own. Moreover, as in nouns, so in verbs, some of the terminations may be combined with servile or indicatory letters, which serve to aid the memory, by indicating that where they occur peculiar changes are required in the root. Thus the three terminations which belong to the 1st, 2nd, and 3rd persons of the Present tense, Parasmai-pada, respectively, are *mi*, *si*, *ti*; and these are combined with the letter P (*mi*P, *si*P, *ti*P), to indicate that roots belonging to the second and third groups of classes (see 258, 259, and 290) must be modified in a particular way, before these terminations are affixed.

The annexed tables exhibit, 1st, the scheme of terminations for Parasmai and A'tmane-pada, with the most useful indicatory letters (denoted by Roman capitals), in all the tenses, the four Special tenses being placed first; 2ndly, the same scheme with the substitutions required by certain classes of roots (the numerical figures denoting the classes in which these substitutions occur, see 257).

245. TERMINATIONS OF SPECIAL TENSES.

PARASMAI-PADA. A'TMANE-PADA.

Present tense.

PERS.	SING.	DUAL.	PLURAL.	SING.	DUAL.	PLURAL.
1.	मिप् *mi*P	वस् *vas*	मस् *mas*	ए *e*	वहे *vahe*	महे *mahe*
2.	सिप् *si*P	थस् *thas*	थ *tha*	से *se*	आथे *áthe*	ध्वे *dhve*
3.	तिप् *ti*P	तस् *tas*	अन्ति *anti*	ते *te*	आते *áte*	अन्ते *ante*

* For this reason we prefer to regard the Passive, not as a Voice, but as a distinct derivative from the root. See 461. *a*.

Imperfect or *First Preterite* (requiring the augment *a*, 251).

1. अमप् *amAP*	व *va*	म *ma*	इ *i*	वहि *vahi*	महि *mahi*
2. सिप् *sIP*	तम् *tam*	त *ta*	थास् *thás*	आथाम् *áthám*	ध्वम् *dhvam*
3. दिप् *dIP*	ताम् *tám*	अन् *an*	त *ta*	आताम् *átám*	अन्त *anta*

Potential or *Optative.*

1. याम् *yám*	याव *yáva*	याम *yáma*	ईय *íya*	ईवहि *ívahi*	ईमहि *ímahi*
2. यास् *yás*	यातम् *yátam*	यात *yáta*	ईथास् *íthás*	ईयाथाम् *íyáthám*	ईध्वम् *ídhvam*
3. यात् *yát*	याताम् *yátám*	युस् *yus*	ईत *íta*	ईयाताम् *íyátám*	ईरन् *íran*

Imperative.

1. आनिप् *ániP*	आवप् *ávaP*	आमप् *ámaP*	ऐप् *aiP*	आवहैप् *ávahaiP*	आमहैप् *ámahaiP*
2. हि *hi*	तम् *tam*	त *ta*	स्व *sva*	आथाम् *áthám*	ध्वम् *dhvam*
3. तुप् *tuP*	ताम् *tám*	अन्तु *antu*	ताम् *tám*	आताम् *átám*	अन्ताम् *antám*

TERMINATIONS OF GENERAL TENSES.

Perfect or *Second Preterite* (requiring reduplication, 252).

1. णप् *ṆaP*	व *va*	म *ma*	ए *e*	वहे *vahe*	महे *mahe*
2. थप् *thaP*	अथुस् *athus*	अ *a*	से *se*	आथे *áthe*	ध्वे *dhve* (ढ्वे)
3. णप् *ṆaP*	अतुस् *atus*	उस् *us*	ए *e*	आते *áte*	इरे *ire*

First Future or *Definite Future.*

1. तास्मि *tásmi*	तास्वस् *tásvas*	तास्मस् *tásmas*	ताहे *táhe*	तास्वहे *tásvahe*	तास्महे *tásmahe*
2. तासि *tási*	तास्थस् *tásthas*	तास्थ *tástha*	तासे *táse*	तासाथे *tásáthe*	ताध्वे *tádhve*
3. ता *tá*	तारौ *tárau*	तारस् *táras*	ता *tá*	तारौ *tárau*	तारस् *táras*

Second Future or *Indefinite Future.*

1. स्यामि *syámi*	स्यावस् *syávas*	स्यामस् *syámas*	स्ये *sye*	स्यावहे *syávahe*	स्यामहे *syámahe*
2. स्यसि *syasi*	स्यथस् *syathas*	स्यथ *syatha*	स्यसे *syase*	स्येथे *syethe*	स्यध्वे *syadhve*
3. स्यति *syati*	स्यतस् *syatas*	स्यन्ति *syanti*	स्यते *syate*	स्येते *syete*	स्यन्ते *syante*

Aorist or *Third Preterite* (requiring the augment *a*, 251).

1. सम् *sam*	स्व *sva*	स्म *sma*	सि *si*	स्वहि *svahi*	स्महि *smahi*
2. सीस् *sís*	स्तम् *stam*	स्त *sta*	स्थास् *sthás*	साथाम् *sáthám*	ध्वम् *dhvam* (ढ्वम्)
3. सीत् *sít*	स्ताम् *stám*	सुस् *sus*	स्त *sta*	साताम् *sátám*	सत *sata*

Precative or *Benedictive.*

1. यासम् *yásam*	यास्व *yásva*	यास्म *yásma*	सीय *síya*	सीवहि *sívahi*	सीमहि *símahi*
2. यास् *yás*	यास्तम् *yástam*	यास्त *yásta*	सीष्ठास् *síshṭhás*	सीयास्थाम् *síyásthám*	सीध्वम् *sídhvam*
3. यात् *yát*	यास्ताम् *yástám*	यासुस् *yásus*	सीष्ट *síshṭa*	सीयास्ताम् *síyástám*	सीरन् *síran*

Conditional (requiring the augment *a*, 251).

1. स्यम् *syam*	स्याव *syáva*	स्याम *syáma*	स्ये *sye*	स्यावहि *syávahi*	स्यामहि *syámahi*
2. स्यस् *syas*	स्यतम् *syatam*	स्यत *syata*	स्यथास् *syathás*	स्येथाम् *syethám*	स्यध्वम् *syadhvam*
3. स्यत् *syat*	स्यताम् *syatám*	स्यन् *syan*	स्यत *syata*	स्येताम् *syetám*	स्यन्त *syanta*

246. *The same terminations, with the substitutions required in certain classes.*

TERMINATIONS OF SPECIAL TENSES.

PARASMAI-PADA. ÁTMANE-PADA.

Present tense.

PERS.	SING.	DUAL.	PLURAL.	SING.	DUAL.	PLURAL.
1.	*mi*P	*vas*	*mas*	*i* 1, 4, 6, 10. *e* 2, 3, 7; 5, 8, 9.	*vahe*	*mahe*
2.	*si*P	*thas*	*tha*	*se*	*ithe* 1, 4, 6, 10. *áthe* 2, 3, 7; 5, 8, 9.	*dhve*
3.	*ti*P	*tas*	*nti* 1, 4, 6, 10. *anti* 2, 7; 5, 8, 9. *ati* 3 (2).	*te*	*ite* 1, 4, 6, 10. *áte* 2, 3, 7; 5, 8, 9.	*nte* 1, 4, 6, 10. *ate* 2, 3, 7; 5, 8, 9.

An initial *s*, as in *si*, *se*, &c., is liable to become *sh* by 70.

Imperfect or *First Preterite* (requiring the augment *a*, 251).

PERS.	SING.	DUAL.	PLURAL.	SING.	DUAL.	PLURAL.
1.	*m* 1, 4, 6, 10. *am*P 2, 3, 7; 5, 8, 9.	*va*	*ma*	*i*	*vahi*	*mahi*
2.	*s*P	*tam*	*ta*	*thás*	*ithám* 1, 4, 6, 10. *áthám* 2, 3, 7; 5, 8, 9.	*dhvam*
3.	*t*P	*tám*	*n* 1, 4, 6, 10. *an* 2, 7; 5, 8, 9. *us* 3 (2).	*ta*	*itám* 1, 4, 6, 10. *átám* 2, 3, 7; 5, 8, 9.	*nta* 1, 4, 6, 10. *ata* 2, 3, 7; 5, 8, 9.

Potential or *Optative.*

In 1, 4, 6, 10.

PERS.	SING.	DUAL.	PLURAL.
1.	*iyam*	*iva*	*ima*
2.	*is*	*itam*	*ita*
3.	*it*	*itám*	*iyus*

In 2, 3, 7; 5, 8, 9.

PERS.	SING.	DUAL.	PLURAL.
1.	*yám*	*yáva*	*yáma*
2.	*yás*	*yátam*	*yáta*
3.	*yát*	*yátám*	*yus*

In all the classes.

PERS.	SING.	DUAL.	PLURAL.
1.	*íya*	*ívahi*	*ímahi*
2.	*íthás*	*íyáthám*	*ídhvam*
3.	*íta*	*íyátám*	*íran*

Imperative.

PERS.	SING.	DUAL.	PLURAL.	SING.	DUAL.	PLURAL.
1.	*áni*P	*áva*P	*áma*P	*ai*P	*ávahai*P	*ámahai*P
2.	—1, 4, 6, 10; 5, 8. *hi* 2, 3; 5, 9. *dhi* (*ḍhi*) 2, 3, 7. —after *ána* 9.	*tam*	*ta*	*sva*	*ithám* 1, 4, 6, 10. *áthám* 2, 3, 7; 5, 8, 9.	*dhvam*
3.	*tu*P	*tám*	*ntu* 1, 4, 6, 10. *antu* 2, 7; 5, 8, 9. *atu* 3 (2).	*tám*	*itám* 1, 4, 6, 10. *átám* 2, 3, 7; 5, 8, 9.	*ntám* 1, 4, 6, 10. *atám* 2, 3, 7; 5, 8, 9.

In cl. 9, *hi* is dropped after *ána*, substituted for the conjugational *ní* of the 2nd sing. Impv., Parasmai, in the case of roots ending in consonants. A form तात् *tát* (cf. Latin *to*, Greek τω) may be substituted for *hi* and *tu*, and even for *ta*, to imply benediction, chiefly used in the Vedas.

Terminations of General Tenses.

Perfect or *Second Preterite* (requiring reduplication, 252).

1. *a*P	**iva*	**ima*	*e*	**ivahe*	**imahe*
2. *itha* or *tha*P	*athus*	*a*	**ishe*	*áthe*	**idhve* or **iḍhve*
3. *a*P	*atus*	*us*	*e*	*áte*	*ire*

* Only eight roots, viz. *śru, stu, dru, sru, kṛi, bhṛi, sṛi, vṛi*, reject the initial *i* from the terminations marked with *; and of these eight all but *vṛi* (meaning 'to cover') necessarily reject it also in the 2nd sing. Parasmai. See 369–372.

First Future or *Definite Future.*

1. *tásmi*	*tásvas*	*tásmas*	*táhe*	*tásvahe*	*tásmahe*
2. *tási*	*tásthas*	*tástha*	*táse*	*tásáthe*	*tádhve*
3. *tá*	*tárau*	*táras*	*tá*	*tárau*	*táras*

Many roots prefix *i* to the above terminations; thus, 1. *itásmi*, 2. *itási*, &c. ग्रह् lengthens this *i*; वृ *vṛi* and all roots in long *ṛí* optionally do so.

Second Future or *Indefinite Future.*

1. *syámi*	*syávas*	*syámas*	*sye*	*syávahe*	*syámahe*
2. *syasi*	*syathas*	*syatha*	*syase*	*syethe*	*syadhve*
3. *syati*	*syatas*	*syanti*	*syate*	*syete*	*syante*

Many roots prefix *i* to the above terminations; thus, 1. *ishyámi* (70), 2. *ishyasi*, &c. ग्रह् lengthens this *i*; वृ and all roots in long *ṛí* optionally do so.

Aorist or *Third Preterite* (requiring the augment *a*, 251).

Form I.—Regular terminations of the scheme.

1. *sam*	*sva*	*sma*	*si*	*svahi*	*smahi*
2. *sís*	*stam* or *tam*	*sta* or *ta*	*sthás* or *thás*	*sáthám*	*dhvam*
3. *sít*	*stám* or *tám*	*sus*	*sta* or *ta*	*sátám*	*sata*

ढ्वम् *ḍhvam* is used for *dhvam* after any other vowel but *a* or *á*, or after ड् *ḍ* immediately preceding.

The same terminations with *i* prefixed, except in 2nd and 3rd sing., where initial *s* is rejected.

1. *isham*	*ishva*	*ishma*	*ishi*	*ishvahi*	*ishmahi*
2. *ís*	*ishṭam*	*ishṭa*	*ishṭhás*	*isháthám*	*idhvam*
3. *ít*	*ishṭám*	*ishus*	*ishṭa*	*ishátám*	*ishata*

इढ्वम् *iḍhvam* may be used for *idhvam* when a semivowel or *h* immediately precedes. ग्रह् lengthens the *i* throughout; वृ and all roots in long *ṛí* optionally do so in Átm.

FORM II.—Terminations resembling those of the Imperfect.

1. *am*	*áva* or *va*	*áma* or *ma*	*e* or *i*	*ávahi*	*ámahi*
2. *as* or *s*	*atam* or *tam*	*ata* or *ta*	*athás*	*ethám* or *áthám*	*adhvam*
3. *at* or *t*	*atám* or *tám*	*an* or *us*	*ata*	*etám* or *átám*	*anta* or *ata*

Precative or *Benedictive.*

1. *yásam*	*yásva*	*yásma*	*síya*	*sívahi*	*símahi*
2. *yás*	*yástam*	*yásta*	*síshṭhás*	*síyásthám*	*sídhvam*
3. *yát*	*yástám*	*yásus*	*síshṭa*	*síyástám*	*síran*

Many roots prefix *i* to the Átmane, but not to the Parasmai, of the above; thus, 1. *ishíya*, &c. ग्रह् lengthens the *i* in this tense also, but no other root can do so.

सीढ्वम् *síḍhvam* is used for सीध्वम् *sídhvam* after any other vowel but *a* or *á*, and optionally after the prefixed *i*, when immediately preceded by a semivowel or *h* (see 442).

Conditional (requiring the augment *a*, 251).

1. *syam*	*syáva*	*syáma*	*sye*	*syávahi*	*syámahi*
2. *syas*	*syatam*	*syata*	*syathás*	*syethám*	*syadhvam*
3. *syat*	*syatám*	*syan*	*syata*	*syetám*	*syanta*

Many roots prefix *i* to the above terminations throughout; thus, 1. *ishyam*, 2. *ishyas*, &c. ग्रह् lengthens this *i*; वृ and all roots in long *ṛí* optionally do so.

247. Those terminations which are marked with P will be called the P terminations. They are technically designated *Pit* (i.e. having P for their *it*), and are as follow:

Present, Parasmai, 1, 2, 3 sing. *Impf.*, Par., 1, 2, 3 sing. *Impv.*, Par., 1, 3 sing., 1 du., 1 pl.; Átm., 1 sing., 1 du., 1 pl. In these, however, the P is indicatory only with reference to certain classes of roots (see 244), but in *Perf.*, Par., the indicatory P in 1, 2, 3 sing. applies to all the classes.

Obs.—Instead of Ṇ*a*P, *tha*P, Ṇ*a*P (which are from Vopa-deva), Páṇini gives Ṇ*a*L, *tha*L, Ṇ*a*L; and this L, like the P, has reference to accent.

a. Sometimes, however, it will be convenient to adopt Bopp's expression, 'Strong forms,' in speaking of the form assumed by the stem before the P terminations, these terminations being themselves called Weak.

b. In fact the P or *Pit* terminations are *an-udátta*, 'unaccented;' and when these are added, the stem on which the accent falls is called Strong. In other cases the accent is on the terminations, and the stem is then Weak and unaccented.

c. The terminations of the first four or Special tenses are called by Páṇini *sárva-dhátuka*, 'belonging to the full form of the verbal stem,' which name is also applied to suffixes like *śánać* (i.e. *-ána*), *śatṛi* (i.e. *-at*), having an indicatory *ś* (but not to Vikaraṇas like *śap*, &c.) The term *árdhadhátuka*, 'belonging to the half or shorter form of the verbal stem,' is given to the terminations of the Perfect (*liṭ*), and Precative (*āśir liṅ*), as well as to certain distinctive additions to the root before the terminations of the remaining four tenses (such as *tās* and *sya* in the Futures and Conditional, *s* in the Aorist, *yās* and *sīy* in the Precative), and therefore practically to the terminations of all the six General tenses.

d. If we examine these terminations, we shall find that they are composed of two distinct elements, one marking person, number, and voice; the other, mood and tense. The terminations in which the former element prevails may be called simple, and belong to the Present, Imperfect, Imperative, Perfect, and 2nd form of the Aorist; those which include the second may be called compound, and are peculiar to the other tenses. Thus the terminations of the Potential consist of *i* or *ī* or *yā* as characterizing the mood, and of *am, s, t, va, tam, tām,* &c., as marking person, number, and voice. So, also, in the 2nd Future the syllable *sya* prefixed to all the terminations, characterizes the Future tense, while the *mi, si, ti, vas, thas, tas,* &c., mark person, number, and voice. If, then, such initial parts of every termination as mark mood or tense were left out, an examination of the remaining parts would shew that the Present and Imperfect are the prototypes of the terminations of all the other tenses, that is to say, that the formation of the terminations of every other tense may be referred back to one or other of these two. The Present tense may in this way be connected with the two Futures. These three tenses agree in shewing a certain fulness of form, which is wanting in most of those connected with the Imperfect. The terminations of the Perfect, however, partake of the character of both the Present and Imperfect. In the Ātmane-pada they very closely resemble the Present. Many of them exhibit the same fulness as that tense, while some of the other terminations of the Perfect shew even more lightness than those of the Imperfect *. It should be observed, too, that the terminations of the Imperative, though evidently connected with the Imperfect, are in some instances even more full than those of the Present.

e. Although comparative grammarians have bestowed much labour on investigating the origin of Sanskṛit verbal terminations, the only point that may be asserted with probability is, that they stand in a certain relationship to the pronominal stems *ma, tva, sa, ta*. The *m* of the first persons is related to the stem *ma* (*mad*, 218); the *t, th, sv, s,* of the second persons, to the stem *tva* of the second personal pronoun (Gr. σε); and the *t*, of the third person, to the stem *ta*. We may also observe a community of character between the termination *nti* of the 3rd pl. and the plural of neuter nouns like *dhanavat* (*dhanavanti*). But whether the *v* in the dual is related to a pronominal stem *va* occurring in *ā-vām, va-yam;* whether the *s* of the dual and plural terminations is the result of blending different pronominal stems (e.g. *vas=va-si, mas=ma-si,* 'I and thou'); whether the terminations of the Ātmane-pada are formed from those of the Parasmai-pada by gunation or by composition of the latter with other stems,—these are questions which

* Comparative grammar, however, has established that these terminations are to be referred to the same source as the fuller ones.

cannot be determined with actual certainty. The subject, however, is fully and ably discussed in Schleicher's Compendium of Comparative Grammar, §§ 268–286.

f. Whatever the exact state of the case may be, the student may aid his memory by noting that the letter *m* generally enters into the 1st sing. Par.; *s* into the 2nd sing. Par. and Átm.; and *t* into the 3rd sing. du. and pl. Par. and Átm. of all the tenses. Moreover, that the letter *v* occurs in the 1st du., *m* in the 1st pl. of all the tenses, and *dhv* in every 2nd pl. Átmane. In the Impf. and Pot. Átm., and in the Perf. Par., *th* is admitted, instead of *s*, into the 2nd sing.; and in the 2nd pl. of the last tense, *th* has been dropped, owing to the influence of the heavy reduplication. For the same reason the *m* and *t* are dropped in the 1st and 3rd sing. Perf. Observe also—When the 1st du. Par. is *vas*, the 2nd and 3rd end in *as* (except the 3rd du. 1st Fut.), and the 1st pl. is *mas*. When the 1st du. Par. is *va*, the 2nd and 3rd end in *tam*, *tám* (except in the Perf.), and the 1st pl. in *ma*. When the 1st du. Átm. is *vahe*, the 1st pl. is *mahe*, and the last letter of the remaining terminations is generally *e*. When the 1st du. Átm. is *vahi*, the 2nd and 3rd end in *ám*; the 1st pl. is *mahi*, and the 2nd pl. is *dhvam*.

g. The frequent occurrence of *m* in the 1st sing., of *s* in the 2nd, of *t* in the 3rd, of *mas* and *ma* in the 1st pl., of *ta* in the 2nd pl., and of *ant* in the 3rd pl., suggests a comparison with the Gr. and Lat. verb. We may remark, that *m*, the characteristic of the 1st per. sing., is suppressed in the Pres. Indic. Act. of all Gr. verbs except those in μι (*asmi*=εἰμί, Dor. ἐμμί for εσμι, *dadámi*=δίδωμι), and also in Lat. verbs (except *sum* and *inquam*); but ω and ο answer to the Sk. *á* of *bharámi*=φέρω, *fero*. In the Gr. Middle and Passive, the μι, which originally belonged to all Active verbs, becomes μαι; while the Sanskṛit, on the other hand, here suppresses the *m*, and has *e* for αι; *bhare* (for *bhara-me*)=φέρομαι. In the Impf., Gr. has ν for Sk. and Lat. mute *m*, because μ is not allowed to be final in Greek; *atarpam*=ἔτερπον, *adadám*=ἐδίδων, *astṛiṇavam*=ἐστόρνυν, *avaham*=*vehebam*. Gr. has μι in the 1st sing. Opt.; and in verbs in μι, ν takes the place of the mute *m* of Sk. and Lat.; thus, *bhareyam*=φέροιμι, *feram*; *dadyám*=διδοίην, *dem*; *tishṭheyam*=ἱσταίην, *stem*. In the Gr. First Aorist, *m* is suppressed, so that Sanskṛit *adiksham* (Aor.)=ἔδειξα; but not in the 2nd Aor., so that *adám*=ἔδων. In the Perf., Sk. *a* =Gr. α, *tutopa*=τέτυφα. In the Gr. Middle and Passive Futures, *m* is retained, but not in the Active; *dásyámi*=δώσω, *dekshyámi*=δείξω, *dásye*=δώσομαι. As to the 1st per. pl., Sk. *mas* of the Pres. is μεν (for μες) in Gr., and *mus* in Lat.; *tarpá-mas*=τέρπο-μεν; *sarpá-mas*=ἕρπο-μεν, *serpi-mus*; *dad-mas*=δίδο-μεν, *da-mus*; *tishṭhá-mas*=ἵστα-μεν, *sta-mus*. The Átmane *mahe* answers to Gr. μεθα; *dad-mahe*=διδό-μεθα. As to the other tenses, in Impf. 1st pl. *abhará-ma*=ἐφέρο-μεν, *fereba-mus*; *avahá-ma*=*veheba-mus*; *adad-ma*=ἐδίδο-μεν; *abhará-mahi*=ἐφερόμεθα. In the Pot. 1st pl. *bhare-ma*=φέροι-μεν (-μες), *fera-mus*; *dadyáma*=διδοίημεν (-μες), *demus*; *dadí-mahi*=διδοί-μεθα. In 2nd Fut. *dásyá-mas*=δώσο-μεν, *dekshyá-mas*=δείξο-μεν. In 2nd pers. sing. Act., the characteristic *s* has been preserved in all three languages; thus, in the Present, Sk. *asi* (for original *assi*)=ἐσσί, *es*; *dadá-si*=δίδως, *das*; *bhara-si*=φέρεις, *fers*; *vahasi*=*vehis*. In the Átmane, Sk. *se* (for *sa i*, by 32) answers exactly to Gr. σαι of verbs in μι (*tishṭha-*

se=ἵστα-σαι). In other Gr. verbs, σ has been rejected, and εαι contracted into ῃ, something in the way of Sk. (τύπτῃ for τύπτε-σαι). In 2nd du. *thas*=Gr. τον, and in 2nd pl. *tha*=τε and *tis; bhara-thas*=φέρε-τον; *tishṭha-tha*=ἵστα-τε, *sta-tis; bhara-tha*=φέρε-τε, *fer-tis*. In 2nd pl. Átm. *bhara-dhve*=φέρε-σθε. As to the other tenses, in the 2nd sing. Impf. *atarpas*=ἔτερπες, *avahas*=*vehebas*, &c. So also, *tam*=τον, *adat-tam*=ἐδίδο-τον, *ta*=τε, *adat-ta*=ἐδίδο-τε. In Átm. *thás* is found for *sás* in 2nd sing. Impf. and Pot.; hence *abhara-thás*=ἐφέρε-σο, *adat-thás*=ἐδίδο-σο, *dad-íthás*=δίδ-οι(σ)ο. In 2nd sing. Pot. *tishṭhes*=ἱσταίης, *stes; dadyás*=διδοίης, *des; vahes*=*vehas; bhares*=φέροις, *feras:* in 2nd du. *bhare-tam*=φέροι-τον: in 2nd. pl. *tishṭheta*=ἱσταίητε, *stetis; dadyáta*=διδοίητε, *detis; bhareta*=φέροιτε, *feratis*. In 2nd sing. Impv. *hi* and *dhi* answer to Gr. θι. *Dhi* was originally universal in Sk. (see 291), as in Gr. verbs in μι; *e-dhi*=ἴσ-θι, *vid-dhi*=ἴσ-θι, *de-hi*=δίδο-θι, *śru-dhi*=κλῦ-θι. Many verbs drop the termination *hi* both in Gr. and Sk.; as, भर=φέρε, and compare δείκνυ with *činu*, &c. In 2nd du. Impv. *tam*=τον, and *ta*=τε. In Impv. Átm. *sva*=the old form σο; *bhara-sva*=φέρε-σο (old form of φέρου); *dat-sva*=δίδο-σο; *áthám*=εσθον, &c. In Perf. the *tha* of the 2nd sing.=Latin *sti; dad-itha*=*dedi-sti*, *tasthi-tha*=*steti-sti*, *tutodi-tha*=*tutudi-sti*. In the Aor. *adás*=ἔδως, *avákshís*=*vexisti*. In the 3rd pers. sing. Active, Gr. has dropped the characteristic *t* (except in ἐστί=Sk. *asti*, Lat. *est*); *bharati*=φέρε(τ)ι, *fert; vahati*=*vehit*. Verbs in μι have changed *t* to *s; dadáti*=δίδωσι (for δίδωτι). In Átm. *bharate*=φέρεται. In Impf. *avahat*=*vehebat*, *abharata*=ἐφέρετο. In Pot. *bharet*=φέροι, *dadyát*=διδοίη. In Impv. *bhara-tu* or *bhara-tát*=φερέ-τω, *fer-to*. In Perf. *tutopa*=τέτυφε. In Aor. *avákshít*=*vexit*, *adikshata*=ἐδείξατο. As to 3rd pl., in the above tenses, *bharanti*=φέρουσι, *ferunt; vahunti*=*vehunt; bharante*=φέρονται; *dadati*=διδοῦσι; *tishṭhanti*=*stant; bhareyus*=φέροιεν; *bharantu*=*ferunto; abharan*=ἔφερον; *abharanta*=ἐφέροντο; *ásan*=ἦσαν; *atarpishus*=ἔτερψαν; *dásyante*=δώσονται.

248. The terminations exhibited in the preceding tables are supposed to be applicable to all verbs, whether Primitive or Derivative: and as in nouns, so in verbs, the theory of Indian grammarians is, that before these terminations can be affixed, a stem must be developed out of a root, according to certain rules which vary for the first four tenses in ten different ways, according as a root belongs to one or other of ten classes. Accordingly, ten special rules are propounded for forming verbal stems out of roots in the first four tenses, which are therefore called the four *Special* tenses; while all verbs are arranged under ten classes, according to the form of the stem required by one or other of these rules. In the other tenses there is one general rule for forming the stem, applicable to all verbs of whatever class, and these tenses are therefore called *General.*

Hence the ten classes of roots are sometimes regarded as following one or other of *ten conjugations;* and the four tenses, which alone are affected by these conjugational rules (viz. the Present, Imperfect, Potential, and Imperative), are sometimes called *the conjugational tenses.* It is evident, however, that all Sanskṛit roots, of whatever class, follow one general conjugation for the majority of the tenses of the Primitive verb, although they require a special formation of stem depending on the class of each root for four of the tenses.

249. We begin by giving a brief summary of the ten rules for the forming the stem of the four Special tenses in the ten classes of roots, according to the Indian order of the ten classes.

Obs.—Native grammarians distinguish the ten classes of verbs by the name of the first root in their lists; e. g. cl. 1. *Bhv-ádi,* i. e. Bhú, &c., or the class of roots beginning with *bhú.* Similarly, cl. 2. *Ad-ádi;* cl. 3. *Juhoty-ádi* (i. e. the Hu class); cl. 4. *Div-ádi;* cl. 5. *Sv-ádi* (i. e. the Su class); cl. 6. *Tud-ádi;* cl. 7. *Rudh-ádi;* cl. 8. *Tan-ádi;* cl. 9. *Kry-ádi* (i. e. the Krí class); cl. 10. *Ćur-ádi.*

Cl. 1. Gunate the vowel of the root (unless it be अ *a*, or a long vowel *not final*, or a short vowel followed by a double consonant, 28) before *every termination of the four Special tenses,* and affix अ *a*—lengthened to आ *á* before initial *m** and *v*—to the root thus gunated.

The accent is on the vowel of the root, unless it be thrown on the augment.

Cl. 2. Gunate the vowel of the root (if capable of Guṇa, as in the last) before those terminations only which are marked with P in the scheme at 246. Before all the other terminations the original vowel of the root must be retained.

The accent rests on the vowel of the root, but only when the P terminations are added. In other cases it rests on the first vowel of the Non-P terminations.

Cl. 3. Reduplicate the initial consonant and vowel (see 252) of the root, and gunate the radical but not the reduplicated vowel before the P terminations only, as in cl. 2.

The accent rests on the first syllable of the stem before the Non-P terminations, and before the P terminations beginning with a vowel.

Cl. 4. Affix य *ya*—lengthened to या *yá* before initial *m** and *v*—to the root, the vowel of which is generally left unchanged.

The accent is on the vowel of the root, not on the *ya* (cf. 461).

---

* But not before *m* final, the termination of the 1st sing. Impf. Parasmai.

Cl. 5. Affix नु *nu* to the root, and gunate this *nu* into *no* before the P terminations only.

In this class, as well as in cl. 8 and 9, the accent is on the inserted Vikaraṇa (250. *b*) before the P terminations, and in other cases it rests on the first vowel of the Non-P terminations.

Cl. 6. Affix अ *a*—lengthened to आ *á* before initial *m** and *v*—to the root, which in other respects generally remains unchanged.

The absence of gunation of the radical vowel results from the accent being on the Vikaraṇa *a* (250. *b*).

Cl. 7. Insert न *na* between the vowel and final consonant of the root before the P terminations, and न् *n* before the other terminations.

Observe the peculiarity of this conjugation—that the conjugational *na* or *n* is inserted into the *middle* of the root, and not affixed.

The accent is on the inserted *na* before the P terminations; in other cases it rests on the Non-P terminations.

Cl. 8. Affix उ *u* to the root, and gunate this *u* into *o* before the P terminations only.

Obs.—As nine out of the ten roots in this class end in *n* or *ṇ*, cl. 8 will resemble cl. 5.

Cl. 9. Affix ना *ná* to the root before the P terminations; नी *ní* before all the others, except those beginning with vowels, where only न् *n* is affixed.

Cl. 10. Gunate the radical vowel (if capable of Guṇa) throughout all the persons of all the tenses, and affix अय *aya*—lengthened to अया *ayá* before initial *m** and *v*—to the root thus gunated.

The accent rests on the first vowel of the inserted *aya*.

250. It will appear, from a cursory examination of the above rules, that the object of nearly all of them is to insert either a vowel—sometimes alone, sometimes preceded by *y* or *n*—or a letter of some kind between the modified root and the terminations. The 1st, 4th, 6th, and 10th agree in requiring that the vowel, which is immediately to precede the terminations, shall be *a* or *á*. The 2nd, 3rd, and 7th agree in inserting no vowel between the final of the root and the terminations. The 5th, 8th, and 9th agree in interposing either *u*, *á*, or *í* after the letter *n*.

a. Any letters or syllables required to be inserted by the above

* But not before *m* final, the termination of the 1st sing. Impf. Parasmai.

ten rules, are inserted only in the four Special tenses (except only in the case of cl. 10). In the other six tenses the stem is formed according to one general rule for all roots of whatever class, whence their name of General tenses. But in these also, some letter or syllable has to be inserted (the only exception being in the Perfect).

b. This inserted conjugational vowel, consonant, or syllable is usually called the *vikaraṇa*. Páṇini's technical names for the ten insertions between the modified root and terminations under each of the ten classes, in regular order, are *śap*, *śapo luk*, *ślu*, *śyan*, *śnu*, *śa*, *śnam*, *u*, *śná*, *ṇić*; the last, however, does not strictly contain the *vikaraṇa*, the real insertion in cl. 10 (and in Causals) being *aya* (represented by the *i* of *ṇić*). The above Vikaraṇas (with *ṇić*) hold good before *Kṛit* suffixes containing an indicatory *ś* (such as *śatṛi* or *śánać*, see 247. *c*). In Passives and Neuters the insertion is technically called *yak* (leaving *ya*), to distinguish it from the Vikaraṇa *śyan* of cl. 4. With regard to the six General tenses, the Perfect has strictly no *vikaraṇa* (the almost universally inserted *i* of *iṭ* being called an augment). But in verbs belonging to cl. 10, in Derivative verbs (such as Causals), and in a few Primitive verbs like *íksh*, the syllable *ám* is added to the verbal stem. With regard to the other General tenses the *Ágama iṭ* (or inserted *i*) is by no means universally interposed, but certain letters or syllables are regarded as additions to the root distinct from the terminations; that in the 1st Future is technically called *tási* (=*tás*); that in the 2nd Future and Conditional is *sya*; that in the Aorist is called *ćli* (for which either *sić* or *ksa* or *ćaṇ* or *an* or *ćin* are always substituted); that in the Precative is *yásuṭ* (=*yás*) for Par., and *síyuṭ* (=*síy*) for Átm.; that in the Vedic Leṭ is called *sip*.

THE ÁGAMA OR AUGMENT अ *a*.

251. In classical Sanskṛit (but not always in Vedic) the augment अ *a* (called *ágama*, 'increase') is prefixed to the stems of the Imperfect, Aorist, and Conditional tenses, and when the stem begins with अ *a* or आ *á*, the augment blends with these vowels into आ *á* by 31. (So in Gr. ε and ε become η in ἤγειρον, &c.)

a. But when the augment *a* is prefixed to stems beginning with the vowels इ *i*, उ *u*, and ऋ *ṛi* (short or long), it blends with them into ऐ *ai*, औ *au*, आर् *ár* (against 32, which would require the result to be *e*, *o*, *ar*).

Thus the stem इच्छ *iććha* (fr. rt. *ish*, 'to wish') in 3rd sing. Impf. becomes ऐच्छत् *aiććhat*; the stem ऊह *úha* becomes औहत *auhata* (Impf. Átm.); the stem ऋध्नो *ṛidhno* becomes आर्ध्नोत् *árdhnot*; the stem ओख *okha* becomes औखत् *aukhat*.

b. When a root is compounded with one or more prepositions, the augment is placed between the preposition or prepositions and the root, e.g. *anv-atishṭham* (fr. *anu-sthá*), *upa-sam-aharat* (fr. *upa-saṃ-hṛi*).

When स् *s* is prefixed to the root कृ *kṛi*, after certain prepositions (see 53. *c*), the augment is placed before the *s*, e.g. *sam-askarot*.

Obs.—The augment *a* is thought by some to have been originally a kind of demonstrative particle denoting past time (probably connected with the stem *a* of the demonstrative pronoun *idam*, see 224), while the separable particle *sma* (thought to be an abbreviation of another demonstrative pronominal stem *sa-ma*), also denoting past time, and often discharging the function of the augment *a* (see 878), has remained a detached particle.

REDUPLICATION.

252. After explaining the augment it will be convenient to specify the rules of reduplication (*abhyása*), as these have to be applied in the Special tenses of Primitive verbs of cl. 3, in the Perfect tense of all Primitive verbs, in the Aorist of a few Primitive verbs, and of verbs of cl. 10, and of some Nominals (521), as well as in Desideratives and in Frequentatives.

In reduplication the initial consonant and first vowel of a root are doubled, as in *lilip* fr. rt. *lip*, *dadaridrá* fr. *daridrá*. There are, however, special rules, as follow:

1st, as to consonants, thus:

a. A corresponding unaspirated letter is substituted for an aspirate, as द् *d* for ध् *dh*, in *dadhá* fr. *dhá*. (So in Gr., τ is repeated for θ, as θύω, τέθυκα, &c.)

b. The hard palatal च् *ć* is substituted for the hard gutturals क् *k* or ख् *kh*, as in *ćakhan* fr. *khan*; and the soft palatal ज् *j* for the soft gutturals ग् *g*, घ् *gh*, or ह् *h*, as in *jagam* fr. *gam*, *jaghas* fr. *ghas*, *juhu* fr. *hu*.

Obs.—हन् *han*, 'to kill,' and हि *hi*, 'to go,' substitute घ् *gh* for ह् *h* when reduplicated; as, *jaghan* fr. *han*.

c. If a root begin with a double consonant, the first consonant only or its substitute is repeated; as, च् *ć* for क्ष् *ksh*, in *ćikship* fr. *kship*; स् *s* for स्य् *sy*, in *sasyand* fr. *syand*; ज् *j* for ह्र् *hr*, in *jahras* fr. *hras*.

But if with a double consonant whose first is a sibilant, and whose second is hard, the second or its substitute is reduplicated; as, च् *ć* for स्क् *sk*, as in *ćaskand* fr. *skand*; त् *t* for स्थ् *sth*, as in *tasthá* fr. *sthá*; प् *p* for स्प् *sp*, as in *paspṛiś* fr. *spṛiś*.

2ndly, as to vowels, thus:

d. A short vowel is repeated for a long, and diphthongal sounds are represented by their second element; e.g. अ *a* is reduplicated for आ *á*; इ *i* for ई *í*, ऋ *ṛi*, ॠ *ṛí*, ए *e*, and ऐ *ai*; उ *u* for ऊ *ú*, ओ *o*, and औ *au*.

Obs.—In certain cases इ *i* is also repeated for *a* and *á*, as being a lighter vowel, and *dyut*, 'to shine,' makes *didyut* for *dudyut*.

e. In fact it may be observed, that when a long vowel causes too great weight in the radical syllable, it is generally lightened in the reduplicated syllable.

f. When a form has once been reduplicated, it is never reduplicated again in forming other Derivatives from it (see 517. *a*); and when roots which have to be reduplicated have any changed form, this modified form is taken in the reduplication; thus, स्मृ *smṛi*, 'to remember,' being changed to स्मर् in the Desiderative, the vowel of the root does not appear in the reduplication (सुस्मर्).

VERBS PRIMITIVE, PASSIVE, CAUSAL, DESIDERATIVE, &c.

253. In conjugating a verb, then, two things have to be done: 1st, to form the stem from the root according to ten rules for four of the tenses, and one general rule for the other six; 2ndly, to join the stem so formed with the terminations, according to the regular rules of Sandhi or euphonic *conjugation*. As yet, however, we have only given a general explanation of the formation of the verbal stem of the *Simple* or *Primitive* verb under the ten classes of roots.

There are four other kinds of verbs deducible from all roots, whatever be their class.

254. In fact, every Sanskṛit root serves as a kind of stock out of which the inflective stems of five kinds of verbs may be evolved: 1. of a Primitive, Transitive or Intransitive; 2. of a Passive; 3. of a Causal, having often a Causal and often merely a Transitive signification; 4. of a Desiderative, giving a sense of wishing to the root; and 5. of a Frequentative (or Intensive), implying repetition, or heightening the idea contained in the root (see, however, 507).

255. The first, or Primitive verb, is formed from the root, according to the ten different rules, already given, for the formation of the stem in the first four tenses.

The second, or Passive, is formed according to the rule for the change of the root, required by the 4th class; viz. the addition of *ya* in the first four tenses.

The third, or Causal, is formed according to the rule for the change of the root required by the 10th class; viz. the addition of *aya* to the root in all the tenses excepting the Aorist.

The fourth, or Desiderative, is formed by the addition of *sa* or *isha*, the root also undergoing reduplication.

The fifth, or Frequentative, is formed like the Passive, according to the rule required by cl. 4, and is, in fact, a reduplicated passive verb. It may also be formed analogously to the rule for cl. 3.

Thus, if we take the root शुभ् *śubh*, conveying the idea of 'shining'—from this are developed, 1st, the Primitive verbal stem, *śobha*, 'to shine;' 2ndly, the Passive, *śubhya*, 'to be bright;' 3rdly, the Causal, *śobhaya*, 'to cause to shine' or 'illuminate;' 4thly, the Desiderative, *śuśobhisha*, 'to desire to shine;' 5thly, the Frequentative or Intensive, *śośubhya* or *śośubh*, 'to shine very brightly.'

a. And as every root is the source of five different kinds of Derivative verbs, so there are secondary Derivative verbs developed out of nouns called *Nominal verbs.* An explanation of these will be found after Frequentatives at 518.

256. The subject of verbs, therefore, as of nouns, will divide itself into two heads:

A. The formation of the stem; 1st of Primitive, 2ndly of Passive, 3rdly of Causal, 4thly of Desiderative, 5thly of Frequentative verbs; with their respective Participles.

B. The exhibition of the stem, united to its terminations, under each of the five forms of verbs consecutively.

PRIMITIVE VERBS.

FORMATION OF THE STEM OF THE FIRST FOUR TENSES, IN THE TEN CLASSES.

A brief summary of the ten rules for the formation of the stem of the four Special tenses—viz. the Present, Imperfect, Potential, and Imperative—in the ten classes of roots, has already been given at 249. These ten rules may be collected into three groups, which form three distinct general conjugations, as follow:

257. Group I. Conjugation I. This (like the declension of the first class of nouns whose stems end in *a* and *á*) is by far the most important, as comprising roots of the 1st, 4th, 6th, and 10th classes, which agree in making their stems end in *a* (liable to be lengthened to *á*). These also resemble each other in taking substitutions for some of the terminations, after the analogy of the stems of nouns ending in *a* and *á* at 97. (See the substitutions indicated in the table at 246.)

Note—Of about 2000 roots belonging to the Sanskṛit language, nearly 1300 belong to this 1st conjugation. Besides which, every root in the language may take a Passive and Causal form, and so be conjugated as if it belonged to the 4th and 10th classes.

258. Group II. Conjugation II. This comprises verbs of the 2nd, 3rd, and 7th classes, which agree in affixing the regular terminations

(at 246) to the final letter of the root, without the intervention of a vowel, after the analogy of the last four classes of nouns whose stems end in consonants.

259. GROUP III, Conjugation III, comprising verbs of the 5th, 8th, and 9th classes, also affixes the regular terminations (at 246) to the root; but after the intervention of either *u*, *á*, or *í*, preceded by the consonant *n*.

260. In comparing Sanskṛit verbs with Greek and Latin, it might be shewn that group I, comprising the 1st, 4th, 6th, and 10th classes, answers to the Gr. 1st conjugation in *ω*, the conjugational अ *a* being represented in Gr. by *ο* or *ε* (*tarpámas*=*τέρπομεν*, *tarpatha*=*τέρπετε*); and although the Gr. 1st conjugation contains more subdivisions than the first group in Sk., yet the inflexion of these subdivisions is similar. As to the Sk. 10th class, however, it appears to correspond to Gr. verbs in *αζω* and *ιζω*, which, like the 10th, are generally found in company with other verbs from the same root; thus, *καθαρίζω*, 'I make pure' (*καθαίρω*), *στενάζω*, 'I groan' (*στένω*), where ζ corresponds to य् *y*, as in *ζεά* and यव 'barley.' To this class also may be referred verbs in *αω*, *εω*, *οω*; thus *páraydmi*=*περάω*, where the *y* has been dropped, and the two *a*'s combined. Lat. verbs in *io*, like *audio* &c., seem to be related to the Sk. 4th class, as well as to the 10th; thus *cupio* answers to *kupyámi*; and the *i* of *audiebam* answers to the *aya* of the 10th, just as in Prákṛit *aya* is contracted into ए *e*. The second and third groups of classes in Sk. (viz. the 2nd, 3rd, 7th, 5th, 8th, and 9th) answer to Gr. verbs in *μι*; thus *emi* cl. 2=*εἶμι*, *dadámi* cl. 3=*δίδωμι*. Class 7, however, has no exact parallel in Gr., but many Gr. and Lat. verbs resemble it in inserting a nasal into the middle of the root; see 342.*a*. The 5th and 8th classes answer to Gr. verbs like *δείκ-νυ-μι*, *ζεύγ-νυ-μι*, which agree in inserting *νυ* between the root and termination; in Gr. the vowel *υ* is lengthened before certain terminations, just as *u* is gunated into *o* in Sk.; thus *stṛiṇomi*=*στόρνῡμι*, *stṛiṇoshi*=*στόρνῡς*, *stṛiṇoti*=*στόρνῡσι* (for *στόρνυτι*), *stṛiṇumas*=*στόρνῠμεν* (for *στόρνυμες*), &c. The 9th class answers to Gr. verbs in *νᾱ* (*νη*); thus *kríṇámi*=*πέρνᾱμι* (*πέρνημι*), *kríṇímas*=*πέρνᾰμεν*. Cf. also Lat. forms in *ni*; thus *sternimus*=Sk. *stṛiṇímas*, fr. *stṛi*, cl. 9.

GROUP I.—FORMATION OF STEM IN ROOTS OF CLASSES 1, 4, 6, 10.

261. CLASS 1 (containing about 1000 Primitive verbs).—Rule for the formation of the stem in the four Special tenses.

Gunate the vowel of the root (except when debarred by 28) before *every termination of all the four tenses*, and affix the vowel अ *a* to the root so gunated. Remember, that this अ *a* is lengthened into आ *á* before the initial *m* and *v* of a termination, but not when *m* is final, as in the 1st sing. Impf.

262. Thus, fr. root बुध् *budh*, 'to know,' is formed the stem बोध *bodha*, lengthened

into बोधा *bodhá* before *m* and *v* (Pres. 1.* *bodhá+mi*=बोधामि *bodhámi*, *bodha+si*=बोधसि *bodhasi*, *bodha+ti*=बोधति *bodhati;* Du. 1. *bodhá+vas*=बोधावस् *bodhávas*, &c.; Átm. Pres. *bodha+i*=बोधे *bodhe* by 32, *bodha+se*=बोधसे *bodhase*, &c.) See table at 583.

263. Similarly, fr. जि *ji*, 'to conquer' (see 590), comes the stem जय *jaya* (i.e. *je+a*, see 36. *a*), liable to be lengthened into जया *jayá*, as explained above; fr. नी *ní*, 'to lead,' the stems *naya* and *nayá;* fr. भू *bhú*, 'to be' (φύω, Lat. *fu*), the stems *bhava* (i.e. *bho+a*, 36. *a*) and *bhavá* (Pres. 1. भवामि *bhavámi;* 2. भवसि *bhavasi*, φύεις, &c., see 584); fr. सृप् *sṛip*, 'to creep,' the stems सर्प *sarpa* and *sarpá* (see 27); fr. क्लृप् *klṛip*, 'to fashion,' the stems कल्प *kalpa* and *kalpá*.

Obs.—*Bhú*, 'to be' or 'to become,' is one of the commonest verbs in the language, and like *as*, 'to be,' at 584, 327, is sometimes used as an auxiliary. *Bhú* is conjugated in full at 585.

264. The stem of the Imperfect has the augment अ *a* prefixed by 251 (Impf. 1. *abodha+m*=अबोधम् *abodham*, 2. *abodha+s*=अबोधस् *abodhas*, &c.)

265. In the Potential the final *a* of the stem blends with the initial *i* of the termination into *e* by 32 (Pot. 1. *bodha+iyam*=बोधेयम् *bodheyam*). So also in the Pres. Átm. (बोधे &c.) See table at 583.

266. In the Imperative the termination is rejected in the 2nd sing. (Impv. 1. *bodha+áni*=बोधानि *bodháni*, 2. बोध *bodha*, 3. *bodha+tu* =बोधतु *bodhatu*).

267. Roots like पच् 'to cook,' भिक्ष् 'to beg,' जीव् 'to live' (603), cannot change their radical vowels (see 27. *a*, 28), but, as before, affix अ *a*, liable to be lengthened to आ *á;* (Pres. 1. पचामि &c.; Pres. Átm. 1. भिक्षे &c.; Pres. 1. जीवामि &c.)

268. Some roots ending in the Vṛiddhi ऐ *ai* cannot be gunated, but suffer the usual change of Sandhi before अ *a* and आ *á* by 37; as, from गै 'to sing,' ग्लै 'to be weary,' त्रै Átm. 'to preserve†,' ध्यै 'to meditate,' म्लै 'to fade,' are formed the stems *gáya*, *gláya*, *tráya*, *dhyáya*, *mláya*. See 595. *a*. *b*.

269. Some roots of cl. 1 form their stems in the first four tenses by a change peculiar to themselves, which change is of course discarded in the other tenses; thus, from स्था *sthá*, 'to stand' (587), घ्रा *ghrá*, 'to smell' (588), पा 'to drink' (589), ध्मा 'to blow,' म्ना 'to repeat' or 'think over,' come the bases तिष्ठ *tishṭha*, जिघ्र *jighra*, पिब *piva*, धम *dhama*, मन *mana*, the final *a* being, as before, liable to be lengthened.

a. It should be noted that स्था *sthá* and घ्रा *ghrá* are properly reduplicated verbs of cl. 3 at 330. The reduplicated stem, by 252, would be *tasthá*, *jaghrá:* but as the reduplication is irregular, and the radical *á* gives way to the conjugational *a*,

---

* 1. stands for 1st person singular; Du. 1. for 1st dual; Pl. 1. for 1st plural, &c.

† A form त्राहि, as well as त्रायस्व, is found in Epic poetry for the 2nd sing. Impv. of this root.

grammarians place these roots under cl. 1. The Greek ἵστημι, on the other hand, has not shortened its radical vowel in the singular.

270. Again, दृश् 'to see,' गम् 'to go,' यम् 'to restrain,' ऋ 'to go,' सद् 'to sink,' शद् (Átm. in Special tenses, Par. in others) 'to fall,' 'to perish,' form their stems पश्य *paśya*, गच्छ *gaććha*, यच्छ *yaććha*, ऋच्छ *ṛiććha*, सीद *sída*, शीय *śíya*: (Pres. 1. पश्यामि *paśyámi*, &c.)

a. According to Páṇini (VII. 3, 78), दा 'to give' may sometimes substitute the stem यच्छ *yaććha*; and सृ 'to go,' the stem धाव *dháva*.

b. गुह् 'to conceal' forms गूह; ष्ठिव् 'to spit,' ष्ठीव; मृज् 'to cleanse,' मार्ज: (Pres. 1. गूहामि &c.)

c. क्रम् 'to step,' क्लम् 'to tire,' चम् (with आ) 'to rinse the mouth,' lengthen their medial vowels, but the first only in Parasmai: (Pres. 1. क्रामामि &c., but Átm. क्रमे.)

d. दंश् 'to bite,' रञ्ज् 'to colour,' सञ्ज् 'to adhere,' स्वञ्ज् 'to embrace,' drop their nasals: (Pres. 1. दशामि &c., रजामि &c.)

e. जभ् Átm. 'to yawn' makes its stem जम्भ, and even लभ् Átm. 'to receive' sometimes becomes लम्भ in Epic poetry.

271. कम् Átm. 'to love' forms its stem after the analogy of cl. 10 (Pres. 1. कामये &c.), and some other roots add *áya*: thus, fr. गुप् 'to protect,' गोपाय *gopáya*; fr. धूप् 'to fumigate,' धूपाय; fr. विच्छ् 'to go,' विच्छाय; fr. पण् Átm. (meaning 'to praise,' not 'to wager'), पणाय; fr. पन् Átm. 'to praise,' पनाय.

a. कुर्द् Átm. 'to play,' like all roots containing *ir* and *ur* compounded with another consonant, lengthens the vowel (Pres. 1. कूर्दे &c.)

272. CLASS 4 (containing about 130 Primitive verbs).—Rule for the formation of the stem in the four Special tenses.

Affix य *ya* to the root. The vowel of the root is not gunated, and generally remains unchanged. Remember, that the inserted य *ya* is liable to become या *yá* before an initial *m* and *v* of the terminations (but not before the *m* of the 1st sing. Impf. Par.), as in cl. 1 at 261.

273. Thus, fr. सिध् *sidh*, 'to succeed,' is formed the stem सिध्य *sidhya* (Pres. 1. *sidhyá+mi*=सिध्यामि *sidhyámi*, 2. सिध्यसि *sidhyasi*, &c.; Impf. *asidhya+m*=असिध्यम् *asidhyam*, &c.; Pot. 1. *sidhya+iyam*=सिध्येयम् *sidhyeyam*, 2. सिध्येस् *sidhyes*, &c.; Impv. 1. *sidhya+áni*=सिध्यानि *sidhyáni*, &c. Pres. Átm. 1. *sidhya+i*=सिध्ये *sidhye*, *sidhya+se*=सिध्यसे *sidhyase*, &c.) See 616.

274. Similarly, fr. मा *má*, 'to measure,' the stem माय *máya* (Pres. 1. Átm. *máya+i*=माये *máye*, &c.); fr. क्षिप् *kship*, 'to throw,' क्षिप्य *kshipya*; fr. नृत् *nṛit*, 'to dance,' नृत्य *nṛitya*; fr. डी *ḍí*, 'to fly,' डीय *ḍíya* (Pres. Átm. 1. डीये).

275. Roots ending in *am* and *iv*, and one in *ad*, lengthen the vowel; as, fr. दिव् *div*, 'to play,' दीव्य *dívya*; fr. भ्रम् *bhram* (also cl. 1), 'to wander,' भ्राम्य *bhrámya*; fr. मद् *mad*, 'to be mad,' माद्य *mádya*. Similarly, क्रम् (also cl. 1) 'to step,' क्षम् 'to endure,' क्लम् 'to grow weary,' तम् 'to be afflicted,' दम् 'to be tamed;' but *bhram* may optionally form भ्रम्य *bhramya*.

276. If a root contain a nasal it is generally rejected; as, from भ्रंश् 'to fall,' भ्रश्य *bhraśya*; from रञ्ज् 'to colour,' रज्य; जन् 'to be born' makes जाय *jáya* (Pres. 1. Átm. जाये), lengthening the vowel, to compensate for the loss of *n*.

a. Roots ending in ओ *o* drop this *o* before the conjugational *ya*; thus, सो *so*, 'to end,' makes its stem *sya*. Similarly, छो 'to cut,' शो 'to sharpen,' दो 'to divide.'

277. The following are anomalous. From जॄ 'to grow old,' जीर्य *jírya*; fr. व्यध् 'to pierce,' विध्य *vidhya* (cf. 472); fr. मिद् 'to be viscid,' मेद्य *medya*.

Obs.—Although this class includes only 130 Primitive verbs (generally Intransitive in signification), yet every one of the 2000 roots in the language may have a Passive form which follows the Átmane-pada of this class, differing from it only in the position of the accent, see 461.

278. Class 6 (containing about 140 Primitive verbs).—Rule for the formation of the stem in the four Special tenses.

Affix the vowel अ *a* to the root, which is not gunated, and in other respects generally remains unchanged. Remember, that the inserted अ *a* becomes आ *á* before an initial *m* and *v* of the terminations of the four tenses (but not before the *m* of the 1st sing. Impf.), as in cl. 1 and 4 at 261 and 272.

279. Thus, fr. क्षिप् *kship*, 'to throw,' comes the stem क्षिप *kshipa* (Pres. 1. *kshipá* + *mi* = क्षिपामि *kshipámi*, 2. *kshipa* + *si* = क्षिपसि *kshipasi*; Pot. 1. *kshipa* + *iyam* = क्षिपेयम् *kshipeyam*, &c. Átm. Pres. 1. *kshipa* + *i* = क्षिपे *kshipe*; see 635).

Similarly, fr. तुद् *tud*, 'to strike,' तुद *tuda*; fr. दिश् *diś*, 'to point out,' दिश *diśa*.

280. Roots in इ *i*, उ *u* or ऊ *ú*, ऋ *ṛi* and ॠ *ṛí*, generally change those vowels into इय् *iy*, उव् *uv*, रिय् *riy*, and इर् *ir* respectively; as, fr. रि, 'to go,' comes the stem रिय *riya*; fr. नु 'to praise,' नुव *nuva*; fr. धू 'to agitate,' धुव *dhuva*; fr. मृ 'to die,' म्रिय *mriya* (626); fr. कॄ *kṛí*, 'to scatter,' किर *kira* (627).

a. गॄ 'to swallow' makes either गिर or गिल.

281. A considerable number of roots of the sixth class, ending in consonants, insert a nasal before the final consonant in the four tenses; as, fr. मुच्, 'to let go,' comes the stem मुञ्च *muńća*; fr. लिप् 'to anoint,' लिम्प *limpa*; fr. कृत् 'to cut,' कृन्त *kṛinta*; fr. सिच् 'to sprinkle,' सिञ्च *sińća*; fr. लुप् 'to break,' लुम्प *lumpa*; fr. पिश् 'to form,' पिंश. Similarly, विद् 'to find,' खिद् 'to trouble.'

282. The following are anomalous. From इष्, 'to wish,' comes the stem इच्छ *iććha*; fr. प्रछ् 'to ask,' पृच्छ *pṛiććha*; fr. भ्रज्ज् 'to fry,' भृज्ज *bhṛijja*; fr. व्यच् 'to deceive,' विच *vića*; fr. व्रश्च् 'to cut,' वृश्च *vṛiśća*. Cf. 472.

a. The roots शद् and सद् are sometimes regarded as falling under this class; see their stems at 270.

283. Class 10 (containing a few Primitive verbs, all Causals, and some Nominal verbs, see 521).—Rule for forming the stem in the four Special tenses.

Gunate the vowel of the root throughout every person of all the four tenses (except when debarred by 28), and affix अय *aya* to the root so gunated. This अय *aya* becomes अया *ayá* before initial *m* and *v* of the terminations of the four tenses, but not before *m* of the 1st sing. Impf.

284. Thus, from चुर् *ćur*, 'to steal,' is formed the stem चोरय *ćoraya* (Pres. 1. *ćorayá + mi* = चोरयामि *ćorayámi*, 2. *ćoraya + si* = चोरयसि *ćorayasi*, &c.; Impf. 1. *aćoraya + m* = अचोरयम् *aćorayam*, &c., see 638; Pot. 1. *ćoraya + iyam* = चोरयेयम् *ćorayeyam;* Impv. 1. *ćoraya + áni* = चोरयाणि *ćorayáṇi*, &c., see 58).

285. Roots ending in vowels generally take Vṛiddhi instead of Guṇa (481); as, fr. प्री 'to please,' प्रायय *práyaya* (cf. 485. *a*); fr. धृ 'to hold,' धारय *dháraya*. But वृ 'to choose' makes वरय *varaya*. This last, however, is generally regarded as a Causal.

286. Roots containing the vowel अ *a* before a single consonant generally lengthen this vowel; as, fr. ग्रस् 'to swallow,' ग्रासय *grásaya:* but not before a conjunct consonant; as, fr. अङ्क् 'to mark,' अङ्कय; fr. दण्ड् 'to punish,' दण्डय.

a. The following, however, do not lengthen the medial *a*, though followed by a single consonant: कथ् 'to say' (कथय); गण् 'to count;' अघ् 'to sin;' स्तन् 'to tie;' रच् 'to arrange;' पद Átm. in the sense of 'to surround;' रद् 'to scream;' व्रण् 'to wound;' श्रथ् and श्लथ् in the sense of 'to be lax or weak;' रह् 'to quit;' पद् Átm. 'to go;' गद् 'to sound;' ध्वन्, स्तन्, स्वन्, 'to sound;' कल् 'to count' (also lengthened in Epic poetry); व्यय् 'to spend;' and others less common.

287. कॄत्, 'to celebrate,' 'to praise,' makes कीर्तय *kírtaya* (Pres. कीर्तयामि).

288. A few roots with a medial ऋ *ṛi* retain that vowel unchanged; as, from स्पृह् 'to desire,' स्पृहय; मृग् 'to search,' मृगय; मृष् 'to bear,' मृषय (more commonly मर्षय); गृह् Átm. 'to take,' गृहय (also ग्राहय); कृप् 'to pity,' कृपय; but मृज् 'to wipe' takes Vṛiddhi (मार्जय). Some of these may be regarded as nominals.

a. The following also do not gunate their medial vowels: सुख् 'to make happy,' पुट् 'to bind,' स्फुट् 'to become manifest,' कुण् or गुण् 'to consult.'

b. A few roots of more than one syllable (see 75. *a*) are said to belong to cl. 10, viz. सभाज् 'to worship,' अवधीर् 'to despise,' संग्राम् 'to fight,' कुमार् or कुमाल् 'to play,' गवेष् 'to search,' विडम्ब् 'to imitate,' निवास् 'to put on,' संकेत् 'to invite,' आन्दोल्, हिन्दोल्, हिल्लोल्, प्रेङ्खोल्, 'to swing,' पल्पूल् or पल्पुल् or पल्यूल् 'to cut off.' These and a few monosyllabic roots of cl. 10, such as अंश् 'to divide,' अर्थ् 'to ask,' मिश्र् 'to mix,' अङ्क् 'to mark,' मूत्र् 'to make water,' सूत्र् 'to thread,' वीज् 'to fan,' छिद्र् 'to perforate,' शब्द् 'to sound,' and others less common, can, according to some grammarians, form their stems optionally with *ápaya;* thus, अंश् may make in Pres. 1. अंशापयामि or अंशयामि.

289. It has been shewn that every root may have a Causal form, which follows the rule of conjugation of cl. 10. Indeed, it may be owing to the fact that there are a number of Active Primitive verbs not Causal in their signification, but conjugated like Causals, that a

10th class has arisen distinct from the Causal. In verbs of this class the Causal form will generally be identical with the Primitive.

Again, as some verbs really Causal in their signification are regarded as belonging to cl. 10, there will often be a difficulty in determining whether a verb be a Primitive verb of this class, or a Causal verb. Hence the consideration of cl. 10 must to a great extent be mixed up with that of the Causal form of the root. See the special changes applicable to Causals at 483–488.

a. Observe, that all verbs, whether Primitive or Causal, which belong to cl. 10, have this great peculiarity, viz. that the conjugational *aya* is carried throughout all the tenses of the verb, General as well as Special, except only the Aorist and the Precative, Parasmai-pada. For this reason the formation of the stem of the General tenses of verbs of cl. 10 will not be explained under the head of the General tenses (at 363), but will fall under Causal verbs.

b. Many verbs of cl. 10 are also conjugated in other classes; and many may be regarded as Nominal verbs.

GROUPS II AND III.—FORMATION OF STEM IN ROOTS OF CLASSES 2, 3, 7, AND CLASSES 5, 8, 9.

Preliminary Observations.

290. The formation of the stems of verbs of groups II and III presents more difficulties than that of group I, containing the 1st, 4th, 6th, and 10th classes. In group I the verbal stem, although varying slightly in each class, preserves the form assumed in the singular before all the terminations of every Special tense; but in the last two groups the stem is liable to variation in the various persons and numbers of most of the tenses, such variation being denoted by the letter P and other indicatory letters of the scheme at 246.

a. The object of the P is to shew, that fulness or strength of form is imparted to the root before these weak terminations (see 247. *b*); thus इ *i*, cl. 2, 'to go,' is in the Pres. sing. *emi*, *eshi*, *eti*; in du. *ivas*, *ithas*, *itas*; in pl. *imas*, &c.: just as in Gr. εἶμι, εἶ, εἶσι, ἴτον, ἴτον, ἴμεν, &c.: cf. also φημί (for φᾶμι), φῄς, φησί, φᾰτόν, φᾰτόν, φᾰμέν, φᾰτέ, φασί. So again, *stṛi*, 'to strew,' is in Pres. sing. *stṛiṇomi*, *stṛiṇoshi*, *stṛiṇoti*; in du. *stṛiṇuvas*, *stṛiṇuthas*, *stṛiṇutas*; in pl. *stṛiṇumas*, &c.: just as in Gr. στόρνῡμι, στόρνῡς, στόρνῡσι, στόρνῠτον, στόρνῠτον, στόρνῦμεν, &c. Similarly, *krí*, 'to buy,' is in Pres. sing. *kríṇámi, kríṇási, kríṇáti*; in du. &c. *kríṇívas, kríṇíthas, kríṇítas, kríṇímas*, &c., the *á* being heavier than *í*. Cf. πέρνᾱμι (πέρνημι), πέρνᾱς, πέρνᾱτι, πέρνᾰτον, πέρνᾰτον, &c. The P after the terminations of the first three persons of the Impv., Parasmai and Átmane, indicates that even before these heavy terminations the stem must be full. When a root ending in a consonant is long by nature or position, no additional strength is necessary, and no Guṇa is then possible (see 28); but in place of Guṇa, the stem sometimes remains unmutilated before the light terminations, while mutilation takes place before the heavy. The same holds good in roots ending in *á*; thus *dá* and *dhá* suppress their final vowels before strong terminations, and preserve them before weak; see 335, 336. Similarly, *as*, 'to be,' which by 28 cannot be gunated, drops its initial vowel before the strong terminations, retaining it before the weak; see 327, and compare 324.

291. Another source of difficulty is, that in group II (containing the 2nd, 3rd, and 7th classes) the verbal stem generally ends in a consonant. This group of verbal stems, therefore, will resemble the last four classes of nominal stems; and the combination of the final consonant of a stem with the initial *t*, *th*, *dh*, or *s*, of a termination in the Special tenses of these three classes requires a knowledge of the laws of Sandhi already given, as well as of others about to be explained.

292. With regard to the terminations, a reference to the table at 246 will shew that the last two groups take the regular terminations of the scheme, with few substitutions. But in the 3rd pl. Present and Imperative, Átmane-pada, the nasal is rejected in all six classes; and in the 3rd class, owing to the burden occasioned by reduplication, the nasal is also rejected in the 3rd pl. of the Parasmai-pada in these two tenses; this class also takes *us* for *an* in the 3rd pl. Impf.

293. Moreover, roots *ending in consonants*, of the 2nd and 3rd, and all roots of the 7th, and the root हु *hu* of the 3rd class, take *dhi* (the Greek θι) for *hi* in the 2nd sing. Impv.* (see 246); and roots *ending in vowels*, of the 5th, and all roots of the 8th, and roots ending in consonants of the 9th class, resemble the first group of classes at 257, in rejecting this termination *hi* altogether.

294. Again, roots ending in consonants reject the terminations *s* and *t* of the 2nd and 3rd sing. Impf. by 41. I, changing the final of the root, if a soft consonant, to an unaspirated hard; and in other respects changing a final consonant, as indicated at 41. I–IV. In roots ending in त्, थ्, द्, ध्, the 3rd person rejects the

---

* *Dhi* was originally the only form. Hence in the Vedas श्रुधि (κλῦθι); and in the Mahá-bhárata बभूश्रुधि. *Dhi* then passed into *hi*, as *dhita* passed into *hita*, and *bhúmi* into the Latin *humus*.

termination *t* regularly, and ends therefore in simple त्; the 2nd person optionally rejects either the termination *s*, and ends therefore in *t*, or the final dental of the root, and ends then in *s*, see 308.

295. The following new rules of Sandhi will also apply in forming the Special tenses of the Parasmai-Frequentative (see 514), and in forming the stem of the General tenses of *all* Primitive verbs (except those of cl. 10), and in some of the Participles; for although in most roots ending in consonants the vowel इ *i* (see 391) is inserted before the terminations of these tenses, yet a large class of common roots reject this inserted vowel, leaving the final of the stem to coalesce with the initial consonant of the termination. It will be convenient, therefore, to introduce by anticipation examples from the General tenses and Participles.

EUPHONIC JUNCTION OF CERTAIN VERBAL STEMS WITH TERMINATIONS AND SUFFIXES.

Combination of final च् ć, छ् ćh, ज् j, झ् jh, *with* त् t, थ् th, ध् dh, स् s.

296. Final च् *ć* and ज् *j*, before त् *t*, थ् *th*, ध् *dh*, and स् *s*, are changed to क् *k* (cf. 41. IV), the क् *k* blending with स् *s* into क्ष् *ksh* by 70, and becoming ग् *g* before *dh*; thus, *vać + ti = vakti; vać + thas = vakthas; vać + si = vakshi; moć + syámi = mokshyámi; mući + ta = mukta; tyaj + ta = tyakta; tyaj + syámi = tyakshyámi.* The same applies to final झ् *jh*, but this is not likely to occur.

a. Similarly, final छ् *ćh* before *s*; as, *praćh + syámi = prakshyámi.*

297. But a final छ् *ćh* and ज् *j* sometimes become ष् *sh* before त् *t*, थ् *th*; and त् *t*, थ् *th*, then become ट्, ठ्; thus, मार्ज् + *ti* = मार्ष्टि; मृज् + *thas* = मृष्ठस्; सृज् + *ta* = सृष्ट; प्रछ् + *tá* = प्रष्टा.

a. Similarly, a final ज् *j* may be changed to ड् *ḍ* before ध् *dh*, which then becomes ढ् *ḍh*.

b. भ्रज्ज् 'to fry,' मज्ज् 'to be immersed,' and व्रश्च् 'to cut,' reject their last consonant, and the first two are treated as if ending in ज्, the last as if ending in श्. See 632, 633, 630.

Combination of final ध् dh, भ् bh, *with* त् t, थ् th, स् s.

298. Final ध् *dh* and भ् *bh*, before त् *t* and थ् *th*, are changed, the one to द् *d*, the other to ब् *b*, and both *t* and *th* then become ध् *dh*; thus, *rundh* with *tas* or *thas* becomes equally रुन्द्धस् *runddhas*; *labh + táhe* = लब्धाहे *labdháhe*; *bodh + táhe* = बोद्धाहे.

A similar rule applies to final घ् *gh*, which must be changed to ग् *g*, but this is not likely to occur.

a. When final ध् *dh* is preceded by a conjunct न् *n*, as in *rundh*, then the final *dh*, which has become *d* (before *t* and *th* changed to *dh*), may optionally be rejected; so that *rundh* + *tas* = रुन्द्धस् or रुन्धस्; *rundh* + *tam* = रुन्द्धम् or रुन्धम् (Páṇ. VIII. 4, 65).

b. On the same principle तृण्ढस् is written for तृण्ड्ढस् from तृह् (674).

c. Similarly roots ending in त् *t* and द् *d* may reject these letters before *th*, *t*, and *dhi*, when *n* immediately precedes, hence भिन्ते may be written for भिन्त्ते, भिन्तस् for भिन्त्तस्, भिन्धि for भिन्द्धि.

299. Final ध् *dh* and भ् *bh*, before स् *s*, are changed by 44, the one to त् *t*, the other to प् *p*; thus, रुणध् *ruṇadh* + सि *si* becomes रुणत्सि *ruṇatsi*; *sedh* + *syámi* = *setsyámi*; *labh* + *sye* = *lapsye* (cf. 41. II).

a. If the initial of the syllable containing the final aspirate be *g*, *d*, *b*, or *ḍ*, then the aspirate, which has been rejected in the final, is thrown back on the initial; as, बोध् *bodh* + स्ये *sye* = भोत्स्ये *bhotsye*; दध् *dadh* + *sva* = *dhatsva*: and in the case of दध् the same applies before *t* and *th*, against 298. See 44. *c*, 336, 664. Cf. θρέψω from τρέφω.

b. The aspiration is also thrown back on the initial, when final *dh* is changed to *d*, before the terminations *dhve* and *dhvam*. See 336, 664.

Combinations of final श् ś, ष् sh, स् s, *with* त् t, थ् th, स् s, ध् dh.

300. Final श् *ś*, before त् *t* and थ् *th*, becomes ष् *sh*; and the त् *t*, थ् *th*, take the cerebral form ट्, ठ्; thus, ईश् + *te* = ईष्टे; ऐश् + *thás* = ऐष्ठास्.

301. Similarly, final ष् *sh*, before त् *t* and थ् *th*, requires the change of त् *t*, थ् *th*, to ट्, ठ्; thus, द्वेष् + *ti* = द्वेष्टि; and द्विष् + *thas* = द्विष्ठस्.

302. Final श् *ś* or ष् *sh*, before स् *s*, is changed to क् *k* by 41. V, the स् *s* then becoming ष् *sh* by 70; thus, वश् + *si* = वक्षि; द्वेष् + *si* = द्वेक्षि; द्रश् + *syámi* = द्रक्ष्यामि.

a. Final क्ष् *ksh* is also changed to क् *k*; as, चक्ष् + से = चक्षे.

303. Final श् *ś* or ष् *sh*, before ध् *dh*, is changed to ड् *ḍ*, the ध् *dh* becoming ढ् *ḍh* by 50; thus, द्विष् + *dhi* = द्विड्ढि. Similarly, द्विष् + *dhvam* = द्विड्ढ्वम्. A final ज् *j* may also follow this rule; see 632, 651.

a. Final क्ष् *ksh* also becomes ड् *ḍ*, *k* being dropped; as, चक्ष् + ध्वे = चड्ढ्वे.

304. Final स् *s* is changed to त् *t* before त् *t* in the 3rd sing. Impf. (the termination *t* being rejected), and before ध् *dh*, is either dropped or changed to द् *d*; thus, *ćakás* + *dhi* = either चकाधि *ćakádhi* or चकाद्धि *ćakáddhi*; शास् + *dhi* = शाधि; हिंस् + *dhi* = हिन्धि or हिन्द्धि, see 658, 673.

a. Final स् *s* before स् *s* is changed to त् *t*; as, *vas* + *syámi* = *vatsyámi*. So optionally in 2nd sing. Impf. of शास्, *aśás* + *s* = *aśáts* = *aśát* (or *aśás*).

b. But not in the case of final *s* preceded by *a* or *á* before *si* and *se*.

Combination of final ह् h *with* त् t, थ् th, स् s, ध् dh.

305. In roots beginning with द् *d*, like दुह् *duh*, 'to milk,' final ह् *h* is treated as if it were घ् *gh*, and is changed to ग् *g* before त् *t* and थ् *th*, and both *t* and *th* then become ध् *dh;* thus, दुह् *duh* + *tas* or *thas* becomes equally दुग्धस् *dugdhas;* दह् *dah* + *tásmi* = *dagdhásmi.*

But दृह् + *ta* = दृढ *dṛiḍha.*

Note—In root नह् the final *h* is treated as if it were ध् *dh*, and becomes द् *d*, after which *t* and *th* both become *dh.* See 624.

a. But if a root begin with any other letter than द् *d* or न् *n*, then its final ह् *h* is dropped, and both the त् *t* and थ् *th* of the termination become ढ् *ḍh.* Moreover, to compensate for the rejection of the final *h*, a radical vowel (except *ṛi*), if not gunated, is lengthened, and in the roots सह् *sah* and वह् *vah*, 'to bear,' changed to *o;* as, मुह् + *ta* = मूढ; रुह् + *ta* = रूढ; लेह् + *ti* = लेढि *leḍhi;* रोह् + *tásmi* = रोढास्मि; सह् + *tá* = सोढा; वह् + *tá* = वोढा.

Obs.—But गुह् + *ta* = गूढ, and वृह् + *ta* = वृढ (Páṇ. VI. 3, 111).

b. द्रुह् 'to injure,' मुह् 'to be foolish,' स्निह् 'to love,' स्नुह् 'to vomit,' optionally follow either 305 or 305. *a.*

306. Final ह् *h*, before स् *s*, follows the analogy of final श् *ś* and ष् *sh*, and is changed to क् *k*, which blends with स् *s* into क्ष् *ksh;* thus, लेह् *leh* with *si* becomes लेक्षि; रोह् + *syámi* = रोक्ष्यामि. Similarly, in Latin, final *h* becomes *k* before *s;* as, *veksit* (*vexit*) from *veho.*

a. And if the initial of the syllable ending in ह् *h* be द् *d*, ग् *g*, ब् *b*, or ड् *ḍ* (the two latter, however, are not likely to occur), then the final ह् *h* is still changed to क् *k* before *s;* but the initial द् *d* and ग् *g* are aspirated according to the analogy of 44. *c;* thus, दोह् *doh* + *si* = धोक्षि; दह् *dah* + *syámi* = धक्ष्यामि; अगुह् *aguh* + *sam* = अघुक्षम्.

b. In root नह् *nah* final ह् *h* is treated as if it were *dh*, and becomes त् *t* before स् *s.* Compare 183, and see 624.

c. In roots beginning with द् *d*, like दुह् *duh* and दिह् *dih*, final ह् *h* becomes ग् *g* before *dh;* i.e. before the *dhi* of the 2nd sing. Imperative, and before the terminations *dhve* and *dhvam* (see 306. *d*); thus, दुह् *duh* + *dhi* = दुग्धि *dugdhi.* And in a root beginning with *n*, like नह् *nah*, final *h* becomes *d* before these terminations.

But if the root begin with any other letter than द् *d* or न् *n*, then final ह् *h* is dropped, and the ध् *dh* of the termination becomes ढ् *ḍh*, the radical vowel (except ऋ *ṛi*) being lengthened; thus, लिह् *lih* + *ḍhi*

= लीढि ; *lih* + *dhvam* = लीढ्वम्. An option, however, is allowed in the case of the roots at 305. *b.*

d. And 306. *a.* applies before *dhve* and *dhvam*, when final ह् *h* becomes ग् *g* or is dropped, although not before *dhi* of the Imperative; thus, *duh* + *dhve* = धुग्ध्वे *dhugdhve;* and *aguh* + *dhvam* = अघूढ्वम् *aghúḍhvam.*

e. Obs.—If a root end in ह् *h*, this final *h* becomes क् *k* in the 2nd and 3rd sing. Impf. of roots beginning with द् *d* (the personal terminations *s* and *t* being dropped). In all other roots the final ह् *h* becomes ट् *ṭ* (41. III). In both cases the changed ह् throws back an aspiration on the first consonant of the root in accordance with 306. *a.*

GROUP II. CONJUGATION II.

307. CLASS 2 (containing about 70 Primitive verbs).—Rule for forming the stem in the four Special tenses.

Gunate the vowel of the root (except when debarred by 28) in the *strong forms*, or before those terminations only which are marked with P in the scheme at 246. Before all the other terminations the original vowel of the root must be retained. No vowel is interposed between the root and the terminations. (Cf. Gr. verbs like εἶμι, φημί, &c. See 290. *a.*)

308. Thus, from विद् *vid*, 'to know' (Gr. εἴδω, ἴδον, Lat. *video*), is formed the stem of the singular Present *ved* (1. *ved* + *mi* = वेद्मि *vedmi*, &c.), and the stem of the dual and plural *vid* (Du. 1. *vid* + *vas* = विद्वस् *vidvas*, &c.; Pl. 1. *vid* + *mas* = विद्मस् *vidmas*, &c.) So also the stem of the Impf. *aved* and *avid* (1. *aved* + *am* = *avedam*, 2. *aved* + *s* = *avet* or *aves* by 41. I. and 294); the stem of the Pot. *vid* (1. *vid* + *yám* = विद्याम् *vidyám*, &c.); and the stem of the Impv. *ved* and *vid* (1. *ved* + *áni* = *vedáni*, 2. *vid* + *dhi* = *viddhi* 293, *ved* + *tu* = *vettu;* Du. 1. *ved* + *áva* = *vedáva*, &c. *) See the table at 583.

a. A contracted form of the Perfect of *vid* (365) is sometimes used for the Present; thus, Sing. *veda, vettha, veda;* Du. *vidva, vidathus, vidatus;* Pl. *vidma, vida, vidus;* see 168. *e.* Cf. Gr. οἶδα (for Ϝοῖδα) fr. rt. Ϝιδ (εἴδω), also used with a Present signification; and Lat. *vidi, vidisti,* &c. Cf. also the Present *vidmas* with ἴδμεν (ἴσμεν), *vittha* with ἴστε, and *viddhi* with ἴσθι. Cf. also old English 'to wit.'

309. Similarly, from द्विष्, 'to hate,' come the stems *dvesh* and *dvish* (Pres. 1. द्वेष्मि; Du. 1. द्विष्वस्, &c.; see 657).

---

* The Impv. of *vid* is optionally formed with the syllable *ám* and the auxiliary verb *kṛi* (cf. 385); thus, Sing. 3. विदांकरोतु or विदाङ्करोतु (Páṇ. III. 1, 41). And this root may optionally insert *r* in the 3rd pl. Átm. of the Pres., Impf., and Impv.; thus, विदते or विद्रते, अविदत or अविद्रत, विदताम् or विद्रताम्.

310. So also, from इ *i*, 'to go,' come the stems *e* and *i* (Pres. 1. एमि *emi* (= εἶμι), 2. एषि by 70, 3. एति; Pl. 1. इमस्, ἴμεν, see 645).

a. जागृ 'to awake' makes, in the same way, *jágar* and *jágṛi* (Pres. 1. जागर्मि, &c.; Du. 1. जागृवस्; Pl. 3. जाग्रति; Impf. 2, 3. अजागर् or अजागः; Du. 3. अजागृताम्; Pl. 3. अजागरुस्; Pot. 1. जागृयाम्; Impv. 3. जागर्तु; Pl. 3. जाग्रतु).

Obs.—Roots of cl. 2, having more than one syllable (such as जागृ above, दरिद्रा 'to be poor,' चकास् 'to shine,' all formed by reduplication), as well as शास् 'to rule' (perhaps contracted from a reduplicated शशास्), and जक्ष् 'to eat' (perhaps for जघस्), resemble the reduplicated verbs of cl. 3 in rejecting the nasal from the 3rd pl. Pres. and Impv. Parasmai, and taking *us* for *an* in 3rd pl. Impf. Moreover, a few roots like विद् and द्विष् above, as well as some in *á*, like या 'to go' and पा 'to protect,' optionally take *us* for *an* in Impf., before which a final *á* is dropped.

311. The preposition अधि *adhi*, 'over,' prefixed to the root इ *i*, 'to go,' gives the sense of 'to read' (Átmane-pada only): इ then becomes *iy* (compare 123) and blends with *adhi* into अधीय् *adhíy* before the vowel-terminations of the Pres., Impf., and Pot. Before the consonantal terminations it becomes अधी *adhí*. (Hence Pres. 1. अधीये, 2. अधीषे, 3. अधीते; Du. 1. अधीवहे, &c.; Pl. 3. अधीयते; Impf. 1. *adhi*+*a*+*iy*+*i*=अध्यैयि by 251. *a*, 2. अध्यैथास्, 3. अध्यैत; Du. 1. अध्यैवहि, 2. अध्यैयाथाम्, &c.; Pot. 1. अधीयीय, अधीयीथास्, &c.; Impv. 1. *adhi*+*e*+*ai*=अध्ययै by 36. *a*, 2. अधीष्व, &c.)

a. The preposition आ *á* is prefixed to the root इ *i*, according to the usual rules of Sandhi, and gives the sense of 'to come;' thus, Pres. ऐमि, ऐषि, ऐति; एयस्, &c.; Impf. आयम्, ऐस्, &c.; Pot. एयाम्, एयास्, &c.; Impv. आयानि, एहि, ऐतु, &c. Again, the prep. अप *apa* prefixed gives the sense of 'to go away;' thus, Pres. अपैमि, &c.: and the prep. अव gives the sense of 'to know;' as, Pres. अवैमि.

312. So also other roots in ई *í* and उ *u* or ऊ *ú* change these vowels to *iy* and *uv* (cf. 123, 125. *a*) before the vowel-terminations; as, fr. वी *ví*, 'to go,' come *ve*, *ví*, and *viy* (Pres. 1. वेमि, &c.; Du. 1. वीवस्; Pl. 3. वियन्ति) *. Similarly, सू, 'to bring forth' (Átm. only), makes in Pres. Sing. Du. Pl. 3. सूते, सुवाते, सुवते; and in Impv. Sing. Du. Pl. 1. सुवै, सुवावहै, सुवामहै, Guṇa being suppressed.

313. स्तु *stu* and नु *nu*, 'to praise;' यु *yu*, 'to join,' 'to mix;' and रु *ru*, 'to sound,' follow 312, but take Vṛiddhi instead of Guṇa before the consonantal P terminations †. Hence the stems स्तौ *stau*, स्तु *stu*, and स्तुव् *stuv*; see 648. Before the vowel P terminations both Vṛiddhi and Guṇa are generally (but not always) suppressed, and *uv* substituted, as in सू at 312. Note, that these roots may optionally insert an ई *í* before the consonantal P terminations; and before this vowel Guṇa, not Vṛiddhi, is required. According to some authorities, however, *í* is inserted before *all* the consonantal terminations; and, according to others, before all the consonants, except *y*, *v*, or *m*, not followed by an indicatory P.

314. ब्रू, 'to speak,' can never take Vṛiddhi, like the roots at 313; but inserts

* According to some the 3rd pl. Impf. of वी is अव्यन् as well as अवियन्.

† That is, the terminations marked with P, which begin with consonants.

an ई *í* after Guṇa in the places where those roots optionally insert it, viz. before the consonantal P terminations. Hence the stems *braví, brú, bruv*. See 649.

a. Before the vowel P terminations Guṇa is not suppressed, excepting in the 1st sing. Impf., which may be either अब्रवम् or अब्रुवम्.

315. शी, 'to lie down' (Átm. only), gunates the radical vowel before *all* the terminations, and inserts *r* in the 3rd pl. Pres., Impf., and Impv., after the analogy of the 3rd pl. Pot. See 646.

316. ऊर्णु, 'to cover,' takes either Vṛiddhi or Guṇa of the final *u* before the consonantal P terminations, except before the 2nd and 3rd sing. of the Impf., where Guṇa only is admissible. Before the vowel-terminations it follows 312, but Guṇa is retained before the vowel P terminations, excepting in the 1st sing. Impf. Hence the stems *úrṇau, úrṇo, úrṇu*, and *úrṇuv* (Pres. Par. 1. ऊर्णौमि or ऊर्णोमि; Du. 1. ऊर्णुवस्; Pl. 3. ऊर्णुवन्ति, see 310. Obs.; Impf. 1. और्णवम् or और्णुवम् by 251. *a*, 2. और्णोस्, &c.; Pot. 1. ऊर्णुयाम्; Impv. S. 1. ऊर्णवानि, 3. ऊर्णौतु or ऊर्णोतु. Pres. Átm. 3. ऊर्णुते, ऊर्णुवाते, ऊर्णुवते).

317. या 'to go,' पा 'to protect,' अद् 'to eat' (*edo*), आस् 'to sit,' Átm., and other roots having *a* or *á* for their vowels, cannot be changed, but are themselves the inflective stems (Pres. 1. या *yá+mi=yámi*, see 644; अद् *ad+mi=admi*, 2. *ad+si =atsi*, 3. *ad+ti=atti*; Du. 3. *ad+tas=attas*, &c., see 652). With *atti* compare Lat. *edit*.

a. आस् 'to sit' is similar; thus *ás+e=áse, ás+se=ásse, ás+te=áste*. The final of *ás* is dropped before *dh*, hence Pl. 2. आध्वे *ádhve*, &c.

b. अद् 'to eat,' before the terminations of the 2nd and 3rd sing. Imperfect, inserts the vowel अ *a* by special rule, see 652; and some other roots of this class require peculiar changes, as follows:—

318. दरिद्रा *daridrá*, 'to be poor,' follows 310. Obs., making its stem *daridri* before the consonantal terminations not marked with P, and *daridr* before *ati, us, atu* (Pres. S. Du. Pl. 3. दरिद्राति, दरिद्रितस्, दरिद्रति; Impf. 1. अदरिद्राम्; Pl. 3. अदरिद्रुस्; Pot. 3. दरिद्रियात्; Impv. 1. दरिद्राणि; Du. 1. दरिद्राव; Pl. 3. दरिद्रतु).

319. दीधी *dídhí*, 'to shine' (Átm.), and वेवी 'to go' (Átm.), change their final to *y*, and not to *iy*, before the vowel-terminations (compare 312); but in the Potential the final *í* coalesces with the *í* of the terminations (Pres. Sing. 1. दीध्ये; वेव्ये; Pl. 3. दीध्यते; वेव्यते: Pot. 1. दीधीय, &c.)

320. वच् *vać*, 'to speak,' changes its final palatal to a guttural before all the hard consonantal terminations, in conformity with 176; but not before the soft (except *dh*). It is defective in the 3rd pl. Present and Imperative, where its place must be supplied by ब्रू at 314, 649. Hence the stems *vać* and *vak*. See 650.

321. मृज् *mṛij*, 'to cleanse,' is vriddhied in strong forms, and optionally before the vowel-terminations having no P. Hence the stems *márj* and *mṛij*. See 651.

322. रुद् *rud*, 'to weep,' besides the usual Guṇa change before the P terminations, inserts the vowel इ *i* before all the consonantal terminations except *y*, and optionally *a* or *í* in the 2nd and 3rd sing. Impf. Hence *rodi, rudi, rud*. See 653.

a. स्वप् 'to sleep,' श्वस् and अन् 'to breathe,' and जक्ष् 'to eat,' are similar, but without Guṇa. The last conforms to 310. Obs. In the Epic poems, forms like स्वपामि are found as well as स्वपिमि, while in the Veda other roots (besides the above five) insert *i* (as शोचिमि, वमिति, ज्वलिति, स्वरिति, &c.) See Páṇ. VII. 2, 76. 34.

323. हन् *han*, 'to kill,' makes its stem ह *ha* before *t* or *th* (by 57. *a*); घ्न् *ghn* before *anti*, *an*, *antu*; and ज *ja* before हि. The last change is to avoid the proximity of two aspirates. See 654, and compare 252. *b*. Obs.

324. वश् *vaś*, 'to desire,' 'to choose,' suppresses the *a*, and changes *v* to *u* before the terminations which have no P (see 290. *a*); and उश् *uś* becomes उष् *ush* before *t* and *th* by 300. See 656.

325. ईड् *íḍ*, 'to praise' (Átm.), not gunated by 28, inserts the vowel इ *i* between the root and the terminations of the 2nd person से, स्व, ध्वे, and ध्वम्: Pres. 1. ईडे, 2. ईडिषे, 3. ईट्टे (see 48. *b*. Obs.); Du. 1. ईड्वहे; Pl. 2. ईडिध्वे; Impf. 3. ऐट्ट, &c.; Pot. 1. ईडीय, &c.; Impv. 1. ईडै, 2. ईडिष्व, 3. ईट्टाम्; Pl. 2. ईडिध्वम्.

a. Similarly, ईश् *íś*, 'to rule' (Átm. only): Pres. 1. ईशे, 2. ईशिषे, 3. ईष्टे by 300; Impf. 3. ऐष्ट, &c.; Impv. 3. ईष्टाम्, &c.

326. चक्ष् *ćaksh*, 'to speak' (Átm.), drops the penultimate *k* before all consonantal terminations, except those beginning with *m* or *v* (Pres. 1. चक्षे, 2. चष्+से = चक्षे, 3. चष्टे, &c., see 302. *a*, 303. *a*; Impf. 3. अचष्ट; Pot. 3. चक्षीत). Kátyáyana considers क्शा the original root, whence is formed ख्या; the latter being substituted for चक्ष् in the General tenses.

327. अस् *as*, 'to be' (Parasmai only), a very useful auxiliary verb, follows 290. *a*, and rejects its initial *a*, except before the P terminations. The 2nd pers. sing. Pres. is असि for अस्सि. The Impf. has the character of an Aor., and retains the initial *a* throughout, and inserts ई *í* before the *s* and *t* of the 2nd and 3rd sing.; see 584. The 2nd sing. Impv. substitutes *e* for *as*, and takes the termination *dhi*. This root is found in the Átmane-pada, with the prepositions *vi* and *ati*, when the Present is Sing. व्यतिहे, -से, -स्ते; Du. -स्वहे, -साथे, -साते, -स्महे, -ध्वे, -सते; Pot. व्यतिषीय, &c. (Páṇ. VIII. 3, 87). See 584.

328. शास् *śás*, 'to rule,' in Parasmai (but not in Átmane), changes its vowel to इ *i* before the consonantal terminations having no P, except that of the 2nd sing. Impv. Before that and all vowel-terminations, as well as in the strong forms, the vowel of the root remains unchanged; and, after *i*, स् becomes ष् by 70. Hence the stems शास् and शिष्. See 658.

329. चकास्, 'to shine,' is Pres. 1. चकास्मि, 2. चकास्सि, 3. चकास्ति; Du. 1. चकास्वः; Pl. 3. चकासति (310. Obs.); Impf. 1. अचकासम्, 2. अचकास् or अचकात् (294), 3. अचकात्; Du. 1. अचकास्व; Pl. 3. अचकासुः; Pot. 1. चकास्याम्; Impv. 1. चकासानि, 2. चकाधि or चकाद्धि (304), 3. चकास्तु; Du. 1. चकासाव, 2. चकास्तम्; Pl. 3. चकासतु.

330. दुह् *duh*, 'to milk,' and लिह् *lih*, 'to lick,' form their stems as explained at 305, 306. They are conjugated at 660, 661.

331. CLASS 3 (containing about 20 Primitive verbs).—Rule for forming the stem in the four Special tenses.

Reduplicate the initial consonant and vowel of the root, and gunate the vowel of the *radical syllable* before the P terminations only, as in cl. 2.

Obs.—This class resembles the 2nd in interposing no vowel between the root and terminations. It is the only class that necessarily rejects the nasal in 3rd pl. Pres. and Impv. Parasmai (see 292), and takes *us* for *an* in 3rd pl. Impf. Parasmai, before which *us* Guṇa is generally required. See 292–294.

332. Thus, from भृ *bhṛi*, 'to bear' (*φέρω*, *fero*), is formed the stem of the Present singular बिभर् *bibhar* (1. *bibhar*+*mi*=बिभर्मि), and the stem of the dual and plural बिभृ *bibhṛi* (Du. 1. *bibhṛi*+*vas*=बिभृवस्; Pl. 1. *bibhṛi*+*mas*=बिभृमस्; Pl. 3. *bibhṛi* +*ati*=बिभ्रति by 34 and 292). See the table at 583.

a. Note, that *bibharti* bears the same relation to *bibhṛimas* that *fert* does to *ferimus*, and *vult* to *volumus*.

333. Similarly, from भी *bhí*, 'to fear,' come the two stems *bibhe* and *bibhí*; from हु *hu*, 'to sacrifice,' the two stems *juho* and *juhu*. The former of these roots may optionally shorten the radical vowel before a consonant, when not gunated. See 666. The latter may optionally reject its final before *vas* and *mas*, and is the only root ending in a vowel which takes *dhi* for *hi* in the 2nd sing. Impv. See 662.

a. ह्री, 'to be ashamed,' is like भी, but changes its final ई to इय् *iy* before the vowel-terminations, in conformity with 123. See 666. *a.*

334. ऋ *ṛi*, 'to go,' is the only verb in this class that begins with a vowel. It substitutes *iy* for *ṛi* in the reduplication, and makes its stems इयर् *iyar* and इयृ *iyṛi* (Pres. Sing. Du. Pl. 3. इयर्ति, इयृतस्, इय्रति; Impf. 1. ऐयरम्, 2. ऐयर्, 3. ऐयर्; Du. 3. ऐयृताम्; Pot. 3. इयृयात्; Impv. 1. इयराणि).

335. दा *dá*, 'to give' (*δίδωμι*, *do*), drops its final *á* before all excepting the P terminations. Hence the stems *dadá* and *dad*. It becomes दे *de* before the *hi* of the Impv. See 663.

336. धा *dhá*, 'to place' (*τίθημι*), is similar. Hence the stems *dadhá* and *dadh*; but *dadh* becomes धत् before *t*, *th*, and *s*; and *dhad* before *dhve* and *dhvam* by 299. *a. b*; and *dhe* before the *hi* of the Impv. See 664.

337. हा *há*, 'to abandon,' changes its final *á* to ई *í* before the consonantal terminations not marked with P, and drops the final altogether before the vowel-terminations, and before *y* of the Potential. Hence the stems *jahá*, *jahí*, *jah*. Before *hi* of the Impv. the stem is optionally *jahá*, *jahí*, or *jahi*. According to some authorities, जही may be shortened into जहि in Pres., Impf., and Impv. See 665.

338. मा *má*, 'to measure' (Átm.), and हा *há*, 'to go' (Átm.), make their stems मिमी *mimí* and जिही *jihí* before the consonantal terminations not marked with P. Before the vowel-terminations their stems are *mim* and *jih* (Sing. Du. Pl. 3. जिहीते, जिहाते, जिहते; Impf. 3. अजिहीत; Impv. 3. जिहीताम्). See मा at 664. *a.*

339. जन् *jan*, 'to produce' (Parasmai-pada), rejects the final nasal (see 57. *a*),

and lengthens the radical *a* before *t* and *th* and *hi*, and optionally before *y*. Before consonantal terminations beginning with *m* or *v* the radical *jan* remains, but before vowel-terminations not marked with P the medial *a* is dropped, and the nasal combining with *j* becomes palatal (compare the declension of *rájan* at 148). Hence the three stems *jajan*, *jajá*, and *jajñ*. See 666. *b*.

340. भस् *bhas*, 'to eat,' 'to shine,' like *jan*, rejects the radical *a* before the vowel-terminations not marked with P; and *bh* coalescing with *s* becomes *p* by 44 (Pres. S. Du. Pl. 3. बभस्ति, बभस्तस्, बप्सति). The same contraction takes place before terminations beginning with त, थ, but the final *s* is then dropped, and the usual rules of Sandhi applied; thus, बभ् + तास् = बब्धास् by 298.

341. निज् 'to purify,' विज् 'to shake,' विच् 'to separate' (identified with *vij*), and विष् 'to pervade,' 'to penetrate,' gunate the reduplicated syllable before *all* the terminations, and forbid the usual Guṇa of the radical syllable before terminations beginning with vowels, as in the 1st sing. Impf. and the 1st sing. du. pl. Impv. (Pres. 1. नेनेज्मि, 2. नेनेक्षि, 3. नेनेक्ति; Du. 1. नेनिज्वस्, &c.; Pl. 1. नेनिज्मस्, 3. नेनिजति; Impf. 1. अनेनिजम्, 2. अनेनेक्, &c.; Pl. 3. अनेनिजुस्, &c.; Impv. 1. नेनिजानि; Du. 1. नेनिजाव; Pl. 1. नेनिजाम).

342. Class 7 (containing about 24 Primitive verbs).—Rule for forming the stem in the four Special tenses.

Insert न *na* (changeable to ण *ṇa* after *ṛi* &c. by 58) *between* the vowel and final consonant* of the root before the P terminations, and न् *n* (changeable to ङ्, ञ्, ण्, म्, or Anusvára†, according to the consonant immediately succeeding) before all the other terminations.

Obs.—This class resembles the 2nd and 3rd in interposing no vowel between the final consonant of the root and the terminations.

a. The insertion of nasals is common in other roots besides those of the 7th class (cf. 270. *d*, 281, 487. *b*), and cf. certain Greek and Latin roots; as, μαθ, μανθάνω; λαβ, λαμβάνω; θιγ, θιγγάνω; *scid*, *scindo*; *fid*, *findo*; *tag*, *tango*; *liq*, *linquo*, &c. See 260.

343. Thus, from भिद् *bhid*, 'to divide,' 'to break,' is formed the stem of the Present tense singular भिनद् *bhinad*, and the stem of the dual and plural भिन्द् *bhind*, changeable to *bhinat* and *bhint* by 46 (1. *bhinad* + *mi* = भिनद्मि, 3. *bhinad* + *ti* = भिनत्ति; Du. 1. *bhind* + *vas* = भिन्द्वस्, 3. *bhind* + *tas* = भिन्त्तस् or भिन्तस् (298. *c*); Pl. 3. *bhind* + *anti* = भिन्दन्ति). See the table at 583.

344. Similarly, from रुध् *rudh*, 'to hinder,' the two stems रुणध् *ruṇadh* and रुन्ध् *rundh*, changeable to *ruṇat*, *ruṇad*, and *rund* (1.

---

* All the roots in this class end in consonants.

† The change to Anusvára will take place before sibilants and ह. See 6. *a*.

ruṇadh + *mi* = रुणध्मि, 2. *ruṇadh* + *si* = रुणत्सि, 3. *ruṇadh* + *ti* = रुणद्धि; Du. 3. *rundh* + *tas* = रुन्द्धस्); see 671. So also, from पिष्, 'to grind,' the two stems पिनष् and पिंष् (Pres. 3. पिनष् + ति = पिनष्टि; Impv. 2. पिंष् + धि = पिण्ड्ढि or पिण्ढि).

345. Observe—Roots ending in त् *t* and द् *d* may reject these letters before *th*, *t*, and *dhi*, when *n* immediately precedes; see 298. *a*. *b*. *c*.

346. भुज् 'to eat,' युज् 'to join,' विच् 'to distinguish,' conform to 296. Hence, from *bhuj* come *bhunaj* and *bhuñj*, changeable to *bhunak* and *bhuṅk*; see 668. *a*.

347. भञ्ज् 'to break,' अञ्ज् 'to anoint,' उन्द् 'to moisten,' इन्ध् 'to kindle,' हिंस् 'to injure,' तञ्च् or तञ्ज् 'to contract,' fall under this class; but the nasal belonging to the root takes the place of the conjugational nasal, and becomes न *na* in the strong forms. Hence, from *bhañj* come the two stems *bhanaj* and *bhañj*, changeable to *bhanak* and *bhaṅk*; from *und* come *unad* and *und* (Pres. 3. *unatti*, *untas*, *undanti*; Impf. 1. *aunadam*, 2. *aunas*, 3. *aunat*; Du. 3. *auntám*, &c.) See 669, 668, 673. Similarly, from इन्ध्, Pres. 1. *indhe*, 2. *intse*, 3. *inddhe*; Pl. 3. *indhate*; Impf. 2. *ainddhás*, 3. *ainddha*; Impv. 1. *inadhai*, &c.

348. तृह्, 'to strike,' 'to kill,' inserts णे instead of ण before all the consonantal P terminations (Páṇ. VII. 3, 92), but not before those beginning with vowels. See 674.

GROUP III. CONJUGATION III.

349. Class 5 (containing about 30 Primitive verbs).—Rule for forming the stem in the four Special tenses.

Add नु *nu* (changeable to णु by 58) to the root, which must be gunated into नो *no* (changeable to णो) before the P terminations (290. *a*) *. Roots ending in consonants add *nuv*, instead of *nu*, to the root before the vowel-terminations. Roots ending in *vowels* may drop the *u* of *nu* before initial *v* and *m* (not marked with P), and always reject the termination *hi* of the Imperative. See 293.

350. Thus, from चि *ći*, 'to gather,' are formed the stems *ćino* and *ćinu* (Pres. 1. *ćino*+*mi*=चिनोमि, *ćino*+*si*=चिनोषि by 70; Du. 1. *ćinu*+*vas*=चिनुवस् or चिन्वस्; Pl. 1. *ćinu*+*mas*=चिनुमस् or चिन्मस्, 3. *ćinu*+*anti*=चिन्वन्ति by 34; Impv. 1. *ćino*+*áni*=चिनवानि by 36. *a*, 2. चिनु *ćinu* by 291). See the table at 583.

351. Similarly, fr. दु *du*, 'to burn,' come *duno*, *dunu*, and *dunuv*; fr. आप् *áp*, 'to obtain,' come *ápno*, *ápnu*, and *ápnuv*, see 681; fr. तृप् 'to satisfy,' *tṛipno*, *tṛipnu*, and *tṛipnuv*, see 618.

---

* The change of *nu* to *no* before the P terminations is represented in Gr. by the lengthening of υ before certain terminations, as in ζεύγ-νῡ-μι, δείκ-νῡ-μι, but ζεύγ-νῠ-μεν, δείκ-νῠ-μεν. See 260.

352. श्रु *śru*, 'to hear' (sometimes placed under the 1st class), substitutes शृ *śṛi* for the root, and makes its stems *śṛiṇo* and *śṛiṇu*. See 676.

a. दम्भ् 'to deceive,' स्कम्भ् and स्तम्भ् 'to support,' स्कुम्भ् 'to stop,' and स्तुम्भ् 'to astonish,' reject their nasals in favour of the conjugational *nu*; thus, *dabhnu*, *skabhnu*, &c.

353. Class 8 (containing 10 Primitive verbs).—Rule for forming the stem in the four Special tenses.

Add उ *u* to the root, which must be gunated into ओ *o* before the P terminations (see 290. *a*).

Note—Only ten roots are generally given in this class, and nine of these end in न् *n* or ण् *ṇ*; hence the addition of *u* and *o* will have the same apparent effect as the addition of *nu* and *no* in cl. 5.

354. Thus, from तन् *tan*, 'to stretch,' are formed the stems *tano* and *tanu* (Pres. 1. *tano+mi*=तनोमि, 2. *tano+si*=तनोषि by 70; Du. 1. *tanu+vas*=तनुवस् or तन्वस्; Pl. 1. *tanu+mas*=तनुमस् or तन्मस्; Impv. 1. *tano+áni*=तनवानि by 36. *a*, 2. तनु *tanu*, see 293). Cf. Gr. τάνυμι, τάνυμεν.

a. The root सन् *san*, 'to give,' optionally rejects its *n*, and lengthens the radical *a* before the *y* of the Potential; thus, सन्याम् *sanyám* or सायाम् *sáyám*, &c.

b. When the vowel of a root is capable of Guṇa, it may optionally take it; thus the stem of ऋण् 'to go' may be either ऋणु or अर्णु (1. अर्णोमि or ऋणोमि).

355. One root in this class, कृ *kṛi*, 'to do,' 'to make,' is by far the most common and useful in the language. This root gunates the radical vowel *ṛi*, as well as the conjugational *u*, before the P terminations. Before the other terminations it changes the radical *ṛi* to *ur*. The rejection of the conjugational *u* before initial *m* (not marked with P) and *v*, which is allowable in the 5th class, is in this verb compulsory, and is, moreover, required before initial *y*. Hence the three stems *karo*, *kuru*, and *kur*. See 682.

356. Class 9 (containing about 52 Primitive verbs).—Rule for forming the stem in the four Special tenses.

Add ना *ná* to the root before the P terminations; नी *ní* before all the others, except those beginning with vowels, where only न् *n* is added (see 290. *a*).

Obs.—ना, नी, and न् are changeable to णा, णी, and ण्, by 58.

357. Thus, from यु *yu*, 'to join,' are formed the three stems *yuná*, *yuní*, and *yun* (Pres. 1. *yuná+mi*=युनामि; Du. 1. *yuní+vas*=युनीवस्; Pl. 1. *yuní+mas*=युनीमस्, 3. *yun+anti*=युनन्ति. Pres. Átm. 1. *yun+e*=युने; Impv. 1. *yuná+áni*=युनानि, 2. *yuní+hi*=युनीहि, &c.)

a. Obs.—Roots ending in consonants substitute *ána* for their conjugational sign in 2nd sing. Impv., and reject the termination *hi;* e. g. अशान 'eat thou,' from अश् 'to eat;' पुषाण 'nourish thou,' from पुष्; क्षुभाण 'shake thou,' from क्षुभ्, &c. See 696, 698, 694.

358. री 'to go,' प्ली 'to go,' व्ली 'to go,' 'to choose,' व्री 'to choose,' ली 'to adhere,' भ्री 'to fear,' 'to bear,' क्षी 'to destroy,' धू 'to shake,' पू 'to purify' (583), लू 'to cut' (691), ॠ 'to go,' कॄ 'to hurt,' गॄ 'to sound,' जॄ 'to grow old,' दॄ 'to split,' नॄ 'to lead,' पॄ 'to fill,' भॄ 'to bear,' 'to blame,' मॄ 'to kill,' बॄ or वॄ 'to choose,' शॄ 'to injure,' स्तॄ 'to spread,' स्वॄ or स्नॄ or स्पॄ or सॄ 'to hurt,' shorten the radical vowel in forming their stems; thus, from पू 'to purify' come the stems *puná, puní,* and *pun;* see the table at 583.

a. क्री 'to buy,' प्री 'to love,' श्री 'to cook,' क्ष्णू or क्नू† 'to sound,' दू 'to hurt,' do not shorten their vowels. See 689, 690.

359. ग्रह्, 'to take,' becomes गृह्, and makes its stems गृह्णा, गृह्णी, and गृह्ण्. See 699.

a. ज्या, 'to grow old,' becomes जि, and makes its stems *jiná, jiní,* and *jin.*

360. बन्ध्, ग्रन्थ्, मन्थ्, श्रन्थ्, कुन्थ्, and स्तम्भ् reject the radical nasal in favour of the conjugational; thus, from *bandh* are formed the three stems *badhná, badhní,* and *badhn.* See 692, 693, 695.

361. ज्ञा 'to know,' in the same way, rejects its nasal in favour of the conjugational, and makes its stems *jáná, jání,* and *ján.* See 688.

362. खव्, 'to appear as a spectre,' is said to make its stems *khauná, khauní,* and *khaun.*

PRIMITIVE VERBS OF THE FIRST NINE CLASSES IN THE SIX GENERAL TENSES.

363. The general rules for the formation of the stem in the Perfect, 1st and 2nd Futures, Aorist, Precative, and Conditional, apply to all verbs of the first nine classes indiscriminately; see 250. *a.* The 10th class alone carries its conjugational characteristic into most of the General tenses; for this reason the consideration of its last tenses falls most conveniently under Causal verbs. See 289. *a.*

Reduplicated Perfect (Second Preterite).

Terminations repeated from 246.

Parasmai.			Átmane.		
a (au)	**iva*	**ima*	*e*	**ivahe*	**imahe*
itha or *tha*	*athus*	*a*	**ishe*	*áthe*	**idhve* or **iḍhve*
a (au)	*atus*	*us*	*e*	*áte*	*ire*

† क्नू, however, may optionally shorten it.

364. Rule for forming the stem in verbs of the first nine classes.

In the first place, with regard to reduplication, if a root *begin with a consonant*, double the initial consonant, with its vowel, according to the rules given at 252 (but *a* is reduplicated for a radical *a*, *á*, *ṛi*, *ṛí*, *lṛi*, and even for radical *e*, *ai*, *o*, if final; *i* for *i*, *í*, *e*; *u* for *u*, *ú*, *o*); e.g.

From पच् *paé*, 'to cook,' *papaé*; fr. याच् *yáé*, 'to ask,' *yayáé*; fr. कृ *kṛi*, 'to do,' *éakṛi*; fr. नृत् *nṛit*, 'to dance,' *nanṛit*; fr. तॄ *tṛí*, 'to cross,' *tatṛí*; fr. कॢप् *klṛip*, 'to be able,' *éaklṛip*; fr. मे *me*, 'to change,' *mame*; fr. गै *gai*, 'to sing,' *jagai*; fr. सो *so*, 'to finish,' *saso*; fr. सिध् *sidh*, 'to accomplish,' *sishidh* (70); fr. जीव् *jív*, 'to live,' *jijív*; fr. सेव् *sev*, 'to serve,' *sishev*; fr. द्रु *dru*, 'to run,' *dudru*; fr. पू *pú*, 'to purify,' *pupú*; fr. बुध् *budh*, 'to know,' *bubudh*; fr. लोक् *lok*, 'to see,' *lulok*; fr. स्मि *smi*, 'to smile,' *sishmi*; fr. स्था *sthá*, 'to stand,' *tasthá*.

a. And if it *begin with a vowel*, double the initial vowel; e.g. fr. अस् *as*, 'to be,' comes *a as* = आस् *ás* by 31; fr. आप् *áp*, 'to obtain,' *a áp* = *áp*; fr. इष् *ish*, 'to wish,' *i ish* = *ísh* (see 31).

b. In the second place, with regard to changes of the radical vowel, if the root *end in a consonant*, gunate* the vowel of the radical syllable, if capable of Guṇa (see 28), in 1st, 2nd, and 3rd *sing*. Par.; but leave the vowel unchanged before all other terminations, both Par. and Átm.

c. If the root *end in a simple consonant*, preceded by short *a*, this *a* is lengthened optionally in 1st and necessarily in 3rd sing.; and before the other terminations it is either left unchanged, or is liable to become *e* (see 375. *a*).

d. If the root *end in a vowel*, vriddhi the vowel of the radical syllable in 1st and 3rd *sing*. Par.†, and gunate it in 2nd *sing*. (optionally in 1st sing.) Before all other terminations, Parasmai and Átmane, the root must revert to its original form, but the terminations must be affixed according to euphonic rules‡.

365. Thus, fr. बुध् *budh*, cl. 1, comes the stem of the sing. Parasmai बुबोध् *bubodh*,

---

* The gunation of the vowel is indicated by the P of णप्, थप्, णप्, in the singular terminations. See scheme at 245.

† Vṛiddhi is indicated by the ण् of णप् ṇaP. See scheme at 245.

‡ Greek affords many examples of verbs which suffer a kind of Guṇa or Vṛiddhi change in the Perfect; but this change is not confined to the singular, as in Sanskṛit. Compare λέλοιπα (fr. λείπω, ἔλιπον), πέποιθα (fr. πείθω, ἔπιθον), τέτροφα (fr. τρέφω), τέθεικα (fr. τίθημι), &c.

and the stem of the rest of the tense बुबुध् *bubudh* (1. *bubodh*+*a*=*bubodha*, 2. *bubodh* +*itha*=*bubodhitha*, 3. *bubodh*+*a*=*bubodha*; Du. 1. *bubudh*+*iva*=*bubudhiva*, 2. *bubudh*+*athus*=*bubudhathus*, &c. Átm. 1. *bubudh*+*e*=*bubudhe*, &c.)

Similarly, fr. विद् *vid*, cl. 2, 'to know,' come the two stems विवेद् *vived* and विविद् *vivid* (1. 3. *viveda*; Du. 1. *vividiva*; Pl. 1. *vividima*, &c.*)

From पच्, 'to cook,' the two stems पपाच् *papáć* and पपच् *papać* (1. *papáća* or *papaća*, 3. *papáća*, &c.)

366. Again, fr. कृ *kṛi*, 'to do' (see 684), comes the stem of the 1st and 3rd sing. Par. चकार् *ćakár* (252. *b*), the stem of the 2nd sing. चकर् *ćakar* (which is optionally the stem of the 1st sing. also), and the stem of the rest of the tense चकृ *ćakṛi* (1. *ćakár*+*a*=*ćakára* (or *ćakara*), 2. *ćakar*+*tha*=*ćakartha*, 3. *ćakár*+*a*=*ćakára*; Du. 1. *ćakṛi*+*va*=*ćakṛiva* (369), 2. *ćakṛi*+*athus*=*ćakrathus* by 34. Átm. 1. *ćakṛi* +*e*=*ćakre*; Pl. 2. *ćakṛi*+*ḍhve*=चकृढ्वे. See 684).

a. Observe—The roots enumerated at 390. *a.* reject Guṇa in the 2nd sing.; thus, विज् makes 1. 3. विवेज, but 2. विविजिथ. So कु or कू 'to cry' makes 1. चुकाव or चुकव, 2. चुकुविथ.

367. We have seen at 364. *a.* that if a root, ending in a single consonant, begin with a vowel, this vowel is repeated, and the two similar vowels blend into one long one by 31. But when an initial *i* or *u* is gunated in the sing. Par., then the reduplicated *i* becomes *iy* before *e*, and the reduplicated *u* becomes *uv* before *o*; thus, fr. इष् *ish*, 'to wish,' come the two stems *iyesh* and *ísh* (1. 3. इयेष; Du. 1. ईषिव; see 637); and fr. उख् *ukh*, 'to move,' *uvokh* and *úkh* (1. 3. उवोख; Du. 1. ऊखिव).

a. The same holds good in the root इ *i*, 'to go,' which makes the reduplicated syllable *iy* before the Vṛiddhi and Guṇa of the sing. In the remainder of the tense the stem becomes *iy* (cf. 375. *e*), which is reduplicated into *íy* (1. 3. इयाय, 2. इययिथ or इयेथ; Du. 1. ईयिव). But when the prep. *adhi* is prefixed, the Perf. is formed as if from *gá*, Átm. only (Sing. Du. Pl. 3. *adhijage*, *-jagáte*, *-jagire*).

b. And if a root begin with अ *a*, and end in a *double* consonant, or begin with ऋ *ṛi* and end in a single consonant, the reduplicated syllable is आन् *án*; thus, fr. अर्च् *arć*, 'to worship,' comes the stem आनर्च् *ánarć* (1. 3. आनर्च); fr. ऋध् *ṛidh*, 'to flourish,' comes आनर्ध् *ánardh* (1. 3. आनर्ध; Du. 1. आनृधिव, &c.)

---

* One Greek root agrees very remarkably with the Sanskṛit in restricting Guṇa to the singular, viz. Ϝιδ (εἴδω), 'to know' (= Sk. *vid* above); thus, οἶδα, οἶσθα, οἶδε; ἴστον, ἴστον; ἴσμεν, ἴστε, ἴσασι. Rt. *vid* has a contracted Perf. used for the Present, which agrees exactly with οἶδα; thus, *veda*, *vettha*, &c. See 308. *a.*

c. अश् Átm. 'to pervade,' although ending in a *single* consonant श्, follows the last rule (1. 3. आनशे).

368. Obs.—In the Perfect the 1st and 3rd sing. Par. and Átm. have the same termination, and are generally identical in form; but when Vṛiddhi of a final vowel is required in both, then there is optionally Guṇa in the first; and when a medial *a* is lengthened, this *a* may optionally remain unchanged in the first; thus कृ 'to do' may be in 1st sing. either चकार or चकर, and पच् 'to cook' may be पपाच or पपच in 1st sing.; but in 3rd sing. they can only make चकार and पपाच.

369. By referring back to the scheme at 363, 246, it will be seen that all the terminations of this tense (except optionally the 2nd sing. Par.) begin with vowels. Those which begin with *i* are all (except the 3rd pl. Átm.) distinguished by the mark *, because eight roots only in the language (viz. कृ 'to do†,' भृ 'to bear,' सृ 'to go,' वृ 'to surround,' श्रु 'to hear,' स्तु 'to praise,' द्रु 'to run,' स्रु *sru*, 'to flow') *necessarily* reject the *i* from these terminations.

Some roots, however, optionally reject *i* from these terminations, see क्षम् 371.

Rejection of i *from* itha (*2nd sing. Perfect, Parasmai*).

370. The above eight roots (except वृ *vṛi* when it means 'to cover,' and except कृ *kṛi*, 'to do,' when compounded with the prep. *sam*†) also reject *i* from the 2nd sing. Parasmai.

a. Moreover, the 2nd sing. Parasmai is formed with *tha* instead of *itha* after roots ending in ऋ *ṛi* (except after the root ऋ *ṛi* itself, and वृ *vṛi* and जागृ *jágṛi*, which only allow *itha*; thus, *áritha*, *vavaritha*, *jágaritha*; and except स्वृ at *b*);

b. and optionally with *tha* or *itha* after the root स्वृ *svṛi*, 'to sound' (*sasvartha* or *sasvaritha*);

c. and optionally with *tha* or *itha* after roots ending in आ *á*, ए *e* (except व्ये *vye*, which allows only *itha*), and after roots in ऐ *ai*, ओ *o*, इ *i*, ई *í*, उ *u*, and the root धू 'to shake' (except those indicated at 392, as necessarily inserting *i* in the Futures &c.; e.g. श्रि, which makes *śiśrayitha* only, and so also most roots in ऊ *ú*);

d. and optionally with *tha* or *itha* after those roots enumerated at

† But कृ 'to do,' if स् is inserted after a preposition, as in संस्कृ, does not reject *i*, and follows 374. *k*; thus, 2. संचस्करिथ.

400–414, which have a medial *a*, and which reject *i* either necessarily or optionally from the Futures &c. (e. g. शक्, *śekitha* or *śaśaktha;* क्षम्, *ćakshamitha* or *ćakshantha*, &c.); but not अद् and घस्, which can only make *áditha*, *jaghasitha;*

e. and optionally with *tha* or *itha* after most of the roots enumerated at 415, as optionally inserting *i* in the Futures &c.:

f. but all other roots, which necessarily take *i*, and even most of those (having no medial *a*) at 400–414 which necessarily reject *i* in the Futures &c., must take *itha* only in the 2nd sing. of the Perfect; thus तुद् is तोत्तासि *tottási* in the 2nd sing. 1st Future, but तुतोदिथ *tutoditha* in the 2nd sing. Perfect (Du. 1. *tutudiva*). Some few of these, however, are allowed the alternative of *tha*, as सृज् 'to create' makes ससर्जिथ or सस्रष्ठ; दृश् 'to see,' ददर्शिथ or दद्रष्ठ; both these roots requiring the radical *ṛi* to be changed to र *ra*, instead of gunated, when *tha* is used.

g. मज्ज् 'to dip' and नश् 'to perish,' which belong to 370. *d*, insert a nasal when *tha* is used; thus, ममज्जिथ or ममंक्थ, नेशिथ or ननंष्ठ.

h. तृप् 'to be satisfied' and दृप् 'to be proud,' which belong to 370. *e*, either gunate the radical *ṛi* or change it to र *ra* when *tha* is used (ततर्प्थ or तत्रप्थ or ततर्पिथ).

Obs.—When *tha* is affixed to roots ending in consonants, the rules of Sandhi (296–306) must be applied.

Optional rejection of i, *in certain cases, from the dual and remaining terminations (of the Perfect, Parasmai and Átmane, marked with *).*

371. The roots enumerated at 415, as optionally rejecting or inserting *i* in the Futures &c., may optionally reject it also from the dual and remaining terminations of the Perfect marked with * in the table at 363; thus क्षम् makes चक्षमिव or चक्षण्व, चक्षंसे or चक्षमिषे, चक्षमिवहे or चक्षण्वहे; but the forms with the inserted *i* are the most usual, and all other roots, even those which necessarily reject *i* from the Futures &c. (except the eight enumerated at 369), must take *i* in the dual and remaining terminations of the Perfect marked with *.

Observe—The *i* is never rejected from the 3rd pl. Átmane, except in the Veda.

Substitution of ढ्वे *for* ध्वे *(2nd pl. Perfect, Átmane).*

372. ढ्वे *ḍhve* is used instead of ध्वे *dhve* by the eight roots at 369,

also in certain cases by the roots mentioned at 371. The usual rules of Sandhi must then be observed, as in वव्रश्चिढ्वे from व्रश्च्.

a. इढ्वे for इध्वे may be optionally used by other roots when a semi-vowel or *h* immediately precedes, as लुलुविध्वे or -विढ्वे from लू, चिक्रियिध्वे or -यिढ्वे from क्री.

Anomalies in forming the stem of the Perfect.

373. Roots ending in आ *á* (as दा *dá*, 'to give;' धा *dhá*, 'to place;' या *yá*, 'to go;' स्था *sthá*, 'to stand') drop the *á* before all the terminations except the *tha* of the 2nd sing., and substitute औ *au* for the terminations of the 1st and 3rd sing. Parasmai. Hence, from दा *dá* comes the stem दद् *dad* (1. 3. ददौ, 2. ददिथ or ददाथ; Du. 1. ददिव. Átm. 1. 3. ददे, 2. ददिषे, &c. See 663).

a. दरिद्रा 'to be poor' makes 1. 3. ददरिद्रौ; Du. 3. ददरिद्रतुस्; Pl. 3. ददरिद्रुस्; or more properly takes the periphrastic form of Perfect. See 385.

b. ज्या 'to grow old' has a reduplicated stem जिज्या (1. 3. जिज्यौ, 2. जिज्याथ or जिज्यिथ; Du. 1. जिज्यिव). Similarly, an uncommon root ज्यो Átm. 'to instruct' makes 1. 3. जिज्ये.

c. मि 'to throw,' मी 'to destroy,' 'to perish,' *must* be treated in the sing. as if they ended in *á;* and ली cl. 9, 'to obtain,' *may* optionally be so treated; thus, Sing. 1. ममौ, 2. ममाथ or ममिथ, 3. ममौ; Du. 1. मिम्यिव. But ली is 1. ललौ or लिलाय, 2. ललाथ or ललिथ or लिलेथ or लिलयिथ; Du. 1. लिल्यिव.

d. Most roots ending in the diphthongs ए *e* (except ह्वे, दे, व्ये, वे, &c., see *e. f*), ऐ *ai*, ओ *o*, follow 373, and form their Perfect as if they ended in *á;* thus, धे cl. 1, 'to drink,' 1st and 3rd sing. दधौ, 2. दधिथ or दधाथ, Du. 1. दधिव; गै cl. 1, 'to sing,' 1. 3. जगौ, 2. जगिथ or जगाथ; म्लै cl. 1, 'to fade,' 1. 3. मम्लौ; शो cl. 4, 'to sharpen,' 1. 3. शशौ.

e. But ह्वे 'to call' forms its stem as if from हू, see 595 (1. 3. जुहाव, &c.)

f. दे Átm. 'to pity,' 'to protect,' makes its stem *digi* (1. 3. दिग्ये, 2. दिग्यिषे, &c.)

g. व्ये 'to cover' makes *vivyáy*, *vivyay*, and *vivy* (1. 3. विव्याय, 2. विव्ययिथ; Du. 1. विव्ययिव or विव्यिव, &c.)

h. वे 'to weave' forms its stems as if from *vá* or *vav* or *vay* (1. 3. ववौ or उवाय, 2. वविथ or ववाथ or उवयिथ; Du. 1. वविव or ऊविव or ऊयिव, &c. Átm. 1. 3. ववे or ऊवे or ऊये, &c.)

i. प्यै Átm. 'to be fat' makes regularly पप्ये, पप्यिषे, &c.; but the root प्याय्, meaning the same, and often identified with प्यै, makes पिप्ये, पिप्यिषे, &c.

374. If a root end in इ *i* or ई *í*, this vowel does not blend with the initial *i* of the terminations in du. pl. Parasmai, sing. du. pl. Átmane, but is changed to *y*, in opposition to 31; thus, from चि *ći*, cl. 5, 'to collect,' come the stems *ćićai*, *ćiće*, and *ćići*, changeable to *ćićáy*, *ćićay*, and *ćićy* (1. 3. *ćićáya*, 2. *ćićayitha* or *ćićetha;* Du. 1. चिच्यिव *ćićyiva*, 2. *ćićyathus* by 34. Átm. 1. 3. *ćićye*. See the table at 583). Obs.—चि may also substitute चिकाय for चिचाय and चिक्ये for चिच्ये.

a. Similarly, नी *ní*, 'to lead' (1. 3. *ninдya;* Du. 1. *ninyiva.* Átm. 1. *ninye*, &c.); and ली *lí* (Du. 1. *lilyiva;* Átm. 1. *lilye*).

b. जि *ji*, 'to conquer,' makes its stem जिगि, as if from *gi* (1. 3. जिगाय; Du. 1. जिग्यिव, &c. See 590).

c. हि *hi*, 'to go,' 'to send,' makes जिघि, as if from *ghi* (1. 3. जिघाय).

d. दी Átm. 'to sink,' 'to decay,' makes its stem दिदीय् throughout; thus, 1. 3. दिदीये, 2. दिदीयिषे, &c.

e. But roots ending in इ *i* or ई *í*, and having a double initial consonant, change *i* or *í* to इय् *iy* before all terminations, except those of the sing. Parasmai; hence, from श्रि cl. 1, 'to resort to,' come the three stems *śiśrai, śiśre*, and *śiśriy* (1. 3. शिश्राय, 2. शिश्रयिथ; Du. 1. शिश्रियिव, &c.) So क्री cl. 9, 'to buy' (1. 3. चिक्राय, 2. चिक्रयिथ or चिक्रेथ; Du. 1. चिक्रियिव, &c. See 689).

f. श्वि *śvi*, 'to swell,' like ह्वे at 373. *e*, forms its stem as if from शू, but only optionally; thus, 1. 3. शिश्वाय or शुशाव, 2. शिश्वेथ or शिश्वयिथ or शुशोथ or शुशविथ.

g. And *all roots* ending in उ *u* or ऊ *ú* change *u* or *ú* to उव् *uv* before the terminations of the du. and pl. Parasmai and the whole Átmane (except of course श्रु, स्तु, द्रु, स्रु, in the persons marked with * at 246; and except भू 'to be,' see *i.* below); thus, fr. धू *dhú*, 'to shake,' come the stems *dudhau, dudho*, and *dudhuv* (1. 3. दुधाव, 2. दुधविथ or दुधोथ; Du. 1. दुधुविव. Átm. 1. 3. दुधुवे). Similarly, उ *u*, Átm. 'to sound,' makes 1. 3. ऊवे, 2. ऊविषे.

h. But श्रु makes 1. 3. शुश्राव, 2. शुश्रोथ; Du. 1. शुश्रुव, 2. शुश्रुवथुस्. Átm. 1. 3. शुश्रुवे; and similarly, स्तु, द्रु, and स्रु *sru*.

i. भू 'to be' is anomalous, and makes its stem बभूव् throughout; see 585, 586. So सू 'to bring forth' makes in the Veda ससूव.

j. ऊर्णु 'to cover' (although properly requiring the periphrastic form of Perfect, see 385) is reduplicated into ऊर्णुनु. In the 2nd sing. it may reject Guṇa; thus, ऊर्णुनविथ or ऊर्णुनुविथ, 3rd sing. ऊर्णुनाव; Du. 1. ऊर्णुनुविव, 3. ऊर्णुनुवतुस्; Pl. 3. ऊर्णुनुवुस्.

k. Roots ending in ऋ *ṛi, preceded by a double consonant*, and most roots in long ॠ *ṛí*, instead of retaining this vowel and changing it to *r* by 364. *d*, gunate it into *ar* in the 2nd sing., and throughout the whole tense, except the 1st and 3rd sing. (and even in the 1st there may be optionally Guṇa by 368); e. g. स्मृ *smṛi*, 'to remember,' 1. *sasmára* or *sasmara*, 2. *sasmartha*, 3. *sasmára;* Du. 1. *sasmariva*, &c. Átm. 1. 3. *sasmare.*

l. But धृ *dhṛi*, 'to hold,' not being preceded by a double consonant, makes regularly 1. Sing. Du. Pl. दधार, दध्रिव, दध्रिम.

m. पॄ 'to fill,' शॄ 'to injure,' and दॄ 'to rend,' may *optionally* retain *ṛí*, changeable to *r;* thus, Du. पपरिव or पप्रिव.

n. ऋ *ṛi*, 'to go,' takes Vṛiddhi, and makes its stem आर् *ár* throughout; thus, 1. 3. आर, 2. आरिथ; Du. 1. आरिव.

o. मृ Átm. 'to die,' although properly Átmane, is Parasmai in Perfect; thus, 1. 3. ममार, 2. ममर्थ.

p. जागृ 'to awake,' which properly takes the periphrastic form of Perfect (जागराञ्चकार, see 385), may also take the reduplicated form, and may optionally drop the reduplicated syllable; thus, 1. 3. जजागार or जागार, 2. जजागरिथ or जागरिथ (370. *a*).

q. गृ 'to swallow' may optionally change र् to ल्; thus, जगार or जगाल.

r. तॄ 'to pass' follows 375. *a*, as if it were तर्; thus, 1. 3. ततार, 2. तेरिथ; Du. 1. तेरिव.

s. जॄ 'to grow old' optionally follows 375. *a* (3. जजार, 2. जजरिथ or जेरिथ; Du. 3. जजरतुस् or जेरतुस्).

375. We have already seen, at 364, that roots beginning with any consonant and ending with a single consonant, and enclosing short अ *a*, lengthen this vowel in the 3rd sing. and optionally in the 1st; as, fr. पच् *pać*, 'to cook,' पपाच् *papáć*; fr. *tyaj*, 'to quit,' *tatyáj* (1. 3. *tatyája*, 2. *tatyojitha* or *tatyaktha*; Du. 1. *tatyajiva*, &c.)

a. Moreover, before *itha* and in du. and pl. Parasmai, and all persons of the Átmane, if the initial as well as the final consonant of the root be single, and if the root does not begin with व् *v*, and does not require a substituted consonant in the reduplication, the reduplication is suppressed, and, to compensate for this, the अ *a* is changed to ए *e**; thus, from *pać* come the stems पपाच् *papáć*, *papać*, and पेच् *peć* (1. *papáća* or *papaća*, 2. *pećitha* or *papaktha* by 296, 3. *papáća*; Du. 1. *pećiva*. Átm. 1. 3. *peće*, &c.) Similarly, from लभ् *labh*, cl. 1, Átm. 'to obtain' (cf. λαμβάνω, ἔλαβον), the stem लेभ् *lebh* throughout (*lebhe*, *lebhishe*, *lebhe*, *lebhivahe*, &c.) So नह् *nah*, 'to bind,' makes 1. *nanáha* or *nanaha*, 2. *nehitha* or *nanaddha* by 305, 3. *nanáha*; Du. 1. *nehiva*, &c. Átm. *nehe*, &c.

Similarly, नश् *naś*, 'to perish,' 1. *nanáśa* or *nanaśa*, 2. *neśitha* or *nanaṃshṭha* (ननंष्ठ), 3. *nanáśa*, &c.: see 620, 370. *g*.

b. Roots that require a substituted consonant in the reduplication are excepted from 375. *a* (but not भज् *bhaj* and फल् *phal*, see *g.* below); thus, भण् 'to speak' makes 1. 3. बभाण; Du. 1. बभणिव.

c. वच् 'to speak,' वद् 'to say,' वप् 'to sow,' वश् 'to wish,' वस् 'to dwell,' वह् 'to carry,' beginning with *v*, are also excepted. These require that the reduplicated syllable be उ *u*, or the corresponding vowel of the semivowel, and also change *va* of the root to उ *u* before every termination, except those of the sing. Parasmai, the two *u*'s blending into one long ऊ *ú*; thus, fr. वच् *vać*, 'to speak,' come the two stems उवाच् *uváć* and ऊच् *úć* (1. *uváća* or *uvaća*, 2. *uvaćitha* or *uvaktha*, 3. *uváća*; Du. 3. *úćatus*; Pl. 3. *úćus*).

Obs.—This change of a semivowel to its corresponding vowel is called Samprasáraṇa by native grammarians (Páṇ. 1. 1, 45).

d. वह् *vah*, 'to carry,' changes the radical vowel to ओ *o* before *tha* (see 305. *a*), optionally substituted for *itha* (1. 3. उवाह, 2. उवहिथ or उवोढ). Compare 424.

Obs.—वम् *vam*, 'to vomit,' is excepted from 375. c (thus, 3. *vaváma*, *vavamatus*,

---

* Bopp deduces forms like *pećiva*, from *papaćiva*, by supposing that the second *p* is suppressed, the two *a*'s combined into *á*, and *á* weakened into *e*.

vavamus, Páṇ. vi. 4, 126); it may also, according to Vopadeva, follow 375. *a* (3. *vaváma, vematus, vemus*).

e. यज् *yaj*, 'to sacrifice,' is excepted from 375. *a*, and follows the analogy of 375. *c* (1. 3. *iyája;* Du. 3. *íjatus;* Pl. 3. *íjus*): the 2nd sing. is इयजिथ or इयष्ठ by 297; Átmane 1. 3. ईजे, 2. ईजिषे, see 597. *Yej* is allowed optionally in the weak forms, and optionally in 2nd sing., especially in the Veda.

f. शस् 'to injure' and दद् Átm. 'to give' are excepted from 375. *a* (शशास, शशसिव, ददृदिवहे).

g. भज् 'to honour,' श्रथ् 'to loosen,' त्रप् 'to be ashamed,' फल् 'to bear fruit,' *necessarily* conform to 375. *a*, although properly excepted (thus, भेजिथ, भेजिव, &c.) The following conform to 375. *a. optionally:* फण् 'to go,' स्वन् 'to sound,' (according to some) स्तन् 'to sound,' भ्रम् 'to wander,' वम् 'to vomit,' and (according to some) स्तम् and स्यम् 'to sound,' त्रस् 'to tremble' (thus, पफणिथ or फेणिथ, पफणिथ or फेणिथ, &c.)

h. The following also conform optionally to 375. *a:* ग्रन्थ् 'to tie,' श्रन्थ् 'to loosen,' दम्भ् 'to deceive;' and, when they do so, drop their nasals (thus, जग्रन्थिथ or ग्रेथिथ, जग्रन्थुस् or ग्रेथुस्).

i. The following, although their radical vowel is long, also conform optionally to 375. *a:* राज्, भ्राज् Átm., भ्राश्, and भ्लाश्, all meaning 'to shine' (रराजिव or रेजिव, &c.)

j. राध्, when it signifies 'to injure,' necessarily conforms to 375. *a* (2. रेधिथ; Du. 1. रेधिव, 3. रेधतुस्; Pl. 3. रेधुस्).

k. तॄ 'to pass' follows 375. *a*, and जॄ 'to grow old' may do so. See 374. *r. s.*

376. गम् *gam*, 'to go,' जन् *jan*, 'to be born,' खन् *khan*, 'to dig,' and हन् *han*, 'to kill' (which last forms its Perfect as if from घन् *ghan*), drop the medial *a* before all the terminations, except those of the sing. Par. (cf. the declension of *rájan* at 148). Hence, *gam* makes in sing. du. pl. 3. *jagáma, jagmatus, jagmus; jan* makes *jajána, jajñatus, jajñus; khan* makes *ćakhána, ćakhnatus, ćakhnus;* and *han* makes 1: 3. *jaghána, jaghnatus, jaghnus,* 2. *jaghanitha* or *jaghantha.*

377. घस् *ghas*, 'to eat,' is analogous, making *jaghása, jakshatus, jakshus;* Du. 1. *jakshiva.* See 44 and 70. And in the Veda some other roots follow this analogy; thus, पत् 'to fall' (पप्तिव &c.); तन् 'to stretch' (तत्निषे &c.); भस् 'to eat' (बप्सिव &c.)

378. सञ्ज् 'to adhere,' स्वञ्ज् 'to embrace,' and दंश् 'to bite,' can optionally drop their nasals in du. pl. Parasmai and all the Átmane; thus, ससजिव or ससञ्जिव, सस्वजे or सस्वञ्जे.

379. रध् 'to perish' and जभ् Átm. 'to yawn' may insert a nasal before vowel-terminations (ररन्ध, ररन्धिथ or ररद्ध; Du. 1. ररन्धिव or रेध्व, see 371: 1. 3. जजम्भे).

380. मृज् 'to clean' makes its stem ममार्ज् in sing. Parasmai, and may do so before the remaining terminations (1. 3. ममार्ज, 2. ममार्जिथ or ममार्ष्ठ; Du. 1. ममार्जिव or ममृजिव or ममृज्व, see 651).

381. प्रछ् *praćh*, 'to ask,' makes its stem पप्रछ्* (becoming पप्रच्छ् before a vowel

* This rests on Siddhánta-kaum. 134. Some grammarians make the stem in du. and pl. &c. पपृच्छ्.

by 51) throughout; see 631. भ्रज्ज् *bhrajj*, cl. 6, 'to fry,' makes either बभर्ज्ज् or बभ्रज्ज् throughout. See 632.

a. ऋछ् 'to go' gunates the radical vowel throughout; thus, 1. 3. आनर्छ, 2. आनर्छिथ; Du. 1. आनर्छिव.

382. स्वप् *svap*, 'to sleep,' makes its bases सुष्वाप् and सुषुप्. See 655.

a. ष्ठिव् or ष्ठीव् 'to spit' may substitute त् *t* for ट् *ṭ* in the reduplication; thus, 1. 3. टिष्ठेव or तिष्ठेव, टिष्ठीव or तिष्ठीव.

383. व्यध् 'to pierce,' व्यच् 'to encompass,' 'to deceive,' व्यथ् Átm. 'to be pained,' make their reduplicated syllable *vi*; and the first two roots change *vya* to *vi* before all the terminations, except the sing. Parasmai; thus, from *vyadh* comes sing. du. pl. 3. विव्याध, विविधतुस्, विविधुस्; Átm. विविधे, &c.: from *vyać*, विव्याच, विविचतुस्, विविचुस्: from *vyath*, विव्यथे, विव्यथाते, विव्यथिरे. See 615 and 629.

a. द्युत् cl. 1. Átm., 'to shine,' makes its reduplicated syllable *di* (1. 3. *didyute*).

384. ग्रह् *grah*, cl. 9, 'to take,' makes its stem जग्राह् and जगृह् (S. Du. Pl. 3. जग्राह, जगृहतुस्, जगृहुस्). But sing. 2. जग्रहिथ. See 699.

a. गुह् 'to conceal' lengthens its radical vowel instead of gunating it in the sing. Parasmai, जुगूह, जुगूहिथ, &c.

b. अह् *ah*, 'to say' (only used in Perf.), is defective in sing. du. pl. 1. and pl. 2, and forms 2nd sing. from अत् (2. आत्थ, 3. आह; Du. 2. आहथुस्, 3. आहतुस्; Pl. 3. आहुस्).

c. ब्रू 'to say' has no Perfect of its own, but substitutes either that of वच् (375. *c*) or the above forms from अह्. Again, अद् 'to eat' has a Perfect of its own, but may substitute that of घस् 377. Similarly, अज् 'to drive' (*ago*) may substitute that of वी.

Periphrastic Perfect.

385. Roots which begin with a vowel, long by nature or position (*except the vowel* आ, *as in* आप् '*to obtain,*' 364. *a*, *and in* आञ्छ् '*to stretch;*' *and roots having an initial* अ *before two consonants*, 367. *b*), and all roots of more than one syllable (*except* ऊर्णु '*to cover,*' 374. *j; and except optionally* जागृ '*to awake,*' 374. *p*, *and* दरिद्रा '*to be poor,*' 373. *a*), form their Perfects by adding आम् *ám* to the root or stem (which generally gunates its last vowel if ending in *i*, *u*, *ṛi*, short or long), and affixing the Perfect of one of the auxiliary verbs, अस् *as*, 'to be;' भू *bhú*, 'to be;' कृ *kṛi*, 'to do.'

a. This *ám* may be regarded as the acc. case of a feminine abstract noun formed from the verbal stem. With चकार it becomes आञ्चकार or आंचकार by 59. Thus, ईश्, 'to rule,' makes 1st and 3rd sing. ईशामास or ईशाम्बभूव or ईशाञ्चकार; the last might be translated 'he made ruling,' and in the former cases the acc. may be taken adverbially. So also, चकास्, 'to shine,' makes चकासाञ्चकार 'he made shining.'

Obs.—The stem with *ám* may sometimes be separated from the auxiliary verb; e.g. तं पातयां प्रथमम् आस 'first he caused him to fall' (Raghu-v. IX. 61), and प्रभ्रंशयां यो नहुषं चकार (Raghu-v. XIII. 36).

b. When the Átmane inflexion has to be employed, कृ only is used; thus, ईड् Átm., 'to praise,' makes 1st and 3rd sing. ईडाञ्चक्रे 'he made praising or praised.'

c. Roots of cl. 10 also form their Perfect in this way, the syllable *ám* blending with the final *a* of the stem; thus, from चुर् *ćur*, cl. 10, 'to steal,' *ćorayámása*, 'I have or he has stolen.'

d. Also all Derivative verbs, such as Causals, Desideratives, and Frequentatives. See 490, 504, 513, 516.

e. Also the roots अय् *ay*, 'to go;' दय् *day*, Átm. 'to pity;' आस् *ás*, Átm. 'to sit;' कास् *kás*, 'to cough,' 'to shine' (कासाञ्चक्रे &c.); see Páṇ. III. 1, 37. 35.

And optionally the roots भी *bhí*, cl. 3, 'to fear' (बिभाय or बिभयाञ्चकार); ह्री *hrí*, cl. 3, 'to be ashamed' (जिह्राय or जिह्रयाञ्चकार); भृ *bhṛi*, cl. 3, 'to bear' (बभार or बिभराञ्चकार); हु *hu*, cl. 3, 'to sacrifice' (जुहाव or जुहवाञ्चकार); विद् *vid*, cl. 2, 'to know' (विवेद or विदाञ्चकार); उष् *ush*, cl. 1, 'to burn' (उवोष or ओषाञ्चकार).

f. The roots कम् Átm., गुप्, धूप्, विछ्, पण्, पन्, whose peculiarity of conjugational form is explained at 271, and ऋत् Átm. 'to blame,' may optionally employ a Periphrastic Perfect, not derived from the root, but from the conjugational stem; thus, चकमे or कामयाञ्चक्रे, जुगोप or गोपायाञ्चकार, दुधूप or धूपायाञ्चकार, विविच्छ or विच्छायाञ्चकार, पेणे or पणायाञ्चकार (according to Vopa-deva पणायाञ्चक्रे), पेने or पनायाञ्चकार, आनर्त or ऋतीयाञ्चक्रे.

g. Observe—Stems ending in *i*, *u*, or *ṛi*, short or long, are generally gunated before *ám*; but दीधी 'to shine' and वेवी 'to go' make दीध्याञ्चक्रे, वेव्याञ्चक्रे, &c.

386 *First and Second Future.*

Terminations of First Future repeated from 246.

Parasmai.			Átmane.		
tásmi	*tásvas*	*tásmas*	*táhe*	*tásvahe*	*tásmahe*
tási	*tásthas*	*tástha*	*táse*	*tásáthe*	*tádhve*
tá	*tárau*	*táras*	*tá*	*tárau*	*táras*

Terminations of Second Future repeated from 246.

syámi	*syávas*	*syámas*	*sye*	*syávahe*	*syámahe*
syasi	*syathas*	*syatha*	*syase*	*syethe*	*syadhve*
syati	*syatas*	*syanti*	*syate*	*syete*	*syante*

Obs.—The First Future results from the union of the Nom. case of the noun of agency (formed with the suffix तृ *tṛi*, see 83) with the Present tense of the verb अस् *as*, 'to be;' thus, taking दातृ *dátṛi*, 'a giver' (declined at 127), and combining its Nom. case with अस्मि *asmi* and हे *he*, we have *dátásmi* and *dátáhe*, 'I am a giver,' identical with the 1st pers. sing. Par. and Átm. of the 1st Fut., 'I will give.' So also *dátási* and *dátáse*, 'thou art a giver,' or 'thou wilt give.' In the 1st and 2nd persons du. and pl. the sing. of the noun is joined with the du. and pl. of the auxiliary. In the 3rd pers. the auxiliary is omitted, and the 3rd sing. du. and pl. of the 1st Fut. in both voices is then identical with the Nom. case sing. du. and pl. of the noun of agency; thus, *dátá*, 'a giver,' or 'he will give;' *dátárau*, 'two givers,' or 'they two will give,' &c. *

Hence this tense is sometimes called the Periphrastic Future.

387. The terminations of the Second Future appear also to be derived from the verb अस् joined, as in forming the Passive and 4th class, with the *y* of root या 'to go,' just as in English we often express the Future tense by the phrase 'I am going.'

388. Rule for forming the stem in verbs of the first nine classes.

Gunate the vowel of the root (except as debarred at 28, and except in certain roots of cl. 6, noted at 390, 390. *a*) throughout all the persons of both First and Second Future; and in all roots ending in consonants (except those enumerated at 400–414), and in a few ending in vowels (enumerated at 392), insert the vowel इ *i* between the root so gunated, and the terminations.

389. Thus, from जि *ji*, cl. 1, 'to conquer,' comes the stem जे *je* (1st Fut. *je*+*tásmi*=जेतास्मि, &c.; Átm. *je*+*táhe*=जेताहे. 2nd Fut. *je*+*syámi*=जेष्यामि, &c.; Átm. *je*+*sye*=जेष्ये, by 70). Similarly, from श्रु *śru*, cl. 5, 'to hear,' comes the stem श्रो *śro* (1st Fut. *śro*+*tásmi*=श्रोतास्मि, &c.; 2nd Fut. *śro*+*syámi*=श्रोष्यामि, &c.)

a. So also, from बुध् *budh*, cl. 1, 'to know,' comes the stem बोधि *bodhi* (1st Fut. *bodhi*+*tásmi*=बोधितास्मि, &c.; Átm. *bodhi*+*táhe*=बोधिताहे. 2nd Fut. *bodhi*+*syámi*=बोधिष्यामि, &c.; Átm. *bodhi*+*sye*=बोधिष्ये).

390. The roots ending in उ *u* and ऊ *ú* of cl. 6, forbidding Guṇa, are कु or कू 'to call out,' गु or गू 'to void excrement,' ध्रु or ध्रू 'to be firm,' नु or नू 'to praise,' धू 'to shake.' These generally change their final *ú* to *uv*; thus, कुविताहे &c. from कू, but कुताहे &c. from कु; गुवितास्मि &c. from गू, but गुतास्मि &c. from गु.

a. The roots ending in consonants of cl. 6, *not gunated*, are कुच् 'to contract,' गुज् 'to sound,' कुट् 'to make crooked,' पुट् 'to resist,' चुट् or छुट् 'to cut,' तुट् 'to quarrel,' त्रुट् 'to break,' पुट् 'to embrace,' मुट् or मुड् or तुड् 'to pound,' स्फुट् 'to burst in pieces,' लुट् 'to roll,' कुड् 'to play,' क्रुड् or ब्रुड् 'to be immersed,' खुड्, चुड्, छुड्, पुड्, घुड्, बुड्, थुड्, स्थुड्, स्थुड्, स्फुड्, all meaning 'to cover,' गुड् 'to guard,' घुड् 'to hinder,' जुड् 'to bind,' तुड् 'to strike,' पुड् 'to emit,' लुड् 'to adhere,' हुड् 'to collect,' डिप् 'to throw,' गुर् Átm. 'to make effort,' छुर् 'to cut,' स्फुर् or स्फुल् 'to vibrate,' ध्रुव् 'to be firm,' 'to go,' कृड् 'to eat,'—nearly all uncommon as verbs. To these must be added विज् cl. 7, 'to tremble.'

* The future signification inherent in the noun of agency *dátá*, seems implied in Latin by the relation of *dator* to *daturus*.

b. ऊर्णु 'to cover' may either gunate its final or change it to *uv* (ऊर्णवितास्मि or ऊर्णुवितास्मि, ऊर्णविष्यामि or ऊर्णुविष्यामि).

c. दीधी A'tm. 'to shine,' वेवी A'tm. 'to go,' drop their finals before the inserted *i* (दीधिताहे &c.) Similarly, दरिद्रा 'to be poor' (दरिद्रितास्मि &c., दरिद्रिष्यामि &c.)

d. Roots in ए *e*, ऐ *ai*, ओ *o*, change their finals to *á;* thus, ह्वे 'to call' (ह्वातास्मि, ह्वास्यामि).

e. मि 'to throw,' मी 'to perish,' and दी A'tm. 'to decay,' *must* change, and ली 'to obtain' may optionally change their finals to *á* (मातास्मि, मास्यामि, &c.; दाताहे, &c.; लेतास्मि or लातास्मि, &c.; लेष्यामि or लास्यामि, &c.) Compare 373. *c.*

f. Roots containing the vowel *ṛi*, as सृप् 'to creep,' मृश् 'to handle,' स्पृश् 'to touch,' कृप् 'to draw,' are generally gunated, but may optionally change the vowel *ṛi* to र *ra;* thus, सर्प्तास्मि or स्रप्तास्मि &c., सर्प्स्यामि or स्रप्स्यामि &c.

g. Reversing this principle, भ्रज्ज् 'to fry' may make either भ्रष्टास्मि or भर्ष्टास्मि &c., भ्रक्ष्यामि or भर्क्ष्यामि &c.

h. The alternative is not allowed when *i* is inserted; thus, तृप् 'to be satisfied' makes तर्प्तास्मि or त्रप्तास्मि, but only तर्पितास्मि. Similarly, दृप् 'to be proud.'

i. सृज् 'to let go,' 'to create,' and दृश् 'to see,' necessarily change *ṛi* to *ra;* thus, स्रष्टास्मि, स्रक्ष्यामि, &c.; द्रष्टास्मि, द्रक्ष्यामि, &c.

j. मृज् 'to rub,' 'to clean,' takes Vṛiddhi instead of Guṇa (मार्जितास्मि or मार्ष्टास्मि).

k. मस्ज् 'to be immersed,' and नश् 'to perish' when it rejects *i*, insert a nasal; thus, मंक्तास्मि, मंक्ष्यामि, &c.; नंष्टास्मि, नंक्ष्यामि, &c.; but नशितास्मि &c., नशिष्यामि &c.

l. कम् A'tm., गुप्, धूप्, विछ्, पण्, पन्, ऋत्, at 385. *f*, may optionally carry their peculiar conjugational form into the Futures (कमिताहे or कामयिताहे, गोप्तास्मि or गोपितास्मि or गोपायितास्मि, विच्छितास्मि or विच्छायितास्मि, अर्तिताहे or ऋतीयिताहे, &c.)

m. गुह् 'to conceal' lengthens its vowel when *i* is inserted. See 415. *m.*

n. अस् 'to be,' ब्रू and चक्ष् 'to speak,' have no Futures of their own, and substitute those of भू, वच्, and ख्या respectively; अद् 'to eat' may optionally substitute the Futures of घस्, and अज् 'to drive' of वी (अजितास्मि or वेतास्मि &c.) Cf. 384. *c.*

o. The rules at 296–306 must, of course, be applied to the two Futures; thus, नह् 'to tie' makes नत्स्यामि &c. See 306. *b.*

Observe—The above rules apply generally to the Aorist, Precative (A'tmane), and Conditional, as well as to the two Futures.

RULES FOR INSERTION OR REJECTION OF इ *i* IN THE LAST FIVE TENSES AND DESIDERATIVE.

391. These rules do not apply to form II of the Aorist at 435, nor to the Parasmai of the Precative at 442, which can never insert *i*.

a. The insertion of the vowel *i* (called an *ágama* or 'augment,' and technically styled *iṭ*) before the terminations of the General tenses constitutes one of the most important and intricate subjects of Sanskṛit Grammar. The manifest object of this inserted *i*—which can never be gunated or vriddhied, but may occasionally be lengthened into *í*—is to take the place of the *conjugational vowel*, and prevent the coalition of consonants. Hence it is evident that roots ending in vowels do not properly require the inserted *i*. Nevertheless, even these roots often insert it; and if it were always inserted after roots ending in consonants, there would be no difficulty in forming the last five tenses of the Sanskṛit verb.

Unfortunately, however, its insertion is forbidden in about one hundred roots ending in consonants, and the combination of the final radical consonant with the initial *t* and *s* of the terminations will require a knowledge of the rules already laid down at 296–306.

We now proceed to enumerate, 1st, with regard to roots ending in vowels; 2ndly, with regard to roots ending in consonants: A. those inserting *i*; B. those rejecting *i*; C. those optionally inserting or rejecting *i*. As, however, it is more important to direct attention to those roots (whether ending in vowels or consonants) which reject *i*, the paragraphs under B. will be printed in large type.

Obs.—In the following lists of roots the 3rd sing. will sometimes be given between brackets, and the roots will be arranged generally *in the order of their final vowels and consonants.*

Note that if the 1st Future reject इ *i*, it is generally rejected in form I of Aorist, in Átmane-pada of Precative, in Conditional, Infinitive, Past Passive Participle, Indeclinable Past Participle, Future Participle formed with the suffix *tavya*, and noun of agency formed with the suffix *tṛi*; and often (though not invariably) decides the formation of the Desiderative form of the root by *s* instead of *ish*. So that the learner may always look to the 1st Future as his guide. For example, taking the root *kship*, 'to throw,' and finding the 1st Fut. to be *ksheptásmi*, he knows that *i* is rejected. Therefore he understands why it is that the 2nd Fut. is *kshepsyámi*; Aor. *akshaipsam*; Átmane of Precative, *kshipsíya*; Cond. *akshepsyam*; Infin. *ksheptum*; Past Pass. Part. *kshipta*; Indecl. Part. *kshiptvá*; Fut. Part. *ksheptavya*; noun of agency, *ksheptṛi*; Desid. *ćikshipsámi*. On the other hand, taking root *yáć*, 'to ask,' and finding the 1st Fut. to be *yáćitá*, he knows that *i* is inserted, and therefore the same parts of the verb will be *yáćishyámi*, *ayáćisham*, *yáćishíya*, *ayáćishyam*, *yáćitum*, *yáćita*, *yáćitvá*, *yáćitavya*, *yáćitṛi*, *yiyáćishámi*, respectively.

A. *Roots ending in Vowels* inserting इ i (*except as indicated at* 391).

392. Five in इ *i* and ई *í*, viz. श्रि 'to resort to' (श्रयिता, श्रयिष्यति), श्वि 'to swell,' डी 'to fly,' शी 'to lie down,' स्मि 'to smile' (in Desid. alone).

a. Six in उ *u*, viz. क्षु 'to sneeze,' क्ष्णु 'to sharpen,' नु 'to praise,' यु 'to join,'

रु 'to sound,' स्नु *snu*, 'to drip' (the last only when Parasmai; when inflected in Átm., it may reject *i*).

Obs.—स्तु 'to praise,' and सु 'to pour out,' in the Aorist Parasmai.

b. All in ऊ *ú*, as भू 'to be' (भविता, भविष्यति), except सू and धू (which optionally reject *i*), and except in the Desiderative. See 395, 395. *a.*

c. All in short ऋ *ṛi*, in the 2nd Future and Conditional, &c., but not in the 1st Future, as कृ 'to do' (करिष्यति, but कर्ता).

d. Two in short ऋ *ṛi* (viz. वृ 'to choose' and जागृ 'to awake') also in 1st Future (वरिता, वरिष्यति, जागरिता, &c.)

e. All in long ॠ *ṛí*, as तॄ 'to pass' (तरिता, तरिष्यति).

393. Observe—वृ 'to choose,' and all roots in long ॠ *ṛí*, may optionally lengthen the inserted *i*, except in Aorist Parasmai and Precative Átmane (वरिता or वरीता, वरिष्यति or वरीष्यति, तरिता or तरीता, &c.) See 627, note *.

B. *Roots ending in Vowels* rejecting इ i.

394. All in आ *á*, as दा 'to give' (दाता, दास्यति).

a. Nearly all in इ *i* and ई *í*, as जि 'to conquer,' नी 'to lead' (जेता, जेष्यति, &c.)

b. Nearly all in short उ *u*, as श्रु 'to hear' (श्रोता, श्रोष्यति).

c. Those in long ऊ *ú* generally in the Desiderative only.

d. All in short ऋ *ṛi* (except वृ) in the 1st Future only, as कृ 'to do' (कर्ता, but करिष्यति). See 392. *c.*

e. All in ए *e*, ऐ *ai*, ओ *o*. See 390. *d.*

C. *Roots ending in Vowels* optionally *inserting or rejecting* इ i, *either in all the last five tenses and Desiderative, or in certain of these forms only.*

395. सू or सु cl. 2, 4, Átm. 'to bring forth' (सोता or सविता, सोष्यते or सविष्यते).

a. धू 'to shake' (धविता or धोता, धविष्यति or धोष्यति, &c., but *i* must be inserted in Aor. Par., see 430), पू 'to purify,' optionally in Desid. only (पुपूष्, पिपविष् Átm.)

b. प्यै Átm. 'to grow fat' (प्याता and प्यायिता, प्यास्यते and प्यायिष्यते; but necessarily inserts *i* in Desid.)

c. ऋ 'to go,' स्तृ or स्तॄ 'to spread,' 'to cover,' and स्वृ 'to sound,' all in 1st Fut., and the latter two optionally in Desid. also (अर्ता, अरिता or (?) अरीता; स्तर्ता, स्तरिता or स्तरीता; स्वर्ता or स्वरिता; तिस्तीर्षति or तिस्तरिषति or तिस्तरीषति; सिस्वरिषति or सुस्वूर्षति).

396. दरिद्रा 'to be poor' optionally in Desid. (दिदरिद्रास् or दिदरिद्रिष्).

397. All roots in long ॠ *ṛí* optionally in Desid., as तॄ makes तितरिषति or तितीर्षति.

398. श्रि, यु, भृ, वृ, optionally in Desiderative. Compare 392.

A. *Roots ending in Consonants* inserting इ i.

399. As a general rule, all roots ending in ख् *kh*, ग् *g*, घ् *gh*, झ् *jh*, ट् *ṭ*, ठ् *ṭh*, ड् *ḍ*, ढ् *ḍh*, ण् *ṇ*, त् *t*, थ् *th*, फ् *ph*, ब् *b*, य् *y*, र् *r*, ल् *l*, व् *v*; thus, लिख् 'to write' makes लेखिता, लेखिष्यति, &c.; वल्ग् 'to leap' makes वल्गिता, वल्गिष्यति.

a. ग्रह् 'to take' lengthens the inserted *i* in all the last five tenses, except Prec. Parasmai (ग्रहीता, ग्रहीष्यति), see 699. It rejects *i* in Desid.

B. *Roots ending in Consonants* rejecting इ i.

Obs.—The rules at 296–306 must in all cases be applied. When a number is given after a root, it indicates that the root only rejects *i* if conjugated in the class to which the number refers. When a number is given between brackets, this refers to the rule under which the root is conjugated.

400. One in क् *k*.—शक् 5. 'to be able' (शक्ता, शक्ष्यति 679).

401. Six in च् *ć*.—पच् 'to cook' (पक्ता, पक्ष्यति); वच् 'to speak' (650); रिच् 7. 'to make empty' (रेक्ता, रेक्ष्यति); विच् 7. 3. 'to separate;' सिच् 'to sprinkle;' मुच् 'to loosen' (628).

402. One in छ् *ćh*.—प्रछ्* 'to ask' (प्रष्टा, प्रक्ष्यति 631).

403. Fifteen in ज् *j*.—त्यज् 'to quit' (596); भज् 'to honour;' यज् 'to sacrifice' (597); भ्रस्ज्† 6. 'to fry' (632); मस्ज् 'to be immersed' (633); भञ्ज् 'to break' (669); रञ्ज् 'to colour,' 'to be attached;' सञ्ज् 'to adhere' (597. *a*); स्वञ्ज् 'to embrace;' निज् 'to cleanse' (नेक्ता, नेक्ष्यति); विज्‡ 3. 'to tremble' (वेक्ता, &c.); भुज् 6. 'to bend,' 7. 'to enjoy' (668. *a*); युज् 'to join' (670); रुज् 'to break' (रोक्ता, &c.); सृज् 'to create,' 'to let go' (625).

404. One in त् *t*.—वृत् 'to be,' 'to turn,' but only in 2nd Fut. Par., Cond. Par., Aor. Par., Desid. Par. (This root is generally Átm. and inserts *i*, 598.)

405. Fourteen in द् *d*.—अद् 'to eat' (652); पद् 'to go' (पत्ता, पत्स्यते); शद् 'to perish;' सद् 'to sink;' स्कन्द् 1. Parasmai, 'to leap;' हद् 'to void excrement;' खिद् 'to be troubled' (खेत्ता, &c.); छिद् 'to cut' (667); भिद् 'to break' (583); विद् 7. 'to reason,' 4. 'to be,' 'to exist,' 6. 'to find;' स्विद् 4. 'to sweat;' क्षुद् 'to pound' (क्षोत्ता, क्षोत्स्यति); तुद् 'to strike' (634); नुद् 'to impel.'

406. Thirteen in ध् *dh*.—बन्ध् 'to bind' (692); व्यध् 'to pierce' (615); राध् 'to accomplish' (राद्धा, रात्स्यति); साध् 5. 'to accomplish;' सिध् 4. 'to be accomplished' (616); क्रुध् 'to be angry' (क्रोद्धा, क्रोत्स्यति); क्षुध् 'to be hungry;'

---

* प्रछ् inserts *i* in the Desiderative.

† भ्रस्ज् optionally inserts *i* in the Desiderative.

‡ When विज् belongs to cl. 7, it takes *i*; as, विजिता, विजिष्यति. See 390. *a*.

बुध् 4. A'tm. 'to be aware' (614)*; युध् A'tm. 'to fight;' रुध् 'to obstruct' (671); शुध् 'to be pure;' वृध् 'to increase,' only in 2nd Fut. Par., Cond. Par., Aor. Par.; शृध् 'to break wind,' only in 2nd Fut. Par., Cond. Par., Aor. Par. (both these last insert *i* throughout the A'tmane).

407. Two in न् *n*.—मन् 4. A'tm. 'to think' (617); हन् 'to kill' (654), but the last takes *i* in 2nd Fut. and Conditional.

408. Eleven in प् *p*.—तप् 'to burn' (तप्ता, तप्स्यति); वप् 'to sow;' शप् 'to curse;' स्वप् 'to sleep' (655); आप् 'to obtain' (681); क्षिप् 'to throw' (635); तिप् A'tm. 'to distil;' लिप् 'to anoint;' छुप् 'to touch' (छोप्ता, छोप्स्यति); लुप् 6. 'to break' (लोप्ता, लोप्स्यति); सृप् 'to creep' (390. *f*).

409. Three in भ् *bh*.—यभ् 'to lie with carnally' (यब्धा, यप्स्यति); रभ् A'tm. 'to desire' (with आ 'to begin,' 601. *a*); लभ् A'tm. 'to obtain' (601).

410. Five in म् *m*.—गम् 'to go' (602), but takes *i* in 2nd Fut. and Cond.; नम् 'to bend' (नन्ता, नंस्यति); यम् 'to restrain;' रम् A'tm. 'to sport;' क्रम् 'to walk' in the A'tmane (क्रन्ता, क्रंस्यते).

411. Ten in श् *ś*.—दंश् 'to bite' (दंष्टा, दंक्ष्यति); दिश् 6. 'to point out' (583); विश् 'to enter' (वेष्टा, वेक्ष्यति); रिश् 'to hurt;' लिश् 'to become small;' क्रुश् 'to cry out' (क्रोष्टा, क्रोक्ष्यति); रुश् 6. 'to hurt;' दृश् 1. 'to see' (390. *i*, 604, द्रष्टा, द्रक्ष्यति); मृश् 'to handle' (390. *f*); स्पृश् 6. 'to touch' (390. *f*, 636, स्प्रष्टा, स्प्रक्ष्यति).

412. Eleven in ष् *sh*.—त्विष् 'to shine' (त्वेष्टा, त्वेक्ष्यति); द्विष् 'to hate' (657); पिष् 7. 'to pound;' विष् 'to pervade;' शिष् 7. 'to distinguish' (672); श्लिष् 4. 'to embrace' (301, 302); तुष् 4. 'to be satisfied' (तोष्टा, तोक्ष्यति); दुष् 4. 'to be sinful;' पुष् 4. 'to be nourished†' (पोष्टा, पोक्ष्यति); शुष् 4. 'to become dry' (शोष्टा, शोक्ष्यति); कृष् 'to draw' (390. *f*, 606).

413. Two in स् *s*.—घस् 'to eat' (घस्ता, घत्स्यति); वस् 1. 'to dwell' (607) ‡.

414. Eight in ह् *h*.—दह् 'to burn' (610); नह् 'to tie' (624); वह् 'to carry' (611); दिह् 'to anoint' (659); मिह् 'to make water' (मेढा 305. *a*, मेक्ष्यति); लिह् 2. 'to lick' (661); दुह् 2. 'to milk' (660) ‖; रुह् 'to ascend' (रोढा, रोक्ष्यति).

---

* When बुध् belongs to cl. 1, it inserts *i*.

† When पुष् belongs to cl. 9, it takes *i* (पोषितुम्, पोषिष्यति).

‡ Except in the Past Pass. and Indecl. Participles उषित and उषित्वा (607). वस् cl. 2. A'tm. 'to put on,' 'to wear,' inserts *i* (वसितुम्, वसिष्यते).

‖ दुह् cl. 1, 'to afflict,' inserts *i* (दोहिता, &c.)

C. *Roots ending in Consonants* optionally *inserting or rejecting* इ i, *either in all the last five tenses and Desiderative, or in certain of these forms only.*

Obs.—When no tenses or forms are specified, the option applies to all except to form II of the Aorist and the Precative Parasmai, which can never insert *i*.

415. Two in च् *c*.—तञ्च् or तञ्ज् 7. 'to contract;' व्रश्च् 'to cut' (630).

a. Three in ज् *j*.—अञ्ज् 7. 'to anoint' (668, but necessarily inserts *i* in Desid.); मृज् 'to clean' (390. *j*, 651); भ्रज्ज् 'to fry' (optionally in Desid. only, necessarily rejects *i* in other forms).

b. Four in त् *t*.—पत् 'to fall' (optionally in Desid. only; necessarily inserts *i* in Futures and Cond., and rejects it in Aor.); कृत् 6. 'to cut' (optionally in 2nd Fut., Cond., and Desid.; necessarily inserts *i* in 1st Fut. and Aor.); चृत् 'to kill' (optionally in 2nd Fut., Cond., and Desid.; necessarily inserts *i* in 1st Fut. and Aor.); नृत् 'to dance' (optionally in 2nd Fut. and Desid., necessarily inserts *i* in 1st Fut. and Aor.)

c. Four in द् *d*.—स्यन्द् 'to flow' (optionally in all forms except 2nd Fut. and Cond. Par., and Desid. Par., where *i* is necessarily rejected); क्लिद् 'to be wet,' छृद् 'to shine,' and तृद् 'to injure' (the last two optionally in all forms except 1st Fut., which necessarily inserts *i*).

d. Three in ध् *dh*.—रध् 'to perish;' सिध् 1. 'to restrain;' ऋध् 'to prosper' (the last optionally in Desid. only, necessarily inserts *i* in other forms, see 680).

e. Two in न् *n*.—तन् 'to stretch' and सन् 'to honour' (both optionally in Desid. only, necessarily insert *i* in other forms, see 583).

f. Five in प् *p*.—त्रप् 'to be ashamed;' गुप् 1. 'to defend;' तृप् 4. 'to be satisfied' (618); दृप् 4. 'to be proud;' कृप् 'to be capable' (when it rejects *i*, it is Parasmai only).

g. Two in भ् *bh*.—लुभ् 4. 'to desire' (optionally in 1st Fut., necessarily inserts *i* in other forms *); दम्भ् 'to deceive' (optionally in Desid. only, दिदम्भिषति or धिप्सति or धीप्सति, necessarily inserts *i* in other forms).

h. One in म् *m*.—क्षम् 1. 4. 'to bear' (क्षमिता or क्षन्ता, क्षमिष्यते, -ति, or क्षंस्यते, -ति).

i. All in इव् *iv* (but only optionally in Desid.); as, दिव् 'to play,' ष्ठिव् 'to spit,' सिव् 'to sew.'

j. Two in य् *y*.—चाय् 'to honour;' प्याय् or स्फाय् 'to be fat' (but both necessarily insert *i* in Desid., compare 395. *b*).

k. Three in श् *ś*.—अश् 5. Ātm. 'to pervade †' (but necessarily inserts *i* in Desid., see 681. *a*); नश् 4. 'to perish' (see 390. *k*, and 620); क्लिश् 9. 'to torment' (697).

l. Seven in ष् *sh*.—अक्ष् 'to pervade;' तक्ष् 'to form by cutting,' 'to carve' (तक्षिता or तष्टा, तक्षिष्यति or तक्ष्यति, &c.); त्वक्ष् 'to create;' कुष् with निर् 'to extract' (otherwise necessarily inserts *i*); इष् 6. 'to wish' (637); रिष् 'to injure;' रुष् 1. 'to

---

* Except the Aorist, following form II at 435.

† अश् cl. 9, 'to eat,' inserts *i*.

injure' (the last three optionally in 1st Fut., but necessarily insert *i* in other forms).

m. Twelve in ह् *h.*—सह् Átm. 'to bear' (optionally in 1st Fut. only, necessarily inserts *i* in other forms, see 611. *a*); ग्लह् 'to gamble' (ग्लहिता or ग्लाढा, &c.); गाह् 'to penetrate;' माह् 'to measure' (माहिता or माढा, &c.); स्निह् *snih*, 'to love' (स्नेहिता or स्नेग्धा or स्नेढा, &c.); स्नुह् *snuh*, 'to love,' 'to vomit;' मुह् 'to be perplexed' (612); गुह् 'to conceal' (गूहिता or गोढा, गूहिष्यति or घोक्ष्यति, see 306. *a*, 390. *m*); द्रुह् 'to seek to injure' (623); तृह् 6. 7. or तृंह् 6. 'to kill' (674); वृह् or बृह् 'to raise;' स्तृह् or स्तृंह् 6. 'to kill.'

Aorist (Third Preterite).

This complex and multiform tense, the most troublesome and intricate in the whole Sanskṛit verb, but fortunately less used in classical Sanskṛit than the other past tenses, is not so much one tense, as an aggregation of several, all more or less allied to each other, and all bearing a manifest resemblance to the Imperfect.

416. Grammarians assert that there are seven different varieties of the Sanskṛit Aorist, four of which correspond more or less to the Greek 1st Aorist, and three to the 2nd Aorist, but we shall endeavour to shew that all these varieties may be included under two distinct forms of terminations given in the table at 246, and again below, and at 435.

417. Form I is subdivided like the terminations of all the last five tenses into (A) those which reject *i*, and (B) those which assume it; A belongs to many of those roots at 394, 400–414, which reject *i*; B to most of those at 392, 399, which insert it: but in the latter case the initial *s* becomes *sh* by 70, and in the 2nd and 3rd sing. the initial *s* is rejected, the *i* blending with the *í*, which then becomes the initial of those terminations. Moreover, in the case of roots which insert *i* the stem is formed according to rules different from those which apply in the case of roots which reject *i*.

a. Form II at 435 resembles the terminations of the Imperfect, and belongs, in the first place, to some of those roots rejecting *i*, whose stems in the Imperfect present some important variation from the root (see 436); in the second, to certain of the roots rejecting *i*, which end in श् *ś*, ष् *sh*, or ह् *h*, and which have *i*, *u*, or *ṛi*, for their radical vowel (see 439); in the third, to verbs of cl. 10 and Causals.

FORM I.

418. The terminations are here repeated from 246.

A. *Terminations without* इ i.

PARASMAI.			ÁTMANE.		
1. *sam*	*sva*	*sma*	*si*	*svahi*	*smahi*
2. *sís*	*stam* [*tam*]	*sta* [*ta*]	*sthás* [*thás*]	*sáthám*	*dhvam* or *ḍhvam*
3. *sít*	*stám* [*tám*]	*sus*	*sta* [*ta*]	*sátám*	*sata*

B. *Terminations with* इ i.

PARASMAI.			ÁTMANE.		
1. *isham*	*ishva*	*ishma*	*ishi*	*ishvahi*	*ishmahi*
2. *ís*	*ishṭam*	*ishṭa*	*ishṭhás*	*isháthám*	*idhvam* or *iḍhvam*
3. *ít*	*ishṭám*	*ishus*	*ishṭa*	*ishátám*	*ishata*

419. Observe—The brackets in the A terminations indicate the rejection of initial *s* from those terminations in which it is compounded with *t* and *th*, if the stem ends in any consonant except a nasal or semivowel, or in any *short* vowel such as *a*, *i*, *u*, or *ṛi*. Observe also, that initial *s* is liable to become *sh* by 70, in which case a following *t* or *th* is cerebralized. The substitution of *ḍhvam* for *dhvam* and *iḍhvam* for *idhvam*, in certain cases, is explained in the table at 246.

420. General rule for forming the stem for those verbs of the first nine classes which reject इ *i* and so take the A terminations.

Obs. 1. The augment अ *a* must always be prefixed, as in the Imperfect; but it will be shewn in the Syntax at 889, that when the Aorist is used as a prohibitive Imperative, after the particle *má* or *má sma*, the augment is then rejected. See 242. *a*.

Obs. 2. When a root begins with the vowels इ *i*, उ *u*, or ऋ *ṛi*, short or long, the augment is prefixed in accordance with 251. *a*.

In Parasmai, if a root end in either a vowel or a consonant, vriddhi the radical vowel before *all* the terminations.

In Átmane, if a root end in इ *i*, ई *í*, उ *u*, or ऊ *ú*, gunate the radical vowel; if in ऋ *ṛi* or any consonant, leave the vowel unchanged before *all* the terminations. Final consonants must be joined to the A terminations according to the rules propounded at 296–306.

a. Thus, from नी 'to lead' come the two stems *anai* for Parasmai and *ane* for Átmane (*anai*+*sam*=अनैषम् by 70; Átm. *ane*+*si*=अनेषि, *ane*+*sthás*=अनेष्ठास्, &c.)

b. From कृ cl. 8, 'to make,' come the two stems *akár* for Parasmai and *akṛi* for Átmane (*akár*+*sam*=अकार्षम् by 70, &c.; Átm. *akṛi*+*si*=अकृषि by 70, *akṛi*+*thás*=अकृथास् by 419, *akṛi*+*ta*=अकृत, &c.) See 682.

Similarly, भृ cl. 3, 'to bear.' See the table at 583.

c. So, from युज् 'to join' come the two stems *ayauj* for Parasmai and *ayuj* for A'tmane (Par. *ayauj+sam*=अयौक्षम् by 296, *ayauj+sva*=अयौक्ष्व, *ayauj+tam*=अयौक्तम् by 419; A'tm. *ayuj+si*=अयुक्षि by 296, *ayuj+thás*=अयुक्थास्, *ayuj+ta*=अयुक्त).

d. From रुध् cl. 7, 'to hinder,' the stems *araudh* and *arudh* (Par. *araudh+sam*=अरौत्सम् by 299, Du. *araudh+sva*=अरौत्स्व, *araudh+tam*=अरौद्धम्; A'tm. *arudh+si*=अरुत्सि, *arudh+thás*=अरुद्धास्, &c.)

e. Similarly, from पच् 'to cook' come the stems *apáć* and *apać* (*apáć+sam*=अपाक्षम् by 296; A'tm. *apać+si*=अपक्षि, *apać+thás*=अपक्थास्, &c.)

f. From दह् 'to burn' (610), the stems *adáh* and *adah* (*adáh+sam*=अधाक्षम् by 306. *a*, *adáh+tam*=अदाग्धम् by 305; A'tm. *adah+si*=अधक्षि by 306. *a*, *adah+thás*=अदग्धास्, &c.)

421. By referring to 391. *b*. it will be easy to understand that most roots in *i*, *í*, short *u*, and short *ṛi*, take the A terminations. Most of those in *á*, *e*, *ai*, *o*, do so *in the A'tmane*, and a few of those in *á* also in the Parasmai.

a. स्तॄ or स्तृ 'to spread' takes either A or B; and in A'tmane when it takes A, changes *ṛí* to *ír*. See 678.

b. वॄ or वृ 'to choose,' 'to cover,' changes its vowel to *úr*, under the same circumstances. See 675.

c. Roots in *e*, *ai*, *o*, change these vowels to *á* as in the other General tenses; thus, from व्ये 'to cover,' अव्यासिषम् &c. (see 433), अव्यासि &c. Similarly, मि, मी, दी, and optionally ली, see 390. *e* (अमासिषम् &c., अमासि &c.)

d. दा 'to give' (see 663), धा 'to place' (see 664), स्था 'to stand' (see 587), दे 'to protect,' धे 'to drink' (if in A'tm.), दो or दा 'to cut' (if in A'tm.), change their finals in the A'tmane to *i* (अदिषि, अदिथास् 419, अदित, अदिष्वहि; 2nd pl. अदिढ्वम्). In Parasmai they follow 438.

e. गा used for इ 'to go,' with अधि prefixed, signifying 'to go over,' 'to read' (A'tmane only), changes its final to *í* (अध्यगीषि, -गीष्ठास्, -गीष्ट, &c.)

f. कु A'tm. 'to cry out,' गु 'to void excrement,' and ध्रु 'to be firm,' all cl. 6, preserve their vowels unchanged (अकुषि, &c.; अकुथास्, अकुत, &c.; अगुषम्, &c.); ध्रु may also make अध्रौषम्, and गु may also make अगुविषम्, but the latter root is then generally regarded as गू.

422. The following roots of those rejecting *i*, enumerated at 400–414, take the A terminations only, both for Par. or A'tm.: पच्; मुच्; त्यज्, भज्, भञ्ज्, भ्रज्ज्, मज्ज्, यज्, रञ्ज्, सञ्ज्, स्वञ्ज् A'tm., भुज्, रुज्, सृज्; पद् A'tm., हद् A'tm., खिद्, तुद्, नुद्; बन्ध्, व्यध्, राध्, साध्, युध् 4. A'tm., युध्; मन् 4. A'tm.; तप्, वप्, शप्, स्वप्, क्षिप्, तिप् A'tm., लुप्; यभ्, रभ्, लभ्; दंश्; वस्; दह्, नह्, वह्.

a. The following take in Par. either the A terminations of form I or optionally form II; but in A'tm. usually the A form of I, sometimes form II: रिच्, विच् 3, निज्, विज् 3, स्कन्द्, छिद्, भिद्, क्षुद्, रुध्, दृश्, मृश्, स्पृश्, कृष्.

b. The following take in Par. only form II; but in A'tm. the A form of I, or sometimes the B form of I: शक् (A'tm. doubtful), सिच्, मुच्, विद् 6. 'to find' (A'tm. doubtful), 4. 7. (only A'tm.), शद्, सद्, क्लिद्, स्विद् 4, रध्, सिध् 4, कुप्, क्षुप्, हन् (see

424. *b*; वध् with the B terminations is generally used for Par., but अहनत् occurs in Epic poetry), आप्, लिप्, लुप्, सृप्, गम्, घस्.

423. The following of those inserting or rejecting *i*, enumerated at 415, take either the A or B terminations: तञ्च् or तञ्ज्, व्रश्च्, मृज्, स्यन्द् generally Átm. only, सिध्, क्लप् Átm., गुप्, क्लृप् Átm., तृप्, दृप् (the last three in Par. take also form II), क्षम् generally Átm. (may also follow form II in Par.), प्याय् (or प्यै) Átm., अञ्ज्, अक्ष्, गृह्, गाह्, माह्, तृंह्.

424. The rules at 296–306 must in all cases be applied, as well as the special rules applicable to certain roots in forming the Futures at 390 and 390. *a–o*; thus, व्रश्च् makes अव्राक्षम् by 297. *b* (see 630); मज्ज् makes अमाङ्क्षम् by 390. *k* (see 633); नश् in Átm., अनङ्क्षि or अनशिषि; भ्रज्ज्, अभ्राक्षम् or अभार्क्षम्, अभ्रक्षि or अभर्क्षि by 390. *g*; मृज्, अमार्क्षम् by 390. *j* (also अमार्जिषम्); नह्, अनात्सम् by 306. *b*.

a. पद् Átm. 'to go,' बुध् Átm. 'to awake,' जन् Átm. 'to be born,' may form their 3rd sing. as if they were Passive verbs (see 475); thus, अपादि, Du. 3. अपत्साताम्; अबोधि (or optionally अबुद्ध), Du. 3. अभुत्साताम्; अजनि (or optionally अजनिष्ट).

b. Roots ending in न् and म् must change these letters to Anusvára before *s*, and म् becomes न् before ध्व; thus, मन् makes अमंसि, अमंस्थास्, अमंस्त (or if in cl. 8. अमनिष्ट, or by *c.* below अमत); यम् makes अयंसि &c., Du. 2. अयन्ध्वम्.

हन् (generally Par.) drops its nasal before the Átmane terminations (अहसि, अहथास्, &c.; initial *s* being rejected according to 419).

गम् does so optionally (अगंसि or अगसि, अगंस्थास् or अगथास्, &c.)

c. Roots in न् and ण् of cl. 8, which properly take the B terminations, are allowed an option of dropping the nasal in 2nd and 3rd sing. Átm., in which case initial *s* is rejected (419); e. g. तन् makes 3. अतनिष्ट or अतत (Páṇ. II. 4, 79).

d. Similarly, क्षण् makes 3. अक्षणिष्ट or अक्षत; and ऋण्, आर्णिष्ट or आर्त.

e. सन् 'to give' is allowed the option of lengthening the *a*, when *n* is dropped; thus, Sing. 2. असाथास् or असनिष्ठास्, 3. असात or असनिष्ट. Compare 354. *a*, 339 (Páṇ. II. 4, 79).

f. The nasal of दंश् 'to bite' becomes ङ् before क् and ण् before ड्; thus, अदाङ्क्षम्, Du. 2. अदांष्टम्; Átm. 1. अदङ्क्षि, Du. 2. अदण्ड्ढम्. See 303.

425. वह् 'to carry' (see 611) changes its radical vowel to ओ *o* before those terminations which reject an initial *s* by 305. *a*; thus, *avákSham, avákshís, avákshít* (Lat. *vexit*), *avákshva, avoḍham*, &c.; Átm. *avakshi* (Lat. *vexi*), *avoḍhás, avoḍha*.

a. सह् Átm., 'to bear,' generally takes the B terminations (*asahishi*, &c.), though the form असोढ is also given for the 3rd sing.

426. नह् 'to tie,' 'to fasten,' makes *anátsam, anátsís, anátsít, anátsva, anáddham*, &c.; and Átm. *anatsi, anaddhás*, &c., by 306. *b* (compare 183).

a. वस् 'to dwell' (see 607) makes *avátsam*, &c., by 304. *a*.

427. General rule for forming the stem for those verbs of the first nine classes which assume *i*, and so take the B terminations at 418.

a. If a root end in the vowels इ *i*, ई *í*, उ *u*, ऊ *ú*, ऋ *ṛi*, ॠ *ṛí*, vriddhi those vowels in the Parasmai before *all* the terminations, and gunate them in the A'tmane.

Thus, from पू 'to purify' come the two stems *apau* for Parasmai and *apo* for A'tmane (*apau*+*i*+*sam*=अपाविषम् by 37, *apau*+*i*+*ís*=अपावीस्, *apau*+*i*+*ít*= अपावीत्, &c.; A'tm. *apo*+*i*+*si*=अपविषि, &c., by 36), see 583.

From तॄ cl. 1, 'to cross,' comes the stem *atár* for Parasmai (*atár*+*i*+*sam*= अतारिषम्, &c.)

So, from शी 'to lie down' comes अशयिषि, अशयिषाताम्, &c.; but roots ending in any other vowel than *ú* and long *ṛí* more frequently take the A terminations, as they generally reject *i*.

b. If a root end in a single consonant, gunate the radical vowel in both Parasmai and A'tmane (except as debarred at 28, and except in the roots enumerated at 390. *a*).

Thus, बुध् *budh*, cl. 1, 'to know,' makes its stem *abodh* (*abodhisham*, &c.) See 583.

वृत् *vṛit*, 'to be,' makes *avart* (*avartishi*, &c.)

एध् *edh*, 'to increase,' makes *aidh* (*aidhishi*, &c., 251. *b*). See 600.

428. A medial *a* in roots ending in र् and ल् is lengthened in Parasmai, but not in A'tmane.

Thus, चर् 'to go' makes अचारिषम्; ज्वल् 'to blaze,' अज्वालिषम्. The roots वद् 'to speak' and व्रज् 'to go' also lengthen the *a* in Parasmai (अवादिषम्; but not in A'tmane अवदिषि &c.)

a. But those in म्, य्, ह् never lengthen the *a* in Parasmai; thus, स्यम् 'to sound' makes अस्यमिषम्. The following roots also are debarred from lengthening the *a*: कख्, कग्, रग्, लग्, सग्, स्थग्, ह्रग्, ह्लग्, कट्, क्षण्, चत्, क्षप्, पथ्, मथ्, चट्, वध्, श्वस्, हस्. One or two do so optionally; as, कण् and नद् 'to sound.'

429. Observe, that as the majority of Sanskṛit verbs assume *i*, it follows that rule 427. *a*. *b*. will be more universally applicable than rule 420, especially as the former applies to the Aorist of Intensives, Desideratives, and Nominals, as well as to that of simple verbs.

430. The special rules for the two Futures at 390. *a–o* will of course hold good for the Aorist; thus the roots enumerated at 390 and 390. *a* (कुच् &c.) forbid Guṇa; and गू, धू, धु, नू generally change their finals to *uv* (अकुविषम् &c., अगुविषम् &c.); but when गू is written गु it makes अगुषम् &c., see 421. *f*, and धू may also make अधाविषम्, and नू, अनाविषम्.

a. ऊर्णु makes और्णाविषम् or और्णविषम् or और्णुविषम् &c., and in A'tmane और्णविषि or और्णुविषि.

b. According to 390. *c*. दीधी, वेवी, and दरिद्रा drop their finals (अदीधिषि, अदरिद्रिषम्, &c.; see also 433).

431. In the A'tmane, वृ 'to choose,' 'to cover,' and all roots in long ॠ *ṛí*, such

as स्तॄ 'to spread,' may optionally lengthen the inserted *i*; thus, अवरिषि or अवरीषि &c., अस्तरिषि or अस्तरीषि; but in Parasmai only अवारिषम्, अस्तारिषम्.

432. श्वि 'to swell' and जागृ 'to awake' take Guṇa instead of Vṛiddhi (अश्वयिषम् &c., see also 440. *a*; अजागरिषम् &c.)

a. ग्रह् according to 399. *a.* makes अग्रहीषम्, and by 390. *m.* गुह् makes अगूहिषम्. The latter also conforms to 439 and 439. *b.* See 609.

b. हन् 'to kill' forms its Aorist from वध् (अवधिषम् &c.), but see 422. *b.*

433. Many roots in आ *á*, ए *e*, ओ *o*, and ऐ *ai*, with three in म् *m*, viz. यम् *yam*, रम् *ram*, नम् *nam*, assume *i*, but *in the Parasmai* insert *s* before it; final *e*, *o*, and *ai*, being changed to आ *á*; thus, from या 'to go' comes अयासिषम्, &c. (see 644); from शो 'to sharpen,' अशासिषम्, &c.; from यम् 'to restrain,' अयंसिषम्, &c.

दरिद्रा 'to be poor' makes *adaridrisham* or *adaridrásisham*, &c.

434. In the Átmane these roots reject the *i* and the *s* which precedes it, and follow 418; thus, from मा 'to measure' comes अमासि, &c. (see 664. *a*); from व्ये 'to cover,' अव्यासि (see 421. *c*); from रम् 'to sport,' अरंसि, अरंस्थास्, अरंस्त, &c.

Form II.

435. Resembling the Imperfect.

	Parasmai.			Átmane.	
1. *am*	*áva* [*va*]	*áma* [*ma*]	*e* [*i*]	*ávahi*	*ámahi*
2. *as* [*s*]	*atam* [*tam*]	*ata* [*ta*]	*athás*	*ethám* [*áthám*]	*adhvam*
3. *at* [*t*]	*atám* [*tám*]	*an* [*us*]	*ata*	*etám* [*átám*]	*anta*

436. No confusion arises from the similarity which this form bears to the Imperfect, as in all cases where the above terminations are used for the Aorist, the Imperfect presents some difference in the form of its stem; thus, गम् 'to go' makes *agaććham* for its Impf., *agamam* for its Aor. (see 602); भिद् 'to break' makes *abhinadam* for its Impf., *abhidam* for its Aor. (see 583). So again, cl. 6, which alone can shew a perfect identity of root and stem, never makes use of this form for its Aorist, unless by some special rule the stem of its Imperfect is made to differ from the root; thus, लिप् 'to smear' (cf. ἀλείφω), which makes *alipam* in Aor., is *alimpam* in its Impf.; see 281. (So in Gr., cf. Impf. ἔλειπον with 2nd Aor. ἔλιπον; ἐλάμβανον with ἔλαβον; ἐδάμνην with ἔδαμον, &c.)

Obs.—This form of the Sanskṛit Aorist corresponds to Gr. 2nd Aor. (cf. *asthám*, *asthás*, *asthát*, with ἔστην, ἔστης, ἔστη), and the first form is more or less analogous to the 1st Aor. The substitution of *i* for *e*, and *áthám*, *átám*, for *ethám*, *etám*, in Átm. of form II, is confined to a class of roots mentioned at 439.

437. Rule for forming the stem in verbs of the first nine classes. Prefix the augment, and as a general rule attach the terminations directly to the root.

Thus, in *agamam* &c., *abhidam* &c., see 436. So also, नश् 'to perish' makes अनशम् (also अनेशम्, see 441, 424).

a. Observe, however, that most of the roots which follow this form in Par., follow form I at 418 in Átm.; thus, भिद् 'to break' makes *abhitsi*, &c., in Átm.; see the table at 583: similarly, छिद् 'to cut,' see 667. And a few roots, which are properly restricted to Átm., have a Parasmai Aorist of this 2nd form; thus, रुच् Átm. 'to shine,' 'to be pleasing,' makes Par. *arućam*, as well as Átm. *arocishi*.

b. One or two roots in आ *á*, इ *i*, and ए *e* reject their finals; and one or two in ऋ *ṛi* and ॠ *ṛí* gunate these vowels before the above terminations; thus, ख्या 'to tell' makes अख्यम् &c., अख्ये &c.; श्वि 'to swell,' अश्वम्; ह्वे 'to call' makes अह्वम् (see 595); सृ 'to go,' असरम्; ऋ 'to go,' आरम्; जॄ 'to grow old,' अजरम्.

c. दृश् 'to see' gunates its vowel (अदर्शम्, see 604).

d. Penultimate nasals are generally dropped; thus, स्तम्भ् 'to stop' makes अस्तभम्; स्यन्द् 'to distil,' अस्यदम्; स्कन्द् 'to mount,' अस्कदम्; भ्रंश् 'to fall,' अभ्रशम्.

e. A form अघसम् occurs in the Veda, from घस् 'to eat,' the medial *a* being dropped.

438. In the Parasmai certain roots ending in long आ *á* and ए *e* conform still more closely to the terminations of the Imperfect, rejecting the initial vowel, as indicated by the brackets in the table at 435. In the 3rd pl. they take *us* for *an*.

Thus, दा cl. 3, 'to give,' makes *adám, adás, adát, adáva*, &c.; 3rd pl. *adus*, see 663. So also, धा cl. 3, 'to place,' makes *adhám*, &c., 664; and स्था cl. 1, 'to stand,' makes *asthám*, &c., 587.

a. Similarly, भू cl. 1, 'to be,' except 1st sing. and 3rd pl. (अभूवम्, अभूस्, अभूत्, अभूव, &c.; but 3rd pl. अभूवन्, see 585).

b. Observe, however, that some roots in *á*, like *yá*, 'to go,' follow 433.

c. And some roots in ए *e* and ओ *o*, which follow 433, optionally follow 438; in which case *e* and *o* are changed as before to *á*; thus, धे *dhe*, cl. 1, 'to drink,' makes either *adhásisham* &c., or *adhám* &c., also *adadham*, see 440. *a*; सो *so*, cl. 4, 'to come to an end,' makes either *asásisham* or *asám*, see 613.

d. In the Átmane-pada, roots like दा, धा, स्था, दे, धे, दो follow 421. *d*.

e. इ 'to go' makes its Aorist from a root गा; thus, *agám, agás*, &c.

Note—*Adadám*, Impf. of *dá*, 'to give,' bears the same relation to its Aor. *adám* that ἐδίδων does to ἔδων. So also the relation of *adhám* (Aor. of *dhá*, 'to place') to *adadhám* (Impf.) corresponds to that of ἔθην to ἐτίθην. Cf. also *abhavas* and *abhús* with ἔφυες and ἔφυς.

439. Certain roots ending in श् *ś*, ष् *sh*, ह् *h*, enclosing a medial *i*, *u*, or *ṛi*, form their Aorists according to form II at 435; but whenever confusion is likely to arise between the Imperfect and Aorist, *s* is prefixed to the terminations, before which sibilant the final of the root becomes *k* by 302 and 306.

Thus, दिश् 'to point out,' the Impf. of which is अदिशम्, makes अदिक्षम् &c. in Aor. (cf. Gr. 1st Aor. ἔδειξα). Similarly, द्विष् cl. 2, 'to hate,' makes *adviksham* &c., 657; दुह् cl. 2, 'to milk,' makes अधुक्षम् *adhuksham* &c., by 306. *a*. See 660.

a. This class of roots substitutes *i* for *e*, and *áthám, átám*, for *ethám, etám*, in

Átmane terminations; thus, *adikshi, adikshathás, adikshata, adikshávahi, adikshá-thám*, &c.; 3rd pl. *adikshanta*.

b. A few roots in ह् *h* (viz. लिह्, दिह्, गुह्, दुह्) optionally in the Átmane reject the initial *a* from the terminations of the 2nd and 3rd sing., 1st du., and 2nd pl.; thus, लिह् may make अलिक्षि, अलीढास्, अलीढ; Du. 1. अलिह्वहि; Pl. 2. अलीढ्वम्, 661: and दुह् 'to milk,' अधुक्षि, अदुग्धास्, &c. See 661, 659, 609, 660.

c. According to some authorities, a few roots (e. g. तृप्, दृप्, सृप्) which generally follow form I, A, in Átmane, may optionally conform to form II, taking the terminations *i, áthám, átám*, rejecting initial *a* and *á* from the other terminations, and taking *ata* for *anta*; thus, *atṛipi, atṛipthás, atṛipta, atṛipvahi*, &c.

440. Causal verbs and verbs of cl. 10 make use of form II, but the stem assumes both reduplication and augment (as in the Greek Pluperfect); thus, बुध् cl. 1, 'to know,' makes in the Causal Aorist अबूबुधम्, &c. This will be explained at 492.

a. A few Primitive verbs besides those of cl. 10 take a reduplicated stem, analogous to Causals (see 492).

Thus, श्रि 'to resort to' makes अशिश्रियम् &c.; श्वि 'to swell' makes अशिश्वियम् (also अश्वम् and अश्वयिषम्, see 432, 437. *b*); द्रु cl. 1, 'to run,' अदुद्रुवम्; स्रु 'to flow,' असुस्रुवम्; धे 'to drink,' अदधम्; कम् 'to love,' अचकमे, &c. This last is defective when it belongs to cl. 1, having no Special tenses; but when it belongs to cl. 10 (Pres. कामये, &c.) its Aorist is अचीकमे.

441. The following Primitive verbs take a contracted form of reduplicated stem: वच् cl. 2, 'to speak,' makes अवोचम् *avoćam* (from अवउचम् for अववचम् 650); पत् cl. 1, 'to fall,' अपप्तम् (from अपपतम्; compare Gr. ἔπιπτον); शास् cl. 2, 'to rule,' अशिषम् (from अशिशासम्, but the Átmane follows 427; see 658); अस् cl. 4, 'to throw,' आस्थम् (from आससम्, contracted into आस्सम् for आसम् 304. *a*, whence by transposition आस्थम्); नश् cl. 4, 'to perish,' अनेशम् (from अनइशम् for अननिशम्). See 620, 436.

Precative or *Benedictive.*

Terminations of Precative repeated from 246.

Parasmai.			Átmane.		
yásam	*yásva*	*yásma*	*síya*	*sívahi*	*símahi*
yás	*yástam*	*yásta*	*sishṭhás*	*síyástham*	*sídhvam* or *síḍhvam*
yát	*yástám*	*yásus*	*sishṭa*	*síyástám*	*síran*

442. The terminations of this tense resemble those of the Potential in the scheme at 245. In 2nd and 3rd sing. they are identical. In the other persons of the Parasmai a sibilant is inserted, and in some of the Átmane, both prefixed and inserted. In 2nd pl. Átm. *síḍhvam* is used for *sídhvam* when immediately preceded by any other vowel but *a* or *á*, and optionally *ishíḍhvam* for *ishídhvam* when immediately preceded by a semivowel or *h*. The only difference between the Potential

and Precative of verbs of the 2nd and 3rd groups, at 290, will often be that the Potential will have the conjugational characteristic; thus, *bhid*, cl. 7, 'to break,' will be *bhindyát* in Pot., and *bhidyát* in Prec. (Compare the Optative of the Gr. Aor. δοίην with Optative of the Present διδοίην.)

443. Rule for forming the stem in verbs of the first nine classes.

In Parasmai, as a general rule, either leave the root unchanged before the *y* of the terminations, or make such changes as are required in the Passive (see 465–472), or by the conjugational rule of the 4th class, and never insert *i*.

In Átmane, as a general rule, prefix *i* to the terminations in those roots ending in consonants or vowels which take *i* in the Futures (see 392, 399), and before this *i* gunate the radical vowel. Gunate it also in the Átmane in some roots ending in vowels which reject *i*: but if a root end in a *consonant*, and *reject i*, the radical vowel is generally left unchanged in the Átmane, as well as Parasmai.

444. Thus, from भू cl. 1, 'to be,' come the stem of the Parasmai *bhú*, and the stem of the Átmane *bhavi*, by 36. *a* (*bhú* + *yásam* = भूयासम् &c., *bhavi* + *síya* = भविषीय by 70).

445. Frequently, as already observed, before the *y* of the Parasmai terminations, the root is liable to changes analogous to those which take place before the *y* of cl. 4 at 272, and the *y* of Passive verbs at 465; and not unfrequently it undergoes changes similar to those of the Perfect at 373, &c., as follows:—

446. A final आ *á* is changed to ए *e* in Par., but remains unchanged in Átm., as before the *s* of the 2nd Future terminations; thus, दा cl. 3, 'to give,' makes देयासम् &c. for Par., but दासीय &c. for Átm.; पा 'to drink' makes पेयासम् &c.

a. But ज्या 'to become old' makes जीयासम् &c., and दरिद्रा 'to be poor' drops its final even in Parasmai (दरिद्र्यासम्, दरिद्रिषीय, &c.) Compare 390. *c*.

447. Final इ *i* and उ *u* are lengthened in Par., as before the *y* of Passives, and gunated in Átm., as before the *s* of the 2nd Future; thus, चि 'to gather' makes चीयासम् &c., चेषीय &c.; and हु 'to sacrifice' makes हूयासम् &c., होषीय &c.

a. When इ 'to go' is preceded by a preposition, it is not lengthened (इयासम् &c.; otherwise ईयासम्).

b. दीधी and वेवी drop their finals as at 390. *c* (दीधिषीय &c.)

448. Final ऋ *ṛi* is changed to रि *ri* in Parasmai, but retained in Átmane; thus, कृ 'to do' makes क्रियासम् &c., and कृषीय &c. After a double consonant *ṛi* is gunated in Parasmai, as well as before inserted *i*; thus, स्तृ 'to spread' makes स्तर्यासम् &c., स्तृषीय &c., or स्तरिषीय &c.

a. It is also gunated in ऋ *ṛi*, 'to go,' and जागृ 'to awake' (अर्यासम्, जागर्यासम्, &c.)

b. वृ 'to cover,' 'to choose,' makes व्रियासम् or वूर्यासम्, वृषीय or वरिषीय or वूर्षीय.

449. Final ऋ *ṛi* is changed to ईर् *ír* in both voices, but is gunated before inserted *i* in Átmane; thus, तॄ cl. 1, 'to cross,' makes तीर्यासम् &c., तीर्षीय &c., or तरिषीय &c., or तरीषीय &c.

a. One root, पॄ cl. 10, 'to fill,' makes पूर्यासम् &c. Compare 448. *a.*

450. Of roots in ए *e*, धे 'to drink' makes धेयासम् &c. (which is also the Precative of धा 'to hold'); दे 'to protect,' देयासम्.

a. But ह्वे 'to call' makes हूयासम् &c., and ह्वासीय &c.; व्ये 'to cover' makes वीयासम् &c., and व्यासीय &c.; and वे 'to weave' makes ऊयासम् &c., and वासीय &c. Compare 465. *c.*

451. Final ऐ *ai* and ओ *o* are often treated like final *á* at 446; thus गै 'to sing' makes गेयासम् &c.; सै 'to waste' and सो 'to destroy' make सेयासम्; दो 'to cut,' like दा 'to give' and दे 'to protect,' makes देयासम्. But sometimes they are changed to *á*; thus, त्रै 'to preserve' makes त्रासीय &c.; दै 'to purify' makes दायासम्; ध्यै 'to think' either ध्यायासम् or ध्येयासम्; ग्लै 'to be weary' either ग्लायासम् or ग्लेयासम्.

452. As already stated, if a root end in a consonant, there is no change in Parasmai, except the usual changes before *y*; moreover, unlike the 2nd Future, there is no Guṇa in Átmane, *unless the root take i*; the other changes in Átmane are similar to those applicable before the *s* of the 2nd Future terminations (390. *o*); thus, दुह् 'to milk' makes दुह्यासम् &c., and धुक्षीय &c., by 306. *a*; द्विष् 'to hate' makes द्विष्यासम् &c., and द्विक्षीय &c., by 302; and बुध् 'to know' makes बुध्यासम् &c., and बोधिषीय &c. See 443.

a. Roots of the 10th class, however, retain Guṇa in Par., as well as in Átm., rejecting the conjugational *aya* in Par. only; see under Causals (495).

453. According to the usual changes in cl. 4 and in Passives, roots ending in a double consonant, of which the first member is a nasal, generally reject the nasal; thus, भञ्ज् *bhañj*, cl. 7, makes *bhajyásam*, &c. Compare 469.

a. So again, according to 472, ग्रह् 'to take' makes in Par. गृह्यासम् &c.; प्रछ् 'to ask,' पृच्छ्यासम् &c.; भ्रज्ज् 'to fry,' भृज्ज्यासम् (632); व्रश्च् 'to cut,' वृश्च्यासम् (636); व्यध् 'to pierce,' विध्यासम्; व्यच् 'to deceive,' विच्यासम्; शास् 'to teach,' शिष्यासम् &c. In the Átmane they are regular.

b. So again, इ *i* and उ *u* before *r* and *v* are lengthened; thus, कुर् 'to sound' makes कूर्यासम्; and दिव् 'to play,' दीव्यासम्. Compare 466.

454. वच् 'to speak,' वद् 'to say,' वप् 'to sow,' वश् 'to wish,' वस् 'to dwell,' वह् 'to carry,' and स्वप् 'to sleep,' substitute उ *u* for व *va* in Par., and यज् 'to sacrifice' substitutes *i* for *ya*; thus, उच्यासम्, सुप्यासम्, इज्यासम्, &c.; cf. 471. In the Átmane they are regular; as, वक्षीय from वह्; यक्षीय from यज्.

a. जन्, खन्, and सन् conform to 470; thus, जन्यासम् or जायासम् &c.; cf. 424. *e.*

Observe—In addition to these rules, the other special changes which take place before the *s* of the 2nd Future terminations, noted at 390 and 390. *a–o*, will apply to the Átmane of the Precative; thus, कु or कू at 390 makes कुषीय or कुविषीय; भ्रज्ज् at 390. *g.*

makes भक्षीय or भक्षीय; कम् at 390. *l.* makes कामयिषीय or कमिषीय; and गुप् may be गुप्यासम् or गोपाय्यासम् even in Parasmai.

Conditional.

Terminations of Conditional repeated from 246.

Parasmai.			Átmane.		
syam	*syáva*	*syáma*	*sye*	*syávahi*	*syámahi*
syas	*syatam*	*syata*	*syathás*	*syethám*	*syadhvam*
syat	*syatám*	*syan*	*syata*	*syetám*	*syanta*

455. **Observe, that this tense bears the same relation to the 2nd Future that the Imperfect does to the Present. In its form it is half an Imperfect, half a 2nd Future. It resembles the Imperfect in prefixing the augment अ *a* to the stem (see 251), and in the latter part of its terminations: it resembles the 2nd Future in the first part of its terminations in gunating the radical vowel, in inserting इ *i* in exactly those roots in which the Future inserts *i*, and in the other changes of the stem.**

456. The Conditional is most easily formed from the 2nd Future (388–415) by prefixing the augment *a* and changing *syámi* (*shyámi*) into *syam* (*shyam*); e.g. *karishyámi, akarishyam.*

457. Thus, बुध् cl. 1, 'to know,' makes अबोधिष्यम् &c.; दुह् 'to milk' makes अधोक्ष्यम् &c. (see 414 and 306. *a*); द्विष् 'to hate,' अद्वेक्ष्यम् &c. (see 412); गुह् 'to conceal,' अगूहिष्यम् or अघोक्ष्यम् (415. *m*); मज्ज् 'to be immersed,' अमंक्ष्यम् (390. *k*).

a. The augment will be prefixed to roots beginning with vowels according to the rules given at 251; thus, ऊर्णु 'to cover' makes और्णुविष्यम् or और्णविष्यम्, cf. 390. *b.*

b. इ 'to go,' with अधि prefixed (meaning 'to read'), may optionally form its Conditional from the root गा (अध्येष्ये or अध्यगीष्ये, see 421. *e*).

Infinitive.

458. The termination of the Infinitive is तुम् *tum* (= the *tum* of the Latin Supine). It is used as a verbal noun with the force of the accusative or dative case.

Obs.—The suffix *tum* is probably the accusative of the suffix *tu* (see 82. VIII), of which other cases are used as Infinitives in the Veda.

459. Rule for forming the stem in verbs of the ten classes.

The stem of the Infinitive is identical with the stem of the First Future, and where one inserts इ *i*, the other does also; thus, *budh*, cl. 1, 'to know,' makes बोधितुम् *bodhitum*; क्षिप् *kship*, cl. 6, 'to throw,' makes क्षेप्तुम् *ksheptum.* Moreover, all the rules for the change of the root before the *t* of the Future terminations apply equally before the *t* of the Infinitive. Hence, by substituting *um* for the final *á* of the 3rd pers. sing. of the 1st Future, the Infinitive is at once obtained.

Thus, शक्ता, शक्तुम्; प्रष्टा, प्रष्टुम्; सोढा, सोढुम्; कथयिता, कथयितुम्. So also, दुह् makes दोग्धुम्; द्रुह्, द्रोढुम् or द्रोग्धुम् or द्रोहितुम्; कुच्, कुचितुम्. See 388–415.

a. In the Veda, Infinitives are also formed by the suffixes तवे, तवै, तोस्, स्यै, से, असे, अध्यै, अम्, ए, ऐ, अस्, which are really cases of verbal nouns (see 867. *a. b*).

b. The following examples will shew how remarkably the Sanskṛit Infinitive answers to the Latin Supine. S. स्थातुम् 'to stand,' L. *statum;* S. दातुम् 'to give,' L. *datum;* S. पातुम् 'to drink,' L. *potum;* S. एतुम् 'to go,' L. *itum;* S. स्तर्तुम् 'to strew,' L. *stratum;* S. अंक्तुम् 'to anoint,' L. *unctum;* S. जनितुम् 'to beget,' L. *genitum;* S. स्वनितुम् 'to sound,' L. *sonitum;* S. सर्प्तुम् 'to go,' L. *serptum;* S. वमितुम् 'to vomit,' L. *vomitum.*

DERIVATIVE VERBS.

460. Having explained the formation of the verbal stem in the ten classes of Primitive verbs, we come next to the four kinds of Derivative verbs, viz. Passives, Causals, Desideratives, and Frequentatives.

PASSIVE VERBS.

461. Every root in every one of the ten classes may take a Passive form, conjugated as an Átmane-pada verb of cl. 4, the only difference being in the accent, which in Passives falls on the inserted *ya*, whereas in the Átmane of Primitive verbs of cl. 4, it falls on the radical syllable.

a. It has already been remarked, that the Passive may be regarded as a distinct derivative from the root, formed on one invariable principle, without any necessary community with the conjugational structure of the Active verb. Thus the root *bhid*, cl. 7, 'to divide,' makes *bhinatti* or *bhintte*, 'he divides;' *dvish*, cl. 2, 'to hate,' makes *dveshṭi* or *dvishṭe*, 'he hates;' but the Passive of both is formed according to one invariable rule, by the simple insertion of *ya*, without reference to the conjugational form of the Active; thus, *bhidyate*, 'he is divided;' *dvishyate*, 'he is hated.' See 243. *a.*

b. In fact, a Passive verb is really nothing but a root conjugated according to the rule for cl. 4 restricted to the Átmane-pada: and to say that every root may take a Passive form, is to say that roots of classes 1, 2, 3, 5, 6, 7, 8, 9, and 10 may all belong to cl. 4, when they receive a Passive sense: so that if a root be already of cl. 4, its Passive is frequently identical in form with its own Átmane-pada (the only difference being in the accent).

c. It might even be suspected, that the occasional assumption of an Intransitive signification and a Parasmai-pada inflexion by a Passive verb, was the cause which gave rise to a 4th class of Primitive verbs as distinct from the Passive. Instances are certainly found of Passive verbs taking Parasmai-pada terminations, and some Passive verbs (e. g. *jáyate*, 'he is born,' fr. rt. *jan*; *púryate*, 'he is filled,' fr. *pṛí*; and *tapyate*, 'he is heated,' fr. *tap*) are regarded by native grammarians as Átmane verbs of cl. 4 *. Again, many roots appear in class 4 as Intransitive verbs, which also appear in some one of the other nine as Transitive. For example, *yuj*, 'to join,' when used in a Transitive sense, is conjugated either in cl. 7, or in the Causal; when in an Intransitive, in cl. 4. So also, *push*, 'to nourish;' *kshubh*, 'to agitate;' *kliś*, 'to vex;' *sidh*, 'to accomplish †.'

d. There are said to be three kinds of Passive verbs.

I. The Passive, properly so called (*karman*); as, from तुद्, तुद्यते 'he is struck' (i. e. 'by another'), where the verb implies that the person or thing spoken of suffers some action from another person or thing; e. g. ओदनः पच्यते मया 'rice is cooked by me.'

II. An Impersonal Passive (*bháva*), generally formed from an Intransitive verb, and only occurring in the 3rd singular; गम्यते 'it is gone;' नृत्यते 'it is danced;' पच्यते 'it is cooked' or 'cooking goes on,' where the verb itself implies neither person nor thing as either acting or suffering, but simply expresses a state or condition.

III. A Reflexive Passive (*karma-kartṛi*, 'object-agent' or 'object-containing-agent'), where there is no object as distinct from the subject of the verb, or, in other words, where the subject is both agent and object, as in ओदनः पच्यते 'rice is cooked;' स जायते 'he is born,' &c. In these latter, if a vowel immediately precedes the characteristic *y*, the accent may fall on the radical syllable, as in cl. 4. They may also, in some cases, make use of the Átmane-pada of the Active, and drop the *y* altogether; thus to express 'he is adorned by himself,' it would be right to use भूषते 'he adorns himself.'

Obs.—According to Páṇini the Passive verb is merely an Átmane verb with the Vikaraṇa *yak* in the four tenses, and *karman* merely expresses one idea of the Passive. The object is expressed by the termination of the Passive in such a case as 'the house is built by me,' where the object of the agent *me*, viz. house, is expressed by the terminations of the Passive. But no agent might be mentioned, as simply 'the house is built,' in which case it would be a *bháva*, not a *karman*.

462. Passive verbs take the regular Átmane-pada terminations at 246, making use of the substitutions required in cl. 4.

In the Aorist they take either the A or B terminations of form I at 418, according as the root may admit the inserted इ *i* or not; but they require that in 3rd sing. of both forms the termination be इ *i* in place of *sta* and *ishṭa* (see 475).

---

* The Passive not unfrequently takes the terminations of the Parasmai-pada in Epic poetry; e. g. *ćhidyet* for *ćhidyeta*, 'it may be cut;' *mokshyasi* for *mokshyase*, 'thou shalt be liberated;' *adṛiśyat*, 'he was seen.'

† The forms given for the Aorists of such verbs as *pad*, 'to go,' *budh*, 'to know' (which are said to be Átmane verbs of cl. 4), could only belong to Passive verbs. The forms given by Westergaard are, *apádi*, *abodhi*. See 475.

Special Tenses.

463. Rule for the formation of the stem in the four Special tenses, Átmane-pada, of roots of the first nine classes.

Affix य *ya* *—lengthened to या *yá* before initial *m* and *v*—to the root, the vowel of which is not gunated, and often remains unchanged. (Compare the rule for cl. 4 at 249 and 272.)

464. Thus, from भू cl. 1, 'to be,' comes the stem भूय *bhúya* (Pres. *bhúya*+*i*=भूये, *bhúya*+*se*=भूयसे, &c.; Impf. *abhúya*+*i*=अभूये, &c.; Pot. *bhúya*+*íya*=भूयेय, &c.; Impv. *bhúya*+*ai*=भूयै, &c.); from तुद् cl. 6, 'to strike,' comes *tudya* (Pres. *tudya*+*i*=तुद्ये, &c.)

465. The root, however, often undergoes changes, which are generally analogous to those of cl. 4 and the Precative Parasmai-pada (see 275 and 445); but a final *á* is not changed to *e* as in the Precative.

Six roots in आ *á*, and one or two in ए *e*, ऐ *ai*, and ओ *o*, change their final vowels to ई *í*; thus, दा 'to give,' दे 'to protect,' and दो 'to cut,' make Pres. दीये, दीयसे, दीयते, &c. So also, धा 'to place' (3rd sing. धीयते); स्था 'to stand,' मा 'to measure,' पा 'to drink,' and हा 'to quit;' धे 'to drink' (3rd sing. धीयते, &c.); गै 'to sing' (गीयते); सो 'to destroy' (सीयते).

Obs. 1. दा cl. 2, 'to bind,' makes दायते, as it is not a *ghu* and does not come under Páṇ. VI. 4, 66.

Obs. 2. हा 'to go' (*ohán*) makes *háyate*, though हा 'to quit' (*ohák*) makes *híyate*.

a. But other roots in आ *á* remain unchanged; and most others in *ai* and *o* are changed to *á*; thus, ख्या 'to tell' makes 3rd sing. ख्यायते; and ज्ञा 'to know,' ज्ञायते; पा 'to protect,' पायते; ध्यै 'to meditate,' ध्यायते; शो 'to sharpen,' शायते.

b. दरिद्रा, दीधी, and वेवी drop their final vowels as at 390. *c* (दरिद्र्यते, दीध्यते, &c.); and ज्या 'to become old' makes 1. जीयते. Cf. 446. *a*.

c. ह्वे 'to call,' वे 'to weave,' व्ये 'to cover,' make their stems हूय, ऊय, and वीय (3rd sing. हूयते). Compare 450. *a*.

466. Final इ *i* or उ *u* are lengthened, as also a medial *i* or *u* before *v* or *r*; thus, from जि, हु, दिव्, कुर्, come जीय, हूय, दीव्य, कूर्य. See 447 and 453. *b*.

a. But श्वि 'to swell' makes 3rd sing. शूयते; and शी 'to lie down,' शय्यते.

467. Final ऋ *ri* becomes रि *ri*, but if preceded by a double consonant is gunated; thus, कृ makes 3. क्रियते; वृ, व्रियते; but स्मृ, स्मर्यते. Cf. 448.

a. The roots ऋ (3rd sing. अर्यते) and जागृ are also gunated. Cf. 448. *a*.

468. Final ॠ *rí* becomes ईर् *ír*; thus, कॄ 'to scatter' makes 3. कीर्यते; but पॄ 'to fill,' पूर्यते. See 449 and 449. *a*.

---

* This *ya* is probably derived from *yá*, 'to go,' just as the Causal *aya* is derived from *i*, 'to go.' It is certain that in Bengálí and Hindí the Passive is formed with the root *yá*. Cf. Latin *amatum iri*, &c. See 481.

469. Roots ending in a double consonant, of which the first is a nasal, usually reject the nasal; as, from बन्ध्, स्तम्भ्, सञ्ज्, come the stems बध्य, &c. (बध्ये, &c.)

a. The roots at 390. *l.* carry their peculiarities into the Passive (कम्यते or काम्यते, गुप्यते or गोपाय्यते, विच्छ्यते or विच्छाय्यते, ऋत्यते or ऋतीय्यते).

470. जन् 'to produce,' खन् 'to dig,' तन् 'to stretch,' सन् 'to give,' optionally reject the final nasal, and lengthen the preceding *a*; thus, जायते or जन्यते, &c.

471. वच् 'to speak,' वद् 'to say,' वप् 'to sow,' वश् 'to wish,' वस् 'to dwell,' वह् 'to bear,' स्वप् 'to sleep,' यज् 'to sacrifice,' change the semivowels व, य into their corresponding vowels and accordingly make their stems उच्य, उद्य, उप्य, उश्य, उष्य, उह्य, सुप्य, इज्य respectively, (उच्यते, &c.)

Obs.—This change of a semivowel into its corresponding vowel is technically called Samprasárana.

472. Similarly, ग्रह् 'to take,' प्रछ् 'to ask,' भ्रज्ज् 'to fry,' व्यच् 'to deceive,' व्यध् 'to pierce,' व्रश्च् 'to cut,' make their stems गृह्य, पृच्छ्य, भृज्ज्य, विच्य, विध्य, वृश्च्य respectively, (गृह्यते, &c.)

a. ऊह् 'to reason' shortens its vowel after prepositions (उह्यते; otherwise ऊह्यते).

b. अज् forms its Passive from वी; घस् from अद्; अस् from भू; ब्रू from वच्; and चक्ष् from ख्या.

c. शास् 'to rule' makes its Passive stem शिष्य.

General Tenses.—Perfect of Passives.

473. The stem of this tense in the Passive verb is identical with that of all Primitive verbs, in all ten classes. The stems, therefore, as formed at 364–384, will serve equally well for the Perfect of the Passive, provided only that they be restricted to the Átmane-pada inflexion; thus, बुबुधे, पेचे, &c.

a. When the Periphrastic Perfect has to be employed (see 385) the auxiliaries अस and भू may be used in the Átmane, as well as कृ. Compare 385. *b.*

First and Second Future of Passives.

474. In these and the remaining tenses no variation generally occurs from the stems of the same tenses in the Primitive, Átmane, unless the root end in a vowel. In that case the insertion of इ *i* may take place in the Passive, although prohibited in the Primitive, provided the final vowel of the root be first vriddhied; thus, from चि *ći*, cl. 5, 'to gather,' may come the stem of the 1st and 2nd Fut. Pass. *ćáyi* (*ćáyitáhe* &c., *ćáyishye* &c.), although the stem of the same tenses in the Primitive is *će* (*ćetáhe* &c., *ćeshye* &c.) Similarly, from हु *hu* and कृ *kṛi* may come *hávi* and *kári* (*hávitáhe*, *káritáhe*), although the stems in the Primitive are *ho* and *kar*.

a. In like manner इ *i* may be inserted when the root ends in long आ *á*, or in ए *e*, ऐ *ai*, ओ *o*, changeable to आ *á*, provided that, instead of Vṛiddhi (which is impossible), *y* be interposed between the final *á* and inserted *i*; thus, from दा *dá*, 'to give,' may come the stem of the Fut. Pass. *dáyi* (*dáyitáhe* &c.), although the stem of the same tenses in the Primitive is *dá* (*dátáhe* &c.); from ह्वे *hve*, 'to call,' may come *hváyi*

(ह्वापिताहे &c.), although the stem in the Primitive is *hvá*. But in all these cases the stem of the Primitive may be taken for that of the Passive, so that *ćetáhe* or *ćáyitáhe* may equally stand for the 1st Fut. Pass.; and similarly with the others.

b. In the case of roots ending in consonants, the stem of the two Futures in the Passive will be identical with that of the same tenses in the Primitive verb, the inflexion being that of the Átmane. दृश् 'to see,' however, in the Passive, may be दर्शिताहे, दर्शिष्ये, as well as द्रष्टाहे, द्रक्ष्ये; and हन् 'to kill' may be घानिताहे, घानिष्ये, as well as हन्ताहे, हनिष्ये; and ग्रह् 'to take' may be ग्राहिताहे, ग्राहिष्ये, as well as ग्रहीताहे, ग्रहीष्ये.

c. In verbs of cl. 10 and Causals, deviation from the Átmane form of the Primitive may take place in these and the succeeding tenses. See 496.

Aorist of Passives.

475. In this tense, also, variation from the Primitive may occur when the root ends in a *vowel*. For in that case the insertion of इ *i* may take place, although forbidden in the Primitive verb, provided the final of the root be vriddhied; thus, from चि *ći* may come the stem of the Aor. Pass. *aćáyi* (*aćáyishi* &c., 427), although the stem in the Átmane of the Primitive is *aće* (*aćeshi* &c., 420). So also, from हु *hu* and कृ *kṛi* may come *ahávi* and *akári* (*ahávishi, akárishi,* 427), although the stems in the Átmane of the Primitive are *aho* and *akṛi* (*ahoshi, akṛishi,* 420). Again, *i* may be inserted when the root ends in long आ *á*, or in ए *e*, ऐ *ai*, ओ *o*, changeable to आ *á*, provided that *y* be interposed between final *á* and inserted *i*; thus, from दा 'to give,' दे 'to protect,' दै 'to purify,' दो 'to cut,' may come *adáyi* (*adáyishi* &c.), although the stems in the Átmane of the Primitives are different (as *adishi* &c.) But in all these cases it is permitted to take the stem of the Primitive for that of the Passive (so that the Passive of *ći* may be either *aćáyishi* or *aćeshi*), except in the *3rd pers. sing.*, where the terminations *ishṭa* and *sta* being rejected, the stem, as formed by Vṛiddhi and the inserted *i*, must stand alone; thus, *aćáyi*, 'it was gathered;' *ahávi*, 'it was sacrificed;' *akári*, 'it was done;' *adáyi*, 'it was given,' 'protected,' 'purified,' 'cut.'

a. Sometimes the usual form of the Aorist Átmane is employed throughout (see 461. III). This is the case whenever the sense is that of a Reflexive Passive, not of the real Passive; thus, ख्या 'to tell' in the 3rd sing. Aor. Pass. is अख्यायि, but in the sense of a Reflexive Passive अख्यत; श्रि 'to resort to' makes 1st sing. Aor. Pass. अश्रयिषि, but Reflexive अशिश्रिये; and कम् 'to love' makes 3rd sing. Aor. Pass. अकामि or अकामि, but Reflexive अचकमे.

b. If the root end in a *consonant*, the stem of the Aorist Passive will always be identical with that of the Átmane of the Primitive, except in the 3rd sing., where इ *i* being substituted for the terminations *ishṭa* and *sta* of form I at 418, generally requires before it the lengthening of a medial *a* (if not already long by position), and the *Guṇa* of any other short medial vowel*. Hence, from *tan*, 'to stretch,'

* A medial vowel, long by nature or position, remains unchanged (by 28), and in one or two cases even a short vowel; as, *aśami* for *aśámi*.

1st, 2nd, and 3rd sing. *atanishi, atanishṭhás, atáni;* from *kship*, 'to throw,' *akshipsi, akshipthás, akshepi;* from *vid*, 'to know,' *avedishi, avedishṭhás, avedi*, &c.

c. The lengthening of a medial *a*, however, is by no means universal; and there are other exceptions in the 3rd sing., as follows:—

Nearly all roots ending in *am* forbid the lengthening of the vowel in the 3rd sing.; thus, अक्रमि from क्रम् 'to walk;' अक्षमि from क्षम् 'to bear;' अशमि from शम् 'to be calm' (but in the sense of 'to observe,' अशामि).

d. Similarly, अवधि from वध् and अजनि from जन्. The former may optionally substitute अघानि from हन्.

e. मृज् and गुह् lengthen their vowels (अमार्जि, अगूहि).

f. The roots at 390. *l.* will have two forms, अकमि or अकामि, अगोपि or अगोपायि, अविच्छि or अविच्छायि, &c.

g. रध् 'to perish,' जभ् 'to yawn,' रभ् 'to desire,' insert nasals (अरन्धि, अजम्भि, अरम्भि). Similarly, लभ् 'to receive,' when it has a preposition (e.g. प्रालम्भि), and optionally when it has none (अलम्भि or अलाभि, Páṇ. VII. 1, 69).

h. भञ्ज् 'to break' may drop its nasal, in which case the medial *a* is lengthened (अभञ्जि or अभाजि).

i. हेड् 'to clothe' may either retain the *e* or change it to *í* or *i* (अहेडि or अहिडि or अहीडि).

j. इ 'to go' substitutes गा, and optionally does so when *adhi* is prefixed in the sense of 'to read' (अध्यगायि or अध्यायि).

k. ऋत् 'to blame' makes आर्तीयि or आर्ति.

Precative (or *Benedictive*) *and Conditional of Passives.*

476. In these tenses the same variation is permitted in the case of roots ending in vowels as in the Aorist; that is, the insertion of इ *i* is allowed, provided that, before it, Vṛiddhi take place in a final vowel capable of such a change, and *y* be interposed after final *á;* thus, from चि *ći* may come the stems *ćáyi* and *aćáyi* (*ćáyishíya, aćáyishye*); from हु *hu*, *hávi* and *ahávi;* from कृ *kṛi*, *kári* and *akári;* from दा *dá*, *dáyi* and *adáyi*. But *ćeshíya, aćeshye, hoshíya, ahoshye*, &c., the forms belonging to the Átmane of the Primitive verb, are equally admissible in the Passive.

Passive Infinitive.

477. There is no Passive Infinitive in Sanskṛit distinct in form from the Active. The suffix *tum*, however, is capable of a Passive sense, when joined with certain verbs, especially with the Passive of शक् *śak*, 'to be able.' It is also used passively, in connection with the Participles *árabdha, nirúpita, yukta*, &c. See Syntax, 869.

Passive verbs from roots of the 10*th class.*

478. In forming a Passive verb from roots of cl. 10, although the conjugational अय is rejected in the first four tenses, yet the other conjugational changes of the root are retained before the suffix *ya;* thus, from चुर् cl. 10, 'to steal,' comes the

stem *ćorya* (चोर्यते). In the Perfect अय is retained (see 473. *a*), and in the other General tenses the stem may deviate from the Átmane form of the Primitive by the optional rejection or assumption of अय, especially in the Aorist. See Causal Passives at 496.

CAUSAL VERBS.

479. Every root in every one of the ten classes may take a Causal form, which is conjugated as a verb of the 10th class; and which is not only employed to give a Causal sense to a Primitive verb, but also a Transitive sense to an Intransitive verb; see 289.

Thus, the Primitive verb *bodhati*, 'he knows' (from root *budh*, cl. 1), becomes in the Causal बोधयति *bodhayati*, 'he causes to know,' 'he informs;' and the Intransitive verb *kshubhyati*, 'he shakes,' 'is shaken' (from *kshubh*, cl. 4), becomes क्षोभयति 'he shakes' (transitively).

a. This form may sometimes imply other analogous senses.

Thus, *hárayati*, 'he allows to take;' *náśayati*, 'he suffers to perish;' *abhishećayati*, 'he permits himself to be inaugurated;' *kshamayati*, 'he asks to be forgiven;' अभिषेचय आत्मानम् 'allow yourself to be inaugurated.'

Obs.—To say that every root may take a Causal form, is equivalent to saying that roots of the first nine classes may all belong to the 10th, when they take a Causal sense; and that if a root be originally of the 10th class, no distinct form for its Causal is necessary, the Primitive verb and the Causal being in that case identical (see 289). Possibly the occasional employment of a Causal verb in a Transitive, rather than a Causal sense, was the reason for creating a 10th class of Primitive verbs. Certainly the subject of conjugation would be simplified if the addition of *aya* to the root were considered in all cases as the mark of a Causal verb; especially as *aya* is not the sign of a separate conjugation, in the way of any other conjugational Vikaraṇa (see 250. *b*); for it is retained in most of the other tenses of the verb, not only in the first four, just as the Desiderative *ish* is retained.

480. As to the terminations of Causal verbs, they are the same as those of the scheme at 246; and the same substitutions are required in the first four tenses as in classes 1, 4, 6, and 10.

Special Tenses.

481. General rule for forming the stem in the four Special tenses of roots of the ten classes.

If a root end in a vowel, vriddhi that vowel; if in a consonant, gunate the radical vowel before *all* the terminations, and affix अय *aya* *

* This may be derived from root इ *i*, 'to go,' just as the Passive *ya* is supposed to be derived from root *yá*. See 463, note *.

(changeable to *ayá* before initial *m* and *v*, but not before simple *m*) to the root so vriddhied or gunated.

482. Thus, from नी 'to lead' comes the stem नायय by 37 (Pres. *náyayá+mi*= नाययामि, *náyaya+si*=नाययसि &c.; Impf. *anáyaya+m*=अनाययम् &c.; Pot. *náyaya+iyam*=नाययेयम् &c.; Impv. *náyaya+áni*=नाययानि &c. Átm. Pres. *náyaya+i*=नायये &c. In Epic poetry a doubtful form नापयामि is found). Similarly, from शी 'to lie down' comes शायय *śáyaya* (शाययामि &c.); from भू *bhú*, 'to be,' comes भावय *bhávaya* (भावयामि &c.); and from कृ 'to do' and कॄ 'to scatter' the stem कारय *káraya*.

But from बुध् 'to know' comes the gunated बोधय *bodhaya* (बोधयामि); and from सृप् cl. 1, 'to creep,' the gunated सर्पय *sarpaya*.

Obs.—कॄत् 'to celebrate,' and other verbs of the 10th class, will take the changes already explained at 285–289.

483. Roots ending in आ *á*, or in ए *e*, ऐ *ai*, ओ *o*, changeable to आ *á*, cannot be vriddhied, but frequently insert प् *p* between the root and the suffix *aya*; thus, दा 'to give,' दे 'to love,' and दो 'to cut,' all make दापयामि *dápayámi*, &c.; धे 'to drink,' धापयामि *dhápayámi*, &c.; गै 'to sing,' गापयामि *gápayámi*, &c. See 484.

a. So also other roots in *á* insert *p*, except पा cl. 1, 'to drink,' which inserts य् *y* (पाययामि &c.); and पा cl. 2, 'to preserve,' which inserts ल् *l* (पालयामि &c.); and वा cl. 2, in the sense of 'to agitate,' which inserts ज (वाजयामि &c.)

b. So also other roots in *ai* insert *p*, but most others in *e* and *o* insert *y*; thus, ह्वे 'to call' makes ह्वाययामि &c. Similarly, वे 'to weave,' व्ये 'to put on.' शो 'to sharpen' makes शाययामि &c. Similarly, छो 'to cut,' सो 'to destroy.'

484. ज्ञा 'to know,' श्रा or श्रै 'to stew,' स्ना 'to bathe,' and ग्लै 'to languish,' may optionally shorten the *á*, the last two only when not joined with prepositions; thus, ज्ञापयामि &c., or ज्ञपयामि &c.; ग्लापयामि &c., or ग्लपयामि &c. (but with परि only, परिग्लापयामि). क्षै 'to waste away' makes only क्षपयामि.

485. Some roots in *i*, *í*, *ṛi*, also insert *p*, after changing the final vowel to *á*; thus, जि 'to conquer' makes जापयामि &c. Similarly, मि 'to throw,' मी 'to perish,' क्री 'to buy' (मापयामि, क्रापयामि, &c.)

a. स्मि 'to smile' makes स्माययामि &c., and स्मापये &c.

b. चि 'to collect' has four forms; 1. चापयामि &c., 2. चपयामि &c., 3. चाययामि &c., 4. चययामि &c.

c. भी cl. 3, 'to fear,' has three forms; 1. भाययामि &c., 2. भापये &c., Átm. only, 3. भीषये &c., Átm. only.

d. इ cl. 2, 'to go,' makes आपयामि &c., especially with the preposition अधि 'over,' अध्यापयामि 'I cause to go over,' 'I teach.'

e. Three roots insert *n*; ली cl. 4, 'to embrace,' 'to adhere,' making (with prep. वि in the sense of 'to dissolve') -लीनयामि &c., as well as -लापयामि, -लाययामि, and -लालयामि &c.; in some senses, however, लापयामि only can be used: प्री cl. 9, 'to please,' makes प्रीणयामि (also प्राययामि); and धू cl. 5 and 9, 'to shake,' धूनयामि.

486. ह्री cl. 3, 'to be ashamed,' री 'to flow,' व्री 'to choose,' and ऋ cl. 1, 'to go,' insert *p* after gunation; thus, ह्रेपयामि &c., अर्पयामि &c.

a. दीधी and वेवी and दरिद्रा (see 390. *c*) drop their finals (दीधयामि, वेवयामि, दरिद्रयामि, &c.)

b. जागृ 'to awake,' स्मृ in the sense of 'to long for,' जॄ cl. 4, 'to grow old,' दॄ in the sense of 'to fear,' नॄ 'to lead,' take Guṇa (जागरयामि). But दॄ 'to tear,' दारयामि.

c. गॄ 'to swallow' makes गारयामि or गालयामि.

487. Roots ending in single consonants, enclosing a medial अ *a*, generally lengthen the *a*; thus, पच् cl. 1, 'to cook,' makes पाचयामि &c. There are, however, many exceptions; thus, ज्वर् 'to be sick,' त्वर् 'to hasten,' &c., do not lengthen the vowel. In ज्वल् 'to blaze,' and some others, the lengthening is optional.

a. Roots in *m* generally do not lengthen the *a*; thus, गम् cl. 1, 'to go,' makes गमयामि &c.; क्लम् 'to be weary,' क्लमयामि &c. Some, however, optionally do so; as, नम् 'to bend,' &c. One or two always lengthen the *a*; as, कम् 'to love' makes कामयामि.

b. The roots रध्, जभ्, रभ्, and लभ् (see 475. *g*) insert nasals (रन्धयामि &c.)

488. Other anomalies.—रुह् 'to grow' makes रोहयामि or रोपयामि; क्नूय् or क्नू 'to sound,' क्नोपयामि; दुष् 'to be corrupt,' दूषयामि; हन् 'to kill,' घातयामि; शद् 'to fall,' 'to perish,' शातयामि; स्फुर् 'to quiver,' स्फारयामि or स्फोरयामि; स्फाय् 'to increase,' स्फावयामि; क्ष्माय् 'to shake' as the earth, क्ष्मापयामि &c.; मृज् 'to rub,' मार्जयामि (390. *j*); गुह् 'to conceal,' गूहयामि (390. *m*).

a. The roots गुप्, विछ्, धूप्, पण्, पन्, ऋत्, at 390. *l*, will have two forms (गोपयामि or गोपाययामि &c., see 390. *l*).

b. सिध् 'to be finished' makes its Causal either साधयामि or, with reference to sacred rites, सेधयामि; भ्रज्ज् 'to fry' either भ्रज्जयामि or भर्जयामि; but the last form may be from भृज्.

c. हेड् 'to clothe' makes हिडयामि; रञ्ज् in the sense of 'to hunt,' रजयामि.

Obs.—The Causal of verbs of cl. 10 will be identical with the Primitive; see 289. The Causals of Causals will also be identical with the Causals themselves.

General Tenses.

489. The changes of the root required to form the stem of the Special tenses are continued in the General. Moreover, *aya* is retained in all these tenses, except the Aorist and except the Precative, Parasmai; but the last *a* of *aya* is dropped before the inserted इ *i*, which is invariably assumed in all other General tenses.

Perfect of Causals.

490. This tense must be of the Periphrastic form, as explained at 385; that is, आम् *ám* added to the Causal stem is prefixed to the Perfect of one of the three auxiliary verbs, अस् 'to be,' भू 'to be,' or कृ 'to do;' thus, बुध् 'to know' makes in Causal Perfect बोधयाञ्चकार or

बोधयामास or बोधयाम्बभूव. शम् makes in Caus. Perf. 3rd pl. शमयाम्बभूवुः 'they extinguished' (Raghu-v. VII. 45).

First and Second Future of Causals.

491. In these tenses the inserted इ *i* is invariably assumed between the stem, as formed in the Special tenses, and the usual terminations; thus, बुध् makes बोधयितास्मि &c., बोधयिष्यामि &c.

Aorist of Causals and verbs of cl. 10.

492. The terminations are those of form II at 435. In the formation of the stem of this tense, the suffix *ay* is rejected; but any other change that may take place in the Special tenses, such as the insertion of *p* or *y*, is preserved. The stem is a reduplicated form of this change, and to this reduplication the augment अ *a* is prefixed.

Thus, taking the stems *bodhay* and *jápay* (Causal stems of *budh*, 'to know,' and *ji*, 'to conquer'), and rejecting *ay*, we have *bodh* and *jáp:* and from these are formed the stems of the Aorist *abúbudh* and *ajíjap* (अबूबुधम् *abúbudham* &c., अबूबुधे *abúbudhe* &c., अजीजपम् *ajíjapam* &c., अजीजपे *ajíjape* &c., cf. the Greek Pluperfect).

493. The rule for this reduplication is as follows:—The initial consonant of the root, with its vowel, is reduplicated, and the reduplicated consonant follows the rules given at 252; but the reduplication of the vowel is peculiar.

Reduplication of the vowel of the initial consonant in the Causal Aorist.

a. Causal stems, after rejecting *ay*, will generally end in *áy*, *áv*, *ár*, or a consonant preceded by *a*, *á*, *e*, *o*, or *ar*. The usual reduplicated vowel for all these, except *o*, is इ *i*. But उ *u* is reduplicated for *o*, and sometimes also for *áv*. The rule is, that either the reduplicated or stem syllable must be long either by nature or position; and in general the reduplicated vowel *i* or *u* is made long, and, to compensate for this, the long vowel of the Causal stem shortened, or, if it be Guṇa, changed to its corresponding short vowel; thus, the Causal stem *náy* (from नी, rejecting *ay*) makes the stem of the Aorist *anínay* (अनीनयम् *anínayam* &c.); the Causal stem *bháv* (from भू) makes *abíbhav* (अबीभवम् &c.); the Causal stem *kár* (from कृ), *aćíkar;* *gam* (from गम्), *ajígam;* *páć* (from पच्), *apípać;* *pál* (from पा), *apípal;* *ved* (from विद्), *avívid*. But *bodh* (from बुध्), *abúbudh;* and *sáv* (from सु), *asúshav*.

b. Sometimes the reduplicated vowel is only long by position before two consonants, the radical vowel being still made short; as, *śráv* (from श्रु) makes *aśiśrav* or *aśuśrav;* *dráv* (from द्रु), *adudrav* or *adidrav;* भ्राज्, *abibhraj* (also *ababhráj*).

c. Sometimes the reduplicated vowel remains short, whilst the vowel of the Causal stem, which must be long either by nature or position, remains unchanged;

thus, the Causal stem *jív* (from जीव्) may make अजिजीव् (also अजीजिव्); *ćint*, *aćićint*; *kalp*, *aćikalp*. In such cases *a* is generally reduplicated for *a* or *á*; as, *laksh* makes *alalaksh*; *yáć*, *ayayáć*; *vart* (from *vṛit*), *avavart*, &c.

d. Obs.—If the stem has *ar*, *ár*, *ír*, *al* (from radical *ṛi*, *ṛí*, or *lṛi*), these are either left unchanged or *ar*, *ár*, *ír* may be changed to ऋ *ṛi*, and *al* to ऌ *lṛi*; thus, *vart* (from वृत्) may make *avívṛit* as well as *avavart*; *kírt* (from कृत्) either *aćikírt* or *aćíkṛit*, &c.

e. The following are other examples, some of which are anomalous: from *páy* (Caus. of *pá*, 'to drink'), अपीप्यम् &c.; from *stháp* (Caus. of *sthá*, 'to stand'), अतिष्ठिपम् &c.; from *ghráp* (Caus. of *ghrá*, 'to smell'), अजिघ्रिपम् &c., and अजिघ्रपम् &c.; from *adhyáp* (Caus. of *i*, 'to go,' with *adhi*), अध्यजीगपम् &c.; from *ćesht* (Caus. of *ćesht*, 'to make effort'), अचचेष्टम् or अचिचेष्टम्; from *hváy* (Caus. of *hve*, 'to call'), अजुहावम् or अजूहवम्; from *tvar* (Caus. of *tvar*, 'to hasten'), अतत्वरम्; from *stár* (Caus. of *stṛi* or *stṛí*, 'to spread'), अतस्तरम् or अतिस्तरम्; from *dár* (Caus. of *dṛí*, 'to tear'), अददरम्; from *dyot* (Caus. of *dyut*, 'to shine'), अदिद्युतम्; from *śváy* (Caus. of *śvi*, 'to swell'), अशूशवम् or अशिश्वयम्; from *smár* (Caus. of *smṛi*, 'to remember'), असस्मरम्; from *sváp* (Caus. of स्वप् 'to sleep'), असूषुपम्; from *kath* (cl. 10, 'to tell'), अचकथम् or अचीकथम्; from गण् (cl. 10, 'to count'), अजगणम् or अजीगणम्; from *prath* (Caus. of प्रथ् 'to spread'), अपप्रथम्.

Reduplication of an initial vowel in the Causal Aorist.

494. Roots beginning with vowels, and ending with single consonants, form their Causal Aorists by a peculiar reduplication of the root (after rejecting अय). The rule is that not only the initial vowel, as in the Perfect at 364. *a*, but the final consonant also be reduplicated. In fact, the whole root is doubled, as it would be if it began with a consonant, and ended with a vowel; the consonant is reduplicated according to the rules at 252, but the second vowel is generally इ *i*. This *i* (which probably results from a weakening of *a*) takes the place of the stem vowel, which then becomes the initial of the reduplicated syllable, and combines with the augment अ *a*, according to 251. *a*; thus, ऊह् 'to infer' makes the stem of its Causal Aorist ऊजिह् *újih*; and with अ prefixed, औजिह् (औजिहम् 'I caused to infer'). So also, आप् cl. 5, 'to obtain,' makes आपिपम् 'I caused to obtain;' ईड् cl. 2, 'to praise,' makes ऐडिडम् 'I caused to praise.' Cf. Gr. 2nd Aor. ἤγαγον from ἄγω, and ὤρορον from ὄρνυμι.

a. If a root end in a conjunct consonant, the first member of which is a nasal or *r*, this nasal or *r* is rejected from the final, but not from the reduplicated letter; thus, अर्ह् 'to be worthy' makes आर्जिहम् 'I caused to be worthy,' 'I honoured;' so अर्ध्, Causal stem from ऋध् 'to prosper,' makes आर्दिधम् 'I caused to prosper;' and उन्द् 'to moisten' makes औन्दिदम् 'I caused to moisten.'

b. But when the first member of the compound is any other letter, then the corresponding consonant to this first member of the compound is reduplicated by 252. *c*; thus, ईक्ष् 'to see' makes ऐचिक्षम् *aićiksham*, 'I caused to see;' अक्ष् 'to go' makes आचिक्षम् 'I caused to go.'

c. Roots consisting of a single vowel, form their Causal Aorists from the Causal stem (after rejecting *aya*); thus, the root ऋ 'to go' makes its Causal stem *arp*, 'to deliver over;' and its Causal Aorist आर्पिपम् 'I caused to deliver.'

d. ऊर्णु 'to cover' makes its Causal Aorist और्णुनुवम्; अन्ध् cl. 10, 'to be blind,' आन्दधम्; and ऊन् cl. 10, 'to diminish,' औननम्.

e. When the consonant which follows the initial vowel has another vowel after it, this vowel must appear in the reduplication; thus, from अवधीर् cl. 10, 'to despise,' comes the Aorist आववधीरम्.

Precative (or *Benedictive*) *and Conditional of Causals.*

495. The stem of the Causal Precative Átmane, and of the Causal Conditional in both voices, does not differ from that of the General tenses; but the last *a* of *aya* is dropped before the inserted इ *i*, which is always assumed. In the Precative Parasmai both *aya* and *i* are rejected, but any other change of the root is retained; thus, बुध् 'to know' makes in Caus. Prec. *bodhyásam* &c., *bodhayishíya* &c.; in Cond., *abodhayishyam* &c., *abodhayishye* &c.

Infinitive of Causals.

a. The Infinitive may be most easily formed from the 3rd sing. 1st Future, as explained at 459; thus, from बुध् comes बोधयिता 'he will cause to know,' बोधयितुम् 'to cause to know.'

Passive of Causals.

496. In forming a Passive verb from a Causal stem, the Causal suffix अय is rejected, but the other Causal changes of the root are retained before the Passive suffix *ya*.

Thus, from Caus. stem पातय *pátaya* (from पत् 'to fall') comes the Pass. पात्य *pátya*, making 1st sing. पात्ये 'I am made to fall,' 3rd sing. पात्यते 'he is made to fall.' Similarly, स्था 'to stand' makes स्थापयति 'he causes to stand,' स्थाप्यते 'he is caused to stand;' and ज्ञा 'to know' makes ज्ञपयति 'he causes to know,' and ज्ञप्यते 'he is caused to know,' 'he is informed.'

a. In the General tenses, the stem of all the tenses, excepting the Perfect, may vary from the Átmane form by the optional rejection of the conjugational अय. But in the Perfect, the Átmane of the usual form with *ám* and the auxiliaries (490, 385) is admitted for the Passive. In the Aorist, the usual reduplicated form (492) gives place to the Átmane form which belongs to those verbs of the first nine classes which assume *i*.

Thus, from भावय, the Causal stem of भू 'to be,' come the Passive Perfect भावयाञ्चक्रे or भावयामासे or भावयाम्बभूवे; 1st Fut. भावयिताहे or भाविताहे; 2nd Fut. भावयिष्ये or भाविष्ये; Aor. अभावयिषि or अभाविषि, 3rd sing. अभावि; Prec. भावयिषीय or भाविषीय; Cond. अभावयिष्ये or अभाविष्ये.

b. Similarly, from बोधय, Causal stem of बुध् 'to know,' come Passive Perfect बोधयाञ्चक्रे &c. 'I have been caused to know;' 1st Fut. बोधयिताहे or बोधिताहे &c. 'I shall be caused to know;' 2nd Fut. बोधयिष्ये or बोधिष्ये &c.; Aor. अबोधयिषि or अबोधिषि 'I have been caused to know,' 2. अबोधयिष्ठास् or अबोधिष्ठास्, 3. अबोधि &c.

c. So also, from शमय, Causal stem of शम् 'to cease,' come the Passive Perfect शमयाञ्चक्रे or शमयामासे &c. 'I have been caused to cease,' &c.; 1st Fut. शमयिताहे or शमिताहे; 2nd Fut. शमयिष्ये or शमिष्ये; Aor. अशमयिषि or अशमिषि, 3rd sing. अशमि; Prec. शमयिषीय &c.: and the radical *a* may be optionally lengthened; thus, 1st Fut. शमयिताहे or शामयिताहे &c.

d. So also, अघापि or अघापि, 3rd sing. Aor., from Causal of घै.

Obs.—Even रञ्ज्, कन्द्, क्रन्द्, and some other roots which end in a double consonant, may optionally lengthen the medial *a*; thus, Aor. 3rd sing. अरञ्जि or अराञ्जि.

Desiderative of Causals.

497. When Causals and verbs of cl. 10 take a Desiderative form (see 498), they retain *ay*, and are all formed with *isha*; thus, पातयामि 'I cause to fall' makes पिपातयिषामि 'I desire to cause to fall;' स्वापयामि 'I cause to sleep' makes सुष्वापयिषामि 'I desire to cause to sleep;' चुर् cl. 10, 'to steal,' makes चुचोरयिषामि 'I wish to steal.'

a. The Desiderative stem of the Causal of अधी, 'to go over,' is either अध्यापिपयिष or अधिजिगापयिष; of the Causal of ह्वे 'to call,' जुहावयिष (as if from हावय); of the Causal of ज्ञा 'to know,' ज्ञीप्स (or regularly जिज्ञापयिष or जिज्ञपयिष); of the Causal of श्वि 'to swell,' शुशावयिष (or regularly शिश्वाययिष).

DESIDERATIVE VERBS.

498. Every root in the ten classes may take a Desiderative form.

a. Although this form of the root is not often used, in classical composition, in its character of a verb, yet nouns and participles derived from the Desiderative stem are not uncommon (see 80. I, and 82. VII). Moreover, there are certain Primitive roots which take a Desiderative form, without yielding a Desiderative sense; and these, as equivalent to Primitive verbs (amongst which they are generally classed), may occur in classical Sanskṛit; e. g. *jugups*, 'to blame,' from गुप् *gup*; *ćikits*, 'to çure,' from कित् *kit*; *titiksh*, 'to bear,' from तिज् *tij*; मीमांस् *mímáns*, 'to reason,' from मन् *man*; *bíbhats*, 'to abhor,' from बाध् or बध्.

499. Desideratives take the terminations at 246, with the substitutions required in classes 1, 4, 6, and 10; and their inflexion, either in Parasmai or Átmane, is generally determined by the practice of the Primitive verb.

Thus, root बुध् *budh*, cl. 1, 'to know,' taking both inflexions in the Primitive, may take both in the Desiderative (*bubodhishámi* &c., or *bubodhishe* &c., 'I desire to know'); and लभ् *labh*, 'to obtain,' taking only the Átmane in the Primitive, may take only the Átmane in the Desiderative (*lipse* &c., 'I desire to obtain').

500. Rule for forming the stem in the four Special tenses.

Reduplicate the initial consonant and vowel of the root, and generally, though not invariably, if the Primitive verb inserts इ *i* (see 392–415), affix इष् *ish* or in a few roots ईष् (see 393); if it rejects *i*, then simply स् *s*, changeable to ष् *sh* (by 70; see, however, *f*), to the root so reduplicated. The vowel *a* is then added, as in classes 1, 4, 6, and 10; and, agreeably to the rule in those classes, this *a* becomes *á* before terminations beginning with *m* and *v* (but not before simple *m*).

a. Thus, from क्षिप् *kship*, 'to throw,' comes the stem *ćikshipsa* (*ćikshipsá*+*mi*=चिक्षिप्सामि *ćikshipsámi* &c., 'I desire to throw'); but from विद् *vid*, 'to know,' taking inserted *i*, comes *vividisha* (*vividishá*+*mi*=विविदिषामि *vividishámi* &c. In Átm. the stem is *vivitsa*).

b. Some roots, however, which reject the inserted *i* in other forms, assume it in the Desiderative, and *vice versa*. Some, again, allow an option; thus, वृत् 'to be' makes विवर्तिषे &c. or विवृत्सामि &c. See the lists at 392–415.

c. The reduplication of the consonant is in conformity with the rules at 252; that of the vowel belonging to the initial consonant follows the analogy of Causal Aorists at 493; that is, the vowel इ *i* is reduplicated for *a*, *á*, *i*, *í*, *ṛi*, *ṛí*, *lṛi*, *e*, or *ai*; but the vowel उ *u* for *u*, *ú*, and *o*; and also for the *a* of *av* or *áv* preceded by any consonant except *j*, a labial or a semivowel; thus, fr. पच् 'to cook' comes Desid. stem *pipaksha* by 296; fr. याच् 'to ask,' *yiyáćisha*; fr. जीव् 'to live,' *jijívisha*; fr. दृश् 'to see,' *didṛiksha*; fr. सेव् 'to serve,' *sisevisha*; fr. गै 'to sing,' *jigása*; fr. ज्ञा 'to know,' *jijńása* (γιγνώσκω): but fr. युज् 'to join' comes *yuyuksha*; fr. पू 'to purify,' *pupúsha*; fr. बुध् cl. 4, 'to know,' बुभुत्स *bubhutsa*, see 299. *a*; fr. नावय, Causal stem of नु 'to praise,' *nunávayisha*; fr. पावय, Causal stem of पू 'to purify,' *pipávayisha*.

d. And if the root begin with a vowel the reduplication still follows the analogy of the same tense at 494; thus, from अश् comes अशिशश्; and with *isha* added, अशिशिष. Similarly, from अर्ह् comes *arjihisha*; from ऊह्, *újihisha*; from ईक्ष्, *íćikshisha*; from उन्द्, *undidisha*; see 494.

Obs.—In reduplication the vowel *i* takes the place of *a*, as being lighter; see 252. *d*. Obs. It is probably the result of a weakening of *a*.

e. In Desiderative stems formed from the Causals of च्यु 'to fall,' द्रु 'to run,' प्रु 'to go,' प्लु 'to leap,' श्रु 'to hear,' स्रु 'to distil,' and स्रु 'to flow,' *a* or *á* may be represented by either *u* or *i*; thus, the Causal of च्यु makes चिच्यावयिष or चुच्यावयिष.

f. Observe—When the inserted *s* becomes *sh* by 70, the initial स् of a root will not be affected by the vowel of the reduplicated syllable; thus, *sić* makes *sisiksha*, not *sishiksha*; and *sev* makes *sisevisha*. Except, however, स्तु, which makes तुष्टूष; and except the Desid. of Causals, as सिषेधयिष fr. Caus. of सिध्.

501. When a root takes the inserted *i* or *í* (393), and forms its Desiderative with *isha* or *ísha*, then the final ॠ *ṛí* is gunated.

Thus, तॄ 'to cross' makes *titarisha* or *titarísha* (also *titírsha*, see 502).

a. Moreover, initial and medial *i*, *u*, *ṛi* are often, but not always, gunated if followed by a single consonant.

Thus, उख् 'to go' makes *oćikhisha*; इष् 'to wish,' *eshishisha*; दिव् 'to play,' *didevisha*; नृत् 'to dance,' *ninartisha*: but विद् 'to know,' *vividisha*.

b. An option, as to Guṇa, is however generally allowed to medial *i* and *u*; thus, मुद् 'to rejoice' makes either *mumodisha* or *mumudisha*; क्लिद् 'to become moist' either *ćiklidisha* or *ćikledisha*; but roots in *iv* (e.g. *siv*) are peculiar, see 502. *b*.

c. इ 'to go' and उ 'to sound,' having no consonant, reduplicate the characteristic letter of the Desiderative with *i*; thus, ईषिष (used with the prepositions *adhi* and *prati*), so ऊषिष.

502. When a root rejects *i* and forms its Desiderative with स *sa*, this *sa*, if affixed to roots ending in vowels, has the effect of lengthening a final इ *i* or उ *u*; of changing ए *e*, ऐ *ai*, ओ *o*, to आ *á*; ऋ *ṛi* or ॠ *ṛí* to ईर् *ír*, or after a labial to ऊर् *úr*.

Thus, from चि comes *ćićísha*; from श्रु, *śuśrúsha*; from कृ, *ćikírsha*; from गै, *jigása*; from तॄ, *titírsha*; from पॄ, *pupúrsha*; from भृ, *bubhúrsha*; from मृ, *mumúrsha*.

a. When it is affixed to roots ending in consonants, the radical vowel generally remains unchanged, but the final consonant combines with the initial sibilant, in accordance with the rules at 296.

As, from युध् comes *yuyutsa* (299); from दह् comes *didhaksha* (306. *a*); from दुह्, *dudhuksha*; from भुज्, *bubhuksha*.

b. A medial long *ṛí* becomes *ír*, and final *iv* becomes *yú* or is gunated; thus, from कॄत् comes *ćikírtayisha*; from सिव्, *susyúsha* or *sisevisha*.

c. Many of the special rules for forming the stem in the last five tenses at 390. *a*–*o* apply to the Desiderative; thus the roots at 390. *a*. generally forbid Guṇa (*ćukućisha* &c.)

d. So भ्रस्ज् makes *bibhraksha* or *bibharksha* or *bibhrajjisha* or *bibharjisha* (390. *g*); मस्ज् and नश्, *mimanksha* and *ninanksha* (390. *k*); नह्, *ninatsa* (390. *o*); दरिद्रा,

didaridrisha (390. *c*, but makes also *didaridrása*); कम्, *ćikamisha* or *ćikámayisha*; गुप्, *jugopisha* or *jugopáyisha* or *jugupsa* (390. *l*).

503. The following is an alphabetical list of other Desiderative stems, some of them anomalous: अटिटिष fr. अट् 'to wander;' अट्टिटिष fr. अट्ट् 'to transgress;' अरिरिष fr. ऋ 'to go;' ईप्स fr. आप् 'to obtain;' ईर्त्स (or regularly अर्दिधिष) fr. ऋध् 'to prosper;' ईर्ष्यियिष or ईर्ष्यिषिष fr. ईर्ष्य् 'to envy;' ऊर्णुनूष or ऊर्णुनविष or ऊर्णुनुविष (390. *b*) fr. ऊर्णु 'to cover;' चिकीष (or regularly चिचीष) fr. चि 'to collect;' जिगांस (or regularly जिगमिष) fr. गम् 'to go;' जिगल्लिष (or regularly जिगरिष) fr. गॄ 'to swallow' (cf. 375. *q*); जिगीष fr. जि 'to conquer;' जिघत्स fr. घस् 'to eat' (used as Desid. of अद्); जिघांस fr. हन् 'to kill;' जिघीष fr. हि 'to send;' जिघृक्ष fr. ग्रह् 'to take;' जुहूष fr. ह्वे 'to call;' तितांस (or regularly तितनिष) fr. तन् 'to stretch;' तितृक्ष fr. तृंह् 'to kill;' दित्स fr. दा 'to give,' दे 'to love,' and दो 'to cut;' दिदरिष fr. दृ 'to respect;' दिदरिष or दिदरीष or दिदीर्षं fr. दॄ 'to tear;' दिद्युतिष or दिद्योतिष fr. द्युत् 'to shine;' दिधरिष fr. धृ 'to hold;' दुद्यूष (or regularly दिदेविष) fr. दिव् 'to play;' धित्स fr. धा 'to place' and धे 'to drink;' धिप्स or धीप्स (or दिदम्भिष) fr. दम्भ् 'to deceive;' पित्स (or पिपतिष) fr. पत् 'to fall' and पद् 'to go;' पिपविष or पुपूष fr. पू 'to purify;' पिपृच्छिष fr. प्रछ् 'to ask;' बिभरिष or बुभूर्षं fr. भृ 'to bear;' मित्स fr. मा 'to measure,' मि 'to throw,' मी 'to perish,' and मे 'to change;' मिमार्जिष or मिमृक्ष fr. मृज् 'to rub;' मोक्ष fr. मुच् (in the sense of 'desiring release from mundane existence,' otherwise मुमुक्ष); यियविष or युयूष fr. यु 'to join;' रित्स fr. राध् 'to accomplish;' रिप्स fr. रभ् 'to take;' लिप्स fr. लभ् 'to obtain;' विवरिष or विवरीष or वुवूर्षं fr. वृ 'to choose;' विव्रक्ष fr. व्रश्च् 'to cut;' शिक्ष fr. शक् 'to be able;' शिश्रयिष (or शिश्रीष) fr. श्रि 'to have recourse to;' सिषास (or सिसनिष) fr. सन् 'to obtain,' 'to give;' सिस्मयिष fr. स्मि 'to smile;' सिस्वरिष (or सुस्वूर्षं) fr. स्वृ 'to sound;' सुषुप्स fr. स्वप् 'to sleep.'

General Tenses of Desideratives.

504. The Perfect must be of the Periphrastic form as explained at 385; that is, आम् *ám* added to the Desiderative stem, as already formed, with *sa*, *isha*, or *ísha* (500), is prefixed to the Perfect of one of the auxiliaries *kṛi*, *as*, or *bhú* (see 385); thus, from *pipaksha* (root *pać*, 'to cook') comes the Perfect *pipakshánćakára*, 'I wished to cook;' from *bubodhisha* (root *budh*, 'to know') comes *bubodhishánćakára*, *bubodhishámása*, *bubodhishámbabhúva*, 'I wished to know.'

a. In all the remaining tenses it is a universal rule, that inserted *i* be assumed after the Desiderative stem, whether formed by *sa* or *isha*, except in the Precative Parasmai; thus, from *pać* comes 1st Fut. *pipakshitásmi* &c.; 2nd Fut. *pipakshishyámi* &c.; Aor. *apipakshisham* &c. (form I, B, at 418); Prec. Par. *pipakshyásam* &c.; Átm. *pipakshishíya* &c.; Cond. *apipakshishyam* &c. So also, taking *vividish* (formed with *isha* from *vid*, 'to know'), the 1st Fut. is *vividishitásmi*; 2nd Fut. *vividishishyámi*; Aor. *avividishisham* &c. Similarly, from *bubodhisha*, 1st Fut. *bubodhishitásmi* &c.; 2nd Fut. *bubodhishishyámi*; Aor. *abubodhishisham* &c.

b. The Infinitive may be formed regularly from the 1st Future; thus, from *bubodhishitá*, 'he will wish to know,' comes *bubodhishitum*, 'to wish to know.'

Passive of Desideratives.

505. Desideratives may take a Passive form by adding *ya* to the Desiderative stem after rejecting final *a*; thus, from *bubodhisha* comes *bubodhishye*, 'I am wished to know,' &c. The General tenses will not vary from the Active Átmane-pada form of Desiderative except in the Aor. 3rd sing., which will be *abubodhishi* instead of *abubodhishishṭa*.

Causal of Desideratives.

506. Desiderative verbs may take a Causal form; thus, *dudyúshámi*, 'I desire to play' (from *div*), makes in Caus. *dudyúshayámi*, 'I cause to desire to play,' &c.

FREQUENTATIVE OR INTENSIVE VERBS.

507. Most roots may take a Frequentative form, except polysyllabic roots, and except those of cl. 10, and except certain roots beginning with vowels.

Obs.—ऊर्णु 'to cover,' however, has forms ऊर्णोनूय and ऊर्णोनु. Some few roots also beginning with vowels take the Átmane form of Frequentative; see examples at 511. *a. b*, 681. *a.*

a. The Frequentative form is even less common in classical composition than the Desiderative. In the Pres. Part., however, and in nouns, it not unfrequently appears (see 80. VI). It either expresses repetition or gives intensity to the radical idea; thus, fr. दीप् 'to shine' comes the Frequent. stem *dedípya* (Pres. 3rd sing. *dedípyate*, 'it shines brightly'), and the Pres. Part. *dedípyamána*, 'shining brightly:' so also, fr. शुभ् 'to be beautiful,' *śośubhya* and *śośubhyamána*; fr. रुद् 'to weep,' *rorudya* and *rorudyamána*.

508. There are two kinds of Frequentative verb, the one a reduplicated Átmane-pada verb, with *ya* affixed, conforming, like Intransitive and Passive verbs, to the conjugation of cl. 4, and usually, though not always, yielding an Intransitive signification; the other a reduplicated Parasmai-pada verb, following the conjugation of cl. 3. The latter is less common in classical Sanskṛit than the former, and will therefore be considered last*.

a. The terminations for the first form of Frequentative will be those of the Átmane at 246, with the usual substitutions required for the 4th class of verbs. For the second form they will be the regular Parasmai-pada terminations of the scheme at 246.

---

* Intensive or Frequentative forms are found in Greek, such as παιπάλλω, δαιδάλλω, μαιμάζω or μαιμάω, παμφαίνω, ἀλαλάζω.

ÁTMANE-PADA FREQUENTATIVES, FORMED BY REDUPLICATION AND ADDING *ya*.

509. Rule for forming the stem in the four Special tenses.

Reduplicate the initial consonant and vowel of the Passive stem according to the rules for reduplicating consonants at 252, and gunate the reduplicated vowel (if capable of Guṇa), *whether it be a long or short vowel.*

Thus, from the Passive stem दीय (of *dá*, 'to give') comes the Frequent. stem *dedíya* (Pres. 1. *dedíya+i*=देदीये, 2. *dedíya+se*=देदीयसे &c.); fr. हीय (Pass. of *há*, 'to quit') comes *jehíya* (*jehíye* &c.); fr. स्तीर्य (of स्तॄ 'to spread') comes *testírya* (also *tástarya*); fr. पूय (of पू 'to purify'), *popúya;* fr. विद्य (of विद् 'to know'), *vevidya;* fr. बुध्य (of बुध् 'to know'), *bobudhya* (Pres. बोबुध्ये, बोबुध्यसे, बोबुध्यते, &c.) The conjugation of all four tenses corresponds exactly to that of the Passive.

510. As to the reduplication of the vowel, if the Passive stem contain a medial अ *a*, long *á* is substituted; thus, *pápaćya* from *paćya;* *sásmarya* from *smarya.*

a. If it contain a medial आ *á*, ए *e*, or ओ *o*, the same are reduplicated; as, *yáyáćya* from *yáćya;* *seshevya* from *sevya;* *loloćya* from *loćya.*

b. If it contain a medial ऋ *ṛi*, then अरी *arí** is substituted in the reduplication; as, दरीदृश्य from *dṛiśya;* परीस्पृश्य from *spṛiśya*, &c.; वरीवृश्च्य from व्रश्च्; बरीभृज्ज्य from भ्रज्ज्. Similarly, *alí* is substituted for ऌ *ḷri*, in क्लृप् making चलीक्लृप्य.

511. If a Passive stem has रि *ri* before *ya*, this रि *ri* becomes री *rí* in the Frequentative stem; as, चेक्रीय from क्रिय (Passive of कृ 'to do').

a. If the stem begin with अ *a*, as in अट्य *aṭya* (from अट् 'to wander'), the initial *aṭ* is repeated, and the radical *a* lengthened; thus, अटाट्य *aṭáṭya* (3rd sing. अटाट्यते). Similarly, अशाश्य from अश् 'to pervade.'

b. ऋ *ṛi*, 'to go,' makes its stem अरार्य *arárya.*

512. If the Passive stem contain a nasal after short *a*, this nasal generally appears in the reduplicated syllable, and is treated as final म् *m;* thus, fr. गम् 'to go' comes जङ्गम्य 'to walk crookedly;' fr. भ्रम् 'to wander,' बम्भ्रम्य; fr. हन् 'to kill,' चङ्घन्य.

a. The Passive stems जप्य, जभ्य, दह्य, and some others formed from roots containing nasals (as दश्य, भज्य), may insert nasals, instead of lengthening the vowel in the reduplication; thus, जञ्जप्य, जञ्जभ्य, दन्दह्य, &c.

b. Anomalous forms.—पद् 'to go' (making पद्य) inserts नी *ní;* thus, पनीपद्य. Similarly, पत् 'to fall,' कस् or कश् 'to go,' भ्रंश् 'to fall,' स्रंस् 'to drop,' ध्वंस् 'to fall,' स्कन्द् 'to go,' वञ्च् 'to deceive' (पनीपत्य, चनीकस्य, बनीभ्रश्य, सनीस्रस्य, दनीध्वस्य, चनीस्कद्य, &c.) चर् 'to go' makes चञ्चूर्य.

c. हन् 'to kill' makes जेघ्नीय; घ्रा 'to smell,' जेघ्रीय; ध्मा 'to blow,' देध्मीय (देध्मीये &c.); गॄ 'to swallow,' जेगिल्य.

---

* This seems to support the idea that the original Guṇa of *ṛi* is *aṛi*. See 29. *b*.

General Tenses of Átmane-pada Frequentatives.

513. In these tenses Frequentatives follow the analogy of Passives, and reject the suffix य *ya*. Since, however, the stem of the Perfect is formed by affixing आम् *ám* (as usual in all polysyllabic forms, see 385), and since, in all the other tenses, inserted *i* is assumed, a coalition of vowels might arise were it not allowed to retain *y* in all cases in which a vowel immediately precedes that letter *; thus, from देदीप्य is formed the Perfect 1st sing. देदीपाञ्चक्रे &c., rejecting *ya;* but from देदीय comes देदीयाञ्चक्रे &c., retaining *y*. Similarly in the other tenses: 1st Fut. *dedípitáhe, dedíyitáhe*, &c.; 2nd Fut. *dedípishye, dedíyishye*, &c.; Aor. *adedípishi, adedíyishi*, &c.; Prec. *dedípishíya, dedíyishíya*, &c.; Cond. *adedípishye, adedíyishye*, &c. In the 3rd sing. of the Aor. इ *i* is not allowed to take the place of the regular terminations, as in the Passive form.

a. The Infinitive, as formed in the usual manner (459), will be *dedípitum*, &c.

PARASMAI-PADA FREQUENTATIVES.

514. Rule for forming the stem in the four Special tenses. The stem is here also formed by a reduplication similar to that of Átmane-pada Frequentatives; not, however, from the Passive, but from the root; thus, from root पच् *pać* comes *pápać;* fr. विद् *vid* comes *vevid;* fr. दृश् comes *daríḍṛiś;* fr. कृ comes *ćaríkṛi*.

a. But in the Parasmai form of Frequentative, अरि *ari* and अर् *ar* as well as अरी *arí* may be reduplicated for the vowel ऋ *ṛi;* so that दृश् may make दरीदृश् or दरिदृश् or दर्दृश्; and कृ, चरीकृ or चरिकृ or चर्कृ (Páṇ. VII. 4, 92).

Similarly, क्लृप् may make चलीक्लृप् or चलिक्लृप् or चल्क्लृप्.

b. Again, in roots ending in long ॠ *ṝí*, *á* is reduplicated for ॠ *ṝí*, and this *á* is retained even when *ṝí* becomes *ir;* thus, कॄ *kṝí*, 'to scatter,' makes 1. *ćákarmi;* Pl. 3. *ćákirati*. Similarly, from तॄ 'to cross' come *tátarmi* and *tátirati*.

c. In the Special tenses Parasmai, these Frequentatives follow the conjugation of cl. 3, and in accordance with the rules for the 2nd and 3rd class (307, 331), the radical vowel is gunated before the P terminations of the scheme at 246. Hence, from *vid* come the two stems *veved* and *vevid* (Pres. *vevedmi, vevetsi, vevetti;* du. *vevidvas*, &c.; Impf. *avevedam, avevet, avevet, avevidva*, &c.; 3rd pl. *avevidus;* Pot. *vevidyám*, &c.; Impv. *vevedáni, veviddhi, vevettu, veveddva, vevittam*, &c.)

d. Again, the stem will vary in accordance with the rules of combination at 296–306, as in बुध् *budh* (Pres. *bobodhmi, bobhotsi, boboddhi, bobudhvas*, &c.; see 298). So also, वह् *vah* makes in 3rd sing. वावोढि *vávoḍhi* (see 305. *a*); दुह् makes दोदोग्धि (305); नह् makes नानद्धि (305 note); द्रुह् makes दोद्रोढि or दोद्रोग्धि; and स्निह्, सेष्णेढि or सेष्णेग्धि (305. *b*).

e. And in further analogy to cl. 2 (313, 314) long *í* is often optionally inserted

---

* In Passives this coalition of vowels is avoided by the change of a final vowel to Vṛiddhi, as of *ći* to *ćáy*, of *hu* to *háv*, and of *kṛi* to *kár;* and by the change of final *á* to *áy*, as of *dá* to *dáy;* see 474.

before the consonantal P terminations (Pres. *vevedími, vevedíshi, vevedíti;* du. *vevidvas*, &c.; Impf. *avevedam, avevedís, avevedít, avevidva*, &c.; Impv. *vevedáni, veviddhi, vevedítu*).

515. Lastly, when the root ends in a vowel, the usual changes take place of *i* and *í* to *y* or *iy;* of *u* and *ú* to *uv;* and of *ṛi* to *r* (see 312): as in the roots भी *bhí*, भू *bhú*, कृ *kṛi* (Pres. 1st sing. *bebhemi, bobhomi, ćarkarmi;* 3rd pl. *bebhyati, bobhuvati, ćarkrati*).

a. Observe—Many of the anomalous formations explained under Átmane-pada Frequentatives must be understood as belonging also to the Parasmai-pada; thus, पद् (512. *b*) makes in Parasmai पनीपद्मि, पनीपत्सि, पनीपत्ति, &c.; and so with the other roots at 512. *b*.

b. हन् 'to kill,' गॄ 'to swallow' (512. *c*), and some others have a separate Parasmai-pada form (जङ्घन्मि, जागर्मि; the last identical with Pres. of जागृ).

General Tenses of Parasmai-pada Frequentatives.

516. The Perfect follows the usual rule for polysyllabic roots (385), and affixes आम् *ám* with the auxiliaries; thus, from बुध् *budh*, 'to know,' comes *bobudhámása, bobudhámbabhúva, bobudhánćakára;* from विद् *vid*, 'to know,' comes *vevidámása*. Guṇa of a final and sometimes of a penultimate vowel is required before *ám;* thus, *bobhú* (from भू) becomes *bobhavámása*. So also, वृत् makes *vávartámása*. In the other tenses, excepting the Precative, inserted *i* is invariably assumed; and before this inserted *i* some roots are said to forbid the usual Guṇa change of the radical vowel in the 1st Fut. &c.; thus, *budh* is said to make *bobudhitásmi; bhí*, 'to fear,' *bebhyitásmi*, &c. (374); 2nd Fut. *bobudhishyámi, bebhyishyámi*, &c.; Aor. *abobudhisham, abebháyisham*, &c.; Prec. *bobudhyásam, bebhíyásam*, &c.; Cond. *abobudhishyam, abebhyishyam*, &c. The rejection of Guṇa from the radical syllable, however, admits of question; thus, *bhú*, 'to be,' makes, according to the best authorities, *bobhavitásmi*, &c.

a. The Infinitive will be formed in the usual way from the 1st Fut., see 513. *a*.

Passive, Causal, Desiderative, and Desiderative Causal form of Frequentatives.

517. Frequentatives are capable of all these forms. The Passive, when the root ends in a consonant, will be identical with the Átmane-pada Frequentative formed by reduplication and the suffix *ya;* thus, fr. Frequent. stem *totuda*, 'to strike often,' comes *totudye*, 'I am struck often;' but fr. *lolúya* (*lú*, 'to cut'), *lolúyye*, &c. Again, fr. *totuda* comes *totudayámi*, 'I cause to strike often;' *totudishámi*, 'I desire to strike often;' *totudayishámi*, 'I desire to cause to strike often.'

a. The *ya* of the Átmane-pada Frequentative if preceded by a consonant is rejected; but not if preceded by a vowel; thus, *lolúya*, Frequentative stem of *lú*, 'to cut,' makes *lolúyishámi*, 'I desire to cut often.' See 252. *f*.

NOMINAL VERBS, OR VERBS DERIVED FROM NOUNS.

518. These are formed by adding certain suffixes to the stem of nouns. They are not in very common use, but, theoretically, there is no limit to their formation. They might be classed according to their meaning; viz. 1st, Transitive Nominals, yielding the sense of performing, practising, making or using the thing or quality expressed by the noun; 2nd, Intransitive Nominals, giving a sense of behaving like, becoming like, acting like the person or thing expressed by the noun; 3rd, Desiderative Nominals, yielding the sense of wishing for the thing expressed by the noun. It will be more convenient, however, to arrange them under five heads, according to the suffixes by which they are formed, as follows:—

519. 1st, Those formed by affixing अ *a* (changeable to *á* before a syllable beginning with *m* and *v*) to a nominal stem, after Guṇa of its final vowel (if capable of Guṇa). When the stem ends in *a*, this vowel takes the place of the suffix *a*. A final *á* absorbs the suffix.

Obs.—The terminations of Nominals will be those of the scheme at 246, both for Par. and Átm., requiring the substitutions of the 1st, 4th, 6th, and 10th classes.

a. Thus, from कृष्ण 'Kṛishṇa,' Pres. 1. कृष्णामि 'I act like Kṛishṇa,' 2. कृष्णसि, 3. कृष्णति, &c. So, from कवि 'a poet,' Pres. 1. कवयामि 'I act the poet,' 2. कवयसि, &c.; and from पितृ 'a father,' Pres. 1. पितरामि 'I act like a father,' 2. पितरसि, 3. पितरति; Átm. Pres. 1. पितरे, &c.: from माला 'a garland,' Pres. 1. मालामि, 2. मालासि, 3. मालाति; Impf. 1. अमालाम्, 2. अमालास्, &c.; Pot. मालेयम्, &c.: from स्व 'own,' Pres. 3. स्वति 'he acts like himself.' Sometimes a final *i* or *u* is not gunated; as, from कवि 'a poet,' Pres. कव्यामि, कव्यसि, &c. (Páṇ. VII. 4, 39). Words ending in nasals preserve the nasals, and lengthen the preceding vowels; as, राजानति 'he acts like a king,' पथीनति 'it serves as a road,' इदामति 'he acts like this.'

520. 2ndly, Those formed by affixing य *ya* to a nominal stem.

a. If a word end in a consonant, *ya* is generally affixed without change; as, from वाच् 'a word,' वाच्यति 'he wishes for words;' from दिव् 'heaven,' दिव्यति 'he wishes for heaven' (or, according to some, दीव्यति); from तपस् 'penance,' तपस्यति 'he does penance;' from नमस् 'reverence,' नमस्यति 'he does reverence.' Final *n* is dropped, and the next rule then applied; thus, from राजन् 'a king,' Pres. राजीयामि, Pot. राजीयेयम्; from धनिन् 'rich,' धनीयामि, &c.

b. A final अ *a* or आ *á* is generally changed to ई *í*; final इ *i* or उ *u* lengthened; final ऋ *ṛi* changed to री *rí*; ओ *o* to *av*; औ *au* to *áv*.

Thus, from पुत्र 'a son,' Pres. 1. पुत्रीयामि 'I desire a son,' 2. पुत्रीयसि, &c.; from पति 'a husband,' Pres. 1. पतीयामि 'I desire a husband,' &c. So also, from मातृ 'a mother' comes मात्रीयामि, &c.

c. This form of Nominal has not always a Desiderative meaning. The following are examples of other meanings, some of which properly belong to the next form: प्रासादीयति 'he fancies himself in a palace;' कवीयति 'he acts like a poet;' कण्डूयति or -ते 'he scratches;' मन्तूयति or -ते 'he sins' or 'he is angry;' मित्रीयते 'he acts the part of a friend;' पुत्रीयति छात्रम् 'he treats the pupil as a son;' विष्णूयति द्विजम् 'he treats the Bráhman as if he were Vishṇu;' तिरस्यति 'he vanishes;' गव्यति 'he seeks cows' (from गो 'a cow').

d. In the sense of 'behaving like,' 'acting like,' 'doing like,' a final अ *a* is generally lengthened, a final आ *á* retained, and a final न् *n*, स् *s*, or त् *t* dropped; thus, from पण्डित 'a wise man,' Pres. 1. पण्डिताये 'I act the part of a wise man,' 2. पण्डितायसे, 3. पण्डितायते, &c.; from द्रुम 'a tree,' Pres. 1. द्रुमाये, &c.; from शब्द 'a noise,' Pres. शब्दाये 'I am noisy;' from राजन् 'a king,' Pres. 1. राजाये, &c.; from उन्मनस् 'sorrowful,' Pres. उन्मनाये, &c.; from बृहत् 'great,' Pres. बृहाये, &c.

e. This Nominal is sometimes found with a Transitive sense, especially when derived from nouns expressive of colour; as, from कृष्ण 'black,' कृष्णायते or -ति 'he blackens:' and sometimes in the Parasmai with an Intransitive sense; as, from जिह्म 'crooked,' जिह्मायति 'it is crooked;' from दास 'a slave,' दासायति 'he is a slave.' It corresponds to Greek Desiderative Denominatives in ιαω, as θανατιάω &c.

521. 3rdly, Those formed by affixing अय *aya* to a nominal stem. This form is similar to that of Causals and verbs of the 10th class, with which it is sometimes confounded. Like them it has generally an Active sense. A final vowel must be dropped before *aya;* and if the nominal stem have more than one syllable, and end in a consonant, both the consonant and its preceding vowel must be dropped.

a. Thus, from वस्त्र 'cloth,' Pres. 1. वस्त्रयामि 'I clothe,' 2. वस्त्रयसि, 3. वस्त्रयति, &c.; from वर्मन् 'armour,' Pres. 1. वर्मयामि 'I put on armour,' &c.; from प्रमाण 'authority,' प्रमाणयामि 'I propose as authority;' from स्रज् 'a garland,' स्रजयामि 'I crown;' from घट 'a jar,' घटयामि 'I make a jar' or 'I call it a jar,' &c.

b. In further analogy to Causals, प् *p* is sometimes inserted between the stem and *aya*, especially if the noun be monosyllabic, and end in *a*. Before this प् *p*, Vṛiddhi is required; thus, from स्व 'own,' Pres. स्वापयामि 'I make my own.' There are one or two examples of dissyllabic nouns; thus, from सत्य 'true,' सत्यापयामि, &c.; and from अर्थ 'substance,' अर्थापयामि, &c.

c. If the stem be monosyllabic, and end in a consonant, Guṇa may take place; as, from क्षुध् 'hunger,' क्षोधयामि.

d. Whatever modifications adjectives undergo before the suffixes *íyas* and *ishṭha* at 194, the same generally take place before *aya;* thus, from दीर्घ 'long,' द्राघयामि 'I lengthen;' from अन्तिक 'near,' नेदयामि 'I make near,' &c.

e. This form of Nominal is sometimes Intransitive, as चिरयति 'he delays' (from चिर 'long'). According to Bopp, Greek Denominatives in αω, εω, οω, ιζω correspond to this form; as, πολεμ-όω, γυναικ-ίζω.

522. 4thly, Those formed by affixing स्य *sya* or अस्य *asya* to a nominal stem, giving it the form of a Future tense, generally with the sense of 'desiring,' 'longing for.'

a. Thus, fr. क्षीर 'milk,' Pres. 1. क्षीरस्यामि 'I desire milk,' 2. क्षीरस्यसि, &c.; fr. वृष 'a bull,' वृषस्यति '(the cow) desires the bull;' fr. दधि 'curds,' दध्यस्यामि 'I desire curds,' &c. Cf. Greek Desideratives in σειω.

523. 5thly, Those formed by affixing काम्य *kámya* (derived from *kam*, 'to desire') to a nominal stem; as, from पुत्र 'a son,' Pres. 1. पुत्रकाम्यामि 'I desire a son,' 2. पुत्रकाम्यसि, 3. पुत्रकाम्यति, &c.; from यशस् 'fame,' यशस्काम्यामि 'I desire fame.'

a. The General tenses of these Nominals will be formed analogously to those of other verbs; thus, from स्वामि 'I act like self' comes Perf. सस्वौ; from कुमारयामि 'I play like a boy' comes Aor. अचुकुमारम्, &c. A long vowel in the stem generally remains unchanged, and is not shortened; thus, मालयामि (from माला 'a garland') makes अममालम्. So also, समिध्यिता 'he will wish for fuel' (Guṇa being omitted), पुत्रकाम्यिता 'he will wish for a son.'

b. Nominal verbs may take Passive, Causal, Desiderative, and Frequentative forms. The Causal of those formed with *aya* will be identical with the Primitive Nominal; thus, वर्मयामि 'I put on armour' or 'I cause to put on armour.' In reduplicating for the Desiderative or Frequentative, sometimes the last syllable is repeated, sometimes the first; thus, कण्डूय 'to scratch' makes its Desiderative stem कण्डूयियिष, and पुत्रीय 'to treat as a son' makes पुपुत्रीयिष or पुत्रीयियिष. According to some, the middle syllable may be reduplicated; thus, पुतित्रीयिष.

PARTICIPLES.

PRESENT PARTICIPLES; PARASMAI-PADA.—FORMATION OF STEM.

524. Present Participles are the only Participles the formation of which is connected with the conjugational class of the verb. The stem in the Parasmai may be most easily formed by dropping the final *i* of the 3rd pers. pl. Pres. Par. and rejecting the nasal in certain cases (see 141. *a*, 84. I); e.g.

From पचन्ति *paćanti*, 'they cook' (3rd pl. Pres. of पच्, cl. 1), comes पचत् *paćat*, 'cooking;' fr. घ्नन्ति *ghnanti*, 'they kill' (3rd pl. of *han*, cl. 2), comes घ्नत् *ghnat*, 'killing;' fr. सन्ति *santi*, 'they are' (3rd pl. of *as*, cl. 2, 'to be'), comes सत् *sat*, 'being;' fr. यन्ति *yanti*, 'they go' (3rd pl. of इ, cl. 2), यत् *yat*, 'going;' fr. यान्ति

yánti, 'they go' (3rd pl. of या, cl. 2), यात् *yát*; fr. जुह्वति *juhvati*, 'they sacrifice' (3rd pl. of *hu*, cl. 3), जुह्वत् *juhvat*; fr. नृत्यन्ति *nrityanti*, 'they dance,' cl. 4, नृत्यत् *nrityat*; fr. चिन्वन्ति *ćinvanti*, 'they gather,' cl. 5, चिन्वत् *ćinvat*; fr. आप्नुवन्ति *ápnuvanti*, 'they obtain,' cl. 5, आप्नुवत् *ápnuvat*; fr. तुदन्ति *tudanti*, 'they strike,' cl. 6, *tudat*; fr. रुन्धन्ति *rundhanti*, 'they hinder,' cl. 7, *rundhat*; fr. कुर्वन्ति *kurvanti*, 'they do,' cl. 8, *kurvat*; fr. पुनन्ति *punanti*, 'they purify,' cl. 9, *punat*.

525. The same holds good in Derivative and Nominal verbs; e. g.

From Caus. बोधयन्ति 'they cause to know' (479) comes बोधयत् 'causing to know;' fr. Desid. बुबोधिषन्ति (499) comes बुबोधिषत् 'desiring to know;' fr. दित्सन्ति (503) comes दित्सत् 'desiring to give;' fr. Frequent. चेक्षिपति comes चेक्षिपत् 'throwing frequently;' from the Nominal कृष्णन्ति 'they act like Krishṇa,' कृष्णात् 'acting like Krishṇa;' fr. तपस्यन्ति 'they do penance,' तपस्यत् 'doing penance.'

a. In corroboration of the remark made at 461. *c*, that the Passive verb appears in a few rare instances to assume a Parasmai-pada inflexion, and that many of the Intransitive verbs placed under cl. 4 might be regarded (except for the accent) as examples of this form of the Passive, it is certain that a Parasmai-pada Present Participle derivable from a Passive stem is occasionally found; thus, दृश्यत् 'being seen,' from the Passive stem दृश्य *driśya*; चीयत् 'being gathered,' from चीय *ćíya* (Passive stem of *ći*).

b. The inflexion of Parasmai-pada Present Participles is explained at 141. The first five or strong inflexions (see 135. *a*) of this participle in nine conjugational classes retain the nasal, shewing that the stem in all the classes, except the third, and a few other verbs (141. *a*), ends in *ant* as well as in *at*. The Parasmai-pada Frequentative, as conforming to the conjugational rule for cl. 3, also rejects the nasal.

Obs.—In the cognate languages the *n* is preserved throughout. Cf. Sk. *bharan*, *bharantam* (fr. *bhri*), with φέρων, φέροντα, *ferentem*; also, *bharantau* (Ved. *bharantá*) with φέροντε; *bharantas* with φέροντες, *ferentes*; *bharatas* with φέροντας; Gen. sing. *bharatas* with φέροντος, *ferentis*. So also, Sk. *vahan*, *vahantam*, with Lat. *vehens*, *vehentem*; and *san*, *santam* (fr. *as*, 'to be'), with Lat. *-sens* of *ab-sens*, *præ-sens*. Cf. also the strong stem *striṇvant-* with στορνυντ-.

PRESENT PARTICIPLES; ÁTMANE-PADA.—FORMATION OF STEM.

526. The stem is formed by substituting मान *mána* for न्ते *nte*, the termination of the 3rd pl. Pres. Átm. of verbs of the 1st, 4th, 6th, and 10th classes, and Derivative verbs (see 527, 528, below); and by substituting आन *ána* for अते *ate*, the termination of the 3rd pl. Pres. Átm. of verbs of the other classes (see 246); e. g.

From पचन्ते *paćante* (cl. 1) comes पचमान *paćamána*, 'cooking;' fr. तिष्ठन्ते (*sthá*, cl. 1), तिष्ठमान 'standing;' fr. नृत्यन्ते (cl. 4), नृत्यमान; fr. लिम्पन्ते (*lip*, cl. 6), लिम्पमान.

a. But from ब्रुवते *bruvate* (ब्रू cl. 2), ब्रुवाण *bruváṇa* (58); fr. निघ्नते (हन् with नि cl. 2), निघ्नान; fr. दधते (*dhá*, cl. 3), दधान; fr. चिन्वते (cl. 5), चिन्वान; fr. युञ्जते (cl. 7), युञ्जान; fr. कुर्वते (cl. 8), कुर्वाण; fr. पुनते (cl. 9), पुनान. Root आस् cl. 2, 'to sit,' makes आसीन for आसान; and शी cl. 2 is शेरते in 3rd pl. (see 315), but शयान in Pres. Part.

Obs.—The real suffix for the Pres. Part. Átm. is *mána*, of which *ána* is probably an abbreviation. Cf. Gr. -μενο- in φερό-μενο-ς=*bhara-máṇa* (58).

527. Verbs of class 10 and Causals substitute मान *mána;* as, fr. बोधयन्ते *bodhayante* comes बोधयमान *bodhayamána:* but occasionally आन *ána;* as, fr. दर्शयन्ते, दर्शयान; fr. वेदयन्ते, वेदयान; fr. चिन्तयन्ते, चिन्तयान; fr. पूजयन्ते, पूजयान.

528. Passives, Desideratives, Frequentatives, &c. substitute मान *mána* for the Átmane; thus, from क्रियन्ते 'they are made' comes क्रियमाण 'being made' (58); from दीयन्ते 'they are given,' दीयमान 'being given;' from the Desiderative दित्सन्ते 'they desire to give,' दित्समान 'desiring to give;' from जिघांसन्ते 'they desire to kill,' जिघांसमान 'desiring to kill;' from the Frequentative बोबुध्यन्ते 'they know repeatedly,' बोबुध्यमान 'knowing repeatedly.'

529. The inflexion of Pres. Participles Átmane follows that of adjectives at 187; as, N. sing. m. f. n. पचमानस्, पचमाना, पचमानम्.

PAST PARTICIPLES.

PAST PASSIVE PARTICIPLES.—FORMATION OF STEM.

530. This is the most common and useful of all Participles. In general the stem is formed by adding त *ta* directly to roots ending in vowels, and to most roots ending in consonants; as, fr. या *yá*, 'to go,' यात *yáta*, 'gone;' fr. जि 'to conquer,' जित 'conquered;' fr. नी 'to lead,' नीत 'led;' fr. क्षिप् *kship*, 'to throw,' क्षिप्त *kshipta*, 'thrown;' fr. कृ 'to do,' कृत 'done' (see 80. XVII).

a. But if the root end in ॠ *ṛí*, by adding न *na*, changeable to ण *ṇa* (58); as, fr. कॄ *kṛí*, 'to scatter,' कीर्ण *kírṇa*, 'scattered,' see 534.

531. Some roots in आ *á*, ई *í*, and ऊ *ú*, some in ऐ *ai* preceded by two consonants, with some of those in द् *d*, र् *r*, ज् *j*, one in ग् *g* (लग्), and one or two in च् *ć*, छ् *ćh* (see 541, 544), also take *na* instead of *ta;* see 80. XXIV, 532, 536, 540, &c.

532. Roots ending in vowels do not generally admit inserted इ *i* in this Participle, even when they admit it in the Futures (392, 395, &c.), but attach *ta* or *na* directly to the root; as, fr. पा 'to

protect,' पात; fr. श्रि 'to resort to,' श्रित; fr. श्रु 'to hear,' श्रुत; भू 'to become,' भूत; कृ 'to do,' कृत; घ्रा 'to smell,' घ्राण (58); डी 'to fly,' डीन; दी 'to decay,' दीन; मी 'to perish,' मीन; ली 'to embrace,' लीन; ह्री 'to be ashamed,' ह्रीण; लू 'to cut,' लून; दु 'to be afflicted,' दून; श्वि 'to swell,' शून.

a. But when they do retain *i*, gunation of the final vowel is required as in the Future; thus, शी 'to lie down' makes शयित; and पू 'to purify,' पवित (also पूत); and जागृ 'to awake,' जागरित.

533. In certain cases the final vowel of the root is changed; thus, some roots in आ *á* change *á* to *i* before *ta;* as, from स्था *sthá*, 'to stand,' स्थित *sthita;* from मा 'to measure,' मित; from दरिद्रा 'to be poor,' दरिद्रित.

a. धा 'to place' becomes हित; दा 'to give,' दत्त.

Obs.—When prepositions are prefixed to *datta*, the initial *da* may be rejected; thus, *átta* for *ádatta*, 'taken;' *pratta* for *pradatta*, 'bestowed;' *vyátta* for *vyádatta*, 'expanded;' *nítta* for *nidatta*, 'given away;' *parítta* for *paridatta*, 'delivered over;' *sútta* for *sudatta*, 'well given,' the *i* and *u* being lengthened.

b. पा 'to drink' makes पीत; but हा 'to quit,' हीन; and ज्या 'to grow old,' जीन; हा 'to go,' हान.

c. Some roots in *á* take both *na* and *ta;* as, fr. घ्रा 'to smell,' घ्राण and घ्रात; fr. वा 'to blow,' with prep. निर्, निर्वाण and निर्वात; fr. श्रा (or श्रै) 'to cook,' श्राण or श्रित.

534. Roots in ॠ *ṛí* change *ṛí* to *ír* before *na*, which passes into ण *ṇa* by 58; as, from तॄ 'to pass,' तीर्ण 'passed.' But when a labial precedes, *ṛí* becomes *úr;* as, from पॄ or पूर, पूर्त or पूर्ण 'full,' 'filled.'

535. The root धे *dhe*, 'to suck,' forms धीत; ह्वे *hve*, 'to call,' हूत; वे *ve*, 'to weave,' उत; व्ये *vye*, 'to cover,' वीत; मे 'to barter,' मित.

536. Roots in ऐ *ai* generally change *ai* to *á* before *na* or *ta;* as, from म्लै *mlai*, 'to fade,' म्लान *mlána;* from ध्यै 'to meditate,' ध्यात (in the Veda धीत); from दै 'to purify,' दात; from त्रै 'to rescue,' त्राण or त्रात; from प्यै 'to grow fat,' प्यान, &c.

a. But fr. गै 'to sing,' गीत; fr. सै 'to waste,' सीत; fr. क्षै 'to waste,' क्षाम, see 548; fr. श्यै 'to coagulate,' शीत or शीन or श्यान; fr. स्त्यै 'to accumulate,' स्त्यान, (with प्र) स्तीत or स्तीम.

537. Of the four or five roots in ओ *o*, सो 'to destroy' makes सित (as also सि 'to bind'); शो 'to sharpen,' शित or शात; दो 'to tie,' दित; छो 'to cut,' छात and छित; ज्यो 'to instruct,' जीत.

538. Those roots ending in consonants which take the inserted *i* in the last five tenses (399), generally take this vowel also in the Past Pass. Part., but not invariably (see 542); and when *i* is assumed, *ta* is generally affixed, and not *na;* as, from पत् *pat*, 'to fall,' पतित *patita*, 'fallen.'

a. इ *i*, उ *u*, or ऋ *ṛi* preceding the final consonant of a root may occasionally take Guṇa, especially if the Participle be used impersonally; as, fr. स्विद् 'to sweat,' स्वेदित or स्विन्न; fr. क्ष्विद् 'to be unctuous,' क्ष्वेदित or क्ष्विण्ण; fr. द्युत् 'to shine,' द्योतित or द्युतित; fr. मृष् 'to bear,' मर्षित; fr. मृष् 'to sprinkle,' मृष्ट. See Syntax, 895.

b. ग्रह् 'to take' lengthens the inserted *i*, making गृहीत. See 399. *a.*

539. Roots ending in consonants which reject the inserted *i* in the last five tenses (400–415), generally reject it in the Past Pass. Part. They must be combined with *ta*, agreeably to the rules of Sandhi at 296, &c. Whatever change, therefore, the final consonant undergoes before the termination *tá* of the 1st Fut. (see 400–415), the same will often be preserved before the *ta* of the Past Part.; so that, in many cases, the form of this Participle resembles that of the 3rd sing. 1st Fut., provided the final *á* be shortened, and the vowel of the root preserved unaltered; thus, taking some of the roots at 400–415; शक् (शक्ता), शक्त; सिच् (सेक्ता), सिक्त; मुच् (मोक्ता), मुक्त; त्यज्, त्यक्त; युज्, युक्त; सृज्, सृष्ट; मृज् and मृश्, मृष्ट; सिध्, सिद्ध; बुध्, बुद्ध; युध्, युद्ध; क्षिप्, क्षिप्त; लुप्, लुप्त; सृप्, सृप्त; क्लृप्, क्लृप्त; लभ्, लब्ध; लुभ्, लुब्ध; विश्, विष्ट; दृश्, दृष्ट; क्रुश्, क्रुष्ट; श्लिष्, श्लिष्ट; दुष्, दुष्ट; कृष्, कृष्ट; इष्, इष्ट; दह्, दग्ध; सह्, सोढ (415. *m*); नह्, नद्ध (414); गाह्, गाढ (415. *m*); लिह्, लीढ; दिह्, दिग्ध; स्निह्, स्निग्ध; रुह्, रूढ; मुह्, मूढ or मुग्ध (415. *m*); दुह्, दुग्ध; गुह्, गूढ (415. *m*).

540. Most roots ending in द् *d*, forbidding the inserted इ *i* (405), take *na* instead of *ta*, and are combined with *na*, agreeably to 47; as, fr. पद् 'to go,' पन्न; fr. विद् 'to find,' विन्न (also वित्त); fr. नुद् 'to impel,' नुन्न (also नुत्त); fr. भिद् 'to break,' भिन्न; fr. सद् 'to sit,' 'to sink,' सन्न, with वि, विषण्ण (70, 58); fr. क्षुद् 'to pound,' क्षुण्ण; fr. छृद् 'to play,' 'to vomit,' छृण्ण; fr. अद् 'to eat,' अन्न (unless जग्ध be substituted). ह्लाद् 'to rejoice' makes ह्लन्न.

541. Roots ending in च् *ć* or ज् *j* of course change these letters to *k* before *ta*; see examples at 539. Similarly, those which take *na*, change *ć* and *j* to *g* before *na*; as, fr. नज् 'to be ashamed,' नग्न 'naked;' fr. विज् 'to tremble,' विग्न; fr. रुज् 'to break,' रुग्ण; fr. स्फूर्ज् 'to thunder,' स्फूर्ग्ण; fr. अञ्च् 'to move' (in some senses), अक्न. So, fr. मस्ज् 'to be immersed,' rejecting one *j*, मग्न; from लस्ज् 'to be ashamed,' लग्न (as well as लज्जित). लग् 'to adhere' also makes लग्न. But स्फुर्छ् 'to forget,' स्फूर्ण; हुर्छ् 'to be crooked,' हूर्ण.

542. Some roots which admit *i* necessarily or optionally in one or both of the Futures, reject it in this participle; thus, धृष् 'to be bold' makes धृष्ट. According to Páṇ. VII. 2. 24, अर्द् 'to move' makes अर्ण *arṇa* after the prepositions *sam*, *ni*, and *vi*, and in every other case अर्दित *ardita*, so that after *á* prefixed, it becomes आर्दित

(आर्त 'pained' is thought by some to be *ṛita*, fr. rt. *ṛi*, with prep. *á* prefixed, and by others is regarded as an anomalous form of rt. *ard;* by native grammarians a form अर्त्त *artta* is referred to rt. ऋत्); दृंह् 'to make firm,' दृढ; वृह् 'to extol,' वृढ; मद् 'to be mad,' मत्त; दीप् 'to shine,' दीप्त; नश् 'to perish,' नष्ट; मुर्छ् 'to faint,' मूर्त्त as well as मूर्च्छित; म्लेच्छ् 'to speak barbarously,' म्लिष्ट as well as म्लेच्छित; नृत् 'to dance,' नृत्त; यत् 'to strive,' यत्त.

543. If in forming the Passive stem (471), the *v* or *y* contained in a root is changed to its semivowel *u* or *i*, the same change takes place in the Past Pass. Part.; as, fr. वच् *vać*, 'to say,' उक्त *ukta;* fr. वद् 'to speak,' उदित; fr. वश् 'to wish,' उशित; fr. वस् 'to dwell,' उषित; fr. वप् 'to sow,' उप्त; fr. वह् 'to carry,' ऊढ (with प्र, प्रौढ, 38. *n*); fr. स्वप् 'to sleep,' सुप्त; fr. यज् 'to sacrifice,' इष्ट.

Obs.—This change of a semivowel to its corresponding vowel is called Sampra-sáraṇa by native grammarians (Páṇ. I. I, 45).

a. Some roots change व् with a preceding or following vowel into ऊ; as, ज्वर् 'to be feverish,' जूर्ण; त्वर् 'to hasten,' तूर्ण; स्रिव् 'to dry,' स्रूत; अव् 'to protect,' ऊत; मव् 'to bind,' मूत.

b. Some roots ending in व् also substitute ऊ for व्; as, दिव् 'to play,' द्यूत and द्यून (the former only in the sense of 'to gamble'); सिव् 'to sew,' स्यूत; ष्ठिव् or ष्ठीव् 'to spit,' ष्ठ्यूत; ष्ठिव् or ष्ठीव् 'to spit,' ष्ठ्यूत.

544. Some other changes which take place in forming the Passive stem (472) are preserved before *ta;* thus, fr. शास् 'to rule,' शिष्ट; fr. व्यध् 'to pierce,' विद्ध; fr. व्यच् 'to deceive,' विचित; fr. भ्रस्ज् 'to fry,' भृष्ट; fr. प्रछ् 'to ask,' पृष्ट; fr. व्रश्च् 'to cut,' वृक्ण (58).

a. When a root ends in a conjunct consonant, of which the first is a nasal, this nasal is generally rejected before *ta;* as, fr. बन्ध् 'to bind,' बद्ध; fr. भ्रंश् 'to fall,' भ्रष्ट; fr. ध्वंस् 'to fall,' ध्वस्त; fr. अञ्च् 'to move' and अञ्ज् 'to anoint,' अक्त; fr. सञ्ज् 'to adhere,' सक्त; fr. रञ्ज् 'to colour,' रक्त; fr. इन्ध् 'to kindle,' इद्ध; fr. उन्द् 'to be wet,' उत्त or उन्न; fr. स्यन्द् 'to flow,' स्यन्न; fr. स्कन्द् 'to ascend,' स्कन्न; fr. स्कम्भ् 'to stop,' स्कब्ध; fr. स्तम्भ् 'to stop,' स्तब्ध; fr. दम्भ् 'to deceive,' दब्ध; fr. भञ्ज् 'to break,' भग्न; fr. दंश् 'to bite,' दष्ट; fr. तञ्च् 'to contract,' तक्त.

b. But not if इ *i* is inserted; as, fr. खण्ड् 'to break,' खण्डित; fr. क्रन्द्, क्रन्दित (except मन्थ् 'to churn,' making मथित; and ग्रन्थ् 'to tie,' ग्रथित).

545. Many roots ending in म् *m*, न् *n*, or ण् *ṇ* reject these nasals before *ta* if *i* is not inserted; as, गम् *gam*, 'to go,' गत *gata;* यम् *yam*, 'to restrain,' यत *yata;* रम् 'to sport,' रत; तन् 'to stretch,' तत; हन् 'to kill,' हत; नम् 'to bend,' नत; मन् 'to think,' मत; क्षण् 'to hurt,' क्षत: but अन् 'to breathe' and अम् 'to go' make आन्त (the latter also अमित); and स्वन् 'to sound,' स्वनित (also स्वान्त with prep.)

a. जन् 'to be born' makes जात; and खन् 'to dig,' खात; सन् 'to give,' सात; medial *a* being lengthened.

546. Those roots ending in म् *m*, of the 4th class, which lengthen a medial *a* before the conjugational suffix *ya*, also lengthen it before *ta*, changing *m* to *n* as in the Futures; thus, fr. क्रम् 'to step,' क्रान्त; fr. भ्रम् 'to wander,' भ्रान्त; fr. शम् 'to

be appeased,' शान्त; fr. दम् 'to tame,' दान्त (also दमित); fr. क्षम् 'to be patient,' क्षान्त; fr. क्लम् 'to be sad,' क्लान्त.

a. Similarly, वम् 'to vomit,' वान्त; कम् 'to love,' कान्त; चम् 'to eat,' चान्त.

547. From स्फाय् 'to swell' is formed स्फीत; fr. क्ष्माय् 'to shake,' क्ष्मात; fr. पूय् 'to be putrid,' पूत; from ऊय् 'to weave,' ऊत; fr. प्याय् 'to be fat,' पीन (with आ and प्र, -प्यान); fr. क्नूय् 'to stink,' क्नूत.

a. गुर् or गूर् 'to make effort' forms गूर्ण; तुर्व् 'to kill,' like त्वर् 'to hasten,' तूर्ण; मुर्व् 'to bind or tie' makes मूर्ण; धाव् 'to wash,' धौत.

b. फल् 'to open' makes फुल्ल (Páṇ. VIII. 2, 55); and घस् 'to eat,' जग्ध (fr. जक्ष्).

Obs.—From the above examples it appears that sometimes several roots have the same form of Past Pass. Part. The following may also be noted: पूय् 'to stink' and पू 'to purify' make पूत; मा 'to measure' and मे 'to barter,' मित; मृज् 'to wipe,' मृश् 'to touch,' and मृष् 'to sprinkle,' all make मृष्ट (मृष् 'to bear' making मर्षित by Páṇ. I. 2, 20); शंस् 'to recite' and शस् 'to kill,' शस्त; शास् 'to rule' and शिष् 'to distinguish,' शिष्ट; सो 'to destroy' and सि 'to tie,' सित. On the other hand, भुज् 'to enjoy' makes भुक्त; but भुज् 'to bend,' भुग्न.

548. The following, though regarded as Participles by native grammarians, are more properly adjectives: पक्व, fr. पच् *pać*, 'to cook;' शुष्क, fr. शुष् 'to dry;' क्षीव, fr. क्षीव् 'to be drunk;' कृश, fr. कृश् 'to grow thin;' क्षाम, fr. क्षै 'to waste.'

549. In forming the Past Pass. Part. of Causals, the Causal suffix अय *aya* is rejected, but the inserted इ *i* is always assumed; as, fr. कारय, Causal of कृ 'to make,' comes कारित *kárita*, 'caused to be made;' fr. स्थापय, Causal of स्था 'to stand,' स्थापित *sthápita*, 'placed;' fr. आप्याय (प्यै with आ), आप्यायित 'increased,' 'refreshed.'

550. In adding त *ta* to a Desiderative or Frequentative stem, the inserted इ *i* is assumed, final *a* of the stem being dropped; and in the case of roots ending in consonants, final *ya* being dropped; as, fr. पिपास 'to desire to drink' comes पिपासित; fr. चिकीर्ष 'to desire to do,' चिकीर्षित; fr. ईप्स 'to desire to obtain,' ईप्सित, &c.; fr. लोलूय 'to cut often,' लोलूयित; fr. बेभिद्य 'to break frequently,' बेभिदित.

551. त *ta* with *i* is added to nominal stems, final *a* being dropped; as, fr. शिथिल 'loose,' शिथिलित 'loosened;' fr. जिह्म 'crooked,' जिह्मित 'curved.' These may be regarded as Past Passive Participles of the Transitive Nominal verbs शिथिलयति, जिह्मयति (521). So again, from नमस्य 'to do reverence' comes नमस्यित or नमसित.

Obs.—Moreover, as *na* sometimes takes the place of *ta*, so *ina* is added to some nouns instead of *ita*: e.g. मलिन 'soiled,' fr. मल 'dirt;' शृङ्गिण (58) 'horned,' from शृङ्ग 'a horn.' See 80. XLIII.

a. Corresponding forms in Latin are *barbatus*, *alatus*, *cordatus*, *turritus*, &c.; and in Greek, ὀμφαλωτός, κροκωτός, αὐλωτός, &c.

552. The inflexion of Past Passive Participles follows that of adjectives at 187; thus exhibiting a perfect similarity to the declension of Latin participles in *tus;* thus, कृत *kṛita,* Nom. sing. masc. fem. neut. कृतस्, कृता, कृतम्.

a. The resemblance between Sanskṛit Past Passive Participles in *ta,* Latin Participles in *tu-s,* and Greek verbals in *το-ς,* may be seen in the following examples: Sk. *jñáta-s* = Lat. *(g)notu-s (ignotus), γνωτό-ς;* Sk. *datta-s* = Lat. *datus, δοτός; śruta-s=clutus, κλυτό-ς; bhúta-s=φυτό-ς; yukta-s=junctu-s, ζευκτό-ς; labdha-s =ληπτό-ς; píta-s=πότο-ς; bhṛita-s=φερτό-ς; dishṭa-s=dictu-s, δεικτό-ς.* And, like Sanskṛit, Latin often inserts an *i,* as in *domitu-s* (=Sk. *damita-s*), *monitu-s,* &c. This is not the case in Greek, but *ε* is inserted in forms like *μενετό-ς, ἑρπετό-ς.* There are also examples of Latin and Greek formations in *nu-s* and *νο-ς,* corresponding to the Sanskṛit participle in *na;* thus, *plenu-s* (=*púrṇa-s*), *magnu-s* (cf. Sk. rt. *mah*), *dignu-s* (cf. Sk. *diś, dik,* Gr. *δεικ*); and *στυγνό-ς, στεγνό-ς, σεμνό-ς,* &c.

PAST ACTIVE PARTICIPLES.

These are of two kinds: A. those derived from the Past Passive Participle; B. those belonging to the Reduplicated Perfect. The former frequently supply the place of a Perfect tense Active (see 897).

553. A. The stem of these Participles is formed by adding वत् *vat* to that of the Past Passive Participle; e.g.

From कृत 'made,' कृतवत् 'having made,' 'who or what has made;' fr. दग्ध 'burnt,' दग्धवत् 'having burnt;' fr. उक्त 'said,' उक्तवत् 'having said;' fr. भिन्न 'broken,' भिन्नवत् 'having broken;' fr. स्थापित 'placed,' स्थापितवत् 'having placed,' &c.

a. For the declension of these Participles see 140. *a. b. c.*

554. B. In these Participles, either वस् *vas* or इवस् *ivas* is generally added to the stem of the Reduplicated Perfect, as formed in the dual and plural. *Vas* is added when the stem in the dual and plural (as it appears in its unchanged form before the terminations are added) consists of more than one syllable; thus, from *ćakṛi* (root *kṛi,* 'to do'), *ćakṛivas;* from *ćići* (374), *ćićivas;* from *nanṛit* (364, compare 45. *a*), *nanṛitvas;* from *sasmar* (374. *k*), *sasmarvas.*

a. And *ivas* is added when the stem in the dual and plural consists of one syllable only; as, from *ten* (375. *a*), *tenivas;* from *ghas* (377), *jakshivas.*

Obs.—Certain roots are said optionally to form this Perf. Part. with *ivas* or *vas,* whether the stem in dual and plural consists of one syllable or two (see Páṇ. VII. 2, 68); e.g. fr. *gam* (376), *jagmivas* or *jaganvas;* fr. *han, jaghnivas* or *jaghanvas;* fr. *vid,* cl. 6, 'to find,' *vividvas* or *vividivas;* fr. *viś, viviśvas* or *viviśivas;* fr. *dṛiś, dadṛiśvas* or *dadṛiśivas.*

b. When *vas* is affixed, it will be necessary to restore to its original state the final of a root ending in *i, í, u, ú,* or *ṛi,* if changed before the terminations of the du. and pl. to *y, v, r, iy, uv,* or *úv;* thus, श्रि *śri,* changed by 374. *e.* to *śiśriy,* becomes शिश्रिवस्; क्री, changed to *ćikriy,* becomes चिक्रीवस् *ćikrívas;* भू, changed by 374. *g.* to *dudhuv*, becomes दुधूवस् *dudhúvas;* भू, changed by 374. *i.* to *babhúv*, becomes बभूवस् *babhúvas*. In declension, the 3rd pers. pl. with its termination *us* is the form of the stem in the weakest cases (135. *a*), and in the fem. final *s* becoming *sh* by 70; e. g. 3rd pl. *jagmus*, I. *jagmushá;* 3rd pl. *tenus*, I. *tenushá*, &c. See 168.

c. Roots which take the Periphrastic Perfect (see 385) form the Participles of this tense by adding the Perfect Participles of *kṛi*, *bhú*, and *as*, to *ám;* thus, from *ćur*, cl. 10, *ćorayám-babhúvas*, *ćorayáṅ-ćakṛivas*, *ćorayám-ásivas*.

d. There is an Átmane-pada Participle of the Reduplicated Perfect most easily formed by changing *ire*, the termination of the 3rd pl., into *ána;* thus, *vividána*, *ćićyána*, *jagmána*. See 526. *a;* and cf. Greek Perf. Part. in μενο (τετυμμένος = *tutupána*).

e. The Parasmai-pada form of these Participles is inflected at 168. Those of the Átmane-pada follow the inflexion of adjectives like *śubha* at 187.

PAST INDECLINABLE PARTICIPLES.

555. These are of the nature of Gerunds, as 'carrying on the action of the verb.' They fall under two heads: 1st, as formed by affixing त्वा *tvá* to *uncompounded* roots; as, fr. भू *bhú*, 'to be,' भूत्वा *bhútvá*, 'having been' (sec 80. XXI): 2ndly, as formed by affixing य *ya* to roots *compounded* with prepositions or other adverbial prefixes; thus, fr. अनुभू *anubhú*, 'to perceive,' अनुभूय *anubhúya*, 'having perceived;' fr. सज्जीभू *sajjíbhú*, 'to become ready,' सज्जीभूय *sajjíbhúya*, 'having become ready.' The sense involved in them is generally expressed by the English 'when,' 'after,' 'having,' or 'by;' thus, तत् कृत्वा *tat kṛitvá*, 'when he had done that,' 'after he had done that,' 'having done that,' 'by doing that.' See Śyntax, 898.

a. The suffix *tvá* of this participle is thought by some to be the instrumental case of a suffix *tva* (see 80. XXI). The Indeclinable Participle has certainly much of the character of an instrumental case (see Syntax, 901).

Obs.—In the Veda त्वाय, त्वानम्, त्वीनम् or त्वी are sometimes used for त्वा.

Indeclinable Participles formed with tvá *from uncompounded roots.*

556. When the root stands alone and uncompounded, the Indeclinable Participle is formed with त्वा *tvá*.

This suffix is closely allied to the त *ta* of the Past Passive Participle at 531, so that the rules for the affixing of त *ta* to the root generally apply also to the Indeclinable suffix त्वा *tvá*, and the formation of one Participle then involves that of the other.

Thus, क्षिप्त *kshipta*, 'thrown,' क्षिप्त्वा *kshiptvá*, 'having thrown;' कृत 'done' (rt. कृ), कृत्वा 'having done;' स्थित (rt. स्था), स्थित्वा; दृष्ट (rt. दृश्), दृष्ट्वा; दत्त (rt. दा), दत्त्वा;

पीत (rt. पा), पीत्वा; क्रान्त (rt. क्रम्), क्रान्त्वा; गृहीत (rt. ग्रह्), गृहीत्वा; उषित (rt. वस्), उषित्वा; उक्त (rt. वच्), उक्त्वा; बुद्ध (rt. बुध्), बुद्ध्वा; ऊढ (rt. वह्), ऊढ्वा; हित (rt. धा), हित्वा; जग्ध (rt. घस्), जग्ध्वा; गत (rt. गम् 545), गत्वा.

a. Where *i* is inserted, there is generally gunation of final *i*, *í*, *u*, *ú*, and of final ॠ *ṛí* and of medial ऋ *ṛi;* and optional gunation of medial *i*, *u* (except as debarred by 28).

Thus, शयित्वा fr. शी; पवित्वा (also पूत्वा) fr. पू; जरित्वा or जरीत्वा fr. जॄ; लिखित्वा or लेखित्वा fr. लिख्; द्युतित्वा or द्योतित्वा fr. द्युत्; मृषित्वा or मर्षित्वा fr. मृष्.

b. But from दिव्, देवित्वा and द्यूत्वा; from सिव्, सेवित्वा and स्यूत्वा. So ष्ठिव् &c. The root जागृ makes जागरित्वा (532. *a*); and initial *i*, *u*, before single consonants, must be gunated; as, इष् makes एषित्वा.

c. The roots in the list at 390. *a.* do not admit Guṇa; thus, विज् can make only विजित्वा.

d. When there are two forms of the Passive Participle, there is often only one of the Indeclinable; thus, नृत् makes नृत्त and नर्तित, but only नर्तित्वा; लज्ज्, लग्न and लज्जित, but only लज्जित्वा; and, *vice versa,* वस् (543) only उषित, but उषित्वा and उष्ट्वा; सह्, सोढ, but सहित्वा and सोढ्वा; मृज्, मृष्ट, but मार्जित्वा and मृष्ट्वा. So, some roots in nasals optionally insert *i;* तन्, तत्वा or तनित्वा; क्षण्, क्षत्वा or क्षणित्वा; कम्, कान्त्वा or कमित्वा; क्रम्, क्रान्त्वा or क्रन्त्वा or क्रमित्वा; खन्, खात्वा or खनित्वा.

e. The penultimate nasal, which is rejected before *ta* (544. *a*), is optionally so rejected before *tvá* in रञ्ज्, सञ्ज्, स्वञ्ज्, तञ्च् or तञ्ज्, and भञ्ज्; thus, from रञ्ज् comes रक्त, but रंक्त्वा or रक्त्वा; from भञ्ज्, भञ्जित्वा, भंक्त्वा or भक्त्वा.

f. मस्ज् and नश् optionally insert nasals; मक्त्वा or मंक्त्वा, नष्ट्वा or नंष्ट्वा, 390. *k.*

g. Some few roots necessarily retain their nasals; thus, स्कन्द् makes स्कन्त्वा; and स्यन्द्, स्यन्त्वा or स्यन्दित्वा.

557. The only important variation from the Past Passive Participle occurs in those roots, at 531. *a*, which take *na* for *ta*. The change of *ṛí* to *ír* and *úr* (534) is preserved (unless *i* be inserted), but *tvá* never becomes *nvá;* thus, जॄ, जीर्ण, but जरित्वा (or जरीत्वा); from तॄ, तीर्ण, but तीर्त्वा; from पॄ, पूर्ण, but पूर्त्वा; from छिद्, छिन्न, but छित्त्वा; from भञ्ज्, भग्न, but भंक्त्वा or भक्त्वा (556. *e*); from रुज्, रुग्ण, but रुक्त्वा; from हा, हीन, but हित्वा 'having quitted' (not distinguishable in form from हित्वा 'having placed,' root धा).

558. Observe, moreover, that verbs of cl. 10 and Causals, which reject the characteristic *aya* before the *ita* of the Past Pass. Part., retain *ay* before *itvá;* thus, स्थापित 'made to stand' (fr. Caus. stem स्थापय), but स्थापयित्वा 'having made to stand;' चिन्तित 'thought' (fr. चिन्त् cl. 10, 'to think'), but चिन्तयित्वा 'having thought.'

a. All Derivative verbs of course assume *i*, and form their Indeclinable Participles analogously to Causals; thus, बुबोधिषित्वा (fr. Desid. of बुध्), and बोबुधित्वा (fr. Freq. of बुध्). In regard to the Átmane Frequentatives, लोलूयित्वा is formed fr. लोलूय, and देदीप्यित्वा fr. देदीप्य (*ya* in the latter being preceded by a consonant).

b. There are one or two instances of compounded roots formed with *tvá;* thus, अनुध्यात्वा (fr. ध्यै), Rámáy. I. 2, 20; also अप्रतुक्त्वा, Rámáy. I. 74, 23. Especially in the case of Causals; as, निवर्तयित्वा.

c. When अ *a*, 'not,' is prefixed, *tvá* is always used; as, अकृत्वा 'not having done,' 'without having done;' अदत्त्वा 'not having given.'

Indeclinable Participles formed with ya *from compounded roots.*

559. When a root is compounded with a preposition or any indeclinable prefix (except अ *a*, 'not,' see 558. *c*), the Indeclinable Participle is formed by affixing य *ya*, and the rules for annexing it to the root are some of them analogous to those which prevail in other cases in which *ya* is affixed; see the rules for forming the Special tenses in cl. 4 (272), for Passives (461), and for the Precative (443).

560. But if a root end in a short vowel, instead of lengthening this vowel, त् *t* is interposed; as, fr. आश्रि *áśri*, 'to take refuge' (rt. श्रि with आ), आश्रित्य *áśritya*, 'having taken refuge;' fr. निश्रि (rt. चि with निस्), निश्चित्य; fr. उत्सु, उत्सुत्य; from संस्कृ (rt. कृ with सम्), संस्कृत्य; fr. निःसृ, निःसृत्य. The lengthening of the radical vowel by coalition does not prevent this rule; as, fr. अती *atí* (rt. इ with अति), अतीत्य *atítya*.

a. जागृ 'to awake' gunates its final as in उज्जागर्य; and क्षि 'to destroy,' 'to waste,' lengthens its final as in प्रक्षीय, उपक्षीय.

561. If a root end in long आ *á*, ई *í*, or ऊ *ú*, no change generally takes place; as, fr. विहा, विहाय; fr. उपक्री, उपक्रीय; fr. विधू, विधूय.

a. If it end in long ॠ *ṛí*, this vowel becomes *ír*, and after labial letters *úr;* thus, fr. अवकॄ, अवकीर्य 'having scattered;' fr. आपॄ (root पॄ 'to fill'), आपूर्य (compare 534).

562. Final diphthongs pass into आ *á;* as, fr. परिव्ये, परिव्याय (also परिवीय); fr. अभिध्यै, अभिध्याय; fr. अवसो, अवसाय.

a. But ह्वे with आ makes आहूय. In Epic poetry, सो with व्यव makes व्यवस्य.

b. मि 'to throw,' मी 'to kill,' मा 'to measure,' and मे 'to barter,' all make -माय. Similarly, दी 'to decay,' -दाय; but ली 'to adhere,' -लाय or -लीय (see 390. *e*). श्वि and शी conform to the rule for the Passive (-शूय, -शय्य), अधिशय्य 'having reclined upon,' Kirát. I, 38.

563. A penultimate nasal is generally rejected, as in Passives (see 469); as, fr. समासञ्ज् *samásañj*, समासज्य *samásajya;* fr. प्रमन्थ्, प्रमथ्य (used adverbially in the sense 'violently').

a. Some few roots retain the nasal; thus, आशङ्क् makes आशङ्क्य; and आलिङ्ग्, आलिङ्ग्य.

b. लभ् 'to acquire' may insert a nasal after the prepositions आ and उप; thus, आलभ्य &c. (otherwise -लभ्य).

564. If a root end in a consonant the general rule is, that no change takes place;

as, from निक्षिप् *nikship*, निक्षिप्य *nikshipya*; from प्राप् (root आप् with प्र), प्राप्य; from वीक्ष् (root ईक्ष् with वि), वीक्ष्य.

a. But roots in र् or व्, preceded by *i* or *u*, lengthen these vowels, as in प्रतिदीव्य from दिव्, विस्फूर्य from स्फुर्.

b. Four roots in अम् (गम्, नम्, यम्, रम्) optionally reject the nasal, and interpose *t* between the final *a* and *ya*; as, from निर्गम्, निर्गत्य or निर्गम्य. The roots हन्, मन्, तन्, वन्, क्षण्, क्षिण्, ऋण्, घृण्, वृण्, तृण् always reject the nasal; as, from निहन्, निहत्य.

c. खन्, जन्, and सन् optionally reject the न्; but instead of interposing *t*, lengthen the final *a*, as in Passives (see 470); thus, from उत्खन्, उत्खाय (or उत्खन्य).

565. The changes which take place in certain roots before the *ya* of the Passive (471, 472) are preserved before *ya*; as, from निवप्, न्युप्य; from विवस्, व्युष्य; from प्रवस्, प्रोष्य; from अनुवद्, अनूद्य; from विग्रह्, विगृह्य; from आप्रच्छ्, आपृच्छ्य; from आव्यध्, आविध्य; and so with all the roots at 471, 472.

a. The roots at 390. *l.* have two forms; thus, from गुप् comes -गोपाय्य and -गुप्य, &c.

b. There are one or two instances in which an uncompounded root takes य; as, अर्च्य 'having reverenced,' Manu I. 4; VII. 145: Mahá-bh. iii. 8017. उष्य 'having resided,' Nala v. 41 (from वस्); गृह्य 'having taken,' Astra-śikshá 21.

566. In affixing य *ya* to the stems of Causal verbs of cl. 10, and the 3rd class of Nominals (521), the characteristic अय is generally rejected; as, fr. प्रबोधय *prabodhaya*, प्रबोध्य *prabodhya*; fr. प्रसारय, प्रसार्य; fr. सन्दर्शय, सन्दर्श्य; fr. विचारय, विचार्य.

a. It is, however, retained when the root ends in a single consonant and encloses short *a*; thus, विगणय्य 'having calculated' (गण् with वि); आकलय्य 'having imagined' (कल् with आ); सङ्कथय्य 'having narrated' (कथ् with सम्): and also sometimes in other cases; e. g. प्रापय्य 'having conducted,' Raghu-v. XIV. 45.

b. The final *a* of Frequentative stems is of course dropped, and the final *ya* of both Frequentatives and Nominals, if preceded by a consonant; as, from लोलूय comes -लोलूय्य; from बोबुध्य, -बोबुध्य; from तपस्य, -तपस्य.

Adverbial Indeclinable Participle.

567. There is another Indeclinable Participle yielding the same sense as those formed with *tvá* and *ya*, but of rare occurrence. It is equivalent to the accusative case of a noun derived from a root, used adverbially; and is formed by adding अम् *am* to the root, before which suffix changes of the radical vowel take place, similar to those required before the Causal suffix अय (481) or before the 3rd sing. Aorist Passive (see 475); thus, from नी *ní*, 'to lead,' नायम् *náyam*, 'having led;' from पा 'to drink,' पायम् 'having drunk;' from ह्वे, ह्वायम्; from पच्, पाचम्; from क्षिप्, क्षेपम्; from हन् 'to kill,' घातम्. It often occupies the last place in a compound; as in the expression समूलघातम् 'having totally exterminated;' and in the following passage from Bhaṭṭi-k. ii. 11:

लतानुपातं कुसुमान्यगृह्णात् स नद्यवस्कन्दमुपास्पृशच्च ।
कुतूहलाच्चारुशिलोपवेशं काकुत्स्थ ईषत्स्मयमान आस्त ॥

'The descendant of Kakutstha, smiling softly, repeatedly bending down the creepers, would pluck the blossoms; descending to the streams, would sip (the waters); seating himself on some variegated rock, would recline in admiration (of the scene).' Compare also S'akuntalá, Act V, verse 131, बाहूत्क्षेपं क्रन्दितुं प्रवृत्ता 'repeatedly throwing up her arms she began to weep.' Other examples are नामग्राहम् 'mentioning by name,' and जीवग्राहम् 'taking alive.'

a. These Participles generally imply repetition of the action, as above, and in this sense are themselves often repeated; as, *dáyam, dáyam,* 'having repeatedly given.'

FUTURE PASSIVE PARTICIPLES.

568. These are gerundive in their character, and may be called verbal adjectives. They may be classed under three heads: 1st, as formed with the suffix तव्य *tavya* (80. XVIII); 2ndly, as formed with अनीय *aníya* (80. V); 3rdly, as formed with य *ya* (80. XXVIII). These suffixes yield a sense corresponding to the Latin Fut. Pass. Part. in *dus*, and the English *able* and *ible*, and most commonly denote 'obligation' or 'propriety' and 'fitness.'

a. In some of the Latin formations with *tivus*, the Passive sense is preserved, as in *captivus, nativus, coctivus.* Cf. Sk. *dátavya* with *dativus* (*dandus*), δοτέος; *yoktavya* with (*con*)*junctivus* (*jungendus*); *janitavya* with *genitivus* (*gignendus*); *dhátavya* with θετέος, &c.

Future Passive Participles formed with तव्य (80. XVIII).

569. These may be formed by substituting तव्य *tavya* for ता *tá*, the termination of the 3rd pers. sing. of the 1st Future; e. g.

From क्षेप्ता *ksheptá*, 'he will throw,' क्षेप्तव्य *ksheptavya*, 'to be thrown;' कर्ता 'he will do,' कर्तव्य 'to be done;' fr. भविता 'he will be,' भवितव्य 'about to be;' fr. कुषिता, कुषितव्य (see 390. *a*); fr. विजिता, विजितव्य.

Obs.—In the case of those roots ending in consonants which reject *i*, whatever changes take place before *tá*, the same take place before *tavya*, and the special rules at 390. *a–o* will equally apply to this suffix.

Thus, त्यक्ता, त्यक्तव्य (*relinquendus*); प्रष्टा, प्रष्टव्य; द्रष्टा, द्रष्टव्य; वोढा, वोढव्य; दग्धा, दग्धव्य; सोढा, सोढव्य; कमिता or कामयिता, कमितव्य or कामयितव्य; दीधिता, दीधितव्य; मार्ष्टा or मार्जिता, मार्ष्टव्य or मार्जितव्य; and from Causal कारयिता, कारयितव्य; from Desid. बुबोधिषिता, बुबोधिषितव्य; from Frequentative बोबुधिता, बोबुधितव्य; from बोभविता, बोभवितव्य. See the rules at 388, 390, 491, 505, 513, 516.

Future Passive Participles formed with अनीय (80. V).

570. This suffix is added directly to the root, and generally without other change than gunation (if Guṇa is admissible).

Thus, fr. चि *ći*, 'to gather,' चयनीय *ćayaníya*, 'to be gathered;' fr. भू, भवनीय; fr. कृ, करणीय (58); fr. लिख्, लेखनीय; fr. शुध्, शोधनीय; fr. स्पृश्, स्पर्शनीय; fr. कृष्, कर्षणीय; fr. चुर् (cl. 10), चोरणीय: but मृज्, मार्जनीय; गुह्, गूहनीय; दीधी, दीध्यनीय; कम्, कमनीय and कामनीय; गुप्, गोपनीय and गोपायनीय, &c. See 390. *j. l. m.*

a. A final diphthong is changed to आ *á*, which blends with the initial *a* of *aníya;* as, from ध्यै, ध्यानीय; from गै, गानीय.

b. The roots at 390, 390. *a.* of course forbid Guṇa; thus, कुचनीय from कुच्; गुवनीय from गु, &c.

c. As to Derivative verbs, *aya* is rejected from a Causal stem, and *a* from the stems of other Derivative verbs, and *ya*, if a consonant precedes.

Thus, बोधनीय from the Causal stem बोधय; बुबोधिषणीय from the Desid. बुबोधिष; also बोभूयनीय, चेक्षिपणीय, fr. the Frequentatives बोभूय, चेक्षिप्य; and तपस्यनीय or तपसनीय fr. the Nominal तपस्य.

Future Passive Participles formed with य (80. XXVIII).

571. Before this suffix, as before all others beginning with *y*, certain changes of final vowels become necessary.

a. If a root end in आ *á*, or in ए *e*, ऐ *ai*, ओ *o*, changeable to आ *á*, this vowel becomes ए *e* (compare 446); e. g.

From मा *má*, 'to measure,' मेय *meya*, 'to be measured,' 'measurable;' fr. हा *há*, 'to quit,' हेय *heya;* fr. ध्यै *dhyai*, 'to meditate,' ध्येय *dhyeya;* fr. ग्लै 'to be weary,' ग्लेय; fr. दा 'to give,' दे 'to pity,' and दो 'to cut,' देय.

b. If in इ *i*, ई *í*, उ *u*, or ऊ *ú*, these vowels are gunated; e. g.

From चि *ći*, चेय *ćeya* (in the Veda चाय्य with उप); but नी with उद्, -नीय.

But the Guṇa ओ *o* is changed to *av*, and sometimes ए *e* to *ay*, before *ya* (as if before a vowel); thus, from भू, भव्य; from जि 'to conquer,' जय्य; from क्री 'to buy,' क्रय्य; from क्षि 'to destroy,' क्षय्य.

And the Guṇa ओ *o* passes into *áv* before *y*, especially when it is intended to lay emphasis on the meaning; as, from श्रु, श्राव्य; from स्रु, स्राव्य; from भू, भाव्य. But धू 'to shake' makes धूय.

c. If in ऋ *ṛi* or ॠ *ṛí*, these vowels are vriddhied; e. g.

From कृ 'to do,' कार्य; from भृ 'to support,' भार्य (also भृत्य, see 572); fr. वृ 'to choose,' वार्य (also वृत्य).

d. The roots at 390. *c.* drop their finals (दीध्य, दरिद्र्य).

572. Sometimes if a root end in a short vowel no change takes place, but *t* is interposed, after the analogy of the Indeclinable Participle formed with *ya* at 560;

so that the stem of the Future Participle is often not distinguishable from the Indeclinable; thus, from जि *ji*, 'to conquer,' जित्य *jitya* (also *jeya*), 'conquerable;' from स्तु *stu*, 'to praise,' स्तुत्य *stutya*, 'laudable;' from कृ *kṛi*, 'to do,' कृत्य *kṛitya* (as well as कार्य), 'practicable;' from इ 'to go,' इत्य 'to be gone;' from आदृ 'to honour,' आदृत्य 'to be honoured.'

573. If a root end in a single consonant with a medial *a*, the latter may be vriddhied; as, fr. ग्रह् *grah*, 'to take,' ग्राह्य *gráhya;* fr. त्रप् 'to be ashamed,' त्राप्य; fr. कम् 'to love,' काम्य: but not always; as, fr. शक्, शक्य; fr. सह्, सह्य; fr. वध्, वध्य; fr. यत्, यत्य: and not if the final is a labial (except त्रप्, रप्, लप्); as, fr. गम्, गम्य; fr. शप्, शप्य; fr. लभ् 'to receive,' लभ्य (and लम्भ्य). The root मद् 'to be mad' makes माद्य after prepositions, but otherwise मद्य. Similarly, गद् and चर्. The root भज् 'to serve' makes भज्य and भाग्य (see 574).

a. If with a medial इ *i* or उ *u*, these are generally gunated; as, from भुज्, भोज्य; from लिह्, लेह्य; but जुष्, जुष्य: and sometimes only optionally; as, गुह् makes गुह्य as well as गोह्य; and दुह्, दुह्य and दोह्य.

b. If with a medial ऋ *ṛi*, no change generally takes place; as, fr. स्पृश्, स्पृश्य; fr. दृश्, दृश्य; fr. सृज्, सृज्य (after अव and सम्, सर्ग्य); fr. मृज्, मृज्य (also मार्ग्य): but fr. वृष्, वृष्य or वर्ष्य.

c. The roots at 390, 390. *a*. are, as usual, debarred from Guṇa; thus, कुच्य, &c.

574. A final च् *ć* may sometimes be changed to क् *k*, and final ज् *j* to ग् *g*, when the Past Passive Participle rejects *i;* as, from पच् *pać*, पाक्य *pákya* and पाच्य *páćya;* from युज्, योग्य or युग्य. When the final is unchanged, as in *páćya*, the obligation implied is said to be more absolute; but the two forms may have distinct meanings; thus, *bhojya* (fr. *bhuj*) means 'to be eaten,' but *bhogya*, 'to be enjoyed;' *váćya* (fr. *vać*) means 'proper to be said,' but *vákya*, 'that which is actually to be said.'

a. Again, त्याज्य (fr. त्यज्) is used after the prepositions नि and प्र, otherwise त्याग्य. Similarly, योज्य (fr. युज्) after नि and प्र, and यज्य or याज्य (fr. यज्) after the same prepositions.

b. Other anomalous changes may take place, some of which are similar to those before the *ya* of Passives; thus, fr. ग्रह्, गृह्य as well as ग्राह्य (472); fr. वद्, उद्य (471, also वद्य); fr. यज्, इज्य (471); fr. शास्, शिष्य (472. *c*); fr. खन् 'to dig,' खेय; fr. शंस् 'to praise,' शस्य or शंस्य; fr. भ्रज्ज् 'to fry,' भर्ज्य or भ्रज्ज्य; fr. हन्, वध्य or घात्य.

c. The roots beginning with गुप् at 390. *l*. have two forms; thus, गोप्य or गोपाय्य.

575. Many of these Participles are used as substantives; thus, वाक्य n. 'speech;' भोज्य n. 'food;' भोग्या f. 'a harlot;' इज्या f. 'sacrifice;' खेय n. 'a ditch;' भार्या f. 'a wife,' fr. भृ 'to support,' &c.

576. The suffix *ya* may be added to Desiderative, Frequentative, and Nominal stems in the same way as *aníya* (570); thus, बुबोधिष्य, बोभूय्य, चेछिद्य, तपस्य. So also, from मुसल 'a pestle,' मुसल्य 'to be pounded with a pestle.'

a. अ *a* added to a root after gunation (if Guṇa is possible) gives the sense of a Future Passive Participle when in composition with

सु, दुस्, and ईषत्; as, सुकर 'easy to be done,' दुष्कर 'difficult to be done,' दुस्तर 'difficult to be crossed.' See 80. I.

b. Again, a suffix एलिम added to a few roots has the same force as the suffixes of the Future Passive Participle; e.g. पचेलिम 'fit to ripen' or 'to be cooked,' भिदेलिम 'to be broken.'

577. The inflexion of Future Passive Participles follows that of adjectives at 187; thus, कर्तव्य 'to be done;' N. sing. m. f. n. *karta-vyas, -á, -am.* Similarly, *karaṇíyas, -á, -am;* and *káryas, -á, -am.*

PARTICIPLES OF THE SECOND FUTURE.—FORMATION OF STEM.

578. These are not common. They are of two kinds, either Parasmai-pada or Átmane-pada; and, like Present Participles, are most easily formed by changing अन्ति *anti,* the termination of the 3rd pl. of the 2nd Fut., into अत् *at,* for the Par.; and by changing अन्ते *ante* into अमान *amána,* for the Átm.; thus, from करिष्यन्ति *karishyanti* and करिष्यन्ते *karishyante,* 'they will do,' come करिष्यत् *karishyat* and करिष्यमाण *karishyamáṇa* (58), 'about to do;' from the Passive 2nd Fut. वक्ष्यन्ते 'they will be said' comes वक्ष्यमाण 'about to be said' (see 84. I. and 80. XXVII).

a. In their inflexion (see 141), as well as in their formation, they resemble Present Participles; see 524 and 526.

Obs.—Cf. Greek in δωσό-μενο-ς=*dásya-mána-s.*

PARTICIPIAL NOUNS OF AGENCY.

579. These have been already incidentally noticed at 80, 83, 84, 85, 87. As, however, they partake of the nature of Participles, and are often used as Participles (see Syntax, 909–911), a fuller explanation of them is here given. They may be classed under three heads: 1st, as formed from the root; 2ndly, as formed from the same stem as the 1st Future; 3rdly, as formed from the root by changes similar to those which form the Causal stem.

580. The stem of the first class is often identical with the root itself; that is, the unchanged root is frequently used at the end of compounds as a noun of agency, *t* being added if it ends in a short vowel; see examples at 84. III. and 87.

a. Another common noun of agency is formed from the root by affixing अ *a* (as in the first group of conjugational classes at 257), before which *a,* Guṇa, and rarely Vṛiddhi, of a final vowel is required; as, from जि *ji,* 'to conquer,' जय *jaya,* 'conquering.' Medial vowels are generally unchanged; as, from वद् *vad,* 'to say,' वद *vada,* 'saying;' from तुद् *tud,* 'to vex,' तुद *tuda,* 'vexing' (see 80. I).

b. And final आ *á,* अम् *am,* or अन् *an* are dropped; as, from दा

dá, 'to give,' द *da*, 'giving;' from गम् *gam*, 'to go,' ग *ga*, 'going;' from जन् *jan*, 'to be born,' ज *ja*, 'being born.' Their declension follows that of adjectives at 187.

581. The stem of the second class (see 83) may be always inferred from the 3rd pers. sing. of the 1st Fut. of Primitive verbs, the vowel ऋ *ṛi* being substituted for the final vowel *á*, the nominative case being therefore *identical* with the 3rd pers. sing. of that tense (see 386).

Thus, भोक्ता *bhoktá*, 'he will eat,' भोक्तृ *bhoktṛi*, 'an eater;' योद्धा 'he will fight,' योद्धृ 'a fighter;' याचिता 'he will ask,' याचितृ 'an asker;' सोढा 'he will bear,' सोढृ 'a bearer,' &c. They are inflected at 127.

582. The stem of the third class is formed in three ways.

a. By adding इन् *in* to the root (see 85. II), before which suffix changes take place similar to those required before the Causal suffix *aya* (481, 482, 483); as, from कृ, कारिन् *kárin*, 'a doer;' from हन् (488), घातिन् *ghátin*, 'a killer;' from शी, शायिन् 'a sleeper:' *y* being inserted after roots in *á* (483); as, from पा, पायिन् 'a drinker;' from दा, दायिन् *dáyin*, 'a giver.' They are inflected at 159.

b. By adding अक *aka* to the root (see 80. II), before which suffix changes take place analogous to those before the Causal *aya* (481, 482, 483); as, fr. कृ, कारक *káraka*, 'a doer,' 'doing;' fr. नी, नायक *náyaka*, 'a leader,' 'leading;' fr. ग्रह्, ग्राहक *gráhaka*; fr. सिध्, साधक; fr. हन्, घातक; fr. दुष्, दूषक; fr. क्रम्, क्रमक; fr. नन्द्, नन्दक; fr. स्था, स्थापक.

c. By adding अन *ana* to some few roots ending in consonants (see 80. IV), after changes similar to those required in forming the Causal stem; as, fr. नन्द्, नन्दन *nandana*, 'rejoicing;' fr. दुष्, दूषण 'vitiating;' fr. शुध्, शोधन 'cleansing.'

The inflexion of the last two follows that of adjectives at 187.

EXAMPLES OF INFLECTED VERBS.

583. The following tables give a synopsis of the inflexion of the Primitive forms of the ten roots: बुध् *budh*, cl. 1, 'to know;' नृत् *nṛit*, cl. 4, 'to dance;' दिश् *diś*, cl. 6, 'to point out;' युज् *yuj*, cl. 10, 'to unite;' विद् *vid*, cl. 2, 'to know;' भृ *bhṛi*, cl. 3, 'to bear;' भिद् *bhid*, cl. 7, 'to break;' चि *ći*, cl. 5, 'to gather;' तन् *tan*, cl. 8, 'to stretch;' पू *pú*, cl. 9, 'to purify:' classes 1, 4, 6, and 10; 2, 3, and 7; and 5, 7, and 9, being grouped together as at 257–259. Then the Passive forms of these ten roots are given, followed by the Present tense of the Causal, Desiderative, and Frequentative forms, and the Participles.

INFLEXION OF THE STEM OF PRIMITIVE VERBS OF THE TEN CLASSES OR CONJUGATIONS.

PRESENT.

	Parasmai-pada.									Átmane-pada.								
ROOT.	SING.			DUAL.			PLURAL.			SING.			DUAL.			PLURAL.		
1. *Budh*	*bodhá*	*bodha*	*bodha*	*bodhá*	*bodha*	*bodha*	*bodhá*	*bodha*	*bodha*	*bodha*	*bodha*	*bodha*	*bodhá*	*bodha*	*bodha*	*bodhá*	*bodha*	*bodha*
4. *Nṛit*	*nṛityá*	*nṛitya*	*nṛitya*	*nṛityá*	*nṛitya*	*nṛitya*	*nṛityá*	*nṛitya*	*nṛitya*	*nṛitya*	*nṛitya*	*nṛitya*	*nṛityá*	*nṛitya*	*nṛitya*	*nṛityá*	*nṛitya*	*nṛitya*
6. *Diś*	*diśá*	*diśa*	*diśa*	*diśá*	*diśa*	*diśa*	*diśá*	*diśa*	*diśa*	*diśa*	*diśa*	*diśa*	*diśá*	*diśa*	*diśa*	*diśá*	*diśa*	*diśa*
10. *Yuj*	*yojayá*	*yojaya*	*yojaya*	*yojayá*	*yojaya*	*yojaya*	*yojayá*	*yojaya*	*yojaya*	*yojaya*	*yojaya*	*yojaya*	*yojayá*	*yojaya*	*yojaya*	*yojayá*	*yojaya*	*yojaya*
2. *Vid*	*ved*	*vet* *	*vet*	*vid*	*vit*	*vit*	*vid*	*vit*	*vid*	*vid*	*vit* *	*vit*	*vid*	*vid*	*vid*	*vid*	*vid*	*vid*
3. *Bhṛi*	*bibhar*	*bibhar*	*bibhar*	*bibhṛi*	*bibhṛi*	*bibhṛi*	*bibhṛi*	*bibhṛi*	*bibhr* *	*bibhr*	*bibhṛi*	*bibhṛi*	*bibhṛi*	*bibhr*	*bibhr*	*bibhṛi*	*bibhṛi*	*bibhr*
7. *Bhid*	*bhinad*	*bhinat**	*bhinat*	*bhind*	*bhint*	*bhint*	*bhind*	*bhint*	*bhind*	*bhind*	*bhint* *	*bhint*	*bhind*	*bhind*	*bhind*	*bhind*	*bhind*	*bhind*
5. *Ći*	*ćino*	*ćino*	*ćino*	*ćinu*	*ćinu*	*ćinu*	*ćinu*	*ćinu*	*ćinv*	*ćinv*	*ćinu*	*ćinu*	*ćinu*	*ćinv*	*ćinv*	*ćinu*	*ćinu*	*ćinv*
8. *Tan*	*tano*	*tano*	*tano*	*tanu*	*tanu*	*tanu*	*tanu*	*tanu*	*tanv*	*tanv*	*tanu*	*tanu*	*tanu*	*tanv*	*tanv*	*tanu*	*tanu*	*tanv*
9. *Pú*	*puná*	*puná* *	*puná*	*puní*	*puní*	*puní*	*puní*	*puní*	*pun*	*pun*	*puní*	*puní*	*puní*	*pun*	*pun*	*puní*	*puní*	*pun*
1. 4. 6. 10.		* *si*							*nti*	*i*	* *se*			*ithe*	*ite*			*nte*
	mi		*ti*	*vas*	*thas*	*tas*	*mas*	*tha*				*te*	*vahe*			*mahe*	*dhve*	
2. 3. 7. 5. 8. 9.		*shi*							*anti* * *ati*	*e*	*she*			*áthe*	*áte*			*ate*

Observe—The stem is to be united with the terminations: thus, 1st sing. Pres. Parasmai, *bodhá+mi=bodhámi*, 2d sing. *bodha+si=bodhasi*, 3d sing. *bodha+ti=bodhati*; 1st dual, *bodhá+vas=bodhávas*, &c. Átmane, *bodha+i=bodhe*, *bodha+se=bodhase*, &c. Whenever the terminations of the 1st, 4th, 6th, and 10th classes differ from those of the others, they are placed in the upper line. As to the optional dropping of the *u* of *ćinu* and *tanu*, see 349.

IMPERFECT OR FIRST PRETERITE.

	Parasmai-pada.									Átmane-pada.								
Root.	Sing.			Dual.			Plural.			Sing.			Dual.			Plural.		
1. *Budh*	*abodha*	*abodha*	*abodha*	*abodhá*	*abodha*	*abodha*	*abodhá*	*abodha*	*abodha*	*abodha*	*abodha*	*abodha*	*abodhá*	*abodha*	*abodha*	*abodhá*	*abodha*	*abodha*
4. *Nṛit*	*anṛitya*	*anṛitya*	*anṛitya*	*anṛityá*	*anṛitya*	*anṛitya*	*anṛityá*	*anṛitya*	*anṛitya*	*anṛitya*	*anṛitya*	*anṛitya*	*anṛityá*	*anṛitya*	*anṛitya*	*anṛityá*	*anṛitya*	*anṛitya*
6. *Diś*	*adiśa*	*adiśa*	*adiśa*	*adiśá*	*adiśa*	*adiśa*	*adiśá*	*adiśa*	*adiśa*	*adiśa*	*adiśa*	*adiśa*	*adiśá*	*adiśa*	*adiśa*	*adiśá*	*adiśa*	*adiśa*
10. *Yuj*	*ayojaya*	*ayojaya*	*ayojaya*	*ayojayá*	*ayojaya*	*ayojaya*	*ayojayá*	*ayojaya*	*ayojaya*	*ayojaya*	*ayojaya*	*ayojaya*	*ayojayá*	*ayojaya*	*ayojaya*	*ayojayá*	*ayojaya*	*ayojaya*
2. *Vid*	*aved*	*avet*	*avet*	*avid*	*avit*	*avit*	*avid*	*avit*	*avid**	*avid*	*avit*	*avit*	*avid*	*avid*	*avid*	*avid*	*avid*	*avid*
3. *Bhṛi*	*abibhar*	*abibhar*	*abibhar*	*abibhṛi*	*abibhṛi*	*abibhṛi*	*abibhṛi*	*abibhṛi*	*abibhar**	*abibhr*	*abibhṛi*	*abibhṛi*	*abibhṛi*	*abibhr*	*abibhr*	*abibhṛi*	*abibhṛi*	*abibhr*
7. *Bhid*	*abhinad*	*abhinat*	*abhinat*	*abhind*	*abhint*	*abhint*	*abhind*	*abhint*	*abhind*	*abhind*	*abhint*	*abhint*	*abhind*	*abhind*	*abhind*	*abhind*	*abhind*	*abhind*
5. *Ći*	*aćinav*	*aćino*	*aćino*	*aćinu*	*aćinu*	*aćinu*	*aćinu*	*aćinu*	*aćinv*	*aćinv*	*aćinu*	*aćinu*	*aćinu*	*aćinv*	*aćinv*	*aćinu*	*aćinu*	*aćinv*
8. *Tan*	*atanav*	*atano*	*atano*	*atanu*	*atanu*	*atanu*	*atanu*	*atanu*	*atanv*	*atanv*	*atanu*	*atanu*	*atanu*	*atanv*	*atanv*	*atanu*	*atanu*	*atanv*
9. *Pú*	*apuná*	*apuná*	*apuná*	*apuní*	*apuní*	*apuní*	*apuní*	*apuní*	*apun*	*apun*	*apuní*	*apuní*	*apuní*	*apun*	*apun*	*apuní*	*apuní*	*apun*
1. 4. 6. 10.	*m*								*n*					*ithám*	*itám*			*nta*
		s	*t*	*va*	*tam*	*tám*	*ma*	*ta*		*i*	*thás*	*ta*	*vahi*			*mahi*	*dhvam*	
2. 3. 7. 5. 8. 9.	*am*								*an* *us					*áthám*	*átám*			*ata*

Observe—In the 2d and 3d sing., Parasmai, the roots of the 2d group reject the terminations by 294: thus, 2d and 3d sing., *avet*, *abibhar*, *abhinat*. In the Átmane the final *a* of the stems of the roots of the 1st group will blend with the initial *i* of a termination into *e* by 32. As to the optional dropping of the *u* of *aćinu* and *atanu*, see 349.

POTENTIAL.

	Parasmai-pada.									Átmane-pada.								
ROOT.	SING.			DUAL.			PLURAL.			SING.			DUAL.			PLURAL.		
1. *Budh*	*bodha*	*bodha*	*bodha*	*bodha*	*bodha*	*bodha*	*bodha*	*bodha*	*bodha*	*bodha*	*bodha*	*bodha*	*bodha*	*bodha*	*bodha*	*bodha*	*bodha*	*bodha*
4. *Nṛit*	*nṛitya*	*nṛitya*	*nṛitya*	*nṛitya*	*nṛitya*	*nṛitya*	*nṛitya*	*nṛitya*	*nṛitya*	*nṛitya*	*nṛitya*	*nṛitya*	*nṛitya*	*nṛitya*	*nṛitya*	*nṛitya*	*nṛitya*	*nṛitya*
6. *Diś*	*diśa*	*diśa*	*diśa*	*diśa*	*diśa*	*diśa*	*diśa*	*diśa*	*diśa*	*diśa*	*diśa*	*diśa*	*diśa*	*diśa*	*diśa*	*diśa*	*diśa*	*diśa*
10. *Yuj*	*yojaya*	*yojaya*	*yojaya*	*yojaya*	*yojaya*	*yojaya*	*yojaya*	*yojaya*	*yojaya*	*yojaya*	*yojaya*	*yojaya*	*yojaya*	*yojaya*	*yojaya*	*yojaya*	*yojaya*	*yojaya*
2. *Vid*	*vid*	*vid*	*vid*	*vid*	*vid*	*vid*	*vid*	*vid*	*vid*	*vid*	*vid*	*vid*	*vid*	*vid*	*vid*	*vid*	*vid*	*vid*
3. *Bhṛi*	*bibhṛi*	*bibhṛi*	*bibhṛi*	*bibhṛi*	*bibhṛi*	*bibhṛi*	*bibhṛi*	*bibhṛi*	*bibhṛi*	*bibhr*	*bibhr*	*bibhr*	*bibhr*	*bibhr*	*bibhr*	*bibhr*	*bibhr*	*bibhr*
7. *Bhid*	*bhind*	*bhind*	*bhind*	*bhind*	*bhind*	*bhind*	*bhind*	*bhind*	*bhind*	*bhind*	*bhind*	*bhind*	*bhind*	*bhind*	*bhind*	*bhind*	*bhind*	*bhind*
5. *Ći*	*ćinu*	*ćinu*	*ćinu*	*ćinu*	*ćinu*	*ćinu*	*ćinu*	*ćinu*	*ćinu*	*ćinv*	*ćinv*	*ćinv*	*ćinv*	*ćinv*	*ćinv*	*ćinv*	*ćinv*	*ćinv*
8. *Tan*	*tanu*	*tanu*	*tanu*	*tanu*	*tanu*	*tanu*	*tanu*	*tanu*	*tanu*	*tanv*	*tanv*	*tanv*	*tanv*	*tanv*	*tanv*	*tanv*	*tanv*	*tanv*
9. *Pú*	*puní*	*puní*	*puní*	*puní*	*puní*	*puní*	*puní*	*puní*	*puní*	*pun*	*pun*	*pun*	*pun*	*pun*	*pun*	*pun*	*pun*	*pun*
1. 4. 6. 10.	*iyam*	*is*	*it*	*iva*	*itam*	*itám*	*ima*	*ita*	*iyus*	*íya*	*íthás*	*íta*	*ívahi*	*íyáthám*	*íyátám*	*ímahi*	*ídhvam*	*íran*
2. 3. 7. 5. 8. 9.	*yám*	*yás*	*yát*	*yáva*	*yátam*	*yátám*	*yáma*	*yáta*	*yus*									

Observe—As the stem in the 1st group of classes ends in *a*, and the terminations begin with *i*, these two vowels will blend into *e* by 32: thus, *bodha* + *iyam* = *bodheyam*, *bodha* + *is* = *bodhes*, &c.; Átmane, *bodha* + *íya* = *bodheya*.

IMPERATIVE.

	Parasmai-pada.									Átmane-pada.								
ROOT.	SING.			DUAL.			PLURAL.			SING.			DUAL.			PLURAL.		
1. **Budh**	bodha	bodha	bodha	bodha	bodha	bodha	bodha	bodha	bodha	bodha	bodha	bodha	bodha	bodha	bodha	bodha	bodha	bodha
4. **Nṛit**	nṛitya	nṛitya	nṛitya	nṛitya	nṛitya	nṛitya	nṛitya	nṛitya	nṛitya	nṛitya	nṛitya	nṛitya	nṛitya	nṛitya	nṛitya	nṛitya	nṛitya	nṛitya
6. **Diś**	diśa	diśa	diśa	diśa	diśa	diśa	diśa	diśa	diśa	diśa	diśa	diśa	diśa	diśa	diśa	diśa	diśa	diśa
10. **Yuj**	yojaya	yojaya	yojaya	yojaya	yojaya	yojaya	yojaya	yojaya	yojaya	yojaya	yojaya	yojaya	yojaya	yojaya	yojaya	yojaya	yojaya	yojaya
2. **Vid**	ved	vid †	vet	ved	vit	vit	ved	vit	vid	ved	vit *	vit	ved	vid	vid	ved	vid	vid
3. **Bhṛi**	bibhar	bibhṛi	bibhar	bibhar	bibhṛi	bibhṛi	bibhar	bibhṛi	bibhr *	bibhar	bibhṛi	bibhṛi	bibhar	bibhr	bibhr	bibhar	bibhṛi	bibhr
7. **Bhid**	bhinad	bhind†	bhinat	bhinad	bhint	bhint	bhinad	bhint	bhind	bhinad	bhint *	bhint	bhinad	bhind	bhind	bhinad	bhind	bhind
5. **Ći**	ćinav	ćinu *	ćino	ćinav	ćinu	ćinu	ćinav	ćinu	ćinv	ćinav	ćinu	ćinu	ćinav	ćinv	ćinv	ćinav	ćinu	ćinv
8. **Tan**	tanav	tanu *	tano	tanav	tanu	tanu	tanav	tanu	tanv	tanav	tanu	tanu	tanav	tanv	tanv	tanav	tanu	tanv
9. **Pú**	puná	puní	puná	puná	puní	puní	puná	puní	pun	puná	puní	puní	puná	pun	pun	puná	puní	pun
1. 4. 6. 10.		* —							ntu		* sva			ithám	itám			ntám
	áni		tu	áva	tam	tám	áma	ta		ai		tám	ávahai			ámahai	dhvam	
2. 3. 7. 5. 8. 9.		hi † dhi							antu * atu		shva			áthám	átám			atám

Observe—In the 2d sing., Parasmai, the roots of the 5th and 8th class are like those of the 1st group, and make *ćinu, tanu*, rejecting the termination. The 2d and 7th take *dhi* for *hi* by 293, and make *viddhi, bhinddhi*. *Bhṛi* makes *bibhratu* for *bibhrantu* in 3d pl. by 292. In the Átmane, *bodha* + *ai* = *bodhai* and *puná* + *ai* = *punai* by 33, *bodha* + *ithám* = *bodhethám* by 32.

PERFECT OR SECOND PRETERITE.

Parasmai-pada.

ROOT.	SING.			DUAL.			PLURAL.		
1. *Budh*	*bubodh*	*bubodh*	*bubodh*	*bubudh*	*bubudh*	*bubudh*	*bubudh*	*bubudh*	*bubudh*
4. *Nṛit*	*nanart*	*nanart*	*nanart*	*nanṛit*	*nanṛit*	*nanṛit*	*nanṛit*	*nanṛit*	*nanṛit*
6. *Diś*	*dideś*	*dideś*	*dideś*	*didiś*	*didiś*	*didiś*	*didiś*	*didiś*	*didiś*
10. *Yuj*	*yojay*†	*yojay*†	*yojay*†	*yojay*†	*yojay*†	*yojay*†	*yojay*†	*yojay*†	*yojay*†
2. *Vid*	*vived*	*vived*	*vived*	*vivid*	*vivid*	*vivid*	*vivid*	*vivid*	*vivid*
3. *Bhṛi**	*babhár*	*babhar**	*babhár*	*babhṛi**	*babhr*	*babhr*	*babhṛi**	*babhr*	*babhr*
7. *Bhid*	*bibhed*	*bibhed*	*bibhed*	*bibhid*	*bibhid*	*bibhid*	*bibhid*	*bibhid*	*bibhid*
5. *Ći*	*ćićáy*	*ćićay*	*ćićáy*	*ćićy*	*ćićy*	*ćićy*	*ćićy*	*ćićy*	*ćićy*
8. *Tan*	*tatán*	*ten*	*tatán*	*ten*	*ten*	*ten*	*ten*	*ten*	*ten*
9. *Pú*	*pupáv*	*pupav*	*pupáv*	*pupuv*	*pupuv*	*pupuv*	*pupuv*	*pupuv*	*pupuv*
	a	*itha* **tha*	*a*	*iva* **va*	*athus*	*atus*	*ima* **ma*	*a*	*us*

Ātmane-pada.

ROOT.	SING.			DUAL.			PLURAL.		
1. *Budh*	*bubudh*	*bubudh*	*bubudh*	*bubudh*	*bubudh*	*bubudh*	*bubudh*	*bubudh*	*bubudh*
4. *Nṛit*	*nanṛit*	*nanṛit*	*nanṛit*	*nanṛit*	*nanṛit*	*nanṛit*	*nanṛit*	*nanṛit*	*nanṛit*
6. *Diś*	*didiś*	*didiś*	*didiś*	*didiś*	*didiś*	*didiś*	*didiś*	*didiś*	*didiś*
10. *Yuj*	*yojay*†	*yojay*†	*yojay*†	*yojay*†	*yojay*†	*yojay*†	*yojay*†	*yojay*†	*yojay*†
2. *Vid*	*vivid*	*vivid*	*vivid*	*vivid*	*vivid*	*vivid*	*vivid*	*vivid*	*vivid*
3. *Bhṛi**	*babhr*	*babhṛi**	*babhr*	*babhṛi**	*babhr*	*babhr*	*babhṛi**	*babhṛi**	*babhr*
7. *Bhid*	*bibhid*	*bibhid*	*bibhid*	*bibhid*	*bibhid*	*bibhid*	*bibhid*	*bidhid*	*bibhid*
5. *Ći*	*ćićy*	*ćićy*	*ćićy*	*ćićy*	*ćićy*	*ćićy*	*ćićy*	*ćićy*	*ćićy*
8. *Tan*	*ten*	*ten*	*ten*	*ten*	*ten*	*ten*	*ten*	*ten*	*ten*
9. *Pú*	*pupuv*	*pupuv*	*pupuv*	*pupuv*	*pupuv*	*pupuv*	*pupuv*	*pupuv*	*pupuv*
	e	*ishe* **she*	*e*	*ivahe* **vahe*	*áthe*	*áte*	*imahe* **mahe*	*idhve* **dhve*	*ire*

† The syllable *ám* must be added to *yojay* throughout; and the stem of the second preterites of *as*, *bhú*, or *kṛi*, must be affixed to *yojayám*: thus, 1st sing. *yojayámás*+*a* or *yojayámbabhúv*+*a* or *yojayáńćakár*+*a*; see 385. *a*. *Ći* may optionally take *tha* as well as *itha* in the 2d sing.; thus, *ćićayitha* or *ćićetha*: but *bhṛi* makes only *babhartha*, see pp. 139 and 171. As to the alternative *ćićay*, *tatan*, *pupav*, in the stems of 1st sing., see 368. As to *iḍhve*, see 372. *a*.

FIRST FUTURE.

ROOT.	STEM.	PAR. TERM.	ÁTM. TERM.
1. *Budh*	*bodhi**	*tásmi*	*táhe*
4. *Nṛit*	*narti*	*tási*	*táse*
6. *Diś*	*desh**	*tá*	*tá*
10. *Yuj*	*yojayi*		
		tásvas	*tásvahe*
2. *Vid*	*vedi*	*tásthas*	*tásáthe*
3. *Bhṛi*	*bhar*	*tárau*	*tárau*
7. *Bhid*	*bhet*		
		tásmas	*tásmahe*
5. *Ći*	*će*	*tástha*	*tádhve*
8. *Tan*	*tani*	*táras*	*táras*
9. *Pú*	*pavi*		

* Note, that *budh* also forms *boddháhe* &c. in Átm. by 406. After *desh* the *t* of the terminations will become *ṭ* by 300.

SECOND FUTURE.

ROOT.	STEM.	PAR. TERM.	ÁTM. TERM.
1. *Budh*	*bodhi**	*shyámi*	*shye*
4. *Nṛit*	*narti*	*shyasi*	*shyase*
6. *Diś*	*dek*	*shyati*	*shyate*
10. *Yuj*	*yojayi*		
		shyávas	*shyávahe*
2. *Vid*	*vedi*	*shyathas*	*shyethe*
3. *Bhṛi*	*bhari*	*shyatas*	*shyete*
7. *Bhid*	*bhet**		
		shyámas	*shyámahe*
5. *Ći*	*će*	*shyatha*	*shyadhve*
8. *Tan*	*tani*	*shyanti*	*shyante*
9. *Pú*	*pavi*		

* Note, that *budh* also forms *bhotsye* &c. in Átm. by 406; and that after *bhet* the terminations will be *syámi* &c.

AORIST OR THIRD PRETERITE.

Form I.

Root.	Stem.	Par. Term.	Átm. Term.
1. *Budh*	*abodhi* †	*sham*	*shi*
		shís or †*ís*	*shṭhás* or *thás*
4. *Nṛit*	*anarti* †	*shít* or †*ít*	*shṭa* or *ta*
		shva	*shvahi*
2. *Vid*	*avedi* †	*shṭam*	*sháthám*
		shṭám	*shátám*
3. *Bhṛi*	Par. *abhár*; Átm. *abhṛi**	*shma*	*shmahi*
5. *Ći*	Par. *aćai*; Átm. *aće**	*shṭa*	*dhvam* or **ḍhvam*
		shus	*shata*
8. *Tan*	Par. *atáni* †; Átm. *atani*		
9. *Pú*	Par. *apávi* †; Átm. *apavi**		

Note, that *bhṛi* makes *abhṛithás*, *abhṛita*. *Bhid*, 7th c., follows this form in Átm., and makes *abhitsi*, *abhitthás*, *abhitta*, &c., by 419. *Tan* may make *atathás*, *atata*, as well as *atanishṭhás*, &c., by 424. c.

Form II.

Root.	Stem.	Par. Term.	Átm. Term.
6. *Diś*	*adiksh*	*am*	*i* or **e*
		as	*athás*
10. *Yuj*	*ayúyuj**	*at*	*ata*
7. *Bhid* follows this form in Parasmai, but not in Átmane; see note under form I.	*abhid*	*áva*	*ávahi*
		atam	*áthám* or **ethám*
		atám	*átám* or **etám*
		áma	*ámahi*
		ata	*adhvam*
		an	*anta*

PRECATIVE OR BENEDICTIVE.

ROOT.	STEM.	PAR. TERM.	STEM.	ÁTM. TERM.
1. *Budh*	*budh*	*yásam*	*bodhi*	*shíya*
4. *Nṛit*	*nṛit*	*yás*	*narti*	*shíshṭhás*
6. *Diś*	*diś*	*yát*	*dik*	*shíshṭa*
10. *Yuj*	*yuj*	*yásva*	*yojayi*	*shívahi*
		yástam		*shíyásthám*
2. *Vid*	*vid*	*yástám*	*vedi*	*shíyástám*
3. *Bhṛi*	*bhṛi*		*bhṛi*	*shímahi*
7. *Bhid*	*bhid*	*yásma*	*bhit* *	*shídhvam*
		yásta		*shíran*
5. *Ći*	*ći*	*yásus*	*će*	
8. *Tan*	*tan*		*tani*	
9. *Pú*	*pú*		*pavi*	

* Note, that after *bhit* the terminations will be *síya* &c. As to *shíḍhvam*, see p. 193.

CONDITIONAL.

ROOT.	STEM.	PAR. TERM.	ÁTM. TERM.
1. *Budh*	*abodhi*	*shyam*	*shye*
4. *Nṛit*	*anarti*	*shyas*	*shyathás*
6. *Diś*	*adek*	*shyat*	*shyata*
10. *Yuj*	*ayojayi*	*shyáva*	*shyávahi*
		shyatam	*shyethám*
2. *Vid*	*avedi*	*shyatám*	*shyetám*
3. *Bhṛi*	*abhari*		
7. *Bhid*	*abhet* *	*shyáma*	*shyámahi*
		shyata	*shyadhvam*
5. *Ći*	*aće*	*shyan*	*shyanta*
8. *Tan*	*atani*		
9. *Pú*	*apavi*		

* Note, that after *abhet* the terminations will be *syam* &c.

INFINITIVE.

ROOT.	STEM.	TERM.
1. *Budh*	*bodhi*	
4. *Nṛit*	*narti*	
6. *Diś*	*desh* *	
10. *Yuj*	*yojayi*	
		tum
2. *Vid*	*vedi*	or **ṭum*
3. *Bhṛi*	*bhar*	after *desh*
7. *Bhid*	*bhet*	by 300.
5. *Ći*	*će*	
8. *Tan*	*tani*	
9. *Pú*	*pavi*	

INFLEXION OF THE STEM OF PASSIVE VERBS FROM THE SAME TEN ROOTS.

PRESENT.

ROOT.	STEM.	TERM.
1. *Budh*	*budhya* / *budhyá**	*i*
4. *Nṛit*	*nṛitya* / *nṛityá**	*se*
6. *Diś*	*diśya* / *diśyá**	*te*
10. *Yuj*	*yojya* / *yojyá**	**vahe*
2. *Vid*	*vidya* / *vidyá**	*ithe*
3. *Bhṛi*	*bhriya* / *bhriyá**	*ite*
7. *Bhid*	*bhidya* / *bhidyá**	
5. *Ći*	*ćíya* / *ćíyá**	**mahe*
8. *Tan*	*tanya* / *tanyá**	*dhve*
9. *Pú*	*púya* / *púyá**	*nte*

IMPERFECT.

ROOT.	STEM.	TERM.
1. *Budh*	*abudhya* / *abudhyá**	*i*
4. *Nṛit*	*anṛitya* / *anṛityá**	*thás*
6. *Diś*	*adiśya* / *adiśyá**	*ta*
10. *Yuj*	*ayojya* / *ayojyá**	**vahi*
2. *Vid*	*avidya* / *avidyá**	*ithám*
3. *Bhṛi*	*abhriya* / *abhriyá**	*itám*
7. *Bhid*	*abhidya* / *abhidyá**	
5. *Ći*	*aćíya* / *aćíyá**	**mahi*
8. *Tan*	*atanya* / *atanyá**	*dhvam*
9. *Pú*	*apúya* / *apúyá**	*nta*

POTENTIAL.

ROOT.	STEM.	TERM.
1. *Budh*	*budhya*	*íya*
4. *Nṛit*	*nṛitya*	*íthás*
6. *Diś*	*diśya*	*íta*
10. *Yuj*	*yojya*	*ívahi*
2. *Vid*	*vidya*	*íyáthám*
3. *Bhṛi*	*bhriya*	*íyátám*
7. *Bhid*	*bhidya*	
5. *Ći*	*ćíya*	*ímahi*
8. *Tan*	*tanya*	*ídhvam*
9. *Pú*	*púya*	*íran*

IMPERATIVE.

ROOT.	STEM.	TERM.
1. *Budh*	*budhya*	*ai*
4. *Nṛit*	*nṛitya*	*sva*
6. *Diś*	*diśya*	*tám*
10. *Yuj*	*yojya*	*ávahai*
2. *Vid*	*vidya*	*ithám*
3. *Bhṛi*	*bhriya*	*itám*
7. *Bhid*	*bhidya*	
5. *Ći*	*ćíya*	*ámahai*
8. *Tan*	*tanya*	*dhvam*
9. *Pú*	*púya*	*ntám*

PERFECT, Passive.

ROOT.	STEM.	TERM.
1. *Budh*	*bubudh*	*e*
4. *Nṛit*	*nanṛit*	* *ishe*
6. *Diś*	*didiś*	*e*
10. *Yuj*	*yojayámás*	* *ivahe*
2. *Vid*	*vivid*	*áthe*
3. *Bhṛi*	*babhr* / *babhṛ* *	*áte*
7. *Bhid*	*bibhid*	* *imahe*
5. *Ći*	*ćićy*	* *idhve*, 372.a.
8. *Tan*	*ten*	*ire*
9. *Pú*	*pupuv*	

FIRST FUTURE, Passive.

ROOT.	STEM.	TERM.
1. *Budh*	*bodhi*	*táhe*
4. *Nṛit*	*narti*	*táse*
6. *Diś*	*desh* (300)	*tá*
10. *Yuj*	*yojayi* or *yoji*	*tásvahe*
2. *Vid*	*vedi*	*tásáthe*
3. *Bhṛi*	*bhári* or *bhar*	*tárau*
7. *Bhid*	*bhet*	*tásmahe*
5. *Ći*	*ćáyi* or *će*	*tádhve*
8. *Tan*	*tani*	*táras*
9. *Pú*	*pávi* or *pavi*	

SECOND FUTURE, Passive.

ROOT.	STEM.	TERM.
1. *Budh*	*bodhi*	*shye*
4. *Nṛit*	*narti*	*shyase*
6. *Diś*	*dek* (302)	*shyate*
10. *Yuj*	*yojayi* or *yoji*	*shyávahe*
2. *Vid*	*vedi*	*shyethe*
3. *Bhṛi*	*bhári* or *bhari*	*shyete*
7. *Bhid*	*bhet*	*shyámahe*
5. *Ći*	*ćáyi* or *će*	*shyadhve*
8. *Tan*	*tani*	*shyante*
9. *Pú*	*pávi* or *pavi*	

AORIST, Passive.

ROOT.	STEM.	TERM.	STEM OF 3D SING.
1. *Budh*	*abodhi*	*shi*	*abodh*
4. *Nṛit*	*anarti*	*shṭhás*	*anart*
6. *Diś*	*adik* *		*adeś*
10. *Yuj*	*ayojayi* (496.*a*) or *ayoji*	— — *shvahi*	*ayoj*
2. *Vid*	*avedi*	*sháthám*	*aved*
3. *Bhṛi*	*abhári* or *abhṛi* (475)	*shátám*	*abhár*
7. *Bhid*	*abhit* *	—— *shmahi*	*abhed*
5. *Ći*	*aćáyi* or *aće*	*dhvam*	*aćáy*
8. *Tan*	*atani*	*shata*	*atán*
9. *Pú*	*apávi* or *apavi*		*apáv*

TERM. *i*

* Observe—After *abhit* the initial *sh* of the termination takes the dental form *s*, in this and the following tenses. Again, *adik* and *abhit* reject the sibilant from *shṭhás*, and become *adig* and *abhid* before *dhvam*: thus, *adikshi*, *adikthás*, *adeśi*, *adikshvahi*, *adiksháthám*, *adikshátám*, *adikshmahi*, *adigdhvam*, *adikshata*. So, *abhitsi*, *abhitthás*, *abhedi*, *abhitsvahi*, &c. See also 419, 475. *b*.

PRECATIVE, Passive.

ROOT.	STEM.	TERM.
1. *Budh*	*bodhi*	*shíya*
4. *Nṛit*	*narti*	*shíshṭhás*
6. *Diś*	*dik*	*shíshṭa*
10. *Yuj*	*yojayi* or *yoji*	—— *shívahi*
2. *Vid*	*vedi*	*shíyásthám*
3. *Bhṛi*	*bhári* or *bhṛi*	*shíyástám*
7. *Bhid*	*bhit*	—— *shímahi*
5. *Ći*	*ćáyi* or *će*	*shídhvam*, p. 193.
8. *Tan*	*tani*	*shíran*
9. *Pú*	*pávi* or *pavi*	

CONDITIONAL, Passive.

ROOT.	STEM.	TERM.
1. *Budh*	*abodhi*	*shye*
4. *Nṛit*	*anarti*	*shyathás*
6. *Diś*	*adek*	*shyata*
10. *Yuj*	*ayojayi* or *ayoji*	—— *shyávahi*
2. *Vid*	*avedi*	*shyethám*
3. *Bhṛi*	*abhári* or *abhari*	*shyetám*
7. *Bhid*	*abhet*	—— *shyámahi*
5. *Ći*	*aćáyi* or *aće*	*shyadhvam*
8. *Tan*	*atani*	*shyanta*
9. *Pú*	*apávi* or *apavi*	

CAUSAL FORM.
PRESENT TENSE.

ROOT.	STEM.	PAR. TERM.	ÁTM. TERM.
1. *Budh*	*bodhaya* / *bodhayá**	**mi*	*i*
4. *Nṛit*	*nartaya* / *nartayá**	*si*	*se*
6. *Diś*	*deśaya* / *deśayá**	*ti*	*te*
10. *Yuj*	*yojaya* / *yojayá**	**vas*	**vahe*
2. *Vid*	*vedaya* / *vedayá**	*thas*	*ithe*
3. *Bhṛi*	*bháraya* / *bhárayá**	*tas*	*ite*
7. *Bhid*	*bhedaya* / *bhedayá**	**mas*	**mahe*
5. *Ći*	*ćápaya* / *ćápayá**	*tha*	*dhve*
8. *Tan*	*tánaya* / *tánayá**	*nti*	*nte*
9. *Pú*	*pávaya* / *pávayá**		

Note—*Ći* also makes *ćáyaya*, &c. See 485. *b*.

DESIDERATIVE FORM.
PRESENT TENSE.

ROOT.	STEM.	PAR. TERM.	ÁTM. TERM.
1. *Budh*	*bubodhisha* / *bubodhishá**	**mi*	*i*
4. *Nṛit*	*ninartisha* / *ninartishá**	*si*	*se*
6. *Diś*	*didiksha* / *didikshá**	*ti*	*te*
10. *Yuj*	*yuyojayisha* / *yuyojayishá**	**vas*	**vahe*
2. *Vid*	*vividisha* / *vividishá**	*thas*	*ithe*
3. *Bhṛi*	*bibharisha* / *bibharishá**	*tas*	*ite*
7. *Bhid*	*bibhitsa* / *bibhitsá**	**mas*	**mahe*
5. *Ći*	*ćićísha* / *ćićíshá**	*tha*	*dhve*
8. *Tan*	*titanisha* / *titanishá**	*nti*	*nte*
9. *Pú*	*pipavisha* / *pipavishá**		

Observe—*Nṛit* also makes its stem *ninṛitsa*; *bhṛi*, *bubhúrsha*; *ći*, *ćikísha*; *tan*, *titaṃsa* or *titáṃsa*; *pú*, *pupúsha*—in both Átmane and Parasmai: and *budh* and *vid* may respectively make their stems *bubhutsa* (299. *a*) and *vivitsa*, but in Átmane only.

FREQUENTATIVE FORM.
PRESENT ÁTMANE.

ROOT.	STEM.	TERM.
1. *Budh*	*bobudhya* / *bobudhyá**	*i*
4. *Nṛit*	*narínṛitya* / *narínṛityá**	*se*
6. *Diś*	*dediśya* / *dediśyá**	*te*
10. *Yuj*†		**vahe*
2. *Vid*	*vevidya* / *vevidyá**	*ithe*
3. *Bhṛi*	*bebhríya* / *bebhríyá**	*ite*
7. *Bhid*	*bebhidya* / *bebhidyá**	**mahe*
5. *Ći*	*ćećíya* / *ćećíyá**	*dhve*
8. *Tan*	*tantanya* / *tantanyá**	*nte*
9. *Pú*	*popúya* / *popúyá**	

† Observe—The 10th class has no frequentative form.

PARTICIPLES.

ROOT.	PRES. PARASM.	PRES. ÁTMANE.	PRES. PASSIVE.	PAST PASSIVE.	PAST ACTIVE.	PERFECT PARASMAI.	PERFECT ÁTMANE.	PAST INDECL.	FUTURE PASS. 1.	FUTURE PASS. 2.	FUTURE PASS. 3.	2D FUT. PARASMAI.	2D FUT. ÁTMANE OR PASSIVE.
1. *Budh*	*bodhat*	*bodhamána*	*budhyamána*	*buddha*	*buddhavat*	*bubudhvas*	*bubudhána*	*buddhvá*	*boddhavya*	*bodhaníya*	*bodhya*	*bodhishyat*	*bodhishyamáṇa*
4. *Nṛit*	*nṛityat*	*nṛityamána*	*nṛityamána*	*nṛitta* or *nartita*	*nṛittavat* or *nartitavat*	*nanṛitvas*	*nanṛitána*	*nartitvá*	*nartitavya*	*nartaníya*	*nṛitya*	*nartishyat*	*nartishyamáṇa*
6. *Diś*	*diśat*	*diśamána*	*diśyamána*	*dishṭa*	*dishṭavat*	*didiśvas*	*didiśána*	*dishṭvá*	*deshṭavya*	*deśaníya*	*deśya*	*dekshyat*	*dekshyamáṇa*
10. *Yuj*	*yojayat*	*yojayána*	*yojyamána*	*yojita*	*yojitavat*	*yojayáṅ* †	*yojayáṅ* †	*yojayitvá*	*yojayitavya*	*yojaníya*	*yojya*	*yojayishyat*	*yojayishyamáṇa*
2. *Vid*	*vidat*	*vidána*	*vidyamána*	*vidita*	*viditavat*	*vividvas*	*vividána*	*viditvá*	*veditavya*	*vedaníya*	*vedya*	*vedishyat*	*vedishyamáṇa*
3. *Bhṛi*	*bibhrat*	*bibhráṇa*	*bhriyamáṇa*	*bhṛita*	*bhṛitavat*	*babhṛivas*	*babhráṇa*	*bhṛitvá*	*bhartavya*	*bharaṇíya*	*bhárya*	*bharishyat*	*bharishyamáṇa*
7. *Bhid*	*bhindat*	*bhindána*	*bhidyamána*	*bhinna*	*bhinnavat*	*bibhidvas*	*bibhidána*	*bhittvá*	*bhettavya*	*bhedaníya*	*bhedya*	*bhetsyat*	*bhetsyamána*
5. *Ći*	*ćinvat*	*ćinvána*	*ćíyamána*	*ćita*	*ćitavat*	*ćićivas*	*ćićyána*	*ćitvá*	*ćetavya*	*ćayaníya*	*ćeya*	*ćeshyat*	*ćeshyamáṇa*
8. *Tan*	*tanvat*	*tanvána*	*tanyamána*	*tata*	*tatavat*	*tenivas*	*tenána*	*tanitvá*	*tanitavya*	*tananíya*	*tánya*	*tanishyat*	*tanishyamáṇa*
9. *Pú*	*punat*	*punána*	*púyamána*	*púta*	*pútavat*	*pupúvas*	*pupuvána*	*pútvá*	*pavitavya*	*pavaníya*	*pávya*	*pavishyat*	*pavishyamáṇa*

† *Ćakṛivas* is added to *yojayáṅ* for the participle of the perfect Parasmai, and *ćakráṇa* for that of the perfect Átmane.

PARASMAI-PADA (see 327).

584. Although this root belongs to cl. 2, its inflexion is exhibited here, both because it is sometimes used as an auxiliary, and because it is desirable to study its inflexion together with that of the other substantive verb भू *bhú*, 'to be' (585), which supplies many of the tenses in which अस् is defective. Two other roots are sometimes employed as substantive verbs, with the sense 'to be,' viz. स्था cl. 1, 'to stand' (see 269, 587), and आस् cl. 2, 'to sit' (see 317. *a*). Indeed, the root अस् *as*, here inflected, is probably only an abbreviation of आस् *ás*.

The cognate languages have two roots similar to the Sanskṛit for the substantive verb 'to be.' Cf. φῦ and ἐσ in Greek, *es* (*sum*) and *fu* (*fui*) in Latin; and observe how the different parts of the Sanskṛit verbs correspond to the Greek and Latin; thus, *asmi, asi, asti*; ἐμμί, ἐσσί, ἐστί; *sum, es, est*. Cf. also *santi* with *sunt*; *ástam, ástám*, with ἦστον, ἥστην; *ásma, ásta, ásan*, with ἦμεν, ἦστε, ἦσαν, &c.

	Present, 'I am.'			*Potential*, 'I may be,' &c.		
PERS.	SING.	DUAL.	PLURAL.	SING.	DUAL.	PLURAL.
1st,	अस्मि *asmi*	स्वस् *svas*	स्मस् *smas*	स्याम् *syám*	स्याव *syáva*	स्याम *syáma*
2nd,	असि *asi*	स्थस् *sthas*	स्थ *stha*	स्यास् *syás*	स्यातम् *syátam*	स्यात *syáta*
3rd,	अस्ति *asti*	स्तस् *stas*	सन्ति *santi*	स्यात् *syát*	स्याताम् *syátám*	स्युस् *syus*

Imperfect, 'I was.'			*Imperative*, 'Let me be.'		
आसम् *ásam*	आस्व *ásva*	आस्म *ásma*	असानि *asáni*	असाव *asáva*	असाम *asáma*
आसीस् *ásís*	आस्तम् *ástam*	आस्त *ásta*	एधि *edhi*	स्तम् *stam*	स्त *sta*
आसीत् *ásít*	आस्ताम् *ástám*	आसन् *ásan*	अस्तु *astu*	स्ताम् *stám*	सन्तु *santu*

Perfect *, 'I have been,' &c.

PARASMAI.			ÁTMANE.		
आस *ása*	आसिव *ásiva*	आसिम *ásima*	आसे *áse*	आसिवहे *ásivahe*	आसिमहे *ásimahe*
आसिथ *ásitha*	आसथुस् *ásathus*	आस *ása*	आसिषे *ásishe*	आसाथे *ásáthe*	आसिध्वे *ásidhve*
आस *ása*	आसतुस् *ásatus*	आसुस् *ásus*	आसे *áse*	आसाते *ásáte*	आसिरे *ásire*

Obs.—The root *as*, 'to be,' has no Derivative forms, and only two Participles, viz. सत् *sat*, Pres. Par., सान *sána*, Pres. Átm. (see 524, 526). The Special tenses have an Átmane-pada, which is not used unless the root is compounded with prepositions. In this Pada ह् *h* is substituted for the root in 1st sing. Pres., and स् *s* is dropped before *dh* in 2nd pl.; thus, Pres. *he, se, ste*; *svahe, sáthe, sáte*; *smahe, dhve, sate*: Impf. *ási, ásthás, ásta*; *ásvahi, ásáthám, ásátám*; *ásmahi, ádhvam, ásata*: Pot. *síya, síthás, síta*; *sívahi, síyáthám, síyátám*; *símahi, sídhvam, síran*: Impv. *asai, sva, stám*; *asávahai, sáthám, sátám*; *asámahai, dhvam, satám*: see 327.

* The Perfect of *as* is not used by itself, but is employed in forming the Perfect of Causals and some other verbs, see 385, 490; in which case the Átmane may be used. The other tenses of *as* are wanting, and are supplied from *bhú* at 585.

GROUP I. CLASS I.

EXAMPLES OF PRIMITIVE VERBS OF THE FIRST CLASS, EXPLAINED AT 261.

585. Root भू *bhú.* Infin. भवितुम् *bhavitum,* 'to be' or 'become.'

PARASMAI-PADA. *Present Tense,* 'I am' or 'I become.'

PERS.	SING.	DUAL.	PLURAL.
1st,	भवामि *bhavámi*	भवावस् *bhavávas*	भवामस् *bhavámas*
2nd,	भवसि *bhavasi*	भवथस् *bhavathas*	भवथ *bhavatha*
3rd,	भवति *bhavati*	भवतस् *bhavatas*	भवन्ति *bhavanti*

Imperfect, 'I was.'

अभवम् *abhavam*	अभवाव *abhaváva*	अभवाम *abhaváma*
अभवस् *abhavas*	अभवतम् *abhavatam*	अभवत *abhavata*
अभवत् *abhavat*	अभवताम् *abhavatám*	अभवन् *abhavan*

Potential, 'I may be.'

भवेयम् *bhaveyam*	भवेव *bhaveva*	भवेम *bhavema*
भवेस् *bhaves*	भवेतम् *bhavetam*	भवेत *bhaveta*
भवेत् *bhavet*	भवेताम् *bhavetám*	भवेयुस् *bhaveyus*

Imperative, 'Let me be.'

भवानि *bhaváni*	भवाव *bhaváva*	भवाम *bhaváma*
भव *bhava*	भवतम् *bhavatam*	भवत *bhavata*
भवतु *bhavatu*	भवताम् *bhavatám*	भवन्तु *bhavantu*

Perfect, 'I have been,' 'I was.'

बभूव *babhúva*	बभूविव *babhúviva*	बभूविम *babhúvima*
बभूविथ *babhúvitha*	बभूवथुस् *babhúvathus*	बभूव *babhúva*
बभूव *babhúva*	बभूवतुस् *babhúvatus*	बभूवुस् *babhúvus*

First Future, 'I shall or will be.'

भवितास्मि *bhavitásmi*	भवितास्वस् *bhavitásvas*	भवितास्मस् *bhavitásmas*
भवितासि *bhavitási*	भवितास्थस् *bhavitásthas*	भवितास्थ *bhavitástha*
भविता *bhavitá*	भवितारौ *bhavitárau*	भवितारस् *bhavitáras*

Second Future, 'I shall or will be.'

भविष्यामि *bhavishyámi*	भविष्यावस् *bhavishyávas*	भविष्यामस् *bhavishyámas*
भविष्यसि *bhavishyasi*	भविष्यथस् *bhavishyathas*	भविष्यथ *bhavishyatha*
भविष्यति *bhavishyati*	भविष्यतस् *bhavishyatas*	भविष्यन्ति *bhavishyanti*

Aorist, 'I was' or 'had been,' &c.

अभूवम् *abhúvam*	अभूव *abhúva*	अभूम *abhúma*
अभूस् *abhús*	अभूतम् *abhútam*	अभूत *abhúta*
अभूत् *abhút*	अभूताम् *abhútám*	अभूवन् *abhúvan*

Precative or *Benedictive*, 'May I be.'

भूयासम् *bhúyásam*	भूयास्व *bhúyásva*	भूयास्म *bhúyásma*
भूयास् *bhúyás*	भूयास्तम् *bhúyástam*	भूयास्त *bhúyásta*
भूयात् *bhúyát*	भूयास्ताम् *bhúyástám*	भूयासुस् *bhúyásus*

Conditional, (If) 'I should be.'

अभविष्यम् *abhavishyam*	अभविष्याव *abhavishyáva*	अभविष्याम *abhavishyáma*
अभविष्यस् *abhavishyas*	अभविष्यतम् *abhavishyatam*	अभविष्यत *abhavishyata*
अभविष्यत् *abhavishyat*	अभविष्यताम् *abhavishyatám*	अभविष्यन् *abhavishyan*

586. Átmane-pada. *Present Tense*, 'I am,' &c.

भवे *bhave*	भवावहे *bhavávahe*	भवामहे *bhavámahe*
भवसे *bhavase*	भवेथे *bhavethe*	भवध्वे *bhavadhve*
भवते *bhavate*	भवेते *bhavete*	भवन्ते *bhavante*

Imperfect, 'I was.'

अभवे *abhave*	अभवावहि *abhavávahi*	अभवामहि *abhavámahi*
अभवथास् *abhavathás*	अभवेथाम् *abhavethám*	अभवध्वम् *abhavadhvam*
अभवत *abhavata*	अभवेताम् *abhavetám*	अभवन्त *abhavanta*

Potential, 'I may be,' &c.

भवेय *bhaveya*	भवेवहि *bhavevahi*	भवेमहि *bhavemahi*
भवेथास् *bhavethás*	भवेयाथाम् *bhaveyáthám*	भवेध्वम् *bhavedhvam*
भवेत *bhaveta*	भवेयाताम् *bhaveyátám*	भवेरन् *bhaveran*

Imperative, 'Let me be.'

भवै *bhavai*	भवावहै *bhavávahai*	भवामहै *bhavámahai*
भवस्व *bhavasva*	भवेथाम् *bhavethám*	भवध्वम् *bhavadhvam*
भवताम् *bhavatám*	भवेताम् *bhavetám*	भवन्ताम् *bhavantám*

Perfect, 'I have been,' 'I was,' &c.

बभूवे *babhúve*	बभूविवहे *babhúvivahe*	बभूविमहे *babhúvimahe*
बभूविषे *babhúvishe*	बभूवाथे *babhúváthe*	बभूविध्वे (ढ्वे) *babhúvidhve*
बभूवे *babhúve*	बभूवाते *babhúváte*	बभूविरे *babhúvire*

First Future, 'I shall or will be,' &c.

भविताहे *bhavitáhe*	भवितास्वहे *bhavitásvahe*	भवितास्महे *bhavitásmahe*
भवितासे *bhavitáse*	भवितासाथे *bhavitásáthe*	भविताध्वे *bhavitádhve*
भविता *bhavitá*	भवितारौ *bhavitárau*	भवितारस् *bhavitáras*

Second Future, 'I shall or will be,' &c.

भविष्ये *bhavishye*	भविष्यावहे *bhavishyávahe*	भविष्यामहे *bhavishyámahe*
भविष्यसे *bhavishyase*	भविष्येथे *bhavishyethe*	भविष्यध्वे *bhavishyadhve*
भविष्यते *bhavishyate*	भविष्येते *bhavishyete*	भविष्यन्ते *bhavishyante*

Aorist, 'I was' or 'had been,' &c.

अभविषि *abhavishi*	अभविष्वहि *abhavishvahi*	अभविष्महि *abhavishmahi*
अभविष्ठास् *abhavishṭhás*	अभविषाथाम् *abhavisháthám*	अभविध्वम् (ढ्वम्) *abhavidhvam*
अभविष्ट *abhavishṭa*	अभविषाताम् *abhavishátám*	अभविषत *abhavishata*

Precative or *Benedictive*, 'I wish I may be.'

भविषीय *bhavishíya*	भविषीवहि *bhavishívahi*	भविषीमहि *bhavishímahi*
भविषीष्ठास् *bhavishíshṭhás*	भविषीयास्थाम् *bhavishíyásthám*	भविषीध्वम्(ढ्वम्) *bhavishídhvam*
भविषीष्ट *bhavishíshṭa*	भविषीयास्ताम् *bhavishíyástám*	भविषीरन् *bhavishíran*

Conditional, (If) 'I should be,' &c.

अभविष्ये *abhavishye*	अभविष्यावहि *abhavishyávahi*	अभविष्यामहि *abhavishyámahi*
अभविष्यथास् *abhavishyathás*	अभविष्येथाम् *abhavishyethám*	अभविष्यध्वम् *abhavishyadhvam*
अभविष्यत *abhavishyata*	अभविष्येताम् *abhivishyetám*	अभविष्यन्त *abhavishyanta*

Passive (461), *Pres.* भूये, भूयसे, &c.; *Aor.* *3rd sing.* (475) अभावि. Causal (479), *Pres.* भावयामि, भावयसि, &c.; *Aor.* (492) अबीभवम्, &c. *Desiderative form of Causal* (497) बिभावयिषामि, &c. Desiderative (498), *Pres.* बुभूषामि, बुभूषसि, &c. Frequentative (507), *Pres.* बोभूये, बोभोमि or बोभवीमि*. Participles, *Pres.* भवत् (524); *Past Pass.* भूत (531); *Past Indecl.* भूत्वा (556), -भूय (559); *Fut. Pass.* भवितव्य (569), भवनीय (570), भाव्य or भव्य (571).

Obs.—The following examples are given in the order of their final letters.

587. Root स्था (special stem तिष्ठ, 269, 269. *a*). *Inf.* स्थातुम् 'to stand.' Par. and Átm. *Pres.* तिष्ठामि, तिष्ठसि, तिष्ठति; तिष्ठावस्, तिष्ठथस्, तिष्ठतस्; तिष्ठामस्, तिष्ठथ, तिष्ठन्ति. Átm. तिष्ठे, तिष्ठसे, तिष्ठते; तिष्ठावहे, तिष्ठेथे, तिष्ठेते; तिष्ठामहे, तिष्ठध्वे, तिष्ठन्ते. *Impf.* अतिष्ठम्, अतिष्ठस्, &c. Átm. अतिष्ठे, &c. *Pot.* तिष्ठेयम्, तिष्ठेस्, तिष्ठेत्; तिष्ठेव, &c. Átm. तिष्ठेय, तिष्ठेथास्, तिष्ठेत; तिष्ठेवहि, तिष्ठेयाथाम्, &c. *Impv.* तिष्ठानि, तिष्ठ, तिष्ठतु; तिष्ठाव, &c. Átm. तिष्ठै, तिष्ठस्व, तिष्ठताम्; तिष्ठावहै, &c. *Perf.* तस्थौ (373), तस्थिथ or तस्थाथ, तस्थौ; तस्थिव,

* These Derivative verbs will be inflected at full at 703, 705, 706, 707.

तस्थथुस्, तस्थतुस्; तस्थिम, तस्थ, तस्थुस्. Átm. तस्थे, तस्थिषे, तस्थे; तस्थिवहे, तस्थाथे, तस्थाते; तस्थिमहे, तस्थिध्वे, तस्थिरे. *1st Fut.* स्थातास्मि, स्थातासि, &c. Átm. स्थाताहे, स्थातासे, &c. *2nd Fut.* स्थास्यामि, स्थास्यसि, स्थास्यति, &c. Átm. स्थास्ये, स्थास्यसे, स्थास्यते, &c. *Aor.* (438) अस्थाम्, अस्थास्, अस्थात्; अस्थाव, अस्थातम्, अस्थाताम्; अस्थाम, अस्थात, अस्थुस्. Átm. (438. *d*, 421. *d*) अस्थिषि, अस्थिथास्, अस्थित; अस्थिष्वहि, अस्थिषाथाम्, -षाताम्; अस्थिष्महि, अस्थिढ्वम्, अस्थिषत. *Prec.* स्थेयासम्, स्थेयास्, &c. Átm. स्थासीय, स्थासीष्ठास्, &c. *Cond.* अस्थास्यम्, अस्थास्यस्, &c. Átm. अस्थास्ये, अस्थास्यथास्, &c. Pass., *Pres.* स्थीये (465); *Aor. 3rd sing.* अस्थायि. Caus., *Pres.* स्थापयामि, -ये; *Aor.* अतिष्ठिपम्, अतिष्ठिपे. Des. तिष्ठासामि, &c. Freq. तेष्ठीये or तास्थेमि or तास्थामि. Part., *Pres.* तिष्ठत् (141. Obs. 1); *Past Pass.* स्थित; *Past Indecl.* स्थित्वा, -स्थाय, -ष्ठाय; *Fut. Pass.* स्थातव्य, स्थानीय, स्थेय.

588. Root घ्रा (special stem जिघ्र, 269). *Inf.* घ्रातुम् 'to smell.' Par. *Pres.* जिघ्रामि, जिघ्रसि, &c. *Impf.* अजिघ्रम्, अजिघ्रस्, &c. *Pot.* जिघ्रेयम्, जिघ्रेस्, &c. *Impv.* जिघ्राणि (58), जिघ्र, &c. *Perf.* जघ्रौ (373), जघ्रिथ or जघ्राथ, जघ्रौ; जघ्रिव, जघ्रथुस्, जघ्रतुस्; जघ्रिम, जघ्र, जघ्रुस्. *1st Fut.* घ्रातास्मि, घ्रातासि, &c. *2nd Fut.* घ्रास्यामि, घ्रास्यसि, &c. *Aor.* (438) अघ्राम्, अघ्रास्, अघ्रात्; अघ्राव, अघ्रातम्, अघ्राताम्; अघ्राम, अघ्रात, अघ्रुस्. Or by 433, अघ्रासिषम्, अघ्रासीस्, अघ्रासीत्; अघ्रासिष्व, अघ्रासिष्टम्, -सिष्टाम्; अघ्रासिष्म, -सिष्ट, -सिषुस्. *Prec.* घ्रायासम्, घ्रायास्, &c. Or घ्रेयासम्, &c. *Cond.* अघ्रास्यम्, अघ्रास्यस्, &c. Pass., *Pres.* घ्राये (465. *a*); *Aor. 3rd sing.* अघ्रायि. Caus., *Pres.* घ्रापयामि; *Aor.* अजिघ्रपम् or अजिघ्रिपम्. Des. जिघ्रासामि. Freq. जेघ्रीये, जाघ्रामि or जाघ्रेमि. Part., *Pres.* जिघ्रत्; *Past Pass.* घ्रात or घ्राण; *Past Indecl.* घ्रात्वा, -घ्राय; *Fut. Pass.* घ्रातव्य, घ्राणीय, घ्रेय.

589. Root पा (special stem पिब, 269). *Inf.* पातुम् 'to drink.' Par. *Pres.* पिबामि, पिबसि, &c. *Impf.* अपिबम्, अपिबस्, &c. *Pot.* पिबेयम्, पिबेस्, &c. *Impv.* पिबानि, पिब, &c. *Perf.* (373) पपौ, पपिथ or पपाथ, पपौ; पपिव, पपथुस्, पपतुस्; पपिम, पप, पपुस्. *1st Fut.* पातास्मि, पातासि, &c. *2nd Fut.* पास्यामि, पास्यसि, &c. *Aor.* (438) अपाम्, अपास्, अपात्; अपाव, अपातम्, अपाताम्; अपाम, अपात, अपुस्. *Prec.* पेयासम्, पेयास्, &c. *Cond.* अपास्यम्, अपास्यस्, &c. Pass., *Pres.* पीये (465); *Aor. 3rd sing.* अपायि (475). Caus., *Pres.* पाययामि, -ये; *Aor.* अपीप्यम् (493. *e*). Des. पिपासामि. Freq. पेपीये, पापेमि or पापामि. Part., *Pres.* पिबत्; *Past Pass.* पीत (533. *b*); *Past Indecl.* पीत्वा, -पाय; *Fut. Pass.* पातव्य, पानीय, पेय.

590. Root जि (special stem जय, 263). *Inf.* जेतुम् 'to conquer.' Par.*

---

* जि is not generally used in the Átmane, excepting with the prepositions *vi* or *pará*. See 786.

Pres. जयामि, जयसि, जयति; जयावस्, जयथस्, जयतस्; जयामस्, जयथ, जयन्ति. *Impf.* अजयम्, अजयस्, अजयत्; अजयाव, अजयतम्, अजयताम्; अजयाम, अजयत, अजयन्. *Pot.* जयेयम्, जयेस्, जयेत्; जयेव, जयेतम्, जयेताम्; जयेम, जयेत, जयेयुस्. *Impv.* जयानि, जय, जयतु; जयाव, जयतम्, जयताम्; जयाम, जयत, जयन्तु. *Perf.* जिगाय (368, 374. *b*), जिगयिथ or जिगेथ, जिगाय; जिग्यिव (374), जिग्यथुस्, जिग्यतुस्; जिग्यिम, जिग्य, जिग्युस्. *1st Fut.* जेतास्मि, जेतासि, जेता; जेतास्वस्, जेतास्थस्, जेतारौ; जेतास्मस्, जेतास्थ, जेतारस्. *2nd Fut.* जेष्यामि, जेष्यसि, जेष्यति; जेष्यावस्, जेष्यथस्, जेष्यतस्; जेष्यामस्, जेष्यथ, जेष्यन्ति. *Aor.* अजैषम् (420), अजैषीस्, अजैषीत्; अजैष्व, अजैष्टम्, अजैष्टाम्; अजैष्म, अजैष्ट, अजैषुस्. *Prec.* जीयासम्, जीयास्, जीयात्; जीयास्व, जीयास्तम्, जीयास्ताम्; जीयास्म, जीयास्त, जीयासुस्. *Cond.* अजेष्यम्, अजेष्यस्, अजेष्यत्; अजेष्याव, अजेष्यतम्, अजेष्यताम्; अजेष्याम, अजेष्यत, अजेष्यन्. Pass., *Pres.* जीये, &c.; *Aor. 3rd sing.* अजायि. Caus., *Pres.* जापयामि; *Aor.* अजीजपम्. Des. जिगीषामि. Freq. जेजीये, जेजेमि or जेजयीमि. Part., *Pres.* जयत्; *Past Pass.* जित; *Past Indecl.* जित्वा, -जित्य; *Fut. Pass.* जेतव्य, जयनीय, जेय or जित्य or जय्य (571, 572).

a. Like जि may be conjugated नी. *Inf.* नेतुम् 'to lead.' But the Causal is नाययामि; Caus., *Aor.* अनीनयम्; Des. निनीषामि. In Epic poetry the *Perfect* is sometimes नयामास for निनाय, and the *2nd Fut.* नयिष्यामि for नेष्यामि (especially when preceded by the prep. आ).

591. Root स्मि (special stem स्मय). *Inf.* स्मेतुम् 'to smile.' Átm. *Pres.* स्मये, स्मयसे, &c. *Impf.* अस्मये, अस्मयथास्, &c. *Pot.* स्मयेय, स्मयेथास्, &c. *Impv.* स्मयै, स्मयस्व, &c. *Perf.* (374. *e*) सिष्मिये*, सिष्मियिषे, सिष्मिये; सिष्मियिवहे, सिष्मियाथे, सिष्मियाते; सिष्मियिमहे, सिष्मियिध्वे or -यिढ्वे, सिष्मियिरे. *1st Fut.* स्मेताहे, स्मेतासे, &c. *2nd Fut.* स्मेष्ये, स्मेष्यसे, &c. *Aor.* अस्मेषि, अस्मेष्ठास्, अस्मेष्ट; अस्मेष्वहि, अस्मेषाथाम्, -षाताम्; अस्मेष्महि, अस्मेढ्वम्, अस्मेषत. *Prec.* स्मेषीय, &c. *Cond.* अस्मेष्ये, &c. Pass., *Pres.* स्मीये; *Aor. 3rd sing.* अस्मायि. Caus., *Pres.* स्माययामि or स्मापयामि; *Aor.* असिष्मयम् or असिष्मपम्. Des. सिस्मयिषे. Freq. सेष्मीये, सेष्मेमि or सेष्मयीमि. Part., *Pres.* स्मयमान; *Past Pass.* स्मित; *Past Indecl.* स्मित्वा, -स्मित्य; *Fut. Pass.* स्मेतव्य, स्मयनीय, स्मेय.

592. Root द्रु (special stem द्रव). *Inf.* द्रोतुम् 'to run.' Par. *Pres.* द्रवामि, द्रवसि, द्रवति; द्रवावस्, द्रवथस्, द्रवतस्; द्रवामस्, द्रवथ, द्रवन्ति. *Impf.* अद्रवम्, अद्रवस्, &c. *Pot.* द्रवेयम्, द्रवेस्, &c. *Impv.* द्रवाणि (58), द्रव, &c. *Perf.* दुद्राव, दुद्रोथ, दुद्राव; दुद्रुव (369), दुद्रुवथुस् (374. *g*), दुद्रुवतुस्; दुद्रुम, दुद्रुव, दुद्रुवुस्. *1st Fut.* द्रोतास्मि. *2nd Fut.* द्रोष्यामि, द्रोष्यसि, &c. *Aor.*

---

* When वि is prefixed, the Perfect is विसिस्मिये against 70.

अदुद्रुवम् (440. *a*), अदुद्रुवस्, अदुद्रुवत्; अदुद्रुवाव, अदुद्रुवतम्, अदुद्रुवताम्; अदुद्रुवाम, अदुद्रुवत, अदुद्रुवन्. *Prec.* द्रूयासम्, द्रूयास्, &c. *Cond.* अद्रोष्यम्. Pass., *Pres.* द्रूये; *Aor. 3rd sing.* अद्रावि. Caus., *Pres.* द्रावयामि; *Aor.* अदुद्रवम् or अदिद्रवम्. Des. दुद्रूषामि. Freq. दोद्रूये, दोद्रोमि or दोद्रवीमि. Part., *Pres.* द्रवत्; *Past Pass.* द्रुत; *Past Indecl.* द्रुत्वा, -द्रुत्य; *Fut. Pass.* द्रोतव्य, द्रवणीय, द्राव्य or द्रव्य.

a. Like द्रु may be conjugated स्रु (sometimes written श्रु). *Inf.* स्रोतुम् 'to flow.'

593. Root हृ (special stem हर). *Inf.* हर्तुम् 'to seize,' 'to take.' Par. and Átm. *Pres.* हरामि. Átm. हरे, हरसे, हरते; हरावहे, &c. *Impf.* अहरम्, अहरस्, अहरत्; अहराव, &c. Átm. अहरे, अहरथास्, अहरत; अहरावहि, &c. *Pot.* हरेयम्. Átm. हरेय, हरेथास्, &c. *Impv.* हराणि (58), हर, &c. Átm. हरै, हरस्व, &c. *Perf.* जहार, जहर्थ (370. *a*), जहार; जह्रिव, जह्रथुस्, जह्रतुस्; जह्रिम, जह्र, जह्रुस्. Átm. जह्रे, जह्रिषे, जह्रे; जह्रिवहे, जह्राथे, जह्राते; जह्रिमहे, जह्रिध्वे or जह्रिढ्वे, जह्रिरे. *1st Fut.* हर्तास्मि. Átm. हर्ताहे, हर्तासे, &c. *2nd Fut.* हरिष्यामि. Átm. हरिष्ये, हरिष्यसे, &c. *Aor.* अहार्षम्, अहार्षीस्, अहार्षीत्; अहार्ष्व, अहार्ष्टम्, अहार्ष्टाम्; अहार्ष्म, अहार्ष्ट, अहार्षुस्. Átm. अहृषि, अहृथास्, अहृत; अहृष्वहि, अहृषाथाम्, अहृषाताम्; अहृष्महि, अहृढ्वम्, अहृषत. *Prec.* ह्रियासम्. Átm. हृषीय, हृषीष्ठास्, &c. *Cond.* अहरिष्यम्. Átm. अहरिष्ये, अहरिष्यथास्, &c. Pass., *Pres.* ह्रिये; *Aor. 3rd sing.* अहारि. Caus., *Pres.* हारयामि, -ये; *Aor.* अजीहरम्. Des. जिहीर्षामि, -र्षे. Freq. जेह्रीये, जर्हरीमि or जरीहरीमि or जरिहरीमि or जरीहर्मि or जरि- or जर्हर्मि. Part., *Pres.* हरत्; *Pass.* ह्रियमाण; *Past Pass.* हृत; *Past Indecl.* हृत्वा, -हृत्य; *Fut. Pass.* हर्तव्य, हरणीय, हार्य.

594. Root स्मृ (special stem स्मर). *Inf.* स्मर्तुम् 'to remember.' Par. and Átm. *Pres.* स्मरामि. Átm. स्मरे. *Impf.* अस्मरम्, अस्मरस्, &c. Átm. अस्मरे. *Pot.* स्मरेयम्. Átm. स्मरेय, &c. *Impv.* स्मराणि (58). Átm. स्मरै, स्मरस्व, &c. *Perf.* सस्मार, सस्मर्थ (370. *a*), सस्मार; सस्मरिव, सस्मरथुस्, सस्मरतुस्; सस्मरिम, सस्मर, सस्मरुस्. Átm. सस्मरे, सस्मरिषे, सस्मरे; सस्मरिवहे, सस्मराथे, सस्मराते; सस्मरिमहे, सस्मरिध्वे or -रिढ्वे, सस्मरिरे. *1st Fut.* स्मर्तास्मि. Átm. स्मर्ताहे. *2nd Fut.* स्मरिष्यामि. Átm. स्मरिष्ये. *Aor.* अस्मार्षम्, &c. (see हृ at 593). Átm. अस्मृषि, अस्मृथास् (see हृ at 593). *Prec.* स्मर्यासम्. Átm. स्मृषीय or स्मरिषीय. *Cond.* अस्मरिष्यम्. Átm. अस्मरिष्ये. Pass., *Pres.* स्मर्ये; *Aor. 3rd sing.* अस्मारि. Caus., *Pres.* स्मारयामि, -ये; *Aor.* असस्मरम्. Des. सुस्मूर्षे. Freq. सास्मर्ये, सास्मर्मि or सास्मरीमि. Part., *Pres.* स्मरत्; *Past Pass.* स्मृत; *Past Indecl.* स्मृत्वा, -स्मृत्य; *Fut. Pass.* स्मर्तव्य, स्मरणीय, स्मार्य.

595. Root ह्वे (special stem ह्वय). *Inf.* ह्वातुम् 'to call.' Par. and Átm. *Pres.* ह्वयामि. Átm. ह्वये. *Impf.* अह्वयम्, &c. Átm. अह्वये.

Pot. ह्वयेयम्. Átm. ह्वयेय. *Impv.* ह्वयानि. Átm. ह्वयै. *Perf.* (373. *e*) जुहाव, जुहविथ or जुहोथ, जुहाव; जुहुविव, जुहुवथुस्, जुहुवतुस्; जुहुविम, जुहुव, जुहुवुस्. Átm. जुहुवे, जुहुविषे, जुहुवे; जुहुविवहे, जुहुवाथे, जुहुवाते; जुहुविमहे, जुहुविध्वे or -विढ्वे, जुहुविरे. *1st Fut.* ह्वातास्मि. Átm. ह्वाताहे. *2nd Fut.* ह्वास्यामि. Átm. ह्वास्ये. *Aor.* (438. *c*) अह्वम्, अह्वस्, अह्वत्; अह्वाव, अह्वतम्, अह्वताम्; अह्वाम, अह्वत, अह्वन्. Átm. अह्वे, अह्वथास्, अह्वत; अह्वावहि, अह्वेथाम्, अह्वेताम्; अह्वामहि, अह्वध्वम्, अह्वन्त. Or अह्वासि (434), अह्वास्थास्, अह्वास्त; अह्वास्वहि, अह्वासाथाम्, अह्वासाताम्; अह्वास्महि, अह्वाध्वम्, अह्वासत. *Prec.* हूयासम्. Átm. ह्वासीय. *Cond.* अह्वास्यम्. Átm. अह्वास्ये. Pass. हूयते (465. *c*); *Aor. 3rd sing.* अह्वायि or अह्वायिष्ट or अह्वत or अह्वास्त. *2nd Fut.* ह्वास्यते or ह्वायिष्यते (474. *a*). Caus., *Pres.* ह्वाययामि (483. *b*); *Aor.* अजूहवम्. Des. जुहूषामि, जुहूषे. Freq. जोहूये, जोहोमि or जोहवीमि. Part., *Pres.* ह्वयत्; *Pass.* हूयमान; *Past Pass.* हूत; *Past Indecl.* हूत्वा, -हूय; *Fut. Pass.* ह्वातव्य, ह्वानीय, ह्वेय.

a. गै (special stem गाय, 268), *Inf.* गातुम् 'to sing,' follows the analogy of ह्वे, the final diphthong being changed to *á* before all terminations beginning with *t* or *s*. *Pres.* गायामि. *Impf.* अगायम्, &c. *Pot.* गायेयम्. *Impv.* गायानि. *Perf.* (373. *d*) जगौ, जगिथ or जगाथ, जगौ; जगिव, जगथुस्, जगतुस्; जगिम, जग, जगुस्. *1st Fut.* गातास्मि. *2nd Fut.* गास्यामि. *Aor.* (433) अगासिषम्, अगासीस्, अगासीत्; अगासिष्व, अगासिष्टम्, अगासिष्टाम्; अगासिष्म, अगासिष्ट, अगासिषुस्. *Prec.* गेयासम् (451). *Cond.* अगास्यम्. Pass. गीयते (465); *Aor. 3rd sing.* अगायि. Caus., *Pres.* गापयामि (483); *Aor.* अजीगपम्. Des. जिगासामि. Freq. जेगीये, जागेमि or जागामि. Part., *Pres.* गायत्; *Pass.* गीयमान; *Past Pass.* गीत; *Past Indecl.* गीत्वा, -गाय; *Fut. Pass.* गातव्य, गानीय, गेय.

b. Like गै may be conjugated ग्लै 'to be weary;' ध्यै 'to meditate;' म्लै 'to fade;' and all other roots in *ai* (see 268).

c. Root पच् (special stem पच). *Inf.* पक्तुम् 'to cook.' Par. and Átm. *Pres.* पचामि. Átm. पचे. *Impf.* अपचम्, अपचस्, &c. Átm. अपचे. *Pot.* पचेयम्, पचेस्, &c. Átm. पचेय. *Impv.* पचानि, पच, &c. Átm. पचै. *Perf.* पपाच or पपच, पपक्थ or पेचिथ (370. *d*), पपाच; पेचिव, पेचथुस्, पेचतुस्; पेचिम, पेच, पेचुस्. Átm. पेचे, पेचिषे, पेचे; पेचिवहे, पेचाथे, पेचाते; पेचिमहे, पेचिध्वे, पेचिरे. *1st Fut.* पक्तास्मि. Átm. पक्ताहे. *2nd Fut.* पक्ष्यामि. Átm. पक्ष्ये. *Aor.* (420. *e*) अपाक्षम्, अपाक्षीस्, अपाक्षीत्; अपाक्ष्व, अपाक्तम्, अपाक्ताम्; अपाक्ष्म, अपाक्त, अपाक्षुस्. Átm. अपक्षि, अपक्थास्, अपक्त; अपक्ष्वहि, अपक्षाथाम्, अपक्षाताम्; अपक्ष्महि, अपग्ध्वम्, अपक्षत. *Prec.* पच्यासम्. Átm. पक्षीय. *Cond.* अपक्ष्यम्. Átm. अपक्ष्ये. Pass., *Pres.* पच्ये; *Impf.* अपच्ये; *Aor. 3rd sing.* अपाचि. Caus., *Pres.* पाचयामि, पाचये; *Aor.* अपीपचम्.

Des. पिपक्षामि, पिपक्षे. Freq. पापच्ये, पापच्मि or पापचीमि. Part., *Pres.* पचत्; Átm. पचमान; *Pass.* पच्यमान; *Past Pass.* पक्व (548); *Past Indecl.* पक्त्वा, -पच्य; *Fut. Pass.* पक्तव्य, पचनीय, पाच्य or पाक्य (574).

d. Root याच् (special stem याच). *Inf.* याचितुम् 'to ask.' Par. and Átm. *Pres.* याचामि. Átm. याचे. *Impf.* अयाचम्, अयाचस्, &c. Átm. अयाचे. *Pot.* याचेयम्, याचेस्, &c. Átm. याचेय. *Impv.* याचानि, याच, &c. Átm. याचै. *Perf.* ययाच, ययाचिथ, ययाच; ययाचिव, ययाचथुस्, ययाचतुस्; ययाचिम, ययाच, ययाचुस्. Átm. ययाचे, ययाचिषे, ययाचे; ययाचिवहे, ययाचाथे, ययाचाते; ययाचिमहे, ययाचिध्वे, ययाचिरे. *1st Fut.* याचितास्मि. Átm. याचिताहे. *2nd Fut.* याचिष्यामि. Átm. याचिष्ये. *Aor.* (427) अयाचिषम्, अयाचीस्, अयाचीत्; अयाचिष्व, अयाचिष्टम्, -ष्टाम्; अयाचिष्म, -चिष्ट, -चिषुस्. Átm. अयाचिषि, अयाचिष्ठास्, अयाचिष्ट; अयाचिष्वहि, अयाचिषाथाम्, -षाताम्; अयाचिष्महि, अयाचिढ्वम्, अयाचिषत. *Prec.* याच्यासम्. Átm. याचिषीय. *Cond.* अयाचिष्यम्. Pass., *Pres.* याच्ये. Caus., *Pres.* याचयामि; *Aor.* अययाचम्. Des. यियाचिषामि, -षे. Freq. यायाच्ये, यायाच्मि (*3rd sing.* यायाक्ति). Part., *Pres.* याचत्; Átm. याचमान; *Past Pass.* याचित; *Past Indecl.* याचित्वा; *Fut. Pass.* याचितव्य, याचनीय, याच्य.

e. Root शुच् (special stem शोच). *Inf.* शोचितुम् 'to grieve.' Par. (Ep. rarely Átm.) *Pres.* शोचामि. *Impf.* अशोचम्, अशोचस्, &c. *Pot.* शोचेयम्, शोचेस्, &c. *Impv.* शोचानि, शोच, &c. *Perf.* शुशोच, शुशोचिथ, शुशोच; शुशुचिव, शुशुचथुस्, शुशुचतुस्; शुशुचिम, शुशुच, शुशुचुस्. *1st Fut.* शोचितास्मि. *2nd Fut.* शोचिष्यामि. *Aor.* (427. *b*) अशोचिषम्, अशोचीस्, अशोचीत्; अशोचिष्व, अशोचिष्टम्, अशोचिष्टाम्; अशोचिष्म, अशोचिष्ट, अशोचिषुस्. *Prec.* शुच्यासम्. *Cond.* अशोचिष्यम्. Pass., *Pres.* शुच्ये; *Aor. 3rd sing.* अशोचि. Caus., *Pres.* शोचयामि; *Aor.* अशूशुचम्. Des. शुशुचिषामि or शुशोचिषामि. Freq. शोशुच्ये, शोशोच्मि (*3rd sing.* शोशोक्ति). Part., *Pres.* शोचत्; *Pass.* शुच्यमान; *Past Pass.* शुचित and शोचित; *Past Indecl.* शुचित्वा or शोचित्वा, -शुच्य; *Fut. Pass.* शोचितव्य, शोचनीय, शोच्य.

596. Root त्यज्. *Inf.* त्यक्तुम् 'to abandon,' 'to quit.' Par. *Pres.* त्यजामि. *Impf.* अत्यजम्, अत्यजस्, &c. *Pot.* त्यजेयम्. *Impv.* त्यजानि, त्यज, &c. *Perf.* तत्याज, तत्यजिथ or तत्यक्थ (370. *d*), तत्याज; तत्यजिव, तत्यजथुस्, तत्यजतुस्; तत्यजिम, तत्यज, तत्यजुस्. *1st Fut.* त्यक्तास्मि. *2nd Fut.* त्यक्ष्यामि. *Aor.* (422, 296) अत्याक्षम्, अत्याक्षीस्, अत्याक्षीत्; अत्याक्ष्व, अत्याक्तम्, अत्याक्ताम्; अत्याक्ष्म, अत्याक्त, अत्याक्षुस्. *Prec.* त्यज्यासम्. *Cond.* अत्यक्ष्यम्, &c. Pass., *Pres.* त्यज्ये; *Aor. 3rd sing.* अत्याजि. Caus., *Pres.* त्याजयामि; *Aor.* अतित्यजम्. Des. तित्यक्षामि. Freq. तात्यज्ये, तात्यज्मि or तात्यजीमि. Part., *Pres.* त्यजत्; *Past Pass.* त्यक्त; *Past Indecl.* त्यक्त्वा, -त्यज्य; *Fut. Pass.* त्यक्तव्य, त्यजनीय, त्याज्य (573).

597. Root यज्. *Inf.* यष्टुम् 'to sacrifice,' 'to worship.' Par. and Átm. *Pres.* यजामि. Átm. यजे. *Impf.* अयजम्, अयजस्, &c. Átm. अयजे. *Pot.* यजेयम्. Átm. यजेय. *Impv.* यजानि, यज, &c. Átm. यजै. *Perf.* (375. *e*) इयाज, इयजिथ or येजिथ or इयष्ठ (297), इयाज; ईजिव, ईजथुस्, ईजतुस्; ईजिम, ईज, ईजुस्. Átm. ईजे, ईजिषे, ईजे; ईजिवहे, ईजाथे, ईजाते; ईजिमहे, ईजिध्वे, ईजिरे. *1st Fut.* यष्टास्मि (403). Átm. यष्टाहे. *2nd Fut.* यक्ष्यामि (403). Átm. यक्ष्ये. *Aor.* (422) अयाक्षम्, अयाक्षीस्, अयाक्षीत्; अयाक्ष्व, अयाष्टम्, अयाष्टाम्; अयाक्ष्म, अयाष्ट, अयाक्षुस्. Átm. अयक्षि, अयष्ठास्, अयष्ट; अयक्ष्वहि, अयक्षाथाम्, अयक्षाताम्; अयक्ष्महि, अयड्ढ्वम्, अयक्षत. *Prec.* इज्यासम्. Átm. यक्षीय. *Cond.* अयक्ष्यम्. Átm. अयक्ष्ये. Pass., *Pres.* इज्ये (471); *Impf.* ऐज्ये (251. *a*); *Aor. 3rd sing.* अयाजि. Caus., *Pres.* याजयामि, -ये; *Aor.* अयीयजम्. Des. यियक्षामि, -क्षे. Freq. यायज्ये, यायज्मि or यायजीमि. Part., *Pres.* यजत्; Átm. यजमान; *Pass.* इज्यमान; *Past Pass.* इष्ट; *Past Indecl.* इष्ट्वा, -इज्य; *Fut. Pass.* यष्टव्य, यजनीय, याज्य or यज्य.

a. Root सञ्ज् (special stem सज, 270. *d*). *Inf.* संक्तुम् 'to adhere.' Par. *Pres.* सजामि*. *Impf.* असजम्. *Pot.* सजेयम्. *Impv.* सजानि. *Perf.* ससञ्ज, ससञ्जिथ or ससंक्थ, ससञ्ज; ससञ्जिव, ससञ्जथुस्, ससञ्जतुस्; ससञ्जिम, ससञ्ज, ससञ्जुस्. *1st Fut.* संक्तास्मि, &c. *2nd Fut.* संक्ष्यामि, &c. *Aor.* असांक्षम्, -क्षीस्, -क्षीत्; असांक्ष्व, असांक्तम्, -क्ताम्; असांक्ष्म, असांक्त, असांक्षुस्. *Prec.* सज्यासम्, &c. *Cond.* असंक्ष्यम्, &c. Pass., *Pres.* सज्ये. Caus., *Pres.* सञ्जयामि; *Aor.* अससञ्जम्. Des. सिसंक्षामि, &c. Freq. सासज्ये, सासञ्ज्मि. Part., *Pres.* सजत्; *Pass.* सज्यमान; *Past Pass.* सक्त; *Past Indecl.* सक्त्वा or संक्त्वा, -सज्य; *Fut. Pass.* संक्तव्य, सञ्जनीय, संग्य or संज्य.

b. Root द्युत् (special stem द्योत). *Inf.* द्योतितुम् 'to shine.' Átm. (and Par. in *Aor.*) *Pres.* द्योते. *Impf.* अद्योते. *Pot.* द्योतेय. *Impv.* द्योतै. *Perf.* दिद्युते (383. *a*), -तिषे, -ते; दिद्युतिवहे, -ताथे, -ताते; दिद्युतिमहे, -तिध्वे, -तिरे. *1st Fut.* द्योतिताहे. *2nd Fut.* द्योतिष्ये. *Aor.* अद्योतिषि, अद्योतिष्ठास्, अद्योतिष्ट; अद्योतिष्वहि, -तिषाथाम्, -तिषाताम्; -तिष्महि, -तिध्वम्, -तिषत. *Par.* अद्युतम्, -तस्, -तत्; -ताव, -ततम्, तताम्; -ताम, -तत, -तन्. *Prec.* द्योतिषीय. *Cond.* अद्योतिष्ये. Pass., *Pres.* द्युत्ये; *Aor. 3rd sing.* अद्योति. Caus., *Pres.* द्योतयामि; *Aor.* अदिद्युतम्. Des. दिद्युतिषे or दिद्योतिषे. Freq. देद्युत्ये, देद्योत्मि or देद्युतीमि. Part., *Pres.* द्योतमान; *Past Pass.* द्युतित or द्योतित; *Past Indecl.* द्युतित्वा or द्योतित्वा, -द्युत्य; *Fut. Pass.* द्योतितव्य, द्योतनीय, द्योत्य.

c. Root पत्. *Inf.* पतितुम् 'to fall.' Par. *Pres.* पतामि. *Impf.* अपतम्. *Pot.* पतेयम्. *Impv.* पतानि. *Perf.* पपात or पपत (368), पेतिथ, पपात;

---

* The final *j* is sometimes incorrectly doubled (Pres. सज्जामि, सज्जसि, सज्जति, &c.); but the root must not, therefore, be confounded with an uncommon root सज्ज् or सस्ज्, meaning 'to go,' 'to move,' also cl. 1, and making सज्जामि, &c.

पेतिव, पेतथुस्, पेततुस्; पेतिम, पेत, पेतुस्. *1st Fut.* पतितास्मि. *2nd Fut.* पतिष्यामि. *Aor.* अपप्तम् (441), अपप्तस्, अपप्तत्; अपप्ताव, अपप्ततम्, अपप्तताम्; अपप्ताम, अपप्तत, अपप्तन्. *Prec.* पत्यासम्. *Cond.* अपतिष्यम्. Pass., *Pres.* पत्ये; *Impf.* अपत्ये; *Aor. 3rd sing.* अपाति. Caus., *Pres.* पतयामि, पतये and पातयामि, पातये; *Aor.* अपीपतम्. Des. पिपतिषामि or पित्सामि. Freq. पनीपत्ये, पनीपत्मि or पनीपतीमि. Part., *Pres.* पतत्; *Pass.* पत्यमान; *Past Pass.* पतित; *Past Indecl.* पतित्वा, -पत्य; *Fut. Pass.* पतितव्य, पतनीय, पात्य or पत्य.

598. Root वृत् (special stem वर्त). *Inf.* वर्तितुम् 'to be,' 'to exist.' Átm. (and optionally Par. in *2nd Fut., Aor.,* and *Cond.,* when it rejects *i*). *Pres.* वर्ते. *Impf.* अवर्ते. *Pot.* वर्तेय. *Impv.* वर्तै. *Perf.* ववृते, ववृतिषे, ववृते; ववृतिवहे, ववृताथे, ववृताते; ववृतिमहे, ववृतिध्वे, ववृतिरे. *1st Fut.* वर्तिताहे. *2nd Fut.* वर्तिष्ये. *Aor.* अवर्तिषि, अवर्तिष्ठास्, अवर्तिष्ट; अवर्तिष्वहि, -र्तिषाथाम्, -र्तिषाताम्; -र्तिष्महि, -र्तिढ्वम्, -र्तिषत. Par. अवृतम्, -तस्, -तत्; -ताव, -ततम्, -तताम्; -ताम, -तत, -तन्. *Prec.* वर्तिषीय. *Cond.* अवर्तिष्ये or अवर्त्स्यम्. Pass., *Pres.* वृत्ये. Caus., *Pres.* वर्तयामि; *Aor.* अवीवृतम् or अववर्तम्. Des. विवर्तिषे or विवृत्सामि. Freq. वरीवृत्ये, वरीवर्त्मि or वरीवृतीमि. Part., *Pres.* वर्तमान; *Past Pass.* वृत्त; *Past Indecl.* वर्तित्वा or वृत्त्वा, -वृत्य; *Fut. Pass.* वर्तितव्य, वर्तनीय, वृत्य.

599. Root वद्. *Inf.* वदितुम् 'to speak.' Par. *Pres.* वदामि. *Impf.* अवदम्, अवदस्, &c. *Pot.* वदेयम्. *Impv.* वदानि. *Perf.* (375. *c*) उवाद, उवदिथ, उवाद; ऊदिव, ऊदथुस्, ऊदतुस्; ऊदिम, ऊद, ऊदुस्. *1st Fut.* वदितास्मि, वदितासि, &c. *2nd Fut.* वदिष्यामि, वदिष्यसि, &c. *Aor.* (428) अवादिषम्, अवादीस्, अवादीत्; अवादिष्व, अवादिष्टम्, अवादिष्टाम्; अवादिष्म, अवादिष्ट, अवादिषुस्. *Prec.* उद्यासम्, उद्यास्, &c. *Cond.* अवदिष्यम्, अवदिष्यस्, &c. Pass., *Pres.* उद्ये (471); *Aor. 3rd sing.* अवादि. Caus., *Pres.* वादयामि; *Aor.* अवीवदम्. Des. विवदिषामि, -षे. Freq. वावद्ये, वावद्मि or वावदीमि. Part., *Pres.* वदत्; *Pass.* उद्यमान; *Past Pass.* उदित (543); *Past Indecl.* उदित्वा, -उद्य; *Fut. Pass.* वदितव्य, वदनीय, वाद्य or उद्य.

a. Root सद् (special stem सीद, 270). *Inf.* सत्तुम् 'to sink.' Par. *Pres.* सीदामि. *Impf.* असीदम्. *Pot.* सीदेयम्. *Impv.* सीदानि. *Perf.* ससाद, सेदिथ (375. *a*) or ससत्थ, ससाद; सेदिव, सेदथुस्, सेदतुस्; सेदिम, सेद, सेदुस्. *1st Fut.* सत्तास्मि. *2nd Fut.* सत्स्यामि. *Aor.* असदम् (436, 437), असदस्, असदत्; असदाव, असदतम्, असदताम्; असदाम, असदत, असदन्. *Prec.* सद्यासम्. *Cond.* असत्स्यम्. Pass., *Pres.* सद्ये; *Aor. 3rd sing.* असादि. Caus., *Pres.* सादयामि; *Aor.* असीषदम्. Des. सिषत्सामि. Freq. सासद्ये, सासद्मि or सासदीमि. Part., *Pres.* सीदत्; *Past Pass.* सन्न (540); *Past Indecl.* सत्त्वा, -सद्य; *Fut. Pass.* सत्तव्य, सदनीय, साद्य.

b. Root वृध् (special stem वर्ध). *Inf.* वर्धितुम् 'to increase.' Átm. (and Par. in *Fut.*, *Cond.*, and *Aor.*) *Pres.* वर्धे. *Impf.* अवर्धे, अवर्धथास्, &c. *Pot.* वर्धेय. *Impv.* वर्धै, वर्धस्व, &c. *Perf.* ववृधे, ववृधिषे, ववृधे; ववृधिवहे, ववृधाथे, ववृधाते; ववृधिमहे, ववृधिध्वे, ववृधिरे. *1st Fut.* वर्धिताहे. Par. वर्धितास्मि. *2nd Fut.* वर्धिष्ये. Par. वर्त्स्यामि. *Aor.* अवर्धिषि, अवर्धिष्ठास्, अवर्धिष्ट; अवर्धिष्वहि, अवर्धिषाथाम्, अवर्धिषाताम्; अवर्धिष्महि, अवर्धिढ्वम्, अवर्धिषत. Par. अवृधम्, अवृधस्, अवृधत्; अवृधाव, अवृधतम्, अवृधताम्; अवृधाम, अवृधत, अवृधन्. *Prec.* वर्धिषीय. *Cond.* अवर्धिष्ये. Par. अवर्त्स्यम्, अवर्त्स्यस्, &c. Pass., *Pres.* वृध्ये; *Impf.* अवृध्ये; *Aor. 3rd sing.* अवर्धि. Caus., *Pres.* वर्धयामि; *Aor.* अवीवृधम् and अववर्धम्. Des. विवर्धिषे, विवृत्सामि. Freq. वरीवृध्ये, वरीवर्ध्मि or वरीवृधीमि. Part., *Pres.* वर्धमान; *Pass.* वृध्यमान; *Past Pass.* वृद्ध; *Past Indecl.* वर्धित्वा, वृद्ध्वा, -वृध्य; *Fut. Pass.* वर्धनीय, वर्धितव्य, वृध्य.

600. Root एध्. *Inf.* एधितुम् 'to increase,' 'to flourish.' Átm. *Pres.* एधे, एधसे, &c. *Impf.* ऐधे (251), ऐधथास्, &c. *Pot.* एधेय. *Impv.* एधै, एधस्व, &c. *Perf.* (385) एधाञ्चक्रे, एधाञ्चकृषे, एधाञ्चक्रे; एधाञ्चकृवहे, एधाञ्चक्राथे, एधाञ्चक्राते; एधाञ्चकृमहे, एधाञ्चकृढ्वे, एधाञ्चक्रिरे. *1st Fut.* एधिताहे. *2nd Fut.* एधिष्ये. *Aor.* ऐधिषि (427. *b*, 251), ऐधिष्ठास्, ऐधिष्ट; ऐधिष्वहि, ऐधिषाथाम्, ऐधिषाताम्; ऐधिष्महि, ऐधिढ्वम्, ऐधिषत. *Prec.* एधिषीय. *Cond.* ऐधिष्ये (251). Pass. एध्ये; *Aor. 3rd sing.* ऐधि. Caus., *Pres.* एधयामि; *Aor.* ऐदिधम् (494). Des. एदिधिषे (500. *b*). Part., *Pres.* एधमान; *Past Pass.* एधित; *Past Indecl.* एधित्वा, -एध्य; *Fut. Pass.* एधितव्य, एधनीय, एध्य.

a. Root तप्. *Inf.* तप्तुम् 'to burn.' Par. and Átm. *Pres.* तपामि. Átm. तपे. *Impf.* अतपम्. Átm. अतपे. *Pot.* तपेयम्. Átm. तपेय. *Impv.* तपानि, तप, &c. Átm. तपै. *Perf.* तताप or ततप, ततप्थ or तेपिथ, तताप; तेपिव, तेपथुस्, तेपतुस्; तेपिम, तेप, तेपुस्. Átm. तेपे, तेपिषे, तेपे; तेपिवहे, तेपाथे, तेपाते; तेपिमहे, तेपिध्वे, तेपिरे. *1st Fut.* तप्तास्मि, &c. Átm. तप्ताहे, &c. *2nd Fut.* तप्स्यामि (Ep. also तपिष्यामि). Átm. तप्स्ये. *Aor.* अताप्सम्, अताप्सीस्, अताप्सीत्; अताप्स्व, अताप्तम्, अताप्ताम्; अताप्स्म, अताप्त, अताप्सुस्. Átm. अतप्सि, अतप्थास्, अतप्त; अतप्स्वहि, अतप्साथाम्, अतप्साताम्; अतप्स्महि, अतब्ध्वम्, अतप्सत. *Prec.* तप्यासम्. Átm. तप्सीय. *Cond.* अतप्स्यम्. Átm. अतप्स्ये. Pass., *Pres.* तप्ये; *Impf.* अतप्ये; *Aor. 3rd sing.* अतापि. Caus., *Pres.* तापयामि, तापये; *Aor.* अतीतपम्, अतीतपे. Des. तितप्सामि, तितप्से. Freq. तातप्ये, तातप्मि or तातपीमि. Part., *Pres.* तपत्; Átm. तपमान; *Pass.* तप्यमान; *Past Pass.* तप्त; *Past Indecl.* तप्त्वा, -तप्य; *Fut. Pass.* तप्तव्य, तपनीय, तप्य.

601. Root लभ् (270. *e*). *Inf.* लब्धुम् 'to take.' Átm. *Pres.* लभे, लभसे, लभते; लभावहे, लभेथे, लभेते; लभामहे, लभध्वे, लभन्ते. *Impf.* अलभे, अलभथास्, अलभत; अलभावहि, अलभेथाम्, अलभेताम्; अलभामहि, अलभध्वम्, अलभन्त. *Pot.* लभेय, लभेथास्, लभेत; लभेवहि, लभेयाथाम्, लभेयाताम्; लभेमहि,

लभेध्वम्, लभेरन्. *Impv.* लभै, लभस्व, लभताम्; लभावहै, लभेथाम्, लभेताम्; लभामहै, लभध्वम्, लभन्ताम्. *Perf.* लेभे (375. *a*), लेभिषे, लेभे; लेभिवहे, लेभाथे, लेभाते; लेभिमहे, लेभिध्वे, लेभिरे. *1st Fut.* लब्धाहे (409), लब्धासे, लब्धा, &c. *2nd Fut.* लप्स्ये (299), लप्स्यसे, &c. *Aor.* अलप्सि (420, 299), अलब्धास् (298), अलब्ध; अलप्स्वहि, अलप्साथाम्, अलप्साताम्; अलप्स्महि, अलब्ध्वम्, अलप्सत. *Prec.* लप्सीय, लप्सीष्ठास्, लप्सीष्ट, &c. *Cond.* अलप्स्ये, &c. Pass., *Pres.* लभ्ये; *Aor.* अलम्भि, अलब्धास्, अलाभि (475) or अलम्भि, &c. Caus., *Pres.* लम्भयामि, &c.; *Aor.* अललम्भम्. Des. लिप्से (503). Freq. लालभ्ये, लालभ्भीमि. Part., *Pres.* लभमान; *Past Pass.* लब्ध; *Past Indecl.* लब्ध्वा, -लभ्य; *Fut. Pass.* लब्धव्य, लभनीय, लभ्य.

a. Like लभ् is conjugated रभ् (with prep. आ), आरब्धुम् 'to begin.'

602. Root गम् (special stem गच्छ, 270). *Inf.* गन्तुम् 'to go.' Par. *Pres.* गच्छामि, गच्छसि, गच्छति; गच्छावस्, गच्छथस्, गच्छतस्; गच्छामस्, गच्छथ, गच्छन्ति. *Impf.* अगच्छम्, अगच्छस्, &c. *Pot.* गच्छेयम्, गच्छेस्, &c. *Impv.* गच्छानि, गच्छ, &c. *Perf.* (376) जगाम, जगमिथ or जगन्थ, जगाम; जग्मिव, जग्मथुस्, जग्मतुस्; जग्मिम, जग्म, जग्मुस्. *1st Fut.* गन्तास्मि. *2nd Fut.* गमिष्यामि, गमिष्यसि, गमिष्यति, &c. *Aor.* (436) अगमम्, अगमस्, अगमत्; अगमाव, अगमतम्, अगमताम्; अगमाम, अगमत, अगमन्. *Prec.* गम्यासम्. *Cond.* अगमिष्यम्. Pass., *Pres.* गम्ये; *Aor. 3rd sing.* अगामि. Caus., *Pres.* गमयामि; *Aor.* अजीगमम्. Des. जिगमिषामि. Freq. जङ्गम्ये, जङ्गम्मि or जङ्गमीमि; see 709. Part., *Pres.* गच्छत्; *Past Pass.* गत; *Past Indecl.* गत्वा, -गम्य, -गत्य (563. *a*, 560); *Fut. Pass.* गन्तव्य, गमनीय, गम्य.

a. Root नम्. *Inf.* नन्तुम् 'to bend.' Par. and Átm. ('to bow one's self'). *Pres.* नमामि. Átm. नमे. *Impf.* अनमम्. Átm. अनमे. *Pot.* नमेयम्. Átm. नमेय. *Impv.* नमानि. Átm. नमै. *Perf.* (375. *a*) ननाम or ननम, ननन्थ or नेमिथ, ननाम; नेमिव, नेमथुस्, नेमतुस्; नेमिम, नेम, नेमुस्. Átm. नेमे, नेमिषे, नेमे; नेमिवहे, नेमाथे, नेमाते; नेमिमहे, नेमिध्वे, नेमिरे. *1st Fut.* नन्तास्मि. Átm. नन्ताहे. *2nd Fut.* नंस्यामि. Átm. नंस्ये. *Aor.* अनंसिषम्, अनंसीस्, अनंसीत्; अनंसिष्व, अनंसिष्टम्, अनंसिष्टाम्; अनंसिष्म, अनंसिष्ट, अनंसिषुस्. Átm. अनंसि, अनंस्थास्, अनंस्त; अनंस्वहि, अनंसाथाम्, अनंसाताम्; अनंस्महि, अनन्ध्वम्, अनंसत. *Prec.* नम्यासम्. Átm. नंसीय. *Cond.* अनंस्यम्. Átm. अनंस्ये. Pass., *Pres.* नम्ये; *Impf.* अनम्ये; *Aor. 3rd sing.* अनमि or अनामि. Caus. नमयामि or नामयामि; *Aor.* अननमम् or अनीनमम्. Des. निनंसामि. Freq. नन्नम्ये, नन्नमीमि or नन्नन्मि. Part., *Pres.* नमत्; Átm. नममान; *Pass.* नम्यमान; *Past Pass.* नत; *Past Indecl.* नत्वा, -नम्य or -नत्य; *Fut. Pass.* नन्तव्य, नमनीय, नाम्य or नम्य.

b. Root चल्. *Inf.* चलितुम् 'to move.' Par. *Pres.* चलामि. *Impf.* अचलम्. *Pot.* चलेयम्. *Impv.* चलानि, चल, &c. *Perf.* चचाल or चचल,

चेलिथ, चचाल; चेलिव, चेलथुस्, चेलतुस्; चेलिम, चेल, चेलुस्. *1st Fut.* चलितास्मि. *2nd Fut.* चलिष्यामि. *Aor.* अचालिषम्, अचालीस्, अचालीत्; अचालिष्व, अचालिष्टम्, -ष्टाम्; अचालिष्म, -लिष्ट, -लिषुस्. *Prec.* चल्यासम्. *Cond.* अचलिष्यम्. Pass., *Pres.* चल्ये. Caus., *Pres.* चलयामि or चालयामि. Des. चिचलिषामि. Freq. चाचल्ये, चाचल्मि. Part., *Pres.* चलत्; *Past Pass.* चलित; *Past Indecl.* चलित्वा, -चल्य; *Fut. Pass.* चलितव्य, चलनीय, चाल्य.

603. Root जीव्. *Inf.* जीवितुम् 'to live.' Par. *Pres.* जीवामि. *Impf.* अजीवम्. *Pot.* जीवेयम्. *Impv.* जीवानि, जीव, &c. *Perf.* जिजीव, जिजीविथ, जिजीव; जिजीविव, जिजीवथुस्, जिजीवतुस्; जिजीविम, जिजीव, जिजीवुस्. *1st Fut.* जीवितास्मि. *2nd Fut.* जीविष्यामि. *Aor.* अजीविषम्, अजीवीस्, अजीवीत्; अजीविष्व, अजीविष्टम्, अजीविष्टाम्; अजीविष्म, अजीविष्ट, अजीविषुस्. *Prec.* जीव्यासम्. *Cond.* अजीविष्यम्. Pass., *Pres.* जीव्ये; *Aor. 3rd sing.* अजीवि. Caus., *Pres.* जीवयामि; *Aor.* अजिजीवम् or अजीजिवम्. Dcs. जिजीविषामि. Freq. जेजीव्ये. Part:, *Pres.* जीवत्; *Past Pass.* जीवित; *Past Indecl.* जीवित्वा, -जीव्य; *Fut. Pass.* जीवितव्य, जीवनीय, जीव्य.

a. Root धाव्. *Inf.* धावितुम् 'to run,' 'to wash.' Par. and Átm. *Pres.* धावामि. Átm. धावे. *Impf.* अधावम्. Átm. अधावे. *Pot.* धावेयम्. Átm. धावेय. *Impv.* धावानि. Átm. धावै. *Perf.* दधाव, दधाविथ, दधाव; दधाविव, दधावथुस्, -वतुस्; दधाविम, दधाव, दधावुस्. *1st Fut.* धावितास्मि. Átm. धाविताहे. *2nd Fut.* धाविष्यामि. Átm. धाविष्ये. *Aor.* अधाविषम्, अधावीस्, अधावीत्; अधाविष्व, -विष्टम्, -विष्टाम्; अधाविष्म, -विष्ट, -विषुस्. Átm. अधाविषि, -विष्ठास्, -विष्ट; अधाविष्वहि, &c. *Prec.* धाव्यासम्. Átm. धाविषीय. *Cond.* अधाविष्यम्. Átm. अधाविष्ये. Pass., *Pres.* धाव्ये. Caus., *Pres.* धावयामि; *Aor.* अदीधवम्. Des. दिधाविषामि, -षे. Freq. दाधाव्ये. Part., *Pres.* धावत्, धावमान; *Past Pass.* धावित, धौत ('washed'); *Past Indecl.* धावित्वा or धौत्वा; *Fut. Pass.* धावितव्य, धावनीय, धाव्य.

604. Root दृश् (special stem पश्य, 270). *Inf.* द्रष्टुम् 'to see.' Par. *Pres.* पश्यामि, पश्यसि, पश्यति; पश्यावस्, पश्यथस्, पश्यतस्; पश्यामस्, पश्यथ, पश्यन्ति. *Impf.* अपश्यम्, अपश्यस्, अपश्यत्; अपश्याव, &c. *Pot.* पश्येयम्, पश्येस्, पश्येत्; पश्येव, &c. *Impv.* पश्यानि, पश्य, पश्यतु; पश्याव, &c. *Perf.* ददर्श, ददर्शिथ or दद्रष्ठ (370. *f*), ददर्श; ददृशिव, ददृशथुस्, ददृशतुस्; ददृशिम, ददृश, ददृशुस्. *1st Fut.* द्रष्टास्मि. *2nd Fut.* द्रक्ष्यामि. *Aor.* (437. *c*) अदर्शम्, अदर्शस्, अदर्शत्; अदर्शाव, अदर्शतम्, अदर्शताम्; अदर्शाम, अदर्शत, अदर्शन्. Or अद्राक्षम् (420, 390. *f*), अद्राक्षीस्, अद्राक्षीत्; अद्राक्ष्व, अद्राष्टम्, अद्राष्टाम्; अद्राक्ष्म, अद्राष्ट, अद्राक्षुस्. *Prec.* दृश्यासम्. *Cond.* अद्रक्ष्यम्. Pass., *Pres.* दृश्ये; *Aor. 3rd sing.* अदर्शि. Caus., *Pres.* दर्शयामि; *Aor.* अदीदृशम् or अददर्शम्; see 703. Des. दिदृक्षे. Freq. दरीदृश्ये, दर्दर्शिम.

Part., *Pres.* पश्यत्; *Past Pass.* दृष्ट; *Past Indecl.* दृष्ट्वा, -दृश्य; *Fut. Pass.* द्रष्टव्य, दर्शनीय, दृश्य.

605. Root ईक्ष्. *Inf.* ईक्षितुम् 'to see.' Átm. *Pres.* ईक्षे. *Impf.* ऐक्षे (251). *Pot.* ईक्षेय. *Impv.* ईक्षै. *Perf.* ईक्षाञ्चक्रे, &c. (385, and compare एध् at 600). 1*st Fut.* ईक्षिताहे. 2*nd Fut.* ईक्षिष्ये. *Aor.* ऐक्षिषि (251), ऐक्षिष्ठास्, ऐक्षिष्ट; ऐक्षिष्वहि, ऐक्षिषाथाम्, ऐक्षिषाताम्; ऐक्षिष्महि, ऐक्षिध्वम्, ऐक्षिषत. *Prec.* ईक्षिषीय, &c. *Cond.* ऐक्षिष्ये. Pass. ईक्ष्ये; *Aor. 3rd sing.* ऐक्षि. Caus., *Pres.* ईक्षयामि; *Aor.* ऐचिक्षम् (494). Des. ईचिक्षिषे (500. *b*). Part., *Pres.* ईक्षमाण; *Past Pass.* ईक्षित; *Past Indecl.* ईक्षित्वा, -ईक्ष्य; *Fut. Pass.* ईक्षितव्य, ईक्षणीय, ईक्ष्य.

606. Root कृष्* (special stem कर्ष). *Inf.* कर्ष्टुम् or क्रष्टुम् 'to draw,' 'to drag.' Par. and Átm. *Pres.* कर्षामि. Átm. कर्षे. *Impf.* अकर्षम्. Átm. अकर्षे. *Pot.* कर्षेयम्. Átm. कर्षेय. *Impv.* कर्षाणि. Átm. कर्षै. *Perf.* चकर्ष, चकर्षिथ, चकर्ष; चकृषिव, चकृषथुस्, चकृषतुस्; चकृषिम, चकृष, चकृषुस्. Átm. चकृषे, चकृषिषे, चकृषे; चकृषिवहे, चकृषाथे, चकृषाते; चकृषिमहे, चकृषिध्वे, चकृषिरे. 1*st Fut.* कर्ष्टास्मि. Átm. कर्ष्टाहे or क्रष्टाहे. 2*nd Fut.* कर्क्ष्यामि or क्रक्ष्यामि. Átm. कर्क्ष्ये or क्रक्ष्ये. *Aor.* अकार्क्षम्, अकार्क्षीस्, अकार्क्षीत्; अकार्क्ष्व, अकार्ष्टम्, अकार्ष्टाम्; अकार्क्ष्म, अकार्ष्ट, अकार्क्षुस्. Or अक्राक्षम्, अक्राक्षीस्, &c. Or अकृक्षम्, अकृक्षस्, अकृक्षत्; अकृक्षाव, अकृक्षतम्, अकृक्षताम्; अकृक्षाम, अकृक्षत, अकृक्षन्. Átm. अकृक्षि, अकृक्षथास् or अकृष्ठास्, अकृक्षत or अकृष्ट; अकृक्षावहि or अकृक्ष्वहि, अकृक्षाथाम्, अकृक्षाताम्; अकृक्षामहि or अकृक्ष्महि, अकृक्षध्वम् or अकृड्ढ्वम्, अकृक्षन्त or अकृक्षत. *Prec.* कृष्यासम्. Átm. कृक्षीय. *Cond.* अकर्क्ष्यम् or अक्रक्ष्यम्. Átm. अकर्क्ष्ये or अक्रक्ष्ये. Pass., *Pres.* कृष्ये; *Aor. 3rd sing.* अकर्षि. Caus., *Pres.* कर्षयामि; *Aor.* अचकर्षम् or अचीकृषम्. Des. चिकृक्षामि, -क्षे. Freq. चरीकृष्ये, चरीकर्ष्मि or चरीक्रष्मि. Part., *Pres.* कर्षत्; *Past Pass.* कृष्ट; *Past Indecl.* कृष्ट्वा, -कृष्य; *Fut. Pass.* कर्ष्टव्य or क्रष्टव्य, कर्षणीय, कृष्य.

a. Root भाष्. *Inf.* भाषितुम् 'to speak.' Átm. *Pres.* भाषे. *Impf.* अभाषे. *Pot.* भाषेय. *Impv.* भाषै. *Perf.* बभाषे, बभाषिषे, बभाषे; बभाषिवहे, -षाथे, -षाते; बभाषिमहे, -षिध्वे, -षिरे. 1*st Fut.* भाषिताहे. 2*nd Fut.* भाषिष्ये. *Aor.* अभाषिषि, -षिष्ठास्, -षिष्ट; अभाषिष्वहि, -षिषाथाम्, -षिषाताम्; अभाषिष्महि, -षिध्वम्, -षिषत. *Prec.* भाषिषीय. *Cond.* अभाषिष्ये. Pass., *Pres.* भाष्ये; *Aor. 3rd sing.* अभाषि. Caus. भाषयामि; *Aor.* अबभाषम् and अबीभषम्. Des. बिभाषिषे. Freq. बाभाष्ये, बाभाष्मि (*3rd sing.* बाभाष्टि). Part., *Pres.* भाषमाण; *Past Pass.* भाषित; *Past Indecl.* भाषित्वा, -भाष्य; *Fut. Pass.* भाषितव्य, भाषणीय, भाष्य.

---

* This root is also conjugated in cl. 6: Pres. कृषामि, &c.; Pot. कृषेयम्, &c.

b. Root रक्ष्. *Inf.* रक्षितुम् 'to preserve,' 'to defend.' Par. *Pres.* रक्षामि. *Impf.* अरक्षम्. *Pot.* रक्षेयम्. *Impv.* रक्षाणि (58), रक्ष, &c. *Perf.* ररक्ष, ररक्षिथ, ररक्ष; ररक्षिव, ररक्षथुस्, ररक्षतुस्; ररक्षिम, ररक्ष, ररक्षुस्. *1st Fut.* रक्षितास्मि. *2nd Fut.* रक्षिष्यामि. *Aor.* अरक्षिषम्, अरक्षीस्, अरक्षीत्; अरक्षिष्व, अरक्षिष्टम्, अरक्षिष्टाम्; अरक्षिष्म, अरक्षिष्ट, अरक्षिषुस्. *Prec.* रक्ष्यासम्. *Cond.* अरक्षिष्यम्. Pass., *Pres.* रक्ष्ये. Caus., *Pres.* रक्षयामि, &c.; *Aor.* अररक्षम्. Des. रिरक्षिषामि, &c. Freq. रारक्ष्ये, रारक्ष्मि. Part., *Pres.* रक्षत्; *Past Pass.* रक्षित; *Past Indecl.* रक्षित्वा, -रक्ष्य; *Fut. Pass.* रक्षितव्य, रक्षणीय, रक्ष्य.

607. Root वस्. *Inf.* वस्तुम् 'to dwell.' Par. *Pres.* वसामि. *Impf.* अवसम्. *Pot.* वसेयम्. *Impv.* वसानि, वस, &c. *Perf.* उवास (368), उवसिथ or उवस्थ, उवास; ऊषिव, ऊषथुस्, ऊषतुस्; ऊषिम, ऊष, ऊषुस्. *1st Fut.* वस्तास्मि. *2nd Fut.* वत्स्यामि (304. *a*). *Aor.* अवात्सम् (304. *a*, 426. *a*), अवात्सीस्, अवात्सीत्; अवात्स्व, अवात्तम्, अवात्ताम्; अवात्स्म, अवात्त, अवात्सुस्. *Prec.* उष्यासम्. *Cond.* अवत्स्यम् (304. *a*). Pass., *Pres.* उष्ये (471); *Aor. 3rd sing.* अवासि. Caus., *Pres.* वासयामि, -ये; *Aor.* अवीवसम्. Des. विवत्सामि (304. *a*). Freq. वावस्ये, वावस्मि or वावसीमि. Part., *Pres.* वसत्; *Past Pass.* उषित (with वि, उष्ट); *Past Indecl.* उषित्वा, -उष्य (565); *Fut. Pass.* वस्तव्य, वसनीय, वास्य.

608. Root अर्ह्. *Inf.* अर्हितुम् 'to deserve.' Par. *Pres.* अर्हामि. *Impf.* आर्हम्. *Pot.* अर्हेयम्. *Impv.* अर्हाणि (58). *Perf.* (367. *b*) आनर्ह, आनर्हिथ, आनर्ह; आनर्हिव, आनर्हथुस्, आनर्हतुस्; आनर्हिम, आनर्ह, आनर्हुस्. *1st Fut.* अर्हितास्मि. *2nd Fut.* अर्हिष्यामि. *Aor.* आर्हिषम्, आर्हीस्, आर्हीत्; आर्हिष्व, आर्हिष्टम्, आर्हिष्टाम्; आर्हिष्म, आर्हिष्ट, आर्हिषुस्. *Prec.* अर्ह्यासम्. *Cond.* आर्हिष्यम्. Pass., *Pres.* अर्ह्ये; *Aor. 3rd sing.* आर्हि. Caus., *Pres.* अर्हयामि, -ये; *Aor.* आर्जिहम् (494). Des. अर्जिहिषामि, &c. (500. *d*). Part., *Pres.* अर्हत्; *Past Pass.* अर्हित; *Past Indecl.* अर्हित्वा, -अर्ह्य; *Fut. Pass.* अर्हितव्य, अर्हणीय, अर्ह्य.

609. Root गुह् (special stem गूह, 270. *b*). *Inf.* गूहितुम् or गोढुम् 'to hide.' Par. and Átm. *Pres.* गूहामि. Átm. गूहे. *Impf.* अगूहम्. Átm. अगूहे. *Pot.* गूहेयम्. Átm. गूहेय. *Impv.* गूहानि. Átm. गूहै. *Perf.* जुगूह (384. *a*), जुगूहिथ or जुगोढ (305. *a*), जुगूह; जुगुहिव or जुगुह्व (371), जुगुहथुस्, जुगुहतुस्; जुगुहिम or जुगुह्म, जुगुह, जुगुहुस्. Átm. जुगुहे, जुगुहिषे or जुघुक्षे, &c. *1st Fut.* (415. *m*) गूहितास्मि or गोढास्मि (305. *a*). Átm. गूहिताहे or गोढाहे. *2nd Fut.* गूहिष्यामि or घोक्ष्यामि. Átm. गूहिष्ये or घोक्ष्ये. *Aor.* अगूहिषम्, अगूहीस्, अगूहीत्; अगूहिष्व, अगूहिष्टम्, अगूहिष्टाम्; अगूहिष्म, अगूहिष्ट, अगूहिषुस्. Or अघुक्षम् (306. *a*), अघुक्षस्, अघुक्षत्; अघुक्षाव, अघुक्षतम्, अघुक्षताम्; अघुक्षाम, अघुक्षत, अघुक्षन्. Átm. अगूहिषि, अगूहिष्ठास्,

अगूहिष्ट, &c. Or अघुक्षि (439. *b*), अघुक्षथास् or अगूढास्, अघुक्षत or अगूढ; अघुक्षावहि or अगुह्वहि, अघुक्षाथाम्, अघुक्षाताम्; अघुक्षामहि, अघुक्षध्वम् or अघूढ्वम्, अघुक्षन्त. *Prec.* गुह्यासम्. A'tm. गूहिषीय or घुक्षीय (306. *a*). *Cond.* अगूहिष्यम् or अघोक्ष्यम्. A'tm. अगूहिष्ये or अघोक्ष्ये. Pass., *Pres.* गुह्ये; *Aor. 3rd sing.* अगूहि. Caus., *Pres.* गूहयामि; *Aor.* अजूगुहम्. Des. जुघुक्षामि, -क्षे. Freq. जोगुह्ये, जोगोह्मि (*3rd sing.* जोगोढि) or जोगुहीमि. Part., *Pres.* गूहत्; *Past Pass.* गूढ (305. *a*); *Past Indecl.* गूहित्वा or गूढ्वा or गुहित्वा, -गुह्य; *Fut. Pass.* गूहितव्य or गोढव्य, गूहनीय, गुह्य or गोह्य (573. *a*).

610. Root दह्. *Inf.* दग्धुम् 'to burn.' Par. *Pres.* दहामि. *Impf.* अदहम्. *Pot.* दहेयम्, &c. *Impv.* दहानि, दह, &c. *Perf.* ददाह, देहिथ (375. *a*) or ददग्ध (305), ददाह; देहिव, देहथुस्, देहतुस्; देहिम, देह, देहुस्. *1st Fut.* दग्धास्मि. *2nd Fut.* धक्ष्यामि (306. *a*). *Aor.* अधाक्षम् (422), अधाक्षीस्, अधाक्षीत्; अधाक्ष्व, अदाग्धम्, अदाग्धाम्; अधाक्ष्म, अदाग्ध, अधाक्षुस्. *Prec.* दह्यासम्. *Cond.* अधक्ष्यम्. Pass., *Pres.* दह्ये; *Aor. 3rd sing.* अदाहि. Caus., *Pres.* दाहयामि, -ये; *Aor.* अदीदहम्. Des. दिधक्षामि (502. *a*). Freq. दन्दह्ये, दन्दह्मि or दन्दहीमि (*3rd sing.* दन्दग्धि or दन्दहीति). Part., *Pres.* दहत्; *Past Pass.* दग्ध; *Past Indecl.* दग्ध्वा, -दह्य; *Fut. Pass.* दग्धव्य, दहनीय, दाह्य.

611. Root वह्. *Inf.* वोढुम् 'to carry.' Par. and A'tm. *Pres.* वहामि. A'tm. वहे. *Impf.* अवहम्. A'tm. अवहे. *Pot.* वहेयम्. A'tm. वहेय. *Impv.* वहानि, वह, &c. A'tm. वहै. *Perf.* (375. *c*) उवाह (368), उवहिथ or उवोढ, उवाह; ऊहिव, ऊहथुस्, ऊहतुस्; ऊहिम, ऊह, ऊहुस्. A'tm. ऊहे, ऊहिषे, ऊहे; ऊहिवहे, ऊहाथे, ऊहाते; ऊहिमहे, ऊहिध्वे or ऊहिढ्वे, ऊहिरे. *1st Fut.* वोढास्मि. A'tm. वोढाहे. *2nd Fut.* वक्ष्यामि. A'tm. वक्ष्ये. *Aor.* (425) अवाक्षम्, अवाक्षीस्, अवाक्षीत्; अवाक्ष्व, अवोढम्, अवोढाम्; अवाक्ष्म, अवोढ, अवाक्षुस्. A'tm. अवक्षि, अवोढास्, अवोढ; अवक्ष्वहि, अवक्षाथाम्, अवक्षाताम्; अवक्ष्महि, अवोढ्वम्, अवक्षत. *Prec.* उह्यासम्. A'tm. वक्षीय. *Cond.* अवक्ष्यम्. A'tm. अवक्ष्ये. Pass., *Pres.* (471) उह्ये; *Impf.* औह्ये (251. *a*); *Aor. 3rd sing.* अवाहि. Caus., *Pres.* वाहयामि, -ये; *Aor.* अवीवहम्. Des. विवक्षामि, -क्षे. Freq. वावह्ये, वावह्मि (*3rd sing.* वावोढि; cf. 425). Part., *Pres.* वहत्; A'tm. वहमान; *Pass.* उह्यमान; *Past Pass.* ऊढ; *Past Indecl.* ऊढ्वा, -उह्य (565); *Fut. Pass.* वोढव्य, वहनीय, वाह्य.

a. सह्, *Inf.* सोढुम् or सहितुम् 'to bear,' is A'tm. only, and, like *vah*, makes सोढाहे &c. in *1st Fut.*: but in this tense optionally, and in the other General tenses necessarily inserts *i*; thus, *1st Fut.* सहिताहे; *2nd Fut.* सहिष्ये; *Aor.* असहिषि; *Prec.* सहिषीय; *Cond.* असहिष्ये. The *Perf.* is सेहे (375. *a*), सेहिषे, &c. Part., *Fut. Pass.* सोढव्य or सहितव्य, सहनीय, सह्य (573). The other tenses are like the A'tm. of *vah*; thus, *Pres.* सहे, &c.

EXAMPLES OF PRIMITIVE VERBS OF THE FOURTH CLASS, EXPLAINED AT 272.

612. Root मुह् *muh.* Infin. मोहितुम् *mohitum,* 'to be troubled.'

PARASMAI-PADA. *Present Tense,* 'I am troubled.'

मुह्यामि *muhyámi*	मुह्यावस् *muhyávas*	मुह्यामस् *muhyámas*
मुह्यसि *muhyasi*	मुह्यथस् *muhyathas*	मुह्यथ *muhyatha*
मुह्यति *muhyati*	मुह्यतस् *muhyatus*	मुह्यन्ति *muhyanti*

Imperfect, 'I was troubled.'

अमुह्यम् *amuhyam*	अमुह्याव *amuhyáva*	अमुह्याम *amuhyáma*
अमुह्यस् *amuhyas*	अमुह्यतम् *amuhyatam*	अमुह्यत *amuhyata*
अमुह्यत् *amuhyat*	अमुह्यताम् *amuhyatám*	अमुह्यन् *amuhyan*

Potential, 'I may be troubled.'

मुह्येयम् *muhyeyam*	मुह्येव *muhyeva*	मुह्येम *muhyema*
मुह्येस् *muhyes*	मुह्येतम् *muhyetam*	मुह्येत *muhyeta*
मुह्येत् *muhyet*	मुह्येताम् *muhyetám*	मुह्येयुस् *muhyeyus*

Imperative, 'Let me be troubled.'

मुह्यानि *muhyáni*	मुह्याव *muhyáva*	मुह्याम *muhyáma*
मुह्य *muhya*	मुह्यतम् *muhyatam*	मुह्यत *muhyata*
मुह्यतु *muhyatu*	मुह्यताम् *muhyatám*	मुह्यन्तु *muhyantu*

Perfect, 'I have been troubled.'

मुमोह *mumoha*	मुमुहिव *mumuhiva*	मुमुहिम *mumuhima*
मुमोहिथ *mumohitha* *	मुमुहथुस् *mumuhathus*	मुमुह *mumuha*
मुमोह *mumoha*	मुमुहतुस् *mumuhatus*	मुमुहुस् *mumuhus*

First Future †, 'I shall or will be troubled.'

मोहितास्मि *mohitásmi*	मोहितास्वस् *mohitásvas*	मोहितास्मस् *mohitásmas*
मोहितासि *mohitási*	मोहितास्थस् *mohitásthas*	मोहितास्थ *mohitástha*
मोहिता *mohitá*	मोहितारौ *mohitárau*	मोहितारस् *mohitáras*

Second Future †, 'I shall or will be troubled.'

मोहिष्यामि *mohishyámi*	मोहिष्यावस् *mohishyávas*	मोहिष्यामस् *mohishyámas*
मोहिष्यसि *mohishyasi*	मोहिष्यथस् *mohishyathas*	मोहिष्यथ *mohishyatha*
मोहिष्यति *mohishyati*	मोहिष्यतस् *mohishyatas*	मोहिष्यन्ति *mohishyanti*

* Or मुमोढ (305. *a*) or मुमोग्ध (305).

† The 1st and 2nd Futures may optionally reject the inserted *i*; see 415. *m*.

Aorist (435), 'I became troubled.'

अमुहम् *amuham*	अमुहाव *amuháva*	अमुहाम *amuháma*
अमुहस् *amuhas*	अमुहतम् *amuhatam*	अमुहत *amuhata*
अमुहत् *amuhat*	अमुहताम् *amuhatám*	अमुहन् *amuhan*

Precative or *Benedictive*, 'May I be troubled.'

मुह्यासम् *muhyásam*	मुह्यास्व *muhyásva*	मुह्यास्म *muhyásma*
मुह्यास् *muhyás*	मुह्यास्तम् *muhyástam*	मुह्यास्त *muhyásta*
मुह्यात् *muhyát*	मुह्यास्ताम् *muhyástám*	मुह्यासुस् *muhyásus*

Conditional, 'I should be troubled.'

अमोहिष्यम् *amohishyam*	अमोहिष्याव *amohishyáva*	अमोहिष्याम *amohishyáma*
अमोहिष्यस् *amohishyas*	अमोहिष्यतम् *amohishyatam*	अमोहिष्यत *amohishyata*
अमोहिष्यत् *amohishyat*	अमोहिष्यताम् *amohishyatám*	अमोहिष्यन् *amohishyan*

Pass., *Pres.* मुह्ये; *Aor. 3rd sing.* अमोहि. Caus., *Pres.* मोहयामि; *Aor.* अमूमुहम्. Des. मुमोहिषामि or मुमुहिषामि or मुमुक्षामि. Freq. मोमुह्ये, मोमोह्मि (*3rd sing.* मोमोढि or मोमोग्धि, 305). Part., *Pres.* मुह्यत्; *Past Pass.* मूढ (305. *a*) or मुग्ध; *Past Indecl.* मोहित्वा or मुहित्वा or मुग्ध्वा or मूढ्वा, -मुह्य; *Fut. Pass.* मोहितव्य or मोग्धव्य, मोहनीय, मोह्य.

OTHER EXAMPLES OF CL. 4 IN THE ORDER OF THEIR FINAL LETTERS.

613. Root सो (special stem स्य, 276. *a*). *Inf.* सातुम् 'to finish' (with prepositions *vi* and *ava*, 'to determine,' 'to strive'). Par. *Pres.* स्यामि. *Impf.* अस्यम्. *Pot.* स्येयम्. *Impv.* स्यानि. *Perf.* (373. *d*) ससौ, ससिथ or ससाथ, ससौ; ससिव, ससथुस्, ससतुस्; ससिम, सस, ससुस्. *1st Fut.* सातास्मि. *2nd Fut.* सास्यामि. *Aor.* (438. *c*) असाम्, असास्, असात्; असाव, असातम्, असाताम्; असाम, असात, असुस्. Or असासिषम् (433), असासीस्, असासीत्; असासिष्व, असासिष्टम्, असासिष्टाम्; असासिष्म, असासिष्ट, असासिषुस्. *Prec.* सेयासम्. *Cond.* असास्यम्. Pass., *Pres.* सीये; *Aor. 3rd sing.* असायि. Caus., *Pres.* साययामि; *Aor.* असीषयम्. Des. सिषासामि. Freq. सेषीये, सासेमि, सासामि. Part., *Pres.* स्यत्; *Past Pass.* सित; *Past Indecl.* सित्वा, -साय; *Fut. Pass.* सातव्य, सानीय, सेय.

614. Root बुध् (special stem बुध्य). *Inf.* बोद्धुम् 'to perceive*.' Átm. *Pres.* बुध्ये. *Impf.* अबुध्ये. *Pot.* बुध्येय. *Impv.* बुध्यै. *Perf.* बुबुधे; see the tables at 583. *1st Fut.* बोद्धाहे. *2nd Fut.* भोत्स्ये (299. *a*). *Aor.* (420, 299. *a*) अभुत्सि, अबुद्धास्, अबुद्ध or अबोधि (424. *a*); अभुत्स्वहि, अभुत्साथाम्, अभुत्साताम्; अभुत्स्महि, अभुद्ध्वम् (299. *b*), अभुत्सत. *Prec.* भुत्सीय. *Cond.* अभोत्स्ये. For the other forms, see बुध् at 583.

* बुध् is also conjugated in the 1st class. See the tables at 583.

615. Root व्यध् (special stem विध्य, 277). *Inf.* व्यद्धुम् 'to pierce.' Par. *Pres.* विध्यामि. *Impf.* अविध्यम्. *Pot.* विध्येयम्. *Impv.* विध्यानि. *Perf.* (383) विव्याध, विव्यधिथ or विव्यद्ध, विव्याध; विविधिव, विविधथुस्, विविधतुस्; विविधिम, विविध, विविधुस्. *1st Fut.* व्यद्धास्मि (298). *2nd Fut.* व्यत्स्यामि (299). *Aor.* (420) अव्यात्सम्, अव्यात्सीस्, अव्यात्सीत्; अव्यात्स्व, अव्याद्धम् (419, 298), अव्याद्धाम्; अव्यात्स्म, अव्याद्ध, अव्यात्सुस्. *Prec.* विध्यासम्. *Cond.* अव्यत्स्यम्. Pass., *Pres.* विध्ये; *Aor. 3rd sing.* अव्याधि. Caus., *Pres.* व्याधयामि; *Aor.* अविव्यधम्. Des. विव्यत्सामि. Freq. वेविध्ये, वाव्यध्मि. Part., *Pres.* विध्यत्; *Past Pass.* विद्ध; *Past Indecl.* विद्ध्वा, -विध्य; *Fut. Pass.* व्यद्धव्य, व्यधनीय, वेध्य or व्याध्य.

616. Root सिध् (special stem सिध्य, 273). *Inf.* सेद्धुम् 'to succeed.' Par. *Pres.* सिध्यामि. *Impf.* असिध्यम्. *Pot.* सिध्येयम्. *Impv.* सिध्यानि. *Perf.* सिषेध, सिषेधिथ or सिषेद्ध, सिषेध; सिषिधिव, सिषिधथुस्, सिषिधतुस्; सिषिधिम, सिषिध, सिषिधुस्. *1st Fut.* सेद्धास्मि (298)*. *2nd Fut.* सेत्स्यामि (299)*. *Aor.* असिधम्*, असिधस्, असिधत्; असिधाव, असिधतम्, असिधताम्; असिधाम, असिधत, असिधन्. *Prec.* सिध्यासम्. *Cond.* असेत्स्यम्. Pass., *Pres.* सिध्ये; *Aor. 3rd sing.* असेधि. Caus., *Pres.* सेधयामि or साधयामि; *Aor.* असीषिधम्. Des. सिषित्सामि. Freq. सेषिध्ये, सेषेध्मि. Part., *Pres.* सिध्यत्; *Past Pass.* सिद्ध; *Past Indecl.* सिद्ध्वा or सेधित्वा or सिधित्वा, -सिध्य; *Fut. Pass.* सेद्धव्य, सेधनीय, सेध्य.

617. Root मन्† (special stem मन्य). *Inf.* मन्तुम् 'to think,' 'to imagine.' Ātm. *Pres.* मन्ये. *Impf.* अमन्ये. *Pot.* मन्येय. *Impv.* मन्यै. *Perf.* मेने (375. *a*), मेनिषे, मेने; मेनिवहे, मेनाथे, मेनाते; मेनिमहे, मेनिध्वे, मेनिरे. *1st Fut.* मन्ताहे. *2nd Fut.* मंस्ये. *Aor.* (424. *b*) अमंसि†, अमंस्थास्, अमंस्त; अमंस्वहि, अमंसाथाम्, अमंसाताम्; अमंस्महि, अमन्ध्वम्, अमंसत. *Prec.* मंसीय. *Cond.* अमंस्ये. Pass., *Pres.* मन्ये; *Aor. 3rd sing.* अमानि. Caus., *Pres.* मानयामि; *Aor.* अमीमनम्. Des. मिमंसे or मीमांसे or मिमनिषे. Freq. मन्मन्ये, मन्मन्मि. Part., *Pres.* मन्यमान; *Past Pass.* मत; *Past Indecl.* मत्वा, -मत्य; *Fut. Pass.* मन्तव्य, मननीय, मान्य.

a. जन्, *Inf.* जनितुम् 'to be born,' makes *Pres.* जाये; *Impf.* अजाये, &c.; *Pot.* जायेय; *Impv.* जायै. But these may be regarded as coming from Passive of *jan*, cl. 3. See 667.

618. Root तृप्‡ (special stem तृप्य). *Inf.* तर्प्तुम् or त्रप्तुम् or तर्पितुम्

---

* When सिध् belongs to cl. 1, it optionally inserts इ *i*; सेद्धास्मि or सेधितास्मि, सेत्स्यामि or सेधिष्यामि, असेधिषम् or असैत्सम्.

† The root मन् is rarely conjugated in cl. 8, Ātmane (see 684), when the Aorist is अमनिषि, अमनिष्ठास् or अमथास्, अमनिष्ट or अमत, &c. See 424. *b*.

‡ Also conjugated in cl. 5, Par. तृप्नोति, &c.

'to be satisfied.' Par. *Pres.* तृप्यामि. *Impf.* अतृप्यम्. *Pot.* तृप्येयम्. *Impv.* तृप्याणि. *Perf.* ततर्प, ततर्पिथ or ततर्प्थ or तत्रप्थ, ततर्प; ततृपिव or ततृप्व, ततृपथुस्, ततृपतुस्; ततृपिम or ततृप्म, ततृप, ततृपुस्. *1st Fut.* (390. *f*) तर्प्तास्मि or त्रप्तास्मि or तर्पितास्मि (390. *h*). *2nd Fut.* तर्प्स्यामि or त्रप्स्यामि or तर्पिष्यामि, &c. *Aor.* (420) अतार्प्सम्, अतार्प्सीस्, अतार्प्सीत्; अतार्प्स्व, अतार्प्तम्, अतार्प्ताम्; अतार्प्स्म, अतार्प्त, अतार्प्सुस्. Or अत्राप्सम्, अत्राप्सीस्, अत्राप्सीत्, &c. Or अतर्पिषम्, अतर्पीस्, अतर्पीत्, &c. Or अतृपम्, अतृपस्, अतृपत्; अतृपाव, अतृपतम्, अतृपताम्; अतृपाम, अतृपत, अतृपन्. *Prec.* तृप्यासम्. *Cond.* अतर्प्स्यम् or अत्रप्स्यम् or अतर्पिष्यम्. Pass., *Pres.* तृप्ये; *Aor. 3rd sing.* अतर्पि. Caus., *Pres.* तर्पयामि; *Aor.* अतीतृपम् or अततर्पम्. Des. तितृप्सामि or तित्रप्सामि or तितर्पिषामि. Freq. तरीतृप्ये, तरीतर्प्मि or तरीत्रप्मि. Part., *Pres.* तृप्यत्; *Past Pass.* तृप्त; *Past Indecl.* तृप्त्वा, -तृप्य; *Fut. Pass.* तर्प्तव्य, तर्पणीय, तृप्य.

619. Root शम् (special stem शाम्य, 275). *Inf.* शमितुम् 'to be appeased.' Par. *Pres.* शाम्यामि. *Impf.* अशाम्यम्. *Pot.* शाम्येयम्. *Impv.* शाम्यानि. *Perf.* शशाम (368), शेमिथ (375. *a*), शशाम; शेमिव, शेमथुस्, शेमतुस्; शेमिम, शेम, शेमुस्. *1st Fut.* शमितास्मि. *2nd Fut.* शमिष्यामि. *Aor.* अशमम्, अशमस्, अशमत्; अशमाव, अशमतम्, अशमताम्; अशमाम, अशमत, अशमन्. Or अशमिषम्, अशमीस्, अशमीत्; अशमिष्व, &c. *Prec.* शम्यासम्. *Cond.* अशमिष्यम्. Pass., *Pres.* शम्ये; *Aor. 3rd sing.* अशमि or अशामि. Caus., *Pres.* शमयामि; *Aor.* अशीशमम्. Des. शिशमिषामि. Freq. शंशम्ये, शंशम्मि (*3rd sing.* शंशन्ति). Part., *Pres.* शाम्यत्; *Past Pass.* शान्त; *Past Indecl.* शान्त्वा or शमित्वा, -शम्य; *Fut. Pass.* शमितव्य, शमनीय, शम्य.

620. Root नश् (special stem नश्य). *Inf.* नशितुम् or नंष्टुम् 'to perish.' Par. *Pres.* नश्यामि. *Impf.* अनश्यम्. *Pot.* नश्येयम्. *Impv.* नश्यानि. *Perf.* (375. *a*) ननाश or ननश, नेशिथ or ननंष्ठ (375. *a*), ननाश; नेशिव or नेश्व, नेशथुस्, नेशतुस्; नेशिम or नेश्म, नेश, नेशुस्. *1st Fut.* नशितास्मि or नंष्टास्मि (390. *k*). *2nd Fut.* नशिष्यामि or नंक्ष्यामि. *Aor.* (437) अनशम्, अनशस्, अनशत्; अनशाव, अनशतम्, अनशताम्; अनशाम, अनशत, अनशन्. Or अनेशम्, &c. (437, 441). *Prec.* नश्यासम्. *Cond.* अनशिष्यम् &c. or अनंक्ष्यम्. Pass., *Pres.* नश्ये; *Aor. 3rd sing.* अनाशि. Caus., *Pres.* नाशयामि; *Aor.* अनीनशम्. Des. निनशिषामि, निनंक्षामि. Freq. नानश्ये, नानश्मि (*3rd sing.* नानष्टि or नानंष्टि). Part., *Pres.* नश्यत्; *Past Pass.* नष्ट; *Past Indecl.* नष्ट्वा or नंष्ट्वा, -नश्य; *Fut. Pass.* नशितव्य, नशनीय, नाश्य.

621. Root पुष्* (special stem पुष्य). *Inf.* पोष्टुम् 'to be nourished,' 'to grow fat.' Par. *Pres.* पुष्यामि. *Impf.* अपुष्यम्. *Pot.* पुष्येयम्. *Impv.* पुष्याणि. *Perf.* पुपोष, पुपोषिथ, पुपोष; पुपुषिव, पुपुषथुस्, पुपुषतुस्; पुपुषिम, पुपुष, पुपुषुस्. *1st Fut.* पोष्टास्मि. *2nd Fut.* पोक्ष्यामि. *Aor.* (436)

* This root is also conjugated in the 9th class. See 698.

अपुपम्, अपुपस्, अपुपत्; अपुपाव, अपुपतम्, अपुपताम्; अपुपाम, अपुपत, अपुपन्. *Prec.* पुष्यासम्. *Cond.* अपोक्ष्यम्. Pass., *Pres.* पुष्ये; *Aor. 3rd sing.* अपोषि. Caus., *Pres.* पोषयामि; *Aor.* अपूपुषम्. Des. पुपोषिषामि or पुपुषिषामि or पुपुक्षामि. Freq. पोपुष्ये, पोपोष्मि. Part., *Pres.* पुष्यत्; *Past Pass.* पुष्ट; *Past Indecl.* पुष्ट्वा, -पुष्य; *Fut. Pass.* पोष्टव्य, पोषणीय, पोष्य.

622. Root अस् (special stem अस्य). *Inf.* असितुम् 'to throw.' Par. *Pres.* अस्यामि, &c. *Impf.* आस्यम्. *Pot.* अस्येयम्. *Impv.* अस्यानि. *Perf.* आस, आसिथ, आस; आसिव, आसथुस्, आसतुस्; आसिम, आस, आसुस्. *1st Fut.* असितास्मि. *2nd Fut.* असिष्यामि. *Aor.* (441) आस्थम्, आस्थस्, आस्थत्; आस्थाव, आस्थतम्, आस्थताम्; आस्थाम, आस्थत, आस्थन्. *Prec.* अस्यासम्. *Cond.* आसिष्यम्. Pass., *Pres.* अस्ये; *Aor. 3rd sing.* आसि. Caus., *Pres.* आसयामि; *Aor.* आसिसम्. Des. असिसिषामि. Part., *Pres.* अस्यत्; *Past Pass.* अस्त; *Past Indecl.* असित्वा or अस्त्वा, -अस्य; *Fut. Pass.* असितव्य, असनीय, आस्य.

623. Root द्रुह् (special stem द्रुह्य). *Inf.* द्रोग्धुम् or द्रोहितुम् 'to injure,' 'to bear malice.' Par. *Pres.* द्रुह्यामि. *Impf.* अद्रुह्यम्. *Pot.* द्रुह्येयम्. *Impv.* द्रुह्याणि. *Perf.* दुद्रोह, दुद्रोहिथ or दुद्रोग्ध or दुद्रोढ, दुद्रोह; दुद्रुहिव, दुद्रुहथुस्, दुद्रुहतुस्; दुद्रुहिम, दुद्रुह, दुद्रुहुस्. *1st Fut.* (415. *m*) द्रोग्धास्मि or द्रोढास्मि or द्रोहितास्मि, &c. *2nd Fut.* ध्रोक्ष्यामि (306. *a*) or द्रोहिष्यामि. *Aor.* अद्रुहम्, अद्रुहस्, अद्रुहत्; अद्रुहाव, अद्रुहतम्, अद्रुहताम्; अद्रुहाम, अद्रुहत, अद्रुहन्. *Prec.* द्रुह्यासम्, &c. *Cond.* अध्रोक्ष्यम् (306. *a*) or अद्रोहिष्यम्. Pass., *Pres.* द्रुह्ये; *Aor. 3rd sing.* अद्रोहि. Caus., *Pres.* द्रोहयामि; *Aor.* अदुद्रुहम्. Des. दुद्रोहिषामि or दुद्रुहिषामि or दुध्रुक्षामि (306. *a*). Freq. दोद्रुह्ये, दोद्रोह्मि (*3rd sing.* दोद्रोग्धि or दोद्रोढि, 514. *d*). Part., *Pres.* द्रुह्यत्; *Past Pass.* द्रुग्ध; *Past Indecl.* द्रुग्ध्वा or द्रुहित्वा or द्रोहित्वा, -द्रुह्य; *Fut. Pass.* द्रोग्धव्य, द्रोहणीय, द्रोह्य.

624. Root नह् (special stem नह्य). *Inf.* नद्धुम् 'to tie,' 'to bind,' 'to fasten.' Par. and Átm. *Pres.* नह्यामि. Átm. नह्ये. *Impf.* अनह्यम्. Átm. अनह्ये. *Pot.* नह्येयम्. Átm. नह्येय. *Impv.* नह्यानि. Átm. नह्यै. *Perf.* ननाह or ननह, नेहिथ or ननद्ध, ननाह; नेहिव, नेहथुस्, नेहतुस्; नेहिम, नेह, नेहुस्. Átm. नेहे, नेहिषे, नेहे; नेहिवहे, नेहाथे, नेहाते; नेहिमहे, नेहिध्वे or -ढ्वे, नेहिरे. *1st Fut.* नद्धास्मि. Átm. नद्धाहे. *2nd Fut.* (306. *b*) नत्स्यामि. Átm. नत्स्ये. *Aor.* (426) अनात्सम्, अनात्सीस्, अनात्सीत्; अनात्स्व, अनाद्धम्, अनाद्धाम्; अनात्स्म, अनाद्ध, अनात्सुस्. Átm. अनत्सि, अनद्धास्, अनद्ध; अनत्स्वहि, अनत्साथाम्, अनत्साताम्; अनत्स्महि, अनद्धम्, अनत्सत. *Prec.* नह्यासम्. Átm. नत्सीय. *Cond.* अनत्स्यम्. Átm. अनत्स्ये. Pass., *Pres.* नह्ये; *Aor. 3rd sing.* अनाहि. Caus., *Pres.* नाहयामि; *Aor.* अनीनहम्. Des. निनत्सामि, -त्से. Freq. नानह्ये, नानह्मि (*3rd sing.* नानद्धि). Part., *Pres.* नह्यत्; *Past Pass.* नद्ध; *Past Indecl.* नद्ध्वा, -नह्य; *Fut. Pass.* नद्धव्य, नहनीय, नाह्य.

EXAMPLES OF PRIMITIVE VERBS OF THE SIXTH CLASS, EXPLAINED AT 278.

625. Root सृज् *sṛij.* Infin. स्रष्टुम् *srashṭum*, 'to create,' 'to let go.'

PARASMAI-PADA only.

Present Tense, 'I create.'

सृजामि *sṛijámi*	सृजावस् *sṛijávas*	सृजामस् *sṛijámas*
सृजसि *sṛijasi*	सृजथस् *sṛijathas*	सृजथ *sṛijatha*
सृजति *sṛijati*	सृजतस् *sṛijatas*	सृजन्ति *sṛijanti*

Imperfect, 'I was creating,' or 'I created.'

असृजम् *asṛijam*	असृजाव *asṛijáva*	असृजाम *asṛijáma*
असृजस् *asṛijas*	असृजतम् *asṛijatam*	असृजत *asṛijata*
असृजत् *asṛijat*	असृजताम् *asṛijatám*	असृजन् *asṛijan*

Potential, 'I may create.'

सृजेयम् *sṛijeyam*	सृजेव *sṛijeva*	सृजेम *sṛijema*
सृजेस् *sṛijes*	सृजेतम् *sṛijetam*	सृजेत *sṛijeta*
सृजेत् *sṛijet*	सृजेताम् *sṛijetám*	सृजेयुस् *sṛijeyus*

Imperative, 'Let me create.'

सृजानि *sṛijáni*	सृजाव *sṛijáva*	सृजाम *sṛijáma*
सृज *sṛija*	सृजतम् *sṛijatam*	सृजत *sṛijata*
सृजतु *sṛijatu*	सृजताम् *sṛijatám*	सृजन्तु *sṛijantu*

Perfect, 'I created,' or 'I have created.'

ससर्ज *sasarja*	ससृजिव *sasṛijiva*	ससृजिम *sasṛijima*
ससर्जिथ *sasarjitha* or सस्रष्ठ *	ससृजथुस् *sasṛijathus*	ससृज *sasṛija*
ससर्ज *sasarja*	ससृजतुस् *sasṛijatus*	ससृजुस् *sasṛijus*

First Future, 'I shall or will create.'

स्रष्टास्मि *srashṭásmi* (399. *i*)	स्रष्टास्वस् *srashṭásvas*	स्रष्टास्मस् *srashṭásmas*
स्रष्टासि *srashṭási*	स्रष्टास्थस् *srashṭásthas*	स्रष्टास्थ *srashṭástha*
स्रष्टा *srashṭá*	स्रष्टारौ *srashṭárau*	स्रष्टारस् *srashṭáras*

Second Future, 'I shall or will create.'

स्रक्ष्यामि *srakshyámi*	स्रक्ष्यावस् *srakshyávas*	स्रक्ष्यामस् *srakshyámas*
स्रक्ष्यसि *srakshyasi*	स्रक्ष्यथस् *srakshyathas*	स्रक्ष्यथ *srakshyatha*
स्रक्ष्यति *srakshyati*	स्रक्ष्यतस् *srakshyatas*	स्रक्ष्यन्ति *srakshyanti*

* As to *sasrashṭha*, see 370. *f*.

Aorist, 'I created.'

असाक्षम् *asráksham*	अस्राक्ष्व *asrákshva*	अस्राक्ष्म *asrákshma*
अस्राक्षीस् *asrákshís*	अस्राष्टम् *asráshṭam*	अस्राष्ट *asráshṭa*
अस्राक्षीत् *asrákshít*	अस्राष्टाम् *asráshṭám*	अस्राक्षुस् *asrákshus*

Precative or *Benedictive*, 'May I create.'

सृज्यासम् *sṛijyásam*	सृज्यास्व *sṛijyásva*	सृज्यास्म *sṛijyásma*
सृज्यास् *sṛijyás*	सृज्यास्तम् *sṛijyástam*	सृज्यास्त *sṛijyásta*
सृज्यात् *sṛijyát*	सृज्यास्ताम् *sṛijyástám*	सृज्यासुस् *sṛijyásus*

Conditional, 'I should create.'

अस्रक्ष्यम् *asrakshyam*	अस्रक्ष्याव *asrakshyáva*	अस्रक्ष्याम *asrakshyáma*
अस्रक्ष्यस् *asrakshyas*	अस्रक्ष्यतम् *asrakshyatam*	अस्रक्ष्यत *asrakshyata*
अस्रक्ष्यत् *asrakshyat*	अस्रक्ष्यताम् *asrakshyatám*	अस्रक्ष्यन् *asrakshyan*

Pass., *Pres.* सृज्ये; *Aor. 3rd sing.* असर्जि. Caus., *Pres.* सर्जयामि; *Aor.* अससर्जम् or असीसृजम्. Des. सिसृक्षामि, -क्षे. Freq. सरीसृज्ये. Part., *Pres.* सृजत्; *Past Pass.* सृष्ट; *Past Indecl.* सृष्ट्वा, -सृज्य; *Fut. Pass.* स्रष्टव्य, सर्जनीय, सृज्य.

OTHER EXAMPLES OF CL. 6 IN THE ORDER OF THEIR FINAL LETTERS.

626. Root मृ (special stem म्रिय, 280). *Inf.* मर्तुम् 'to die.' Átm. in Special tenses, also in *Aor.* and *Prec.*; Par. in others. *Pres.* म्रिये. *Impf.* अम्रिये. *Pot.* म्रियेय. *Impv.* म्रियै. *Perf.* ममार, ममर्थ, ममार; मम्रिव, मम्रथुस्, मम्रतुस्; मम्रिम, मम्र, मम्रुस्. Átm. मम्रे, मम्रिषे, मम्रे; मम्रिवहे, मम्राथे, मम्राते; मम्रिमहे, मम्रिध्वे or -ढ्वे, मम्रिरे. *1st Fut.* मर्तास्मि. *2nd Fut.* मरिष्यामि. *Aor.* अमृषि, अमृथास्, अमृत; अमृष्वहि, अमृषाथाम्, अमृषाताम्; अमृष्महि, अमृड्ढ्वम्, अमृषत. *Prec.* मृषीय. *Cond.* अमरिष्यम्. Pass., *Pres.* म्रिये; *Aor. 3rd sing.* अमारि. Caus., *Pres.* मारयामि; *Aor.* अमीमरम्. Des. मुमूर्षामि (502). Freq. मेम्रीये, मरि- or मरी- or मर्मर्मि. Part., *Pres.* म्रियमाण; *Past Pass.* मृत; *Past Indecl.* मृत्वा, -मृत्य; *Fut. Pass.* मर्तव्य, मरणीय, मार्य.

627. Root कॄ (special stem किर, 280). *Inf.* करितुम् or करीतुम् 'to scatter.' Par. *Pres.* किरामि. *Impf.* अकिरम्. *Pot.* किरेयम्. *Impv.* किराणि. *Perf.* (374. *k*) चकार, चकरिथ, चकार; चकरिव, चकरथुस्, चकरतुस्; चकरिम, चकर, चकरुस्. *1st Fut.* (393) करितास्मि or करीतास्मि. *2nd Fut.* (393) करिष्यामि or करीष्यामि, &c. *Aor.* अकारिषम्, अकारीस्, अकारीत्; अकारिष्व, अकारिष्टम्, अकारिष्टाम्; अकारिष्म, अकारिष्ट, अकारिषुस्. *Prec.* कीर्यासम्. *Cond.* अकरिष्यम् or अकरीष्यम्. Pass., *Pres.* कीर्ये; *Aor. 3rd sing.* अकारि. Caus., *Pres.* कारयामि; *Aor.* अचीकरम्. Des. चिकरिषामि*. Freq. चेकीर्ये,

* With regard to 393, 501, कॄ and गॄ are not allowed the option of *ísha*.

चाकर्मि. Part., *Pres.* किरत्; *Past Pass.* कीर्ण (530. *a*); *Past Indecl.* कीर्त्वा, -कीर्य; *Fut. Pass.* करितव्य or करीतव्य, करणीय, कार्य.

628. Root मुच् (special stem मुच, 281). *Inf.* मोक्तुम् 'to loose,' 'to let go.' Par. and Átm. *Pres.* मुञ्चामि. Átm. मुञ्चे. *Impf.* अमुञ्चम्. Átm. अमुञ्चे. *Pot.* मुञ्चेयम्. Átm. मुञ्चेय. *Impv.* मुञ्चानि. Átm. मुञ्चै. *Perf.* मुमोच, मुमोचिथ, मुमोच; मुमुचिव, मुमुचथुस्, मुमुचतुस्; मुमुचिम, मुमुच, मुमुचुस्. Átm. मुमुचे, मुमुचिषे, मुमुचे; मुमुचिवहे, मुमुचाथे, मुमुचाते; मुमुचिमहे, मुमुचिध्वे, मुमुचिरे. *1st Fut.* मोक्तास्मि. Átm. मोक्ताहे. *2nd Fut.* मोक्ष्यामि. Átm. मोक्ष्ये. *Aor.* (436) अमुचम्, अमुचस्, अमुचत्; अमुचाव, अमुचतम्, अमुचताम्; अमुचाम, अमुचत, अमुचन्. Átm. अमुक्षि, अमुक्थास्, अमुक्त; अमुक्ष्वहि, अमुक्षाथाम्, अमुक्षाताम्; अमुक्ष्महि, अमुग्ध्वम्, अमुक्षत. *Prec.* मुच्यासम्. Átm. मुक्षीय (452). *Cond.* अमोक्ष्यम्. Átm. अमोक्ष्ये. Pass., *Pres.* मुच्ये; *Aor. 3rd sing.* अमोचि. Caus., *Pres.* मोचयामि; *Aor.* अमूमुचम्. Des. मुमुक्षामि, -क्षे, मोक्षे (503). Freq. मोमुच्ये, मोमोच्मि (*3rd sing.* मोमोक्ति). Part., *Pres.* मुञ्चत्; *Past Pass.* मुक्त; *Past Indecl.* मुक्त्वा, -मुच्य; *Fut. Pass.* मोक्तव्य, मोचनीय, मोच्य.

629. Root व्यच् (special stem विच, 282). *Inf.* व्यचितुम् 'to deceive.' Par. *Pres.* विचामि. *Impf.* अविचम्. *Pot.* विचेयम्. *Impv.* विचानि. *Perf.* (383) विव्याच, विव्यचिथ, विव्याच; विविचिव, विविचथुस्, विविचतुस्; विविचिम, विविच, विविचुस्. *1st Fut.* व्यचितास्मि. *2nd Fut.* व्यचिष्यामि. *Aor.* (428) अव्यचिषम्, अव्यचीस्, &c., or अव्याचिषम्, &c. *Prec.* विच्यासम्. *Cond.* अव्यचिष्यम्. Pass., *Pres.* विच्ये; *Aor. 3rd sing.* अव्याचि. Caus., *Pres.* व्याचयामि; *Aor.* अविव्यचम्. Des. विव्यचिषामि. Freq. वेविच्ये, वाव्यच्मि or वाव्यचीमि. Part., *Pres.* विचत्; *Past Pass.* विचित; *Past Indecl.* विचित्वा, -विच्य; *Fut. Pass.* व्यचितव्य, विचनीय, व्याच्य.

630. Root व्रश्च् (special stem वृश्च, 282). *Inf.* व्रश्चितुम् 'to cut.' Par. *Pres.* वृश्चामि. *Impf.* अवृश्चम्. *Pot.* वृश्चेयम्. *Impv.* वृश्चानि. *Perf.* वव्रश्च, वव्रश्चिथ or वव्रष्ठ, वव्रश्च; वव्रश्चिव or वव्रश्व (371), वव्रश्चथुस्, वव्रश्चतुस्; वव्रश्चिम or वव्रश्म, वव्रश्च, वव्रश्चुस्. *1st Fut.* (415) व्रश्चितास्मि or व्रष्टास्मि. *2nd Fut.* व्रश्चिष्यामि or व्रक्ष्यामि. *Aor.* अव्रश्चिषम्, अव्रश्चीस्, अव्रश्चीत्; अव्रश्चिष्व, &c., see 427. Or अव्राक्षम् (423), अव्राक्षीस्, अव्राक्षीत्; अव्राक्ष्व, अव्राष्टम् (297), अव्राष्टाम्; अव्राक्ष्म, अव्राष्ट, अव्राक्षुस्. *Prec.* वृश्च्यासम्. *Cond.* अव्रश्चिष्यम् or अव्रक्ष्यम्. Pass., *Pres.* वृश्च्ये (472); *Aor. 3rd sing.* अव्रश्चि (475. *b*). Caus., *Pres.* व्रश्चयामि; *Aor.* अविव्रश्चम्. Des. विव्रश्चिषामि or विव्रक्षामि. Freq. वरीवृश्च्ये, वरीवृश्चीमि. Part., *Pres.* वृश्चत्; *Past Pass.* वृक्ण (544, 58); *Past Indecl.* व्रश्चित्वा, -वृश्च्य (565); *Fut. Pass.* व्रश्चितव्य or व्रष्टव्य, व्रश्चनीय, व्रश्च्य.

a. Root सिच् (special stem सिञ्च, 281). *Inf.* सेक्तुम् 'to sprinkle.' Par. and Átm. *Pres.* सिञ्चामि. Átm. सिञ्चे. *Impf.* असिञ्चम्. Átm. असिञ्चे.

Pot. सिञ्चेयम्. Átm. सिञ्चेय. *Impv.* सिञ्चानि. Átm. सिञ्चै. *Perf.* सिषेच, सिषेचिथ, सिषेच; सिषिचिव, सिषिचथुस्, -चतुस्; सिषिचिम, सिषिच, सिषिचुस्. Átm. सिषिचे, सिषिचिषे, सिषिचे; सिषिचिवहे, &c. *1st Fut.* सेक्तास्मि, सेक्तासि, &c. Átm. सेक्ताहे. *2nd Fut.* सेक्ष्यामि. Átm. सेक्ष्ये. *Aor.* असिचम्, -चस्, -चत्; असिचाव, -चतम्, -चताम्; असिचाम, -चत, -चन्. Átm. असिचे, -चथास्, -चत; असिचावहि, -चेथाम्, -चेताम्; असिचामहि, -चध्वम्, -चन्त, or असिक्षि, असिक्थास्, असिक्त; असिक्ष्वहि, -क्षाथाम्, -क्षाताम्; असिक्ष्महि, असिग्ध्वम्, असिक्षत. *Prec.* सिच्यासम्. Átm. सिक्षीय. *Cond.* असेक्ष्यम्. Átm. असेक्ष्ये. Pass., *Pres.* सिच्ये. Caus., *Pres.* सेचयामि; *Aor.* असीषिचम्. Des. सिसिक्षामि, -क्षे. Freq. सेसिच्ये, सेसेच्मि. Part., *Pres.* सिञ्चत्, सिञ्चमान; *Past Pass.* सिक्त; *Past Indecl.* सिक्त्वा, -सिच्य; *Fut. Pass.* सेक्तव्य, सेचनीय, सेच्य.

631. Root प्रछ् (special stem पृच्छ, 282). *Inf.* प्रष्टुम् 'to ask.' Par. *Pres.* पृच्छामि (51). *Impf.* अपृच्छम्. *Pot.* पृच्छेयम्. *Impv.* पृच्छानि. *Perf.* (381) पप्रच्छ, पप्रच्छिथ or पप्रष्ठ, पप्रच्छ; पप्रच्छिव, पप्रच्छथुस्, पप्रच्छतुस्; पप्रच्छिम, पप्रच्छ, पप्रच्छुस्. *1st Fut.* प्रष्टास्मि. *2nd Fut.* प्रक्ष्यामि. *Aor.* अप्राक्षम्, अप्राक्षीस्, अप्राक्षीत्; अप्राक्ष्व, अप्राष्टम्, अप्राष्टाम्; अप्राक्ष्म, अप्राष्ट, अप्राक्षुस्. *Prec.* पृच्छ्यासम्. *Cond.* अप्रक्ष्यम्. Pass., *Pres.* पृच्छ्ये (472); *Aor. 3rd sing.* अप्राच्छि. Caus., *Pres.* प्रच्छयामि; *Aor.* अपप्रच्छम्. Des. पिपृच्छिषामि. Freq. परीपृच्छ्ये, पाप्रश्मि. Part., *Pres.* पृच्छत्; *Past Pass.* पृष्ट; *Past Indecl.* पृष्ट्वा, -पृच्छ्य (565); *Fut. Pass.* प्रष्टव्य, प्रच्छनीय, प्रच्छ्य.

632. Root भ्रज्ज् or भ्रस्ज् (special stem भृज्ज). *Inf.* भ्रष्टुम् or भर्ष्टुम् 'to fry.' Par. and Átm. *Pres.* भृज्जामि. Átm. भृज्जे. *Impf.* अभृज्जम्. Átm. अभृज्जे. *Pot.* भृज्जेयम्. Átm. भृज्जेय. *Impv.* भृज्जानि. Átm. भृज्जै. *Perf.* (381) बभ्रज्ज, बभ्रज्जिथ or बभ्रष्ठ, बभ्रज्ज; बभ्रज्जिव, बभ्रज्जथुस्, बभ्रज्जतुस्; बभ्रज्जिम, बभ्रज्ज, बभ्रज्जुस्. Or बभर्ज्ज, बभर्ज्जिथ or बभर्ष्ठ, बभर्ज्ज; बभर्ज्जिव, &c. Átm. बभ्रज्जे, बभ्रज्जिषे, &c. Or बभर्ज्जे, बभर्ज्जिषे, &c. *1st Fut.* भ्रष्टास्मि or भर्ष्टास्मि. Átm. भ्रष्टाहे or भर्ष्टाहे. *2nd Fut.* भ्रक्ष्यामि or भर्क्ष्यामि. Átm. भ्रक्ष्ये or भर्क्ष्ये. *Aor.* अभ्राक्षम्, अभ्राक्षीस्, अभ्राक्षीत्; अभ्राक्ष्व, अभ्राष्टम्, अभ्राष्टाम्; अभ्राक्ष्म, अभ्राष्ट, अभ्राक्षुस्. Or अभार्क्षम्. Átm. अभ्रक्षि, अभ्रष्ठास्, अभ्रष्ट; अभ्रक्ष्वहि, अभ्रक्षाथाम्, अभ्रक्षाताम्; अभ्रक्ष्महि, अभ्रड्ढ्वम्, अभ्रक्षत. Or अभर्क्षि, अभर्ष्ठास्, अभर्ष्ट; अभर्क्ष्वहि, अभर्क्षाथाम्, अभर्क्षाताम्; अभर्क्ष्महि, अभर्ड्ढ्वम्, अभर्क्षत. *Prec.* भृज्ज्यासम्. Átm. भ्रक्षीय or भर्क्षीय. *Cond.* अभ्रक्ष्यम् or अभर्क्ष्यम्. Átm. अभ्रक्ष्ये or अभर्क्ष्ये. Pass., *Pres.* भृज्ज्ये (472). Caus., *Pres.* भ्रज्जयामि; *Aor.* अबभ्रज्जम् or अबभर्ज्जम्. Des. बिभ्रक्षामि, -क्षे, or बिभर्क्षामि, -क्षे; or बिभ्रज्जिषामि, -षे, or बिभर्ज्जिषामि, -षे, &c. Freq. बरीभृज्ज्ये, बाभ्रज्जिम (*3rd sing.* बाभ्रष्टि). Part., *Pres.* भृज्जत्; *Past Pass.* भृष्ट; *Past Indecl.* भृष्ट्वा, -भृज्ज्य; *Fut. Pass.* भ्रष्टव्य or भर्ष्टव्य, भर्ज्जनीय or भ्रज्जनीय, भर्ज्ज्य or भ्रज्ज्य.

633. Root मज्ज् or मस्ज् (special stem मज्ज). *Inf.* मंक्तुम् 'to be

immersed,' 'to sink.' Par. *Pres.* मज्जामि. *Impf.* अमज्जम्. *Pot.* मज्जेयम्. *Impv.* मज्जानि. *Perf.* ममज्ज, ममज्जिथ or ममंक्थ, ममज्ज; ममज्जिव, ममज्जथुस्, ममज्जतुस्; ममज्जिम, ममज्ज, ममज्जुस्. *1st Fut.* मंक्तास्मि. *2nd Fut.* मंक्ष्यामि. *Aor.* (424) अमांक्षम्, अमांक्षीस्, अमांक्षीत्; अमांक्ष्व, अमांक्तम्, अमांक्ताम्; अमांक्ष्म, अमांक्त, अमांक्षुस्. *Prec.* मज्ज्यासम्. *Cond.* अमंक्ष्यम्. Pass., *Pres.* मज्ज्ये. Caus., *Pres.* मज्जयामि; *Aor.* अममज्जम्. Des. मिमंक्षामि. Freq. मामज्ज्ये, मामज्ज्मि (*3rd sing.* मामंक्ति). Part., *Pres.* मज्जत्; *Past Pass.* मग्न; *Past Indecl.* मंक्त्वा, मक्त्वा, -मज्ज्य; *Fut. Pass.* मंक्तव्य, मज्जनीय, मज्ज्य.

634. Root तुद्. *Inf.* तोत्तुम् 'to strike,' 'to hurt.' Par. and Átm. *Pres.* तुदामि. Átm. तुदे. *Impf.* अतुदम्. Átm. अतुदे. *Pot.* तुदेयम्. Átm. तुदेय. *Impv.* तुदानि. Átm. तुदै. *Perf.* तुतोद, तुतोदिथ, तुतोद; तुतुदिव, तुतुदथुस्, तुतुदतुस्; तुतुदिम, तुतुद, तुतुदुस्. Átm. तुतुदे, तुतुदिषे, तुतुदे; तुतुदिवहे, तुतुदाथे, तुतुदाते; तुतुदिमहे, तुतुदिध्वे, तुतुदिरे. *1st Fut.* तोत्तास्मि. Átm. तोत्ताहे. *2nd Fut.* तोत्स्यामि. Átm. तोत्स्ये. *Aor.* अतौत्सम्, अतौत्सीस्, अतौत्सीत्; अतौत्स्व, अतौत्तम्, अतौत्ताम्; अतौत्स्म, अतौत्त, अतौत्सुस्. Átm. अतुत्सि, अतुत्थास्, अतुत्त; अतुत्स्वहि, अतुत्सायाम्, अतुत्साताम्; अतुत्स्महि, अतुद्ध्वम्, अतुत्सत. *Prec.* तुद्यासम्. Átm. तुत्सीय (452). *Cond.* अतोत्स्यम्. Átm. अतोत्स्ये. Pass., *Pres.* तुद्ये; *Aor. 3rd sing.* अतोदि. Caus., *Pres.* तोदयामि; *Aor.* अतूतुदम्. Des. तुतुत्सामि, -त्से. Freq. तोतुद्ये, तोतोद्मि (*3rd sing.* तोतोत्ति). Part., *Pres.* तुदत्; *Past Pass.* तुन्न; *Past Indecl.* तुत्त्वा, -तुद्य; *Fut. Pass.* तोत्तव्य, तोदनीय, तोद्य.

635. Root क्षिप्. *Inf.* क्षेप्तुम् 'to throw.' Par. and Átm. *Pres.* क्षिपामि. Átm. क्षिपे. *Impf.* अक्षिपम्. Átm. अक्षिपे. *Pot.* क्षिपेयम्. Átm. क्षिपेय. *Impv.* क्षिपाणि. Átm. क्षिपै. *Perf.* चिक्षेप, चिक्षेपिथ, चिक्षेप; चिक्षिपिव, चिक्षिपथुस्, चिक्षिपतुस्; चिक्षिपिम, चिक्षिप, चिक्षिपुस्. Átm. चिक्षिपे, चिक्षिपिषे, चिक्षिपे; चिक्षिपिवहे, चिक्षिपाथे, चिक्षिपाते; चिक्षिपिमहे, चिक्षिपिध्वे, चिक्षिपिरे. *1st Fut.* क्षेप्तास्मि. Átm. क्षेप्ताहे. *2nd Fut.* क्षेप्स्यामि. Átm. क्षेप्स्ये. *Aor.* अक्षैप्सम्, अक्षैप्सीस्, अक्षैप्सीत्; अक्षैप्स्व, अक्षैप्तम्, अक्षैप्ताम्; अक्षैप्स्म, अक्षैप्त, अक्षैप्सुस्. Átm. अक्षिप्सि, अक्षिप्थास्, अक्षिप्त; अक्षिप्स्वहि, अक्षिप्सायाम्, अक्षिप्साताम्; अक्षिप्स्महि, अक्षिब्ध्वम्, अक्षिप्सत. *Prec.* क्षिप्यासम्, &c. Átm. क्षिप्सीय. *Cond.* अक्षेप्स्यम्. Átm. अक्षेप्स्ये. Pass., *Pres.* क्षिप्ये; *Aor. 3rd sing.* अक्षेपि. Caus., *Pres.* क्षेपयामि; *Aor.* अचिक्षिपम्. Des. चिक्षिप्सामि, -प्से. Freq. चेक्षिप्ये, चेक्षेप्मि (710, 43. *e*). Part., *Pres.* क्षिपत्; *Past Pass.* क्षिप्त; *Past Indecl.* क्षिप्त्वा, -क्षिप्य; *Fut. Pass.* क्षेप्तव्य, क्षेपणीय, क्षेप्य.

a. Root विश्. *Inf.* वेष्टुम् 'to enter.' Par. *Pres.* विशामि, विशसि, &c. *Impf.* अविशम्, अविशस्, &c. *Pot.* विशेयम्, विशेस्, &c. *Impv.* विशानि, विश, &c. *Perf.* विवेश, विवेशिथ, विवेश; विविशिव, विविशथुस्, विविशतुस्; विविशिम, विविश, विविशुस्. *1st Fut.* वेष्टास्मि. *2nd Fut.* वेक्ष्यामि. *Aor.* अविक्षम्, -क्षस्, -क्षत्; अविक्षाव, -क्षतम्, -क्षताम्; अविक्षाम, -क्षत, -क्षन्. *Prec.*

विश्यासम्. *Cond.* अवेक्ष्यम्. Pass., *Pres.* विश्ये; *Aor. 3rd sing.* अवेशि. Caus., *Pres.* वेशयामि; *Aor.* अवीविशम्. Des. विविक्षामि. Freq. वेविश्ये, वेवेश्मि (*3rd sing.* वेवेष्टि). Part., *Pres.* विशत्; *Past Pass.* विष्ट; *Past Indecl.* विष्ट्वा, -विश्य; *Fut. Pass.* वेष्टव्य, वेशनीय, वेश्य.

636. Root स्पृश्. *Inf.* स्प्रष्टुम् or स्पर्ष्टुम् 'to touch.' Par. *Pres.* स्पृशामि. *Impf.* अस्पृशम्. *Pot.* स्पृशेयम्. *Impv.* स्पृशानि. *Perf.* पस्पर्श, पस्पर्शिथ, पस्पर्श; पस्पृशिव, पस्पृशथुस्, पस्पृशतुस्; पस्पृशिम, पस्पृश, पस्पृशुस्. *1st Fut.* स्पर्ष्टास्मि or स्प्रष्टास्मि. *2nd Fut.* स्पर्क्ष्यामि or स्प्रक्ष्यामि. *Aor.* अस्पार्क्षम्, अस्पार्क्षीस्, अस्पार्क्षीत्; अस्पार्क्ष्व, अस्पार्ष्टम्, अस्पार्ष्टाम्; अस्पार्क्ष्म, अस्पार्ष्ट, अस्पार्क्षुस्. Or अस्प्राक्षम्, अस्प्राक्षीस्, &c. Or अस्पृक्षम्, अस्पृक्षस्, अस्पृक्षत्; अस्पृक्षाव, अस्पृक्षतम्, अस्पृक्षताम्; अस्पृक्षाम, अस्पृक्षत, अस्पृक्षन्. *Prec.* स्पृश्यासम्. *Cond.* अस्पर्क्ष्यम् or अस्प्रक्ष्यम्. Pass., *Pres.* स्पृश्ये; *Aor. 3rd sing.* अस्पर्शि. Caus., *Pres.* स्पर्शयामि; *Aor.* अपस्पर्शम् or अपिस्पृशम्. Des. पिस्पृक्षामि. Freq. परीस्पृश्ये, परीस्पर्श्मि or परीस्प्रश्मि. Part., *Pres.* स्पृशत्; *Past Pass.* स्पृष्ट; *Past Indecl.* स्पृष्ट्वा, -स्पृश्य; *Fut. Pass.* स्पर्ष्टव्य or स्प्रष्टव्य, स्पर्शनीय, स्पृश्य.

637. Root इष् (special stem इच्छ, 282). *Inf.* एषितुम् or एष्टुम् 'to wish.' Par. *Pres.* इच्छामि. *Impf.* ऐच्छम्. *Pot.* इच्छेयम्. *Impv.* इच्छानि. *Perf.* (367) इयेष, इयेषिथ, इयेष; ईषिव, ईषथुस्, ईषतुस्; ईषिम, ईष, ईषुस्. *1st Fut.* एषितास्मि or एष्टास्मि. *2nd Fut.* एषिष्यामि. *Aor.* ऐषिषम्, ऐषीस्, ऐषीत्; ऐषिष्व, ऐषिष्टम्, ऐषिष्टाम्; ऐषिष्म, ऐषिष्ट, ऐषिषुस्. *Prec.* इष्यासम्. *Cond.* ऐषिष्यम्. Pass., *Pres.* इष्ये; *Aor. 3rd sing.* ऐषि. Caus., *Pres.* एषयामि; *Aor.* ऐषिषम्. Des. एषिषिषामि. Part., *Pres.* इच्छत्; *Past Pass.* इष्ट; *Past Indecl.* इष्ट्वा or इषित्वा, -इष्य; *Fut. Pass.* एष्टव्य or एषितव्य, एषणीय, एष्य.

EXAMPLES OF PRIMITIVE VERBS OF THE TENTH CLASS, EXPLAINED AT 283.

638. Root चुर् *ćur.* Infin. चोरयितुम् *ćorayitum,* 'to steal.'

PARASMAI-PADA.			ĀTMANE-PADA.		

Present Tense, 'I steal.'

चोरयामि	चोरयावस्	चोरयामस्	चोरये	चोरयावहे	चोरयामहे
चोरयसि	चोरयथस्	चोरयथ	चोरयसे	चोरयेथे	चोरयध्वे
चोरयति	चोरयतस्	चोरयन्ति	चोरयते	चोरयेते	चोरयन्ते

Imperfect, 'I was stealing,' or 'I stole.'

अचोरयम्	अचोरयाव	अचोरयाम	अचोरये	अचोरयावहि	अचोरयामहि
अचोरयस्	अचोरयतम्	अचोरयत	अचोरयथास्	अचोरयेथाम्	अचोरयध्वम्
अचोरयत्	अचोरयताम्	अचोरयन्	अचोरयत	अचोरयेताम्	अचोरयन्त

Potential, 'I may steal.'

चोरयेयम्	चोरयेव	चोरयेम	चोरयेय	चोरयेवहि	चोरयेमहि
चोरयेस्	चोरयेतम्	चोरयेत	चोरयेथास्	चोरयेयाथाम्	चोरयेध्वम्
चोरयेत्	चोरयेताम्	चोरयेयुस्	चोरयेत	चोरयेयाताम्	चोरयेरन्

Imperative, 'Let me steal.'

चोरयाणि	चोरयाव	चोरयाम	चोरयै	चोरयावहै	चोरयामहै
चोरय	चोरयतम्	चोरयत	चोरयस्व	चोरयेथाम्	चोरयध्वम्
चोरयतु	चोरयताम्	चोरयन्तु	चोरयताम्	चोरयेताम्	चोरयन्ताम्

Perfect, 'I stole,' or 'I have stolen.'

चोरयामास	चोरयामासिव	चोरयामासिम	चोरयाञ्चक्रे	-चकृवहे	-चकृमहे
चोरयामासिथ	चोरयामासथुस्	चोरयामास	चोरयाञ्चकृषे	-चक्राथे	-चकृढ्वे
चोरयामास	चोरयामासतुस्	चोरयामासुस्	चोरयाञ्चक्रे	-चक्राते	-चक्रिरे

First Future, 'I shall or will steal.'

चोरयितास्मि	चोरयितास्वस्	चोरयितास्मस्	चोरयिताहे	चोरयितास्वहे	चोरयितास्महे
चोरयितासि	चोरयितास्थस्	चोरयितास्थ	चोरयितासे	चोरयितासाथे	चोरयिताध्वे
चोरयिता	चोरयितारौ	चोरयितारस्	चोरयिता	चोरयितारौ	चोरयितारस्

Second Future, 'I shall or will steal.'

चोरयिष्यामि	चोरयिष्यावस्	चोरयिष्यामस्	चोरयिष्ये	चोरयिष्यावहे	चोरयिष्यामहे
चोरयिष्यसि	चोरयिष्यथस्	चोरयिष्यथ	चोरयिष्यसे	चोरयिष्येथे	चोरयिष्यध्वे
चोरयिष्यति	चोरयिष्यतस्	चोरयिष्यन्ति	चोरयिष्यते	चोरयिष्येते	चोरयिष्यन्ते

Aorist, 'I stole.'

अचूचुरम्	अचूचुराव	अचूचुराम	अचूचुरे	अचूचुरावहि	अचूचुरामहि
अचूचुरस्	अचूचुरतम्	अचूचुरत	अचूचुरथास्	अचूचुरेथाम्	अचूचुरध्वम्
अचूचुरत्	अचूचुरताम्	अचूचुरन्	अचूचुरत	अचूचुरेताम्	अचूचुरन्त

Precative or *Benedictive*, 'May I steal.'

चोर्यासम्	चोर्यास्व	चोर्यास्म	चोरयिषीय	-यिषीवहि	-यिषीमहि
चोर्यास्	चोर्यास्तम्	चोर्यास्त	चोरयिषीष्ठास्	-यिषीयास्थाम्	-यिषीध्वम्
चोर्यात्	चोर्यास्ताम्	चोर्यासुस्	चोरयिषीष्ट	-यिषीयास्ताम्	-यिषीरन्

Conditional, 'I should steal.'

अचोरयिष्यम्	अचोरयिष्याव	अचोरयिष्याम	अचोरयिष्ये	-यिष्यावहि	-यिष्यामहि
अचोरयिष्यस्	अचोरयिष्यतम्	अचोरयिष्यत	अचोरयिष्यथास्	-यिष्येथाम्	-यिष्यध्वम्
अचोरयिष्यत्	अचोरयिष्यताम्	अचोरयिष्यन्	अचोरयिष्यत	-यिष्येताम्	-यिष्यन्त

639. Pass., *Pres.* चोर्ये; *Aor. 3rd sing.* अचोरि. Caus. same as the Primitive verb. Des. चुचोरयिषामि. Part., *Pres.* चोरयत्; *Past Pass.* चुरित or चोरित; *Past Indecl.* चोरयित्वा; *Fut. Pass.* चोरयितव्य, चोरणीय, चोर्य.

OTHER EXAMPLES OF CL. 10 IN THE ORDER OF THEIR FINAL LETTERS.

640. Root पृ or पूर् (stem पूरय). *Inf.* पूरयितुम् 'to fill *.' Par. *Pres.* पूरयामि. *Impf.* अपूरयम्. *Pot.* पूरयेयम्. *Impv.* पूरयाणि. *Perf.* पूरयामास. *1st Fut.* पूरयितास्मि. *2nd Fut.* पूरयिष्यामि. *Aor.* अपूपुरम्. *Prec.* पूर्यासम्. *Cond.* अपूरयिष्यम्. Pass., *Pres.* पूर्ये; *Aor. 3rd sing.* अपूरि or अपूरिष्ट. Caus. like the Primitive. Des. पुपूरयिषामि. Part., *Pres.* पूरयत्; *Past Pass.* पूर्ण or पूरित or पूर्त; *Past Indecl.* पूरयित्वा or पूर्त्वा, -पूर्य; *Fut. Pass.* पूरयितव्य, पूरणीय, पूर्य.

641. Root चिन्त् (stem चिन्तय). *Inf.* चिन्तयितुम् 'to think.' Par. *Pres.* चिन्तयामि. *Impf.* अचिन्तयम्. *Pot.* चिन्तयेयम्. *Impv.* चिन्तयानि. *Perf.* चिन्तयामास. *1st Fut.* चिन्तयितास्मि. *2nd Fut.* चिन्तयिष्यामि. *Aor.* अचिचिन्तम्. *Prec.* चिन्त्यासम्. *Cond.* अचिन्तयिष्यम्. Pass., *Pres.* चिन्त्ये. Caus. like the Primitive. Des. चिचिन्तयिषामि. Part., *Pres.* चिन्तयत्; Átm. चिन्तयान (527); *Past Pass.* चिन्तित; *Past Indecl.* चिन्तयित्वा, -चिन्त्य; *Fut. Pass.* चिन्तयितव्य, चिन्तनीय, चिन्त्य.

642. Root अर्थ् (stem अर्थय). *Inf.* अर्थयितुम् (with prep. प्र, प्रार्थ्, प्रार्थयितुम्) 'to ask,' 'to seek.' Átm. *Pres.* अर्थये. *Impf.* आर्थये. *Pot.* अर्थयेय. *Impv.* अर्थयै. *Perf.* अर्थयाञ्चक्रे. *1st Fut.* अर्थयिताहे. *2nd Fut.* अर्थयिष्ये. *Aor.* आर्तिथे, आर्तिथयास्, &c. *Prec.* अर्थयिषीय. *Cond.* आर्थयिष्ये. Pass., *Pres.* अर्थ्ये. Caus. like the Primitive. Des. अर्तिथयिषामि, -षे. Part., *Pres.* अर्थयान (527); *Past Pass.* अर्थित; *Past Indecl.* अर्थयित्वा, -अर्थ्य; *Fut. Pass.* अर्थयितव्य, अर्थनीय, अर्थ्य.

643. Root कथ् (stem कथय). *Inf.* कथयितुम् 'to say,' 'to tell.' Par. *Pres.* कथयामि. *Impf.* अकथयम्. *Pot.* कथयेयम्. *Impv.* कथयानि. *Perf.* कथयामास. *1st Fut.* कथयितास्मि. *2nd Fut.* कथयिष्यामि. *Aor.* अचकथम् or अचीकथम्. *Prec.* कथ्यासम्. *Cond.* अकथयिष्यम्. Pass. कथ्ये, &c. Caus. like the Primitive. Des. चिकथयिषामि. Part., *Pres.* कथयत्; *Past Pass.* कथित; *Past Indecl.* कथयित्वा, -कथय्य (566. a); *Fut. Pass.* कथयितव्य, कथनीय, कथ्य.

a. Root घुष् (stem घोषय). *Inf.* घोषयितुम् 'to proclaim.' Par. *Pres.* घोषयामि. *Impf.* अघोषयम्. *Pot.* घोषयेयम्. *Impv.* घोषयाणि (58). *Perf.*

---

* This root forms its stem पारय *páraya* from पृ, and पूरय *púraya* from पूर्; but the meaning of पारयामि is rather 'to fulfil,' 'to accomplish,' 'to get through.' The Caus. of पृ *pri*, cl. 3, is also पारयामि 'to carry over,' 'to accomplish.'

गोपयाञ्चकार. 1st *Fut.* गोपयितास्मि. 2nd *Fut.* गोपयिष्यामि. *Aor.* अजूगुपम्. *Prec.* गोप्यासम्. *Cond.* अगोपयिष्यम्. Pass., *Pres.* गोप्ये; *Aor.* 3rd *sing.* अगोपि. Caus. like the Primitive. Des. जुगोपयिषामि. Part., *Pres.* गोपयत्; *Past Pass.* गोपित; *Past Indecl.* गोपयित्वा, -गोप्य; *Fut. Pass.* गोपयितव्य, गोपनीय, गोप्य.

b. Root भक्ष् (stem भक्षय). *Inf.* भक्षयितुम् 'to eat,' 'to devour.' Par. *Pres.* भक्षयामि. *Impf.* अभक्षयम्. *Pot.* भक्षयेयम्. *Impv.* भक्षयाणि. *Perf.* भक्षयामास. 1st *Fut.* भक्षयितास्मि. 2nd *Fut.* भक्षयिष्यामि. *Aor.* अबभक्षम्. *Prec.* भक्ष्यासम्. *Cond.* अभक्षयिष्यम्. Pass., *Pres.* भक्ष्ये. Des. बिभक्षयिषामि. Part., *Pres.* भक्षयत्; *Past Pass.* भक्षित; *Past Indecl.* भक्षयित्वा, -भक्ष्य; *Fut. Pass.* भक्षयितव्य, भक्षणीय, भक्ष्य.

EXAMPLES OF PRIMITIVE VERBS OF THE SECOND CLASS, EXPLAINED AT 307.

644. Root या *yá.* Infin. यातुम् *yátum,* 'to go.'

PARASMAI-PADA only.

Present, 'I go.'

यामि *yámi*	यावस् *yávas*	यामस् *yámas*
यासि *yási*	याथस् *yáthas*	याथ *yátha*
याति *yáti*	यातस् *yátas*	यान्ति *yánti*

Imperfect, 'I was going,' or 'I went.'

अयाम् *ayám*	अयाव *ayáva*	अयाम *ayáma*
अयास् *ayás*	अयातम् *ayátam*	अयात *ayáta*
अयात् *ayát*	अयाताम् *ayátám*	अयान् *ayán* *

Potential, 'I may go.'

यायाम् *yáyám*	यायाव *yáyáva*	यायाम *yáyáma*
यायास् *yáyás*	यायातम् *yáyátam*	यायात *yáyáta*
यायात् *yáyát*	यायाताम् *yáyátám*	यायुस् *yáyus*

Imperative, 'Let me go.'

यानि *yáni*	याव *yáva*	याम *yáma*
याहि *yáhi*	यातम् *yátam*	यात *yáta*
यातु *yátu*	याताम् *yátám*	यान्तु *yántu*

645. Root इ *i* (310). Infin. एतुम् *etum,* 'to go.'

For इ with *adhi, á,* &c., see 311.

Present, 'I go.'

एमि *emi* †	इवस् *ivas*	इमस् *imas*
एषि *eshi*	इथस् *ithas*	इथ *itha*
एति *eti*	इतस् *itas*	यन्ति *yanti* (34)

Imperfect, 'I was going,' or 'I went.'

आयम् *áyam* (37)	ऐव *aiva* (251.*a*)	ऐम *aima*
ऐस् *ais* (33)	ऐतम् *aitam*	ऐत *aita*
ऐत् *ait*	ऐताम् *aitám*	आयन् *áyan* ‡

Potential, 'I may go.'

इयाम् *iyám*	इयाव *iyáva*	इयाम *iyáma*
इयास् *iyás*	इयातम् *iyátam*	इयात *iyáta*
इयात् *iyát*	इयाताम् *iyátám*	इयुस् *iyus*

Imperative, 'Let me go.'

अयानि *ayáni*	अयाव *ayáva*	अयाम *ayáma*
इहि *ihi*	इतम् *itam*	इत *ita*
एतु *etu*	इताम् *itám*	यन्तु *yantu*

* Or अयुस् *ayus* (see 310. Obs.)

† This root is also of the 1st class, making अयामि, अयसि, &c., in Pres. tense.

‡ Foster gives अयन्. See Páṇini (VI. 4. 81), and compare Laghu-kaum. 608.

Perf. ययौ (373), ययाथ or ययिथ, ययौ; ययिव, ययथुस्, ययतुस्; ययिम, यय, ययुस्; *1st Fut.* यातास्मि, यातासि, याता, &c. *2nd Fut.* यास्यामि, यास्यसि, यास्यति; यास्यावस्, &c. *Aor.* अयासिषम् (433), अयासीस्, अयासीत्; अयासिष्व, अयासिष्टम्, अयासिष्टाम्; अयासिष्म, अयासिष्ट, अयासिषुस्. *Prec.* यायासम्, यायास्, यायात्; यायास्व, &c. *Cond.* अयास्यम्, अयास्यस्, अयास्यत्, &c. Pass., *Pres.* याये, &c.; *Aor. 3rd sing.* अयायि. Caus., *Pres.* यापयामि, &c.; *Aor.* अयीयपम्, &c. Des. यियासामि. Freq. यायाये, यायामि or यायेमि (*3rd sing.* यायाति or यायेति). Part., *Pres.* यात् (*Nom. case* यान्); *Past Pass.* यात; *Past Indecl.* यात्वा, -याय; *Fut. Pass.* यातव्य, यानीय, येय.

Perf. इयाय (367. *a*), इययिथ or इयेथ, इयाय; ईयिव, ईयथुस्, ईयतुस्; ईयिम, ईय, ईयुस्. *1st Fut.* एतास्मि, &c. *2nd Fut.* एष्यामि, &c. *Aor.* (438. *e*) अगाम्, अगास्, अगात्; अगाव, अगातम्, अगाताम्; अगाम, अगात, अगुस्. *Prec.* ईयासम्, &c. (see 447. *a*). *Cond.* ऐष्यम्. Pass., *Pres.* ईये; *1st Fut.* एताहे or आयिताहे (474); *2nd Fut.* एष्ये or आयिष्ये; *Aor. 3rd sing.* अगायि or अगासत or आयिषत. Caus., *Pres.* गमयामि (from गम् at 602) or आययामि or आपयामि; *Aor.* अजीगमम् or आयियम् or आपिपम् (with *adhi* prefixed, अध्यजीगपम् 493. *e*). Des. जिगमिषामि (from गम् at 602) or ईषिषामि, -षे. Part., *Pres.* यत् (*Nom.* यन्); *Past Pass.* इत; *Past Indecl.* इत्वा, -इत्य; *Fut. Pass.* एतव्य, अयनीय, इत्य or एय.

a. Like या may be conjugated भा 'to shine:' *Pres.* भामि; *Perf.* बभौ; *1st Fut.* भातास्मि; *Aor.* अभासिषम्, &c.

OTHER EXAMPLES OF CL. 2 IN THE ORDER OF THEIR FINAL LETTERS.

646. Root शी (special stem शे, 315). *Inf.* शयितुम् 'to lie down,' 'to sleep.' Átm. *Pres.* शये, शेषे, शेते (κεῖται); शेवहे, शयाथे, शयाते; शेमहे (κείμεθα), शेध्वे, शेरते. *Impf.* अशयि, अशेथास्, अशेत; अशेवहि, अशयाथाम्, अशयाताम्; अशेमहि, अशेध्वम्, अशेरत. *Pot.* शयीय, शयीथास्, शयीत; शयीवहि, शयीयाथाम्, शयीयाताम्; शयीमहि, शयीध्वम्, शयीरन्. *Impv.* शयै, शेष्व, शेताम्; शयावहै, शयाथाम्, शयाताम्; शयामहै, शेध्वम्, शेरताम्. *Perf.* शिश्ये, शिश्यिषे, शिश्ये; शिश्यिवहे, शिश्याथे, शिश्याते; शिश्यिमहे, शिश्यिध्वे or -श्यिढ्वे, शिश्यिरे. *1st Fut.* शयिताहे. *2nd Fut.* शयिष्ये. *Aor.* अशयिषि, अशयिष्ठास्, अशयिष्ट; अशयिष्वहि, अशयिषाथाम्, अशयिषाताम्; अशयिष्महि, अशयिध्वम् or -यिढ्वम्, अशयिषत. *Prec.* शयिषीय. *Cond.* अशयिष्ये. Pass., *Pres.* शय्ये; *Aor. 3rd sing.* अशायि. Caus., *Pres.* शाययामि; *Aor.* अशीशयम्. Des. शिशयिषे. Freq. शाशय्ये, शेशेमि or शेशयीमि. Part., *Pres.* शयान (526. *a*); *Past Pass.* शयित; *Past Indecl.* शयित्वा, -शय्य; *Fut. Pass.* शयितव्य, शयनीय, शेय.

647. Root सू or सु (special stems सू and सुव्, see 312). *Inf.* सोतुम् or सवितुम् 'to bring forth.' Átm. *Pres.* सुवे, सूषे, सूते; सूवहे, सुवाथे, सुवाते; सूमहे, सूध्वे, सुवते. *Impf.* असुवि, असूथास्, असूत; असूवहि, असुवाथाम्,

असुवाताम्; असूमहि, असूध्वम्, असुवत. *Pot.* सुवीय. *Impv.* सुवै (Páṇ. VII. 3, 88), सूष्व, सूताम्; सुवावहै, सुवाथाम्, सुवाताम्; सुवामहै, सूध्वम्, सुवताम्. *Perf.* सुषुवे, सुषुविषे, सुषुवे; सुषुविवहे, सुषुवाथे, सुषुवाते; सुषुविमहे, सुषुविध्वे or -विढ्वे, सुषुविरे. *1st Fut.* सोताहे or सविताहे. *2nd Fut.* सोष्ये or सविष्ये. *Aor.* असविषि, असविष्ठास्, असविष्ट; असविष्वहि, असविषाथाम्, असविषाताम्; असविष्महि, असविढ्वम् or -ध्वम्, असविषत. Or असोषि, असोष्ठास्, असोष्ट; असोष्वहि, असोषाथाम्, असोषाताम्; असोष्महि, असोढ्वम्, असोषत. *Prec.* सोषीय or सविषीय. *Cond.* असोष्ये or असविष्ये. Pass., *Pres.* सूये; *Aor. 3rd sing.* असावि. Caus., *Pres.* सावयामि; *Aor.* असूषवम्. Des. सुसूषामि, -षे. Freq. सोषूये, सोषोमि or सोषवीमि. Part., *Pres.* सुवान; *Past Pass.* सुत or सूत or सून; *Past Indecl.* सूत्वा or सुत्वा, -सूय; *Fut. Pass.* सोतव्य or सवितव्य, सवनीय, साव्य or सव्य.

648. Root स्तु (special stems स्तौ or स्तवी, स्तु and स्तुव्, see 313). *Inf.* स्तोतुम् 'to praise.' Par. and Átm. *Pres.* स्तौमि or स्तवीमि, स्तौषि or स्तवीषि, स्तौति or स्तवीति; स्तुवस् or स्तुवीवस्*, स्तुथस् or स्तुवीथस्*, स्तुतस् or स्तुवीतस्*; स्तुमस् or स्तुवीमस्*, स्तुथ or स्तुवीथ*, स्तुवन्ति. Átm. स्तुवे, स्तुषे or स्तुवीषे*, स्तुते or स्तुवीते*; स्तुवहे or स्तुवीवहे*, स्तुवाथे, स्तुवाते; स्तुमहे or स्तुवीमहे*, स्तुध्वे or स्तुवीध्वे*, स्तुवते. *Impf.* अस्तुवम् or अस्तवम्, अस्तौस् or अस्तवीस्, अस्तौत् or अस्तवीत्; अस्तुव or अस्तुवीव*, अस्तुतम् or अस्तुवीतम्, अस्तुताम् or अस्तुवीताम्; अस्तुम or अस्तुवीम*, अस्तुत or अस्तुवीत, अस्तुवन्. Átm. अस्तुवि, अस्तुथास् or अस्तुवीथास्, अस्तुत or अस्तुवीत; अस्तुवहि or अस्तुवीवहि*, अस्तुवाथाम्, अस्तुवाताम्; अस्तुमहि or अस्तुवीमहि*, अस्तुध्वम् or अस्तुवीध्वम्*, अस्तुवत. *Pot.* स्तुयाम् or स्तुवीयाम्*. Átm. स्तुवीय. *Impv.* स्तुवानि or स्तवानि, स्तुहि or स्तुवीहि*, स्तौतु or स्तवीतु; स्तवाव, स्तुतम् or स्तुवीतम्, स्तुताम् or स्तुवीताम्; स्तवाम, स्तुत or स्तुवीत, स्तुवन्तु. Átm. स्तवै, स्तुष्व or स्तुवीष्व*, स्तुताम् or स्तुवीताम्; स्तवावहै, स्तुवाथाम्, स्तुवाताम्; स्तवामहै, स्तुध्वम् or स्तुवीध्वम्*, स्तुवताम्. *Perf.* (369) तुष्टाव, तुष्टोथ, तुष्टाव; तुष्टुव, तुष्टुवथुस्, तुष्टुवतुस्; तुष्टुम, तुष्टुव, तुष्टुवुस्. Átm. तुष्टुवे, तुष्टुषे, तुष्टुवे; तुष्टुवहे, तुष्टुवाथे, तुष्टुवाते; तुष्टुमहे, तुष्टुढ्वे (372), तुष्टुविरे. *1st Fut.* स्तोतास्मि. Átm. स्तोताहे. *2nd Fut.* स्तोष्यामि. Átm. स्तोष्ये. *Aor.* (427. *a*) अस्ताविषम्, अस्तावीस्, अस्तावीत्; अस्ताविष्व, अस्ताविष्टम्, अस्ताविष्टाम्; अस्ताविष्म, अस्ताविष्ट, अस्ताविषुस्. Átm. अस्तोषि, अस्तोष्ठास्, अस्तोष्ट; अस्तोष्वहि, अस्तोषाथाम्, अस्तोषाताम्; अस्तोष्महि, अस्तोढ्वम्, अस्तोषत. *Prec.* स्तूयासम्. Átm. स्तोषीय. *Cond.* अस्तोष्यम्. Átm. अस्तोष्ये. Pass., *Pres.* स्तूये; *Aor. 3rd sing.* अस्तावि. Caus., *Pres.* स्तावयामि; *Aor.* अतुष्टवम्. Des. तुष्टूषामि, -षे. Freq. तोष्टूये, तोष्टोमि. Part., *Pres.* स्तुवत्; *Past Pass.* स्तुत; *Past Indecl.* स्तुत्वा, -स्तुत्य; *Fut. Pass.* स्तोतव्य, स्तवनीय, स्तुत्य or स्ताव्य or स्तव्य.

649. Root ब्रू (special stems ब्रवी, ब्रू, ब्रुव्, see 314). *Inf.* वक्तुम्

* Some authorities reject these forms.

(borrowed from वच् at 650) 'to say,' 'to speak.' Par. and Átm. *Pres.* ब्रवीमि, ब्रवीषि*, ब्रवीति*; ब्रूवस्, ब्रूथस्*, ब्रूतस्*; ब्रूमस्, ब्रूथ, ब्रुवन्ति*. Átm. ब्रुवे, ब्रूषे, ब्रूते; ब्रूवहे, ब्रुवाथे, ब्रुवाते; ब्रूमहे, ब्रूध्वे, ब्रुवते. *Impf.* अब्रवम् or अब्रुवम् (314. *a*), अब्रवीस्, अब्रवीत्; अब्रूव, अब्रूतम्, अब्रूताम्; अब्रूम, अब्रूत, अब्रुवन्. Átm. अब्रुवि, अब्रूथास्, अब्रूत; अब्रूवहि, अब्रुवाथाम्, अब्रुवाताम्; अब्रूमहि, अब्रूध्वम्, अब्रुवत. *Pot.* ब्रूयाम्, ब्रूयास्, &c. Átm. ब्रुवीय, ब्रुवीथास्, &c. *Impv.* ब्रवाणि (58), ब्रूहि, ब्रवीतु; ब्रवाव, ब्रूतम्, ब्रूताम्; ब्रवाम, ब्रूत, ब्रुवन्तु. Átm. ब्रवै, ब्रूष्व, ब्रूताम्; ब्रवावहै, ब्रुवाथाम्, ब्रुवाताम्; ब्रवामहै, ब्रूध्वम्, ब्रुवताम्. The other tenses and forms are borrowed from वच्; as, *Perf.* उवाच, &c.; 1*st Fut.* वक्तास्मि, &c.; see वच् at 650. But the *Pres.* participles are ब्रुवत् and ब्रुवाण.

650. Root वच् (320). *Inf.* वक्तुम् 'to say,' 'to speak.' Par. In the General tenses Átm. also. *Pres.* वच्मि, वक्षि, वक्ति; वच्वस्, वक्थस्, वक्तस्; वच्मस्, वक्थ, ब्रुवन्ति (borrowed from ब्रू at 649). *Impf.* अवचम्, अवक् (294), अवक् (294); अवच्व, अवक्तम्, अवक्ताम्; अवच्म, अवक्त, अवचन्†. *Pot.* वच्याम्, वच्यास्, वच्यात्, &c. *Impv.* वचानि, वग्धि, वक्तु; वचाव, वक्तम्, वक्ताम्; वचाम, वक्त, ब्रुवन्तु (borrowed from ब्रू). *Perf.* (375. *c*) उवाच, उवचिथ or उवक्थ, उवाच; ऊचिव, ऊचथुस्, ऊचतुस्; ऊचिम, ऊच, ऊचुस्. Átm. ऊचे, ऊचिषे, ऊचे; ऊचिवहे, ऊचाथे, ऊचाते; ऊचिमहे, ऊचिध्वे, ऊचिरे. 1*st Fut.* वक्तास्मि. Átm. वक्ताहे. 2*nd Fut.* वक्ष्यामि. Átm. वक्ष्ये. *Aor.* (441) अवोचम्, अवोचस्, अवोचत्; अवोचाव, अवोचतम्, अवोचताम्; अवोचाम, अवोचत, अवोचन्. Átm. अवोचे, अवोचथास्, अवोचत; अवोचावहि, अवोचेथाम्, अवोचेताम्; अवोचामहि, अवोचध्वम्, अवोचन्त. *Prec.* उच्यासम्. Átm. वक्षीय. *Cond.* अवक्ष्यम्. Átm. अवक्ष्ये. Pass., *Pres.* उच्ये (471); *Aor.* 3*rd sing.* अवाचि. Caus., *Pres.* वाचयामि; *Aor.* अवीवचम्. Des. विवक्षामि, -क्षे. Freq. वावच्ये, वावच्मि. Part., *Pres.* ब्रुवत्; Átm. ब्रुवाण (borrowed from ब्रू at 649); *Past Pass.* उक्त; *Past Indecl.* उक्त्वा, -उच्य; *Fut. Pass.* वक्तव्य, वचनीय, वाच्य or वाक्य.

651. Root मृज् (special stems मार्ज् and मृज्, 321). *Inf.* मार्ष्टुम् or मार्जितुम् 'to wipe,' 'to rub,' 'to clean.' Par. *Pres.* मार्ज्मि, मार्क्षि (296), मार्ष्टि (297); मृज्वस्, मृष्ठस्, मृष्टस्; मृज्मस्, मृष्ठ, मार्जन्ति or मृजन्ति. *Impf.* अमार्जम्, अमार्ट् (294), अमार्ट्; अमृज्व, अमृष्टम्, अमृष्टाम्; अमृज्म, अमृष्ट, अमार्जन् or अमृजन्. *Pot.* मृज्याम्, मृज्यास्, &c. *Impv.* मार्जानि, मृड्ढि (303), मार्ष्टु; मार्जाव, मृष्टम्, मृष्टाम्; मार्जाम, मृष्ट, मार्जन्तु or मृजन्तु. *Perf.* ममार्ज, ममार्जिथ or ममार्ष्ठ (370. *e*), ममार्ज; ममृजिव or ममार्जिव, ममृजथुस् or ममार्जथुस्, ममृजतुस् or ममार्जतुस्; ममृजिम or

* For these forms are sometimes substituted 2nd sing. आत्थ, 3rd sing. आह; 2nd du. आहथुस्, 3rd du. आहतुस्; 3rd pl. आहुस्; all from the Perfect of a defective root अह्, with a Present signification.

† According to some, the 3rd pl. of the Imperfect is also wanting.

ममार्जिम, ममृज or ममार्ज, ममृजुस् or ममार्जुस्. *1st Fut.* मार्ष्टास्मि or मार्जितास्मि (415.*a*). *2nd Fut.* मार्क्ष्यामि or मार्जिष्यामि. *Aor.* अमार्क्षम्, अमार्क्षीस्, अमार्क्षीत्; अमार्क्ष्व, अमार्ष्टम्, अमार्ष्टाम्; अमार्क्ष्म, अमार्ष्ट, अमार्क्षुस्. Or अमार्जिषम्, अमार्जीस्, अमार्जीत्; अमार्जिष्व, &c. *Prec.* मृज्यासम्. *Cond.* अमार्क्ष्यम् or अमार्जिष्यम्. Pass., *Pres.* मृज्ये; *Aor. 3rd sing.* अमार्जि. Caus., *Pres.* मार्जयामि; *Aor.* अममार्जम् or अमीमृजम्. Des. मिमार्क्षामि or मिमृक्षामि or मिमार्जिषामि. Freq. मरीमृज्ये, मरी- or मरि- or मर्मार्ज्मि (*3rd sing.* -मार्ष्टि). Part., *Pres.* मार्जत्; *Past Pass.* मृष्ट; *Past Indecl.* मृष्ट्वा or मार्जित्वा, -मृज्य; *Fut. Pass.* मार्ष्टव्य or मार्जितव्य, मार्जनीय, मार्ग्य or मृज्य.

652. Root अद् (317). *Inf.* अत्तुम् 'to eat.' Par. *Pres.* अद्मि, अत्सि, अत्ति; अद्वस्, अत्थस्, अत्तस्; अद्मस्, अत्थ, अदन्ति. *Impf.* आदम्, आदस् (317.*b*), आदत् (317.*b*); आद्व, आत्तम्, आत्ताम्; आद्म, आत्त, आदन्. *Pot.* अद्याम्. *Impv.* अदानि, अद्धि, अत्तु; अदाव, अत्तम्, अत्ताम्; अदाम, अत्त, अदन्तु. *Perf.* आद, आदिथ, आद; आदिव, आदथुस्, आदतुस्; आदिम, आद, आदुस्. *1st Fut.* अत्तास्मि. *2nd Fut.* अत्स्यामि. *Aor.* अघसम् (borrowed from root घस्), अघसस्, अघसत्; अघसाव, अघसतम्, अघसताम्; अघसाम, अघसत, अघसन्. *Prec.* अद्यासम्. *Cond.* आत्स्यम्. Pass., *Pres.* अद्ये; *Aor. 3rd sing.* आदि. Caus., *Pres.* आदयामि; *Aor.* आदिदम्. Des. जिघत्सामि (borrowed from घस्). Part., *Pres.* अदत्; *Past Pass.* जग्ध; *Past Indecl.* जग्ध्वा; *Fut. Pass.* अत्तव्य, अदनीय, आद्य.

653. Root रुद् (special stems रोद्, रोदि, रुदि, रुद्, see 322). *Inf.* रोदितुम् 'to weep.' Par. *Pres.* रोदिमि, रोदिषि, रोदिति; रुदिवस्, रुदिथस्, रुदितस्; रुदिमस्, रुदिथ, रुदन्ति. *Impf.* अरोदम्, अरोदस् or अरोदीस्, अरोदत् or अरोदीत् (Páṇ. VII. 3, 98, 99); अरुदिव, अरुदितम्, अरुदिताम्; अरुदिम, अरुदित, अरुदन्. *Pot.* रुद्याम्. *Impv.* रोदानि, रुदिहि, रोदितु; रोदाव, रुदितम्, रुदिताम्; रोदाम, रुदित, रुदन्तु. *Perf.* रुरोद, रुरोदिथ, रुरोद; रुरुदिव, रुरुदथुस्, रुरुदतुस्; रुरुदिम, रुरुद, रुरुदुस्. *1st Fut.* रोदितास्मि. *2nd Fut.* रोदिष्यामि. *Aor.* अरुदम्, अरुदस्, अरुदत्; अरुदाव, अरुदतम्, अरुदताम्; अरुदाम, अरुदत, अरुदन्. Or अरोदिषम्, अरोदीस्, अरोदीत्; अरोदिष्व, अरोदिष्टम्, अरोदिष्टाम्; अरोदिष्म, अरोदिष्ट, अरोदिषुस्. *Prec.* रुद्यासम्. *Cond.* अरोदिष्यम्. Pass., *Pres.* रुद्ये; *Aor. 3rd sing.* अरोदि. Caus., *Pres.* रोदयामि; *Aor.* अरूरुदम्. Des. रुरुदिषामि. Freq. रोरुद्ये, रोरोद्मि (*3rd sing.* रोरोत्ति) or रोरुदीमि. Part., *Pres.* रुदत्; *Past Pass.* रुदित; *Past Indecl.* रुदित्वा, -रुद्य; *Fut. Pass.* रोदितव्य, रोदनीय, रोद्य.

654. Root हन्* (special stems हन्, ह, घ्न, and ज, see 323). *Inf.* हन्तुम् 'to strike,' 'to kill.' Par. *Pres.* हन्मि, हंसि, हन्ति*; हन्वस्, हथस्, हतस्;

* It must be borne in mind (with reference to 323) that *han* only loses its nasal before *t* and *th*, *if not marked with P.* When the prep. आ *á* is prefixed, this root may take the Átmane, in which case the 3rd sing. Pres. will be आहते.

हन्मस्, हथ, घ्नन्ति. *Impf.* अहनम्, अहन्, अहन् (294); अहन्व, अहतम्, अहताम्; अहन्म, अहत, अघ्नन्. *Pot.* हन्याम्, &c. *Impv.* हनानि, जहि, हन्तु*; हनाव, हतम्, हताम्; हनाम, हत, घ्नन्तु. *Perf.* जघान (376), जघनिथ or जघन्थ, जघान; जघ्निव, जघ्नथुस्, जघ्नतुस्; जघ्निम, जघ्न, जघ्नुस्. *1st Fut.* हन्तास्मि. *2nd Fut.* हनिष्यामि. *Aor.* (432. *b*) अवधिषम्, अवधीस्, अवधीत्; अवधिष्व, अवधिष्टम्, अवधिष्टाम्; अवधिष्म, अवधिष्ट, अवधिषुस्. *Prec.* वध्यासम्. *Cond.* अहनिष्यम्. Pass., *Pres.* हन्ये; *Perf.* जघ्ने (473); *Aor. 3rd sing.* अघानि (or अवधि, borrowed from वध्); *1st Fut.* हन्ताहे or घानिताहे; *2nd Fut.* हनिष्ये or घानिष्ये. Caus., *Pres.* घातयामि; *Aor.* अजीघनम्. Des. जिघांसामि. Freq. जेघ्नीये or जङ्घन्ये, जङ्घन्मि or जंहन्मि or जङ्घनीमि; see 708. Part., *Pres.* घ्नत्; *Past Pass.* हत; *Past Indecl.* हत्वा, -हत्य; *Fut. Pass.* हन्तव्य, हननीय, घात्य.

655. Root स्वप् (special stems स्वप् and स्वपि, 322. *a*). *Inf.* स्वप्तुम् 'to sleep.' Par. *Pres.* स्वपिमि, स्वपिषि, स्वपिति; स्वपिवस्, स्वपिथस्, स्वपितस्; स्वपिमस्, स्वपिथ, स्वपन्ति. *Impf.* अस्वपम्, अस्वपस् or अस्वपीस्, अस्वपत् or अस्वपीत्; अस्वपिव, &c. (see रुद् at 653). *Pot.* स्वप्याम्. *Impv.* स्वपानि, स्वपिहि, स्वपितु; स्वपाव, स्वपितम्, स्वपिताम्; स्वपाम, स्वपित, स्वपन्तु. *Perf.* (382) सुष्वाप, सुष्वपिथ or सुष्वप्थ, सुष्वाप; सुषुपिव, सुषुपथुस्, सुषुपतुस्; सुषुपिम, सुषुप, सुषुपुस्. *1st Fut.* स्वप्तास्मि. *2nd Fut.* स्वप्स्यामि. *Aor.* अस्वाप्सम्, अस्वाप्सीस्, अस्वाप्सीत्; अस्वाप्स्व, अस्वाप्तम्, अस्वाप्ताम्; अस्वाप्स्म, अस्वाप्त, अस्वाप्सुस्. *Prec.* सुप्यासम्. *Cond.* अस्वप्स्यम्. Pass., *Pres.* सुप्ये (471); *Aor. 3rd sing.* अस्वापि. Caus., *Pres.* स्वापयामि; *Aor.* असूषुपम्, &c. Des. सुषुप्सामि. Freq. सोषुप्ये, सास्वप्मि or सास्वपीमि. Part., *Pres.* स्वपत्; *Past Pass.* सुप्त; *Past Indecl.* सुप्त्वा, -सुप्य; *Fut. Pass.* स्वप्तव्य, स्वपनीय, स्वप्य.

656. Root वश् (special stems वश् and उश्, 324). *Inf.* वशितुम् 'to wish.' Par. *Pres.* वश्मि, वक्षि (302), वष्टि (300); उश्वस्, उष्ठस्, उष्टस्; उश्मस्, उष्ठ, उशन्ति. *Impf.* अवशम्, अवट् (294), अवट्; औश्व (251. *a*), औष्टम्, औष्टाम्; औश्म, औष्ट, औशन्. *Pot.* उश्याम्, उश्यास्, &c. *Impv.* वशानि, उड्ढि (303), वष्टु; वशाव, उष्टम्, उष्टाम्; वशाम, उष्ट, उशन्तु. *Perf.* (375. *c*) उवाश, उवशिथ, उवाश; ऊशिव, ऊशथुस्, ऊशतुस्; ऊशिम, ऊश, ऊशुस्. *1st Fut.* वशितास्मि. *2nd Fut.* वशिष्यामि. *Aor.* अवाशिषम्, अवाशीस्, अवाशीत्, &c.; or अवशिषम्, -शीस्, -शीत्, &c.; see 427. *Prec.* उश्यासम्. *Cond.* अवशिष्यम्. Pass., *Pres.* उश्ये (471); *Aor. 3rd sing.* अवाशि or अवशि. Caus., *Pres.* वाशयामि; *Aor.* अवीवशम्. Des. विवशिषामि. Freq. वावश्ये, वावश्मि or वावशीमि. Part., *Pres.* उशत्; *Past Pass.* उशित; *Past Indecl.* वशित्वा, -उश्य; *Fut. Pass.* वशितव्य, वशनीय, वाश्य.

---

* It must be borne in mind (with reference to 323) that *han* only loses its nasal before *t* and *th*, if not marked with P.

657. Root द्विष् (special stems द्विष् and द्वेष्, 309). *Inf.* द्वेष्टुम् 'to hate.' Par. and Átm. *Pres.* द्वेष्मि, द्वेक्षि (302), द्वेष्टि (301); द्विष्वस्, द्विष्ठस्, द्विष्टस्; द्विष्मस्, द्विष्ठ, द्विषन्ति. Átm. द्विषे, द्विक्षे, द्विष्टे; द्विष्वहे, द्विषाथे, द्विषाते; द्विष्महे, द्विड्ढ्वे, द्विषते. *Impf.* अद्वेषम्, अद्वेट् (294), अद्वेट्; अद्विष्व, अद्विष्टम्, अद्विष्टाम्; अद्विष्म, अद्विष्ट, अद्विषन् or अद्विषुस्. Átm. अद्विषि, अद्विष्ठास्, अद्विष्ट; अद्विष्वहि, अद्विषाथाम्, अद्विषाताम्; अद्विष्महि, अद्विड्ढ्वम्, अद्विषत. *Pot.* द्विष्याम्. Átm. द्विषीय. *Impv.* द्वेषाणि, द्विड्ढि, द्वेष्टु; द्वेषाव, द्विष्टम्, द्विष्टाम्; द्वेषाम, द्विष्ट, द्विषन्तु. Átm. द्वेषै, द्विक्ष्व, द्विष्टाम्; द्वेषावहै, द्विषाथाम्, द्विषाताम्; द्वेषामहै, द्विड्ढ्वम्, द्विषताम्. *Perf.* दिद्वेष, दिद्वेषिथ, दिद्वेष; दिद्विषिव, दिद्विषथुस्, दिद्विषतुस्; दिद्विषिम, दिद्विष, दिद्विषुस्. Átm. दिद्विषे, दिद्विषिषे, दिद्विषे; दिद्विषिवहे, दिद्विषाथे, दिद्विषाते; दिद्विषिमहे, दिद्विषिढ्वे, दिद्विषिरे. *1st Fut.* द्वेष्टास्मि. Átm. द्वेष्टाहे. *2nd Fut.* द्वेक्ष्यामि. Átm. द्वेक्ष्ये. *Aor.* (439) अद्विक्षम्, -क्षस्, -क्षत्; -क्षाव, -क्षतम्, -क्षताम्; -क्षाम, -क्षत, -क्षन्. Átm. (439. *a*) अद्विक्षि, -क्षथास्, -क्षत; -क्षावहि, -क्षाथाम्, -क्षाताम्; -क्षामहि, -क्षध्वम्, -क्षन्त. *Prec.* द्विष्यासम्. Átm. द्विक्षीय. *Cond.* अद्वेक्ष्यम्. Átm. अद्वेक्ष्ये. Pass., *Pres.* द्विष्ये, &c.; *Aor. 3rd sing.* अद्वेषि. Caus., *Pres.* द्वेषयामि; *Aor.* अदिद्विषम्. Des. दिद्विक्षामि, -क्षे. Freq. देद्विष्ये, देद्वेष्मि or देद्विषीमि. Part., *Pres.* द्विषत्; *Past Pass.* द्विष्ट; *Past Indecl.* द्विष्ट्वा, -द्विष्य; *Fut. Pass.* द्वेष्टव्य, द्वेषणीय, द्वेष्य.

a. Root वस्. *Inf.* वसितुम् 'to wear,' 'to put on (as clothes, &c.)' Átm. *Pres.* वसे, वस्से (62. *b*), वस्ते; वस्वहे, वसाथे, वसाते; वस्महे, वद्ध्वे or वध्वे (304), वसते. *Impf.* अवसि, अवस्थास्, अवस्त; अवस्वहि, अवसाथाम्, अवसाताम्; अवस्महि, अवद्ध्वम् or अवध्वम्, अवसत. *Pot.* वसीय. *Impv.* वसै. *Perf.* ववसे, ववसिषे, &c. *1st Fut.* वसिताहे. *2nd Fut.* वसिष्ये. *Aor.* अवसिषि, अवसिष्ठास्, अवसिष्ट; अवसिष्वहि, अवसिषाथाम्, अवसिषाताम्, &c. *Prec.* वसिषीय. *Cond.* अवसिष्ये. Pass., *Pres.* वस्ये. Caus., *Pres.* वासयामि or -ये. Des. विवसिषे. Freq. वावस्ये, वावस्मि. Part., *Pres.* वसान; *Past Pass.* वसित; *Past Indecl.* वसित्वा, -वस्य; *Fut. Pass.* वसितव्य, वसनीय, वास्य.

658. Root शास् (special stems शास् and शिष्, see 328). *Inf.* शासितुम् 'to rule,' 'to punish.' Par. (With आ 'to bless,' Átm.) *Pres.* शास्मि, शास्सि, शास्ति; शिष्वस्, शिष्ठस्, शिष्टस्; शिष्मस्, शिष्ठ, शासति (310. Obs.) Átm. शासे, शास्से (62. *b*), शास्ते; शास्वहे, शासाथे, शासाते; शास्महे, शाद्ध्वे or शाध्वे (304), शासते. *Impf.* अशासम्, अशात् or अशास् (294, 304. *a*), अशात् (304); अशिष्व, अशिष्टम्, अशिष्टाम्; अशिष्म, अशिष्ट, अशासुस्. Átm. अशासि, &c. *Pot.* शिष्याम्. Átm. शासीय. *Impv.* शासानि, शाधि (304), शास्तु; शासाव, शिष्टम्, शिष्टाम्; शासाम, शिष्ट, शासतु. Átm. शासै. *Perf.* शशास, शशासिथ, शशास; शशासिव, शशासथुस्, शशासतुस्; शशासिम, शशास, शशासुस्. Átm. शशासे, शशासिषे, &c. *1st Fut.* शासितास्मि. Átm. शासिताहे. *2nd Fut.* शासिष्यामि. Átm. शासिष्ये. *Aor.* (441) अशिषम्, अशिषस्, अशिषत्; अशिषाव,

अशिषतम्, अशिषताम्; अशिषाम, अशिषत, अशिषन्. Átm. अशासिषि, अशासिष्ठास्, अशासिष्ट; अशासिष्वहि, अशासिषाथाम्, अशासिषाताम्; अशासिष्महि, अशासिढ्वम्, अशासिषत. *Prec.* शिष्यासम्. Átm. शासिषीय. *Cond.* अशासिष्यम्. Átm. अशासिष्ये. Pass., *Pres.* शिष्ये (472. *c*); *Aor. 3rd sing.* अशासि. Caus., *Pres.* शासयामि; *Aor.* अशशासम्. Des. शिशासिषामि. Freq. शेशिष्ये, शाशास्मि or शाशासीमि. Part., *Pres.* शासत् (141. *a*); *Past Pass.* शिष्ट; *Past Indecl.* शासित्वा or शिष्ट्वा, -शिष्य; *Fut. Pass.* शासितव्य, शासनीय, शिष्य.

659. Root दिह् (special stems दिह् and देह्). *Inf.* देग्धुम् 'to anoint,' 'to smear.' Par. and Átm. *Pres.* देह्मि, धेक्षि (306. *a*), देग्धि (305); दिह्वस्, दिग्धस्, दिग्धस्; दिह्मस्, दिग्ध, दिहन्ति. Átm. दिहे, धिक्षे, दिग्धे; दिह्वहे, दिहाथे, दिहाते; दिह्महे, धिग्ध्वे (306. *d*), दिहते. *Impf.* अदेहम्, अधेक् (294), अधेक्; अदिह्व, अदिग्धम्, अदिग्धाम्; अदिह्म, अदिग्ध, अदिहन्. Átm. अदिहि, अदिग्धास्, अदिग्ध; अदिह्वहि, अदिहाथाम्, अदिहाताम्; अदिह्महि, अधिग्ध्वम्, अदिहत. *Pot.* दिह्याम्, दिह्यास्, &c. Átm. दिहीय. *Impv.* देहानि, दिग्धि, देग्धु; देहाव, दिग्धम्, दिग्धाम्; देहाम, दिग्ध, दिहन्तु. Átm. देहै, धिक्ष्व, दिग्धाम्; देहावहै, दिहाथाम्, दिहाताम्; देहामहै, धिग्ध्वम्, दिहताम्. *Perf.* दिदेह, दिदेहिथ, दिदेह; दिदिहिव, दिदिहथुस्, दिदिहतुस्; दिदिहिम, दिदिह, दिदिहुस्. Átm. दिदिहे, दिदिहिषे, दिदिहे; दिदिहिवहे, दिदिहाथे, दिदिहाते; दिदिहिमहे, दिदिहिढ्वे or -ध्वे, दिदिहिरे. *1st Fut.* देग्धास्मि. Átm. देग्धाहे. *2nd Fut.* धेक्ष्यामि. Átm. धेक्ष्ये. *Aor.* (439) अधिक्षम्, अधिक्षस्, अधिक्षत्; अधिक्षाव, अधिक्षतम्, अधिक्षताम्; अधिक्षाम, अधिक्षत, अधिक्षन्. Átm. (439. *b*) अधिक्षि, अधिक्षथास् or अदिग्धास्, अधिक्षत or अदिग्ध; अधिक्षावहि or अदिह्वहि, अधिक्षाथाम्, अधिक्षाताम्; अधिक्षामहि, अधिक्षध्वम् or अधिग्ध्वम्, अधिक्षन्त. *Prec.* दिह्यासम्. Átm. धिक्षीय. *Cond.* अधेक्ष्यम्. Átm. अधेक्ष्ये. Pass., *Pres.* दिह्ये; *Aor. 3rd sing.* अदेहि. Caus., *Pres.* देहयामि; *Aor.* अदीदिहम्. Des. दिधिक्षामि, -क्षे. Freq. देदिह्ये, देदेह्मि (*3rd sing.* देदेग्धि). Part., *Pres.* दिहत्; Átm. दिहान; *Past Pass.* दिग्ध; *Past Indecl.* दिग्ध्वा, -दिह्य; *Fut. Pass.* देग्धव्य, देहनीय, देह्य.

660. Root दुह् (special stems दुह् and दोह्). *Inf.* दोग्धुम् 'to milk.' Par. and Átm. *Pres.* दोह्मि, धोक्षि (306. *a*), दोग्धि (305); दुह्वस्, दुग्धस्, दुग्धस्; दुह्मस्, दुग्ध, दुहन्ति. Átm. दुहे, धुक्षे, दुग्धे; दुह्वहे, दुहाथे, दुहाते; दुह्महे, धुग्ध्वे (306. *d*), दुहते. *Impf.* अदोहम्, अधोक् (294), अधोक्; अदुह्व, अदुग्धम्, अदुग्धाम्; अदुह्म, अदुग्ध, अदुहन्. Átm. अदुहि, अदुग्धास्, अदुग्ध; अदुह्वहि, अदुहाथाम्, अदुहाताम्; अदुह्महि, अधुग्ध्वम्, अदुहत. *Pot.* दुह्याम्, दुह्यास्, &c. Átm. दुहीय. *Impv.* दोहानि, दुग्धि (306. *c*), दोग्धु; दोहाव, दुग्धम्, दुग्धाम्; दोहाम, दुग्ध, दुहन्तु. Átm. दोहै, धुक्ष्व, दुग्धाम्; दोहावहै, दुहाथाम्, दुहाताम्; दोहामहै, धुग्ध्वम् (306. *d*), दुहताम्. *Perf.* दुदोह, दुदोहिथ, दुदोह; दुदुहिव, दुदुहथुस्, दुदुहतुस्; दुदुहिम, दुदुह, दुदुहुस्. Átm. दुदुहे, दुदुहिषे, दुदुहे; दुदुहिवहे,

दुदुहाथे, दुदुहाते; दुदुहिमहे, दुदुहिध्वे or -ढ्वे, दुदुहिरे. *1st Fut.* दोग्धास्मि. Ātm. दोग्धाहे. *2nd Fut.* धोक्ष्यामि. Ātm. धोक्ष्ये. *Aor.* (439) अधुक्षम्, अधुक्षस्, अधुक्षत्; अधुक्षाव, अधुक्षतम्, अधुक्षताम्; अधुक्षाम, अधुक्षत, अधुक्षन्. Ātm. (439. *b*) अधुक्षि, अधुक्षथास् or अदुग्धास्, अधुक्षत or अदुग्ध; अधुक्षावहि or अदुह्वहि, अधुक्षाथाम्, अधुक्षाताम्; अधुक्षामहि, अधुक्षध्वम् or अधुग्ध्वम्, अधुक्षन्त. *Prec.* दुह्यासम्. Ātm. धुक्षीय. *Cond.* अधोक्ष्यम्. Ātm. अधोक्ष्ये. Pass., *Pres.* दुह्ये; *Aor. 3rd sing.* अदोहि. Caus., *Pres.* दोहयामि; *Aor.* अदूदुहम्. Des. दुधुक्षामि, -क्षे. Freq. दोदुह्ये, दोदोह्मि (*3rd sing.* दोदोग्धि). Part., *Pres.* दुहत्, दुहान; *Past Pass.* दुग्ध; *Past Indecl.* दुग्ध्वा, -दुह्य; *Fut. Pass.* दोग्धव्य, दोहनीय, दोह्य or दुह्य (573. *a*).

661. Root लिह् (special stems लिह् and लेह्). *Inf.* लेढुम् 'to lick.' Par. and Ātm. *Pres.* (329) लेह्मि, लेक्षि (306), लेढि (305. *a*); लिह्वस्, लीढस् (305. *a*), लीढस्; लिह्मस्, लीढ, लिहन्ति. Ātm. लिहे, लिक्षे, लीढे; लिह्वहे, लिहाथे, लिहाते; लिह्महे, लीढ्वे, लिहते. *Impf.* अलेहम्, अलेट् (294), अलेट्; अलिह्व, अलीढम्, अलीढाम्; अलिह्म, अलीढ, अलिहन्. Ātm. अलिहि, अलीढास्, अलीढ; अलिह्वहि, अलिहाथाम्, अलिहाताम्; अलिह्महि, अलीढ्वम्, अलिहत. *Pot.* लिह्याम्, लिह्यास्, &c. Ātm. लिहीय. *Impv.* लेहानि, लीढि (306. *c*), लेढु; लेहाव, लीढम्, लीढाम्; लेहाम, लीढ, लिहन्तु. Ātm. लेहै, लिक्ष्व, लीढाम्; लेहावहै, लिहाथाम्, लिहाताम्; लेहामहै, लीढ्वम् (306. *c*), लिहताम्. *Perf.* लिलेह, लिलेहिथ, लिलेह; लिलिहिव, लिलिहथुस्, लिलिहतुस्; लिलिहिम, लिलिह, लिलिहुस्. Ātm. लिलिहे, लिलिहिषे, &c. *1st Fut.* लेढास्मि. Ātm. लेढाहे. *2nd Fut.* लेक्ष्यामि. Ātm. लेक्ष्ये. *Aor.* (439) अलिक्षम्, -क्षस्, -क्षत्; -क्षाव, -क्षतम्, -क्षताम्; -क्षाम, -क्षत, -क्षन्. Ātm. (439. *b*) अलिक्षि, अलिक्षथास् or अलीढास्, अलिक्षत or अलीढ; अलिक्षावहि or अलिह्वहि, -क्षाथाम्, -क्षाताम्; अलिक्षामहि, अलिक्षध्वम् or अलीढ्वम्, अलिक्षन्त. *Prec.* लिह्यासम्. Ātm. लिक्षीय, &c. *Cond.* अलेक्ष्यम्. Ātm. अलेक्ष्ये, &c. Pass., *Pres.* लिह्ये; *Aor. 3rd sing.* अलेहि. Caus., *Pres.* लेहयामि; *Aor.* अलीलिहम्. Des. लिलिक्षामि, -क्षे. Freq. लेलिह्ये, लेलेह्मि (*3rd sing.* लेलेढि). Part., *Pres.* लिहत्; Ātm. लिहान; *Past Pass.* लीढ; *Past Indecl.* लीढ्वा, -लिह्य; *Fut. Pass.* लेढव्य, लेहनीय, लेह्य.

EXAMPLES OF PRIMITIVE VERBS OF THE THIRD CLASS, EXPLAINED AT 331.

662. Root हु *hu* (333). Infin. होतुम् *hotum*, 'to sacrifice.'

PARASMAI-PADA. *Present Tense*, 'I sacrifice.'

जुहोमि *juhomi*	जुहुवस् *juhuvas* or जुह्वस्	जुहुमस् *juhumas* or जुह्मस्
जुहोषि *juhoshi*	जुहुथस् *juhuthas*	जुहुथ *juhutha*
जुहोति *juhoti*	जुहुतस् *juhutas*	जुह्वति *juhvati*

Imperfect, 'I was sacrificing.'

अजुहवम् *ajuhavam*	अजुहुव *ajuhuva*	अजुहुम *ajuhuma*
अजुहोस् *ajuhos*	अजुहुतम् *ajuhutam*	अजुहुत *ajuhuta*
अजुहोत् *ajuhot*	अजुहुताम् *ajuhutám*	अजुहवुस् *ajuhavus* (331. Obs.)

Potential, 'I may sacrifice.'

जुहुयाम् *juhuyám*	जुहुयाव *juhuyáva*	जुहुयाम *juhuyáma*
जुहुयास् *juhuyás*	जुहुयातम् *juhuyátam*	जुहुयात *juhuyáta*
जुहुयात् *juhuyát*	जुहुयाताम् *juhuyátám*	जुहुयुस् *juhuyus*

Imperative, 'Let me sacrifice.'

जुहवानि *juhaváni*	जुहवाव *juhaváva*	जुहवाम *juhaváma*
जुहुधि *juhudhi* (293)	जुहुतम् *juhutam*	जुहुत *juhuta*
जुहोतु *juhotu*	जुहुताम् *juhutám*	जुह्वतु *juhvatu*

Perf. (374. *g*) जुहाव, जुहविथ or जुहोथ, जुहाव; जुहुविव, जुहुवथुस्, जुहुवतुस्; जुहुविम, जुहुव, जुहुवुस्. Or जुहवाञ्चकार, &c.; see 385. *e.* *1st Fut.* होतास्मि. *2nd Fut.* होष्यामि. *Aor.* अहौषम्, अहौषीस्, अहौषीत्; अहौष्व, अहौष्टम्, अहौष्टाम्; अहौष्म, अहौष्ट, अहौषुस्. *Prec.* हूयासम्. *Cond.* अहोष्यम्. Pass., *Pres.* हूये; *Aor. 3rd sing.* अहावि. Caus., *Pres.* हावयामि; *Aor.* अजूहवम्. Des. जुहूषामि. Freq. जोहूये, जोहोमि or जोहवीमि. Part., *Pres.* जुह्वत्; *Past Pass.* हुत; *Past Indecl.* हुत्वा, -हुत्य; *Fut. Pass.* होतव्य, हवनीय, हव्य or हाव्य.

OTHER EXAMPLES OF CL. 3 IN THE ORDER OF THEIR FINAL LETTERS.

663. Root दा (special stems ददा, दद्, see 335). *Inf.* दातुम् 'to give.' Par. and Ātm. *Pres.* ददामि, ददासि, ददाति; दद्वस्, दत्थस्, दत्तस्; दद्मस्, दत्थ, ददति. Ātm. ददे, दत्से, दत्ते; दद्वहे, ददाथे, ददाते; दद्महे, दद्ध्वे, ददते. *Impf.* अददाम्, अददास्, अददात्; अदद्व, अदत्तम्, अदत्ताम्; अदद्म, अदत्त, अददुस् (331. Obs.) Ātm. अददि, अदत्थास्, अदत्त; अदद्वहि, अददाथाम्, अददाताम्; अदद्महि, अदद्ध्वम्, अददत. *Pot.* दद्याम्. Ātm. ददीय. *Impv.* ददानि, देहि, ददातु; ददाव, दत्तम्, दत्ताम्; ददाम, दत्त, ददतु. Ātm. ददै, दत्स्व, दत्ताम्; ददावहै, ददाथाम्, ददाताम्; ददामहै, दद्ध्वम्, ददताम्. *Perf.* (373) ददौ, ददिथ or ददाथ, ददौ; ददिव, ददथुस्, ददतुस्; ददिम, दद, ददुस्. Ātm. ददे, ददिषे, ददे; ददिवहे, ददाथे, ददाते; ददिमहे, ददिध्वे, ददिरे. *1st Fut.* दातास्मि. Ātm. दाताहे. *2nd Fut.* दास्यामि. Ātm. दास्ये. *Aor.* (438) अदाम्, अदास्, अदात्; अदाव, अदातम्, अदाताम्; अदाम, अदात, अदुस्. Ātm. (438. *d*) अदिषि, अदिथास्, अदित; अदिष्वहि, अदिषाथाम्, अदिषाताम्; अदिष्महि, अदिढ्वम्, अदिषत. *Prec.* देयासम्. Ātm. दासीय. *Cond.* अदास्यम्. Ātm. अदास्ये. Pass., *Pres.* दीये; *Aor. 3rd sing.* अदायि, see 700. Caus., *Pres.* दापयामि (483); *Aor.*

अदीदपम्. Des. (503) दित्सामि, दित्से. Freq. देदीये, दादामि or दादेमि. Part., *Pres.* ददत् (141. *a*); A'tm. ददान; *Past Pass.* दत्त; *Past Indecl.* दत्त्वा, -दाय; *Fut. Pass.* दातव्य, दानीय, देय.

664. Root धा (special stems दधा, दध्, see 336). *Inf.* धातुम् 'to place.' Par. and A'tm. *Pres.* दधामि, दधासि, दधाति; दध्वस्, धत्थस् (299. *a*), धत्तस् (299. *a*); दध्मस्, धत्थ, दधति. A'tm. दधे, धत्से, धत्ते; दध्वहे, दधाथे, दधाते; दध्महे, धद्ध्वे (299. *b*), दधते. *Impf.* अदधाम्, अदधास्, अदधात्; अदध्व, अधत्तम्, अधत्ताम्; अदध्म, अधत्त, अदधुस्. A'tm. अदधि, अधत्थास्, अधत्त; अदध्वहि, अदधाथाम्, अदधाताम्; अदध्महि, अधद्ध्वम् (299. *b*), अदधत. *Pot.* दध्याम्. A'tm. दधीय. *Impv.* दधानि, धेहि, दधातु; दधाव, धत्तम्, धत्ताम्; दधाम, धत्त, दधतु. A'tm. दधै, धत्स्व, धत्ताम्; दधावहै, दधाथाम्, दधाताम्; दधामहै, धद्ध्वम्, दधताम्. *Perf.* (373) दधौ, दधिथ or दधाथ, दधौ; दधिव, दधथुस्, दधतुस्; दधिम, दध, दधुस्. A'tm. दधे, दधिषे, &c. *1st Fut.* धातास्मि. A'tm. धाताहे, &c. *2nd Fut.* धास्यामि. A'tm. धास्ये. *Aor.* (438) अधाम्, अधास्, अधात्; अधाव, अधातम्, अधाताम्; अधाम, अधात, अधुस्. A'tm. (438. *d*) अधिषि, अधिथास्, अधित; अधिष्वहि, अधिषाथाम्, अधिषाताम्; अधिष्महि, अधिढ्वम्, अधिषत. *Prec.* धेयासम्. A'tm. धासीय. *Cond.* अधास्यम्. A'tm. अधास्ये. Pass., *Pres.* धीये; *1st Fut.* धायिताहे or धाताहे; *Aor. 3rd sing.* अधायि. Caus., *Pres.* धापयामि; *Aor.* अदीधपम्. Des. धित्सामि (503). Freq. देधीये, दाधामि or दाधेमि. Part., *Pres.* दधत् (141. *a*); A'tm. दधान; *Past Pass.* हित; *Past Indecl.* हित्वा, -धाय; *Fut. Pass.* धातव्य, धानीय, धेय.

a. Root मा (special stems मिमी, मिम्, see 338). *Inf.* मातुम् 'to measure.' A'tm. *Pres.* मिमे, मिमीषे, मिमीते; मिमीवहे, मिमाथे, मिमाते; मिमीमहे, मिमीध्वे, मिमते. *Impf.* अमिमि, अमिमीथास्, अमिमीत; अमिमीवहि, अमिमाथाम्, अमिमाताम्; अमिमीमहि, अमिमीध्वम्, अमिमत. *Pot.* मिमीय, मिमीथास्, मिमीत, &c. *Impv.* मिमै, मिमीष्व, मिमीताम्; मिमावहै, मिमाथाम्, मिमाताम्; मिमामहै, मिमीध्वम्, मिमताम्. *Perf.* ममे, ममिषे, ममे; ममिवहे, ममाथे, ममाते; ममिमहे, ममिध्वे, ममिरे. *1st Fut.* माताहे. *2nd Fut.* मास्ये. *Aor.* (434) अमासि, अमास्थास्, अमास्त; अमास्वहि, अमासाथाम्, अमासाताम्; अमास्महि, अमाध्वम्, अमासत. *Prec.* मासीय. *Cond.* अमास्ये. Pass., *Pres.* मीये; *Aor. 3rd sing.* अमायि. Caus., *Pres.* मापयामि; *Aor.* अमीमपम्. Des. मित्सामि, -त्से (503). Freq. मेमीये, मामामि or मामेमि. Part., *Pres.* मिमान; *Past Pass.* मित; *Past Indecl.* मित्वा, -माय; *Fut. Pass.* मातव्य, मानीय, मेय.

665. Root हा (special stems जहा, जही, जह्, see 337). *Inf.* हातुम् 'to quit.' Par. *Pres.* जहामि, जहासि, जहाति; जहीवस् (or जहिवस्, see Pán. VI. 4, 116), जहीथस् (or जहिथस्), जहीतस् (or जहितस्); जहीमस् (or जहिमस्), जहीथ (or जहिथ), जहति. *Impf.* अजहाम्, अजहास्, अजहात्; अजहीव (or अजहिव), अजहीतम् (or अजहितम्), अजहीताम् (or अजहिताम्); अजहीम (or अज-

हिम), अजहीत (or अजहित), अजहुस्. *Pot.* जह्याम्, जह्यास्, &c. *Impv.* जहानि, जहीहि (or जहिहि) or जहाहि, जहातु; जहाव, जहीतम् (or जहितम्), जहीताम् (or जहिताम्); जहाम, जहीत (or जहित), जहतु. *Perf.* जहौ, जहिथ or जहाथ, जहौ; जहिव, जहथुस्, जहतुस्; जहिम, जह, जहुस्. *1st Fut.* हातास्मि. *2nd Fut.* हास्यामि. *Aor.* (433) अहासिषम्, अहासीस्, अहासीत्; अहासिष्व, अहासिष्टम्, अहासिष्टाम्; अहासिष्म, अहासिष्ट, अहासिषुस्. *Prec.* हेयासम्. *Cond.* अहास्यम्. Pass., *Pres.* हीये; *Aor. 3rd sing.* अहायि. Caus., *Pres.* हापयामि; *Aor.* अजीहपम्. Des. जिहासामि. Freq. जेहीये, जाहामि or जाहेमि. Part., *Pres.* जहत् (141. *a*); *Past Pass.* हीन; *Past Indecl.* हित्वा, -हाय; *Fut. Pass.* हातव्य, हानीय, हेय.

666. Root भी (special stems बिभे, बिभी, बिभि, see 333). *Inf.* भेतुम् 'to fear.' Par. *Pres.* बिभेमि, बिभेषि, बिभेति; बिभीवस् or बिभिवस्, बिभीथस् or बिभिथस्, बिभीतस् or बिभितस्; बिभीमस् or बिभिमस्, बिभीथ or बिभिथ, बिभ्यति (34). *Impf.* अबिभयम्, अबिभेस्, अबिभेत्; अबिभीव or अबिभिव, अबिभीतम् or अबिभितम्, अबिभीताम् or अबिभिताम्; अबिभीम or अबिभिम, अबिभीत or अबिभित, अबिभयुस् (331. Obs.) *Pot.* बिभीयाम् or बिभियाम्, &c. *Impv.* बिभयानि, बिभीहि or बिभिहि, बिभेतु; बिभयाव, बिभीतम् or बिभितम्, बिभीताम् or बिभिताम्; बिभयाम, बिभीत or बिभित, बिभ्यतु (34). *Perf.* (374) बिभाय, बिभयिथ or बिभेथ, बिभाय; बिभ्यिव, बिभ्यथुस्, बिभ्यतुस्; बिभ्यिम, बिभ्य, बिभ्युस्. Or बिभयाञ्चकार (385. *e*). *1st Fut.* भेतास्मि. *2nd Fut.* भेष्यामि. *Aor.* अभैषम्, अभैषीस्, अभैषीत्; अभैष्व, अभैष्टम्, अभैष्टाम्; अभैष्म, अभैष्ट, अभैषुस्. *Prec.* भीयासम्. *Cond.* अभेष्यम्. Pass., *Pres.* भीये; *Aor. 3rd sing.* अभायि. Caus., *Pres.* भाययामि or -ये, or भापये or भीषये; *Aor.* अबीभयम् or अबीभपम् or अबीभिषम्. Des. बिभीषामि. Freq. बेभीये or बेभेमि or बेभयीमि. Part., *Pres.* बिभ्यत् (141. *a*); *Past Pass.* भीत; *Past Indecl.* भीत्वा, -भीय; *Fut. Pass.* भेतव्य, भयनीय, भेय.

a. Root ह्री (special stems जिह्रे, जिह्री, जिह्रिय्, see 333. *a*). *Inf.* ह्रेतुम् 'to be ashamed.' Par. *Pres.* जिह्रेमि, जिह्रेषि, जिह्रेति; जिह्रीवस्, जिह्रीथस्, जिह्रीतस्; जिह्रीमस्, जिह्रीथ, जिह्रियति (123. *a*). *Impf.* अजिह्रयम्, अजिह्रेस्, अजिह्रेत्; अजिह्रीव, अजिह्रीतम्, अजिह्रीताम्; अजिह्रीम, अजिह्रीत, अजिह्रयुस् (331. Obs.) *Pot.* जिह्रीयाम्. *Impv.* जिह्रयाणि, जिह्रीहि, जिह्रेतु; जिह्रयाव, जिह्रीतम्, जिह्रीताम्; जिह्रयाम, जिह्रीत, जिह्रियतु. *Perf.* जिह्राय, जिह्रयिथ or जिह्रेथ, जिह्राय; जिह्रियिव (374. *e*), जिह्रियथुस्, जिह्रियतुस्; जिह्रियिम, जिह्रिय, जिह्रियुस्. *1st Fut.* ह्रेतास्मि. *2nd Fut.* ह्रेष्यामि. *Aor.* अह्रैषम्, अह्रैषीस्, अह्रैषीत्; अह्रैष्व, -ष्टम्, -ष्टाम्; अह्रैष्म, -ष्ट, -षुस्. *Prec.* ह्रीयासम्. *Cond.* अह्रेष्यम्. Pass., *Pres.* ह्रीये; *Aor. 3rd sing.* अह्रायि. Caus., *Pres.* ह्रेपयामि; *Aor.* अजिह्रिपम्. Des. जिह्रीषामि. Freq. जेह्रीये, जेह्रेमि or जेह्रयीमि. Part., *Pres.* जिह्रियत् (141. *a*); *Past*

Pass. ह्रीण or ह्रीत; *Past Indecl.* ह्रीत्वा; *Fut. Pass.* ह्रेतव्य, ह्रयणीय, ह्रेय.

b. Root जन् (special stems जजन्, जजा, जज्ञ्, see 339). *Inf.* जनितुम् 'to produce.' Par. *Pres.* जजन्मि, जजंसि, जजन्ति; जजन्वस्, जजाथस्, जजातस्; जजन्मस्, जजाथ, जज्ञति. *Impf.* अजजनम्, अजजन् (294), अजजन्; अजजन्व, अजजातम्, अजजाताम्; अजजन्म, अजजात, अजज्ञुस्. *Pot.* जजन्याम् or जजायाम्. *Impv.* जजनानि, जजाहि, जजन्तु; जजनाव, जजातम्, जजाताम्; जजनाम, जजात, जज्ञतु. *Perf.* जजान or जजन, जजनिथ, जजान; जज्ञिव, जज्ञथुस्, जज्ञतुस्; जज्ञिम, जज्ञ, जज्ञुस्. 1st *Fut.* जनितास्मि. 2nd *Fut.* जनिष्यामि. *Aor.* अजानिषम्, अजानीस्, अजानीत्; अजानिष्व, &c. Or अजनिषम्, &c.; see 418. B. *Prec.* जन्यासम् or जायासम्. *Cond.* अजनिष्यम्. Pass., *Pres.* जाये (cf. 617. *a*) or जन्ये; *Aor. 3rd sing.* अजनि. Caus., *Pres.* जनयामि; *Aor.* अजीजनम्. Des. जिजनिषे. Freq. जाजाये or जञ्जन्ये, जञ्जन्मि. Part., *Pres.* जज्ञत् (141. *a*); *Past Pass.* जात, जनित; *Past Indecl.* जनित्वा, -जन्य, -जाय; *Fut. Pass.* जनितव्य, जननीय, जन्य.

EXAMPLES OF PRIMITIVE VERBS OF THE SEVENTH CLASS, EXPLAINED AT 342.

667. Root छिद् *ćhid.* Infin. छेत्तुम् *ćhettum,* 'to cut.'

PARASMAI-PADA. *Present Tense,* 'I cut.'

छिनद्मि *ćhinadmi*	छिन्द्वस् *ćhindvas*	छिन्द्मस् *ćhindmas*
छिनत्सि *ćhinatsi*	छिन्थस् *ćhinthas* (345)	छिन्थ *ćhintha* (345)
छिनत्ति *ćhinatti*	छिन्तस् *ćhintas* (345)	छिन्दन्ति *ćhindanti*

Imperfect, 'I was cutting,' or 'I cut.'

अच्छिनदम् *aććhinadam* (51)	अच्छिन्द्व *aććhindva*	अच्छिन्द्म *aććhindma*
अच्छिनत् *aććhinat* (294)	अच्छिन्तम् *aććhintam* (345)	अच्छिन्त *aććhinta* (345)
अच्छिनत् *aććhinat* (294)	अच्छिन्ताम् *aććhintám* (345)	अच्छिन्दन् *aććhindan*

Potential, 'I may cut.'

छिन्द्याम् *ćhindyám*	छिन्द्याव *ćhindyáva*	छिन्द्याम *ćhindyáma*
छिन्द्यास् *ćhindyás*	छिन्द्यातम् *ćhindyátam*	छिन्द्यात *ćhindyáta*
छिन्द्यात् *ćhindyát*	छिन्द्याताम् *ćhindyátám*	छिन्द्युस् *ćhindyus*

Imperative, 'Let me cut.'

छिनदानि *ćhinadáni*	छिनदाव *ćhinadáva*	छिनदाम *ćhinadáma*
छिन्द्धि *ćhinddhi* (or *ćhindhi,* 345)	छिन्तम् *ćhintam* (345)	छिन्त *ćhinta* (345)
छिनत्तु *ćhinattu*	छिन्ताम् *ćhintám* (345)	छिन्दन्तु *ćhindantu*

Perf. चिच्छेद (51), चिच्छेदिथ, चिच्छेद; चिच्छिदिव, चिच्छिदथुस्, चिच्छिदतुस्; चिच्छिदिम, चिच्छिद, चिच्छिदुस्. *1st Fut.* छेत्तास्मि. *2nd Fut.* छेत्स्यामि. *Aor.* अच्छिदम्, अच्छिदस्, अच्छिदत्; अच्छिदाव, अच्छिदतम्, अच्छिदताम्; अच्छिदाम, अच्छिदत, अच्छिदन्. Or अच्छैत्सम्, अच्छैत्सीस्, अच्छैत्सीत्; अच्छैत्स्व, अच्छैत्तम्, अच्छैत्ताम्; अच्छैत्स्म, अच्छैत्त, अच्छैत्सुस्. *Prec.* छिद्यासम्. *Cond.* अच्छेत्स्यम्.

ÁTMANE-PADA. *Present Tense*, 'I cut.'

छिन्दे *ćhinde*	छिन्द्वहे *ćhindvahe*	छिन्द्महे *ćhindmahe*
छिन्त्से *ćhintse*	छिन्दाथे *ćhindáthe*	छिन्द्ध्वे *ćhinddhve*
छिन्ते *ćhinte* (345)	छिन्दाते *ćhindáte*	छिन्दते *ćhindate*

Imperfect, 'I was cutting,' or 'I cut.'

अच्छिन्दि *aććhindi* (51)	अच्छिन्द्वहि *aććhindvahi*	अच्छिन्द्महि *aććhindmahi*
अच्छिन्थास् *aććhinthás* (345)	अच्छिन्दाथाम् *aććhindáthám*	अच्छिन्द्ध्वम् *aććhinddhvam*
अच्छिन्त *aććhinta* (345)	अच्छिन्दाताम् *aććhindátám*	अच्छिन्दत *aććhindata*

Potential, 'I may cut.'

छिन्दीय *ćhindíya*	छिन्दीवहि *ćhindívahi*	छिन्दीमहि *ćhindímahi*
छिन्दीथास् *ćhindíthás*	छिन्दीयाथाम् *ćhindíyáthám*	छिन्दीध्वम् *ćhindídhvam*
छिन्दीत *ćhindíta*	छिन्दीयाताम् *ćhindíyátám*	छिन्दीरन् *ćhindíran*

Imperative, 'Let me cut.'

छिनदै *ćhinadai*	छिनदावहै *ćhinadávahai*	छिनदामहै *ćhinadámahai*
छिन्त्स्व *ćhintsva*	छिन्दाथाम् *ćhindáthám*	छिन्द्ध्वम् *ćhinddhvam*
छिन्ताम् *ćhintám* (345)	छिन्दाताम् *ćhindátám*	छिन्दताम् *ćhindatám*

Perf. चिच्छिदे, चिच्छिदिषे, चिच्छिदे; चिच्छिदिवहे, चिच्छिदाथे, चिच्छिदाते; चिच्छिदिमहे, चिच्छिदिध्वे, चिच्छिदिरे. *1st Fut.* छेत्ताहे. *2nd Fut.* छेत्स्ये. *Aor.* अच्छित्सि, अच्छित्थास्, अच्छित्त; अच्छित्स्वहि, अच्छित्साथाम्, अच्छित्साताम्; अच्छित्स्महि, अच्छिद्ध्वम्, अच्छित्सत. *Prec.* छित्सीय. *Cond.* अच्छेत्स्ये. Pass., *Pres.* छिद्ये; *Aor. 3rd sing.* अच्छेदि. Caus., *Pres.* छेदयामि; *Aor.* अचिच्छिदम्. Des. चिच्छित्सामि, -त्से. Freq. चेच्छिद्ये, चेच्छेद्मि. Part., *Pres.* छिन्दत्; Átm. छिन्दान; *Past Pass.* छिन्न; *Past Indecl.* छित्त्वा, -छिद्य; *Fut. Pass.* छेत्तव्य, छेदनीय, छेद्य.

OTHER EXAMPLES OF CL. 7 IN THE ORDER OF THEIR FINAL LETTERS.

668. Root अञ्ज् (special stems अनज्, अञ्ज्, see 347). *Inf.* अंक्तुम् 'to anoint,' 'to make clear.' Par. *Pres.* अनज्मि, अनक्षि (296), अनक्ति; अंज्वस्, अंक्थस्, अंक्तस्; अंज्मस्, अंक्थ, अञ्जन्ति. *Impf.* आनजम्, आनक् (294), आनक्; आंज्व, आंक्तम्, आंक्ताम्; आंज्म, आंक्त, आञ्जन्. *Pot.* अंज्याम्. *Impv.*

अनजानि, अंग्धि, अनक्तु; अनजाव, अंक्तम्, अंक्ताम्; अनजाम, अंक्त, अञ्जन्तु. *Perf.* आनञ्ज, आनञ्जिथ or आनंक्थ, आनञ्ज; आनञ्जिव, आनञ्जथुस्, आनञ्जतुस्; आनञ्जिम, आनञ्ज, आनञ्जुस्. *1st Fut.* अंक्तास्मि or अञ्जितास्मि. *2nd Fut.* अंक्ष्यामि or अञ्जिष्यामि. *Aor.* आञ्जिषम्, आञ्जीस्, आञ्जीत्; आञ्जिष्व, &c., see 418.B. *Prec.* अज्यासम् (453). *Cond.* आंक्ष्यम् or आञ्जिष्यम्. Pass., *Pres.* अज्ये (469); *Aor. 3rd sing.* आञ्जि. Caus., *Pres.* अञ्जयामि; *Aor.* आञ्जिजम्. Des. अञ्जिजिषामि. Part., *Pres.* अञ्जत्; *Past Pass.* अक्त; *Past Indecl.* अञ्जित्वा or अंक्त्वा or अक्त्वा, -अज्य; *Fut. Pass.* अंक्तव्य or अञ्जितव्य, अञ्जनीय, अंज्य or अंग्य.

a. Root भुज् (special stems भुनज्, भुञ्ज्, 346). *Inf.* भोक्तुम् 'to eat,' 'to enjoy.' Par. and Átm. *Pres.* भुनज्मि, भुनक्षि, भुनक्ति; भुंज्वस्, भुंक्थस्, भुंक्तस्; भुंज्मस्, भुंक्थ, भुञ्जन्ति. Átm. भुञ्जे, भुंक्षे, भुंक्ते; भुंज्वहे, भुञ्जाथे, भुञ्जाते; भुंज्महे, भुंग्ध्वे, भुञ्जते. *Impf.* अभुनजम्, अभुनक् (294), अभुनक्; अभुंज्व, अभुंक्तम्, अभुंक्ताम्; अभुंज्म, अभुंक्त, अभुञ्जन्. Átm. अभुञ्जि, अभुंक्थास्, अभुंक्त; अभुंज्वहि, अभुञ्जाथाम्, अभुञ्जाताम्; अभुंज्महि, अभुंग्ध्वम्, अभुञ्जत. *Pot.* भुंज्याम्. Átm. भुञ्जीय. *Impv.* भुनजानि, भुंग्धि, भुनक्तु; भुनजाव, भुंक्तम्, भुंक्ताम्; भुनजाम, भुंक्त, भुञ्जन्तु. Átm. भुनजै, भुंक्ष्व, भुंक्ताम्; भुनजावहै, भुञ्जाथाम्, भुञ्जाताम्; भुनजामहै, भुंग्ध्वम्, भुञ्जताम्. *Perf.* बुभोज, बुभोजिथ, बुभोज; बुभुजिव, बुभुजथुस्, बुभुजतुस्; बुभुजिम, बुभुज, बुभुजुस्. Átm. बुभुजे, बुभुजिषे, बुभुजे; -जिवहे, -जाथे, -जाते; -जिमहे, -जिध्वे, -जिरे. *1st Fut.* भोक्तास्मि. Átm. भोक्ताहे. *2nd Fut.* भोक्ष्यामि. Átm. भोक्ष्ये. *Aor.* अभौक्षम्, -क्षीस्, -क्षीत्; अभौक्ष्व, अभौक्तम्, -क्ताम्; अभौक्ष्म, अभौक्त, अभौक्षुस्. Átm. अभुक्षि, अभुक्थास्, अभुक्त; अभुक्ष्वहि, अभुक्षाथाम्, अभुक्षाताम्; अभुक्ष्महि, अभुग्ध्वम्, अभुक्षत. *Prec.* भुज्यासम्. Átm. भुक्षीय. *Cond.* अभोक्ष्यम्. Átm. अभोक्ष्ये. Pass., *Pres.* भुज्ये; *Aor. 3rd sing.* अभोजि. Caus., *Pres.* भोजयामि, -ये; *Aor.* अबूभुजम्. Des. बुभुक्षामि, -क्षे. Freq. बोभुज्ये, बोभोज्मि. Part., *Pres.* भुञ्जत्; Átm. भुञ्जान; *Past Pass.* भुक्त; *Past Indecl.* भुक्त्वा, -भुज्य; *Fut. Pass.* भोक्तव्य, भोजनीय, भोज्य or भोग्य (574).

669. Root भञ्ज् (special stems भनज्, भञ्ज्, 347). *Inf.* भंक्तुम् 'to break.' Par. *Pres.* भनज्मि, भनक्षि, भनक्ति; भंज्वस्, भंक्थस्, भंक्तस्; भंज्मस्, भंक्थ, भञ्जन्ति. *Impf.* अभनजम्, अभनक् (294), अभनक्; अभंज्व, अभंक्तम्, अभंक्ताम्; अभंज्म, अभंक्त, अभञ्जन्. *Pot.* भंज्याम्. *Impv.* भनजानि, भंग्धि, भनक्तु; भनजाव, भंक्तम्, भंक्ताम्; भनजाम, भंक्त, भञ्जन्तु. *Perf.* बभञ्ज, बभञ्जिथ or बभंक्थ, बभञ्ज; बभञ्जिव, बभञ्जथुस्, बभञ्जतुस्; बभञ्जिम, बभञ्ज, बभञ्जुस्. *1st Fut.* भंक्तास्मि. *2nd Fut.* भंक्ष्यामि. *Aor.* अभांक्षम्, -क्षीस्, -क्षीत्; अभांक्ष्व, अभांक्तम्, -क्ताम्; अभांक्ष्म, अभांक्त, अभांक्षुस्. *Prec.* भज्यासम् (453). *Cond.* अभंक्ष्यम्. Pass., *Pres.* भज्ये (469); *Aor. 3rd sing.* अभाजि. Caus., *Pres.* भञ्जयामि; *Aor.* अबभञ्जम्. Des. बिभंक्षामि. Freq. बंभज्ये, बंभज्मि. Part., *Pres.* भञ्जत्; *Past Pass.* भग्न; *Past Indecl.* भंक्त्वा or भक्त्वा, -भज्य; *Fut. Pass.* भंक्तव्य, भञ्जनीय, भंज्य.

670. Root युज् (special stems युनज्, युञ्ज्, see 346). *Inf.* योक्तुम् 'to

join,' 'to unite.' Par. and Átm. *Pres.* युनज्मि, युनक्षि, &c.; like भुज्, 668. *a.* Átm. युञ्जे, युंक्षे, &c. *Impf.* अयुनजम्, अयुनक् (294), अयुनक्; अयुंज्व, &c. Átm. अयुञ्जि, अयुंक्थास्, &c. *Pot.* युंज्याम्. Átm. युञ्जीय. *Impv.* युनजानि, युंग्धि, युनक्तु; युनजाव, &c. Átm. युनजै, युंक्ष्व, युंक्ताम्, &c. *Perf.* युयोज, युयोजिथ, युयोज; युयुजिव, &c.; like भुज्, 668. *a.* Átm. युयुजे. 1*st Fut.* योक्तास्मि. Átm. योक्ताहे. 2*nd Fut.* योक्ष्यामि. Átm. योक्ष्ये. *Aor.* अयुजम्, -जस्, -जत्; -जाव, -जतम्, -जताम्; -जाम, -जत, -जन्. Or अयौक्षम्, -क्षीस्, -क्षीत्; अयौक्ष्व, &c. Átm. अयुक्षि, अयुक्थास्, अयुक्त; अयुक्ष्वहि, &c. *Prec.* युज्यासम्. Átm. युक्षीय. *Cond.* अयोक्ष्यम्. Átm. अयोक्ष्ये. Pass., *Pres.* युज्ये; *Aor. 3rd sing.* अयोजि, see 702. Caus., *Pres.* योजयामि; *Aor.* अयूयुजम्. Des. युयुक्षामि, -क्षे. Freq. योयुज्ये, योयोज्मि. Part., *Pres.* युञ्जत्; Átm. युञ्जान; *Past Pass.* युक्त; *Past Indecl.* युक्त्वा, -युज्य; *Fut. Pass.* योक्तव्य, योजनीय, योग्य or योज्य (574, 574. *a*).

671. Root रुध् (special stems रुणध्, रुन्ध्, 344). *Inf.* रोद्धुम् 'to hinder.' Par. and Átm. *Pres.* रुणध्मि, रुणत्सि, रुणद्धि; रुन्ध्वस्, रुन्द्धस्*, रुन्द्धस्*; रुन्ध्मस्, रुन्द्ध*, रुन्धन्ति. Átm. रुन्धे, रुन्त्से, रुन्द्धे*; रुन्ध्वहे, रुन्धाथे, रुन्धाते; रुन्ध्महे, रुन्द्ध्वे, रुन्धते. *Impf.* अरुणधम्, अरुणत् or अरुणस् (294), अरुणत् (294); अरुन्ध्व, अरुन्द्धम्*, अरुन्द्धाम्*; अरुन्ध्म, अरुन्द्ध*, अरुन्धन्. Átm. अरुन्धि, अरुन्द्धास्*, अरुन्द्ध*; अरुन्ध्वहि, अरुन्धाथाम्, अरुन्धाताम्; अरुन्ध्महि, अरुन्द्ध्वम्, अरुन्धत. *Pot.* रुन्ध्याम्. Átm. रुन्धीय. *Impv.* रुणधानि, रुन्द्धि, रुणद्धु; रुणधाव, रुन्द्धम्*, रुन्द्धाम्*; रुणधाम, रुन्द्ध*, रुन्धन्तु. Átm. रुणधै, रुन्त्स्व, रुन्द्धाम्*; रुणधावहै, रुन्धाथाम्, रुन्धाताम्; रुणधामहै, रुन्द्ध्वम्, रुन्धताम्. *Perf.* रुरोध, रुरोधिथ, रुरोध; रुरुधिव, रुरुधथुस्, रुरुधतुस्; रुरुधिम, रुरुध, रुरुधुस्. Átm. रुरुधे, रुरुधिषे, रुरुधे; रुरुधिवहे, रुरुधाथे, रुरुधाते; रुरुधिमहे, रुरुधिध्वे, रुरुधिरे. 1*st Fut.* रोद्धास्मि. Átm. रोद्धाहे. 2*nd Fut.* रोत्स्यामि. Átm. रोत्स्ये. *Aor.* अरुधम्, -धस्, -धत्; -धाव, -धतम्, -धताम्; -धाम, -धत, -धन्. Or अरौत्सम्, अरौत्सीस्, अरौत्सीत्; अरौत्स्व, अरौद्धम्, अरौद्धाम्; अरौत्स्म, अरौद्ध, अरौत्सुस्. Átm. अरुत्सि, अरुद्धास्, अरुद्ध; अरुत्स्वहि, अरुत्साथाम्, अरुत्साताम्; अरुत्स्महि, अरुद्ध्वम्, अरुत्सत. *Prec.* रुध्यासम्. Átm. रुत्सीय. *Cond.* अरोत्स्यम्. Átm. अरोत्स्ये. Part., *Pres.* रुध्ये; *Aor. 3rd sing.* अरोधि. Caus., *Pres.* रोधयामि; *Aor.* अरूरुधम्. Des. रुरुत्सामि, -त्से. Freq. रोरुध्ये, रोरोध्मि. Part., *Pres.* रुन्धत्; Átm. रुन्धान; *Past Pass.* रुद्ध; *Past Indecl.* रुद्ध्वा, -रुध्य; *Fut. Pass.* रोद्धव्य, रोधनीय, रोध्य.

672. Root शिष् (special stems शिनष्, शिंष्). *Inf.* शेष्टुम् 'to distinguish,' 'to separate,' 'to leave remaining.' Par. *Pres.* शिनष्मि, शिनक्षि, शिनष्टि; शिंष्वस्, शिंष्ठस्, शिंष्टस्; शिंष्मस्, शिंष्ठ, शिंषन्ति. *Impf.* अशिनषम्, अशिनट् (294),

* रुन्धस् may be written for रुन्द्धस्. Similarly, रुन्ध for रुन्द्ध, &c. See 298. *a.*

अशिनट्; अशिंष्व, अशिंष्टम्, अशिंष्टाम्; अशिंष्म, अशिंष्ट, अशिंषन्. *Pot.* शिंष्याम्. *Impv.* शिनषाणि, शिंड्ढि or शिण्ढि (303, compare 345), शिनष्टु; शिनषाव, शिंष्टम्, शिंष्टाम्; शिनषाम, शिंष्ट, शिंषन्तु. *Perf.* शिशेष, शिशेषिथ, शिशेष; शिशिषिव, शिशिषथुस्, शिशिषतुस्; शिशिषिम, शिशिष, शिशिषुस्. *1st Fut.* शेष्टास्मि. *2nd Fut.* शेक्ष्यामि. *Aor.* अशिषम्, -षस्, -षत्; -षाव, -षतम्, -षताम्; -षाम, -षत, -षन्. *Prec.* शिष्यासम्. *Cond.* अशेक्ष्यम्. Pass., *Pres.* शिष्ये; *Aor. 3rd sing.* अशेषि. Caus., *Pres.* शेषयामि; *Aor.* अशीशिषम्. Des. शिशिक्षामि. Freq. शेशिष्ये, शेशेष्मि. Part., *Pres.* शिंषत्; *Past Pass.* शिष्ट; *Past Indecl.* शिष्ट्वा, -शिष्य; *Fut. Pass.* शेष्टव्य, शेषणीय, शेष्य.

673. Root हिंस् (special stems हिनस्, हिंस्). *Inf.* हिंसितुम् 'to injure.' Par. *Pres.* हिनस्मि, हिनस्सि*, हिनस्ति; हिंस्वस्, हिंस्थस्, हिंस्तस्; हिंस्मस्, हिंस्थ, हिंसन्ति. *Impf.* अहिनसम्, अहिनत् or अहिनस् (294, 304. *a*), अहिनत्; अहिंस्व, अहिंस्तम्, अहिंस्ताम्; अहिंस्म, अहिंस्त, अहिंसन्. *Pot.* हिंस्याम्. *Impv.* हिनसानि, हिन्द्धि or हिन्धि (304), हिनस्तु; हिनसाव, हिंस्तम्, हिंस्ताम्; हिनसाम, हिंस्त, हिंसन्तु. *Perf.* जिहिंस, जिहिंसिथ, जिहिंस; जिहिंसिव, जिहिंसथुस्, जिहिंसतुस्; जिहिंसिम, जिहिंस, जिहिंसुस्. *1st Fut.* हिंसितास्मि. *2nd Fut.* हिंसिष्यामि. *Aor.* अहिंसिषम्, अहिंसीस्, अहिंसीत्; अहिंसिष्व, अहिंसिष्टम्, अहिंसिष्टाम्; अहिंसिष्म, अहिंसिष्ट, अहिंसिषुस्. *Prec.* हिंस्यासम्. *Cond.* अहिंसिष्यम्. Pass., *Pres.* हिंस्ये; *Aor. 3rd sing.* अहिंसि. Caus., *Pres.* हिंसयामि; *Aor.* अजिहिंसम्. Des. जिहिंसिषामि. Freq. जेहिंस्ये, जेहिंस्मि. Part., *Pres.* हिंसत्; *Past Pass.* हिंसित; *Past Indecl.* हिंसित्वा, -हिंस्य; *Fut. Pass.* हिंसितव्य, हिंसनीय, हिंस्य.

674. Root तृह् (special stems तृणह्, तृणेह्, तृंह्, see 348). *Inf.* तर्हितुम् or तर्ढुम् 'to injure,' 'to kill.' Par. *Pres.* तृणेह्मि, तृणेक्षि (306), तृणेढि (305. *a*); तृंह्वस्, तृण्ढस्, तृण्ढस् (298. *b*); तृंह्मस्, तृण्ढ, तृंहन्ति. *Impf.* अतृणहम्, अतृणेट् (294), अतृणेट्; अतृंह्व, अतृण्ढम्, अतृण्ढाम्; अतृंह्म, अतृण्ढ, अतृंहन्. *Pot.* तृंह्याम्. *Impv.* तृणहानि, तृण्ढि (see 306. *c*), तृणेढु; तृणहाव, तृण्ढम्, तृण्ढाम्; तृणहाम, तृण्ढ, तृंहन्तु. *Perf.* ततर्ह, ततर्हिथ or ततर्ढ, ततर्ह; ततृहिव, ततृहथुस्, ततृहतुस्; ततृहिम, ततृह, ततृहुस्. *1st Fut.* तर्हितास्मि or तर्ढास्मि. *2nd Fut.* तर्हिष्यामि or तर्क्ष्यामि. *Aor.* अतर्हिषम्, -र्हीस्, -र्हीत्; -र्हिष्व, -र्हिष्टम्, -र्हिष्टाम्; -र्हिष्म, -र्हिष्ट, -र्हिषुस्. Or अतृक्षम्, -क्षस्, -क्षत्; -क्षाव, -क्षतम्, -क्षताम्; -क्षाम, -क्षत, -क्षन्. *Prec.* तृह्यासम्. *Cond.* अतर्हिष्यम् or अतर्क्ष्यम्. Pass., *Pres.* तृह्ये; *Aor. 3rd sing.* अतर्हि. Caus., *Pres.* तर्हयामि; *Aor.* अततर्हम् or अतीतृहम्. Des. तितर्हिषामि or तितृक्षामि. Freq. तरीतृह्ये, तरीतर्ह्मि (*3rd sing.* तरीतर्ढि). Part., *Pres.* तृंहत्; *Past Pass.* (305. *a*) तृढ; *Past Indecl.* तर्हित्वा or तृढ्वा, -तृह्य; *Fut. Pass.* तर्हितव्य or तर्ढव्य, तर्हणीय, तृह्य.

* Final स् *s* preceded by *a* or *ā* remains unchanged before the terminations *si* and *se*; see 62. *b*.

EXAMPLES OF PRIMITIVE VERBS OF THE FIFTH CLASS, EXPLAINED AT 349.

675. Root वृ *vṛi*. Infin. वरितुम् *varitum* or वरीतुम् *varítum*, 'to cover,' 'to enclose,' 'to surround,' 'to choose *.'

Note, that the conjugational नु *nu* becomes णु *ṇu* after वृ *vṛi* by 58.

Parasmai-pada. *Present Tense*, 'I cover.'

वृणोमि *vṛiṇomi*	वृणुवस् *vṛiṇuvas* †	वृणुमस् *vṛiṇumas* ‡
वृणोषि *vṛiṇoshi*	वृणुथस् *vṛiṇuthas*	वृणुथ *vṛiṇutha*
वृणोति *vṛiṇoti*	वृणुतस् *vṛiṇutas*	वृण्वन्ति *vṛiṇvanti*

Imperfect, 'I was covering,' or 'I covered.'

अवृणवम् *avṛiṇavam*	अवृणुव *avṛiṇuva* §	अवृणुम *avṛiṇuma* ‖
अवृणोस् *avṛiṇos*	अवृणुतम् *avṛiṇutam*	अवृणुत *avṛiṇuta*
अवृणोत् *avṛiṇot*	अवृणुताम् *avṛiṇutám*	अवृण्वन् *avṛiṇvan*

Potential, 'I may cover.'

वृणुयाम् *vṛiṇuyám*	वृणुयाव *vṛiṇuyáva*	वृणुयाम *vṛiṇuyáma*
वृणुयास् *vṛiṇuyás*	वृणुयातम् *vṛiṇuyátam*	वृणुयात *vṛiṇuyáta*
वृणुयात् *vṛiṇuyát*	वृणुयाताम् *vṛiṇuyátám*	वृणुयुस् *vṛiṇuyus*

Imperative, 'Let me cover.'

वृणवानि *vṛiṇaváni*	वृणवाव *vṛiṇaváva*	वृणवाम *vṛiṇaváma*
वृणु *vṛiṇu*	वृणुतम् *vṛiṇutam*	वृणुत *vṛiṇuta*
वृणोतु *vṛiṇotu*	वृणुताम् *vṛiṇutám*	वृण्वन्तु *vṛiṇvantu*

Perf. (369) ववार, ववर्थ (Vedic) or ववरिथ (see 370), ववार; ववृव, वव्रथुस्, वव्रतुस्; ववृम, वव्र, वव्रुस् or ववरुस्¶. *1st Fut.* (392. *d*) वरितास्मि or वरीतास्मि (393). *2nd Fut.* वरिष्यामि or वरीष्यामि (393). *Aor.* अवारिषम्, अवारीस्, अवारीत्; अवारिष्व, अवारिष्टम्, अवारिष्टाम्; अवारिष्म, अवारिष्ट, अवारिषुस्. *Prec.* व्रियासम् or वूर्षीसम् (448. *b*). *Cond.* अवरिष्यम् or अवरीष्यम्.

Átmane-pada. *Present Tense*, 'I cover.'

वृण्वे *vṛiṇve*	वृणुवहे *vṛiṇuvahe* **	वृणुमहे *vṛiṇumahe* ††
वृणुषे *vṛiṇushe*	वृण्वाथे *vṛiṇváthe*	वृणुध्वे *vṛiṇudhve*
वृणुते *vṛiṇute*	वृण्वाते *vṛiṇváte*	वृण्वते *vṛiṇvate*

---

* In the sense of 'to choose,' this root generally follows cl. 9; thus, Pres. वृणामि, वृणासि, वृणाति; वृणीवस्, &c. See 686.

† Or वृण्वस् *vṛiṇvas*. ‡ Or वृण्मस् *vṛiṇmas*. § Or अवृण्व *avṛiṇva*.

‖ Or अवृण्म *avṛiṇma*.

¶ वृ *vṛi* is sometimes written with long *ṛí*, in which case 374. *k* may be applied.

** Or वृण्वहे *vṛiṇvahe*. †† Or वृण्महे *vṛiṇmahe*.

Imperfect, 'I was covering,' or 'I covered.'

अवृण्वि *avṛiṇvi*	अवृणुवहि *avṛiṇuvahi* *	अवृणुमहि *avṛiṇumahi* †
अवृणुथास् *avṛiṇuthás*	अवृण्वाथाम् *avṛiṇváthám*	अवृणुध्वम् *avṛiṇudhvam*
अवृणुत *avṛiṇuta*	अवृण्वाताम् *avṛiṇvátám*	अवृण्वत *avṛiṇvata*

Potential, 'I may cover.'

वृण्वीय *vṛiṇvíya*	वृण्वीवहि *vṛiṇvívahi*	वृण्वीमहि *vṛiṇvímahi*
वृण्वीथास् *vṛiṇvíthás*	वृण्वीयाथाम् *vṛiṇvíyáthám*	वृण्वीध्वम् *vṛiṇvídhvam*
वृण्वीत *vṛiṇvíta*	वृण्वीयाताम् *vṛiṇvíyátám*	वृण्वीरन् *vṛiṇvíran*

Imperative, 'Let me cover.'

वृणवै *vṛiṇavai*	वृणवावहै *vṛiṇavávahai*	वृणवामहै *vṛiṇavámahai*
वृणुष्व *vṛiṇushva*	वृण्वाथाम् *vṛiṇváthám*	वृणुध्वम् *vṛiṇudhvam*
वृणुताम् *vṛiṇutám*	वृण्वाताम् *vṛiṇvátám*	वृण्वताम् *vṛiṇvatám*

Perf. वव्रे (369) or ववरे ‡, ववृषे, वव्रे or ववरे; ववृवहे, वव्राथे, वव्राते; ववृमहे, ववृढ्वे, वव्रिरे. 1*st Fut.* वरिताहे or वरीताहे. 2*nd Fut.* वरिष्ये or वरीष्ये. *Aor.* अवरिषि, अवरिष्ठास्, अवरिष्ट; अवरिष्वहि, अवरिषाथाम्, अवरिषाताम्; अवरिष्महि, अवरिढ्वम् or -रिध्वम्, अवरिषत. Or अवरीषि, अवरीष्ठास्, &c. Or अवृषि, अवृथास्, अवृत; अवृष्वहि, अवृषाथाम्, अवृषाताम्; अवृष्महि, अवृढ्वम्, अवृषत. Or अवूर्षि, अवूर्ष्ठास्, अवूर्ष्ट; अवूर्ष्वहि, अवूर्षाथाम्, अवूर्षाताम्; अवूर्ष्महि, अवूर्ढ्वम्, अवूर्षत. *Prec.* वरिषीय or वृषीय or वूर्षीय (448. *b*). *Cond.* अवरिष्ये or अवरीष्ये. Pass., *Pres.* व्रिये; *Aor. 3rd sing.* अवारि. Caus., *Pres.* वरयामि or -ये, or वारयामि or -ये; *Aor.* अवीवरम्. Des. विवरिषामि or -षे, विवरीषामि or -षे, वुवूर्षामि or -षे (503). Freq. वेव्रीये (511) or वोवूर्ये, वर्वर्मि. Part., *Pres.* वृण्वत्; Átm. वृण्वान; *Past Pass.* वृत; *Past Indecl.* वृत्वा, -वृत्य; *Fut. Pass.* वरितव्य or वरीतव्य, वरणीय, वार्य.

OTHER EXAMPLES OF CL. 5 IN THE ORDER OF THEIR FINAL LETTERS.

676. Root श्रु § (special stems शृणो, शृणु, see 352). *Inf.* श्रोतुम् 'to hear.' Par. *Pres.* शृणोमि, शृणोषि, शृणोति; शृणुवस् or शृण्वस्, शृणुथस्, शृणुतस्; शृणुमस् or शृण्मस्, शृणुथ, शृण्वन्ति. *Impf.* अशृणवम्, अशृणोस्, अशृणोत्; अशृणुव or अशृण्व, अशृणुतम्, अशृणुताम्; अशृणुम or अशृण्म, अशृणुत, अशृण्वन्. *Pot.* शृणुयाम्. *Impv.* शृणवानि, शृणु, शृणोतु; शृणवाव, शृणुतम्, शृणुताम्; शृणवाम, शृणुत, शृण्वन्तु. *Perf.* (369) शुश्राव, शुश्रोथ, शुश्राव; शुश्रुव, शुश्रुवथुस्, शुश्रुवतुस्; शुश्रुम, शुश्रुव, शुश्रुवुस्. 1*st Fut.* श्रोतास्मि. 2*nd Fut.* श्रोष्यामि. *Aor.* अश्रौषम्, अश्रौषीस्, अश्रौषीत्; अश्रौष्व, अश्रौष्टम्, -ष्टाम्; अश्रौष्म, अश्रौष्ट,

* Or अवृण्वहि *avṛiṇvahi*. † Or अवृण्महि *avṛiṇmahi*.

‡ वृ is sometimes written with long *ṛí*, in which case 374. *k* may be applied.

§ This root is placed by Indian grammarians under the 1st class.

अश्रौषुस्. *Prec.* श्रूयासम्. *Cond.* अश्रोष्यम्. Pass., *Pres.* श्रूये; *Aor. 3rd sing.* अश्रावि. Caus., *Pres.* श्रावयामि; *Aor.* अशिश्रवम् or अशुश्रवम्. Des. शुश्रूषे. Freq. शोश्रूये, शोश्रोमि or शोश्रवीमि. Part., *Pres.* शृण्वत्; *Past Pass.* श्रुत; *Past Indecl.* श्रुत्वा, -श्रुत्य; *Fut. Pass.* श्रोतव्य, श्रवणीय, श्राव्य.

677. Root धू* (special stems धूनो, धूनु). *Inf.* धवितुम् or धोतुम् 'to shake,' 'to agitate.' Par. and Átm. *Pres.* धूनोमि, धूनोषि, धूनोति; धूनुवस् or धून्वस्, धूनुथस्, धूनुतस्; धूनुमस् or धून्मस्, धूनुथ, धून्वन्ति. Átm. धून्वे; धूनुषे, धूनुते; धूनुवहे or धून्वहे, धून्वाथे, धून्वाते; धूनुमहे or धून्महे, धूनुध्वे, धून्वते. *Impf.* अधूनवम्, अधूनोस्, अधूनोत्; अधूनुव or अधून्व, अधूनुतम्, अधूनुताम्; अधूनुम or अधून्म, अधूनुत, अधून्वन्. Átm. अधून्वि, अधूनुथास्, अधूनुत; अधूनुवहि or अधून्वहि, अधून्वाथाम्, अधून्वाताम्; अधूनुमहि, अधूनुध्वम्, अधून्वत. *Pot.* धूनुयाम्. Átm. धून्वीय. *Impv.* धूनवानि, धूनु, धूनोतु; धूनवाव, धूनुतम्, धूनुताम्; धूनवाम, धूनुत, धून्वन्तु. Átm. धूनवै, धूनुष्व, धूनुताम्; धूनवावहै, धून्वाथाम्, धून्वाताम्; धूनवामहै, धूनुध्वम्, धून्वताम्. *Perf.* (374. *g*) दुधाव, दुधविथ or दुधोथ, दुधाव; दुधुविव, दुधुवथुस्, दुधुवतुस्; दुधुविम, दुधुव, दुधुवुस्. Átm. दुधुवे, दुधुविषे, दुधुवे; दुधुविवहे, दुधुवाथे, दुधुवाते; दुधुविमहे, दुधुविध्वे or -ढ्वे, दुधुविरे. *1st Fut.* धवितास्मि or धोतास्मि. Átm. धविताहे or धोताहे. *2nd Fut.* धविष्यामि or धोष्यामि. Átm. धविष्ये or धोष्ये. *Aor.** अधाविषम्, अधावीस्, अधावीत्; अधाविष्व, अधाविष्टम्, अधाविष्टाम्; अधाविष्म, अधाविष्ट, अधाविषुस्. Or अधौषम्, -षीस्, -षीत्; अधौष्व, अधौष्टम्, -ष्टाम्; अधौष्म, अधौष्ट, अधौषुस्. Átm. अधविषि, अधविष्ठास्, अधविष्ट; अधविष्वहि, अधविषाथाम्, -षाताम्; अधविष्महि, अधविढ्वम् (-ध्वम्), अधविषत. Or अधोषि, अधोष्ठास्, अधोष्ट; अधोष्वहि, अधोषाथाम्, -षाताम्; अधोष्महि, अधोढ्वम्, अधोषत. *Prec.* धूयासम्. Átm. धविषीय or धोषीय. *Cond.* अधविष्यम् or अधोष्यम्. Átm. अधविष्ये or अधोष्ये. Pass., *Pres.* धूये; *Aor. 3rd sing.* अधावि. Caus., *Pres.* धूनयामि or धावयामि; *Aor.* अदूधुनम् or अदूधवम्. Des. दुधूषामि, -षे. Freq. दोधूये, दोधोमि or दोधवीमि. Part., *Pres.* धून्वत्; Átm. धून्वान; *Past Pass.* धूत or धून; *Past Indecl.* धूत्वा, -धूय; *Fut. Pass.* धवितव्य or धोतव्य, धवनीय, धाव्य or धव्य.

a. Like धू may be conjugated सु 'to press out Soma juice,' which in native grammars is the model of the 5th class; thus, *Pres.* सुनोमि, &c. The two Futures reject *i; 1st Fut.* सोतास्मि, &c.

678. Root स्तृ or स्तॄ† (special stems स्तृणो, स्तृणु). *Inf.* स्तरितुम् or

---

* This root may also be धुनोमि &c., and also in the 9th class; Pres. धुनामि, धुनासि, धुनाति; धुनीवस्, &c.; see 686: and in the 6th (धुवामि 280). In the latter case the Aor. is अधुविषम्, &c.; see 430.

† This root may also be conjugated as a verb of the 9th class; thus, Pres. स्तृणामि, स्तृणासि, स्तृणाति; स्तृणीवस्, &c. See 686.

स्तरीतुम् or स्तर्तुम् 'to spread,' 'to cover.' Par. and A'tm. *Pres.* स्तृणोमि, &c.; like वृ at 675. A'tm. स्तृणवे, स्तृणुषे, &c. *Impf.* अस्तृणवम्. A'tm. अस्तृणिव. *Pot.* स्तृणुयाम्. A'tm. स्तृण्वीय. *Impv.* स्तृणवानि. A'tm. स्तृणवै. *Perf.* (252. *c*, 374. *k*) तस्तार, तस्तर्थ, तस्तार; तस्तरिव, तस्तरथुस्, तस्तरतुस्; तस्तरिम, तस्तर, तस्तरुस्. A'tm. तस्तरे, तस्तरिषे, तस्तरे; तस्तरिवहे, तस्तराथे, तस्तराते; तस्तरिमहे, तस्तरिध्वे or -ढ्वे, तस्तरिरे. *1st Fut.* स्तरितास्मि or स्तरीतास्मि or स्तर्तास्मि. A'tm. स्तरिताहे or स्तरीताहे or स्तर्ताहे. *2nd Fut.* स्तरिष्यामि or स्तरीष्यामि. A'tm. स्तरिष्ये or स्तरीष्ये. *Aor.* अस्तारिषम्, -रीस्, -रीत्; अस्तारिष्व, &c.; see 675. Or अस्तार्षम्, -र्षीस्, -र्षीत्; अस्तार्ष्व, -ष्टम्, -ष्टाम्; अस्तार्ष्म, -ष्ट, -र्षुस्. A'tm. अस्तरिषि or अस्तरीषि or अस्तृषि or अस्तीर्षि. *Prec.* स्तर्यासम् or स्तीर्यासम्. A'tm. स्तृषीय or स्तरिषीय or स्तीर्षीय. *Cond.* अस्तरिष्यम् or अस्तरीष्यम्. A'tm. अस्तरिष्ये or अस्तरीष्ये. Pass., *Pres.* (467) स्तर्यें; *Aor. 3rd sing.* अस्तारि. Caus., *Pres.* स्तारयामि; *Aor.* अतिस्तरम् or अतस्तरम्. Des. तिस्तरिषामि, -षे; or तिस्तरीषामि, -षे; or तिस्तीर्षामि, -र्षे. Freq. तास्तर्ये or तेस्तीर्ये, तास्तर्मि or तरीस्तर्मि. Part., *Pres.* स्तृणवत्; A'tm. स्तृणवान; *Past Pass.* स्तृत or स्तीर्ण (534); *Past Indecl.* स्तृत्वा, -स्तीर्य, -स्तृत्य; *Fut. Pass.* स्तरितव्य or स्तरीतव्य or स्तर्तव्य, स्तरणीय, स्तार्य.

679. Root शक्* (special stems शक्नो, शक्नु, शक्नुव्). *Inf.* शक्तुम् 'to be able.' Par. *Pres.* शक्नोमि, शक्नोषि, शक्नोति; शक्नुवस्, शक्नुथस्, शक्नुतस्; शक्नुमस्, शक्नुथ, शक्नुवन्ति. *Impf.* अशक्नवम्, अशक्नोस्, अशक्नोत्; अशक्नुव, अशक्नुतम्, अशक्नुताम्; अशक्नुम, अशक्नुत, अशक्नुवन्. *Pot.* शक्नुयाम्. *Impv.* शक्नवानि, शक्नुहि, शक्नोतु; शक्नवाव, शक्नुतम्, शक्नुताम्; शक्नवाम, शक्नुत, शक्नुवन्तु. *Perf.* शशाक, शेकिथ or शशक्थ, शशाक; शेकिव, शेकथुस्, शेकतुस्; शेकिम, शेक, शेकुस्. *1st Fut.* शक्तास्मि. *2nd Fut.* शक्ष्यामि. *Aor.* अशकम्, -कस्, -कत्; -काव, -कतम्, -कताम्; -काम, -कत, -कन्. Or अशकिषम्, -कीस्, -कीत्; अशकिष्व, -किष्टम्, -ष्टाम्; अशकिष्म, -किष्ट, -किषुस्. *Prec.* शक्यासम्. *Cond.* अशक्ष्यम्. Pass., *Pres.* शक्ये; *Aor. 3rd sing.* अशाकि. Caus., *Pres.* शाकयामि; *Aor.* अशीशकम्. Des. शिशकिषामि or शिक्षामि, -क्षे† (503). Freq. शाशक्ये, शाशक्मि or शाशकीमि. Part., *Pres.* शक्नुवत्; A'tm. शक्नुवान; *Past Pass.* शक्त; *Past Indecl.* शक्त्वा, -शक्य; *Fut. Pass.* शक्तव्य, शकनीय, शक्य.

680. Root ऋध् (special stems ऋध्नो, ऋध्नु, ऋध्नुव्). *Inf.* अर्धितुम् 'to prosper,' 'to flourish,' 'to increase.' Par. *Pres.* ऋध्नोमि, ऋध्नोषि, ऋध्नोति; ऋध्नुवस्, ऋध्नुथस्, ऋध्नुतस्; ऋध्नुमस्, ऋध्नुथ, ऋध्नुवन्ति. *Impf.* (251. *a*)

---

* शक् is also conjugated in the 4th class, Parasmai and A'tmane (Pres. शक्यामि &c., शक्ये); but it may then be regarded as a Passive verb. See 461. *b*.

† This form of the Des. generally means 'to learn,' and is said by some to come from a root शिक्ष्.

आर्ध्नवम्, आर्ध्नोस्, आर्ध्नोत्; आर्ध्नुव, आर्ध्नुतम्, आर्ध्नुताम्; आर्ध्नुम, आर्ध्नुत, आर्ध्नुवन्. *Pot.* ऋध्नुयाम्. *Impv.* ऋध्नवानि, ऋध्नुहि, ऋध्नोतु; ऋध्नवाव, ऋध्नुतम्, -ताम्; ऋध्नवाम, ऋध्नुत, ऋध्नुवन्तु. *Perf.* आनर्ध, आनर्धिथ, आनर्ध; आनृधिव, आनृधथुस्, आनृधतुस्; आनृधिम, आनृध, आनृधुस्. *1st Fut.* अर्धितास्मि. *2nd Fut.* अर्धिष्यामि. *Aor.* आर्धिषम्, आर्धीस्, आर्धीत्; आर्धिष्व, आर्धिष्टम्, -ष्टाम्; आर्धिष्म, आर्धिष्ट, आर्धिषुस्. Or आर्धम्, -र्धस्, -र्धत्; -र्धाव, &c. *Prec.* ऋध्यासम्. *Cond.* आर्धिष्यम्. Pass., *Pres.* ऋध्ये; *Aor. 3rd sing.* आर्धि. Caus., *Pres.* अर्धयामि; *Aor.* आर्दिधम्. Des. अर्दिधिषामि or ईर्त्सामि (503). Part., *Pres.* ऋध्नुवत्; *Past Pass.* ऋद्ध; *Past Indecl.* अर्धित्वा or ऋद्ध्वा, -ऋध्य; *Fut. Pass.* अर्धितव्य, अर्धनीय, ऋध्य.

681. Root आप् (special stems आप्नो, आप्नु, आप्नुव्). *Inf.* आप्तुम् 'to obtain.' Par. *Pres.* आप्नोमि, आप्नोषि, आप्नोति; आप्नुवस्, आप्नुथस्, आप्नुतस्; आप्नुमस्, आप्नुथ, आप्नुवन्ति. *Impf.* आप्नवम्, आप्नोस्, आप्नोत्; आप्नुव, आप्नुतम्, -ताम्; आप्नुम, आप्नुत, आप्नुवन्. *Pot.* आप्नुयाम्. *Impv.* आप्नवानि, आप्नुहि, आप्नोतु; आप्नवाव, आप्नुतम्, -ताम्; आप्नवाम, आप्नुत, आप्नुवन्तु. *Perf.* आप, आपिथ, आप; आपिव, आपथुस्, आपतुस्; आपिम, आप, आपुस्. *1st Fut.* आप्तास्मि. *2nd Fut.* आप्स्यामि. *Aor.* आपम्, आपस्, आपत्; आपाव, आपतम्, -ताम्; आपाम, आपत, आपन्. *Prec.* आप्यासम्. *Cond.* आप्स्यम्. Pass., *Pres.* आप्ये; *Aor. 3rd sing.* आपि. Caus., *Pres.* आपयामि; *Aor.* आपिपम्. Des. (503) ईप्सामि. Part., *Pres.* आप्नुवत्; *Past Pass.* आप्त; *Past Indecl.* आप्त्वा, -आप्य; *Fut. Pass.* आप्तव्य, आपनीय, आप्य.

a. Root अश् (special stems अश्नो, अश्नु, अश्नुव्). *Inf.* अशितुम् or अष्टुम् 'to obtain,' 'to enjoy,' 'to pervade.' Ātm. *Pres.* अश्नुवे, अश्नुषे, अश्नुते; अश्नुवहे, अश्नुवाथे, अश्नुवाते; अश्नुमहे, अश्नुध्वे, अश्नुवते. *Impf.* आश्नुवि, आश्नुथास्, आश्नुत; आश्नुवहि, आश्नुवाथाम्, आश्नुवाताम्; आश्नुमहि, आश्नुध्वम्, आश्नुवत. *Pot.* अश्नुवीय. *Impv.* अश्नवै, अश्नुष्व, अश्नुताम्; अश्नवावहै, अश्नुवाथाम्, अश्नुवाताम्; अश्नवामहै, अश्नुध्वम्, अश्नुवताम्. *Perf.* (367. *c*) आनशे, आनशिषे or आनक्षे, आनशे; आनशिवहे or आनश्वहे (371), आनशाथे, आनशाते; आनशिमहे or आनश्महे, आनशिध्वे or आनड्ढ्वे, आनशिरे. *1st Fut.* अशिताहे or अष्टाहे. *2nd Fut.* अशिष्ये or अक्ष्ये. *Aor.* आक्षि, आष्ठास्, आष्ट; आक्ष्वहि, आक्षाथाम्, आक्षाताम्; आक्ष्महि, आग्ध्वम्, आक्षत. Or आशिषि, आशिष्ठास्, आशिष्ट; आशिष्वहि, आशिषाथाम्, आशिषाताम्; आशिष्महि, आशिढ्वम्, आशिषत. *Prec.* अशिषीय or अक्षीय. *Cond.* आशिष्ये or आक्ष्ये. Pass., *Pres.* अश्ये; *Aor. 3rd sing.* आशि. Caus., *Pres.* आशयामि; *Aor.* आशिशम्. Des. अशिशिषे. Freq. अशाश्ये (511. *a*). Part., *Pres.* अश्नुवान; *Past Pass.* अशित or अष्ट; *Past Indecl.* अशित्वा or अष्ट्वा, -अश्य; *Fut. Pass.* अशितव्य or अष्टव्य, अशनीय, आश्य.

EXAMPLES OF PRIMITIVE VERBS OF THE EIGHTH CLASS, EXPLAINED AT 353.

682. Root कृ *kṛi.* Infin. कर्तुम् *kartum*, 'to do' (355).

PARASMAI-PADA. *Present Tense*, 'I do.'

करोमि *karomi*	कुर्वस्* *kurvas*	कुर्मस्* *kurmas*
करोषि *karoshi*	कुरुथस् *kuruthas*	कुरुथ *kurutha*
करोति *karoti*	कुरुतस् *kurutas*	कुर्वन्ति* *kurvanti*

Imperfect, 'I was doing,' or 'I did.'

अकरवम् *akaravam*	अकुर्व *akurva* (73)	अकुर्म *akurma* (73)
अकरोस् *akaros*	अकुरुतम् *akurutam*	अकुरुत *akuruta*
अकरोत् *akarot*	अकुरुताम् *akurutám*	अकुर्वन् *akurvan*

Potential, 'I may do,' &c.

कुर्याम्* *kuryám*	कुर्याव *kuryáva*	कुर्याम *kuryáma*
कुर्यास् *kuryás*	कुर्यातम् *kuryátam*	कुर्यात *kuryáta*
कुर्यात् *kuryát*	कुर्याताम् *kuryátám*	कुर्युस् *kuryus*

Imperative, 'Let me do,' &c.

करवाणि *karaváṇi*	करवाव *karaváva*	करवाम *karaváma*
कुरु *kuru*	कुरुतम् *kurutam*	कुरुत *kuruta*
करोतु *karotu*	कुरुताम् *kurutám*	कुर्वन्तु* *kurvantu*

Perfect, 'I did,' or 'I have done.'

चकार *ćakára* (368)	चकृव *ćakṛiva*	चकृम *ćakṛima*
चकर्थ *ćakartha*	चक्रथुस् *ćakrathus*	चक्र *ćakra*
चकार *ćakára*	चक्रतुस् *ćakratus*	चक्रुस् *ćakrus*

First Future, 'I will do.'

कर्तास्मि *kartásmi*	कर्तास्वस् *kartásvas*	कर्तास्मस् *kartásmas*
कर्तासि *kartási*	कर्तास्थस् *kartásthas*	कर्तास्थ *kartástha*
कर्ता *kartá*	कर्तारौ *kartárau*	कर्तारस् *kartáras*

Second Future, 'I shall do.'

करिष्यामि *karishyámi*	करिष्यावस् *karishyávas*	करिष्यामस् *karishyámas*
करिष्यसि *karishyasi*	करिष्यथस् *karishyathas*	करिष्यथ *karishyatha*
करिष्यति *karishyati*	करिष्यतस् *karishyatas*	करिष्यन्ति *karishyanti*

* कुर्व्वस्, कुर्म्मस्, कुर्य्याम्, &c., would be equally correct; see 73. An obsolete form कुर्मि for करोमि is found in Epic poetry.

Aorist, 'I did.'

अकार्षम् *akársham*	अकार्ष्व *akárshva*	अकार्ष्म *akárshma*
अकार्षीस् *akárshís*	अकार्ष्टम् *akárshṭam*	अकार्ष्ट *akárshṭa*
अकार्षीत् *akárshít*	अकार्ष्टाम् *akárshṭám*	अकार्षुस् *akárshus*

Precative or *Benedictive*, 'May I do.'

क्रियासम् *kriyásam*	क्रियास्व *kriyásva*	क्रियास्म *kriyásma*
क्रियास् *kriyás*	क्रियास्तम् *kriyástam*	क्रियास्त *kriyásta*
क्रियात् *kriyát*	क्रियास्ताम् *kriyástám*	क्रियासुस् *kriyásus*

Conditional, 'I should do.'

अकरिष्यम् *akarishyam*	अकरिष्याव *akarishyáva*	अकरिष्याम *akarishyáma*
अकरिष्यस् *akarishyas*	अकरिष्यतम् *akarishyatam*	अकरिष्यत *akarishyata*
अकरिष्यत् *akarishyat*	अकरिष्यताम् *akarishyatám*	अकरिष्यन् *akarishyan*

683. Átmane-pada. *Present Tense*, 'I do.'

कुर्वे *kurve* (73)	कुर्वहे *kurvahe*	कुर्महे *kurmahe*
कुरुषे *kurushe*	कुर्वाथे *kurváthe*	कुरुध्वे *kurudhve*
कुरुते *kurute*	कुर्वाते *kurváte*	कुर्वते *kurvate*

Imperfect, 'I was doing,' or 'I did.'

अकुर्वि *akurvi* (73)	अकुर्वहि *akurvahi*	अकुर्महि *akurmahi*
अकुरुथास् *akuruthás*	अकुर्वाथाम् *akurváthám*	अकुरुध्वम् *akurudhvam*
अकुरुत *akuruta*	अकुर्वाताम् *akurvátám*	अकुर्वत *akurvata*

Potential, 'I may do.'.

कुर्वीय *kurvíya*	कुर्वीवहि *kurvívahi*	कुर्वीमहि *kurvímahi*
कुर्वीथास् *kurvíthás*	कुर्वीयाथाम् *kurvíyáthám*	कुर्वीध्वम् *kurvídhvam*
कुर्वीत *kurvíta*	कुर्वीयाताम् *kurvíyátám*	कुर्वीरन् *kurvíran*

Imperative, 'Let me do.'

करवै *karavai*	करवावहै *karavávahai*	करवामहै *karavámahai*
कुरुष्व *kurushva*	कुर्वाथाम् *kurváthám*	कुरुध्वम् *kurudhvam*
कुरुताम् *kurutám*	कुर्वाताम् *kurvátám*	कुर्वताम् *kurvatám*

Perfect, 'I did,' or 'I have done.'

चक्रे *ćakre*	चकृवहे *ćakṛivahe*	चकृमहे *ćakṛimahe*
चकृषे *ćakṛishe*	चक्राथे *ćakráthe*	चकृढ्वे *ćakṛiḍhve*
चक्रे *ćakre*	चक्राते *ćakráte*	चक्रिरे *ćakrire*

First Future, 'I will do.'

कर्ताहे *kartáhe*	कर्तास्वहे *kartásvahe*	कर्तास्महे *kartásmahe*
कर्तासे *kartáse*	कर्तासाथे *kartásáthe*	कर्ताध्वे *kartádhve*
कर्ता *kartá*	कर्तारौ *kartárau*	कर्तारस् *kartáras*

Second Future, 'I shall do.'

करिष्ये *karishye*	करिष्यावहे *karishyávahe*	करिष्यामहे *karishyámahe*
करिष्यसे *karishyase*	करिष्येथे *karishyethe*	करिष्यध्वे *karishyadhve*
करिष्यते *karishyate*	करिष्येते *karishyete*	करिष्यन्ते *karishyante*

Aorist, 'I did.'

अकृषि *akṛishi*	अकृष्वहि *akṛishvahi*	अकृष्महि *akṛishmahi*
अकृथास् *akṛithás*	अकृषाथाम् *akṛisháthám*	अकृढ्वम् *akṛiḍhvam*
अकृत *akṛita*	अकृषाताम् *akṛishátám*	अकृषत *akṛishata*

Precative or *Benedictive*, 'May I do.'

कृषीय *kṛishíya*	कृषीवहि *kṛishívahi*	कृषीमहि *kṛishímahi*
कृषीष्ठास् *kṛishíshṭhás*	कृषीयास्थाम् *kṛishíyásthám*	कृषीध्वम् *kṛishídhvam*
कृषीष्ट *kṛishíshṭa*	कृषीयास्ताम् *kṛishíyástám*	कृषीरन् *kṛishíran*

Conditional, 'I should do.'

अकरिष्ये *akarishye*	अकरिष्यावहि *akarishyávahi*	अकरिष्यामहि *akarishyámahi*
अकरिष्यथास् *akarishyathás*	अकरिष्येथाम् *akarishyethám*	अकरिष्यध्वम् *akarishyadhvam*
अकरिष्यत *akarishyata*	अकरिष्येताम् *akarishyetám*	अकरिष्यन्त *akarishyanta*

Pass., *Pres.* क्रिये; *Aor. 3rd sing.* अकारि (701). Caus., *Pres.* कारयामि; *Aor.* अचीकरम्. Des. चिकीर्षामि, -षे (502). Freq. चेक्रीये, चर्कर्मि or चरिकर्मि or चरीकर्मि or चर्करीमि or चरिकरीमि or चरीकरीमि (Páṇ. VII. 4, 92). Part., *Pres.* कुर्वत्; Átm. कुर्वाण; *Past Pass.* कृत; *Past Indecl.* कृत्वा, -कृत्य; *Fut. Pass.* कर्तव्य, करणीय, कार्य.

684. Only nine other roots are generally given in this class. Of these the commonest is तन् 'to stretch,' conjugated at 583. The others are, ऋण् 'to go,' क्षण् and क्षिण् 'to kill' or 'to hurt,' घृण् 'to shine,' तृण् 'to eat grass,' मन् 'to imagine,' Átm.; वन् 'to ask,' सन् 'to give.' As these end in nasals, their conjugation resembles that of verbs of cl. 5 at 675; thus—

685. Root क्षण् (special stems क्षणो, क्षणु). *Inf.* क्षणितुम् 'to kill,' 'to hurt.' Par. and Átm. *Pres.* क्षणोमि, क्षणोषि, क्षणोति; क्षणुवस्, &c. Átm. क्षण्वे, क्षणुषे, &c. *Impf.* अक्षणवम्, अक्षणोस्, &c. Átm. अक्षण्वि. *Pot.* क्षणुयाम्. Átm. क्षण्वीय. *Impv.* क्षणवानि. Átm. क्षणवै. *Perf.* चक्षाण, चक्षणिथ, चक्षाण; चक्षणिव, चक्षणथुस्, चक्षणतुस्; चक्षणिम, चक्षण, चक्षणुस्. Átm. चक्षणे, चक्षणिषे, चक्षणे; चक्षणिवहे, चक्षणाथे, चक्षणाते; चक्षणिमहे,

चक्षणिध्वे, चक्षणिरे. 1st *Fut.* क्षणितास्मि. Átm. क्षणिताहे. 2nd *Fut.* क्षणिष्यामि. Átm. क्षणिष्ये. *Aor.* अक्षणिषम्, -णीस्, -णीत्; अक्षणिष्व, -णिष्टम्, -ष्टाम्; अक्षणिष्म, -णिष्ट, -णिषुस्. Átm. अक्षणिषि, अक्षणिष्ठास् or अक्षथास् (424. *c*), अक्षणिष्ट or अक्षत; अक्षणिष्वहि, -णिषाथाम्, -णिषाताम्; अक्षणिष्महि, -णिढ्वम्, -णिषत. *Prec.* क्षण्यासम्. Átm. क्षणिषीय. *Cond.* अक्षणिष्यम्. Átm. अक्षणिष्ये. Pass., *Pres.* क्षण्ये; *Aor. 3rd sing.* अक्षाणि. Caus., *Pres.* क्षाणयामि; *Aor.* अचिक्षणम्. Des. चिक्षणिषामि, -षे. Freq. चंक्षण्ये, चंक्षण्मि. Part., *Pres.* क्षण्वत्; Átm. क्षण्वान; *Past Pass.* क्षत; *Past Indecl.* क्षत्वा or क्षणित्वा, -क्षत्य; *Fut. Pass.* क्षणितव्य, क्षणनीय, क्षाण्य.

EXAMPLES OF PRIMITIVE VERBS OF THE NINTH CLASS, EXPLAINED AT 356.

686. Root यु *yu.* Infin. यवितुम् *yavitum,* 'to join,' 'to mix.'

PARASMAI-PADA. *Present Tense,* 'I join.'

युनामि *yunámi*	युनीवस् *yunívas*	युनीमस् *yunímas*
युनासि *yunási*	युनीथस् *yuníthas*	युनीथ *yunítha*
युनाति *yunáti*	युनीतस् *yunítas*	युनन्ति *yunanti*

Imperfect, 'I was joining,' or 'I joined.'

अयुनाम् *ayunám*	अयुनीव *ayuníva*	अयुनीम *ayuníma*
अयुनास् *ayunás*	अयुनीतम् *ayunítam*	अयुनीत *ayuníta*
अयुनात् *ayunát*	अयुनीताम् *ayunítám*	अयुनन् *ayunan*

Potential, 'I may join.'

युनीयाम् *yuníyám*	युनीयाव *yuníyáva*	युनीयाम *yuníyáma*
युनीयास् *yuníyás*	युनीयातम् *yuníyátam*	युनीयात *yuníyáta*
युनीयात् *yuníyát*	युनीयाताम् *yuníyátám*	युनीयुस् *yuníyus*

Imperative, 'Let me join.'

युनानि *yunáni*	युनाव *yunáva*	युनाम *yunáma*
युनीहि *yuníhi*	युनीतम् *yunítam*	युनीत *yuníta*
युनातु *yunátu*	युनीताम् *yunítám*	युनन्तु *yunantu*

Perf. युयाव, युयविथ or युयोथ, युयाव; युयुविव, युयुवथुस्, -वतुस्; युयुविम, युयुव, युयुवुस्. 1st *Fut.* यवितास्मि or योतास्मि*. 2nd *Fut.* यविष्यामि. *Aor.* अयाविषम्, -वीस्, -वीत्; अयाविष्व, -विष्टम्, -विष्टाम्; अयाविष्म, -विष्ट, -विषुस्. *Prec.* यूयासम्. *Cond.* अयविष्यम्.

---

* Some authorities give योतास्मि &c. as the only form. See Laghu-kaum. 724.

687. Átmane-pada. *Present Tense*, 'I join.'

युने *yune*	युनीवहे *yunívahe*	युनीमहे *yunímahe*
युनीषे *yuníshe*	युनाथे *yunáthe*	युनीध्वे *yunídhve*
युनीते *yuníte*	युनाते *yunáte*	युनते *yunate*

Imperfect, 'I was joining,' or 'I joined.'

अयुनि *ayuni*	अयुनीवहि *ayunívahi*	अयुनीमहि *ayunímahi*
अयुनीथास् *ayuníthás*	अयुनाथाम् *ayunáthám*	अयुनीध्वम् *ayunídhvam*
अयुनीत *ayuníta*	अयुनाताम् *ayunátám*	अयुनत *ayunata*

Potential, 'I may join.'

युनीय *yuníya*	युनीवहि *yunívahi*	युनीमहि *yunímahi*
युनीथास् *yuníthás*	युनीयाथाम् *yuníyáthám*	युनीध्वम् *yunídhvam*
युनीत *yuníta*	युनीयाताम् *yuníyátám*	युनीरन् *yuníran*

Imperative, 'Let me join.'

युनै *yunai*	युनावहै *yunávahai*	युनामहै *yunámahai*
युनीष्व *yuníshva*	युनाथाम् *yunáthám*	युनीध्वम् *yunídhvam*
युनीताम् *yunítám*	युनाताम् *yunátám*	युनताम् *yunatám*

Perf. युयुवे, युयुविषे, युयुवे; युयुविवहे, युयुवाथे, युयुवाते; युयुविमहे, युयुविध्वे or -ढ्वे, युयुविरे. 1st *Fut.* यविताहे. 2nd *Fut.* यविष्ये. *Aor.* अयविषि, -विष्ठास्, -विष्ट; अयविष्वहि, अयविषाथाम्, -षाताम्; अयविष्महि, -विध्वम् or -विढ्वम्, -विषत. *Prec.* यविषीय. *Cond.* अयविष्ये. Pass., *Pres.* यूये; 1st *Fut.* याविताहे; *Aor.* 3rd *sing.* अयावि. Caus., *Pres.* यावयामि; *Aor.* अयीयवम्. Des. युयूषामि or यियविषामि. Freq. योयूये, योयोमि or योयवीमि. Part., *Pres.* युनत्; Átm. युनान; *Past Pass.* युत; *Past Indecl.* युत्वा, -युत्य; *Fut. Pass.* यवितव्य, यवनीय, याव्य or यव्य.

OTHER EXAMPLES OF CL. 9 IN THE ORDER OF THEIR FINAL LETTERS.

688. Root ज्ञा (special stems जाना, जानी, जान्, 361). *Inf.* ज्ञातुम् 'to know.' Par. and Átm. *Pres.* जानामि, जानासि, जानाति; जानीवस्, जानीथस्, जानीतस्; जानीमस्, जानीथ, जानन्ति. Átm. जाने, जानीषे, जानीते; जानीवहे, जानाथे, जानाते; जानीमहे, जानीध्वे, जानते. *Impf.* अजानाम्, अजानास्, अजानात्; अजानीव, अजानीतम्, अजानीताम्; अजानीम, अजानीत, अजानन्. Átm. अजानि, अजानीथास्, अजानीत; अजानीवहि, अजानाथाम्, अजानाताम्; अजानीमहि, अजानीध्वम्, अजानत. *Pot.* जानीयाम्. Átm. जानीय. *Impv.* जानानि, जानीहि, जानातु; जानाव, जानीतम्, जानीताम्; जानाम, जानीत, जानन्तु. Átm. जानै, जानीष्व, जानीताम्; जानावहै, जानाथाम्, जानाताम्; जानामहै, जानीध्वम्, जानताम्. *Perf.* (373) जज्ञौ, जज्ञिथ or जज्ञाथ, जज्ञौ; जज्ञिव, जज्ञथुस्, जज्ञतुस्; जज्ञिम, जज्ञ, जज्ञुस्. Átm. जज्ञे, जज्ञिषे, जज्ञे; जज्ञिवहे, जज्ञाथे, जज्ञाते; जज्ञिमहे, जज्ञिध्वे, जज्ञिरे. 1st *Fut.* ज्ञातास्मि. 2nd *Fut.* ज्ञास्यामि. *Aor.* (433) अज्ञासिषम्, अज्ञासीस्,

अज्ञासीत्; अज्ञासिष्व, अज्ञासिष्टम्, -ष्टाम्; अज्ञासिष्म, -सिष्ट, -सिषुस्. Átm. अज्ञासि, अज्ञास्थास्, अज्ञास्त; अज्ञास्वहि, अज्ञासाथाम्, -साताम्; अज्ञास्महि, अज्ञाध्वम्, अज्ञासत. *Prec.* ज्ञेयासम् or ज्ञायासम्. Átm. ज्ञासीय. *Cond.* अज्ञास्यम्. Átm. अज्ञास्ये. Pass., *Pres.* (465. *a*) ज्ञाये; *Perf.* जज्ञे (473); *1st Fut.* ज्ञाताहे or ज्ञायिताहे (474); *2nd Fut.* ज्ञास्ये or ज्ञायिष्ये; *Aor. 3rd sing.* अज्ञायि. Caus., *Pres.* ज्ञापयामि or ज्ञपयामि; *Aor.* अजिज्ञपम्. Des. जिज्ञासे (-सामि, Epic). Freq. जाज्ञाये, जाज्ञामि or जाज्ञेमि. Part., *Pres.* जानत्; Átm. जानान; *Past Pass.* ज्ञात; *Past Indecl.* ज्ञात्वा, -ज्ञाय; *Fut. Pass.* ज्ञातव्य, ज्ञानीय, ज्ञेय.

689. Root क्री (special stems क्रीणा, क्रीणी, क्रीण्, 358. *a*). *Inf.* क्रेतुम् 'to buy.' Par. and Átm. *Pres.* क्रीणामि, क्रीणासि, क्रीणाति; क्रीणीवस्, क्रीणीथस्, क्रीणीतस्; क्रीणीमस्, क्रीणीथ, क्रीणन्ति. Átm. क्रीणे, क्रीणीषे, क्रीणीते; क्रीणीवहे, क्रीणाथे, क्रीणाते; क्रीणीमहे, क्रीणीध्वे, क्रीणते. *Impf.* अक्रीणाम्, अक्रीणास्, अक्रीणात्; अक्रीणीव, अक्रीणीतम्, अक्रीणीताम्; अक्रीणीम, अक्रीणीत, अक्रीणन्. Átm. अक्रीणि, अक्रीणीथास्, अक्रीणीत; अक्रीणीवहि, अक्रीणाथाम्, अक्रीणाताम्; अक्रीणीमहि, अक्रीणीध्वम्, अक्रीणत. *Pot.* क्रीणीयाम्. Átm. क्रीणीय. *Impv.* क्रीणानि, क्रीणीहि, क्रीणातु; क्रीणाव, क्रीणीतम्, क्रीणीताम्; क्रीणाम, क्रीणीत, क्रीणन्तु. Átm. क्रीणै, क्रीणीष्व, क्रीणीताम्; क्रीणावहै, क्रीणाथाम्, क्रीणाताम्; क्रीणामहै, क्रीणीध्वम्, क्रीणताम्. *Perf.* (374. *e*) चिक्राय, चिक्रयिथ or चिक्रेथ, चिक्राय; चिक्रियिव, चिक्रियथुस्, चिक्रियतुस्; चिक्रियिम, चिक्रिय, चिक्रियुस्. Átm. चिक्रिये, चिक्रियिषे, चिक्रिये; चिक्रियिवहे, चिक्रियाथे, -याते; चिक्रियिमहे, चिक्रियिध्वे or -ढ्वे, चिक्रियिरे. *1st Fut.* क्रेतास्मि. Átm. क्रेताहे. *2nd Fut.* क्रेष्यामि. Átm. क्रेष्ये. *Aor.* अक्रैषम्, -षीस्, -षीत्; अक्रैष्व, -ष्टम्, -ष्टाम्; अक्रैष्म, -ष्ट, -षुस्. Átm. अक्रेषि, -ष्ठास्, -ष्ट; अक्रेष्वहि, -षाथाम्, -षाताम्; अक्रेष्महि, अक्रेढ्वम्, अक्रेषत. *Prec.* क्रीयासम्. Átm. क्रेषीय. *Cond.* अक्रेष्यम्. Átm. अक्रेष्ये. Pass., *Pres.* क्रीये; *Aor. 3rd sing.* अक्रायि. Caus., *Pres.* क्रापयामि; *Aor.* अचिक्रपम्. Des. चिक्रीषामि, -षे. Freq. चेक्रीये, चेक्रेमि or चेक्रयीमि. Part., *Pres.* क्रीणत्; Átm. क्रीणान; *Past Pass.* क्रीत; *Past Indecl.* क्रीत्वा, -क्रीय; *Fut. Pass.* क्रेतव्य, क्रयणीय, क्रेय.

690. Like क्री is प्री 'to please.' *Pres.* प्रीणामि; Átm. प्रीणे. Caus., *Pres.* प्रीणयामि or प्राययामि; *Aor.* अपिप्रणम् or अपिप्रीणम्*. Des. पिप्रीषामि. Freq. पेप्रीये.

691. लू (special stems लुना, लुनी, लुन्, 358), 'to cut,' follows पू, 'to purify,' at 583; thus, *Pres.* लुनामि; Átm. लुने. *Pot.* लुनीयाम्; Átm. लुनीय. *Perf.* लुलाव; Átm. लुलुवे. *1st Fut.* लवितास्मि. *2nd Fut.* लविष्यामि. *Aor.* अलाविषम्.

692. Root बन्ध् (special stems बध्ना, बध्नी, बध्न्). *Inf.* बन्द्धुम् 'to bind.'

---

* Forster gives अपिप्रणम्; Westergaard, अपिप्रीणम्.

Par. *Pres.* बध्नामि, बध्नासि, बध्नाति; बध्नीवस्, बध्नीथस्, बध्नीतस्; बध्नीमस्, बध्नीथ, बध्नन्ति. *Impf.* अबध्नाम्, अबध्नास्, अबध्नात्; अबध्नीव, अबध्नीतम्, -ताम्; अबध्नीम, अबध्नीत, अबध्नन्. *Pot.* बध्नीयाम्. *Impv.* बध्नानि, बधान (357. *a*), बध्नातु; बध्नाव, बध्नीतम्, -ताम्; बध्नाम, बध्नीत, बध्नन्तु. *Perf.* बबन्ध, बबन्धिथ or बबन्द्ध or बबन्ध (298. *a*), बबन्ध; बबन्धिव, बबन्धथुस्, बबन्धतुस्; बबन्धिम, बबन्ध, बबन्धुस्. *1st Fut.* बन्द्धास्मि. *2nd Fut.* भन्त्स्यामि (299. *a*). *Aor.* अभान्त्सम् (299. *a*), अभान्त्सीस्, अभान्त्सीत्; अभान्त्स्व, अबान्द्धम्, अबान्द्धाम्; अभान्त्स्म, अबान्द्ध, अभान्त्सुस्. *Prec.* बध्यासम्. *Cond.* अभन्त्स्यम्. Pass., *Pres.* (469) बध्ये. Caus., *Pres.* बन्धयामि; *Aor.* अबबन्धम्. Des. बिभन्त्सामि (299. *a*). Freq. बाबध्ये, बाबन्धिम, बाबन्धीमि. Part., *Pres.* बध्नत्; *Past Pass.* बद्ध; *Past Indecl.* बद्ध्वा, -बध्य; *Fut. Pass.* बन्द्धव्य, बन्धनीय, बन्ध्य.

693. Root ग्रन्थ् (special stems ग्रथ्ना, ग्रथ्नी, ग्रथ्न्, 360). *Inf.* ग्रन्थितुम् 'to string,' 'to tie.' Par. *Pres.* ग्रथ्नामि, ग्रथ्नासि, ग्रथ्नाति; ग्रथ्नीवस्, ग्रथ्नीथस्, ग्रथ्नीतस्; ग्रथ्नीमस्, ग्रथ्नीथ, ग्रथ्नन्ति. *Impf.* अग्रथ्नाम्, अग्रथ्नास्, अग्रथ्नात्; अग्रथ्नीव, अग्रथ्नीतम्, -ताम्; अग्रथ्नीम, अग्रथ्नीत, अग्रथ्नन्. *Pot.* ग्रथ्नीयाम्. *Impv.* ग्रथ्नानि, ग्रथान (257. *a*), ग्रथ्नातु; ग्रथ्नाव, ग्रथ्नीतम्, -ताम्; ग्रथ्नाम, ग्रथ्नीत, ग्रथ्नन्तु. *Perf.* (375. *h*) जग्रन्थ*, जग्रन्थिथ or ग्रेथिथ, जग्रन्थ*; जग्रन्थिव or ग्रेथिव, जग्रन्थथुस् or ग्रेथथुस्, जग्रन्थतुस् or ग्रेथतुस्; जग्रन्थिम or ग्रेथिम, जग्रन्थ or ग्रेथ, जग्रन्थुस् or ग्रेथुस्. *1st Fut.* ग्रन्थितास्मि. *2nd Fut.* ग्रन्थिष्यामि. *Aor.* अग्रन्थिषम्, -न्थीस्, -न्थीत्, &c. *Prec.* ग्रथ्यासम्. *Cond.* अग्रन्थिष्यम्. Pass., *Pres.* (469) ग्रथ्ये. Caus., *Pres.* ग्रन्थयामि; *Aor.* अजग्रन्थम्. Des. जिग्रन्थिषामि. Freq. जाग्रथ्ये, जंग्रन्थ्मि, जंग्रन्थीमि. Part., *Pres.* ग्रथ्नत्; *Past Pass.* ग्रथित; *Past Indecl.* ग्रथित्वा or ग्रन्थित्वा, -ग्रथ्य; *Fut. Pass.* ग्रन्थितव्य, ग्रन्थनीय, ग्रन्थ्य.

a. Like ग्रन्थ् is conjugated श्रन्थ् 'to loosen,' मन्थ् 'to churn.'

694. Root क्षुभ्† (special stems क्षुभ्ना, क्षुभ्नी, क्षुभ्न्). *Inf.* क्षोभितुम् 'to agitate.' Par. *Pres.* क्षुभ्नामि, क्षुभ्नासि, क्षुभ्नाति; क्षुभ्नीवस्, क्षुभ्नीथस्, क्षुभ्नीतस्; क्षुभ्नीमस्, क्षुभ्नीथ, क्षुभ्नन्ति. *Impf.* अक्षुभ्नाम्, अक्षुभ्नास्, अक्षुभ्नात्; अक्षुभ्नीव, अक्षुभ्नीतम्, -ताम्; अक्षुभ्नीम, अक्षुभ्नीत, अक्षुभ्नन्. *Pot.* क्षुभ्नीयाम्. *Impv.* क्षुभ्नानि, क्षुभाण (357. *a*, 58), क्षुभ्नातु; क्षुभ्नाव, क्षुभ्नीतम्, -ताम्; क्षुभ्नाम, क्षुभ्नीत, क्षुभ्नन्तु. *Perf.* चुक्षोभ, चुक्षोभिथ, चुक्षोभ; चुक्षुभिव, चुक्षुभथुस्, -भतुस्; चुक्षुभिम, चुक्षुभ, चुक्षुभुस्. *1st Fut.* क्षोभितास्मि. *2nd Fut.* क्षोभिष्यामि. *Aor.* अक्षोभिषम्, -भीस्, -भीत्, &c. Or अक्षुभम्, -भस्, -भत्; -भाव, -भतम्, -भताम्; -भाम, -भत, -भन्. *Prec.* क्षुभ्यासम्. *Cond.* अक्षोभिष्यम्. Pass., *Pres.* क्षुभ्ये; *Aor. 3rd sing.* अक्षोभि. Caus., *Pres.* क्षोभयामि; *Aor.* अचुक्षुभम्. Des. चुक्षोभिषामि or चुक्षुभिषामि. Freq.

* Some authorities give the option of जग्राथ in the 1st and 3rd of the Perf. Compare 339.

† Also cl. 4, Intransitive, 'to be agitated;' Pres. क्षुभ्यामि, 612.

चोक्षुभ्ये, चोक्षोभ्मि (*3rd sing.* चोक्षोब्धि). Part., *Pres.* क्षुभ्नत्; *Past Pass.* क्षुब्ध or क्षुभित; *Past Indecl.* क्षुब्ध्वा or क्षुभित्वा, -क्षुभ्य; *Fut. Pass.* क्षोभितव्य, क्षोभणीय (58), क्षोभ्य.

695. Root स्तम्भ्* (special stems स्तभ्ना, स्तभ्नी, स्तभ्न्, 360). *Inf.* स्तम्भितुम् 'to stop,' 'to support.' Par. *Pres.* स्तभ्नामि; like क्षुभ्, 694. *Impf.* अस्तभ्नाम्. *Pot.* स्तभ्नीयाम्. *Impv.* स्तभ्नानि, स्तभान (357. *a*), स्तभ्नातु; स्तभ्नाथ, स्तभ्नीतम्, -ताम्; स्तभ्नाम, स्तभ्नीत, स्तभ्नन्तु. *Perf.* तस्तम्भ, तस्तम्भिथ, तस्तम्भ; तस्तम्भिव, तस्तम्भथुस्, -म्भतुस्; तस्तम्भिम, तस्तम्भ, तस्तम्भुस्. *1st Fut.* स्तम्भितास्मि. *2nd Fut.* स्तम्भिष्यामि. *Aor.* अस्तम्भिषम्, -म्भीस्, -म्भीत्, &c. Or अस्तभम्, -भस्, -भत्; -भाव, -भतम्, -भताम्; -भाम, -भत, -भन्. *Prec.* स्तभ्यासम्. *Cond.* अस्तम्भिष्यम्. Pass., *Pres.* स्तभ्ये. Caus., *Pres.* स्तम्भयामि; *Aor.* अतस्तम्भम्. Des. तिस्तम्भिषामि. Freq. तास्तभ्ये, तास्तम्भ्मि or तास्तम्भीमि. Part., *Pres.* स्तभ्नत्; *Past Pass.* स्तब्ध; *Past Indecl.* स्तब्ध्वा or स्तम्भित्वा; *Fut. Pass.* स्तम्भितव्य, स्तम्भनीय, स्तम्भ्य.

696. Root अश्† (special stems अश्ना, अश्नी, अश्न्). *Inf.* अशितुम् 'to eat.' Par. *Pres.* अश्नामि, अश्नासि, अश्नाति; अश्नीवस्, अश्नीथस्, अश्नीतस्; अश्नीमस्, अश्नीथ, अश्नन्ति. *Impf.* आश्नाम्, आश्नास्, आश्नात्; आश्नीव, आश्नीतम्, -ताम्; आश्नीम, आश्नीत, आश्नन्. *Pot.* अश्नीयाम्. *Impv.* अश्नानि, अशान (357. *a*), अश्नातु; अश्नाथ, अश्नीतम्, -ताम्; अश्नाम, अश्नीत, अश्नन्तु. *Perf.* आश, आशिथ, आश; आशिव, आशथुस्, आशतुस्; आशिम, आश, आशुस्. *1st Fut.* अशितास्मि. *2nd Fut.* अशिष्यामि. *Aor.* आशिषम्, आशीस्, आशीत्; आशिष्व, आशिष्टम्, आशिष्टाम्; आशिष्म, आशिष्ट, आशिषुस्. *Prec.* अश्यासम्. *Cond.* आशिष्यम्. Pass., *Pres.* अश्ये. Caus., *Pres.* आशयामि; *Aor.* आशिशम्. Des. अशिशिषामि. Freq. अशाश्ये (511. *a*). Part., *Pres.* अश्नत्; *Past Pass.* अशित; *Past Indecl.* अशित्वा, -अश्य; *Fut. Pass.* अशितव्य, अशनीय, आश्य.

697. Root क्लिश् (special stems क्लिश्ना, क्लिश्नी, क्लिश्न्). *Inf.* क्लेशितुम् or क्लेष्टुम् 'to harass.' Par. *Pres.* क्लिश्नामि; like अश्, 696. *Impf.* अक्लिश्नाम्, अक्लिश्नास्, अक्लिश्नात्; अक्लिश्नीव, अक्लिश्नीतम्, -ताम्; अक्लिश्नीम, अक्लिश्नीत, अक्लिश्नन्. *Pot.* क्लिश्नीयाम्. *Impv.* क्लिश्नानि, क्लिशान, &c. *Perf.* चिक्लेश, चिक्लेशिथ or चिक्लेष्ठ, चिक्लेश; चिक्लिशिव or चिक्लिश्व (371), चिक्लिशथुस्, -शतुस्; चिक्लिशिम or चिक्लिश्म, चिक्लिश, चिक्लिशुस्. *1st Fut.* क्लेशितास्मि or क्लेष्टास्मि. *2nd Fut.* क्लेशिष्यामि or क्लेक्ष्यामि. *Aor.* अक्लेशिषम्, -शीस्, -शीत्; अक्लेशिष्व, -शिष्टम्, -शिष्टाम्; अक्लेशिष्म, -शिष्ट, -शिषुस्. Or अक्लिक्षम्, -क्षस्, -क्षत्; -क्षाव, -क्षतम्, -क्षताम्; -क्षाम, -क्षत, -क्षन् (439). *Prec.* क्लिश्यासम्. *Cond.* अक्लेशिष्यम् or अक्लेक्ष्यम्. Pass., *Pres.* क्लिश्ये; *Aor. 3rd sing.* अक्लेशि. Caus., *Pres.* क्लेशयामि; *Aor.* अचिक्लिशम्. Des. चिक्लिशिषामि or चिक्लेशिषामि or चिक्लिक्षामि. Freq.

---

* This root also follows cl. 5; thus, Pres. स्तभ्नोमि. See 675.

† This is a different root from अश् cl. 5. See 682.

चेक्लिश्ये, चेक्लेश्मि. Part., *Pres.* क्लिश्नत्; *Past Pass.* क्लिष्ट or क्लिशित; *Past Indecl.* क्लिष्ट्वा or क्लिशित्वा, -क्लिश्य; *Fut. Pass.* क्लेशितव्य or क्लेष्टव्य, क्लेशनीय, क्लेश्य.

698. Root पुष् (special stems पुष्णा, पुष्णी, पुष्ण्). *Inf.* पोषितुम् 'to nourish.' Par. *Pres.* पुष्णामि, पुष्णासि, पुष्णाति; पुष्णीवस्, पुष्णीथस्, पुष्णीतस्; पुष्णीमस्, पुष्णीथ, पुष्णन्ति. *Impf.* अपुष्णाम्, अपुष्णास्, अपुष्णात्; अपुष्णीव, अपुष्णीतम्, -ताम्; अपुष्णीम, अपुष्णीत, अपुष्णन्. *Pot.* पुष्णीयाम्. *Impv.* पुष्णानि, पुषाण (357. *a*), पुष्णातु; पुष्णाव, पुष्णीतम्, -ताम्; पुष्णाम, पुष्णीत, पुष्णन्तु. For the rest, see पुष् cl. 4 at 621.

699. Root ग्रह् (special stems गृह्णा, गृह्णी, गृह्ण्, 359; see 399. *a*). *Inf.* ग्रहीतुम् 'to take.' Par. and Átm. *Pres.* गृह्णामि, गृह्णासि, गृह्णाति; गृह्णीवस्, गृह्णीथस्, गृह्णीतस्; गृह्णीमस्, गृह्णीथ, गृह्णन्ति. Átm. गृह्णे, गृह्णीषे, गृह्णीते; गृह्णीवहे, गृह्णाथे, गृह्णाते; गृह्णीमहे, गृह्णीध्वे, गृह्णते. *Impf.* अगृह्णाम्, अगृह्णास्, अगृह्णात्; अगृह्णीव, अगृह्णीतम्, अगृह्णीताम्; अगृह्णीम, अगृह्णीत, अगृह्णन्. Átm. अगृह्णि, अगृह्णीथास्, अगृह्णीत; अगृह्णीवहि, अगृह्णाथाम्, अगृह्णाताम्; अगृह्णीमहि, अगृह्णीध्वम्, अगृह्णत. *Pot.* गृह्णीयाम्. Átm. गृह्णीय. *Impv.* गृह्णानि, गृहाण, गृह्णातु; गृह्णाव, गृह्णीतम्, गृह्णीताम्; गृह्णाम, गृह्णीत, गृह्णन्तु. Átm. गृह्णै, गृह्णीष्व, गृह्णीताम्; गृह्णावहै, गृह्णाथाम्, गृह्णाताम्; गृह्णामहै, गृह्णीध्वम्, गृह्णताम्. *Perf.* (384) जग्राह, जग्रहिथ, जग्राह; जगृहिव, जगृहथुस्, जगृहतुस्; जगृहिम, जगृह, जगृहुस्. Átm. जगृहे, जगृहिषे, जगृहे; जगृहि-वहे, जगृहाथे, जगृहाते; जगृहिमहे, जगृहिध्वे or -ढ्वे, जगृहिरे. *1st Fut.* ग्रहीतास्मि (399. *a*). Átm. ग्रहीताहे. *2nd Fut.* ग्रहीष्यामि. Átm. ग्रहीष्ये. *Aor.* अग्रहीषम्, अग्रहीस्, अग्रहीत्; अग्रहीष्व, अग्रहीष्टम्, अग्रहीष्टाम्; अग्रहीष्म, अग्रहीष्ट, अग्रहीषुस्. Átm. अग्रहीषि, अग्रहीष्ठास्, अग्रहीष्ट; अग्रहीष्वहि, अग्रहीषाथाम्, अग्रहीषाताम्; अग्रहीष्महि, अग्रहीध्वम्, अग्रहीषत. *Prec.* गृह्यासम्. Átm. ग्रहीषीय. *Cond.* अग्रहीष्यम्. Átm. अग्रहीष्ये. Pass., *Pres.* गृह्ये; *Perf.* जगृहे; *1st Fut.* ग्रहीताहे or ग्राहिताहे; *2nd Fut.* ग्रहीष्ये or ग्राहिष्ये; *Aor. 3rd sing.* अग्राहि, *3rd pl.* अग्रहीषत or अग्राहिषत. Caus., *Pres.* ग्राहयामि; *Aor.* अजिग्रहम्. Des. जिघृक्षामि, -क्षे (503). Freq. जरीगृह्ये, जाग्रह्मि (*3rd sing.* जाग्राढि) or जाग्रहीमि (711). Part., *Pres.* गृह्णत्; Átm. गृह्णान; *Past Pass.* गृहीत; *Past Indecl.* गृहीत्वा, -गृह्य; *Fut. Pass.* ग्रहीतव्य, ग्रहणीय, ग्राह्य.

EXAMPLES OF PASSIVE VERBS, EXPLAINED AT 461.

700. Root दा *dá* (465). Infin. दातुम् *dátum*, 'to be given.'

Present Tense, 'I am given.'

दीये *díye*	दीयावहे *díyávahe*	दीयामहे *díyámahe*
दीयसे *díyase*	दीयेथे *díyethe*	दीयध्वे *díyadhve*
दीयते *díyate*	दीयेते *díyete*	दीयन्ते *díyante*

Imperfect, 'I was given.'

अदीये *adíye*	अदीयावहि *adíyávahi*	अदीयामहि *adíyámahi*
अदीयथास् *adíyathás*	अदीयेथाम् *adíyethám*	अदीयध्वम् *adíyadhvam*
अदीयत *adíyata*	अदीयेताम् *adíyetám*	अदीयन्त *adíyanta*

Potential, 'I may be given.'

दीयेय *díyeya*	दीयेवहि *díyevahi*	दीयेमहि *díyemahi*
दीयेथास् *díyethás*	दीयेयाथाम् *díyeyáthám*	दीयेध्वम् *díyedhvam*
दीयेत *díyeta*	दीयेयाताम् *díyeyátám*	दीयेरन् *díyeran*

Imperative, 'Let me be given.'

दीयै *díyai*	दीयावहै *díyávahai*	दीयामहै *díyámahai*
दीयस्व *díyasva*	दीयेथाम् *díyethám*	दीयध्वम् *díyadhvam*
दीयताम् *díyatám*	दीयेताम् *díyetám*	दीयन्ताम् *díyantám*

Perfect, 'I have been given.'

ददे *dade*	ददिवहे *dadivahe*	ददिमहे *dadimahe*
ददिषे *dadishe*	ददाथे *dadáthe*	ददिध्वे *dadidhve*
ददे *dade*	ददाते *dadáte*	ददिरे *dadire*

First Future, 'I shall be given.'

{ दाताहे *dátáhe* or	दातास्वहे *dátásvahe*	दातास्महे *dátásmahe*, &c.
{ दायिताहे *dáyitáhe*	दायितास्वहे *dáyitásvahe*	दायितास्महे *dáyitásmahe*, &c.

Second Future, 'I shall be given.'

{ दास्ये *dásye* or	दास्यावहे *dásyávahe*	दास्यामहे *dásyámahe*, &c.
{ दायिष्ये *dáyishye*	दायिष्यावहे *dáyishyávahe*	दायिष्यामहे *dáyishyámahe*, &c.

Aorist, 'I was given.'

{ अदिषि *adishi* or	अदिष्वहि *adishvahi*	अदिष्महि *adishmahi*
{ अदायिषि *adáyishi*	अदायिष्वहि *adáyishvahi*	अदायिष्महि *adáyishmahi*
{ अदिथास् *adithás* or	अदिषाथाम् *adisháthám*	अदिढ्वम् *adiḍhvam*
{ अदायिष्ठास् *adáyishṭhás*	अदायिषाथाम् *adáyisháthám*	अदायिध्वम् *adáyidhvam* (-ढ्वम्)
अदायि *adáyi*, 'it was given,' {	अदिषाताम् *adishátám*	अदिषत *adishata*
	अदायिषाताम् *adáyishátám*	अदायिषत *adáyishata*

Prec. दासीय or दायिषीय, &c. *Cond.* अदास्ये or अदायिष्ये.

701. Root कृ *kṛi* (467). Infin. कर्तुम् *kartum*, 'to be made' or 'done.'

Present Tense, 'I am made.'			*Imperfect*, 'I was made.'		
क्रिये	क्रियावहे	क्रियामहे	अक्रिये	अक्रियावहि	अक्रियामहि
क्रियसे	क्रियेथे	क्रियध्वे	अक्रियथास्	अक्रियेथाम्	अक्रियध्वम्
क्रियते	क्रियेते	क्रियन्ते	अक्रियत	अक्रियेताम्	अक्रियन्त

Potential, 'I may be made.'

क्रियेय	क्रियेवहि	क्रियेमहि
क्रियेथास्	क्रियेयाथाम्	क्रियेध्वम्
क्रियेत	क्रियेयाताम्	क्रियेरन्

Perfect.

चक्रे	चकृवहे	चकृमहे
चकृषे	चक्राथे	चकृढ्वे
चक्रे	चक्राते	चक्रिरे

Imperative, 'Let me be made.'

क्रियै	क्रियावहै	क्रियामहै
क्रियस्व	क्रियेथाम्	क्रियध्वम्
क्रियताम्	क्रियेताम्	क्रियन्ताम्

First Future.

कर्ताहे कर्तास्वहे कर्तास्महे, &c.
or कारिताहे कारितास्वहे कारितास्महे, &c.

Second Fut. करिष्ये or कारिष्ये, &c.

Aorist.

SING.	DUAL.	PLURAL.
अकृषि or अकारिषि	अकृष्वहि or अकारिष्वहि	अकृष्महि or अकारिष्महि
अकृथास् or अकारिष्ठास्	अकृषाथाम् or अकारिषाथाम्	अकृढ्वम् or अकारिध्वम् (-ढ्वम्)
अकारि 'it was done'	अकृषाताम् or अकारिषाताम्	अकृषत or अकारिषत

Prec. कृषीय or कारिषीय. *Cond.* अकरिष्ये or अकारिष्ये.

702. Example of a Passive from a root ending in a consonant: Root युज् *yuj*. Infin. योक्तुम् *yoktum*, 'to be fitting.'

Pres. युज्ये, युज्यसे, युज्यते, &c. *Impf.* अयुज्ये, अयुज्यथास्, अयुज्यत, &c. *Pot.* युज्येय. *Impv.* युज्यै, युज्यस्व, युज्यताम्, &c. *Perf.* युयुजे, युयुजिषे, युयुजे, &c. *1st Fut.* योक्ताहे, योक्तासे, योक्ता, &c. *2nd Fut.* योक्ष्ये, योक्ष्यसे, &c. *Aor.* अयुक्षि, अयुक्थास्, अयोजि; अयुक्ष्वहि, &c. *Prec.* युक्षीय. *Cond.* अयोक्ष्ये.

EXAMPLE OF CAUSAL VERBS, EXPLAINED AT 479.

703. Root भू *bhú*. Infin. भावयितुम् *bhávayitum*, 'to cause to be.'

PARASMAI-PADA. ÁTMANE-PADA.

Present Tense, 'I cause to be.'

भावयामि	भावयावस्	भावयामस्	भावये	भावयावहे	भावयामहे
भावयसि	भावयथस्	भावयथ	भावयसे	भावयेथे	भावयध्वे
भावयति	भावयतस्	भावयन्ति	भावयते	भावयेते	भावयन्ते

Imperfect, 'I was causing to be,' or 'I caused,' &c.

अभावयम्	अभावयाव	अभावयाम	अभावये	अभावयावहि	अभावयामहि
अभावयस्	अभावयतम्	अभावयत	अभावयथास्	अभावयेथाम्	अभावयध्वम्
अभावयत्	अभावयताम्	अभावयन्	अभावयत	अभावयेताम्	अभावयन्त

Potential, 'I may cause to be.'

भावयेयम्	भावयेव	भावयेम	भावयेय	भावयेवहि	भावयेमहि
भावयेस्	भावयेतम्	भावयेत	भावयेथास्	भावयेयाथाम्	भावयेध्वम्
भावयेत्	भावयेताम्	भावयेयुस्	भावयेत	भावयेयाताम्	भावयेरन्

Imperative, 'Let me cause to be.'

भावयानि	भावयाव	भावयाम	भावयै	भावयावहै	भावयामहै
भावय	भावयतम्	भावयत	भावयस्व	भावयेथाम्	भावयध्वम्
भावयतु	भावयताम्	भावयन्तु	भावयताम्	भावयेताम्	भावयन्ताम्

Perfect, 'I caused to be.'

भावयाञ्चकार	भावयाञ्चकृव	भावयाञ्चकृम	भावयाञ्चक्रे	भावयाञ्चकृवहे	भावयाञ्चकृमहे
भावयाञ्चकर्थ	भावयाञ्चक्रथुस्	भावयाञ्चक्र	भावयाञ्चकृषे	भावयाञ्चक्राथे	भावयाञ्चकृढ्वे
भावयाञ्चकार	भावयाञ्चक्रतुस्	भावयाञ्चक्रुस्	भावयाञ्चक्रे	भावयाञ्चक्राते	भावयाञ्चक्रिरे

First Future, 'I will cause to be.'

भावयितास्मि	भावयितास्वस्	भावयितास्मस्	भावयिताहे	भावयितास्वहे	भावयितास्महे
भावयितासि	भावयितास्थस्	भावयितास्थ	भावयितासे	भावयितासाथे	भावयिताध्वे
भावयिता	भावयितारौ	भावयितारस्	भावयिता	भावयितारौ	भावयितारस्

Second Future, 'I shall or will cause to be.'

भावयिष्यामि	भावयिष्यावस्	भावयिष्यामस्	भावयिष्ये	भावयिष्यावहे	भावयिष्यामहे
भावयिष्यसि	भावयिष्यथस्	भावयिष्यथ	भावयिष्यसे	भावयिष्येथे	भावयिष्यध्वे
भावयिष्यति	भावयिष्यतस्	भावयिष्यन्ति	भावयिष्यते	भावयिष्येते	भावयिष्यन्ते

Aorist, 'I caused to be.'

अबीभवम्	अबीभवाव	अबीभवाम	अबीभवे	अबीभवावहि	अबीभवामहि
अबीभवस्	अबीभवतम्	अबीभवत	अबीभवथास्	अबीभवेथाम्	अबीभवध्वम्
अबीभवत्	अबीभवताम्	अबीभवन्	अबीभवत	अबीभवेताम्	अबीभवन्त

Precative or *Benedictive*, 'May I cause to be.'

भाव्यासम्	भाव्यास्व	भाव्यास्म	भावयिषीय	भावयिषीवहि	भावयिषीमहि
भाव्यास्	भाव्यास्तम्	भाव्यास्त	भावयिषीष्ठास्	भावयिषीयास्थाम्	भावयिषीध्वम्
भाव्यात्	भाव्यास्ताम्	भाव्यासुस्	भावयिषीष्ट	भावयिषीयास्ताम्	भावयिषीरन्

Conditional, 'I should cause to be.'

अभावयिष्यम्	अभावयिष्याव	अभावयिष्याम	अभावयिष्ये	अभावयिष्यावहि	अभावयिष्यामहि
अभावयिष्यस्	अभावयिष्यतम्	अभावयिष्यत	अभावयिष्यथास्	अभावयिष्येथाम्	अभावयिष्यध्वम्
अभावयिष्यत्	अभावयिष्यताम्	अभावयिष्यन्	अभावयिष्यत	अभावयिष्येताम्	अभावयिष्यन्त

704. After this model, and after the model of Primitive verbs of cl. 10 at 638, may be conjugated all Causal verbs.

EXAMPLES OF DESIDERATIVE VERBS, EXPLAINED AT 498.

705. Root भू *bhú*. Infin. बुभूषितुम् *bubhúshitum*, 'to wish to be.'

PARASMAI-PADA. ÁTMANE-PADA.

Present Tense, 'I wish to be.'

बुभूषामि	बुभूषावस्	बुभूषामस्	बुभूषे	बुभूषावहे	बुभूषामहे
बुभूषसि	बुभूषथस्	बुभूषथ	बुभूषसे	बुभूषेथे	बुभूषध्वे
बुभूषति	बुभूषतस्	बुभूषन्ति	बुभूषते	बुभूषेते	बुभूषन्ते

Imperfect, 'I was wishing to be,' or 'I wished,' &c.

अबुभूषम्	अबुभूषाव	अबुभूषाम	अबुभूषे	अबुभूषावहि	अबुभूषामहि
अबुभूषस्	अबुभूषतम्	अबुभूषत	अबुभूषथास्	अबुभूषेथाम्	अबुभूषध्वम्
अबुभूषत्	अबुभूषताम्	अबुभूषन्	अबुभूषत	अबुभूषेताम्	अबुभूषन्त

Potential, 'I may wish to be.'

बुभूषेयम्	बुभूषेव	बुभूषेम	बुभूषेय	बुभूषेवहि	बुभूषेमहि
बुभूषेस्	बुभूषेतम्	बुभूषेत	बुभूषेथास्	बुभूषेयाथाम्	बुभूषेध्वम्
बुभूषेत्	बुभूषेताम्	बुभूषेयुस्	बुभूषेत	बुभूषेयाताम्	बुभूषेरन्

Imperative, 'Let me wish to be.'

बुभूषाणि	बुभूषाव	बुभूषाम	बुभूषै	बुभूषावहै	बुभूषामहै
बुभूष	बुभूषतम्	बुभूषत	बुभूषस्व	बुभूषेथाम्	बुभूषध्वम्
बुभूषतु	बुभूषताम्	बुभूषन्तु	बुभूषताम्	बुभूषेताम्	बुभूषन्ताम्

Perfect, 'I wished to be.'

बुभूषाञ्चकार*	बुभूषाञ्चकृव	बुभूषाञ्चकृम	बुभूषाञ्चक्रे	बुभूषाञ्चकृवहे	बुभूषाञ्चकृमहे
बुभूषाञ्चकर्थ	बुभूषाञ्चक्रथुस्	बुभूषाञ्चक्र	बुभूषाञ्चकृषे	बुभूषाञ्चक्राथे	बुभूषाञ्चकृढ्वे
बुभूषाञ्चकार	बुभूषाञ्चक्रतुस्	बुभूषाञ्चक्रुस्	बुभूषाञ्चक्रे	बुभूषाञ्चक्राते	बुभूषाञ्चक्रिरे

First Future, 'I will wish to be.'

बुभूषितास्मि	बुभूषितास्वस्	बुभूषितास्मस्	बुभूषिताहे	बुभूषितास्वहे	बुभूषितास्महे
बुभूषितासि	बुभूषितास्थस्	बुभूषितास्थ	बुभूषितासे	बुभूषितासाथे	बुभूषिताध्वे
बुभूषिता	बुभूषितारौ	बुभूषितारस्	बुभूषिता	बुभूषितारौ	बुभूषितारस्

Second Future, 'I will or shall wish to be.'

बुभूषिष्यामि	बुभूषिष्यावस्	बुभूषिष्यामस्	बुभूषिष्ये	बुभूषिष्यावहे	बुभूषिष्यामहे
बुभूषिष्यसि	बुभूषिष्यथस्	बुभूषिष्यथ	बुभूषिष्यसे	बुभूषिष्येथे	बुभूषिष्यध्वे
बुभूषिष्यति	बुभूषिष्यतस्	बुभूषिष्यन्ति	बुभूषिष्यते	बुभूषिष्येते	बुभूषिष्यन्ते

Aorist, 'I wished to be.'

अबुभूषिषम्	अबुभूषिष्व	अबुभूषिष्म	अबुभूषिषि	अबुभूषिष्वहि	अबुभूषिष्महि
अबुभूषीस्	अबुभूषिष्टम्	अबुभूषिष्ट	अबुभूषिष्ठास्	अबुभूषिषाथाम्	अबुभूषिढ्वम्
अबुभूषीत्	अबुभूषिष्टाम्	अबुभूषिषुस्	अबुभूषिष्ट	अबुभूषिषाताम्	अबुभूषिषत

Precative or Benedictive, 'May I wish to be.'

बुभूष्यासम्	बुभूष्यास्व	बुभूष्यास्म	बुभूषिषीय	बुभूषिषीवहि	बुभूषिषीमहि
बुभूष्यास्	बुभूष्यास्तम्	बुभूष्यास्त	बुभूषिषीष्ठास्	बुभूषिषीयास्थाम्	बुभूषिषीध्वम्
बुभूष्यात्	बुभूष्यास्ताम्	बुभूष्यासुस्	बुभूषिषीष्ट	बुभूषिषीयास्ताम्	बुभूषिषीरन्

Conditional, 'I should wish to be.'

अबुभूषिष्यम्	अबुभूषिष्याव	अबुभूषिष्याम	अबुभूषिष्ये	अबुभूषिष्यावहि	अबुभूषिष्यामहि
अबुभूषिष्यस्	अबुभूषिष्यतम्	अबुभूषिष्यत	अबुभूषिष्यथास्	अबुभूषिष्येथाम्	अबुभूषिष्यध्वम्
अबुभूषिष्यत्	अबुभूषिष्यताम्	अबुभूषिष्यन्	अबुभूषिष्यत	अबुभूषिष्येताम्	अबुभूषिष्यन्त

* Or बुभूषाञ्चकर.

EXAMPLES OF FREQUENTATIVE OR INTENSIVE VERBS, EXPLAINED AT 507.

706. Root भू *bhú.* Infin. बोभूयितुम् *bobhúyitum,* 'to be repeatedly.'

ĀTMANE-PADA FORM (509).

Present Tense, 'I am repeatedly.'

बोभूये	बोभूयावहे	बोभूयामहे
बोभूयसे	बोभूयेथे	बोभूयध्वे
बोभूयते	बोभूयेते	बोभूयन्ते

Imperfect, 'I was frequently.'

अबोभूये	अबोभूयावहि	अबोभूयामहि
अबोभूयथास्	अबोभूयेथाम्	अबोभूयध्वम्
अबोभूयत	अबोभूयेताम्	अबोभूयन्त

Potential, 'I may be frequently.'

बोभूयेय	बोभूयेवहि	बोभूयेमहि
बोभूयेथास्	बोभूयेयाथाम्	बोभूयेध्वम्
बोभूयेत	बोभूयेयाताम्	बोभूयेरन्

Imperative, 'Let me be frequently.'

बोभूयै	बोभूयावहै	बोभूयामहै
बोभूयस्व	बोभूयेथाम्	बोभूयध्वम्
बोभूयताम्	बोभूयेताम्	बोभूयन्ताम्

Perfect, 'I was frequently.'

बोभूयाञ्चक्रे	बोभूयाञ्चकृवहे	बोभूयाञ्चकृमहे
बोभूयाञ्चकृषे	बोभूयाञ्चक्राथे	बोभूयाञ्चकृढ्वे
बोभूयाञ्चक्रे	बोभूयाञ्चक्राते	बोभूयाञ्चक्रिरे

First Future, 'I will be frequently.'

बोभूयिताहे	बोभूयितास्वहे	बोभूयितास्महे
बोभूयितासे	बोभूयितासाथे	बोभूयिताध्वे
बोभूयिता	बोभूयितारौ	बोभूयितारस्

Second Future, 'I will or shall be frequently.'

बोभूयिष्ये	बोभूयिष्यावहे	बोभूयिष्यामहे
बोभूयिष्यसे	बोभूयिष्येथे	बोभूयिष्यध्वे
बोभूयिष्यते	बोभूयिष्येते	बोभूयिष्यन्ते

Aorist, 'I was frequently.'

अबोभूयिषि	अबोभूयिष्वहि	अबोभूयिष्महि
अबोभूयिष्ठास्	अबोभूयिषाथाम्	अबोभूयिध्वम् or -ढ्वम्
अबोभूयिष्ट	अबोभूयिषाताम्	अबोभूयिषत

Precative or *Benedictive*, 'May I be frequently.'

बोभूयिषीय	बोभूयिषीवहि	बोभूयिषीमहि
बोभूयिषीष्ठास्	बोभूयिषीयास्थाम्	बोभूयिषीध्वम् or -ढ्वम्
बोभूयिषीष्ट	बोभूयिषीयास्ताम्	बोभूयिषीरन्

Conditional, 'I should be frequently.'

अबोभूयिष्ये	अबोभूयिष्यावहि	अबोभूयिष्यामहि
अबोभूयिष्यथास्	अबोभूयिष्येथाम्	अबोभूयिष्यध्वम्
अबोभूयिष्यत	अबोभूयिष्येताम्	अबोभूयिष्यन्त

707. PARASMAI-PADA FORM (514).

Present Tense, 'I am frequently.'

बोभवीमि or बोभोमि	बोभूवस्	बोभूमस्
बोभवीषि or बोभोषि	बोभूथस्	बोभूथ
बोभवीति or बोभोति	बोभूतस्	बोभुवति

Imperfect, 'I was frequently.'

अबोभवम्	अबोभूव	अबोभूम
अबोभवीस् or अबोभोस्	अबोभूतम्	अबोभूत
अबोभवीत् or अबोभोत्	अबोभूताम्	अबोभवुस्

Potential, 'I may be frequently.'

बोभूयाम्	बोभूयाव	बोभूयाम
बोभूयास्	बोभूयातम्	बोभूयात
बोभूयात्	बोभूयाताम्	बोभूयुस्

Imperative, 'May I be frequently.'

बोभवानि	बोभवाव	बोभवाम
बोभूहि	बोभूतम्	बोभूत
बोभवीतु or बोभोतु	बोभूताम्	बोभुवतु

Perfect, 'I was frequently.'

बोभुवाम्बभूव, &c.	बोभुवाम्बभूविव, &c.	बोभुवाम्बभूविम, &c.
or	or	or
बोभाव or बोभूव	बोभुविव or बोभूविव	बोभुविम or बोभूविम
बोभूविथ	बोभुवथुस् or बोभूवथुस्	बोभुव or बोभूव
बोभाव or बोभूव	बोभुवतुस् or बोभूवतुस्	बोभुवुस् or बोभूवुस्

First Future, 'I will be frequently.'

बोभवितास्मि	बोभवितास्वस्	बोभवितास्मस्
बोभवितासि	बोभवितास्थस्	बोभवितास्थ
बोभविता	बोभवितारौ	बोभवितारस्

Second Future, 'I will or shall be frequently.'

बोभविष्यामि	बोभविष्यावस्	बोभविष्यामस्
बोभविष्यसि	बोभविष्यथस्	बोभविष्यथ
बोभविष्यति	बोभविष्यतस्	बोभविष्यन्ति

Aorist, 'I was frequently.'

अबोभूवम्	अबोभूव	अबोभूम
अबोभूस्	अबोभूतम्	अबोभूत
अबोभूत्	अबोभूताम्	अबोभूवन्
or	or	or
अबोभाविषम्	अबोभाविष्व	अबोभाविष्म
अबोभावीस्	अबोभाविष्टम्	अबोभाविष्ट
अबोभावीत्	अबोभाविष्टाम्	अबोभाविषुस्

Precative or *Benedictive*, 'May I be frequently.'

बोभूयासम्	बोभूयास्व	बोभूयास्म
बोभूयास्	बोभूयास्तम्	बोभूयास्त
बोभूयात्	बोभूयास्ताम्	बोभूयासुस्

Conditional, 'I should be frequently.'

अबोभविष्यम्	अबोभविष्याव	अबोभविष्याम
अबोभविष्यस्	अबोभविष्यतम्	अबोभविष्यत
अबोभविष्यत्	अबोभविष्यताम्	अबोभविष्यन्

708. Root हन् 'to kill' (323, 654). Parasmai form of Frequentative, 'to kill repeatedly.' *Pres.* जङ्घन्मि or जङ्घनीमि, जङ्घंसि or जङ्घनीषि, जङ्घन्ति or जङ्घनीति; जङ्घन्वस्, जङ्घथस्, जङ्घतस्; जङ्घन्मस्, जङ्घथ, जङ्घनति or जंघ्नति. *Impf.* अजङ्घनम्, अजङ्घन् or अजङ्घनीस्, अजङ्घन् or अजङ्घनीत्; अजङ्घन्व, अजङ्घतम्, -ताम्; अजङ्घन्म, अजङ्घत, अजङ्घनुस् or अजंघ्नुस्. *Pot.* जङ्घन्याम्. *Impv.* जङ्घनानि, जंघहि, जङ्घन्तु or जङ्घनीतु; जङ्घनाव, जङ्घतम्, -ताम्; जङ्घनाम, जङ्घत, जङ्घनतु or जंघ्नतु. *Perf.* जङ्घनाम्बभूव or जङ्घनाञ्चकार, &c. &c.

709. Root गम् 'to go' (602, 270). Parasmai form of Frequentative, 'to go frequently.' *Pres.* जङ्गन्मि or जङ्गमीमि, जङ्गंसि or जङ्गमीषि, जङ्गन्ति or जङ्गमीति; जङ्गन्वस्, जङ्गथस्, जङ्गतस्; जङ्गन्मस्, जङ्गथ, जङ्गमति or जंग्मति. *Impf.* अजङ्गमम्, अजङ्गन् or अजङ्गमीस्, अजङ्गन् or अजङ्गमीत्; अजङ्गन्व, अजङ्गतम्, -ताम्; अजङ्गन्म, अजङ्गत, अजङ्गमुस् or अजंग्मुस्. *Pot.* जङ्गम्याम्. *Impv.* जङ्गमानि, जङ्गहि, जङ्गन्तु or जङ्गमीतु; जङ्गमाव, जङ्गतम्, जङ्गताम्; जङ्गमाम, जङ्गत, जङ्गमतु or जंग्मतु. *Perf.* जङ्गमाम्बभूव or जङ्गमाञ्चकार, &c. &c.

710. Root क्षिप् 'to throw' (635). Parasmai form of Frequentative. *Pres.* चेक्षेप्मि or चेक्षिपीमि, चेक्षेप्सि or चेक्षिपीषि, चेक्षेप्ति or चेक्षिपीति; चेक्षिप्वस्, चेक्षिप्थस्, चेक्षिप्तस्; चेक्षिप्मस्, चेक्षिप्थ, चेक्षिपति. *Impf.* अचेक्षेपम्,

अचेक्षेप् or अचेक्षिपीस्, अचेक्षेप् or अचेक्षिपीत्; अचेक्षिप्व, अचेक्षिप्तम्, -प्ताम्; अचेक्षिप्म, अचेक्षिप्त, अचेक्षिपुस्. *Pot.* चेक्षिप्याम्, &c. *Impv.* चेक्षेपाणि, चेक्षिप्धि, चेक्षेप्तु or चेक्षिपीतु; चेक्षेपाव, चेक्षिप्तम्, -प्ताम्; चेक्षेपाम, चेक्षिप्त, चेक्षिपतु. *Perf.* चेक्षिपाम्बभूव or चेक्षिपाञ्चकार, &c. &c.

711. Root ग्रह् 'to take' (699, 359). Parasmai form of Frequentative. *Pres.* जाग्रह्मि or जाग्रहीमि, जाघक्षि (306. *a*) or जाग्रहीषि, जाग्राढि (305. *a*) or जाग्रहीति; जागृह्वस्, जागृढस्, जागृढस्; जागृह्मस्, जागृढ, जागृहति. *Impf.* अजाग्रहम्, अजाघट् (306. *e*) or अजाग्रहीस्, अजाघद् or अजाग्रहीत्; अजागृह्व, अजागृढम्, -ढाम्; अजागृह्म, अजागृढ, अजागर्हुस् (331. Obs.) *Pot.* जागृह्याम्. *Impv.* जाग्रहाणि, जागृढि, जाग्राढु or जाग्रहीतु; जाग्रहाव, जागृढम्, -ढाम्; जाग्रहाम, जागृढ, जागृहतु, &c. &c.

CHAPTER VII.

INDECLINABLE WORDS.

712. There are in Sanskṛit a number of words used as nouns having only one inflexion, which may be classed among *indeclinables;* e. g. अस्तम् 'setting,' 'decline;' अस्ति 'what exists,' 'existence;' ओम् 'the sacred syllable *Om;*' अनस् 'satisfaction,' 'food;' नमस् 'reverence;' नास्ति 'non-existence;' बदि or वदि 'the fortnight of the moon's wane;' भुवर् 'sky;' भूर् 'earth;' शम् 'ease;' संवत् 'a year;' सुदि or शुदि 'the fortnight of the moon's increase;' स्वधा an exclamation used on making oblations to the spirits of the dead; स्वर् 'heaven;' स्वस्ति 'salutation' (see Gaṇa *Svarádi* to Páṇ. I. I, 37). Others will be mentioned at 713–717.

ADVERBS.

a. Adverbs (*nipáta*), like nouns and verbs, may be divided into simple and compound. The latter are treated of in the next Chapter on Compound Words. Simple adverbs may be classified under four heads: 1st, those formed from the cases of nouns and obsolete words; 2ndly, other adverbs of less obvious derivation; 3rdly, adverbial suffixes; 4thly, adverbial prefixes.

Formed from the Cases of Nouns and Obsolete Words.

713. The Accusative neuter of many adjectives;

As, सत्यम् 'truly;' बहु 'much;' शीघ्रम्, क्षिप्रम्, 'quickly;' युक्तम् 'fitly;' समीपम्

'near;' ध्रुवम् 'certainly;' लघु 'lightly;' निर्भरम्, अत्यन्तम्, गाढम्, भृशम्, 'exceedingly;' अवश्यम् 'certainly;' नित्यम् 'constantly;' चिरम् 'for a long while;' बलवत् 'strongly;' भूयस् 'again,' 'repeatedly' (194); केवलम् 'only,' 'merely;' बाढम् 'very well.'

a. The Acc. neuter of certain pronouns; as, तत् 'therefore,' 'then;' यत् 'wherefore,' 'when,' 'since;' तावत् 'so long,' 'so soon;' यावत् 'as long as,' 'as soon as;' किम् 'why?'

b. The Acc. neuter of certain substantives and obsolete words; as, रहस् 'secretly;' कामम् 'willingly;' स्वयम् 'of one's own accord,' 'of one's self,' 'spontaneously;' नाम 'by name,' 'that is to say;' वारं वारम् 'repeatedly;' चिरम् 'long ago;' सुखम् 'pleasantly;' साम्प्रतम् 'now;' नक्तम् 'by night' (*noctu*); सायम् 'in the evening' (this last may be an ind. part. of *so*, 'to finish').

714. The Instrumental of nouns, pronouns, and obsolete words;

As, धर्मेण 'virtuously;' दक्षिणेन 'to the right,' 'southwards;' उत्तरेण 'northwards;' व्यतिरेकेण 'without;' उच्चैस् 'above,' 'aloud;' नीचैस् 'below;' शनैस् or शनकैस् 'slowly;' तेन 'therefore;' येन 'wherefore;' अन्तरा or अन्तरेण 'without,' 'except;' क्षणेन 'instantly;' चिरेण 'for a long time;' अचिरेण 'in a short time;' अशेषेण 'entirely;' दिवा 'by day;' दिष्ट्या 'fortunately;' सहसा, अञ्जसा, 'quickly;' अधुना 'now;' विहायसा 'in the air;' पुरा 'formerly;' क्षमा 'on the ground' (χαμαί).

a. The Dative case more rarely;

As, चिराय 'for a long time;' चिररात्राय 'for a period of many nights;' अर्थाय 'for the sake of.'

715. The Ablative case of nouns, pronouns, and obsolete words;

As, बलात् 'forcibly;' हर्षात् 'joyfully;' दूरात् 'at a distance;' तस्मात् 'therefore;' कस्मात् 'wherefore?' अकस्मात् 'without cause,' 'unexpectedly;' उत्तरात् 'from the north;' चिरात् 'for a long time;' पश्चात् 'afterwards;' तत्क्षणात् 'at that instant;' समन्तात् 'from all quarters.'

716. The Locative case of nouns and obsolete words;

As, रात्रौ 'at night;' दूरे 'far off;' प्रभाते 'in the morning;' प्राह्णे 'in the forenoon;' स्थाने 'suitably;' अग्रे 'in front;' एकपदे 'at once;' सपदि 'instantly;' ऋते 'except;' अन्तरे 'within;' दक्षिणे 'towards the south;' समीपे or अभ्यासे 'near;' एकान्ते 'in private;' सायाह्ने 'in the evening;' हेतौ 'by reason of.'

Other Adverbs and Particles of less obvious Derivation.

717. Of *affirmation.*—नूनम्, खलु, किल, एव, अङ्ग, 'indeed;' अथकिम् 'certainly.'

a. Of *negation.*—न, नो, नहि, 'not.' मा, मा स्म are prohibitive; as, मा कुरु, मा कार्षीस्, 'do not.' See 889.

b. Of *interrogation.*—किम्, किमु, कच्चित्, नु, ननु, किमु, किमुत, 'whether?'

c. Of *comparison.*—इव 'like;' एव, एवम्, 'so;' किम्पुनर् 'how much rather;' तथैव (तथा + एव) 'in like manner.'

d. Of *quantity.*—अतीव 'exceedingly;' ईषत् 'a little' (cf. 726. *b*).

e. Of *manner.*—इति, एवम्, 'so,' 'thus;' पुनर् 'again;' प्रायस् 'for the most part;' नाना 'variously;' पृथक् 'separately;' मृषा, मिथ्या, 'falsely;' वृथा, मुधा, 'in vain;' अलम् 'enough;' झटिति, आशु (cf. ὠκύς), 'quickly;' तूष्णीम् 'silently;' मिथस् 'reciprocally,' 'together.'

f. Of *time.*—अद्य 'to-day,' 'now;' श्वस् 'to-morrow;' ह्यस् 'yesterday;' परश्वस् 'the day after to-morrow;' सम्प्रति 'now;' पुरा 'formerly;' पुरस्, पुरस्तात्, प्राक्, 'before;' युगपद् 'at once;' सद्यस् 'instantly;' प्रेत्य 'after death' (lit. 'having departed'); परम् 'afterwards;' जातु 'ever;' न जातु 'never;' अन्येद्युस्, परेद्युस्, 'another day,' 'next day;' सकृत् 'once;' असकृत्, पुनर्, मुहुस्, 'again and again,' 'repeatedly.'

Obs.—स्म is used with a Present tense to denote past time. See 251. *b*, 878.

g. Of *place.*—इह 'here;' क्व 'where?' बहिस् 'without.'

h. Of *doubt.*—स्विद्, किंस्विद्, अपिनाम, उत, उताहो, उताहो स्विद्, आहो स्विद्, 'perhaps,' &c.

i. अपि 'even,' एव 'indeed,' ह 'just,' are placed after words to modify their sense, or for emphatic affirmation. इद्, ईम्, घ are similarly used in the Veda.

Observe—Some of the above are properly conjunctions; see 727.

Adverbial Suffixes.

718. चिद् *ćid*, अपि *api*, and चन *ćana* may form *indefinite* adverbs of *time* and *place*, when affixed to interrogative adverbs;

As, from कदा 'when?' कदाचिद्, कदापि, and कदाचन, 'sometimes;' from कुत्र and क्व 'where?' कुत्रचिद्, कुत्रापि, क्वचिद्, क्वापि, 'somewhere;' from कुतस् 'whence?' कुतश्चिद् and कुतश्चन 'from somewhere;' from कति 'how many?' कतिचिद् 'a few;' from कर्हि 'when?' कर्हिचिद् 'at some time;' from कथम् 'how?' कथमपि, कथञ्चन, 'somehow or other,' 'with some difficulty.' Compare 228, 230.

a. अपि following a word, generally signifies 'even,' but after numerals, 'all,' as त्रयोऽपि 'all three;' सर्वेऽपि 'all together.'

719. तस् *tas* may be added to the stem of any noun, and to some pronouns, to form adverbs;

As, from यत्न, यत्नतस् 'with effort;' from आदि, आदितस् 'from the beginning;' from त (the proper stem of the pronoun तद्), ततस् 'thence,' 'then,' 'thereupon,' 'therefore:' similarly, यतस् 'whence,' 'since,' 'because;' अतस्, इतस्, अमुतस्, 'hence,' 'hereupon.'

Obs.—In affixing *tas* to pronouns, the stem त is used for तद्, अ for एतद्, इ for इदम्, अमु for अदस्, य for यद्, कु for किम्.

a. This suffix usually gives the sense of the preposition 'from,' and is often equivalent to the ablative case; as in मत्तस् 'from me;' त्वत्तस् 'from thee*;' पितृतस् 'from a father;' शत्रुतस् 'from an enemy.'

b. But it is sometimes vaguely employed to express other relations; as, पृष्ठतस् 'behind the back;' अन्यतस् 'to another place,' 'elsewhere;' प्रथमतस् 'in the first place;' इतस्ततस् 'here and there,' 'hither and thither;' समन्ततस् 'on all sides;' समीपतस् 'in the neighbourhood;' पुरतस्, अग्रतस्, 'in front;' अभितस् 'near to;' विभवतस् 'in pomp or state.'

c. तात् is a suffix which generally denotes 'place' or 'direction;' as, from अधस्, अधस्तात् 'downwards;' from उपरि (which becomes उपरिस्), उपरिष्टात् 'above' (cf. 84. V).

720. त्र *tra*, forming adverbs of *place* with a locative sense from stems of pronouns, adjectives, &c.;

As, अत्र 'here;' तत्र 'there;' कुत्र 'where?' यत्र 'where;' सर्वत्र 'everywhere;' अन्यत्र 'in another place;' एकत्र 'in one place;' बहुत्र 'in many places;' अमुत्र 'there,' 'in the next world.'

a. त्रा *trá;* as, देवत्रा 'among the gods;' मनुष्यत्रा 'among men' (Páṇ. v. 4, 56); बहुत्रा 'amongst many.'

721. था *thá* and थम् *tham*, forming adverbs of *manner;*

As, तथा 'so,' 'in like manner;' यथा 'as;' सर्वथा 'in every way,' 'by all means;' अन्यथा 'otherwise;' कथम् 'how?' इत्थम् 'thus.'

722. दा *dá*, र्हि *rhi*, नीम् *ním*, forming adverbs of *time* from pronouns, &c.;

As, तदा 'then;' यदा 'when;' कदा 'when?' एकदा 'once;' नित्यदा 'constantly;' सर्वदा, सदा, 'always;' तर्हि, तदानीम्, 'then;' इदानीम् 'now.'

723. धा *dhá*, forming adverbs of *distribution* from numerals;

As, एकधा 'in one way;' द्विधा 'in two ways;' षोधा 'in six ways;' शतधा 'in a hundred ways;' सहस्रधा 'in a thousand ways;' बहुधा or अनेकधा 'in many ways.'

a. कृत्वस्, signifying 'times,' is added to पञ्च, 'five,' and other numerals, as explained at 215. सकृत्, 'once,' may be a corruption of सकृत्वस् ('this time'); and only स् is added to द्वि, त्रि, and dropped after चतुर् 'four times.'

724. वत् *vat* (technically called *vati*) may be added to any nominal stem to form adverbs of *comparison* or *similitude* (see 922);

As, from सूर्य, सूर्यवत् 'like the sun;' from पूर्व, पूर्ववत् 'as before.' It may be used in connexion with a word in the Accusative case.

a. This suffix often expresses 'according to;' as, विधिवत् 'according to rule;' प्रयोजनवत् 'according to need.' It may also be added to adverbs; as, यथावत् 'truly' (exactly as it took place).

---

* These are the forms generally used for the Ablative case of the personal pronouns, the proper Ablative cases मत्, त्वत् being rarely used.

725. शस् *śas*, forming adverbs of *quantity*, &c.;

As, बहुशस् 'abundantly;' अल्पशस् 'in small quantities;' सर्वशस् 'wholly;' एकशस् 'singly;' शतसहस्रशस् 'by hundreds and thousands;' क्रमशस् 'by degrees;' मुख्यशस् 'principally;' पादशस् 'foot by foot;' द्विशस् 'two by two;' त्रिशस् 'by threes;' अनेकशस् 'in great numbers;' अक्षरशस् 'syllable by syllable;' तावच्छस् 'in so many ways;' कतिशस् 'how many at a time?'

a. सात् is added to nouns in connexion with the roots कृ, अस्, and भू, to denote a complete change *to* the condition of the thing signified by the noun; as, अग्नि-सात् 'to the state of fire.' See 789, and cf. 70. *i.*

Adverbial Prefixes.

726. अ *a*, prefixed to nouns and even to participles with a privative or negative force, corresponding to the Greek α, the Latin *in*, and the English *in*, *im*, *un*; as, from शक्य 'possible,' अशक्य 'impossible;' from स्पृशत् 'touching' (pres. part.), अस्पृशत् 'not touching;' from कृत्वा 'having done' (indecl. part.), अकृत्वा 'not having done.' When a word begins with a vowel, अन् is euphonically substituted; as, from अन्त 'end,' अनन्त 'endless.'

a. अति *ati*, 'excessively,' 'very;' as, अतिमहत् 'very great.'

b. आ *á*, implying 'diminution;' as, आपाण्डु 'somewhat pale.'

ईषत् is prefixed with the same sense; as, ईषदुष्ण 'slightly warm.'

c. का *ká* or कु *ku*, prefixed to words to imply 'disparagement;' as, कापुरुष 'a coward;' कुरूप 'deformed.'

d. दुस् *dus* (or दुर् *dur*), prefixed to imply 'badly' or 'with difficulty;' as, दुष्कृत 'badly done' (see 72); दुर्भेद 'not easily broken.' It is opposed to सु, and corresponds to the Greek δυσ-.

e. निस् *nis* (or निर् *nir*) and वि *vi* are prefixed to nouns like अ *a* with a privative or negative sense; as, निर्बल 'powerless;' निष्फल 'without fruit' (see 72); विशस्त्र 'unarmed:' but not to participles.

f. सु *su*, prefixed to imply 'well,' 'easily;' as, सुकृत 'well done;' सुभेद 'easily broken.' In this sense it is opposed to दुस्, and corresponds to the Greek εὖ. It is also used for अति, to imply 'very,' 'excessively;' as, सुमहत् 'very great.'

CONJUNCTIONS.

Copulative.

727. च *ća*, 'and,' 'also,' corresponding to the Latin *que* and not to *et*. It can never, therefore, stand as the *first word* in a sentence, but follows the word of which it is the copulative. चैव (च एव), 'also,' is a common combination.

a. उत 'and,' 'also,' is sometimes copulative. Sometimes it implies *doubt* or *interrogation.*

b. तथा 'so,' 'thus,' 'in like manner' (see 721), is not unfrequently used for च, in the sense of 'also;' and like च is then generally placed after the word which it connects with another.

c. अथ 'now,' 'and,' अथो 'then,' are inceptive, being frequently used at the commencement of sentences or narratives. अथ is often opposed to इति, which marks the close of a story or chapter.

d. हि, 'for,' is a causal conjunction; like च it is always placed after its word, and never admitted to the first place in a sentence.

e. यदि, चेद्, both meaning 'if,' are conditional conjunctions.

f. ततस् 'upon that,' 'then' (719), तत् 'then,' अन्यच्च, किञ्च, अपरञ्च, परञ्च, अपिच, 'again,' 'moreover,' are all copulatives, used very commonly in narration.

Disjunctive.

728. वा *vá*, 'or' (like *-ve* in Latin), is always placed after its word, being never admitted to the first place in a sentence.

a. तु, किन्तु, 'but;' the former is placed after its word.

b. यद्यपि 'although;' तथापि 'nevertheless,' 'yet,' sometimes used as a correlative to the last; अथवा, किं वा, 'or else;' न वा 'or not;' यदि वा 'whether,' 'whether or no.'

c. अथवा may also be used to correct or qualify a previous thought, when it is equivalent to 'but no,' 'yet,' 'however.'

d. स्म, ह, तु, वै are expletives, often used in poetry to fill up the verse.

PREPOSITIONS.

729. There are about twenty prepositions (see 783), but in later Sanskṛit they are generally prefixes, qualifying the sense of verbs (and then called *upasarga*) or of verbal derivatives (and then called *gati*). About ten may be used separately or detached in government with the cases of nouns (and then called *karma-pravaćaníya*); e.g. आ, प्रति, अनु, अति, अधि, अभि, परि, अप, अपि, and उप; but of these the first three only are commonly found as separable particles in classical Sanskṛit.

730. आ *á*, generally signifying 'as far as,' 'up to,' 'until,' with Abl.; as, आ समुद्रात् 'as far as the ocean;' आ मनोस् 'up to Manu;' आ मणिबन्धनात् 'as far as the wrist;' आ मृत्योस् 'till death;' आ व्रतस्य समापनात् 'till the completion of his vow:' and rarely with Acc.; as, शतम् आ जातीस् 'for a hundred births.'

a. आ *á* may sometimes express 'from;' as, आ मूलात् 'from the beginning;' आ प्रथमदर्शनात् 'from the first sight;' आ जन्मनस् 'from birth.'

b. It may also be compounded with a word in the Accusative neuter forming with it an Avyayí-bháva (see 760); thus, आमेखलम् 'as far as the girdle' (where मेखलम् is for मेखलाम्).

c. प्रति *prati*, generally a postposition, signifying 'at,' 'with regard to,' 'to,' 'towards,' 'against,' with Acc.; as, गङ्गां प्रति 'at the Ganges;' धर्मं प्रति 'with regard to justice;' शत्रुं प्रति 'against an enemy;' मां प्रति 'as far as regards me.' When denoting 'in the place of,' it governs the Ablative.

d. अनु 'after,' with Acc., and rarely with Abl. or Gen.; as, गङ्गाया अनु 'along the Ganges;' तदनु or ततोऽनु 'after that.'

e. प्रति, and more rarely अनु and अभि, may be used distributively to signify 'each,' 'every;' thus, वृक्षमनु 'tree by tree.' They may also be prefixed to form Avyayí-bhávas; प्रतिवत्सरम् or अनुवत्सरम् 'every year,' 'year by year.' See 760.

f. अति, अभि, परि are said to require the Accusative; अधि the Locative or Accusative; अप and परि, in the sense 'except,' the Ablative; उप the Locative and Accusative: but examples of such syntax are not common in classical Sanskṛit.

g. Instances are common of prepositions united with the neuter form or Accusative of nouns, so as to form compounds (760. *b*); as, प्रतिस्कन्धम् 'upon the shoulders;' प्रतिमुखम् 'face to face;' अधिवृक्षम् 'upon the tree;' अनुगङ्गम् 'along the Ganges.'

ADVERBS IN GOVERNMENT WITH NOUNS.

731. There are many adverbs used like the preceding prepositions in government with nouns, and often placed after the nouns which they govern (for examples see 917).

These are, अग्रे 'before,' 'in front of,' with Gen.; अधरेण 'under,' with Gen. or Acc.; अधस् or अधस्तात् 'below,' with Gen. (अधस् is sometimes doubled; thus, अधोऽधस्); अनन्तरम् 'after,' 'afterwards,' with Gen.; अन्तर् 'within,' with Gen. or Loc.; अन्तरेण 'without,' 'except,' 'with regard to,' with Acc.; अन्तिकम् 'near,' with Gen. or Abl.; अभितस् 'on both sides of,' with Acc.; अभिमुखम् 'in front of,' with Gen. or Acc.; अभ्यासे 'near,' with Gen.; अर्थम् or अर्थाय or अर्थे 'on account of,' 'for,' with Gen.; अर्वाक् 'after,' 'beyond,' with Abl.; उत्तरात् 'to the north,' with Gen.; उत्तरेण 'to the north,' with Gen. or Acc.; उपरि 'above,' 'over,' 'upon,' with Gen. or Acc. (sometimes doubled; thus, उपर्युपरि); ऊर्ध्वम् 'above,' 'over,' 'upon,' with Gen. or Acc.; 'after,' 'beyond,' with Abl.; ऋते 'besides,' 'without,' 'except,' with Acc., sometimes with Abl.; कारणात् or कृते 'on account of,' 'for,' with Gen.; दक्षिणात् 'to the south,' with Gen.; दक्षिणेन 'to the right,' 'to the south,' with Gen. or Acc.; निमित्ते 'for the sake of,' 'for,' with Gen.; परतस् 'behind,' with Gen.; परम् or परेण 'after,' 'beyond,' with Abl.; पश्चात् 'after,' with Gen. or Abl.; पारे 'on the further side,' with Gen.; पुरतस् or पुरस् 'before,' 'in the presence of,' with Gen.; पूर्वम् 'before,' with Abl., rarely with Gen. or Acc.; प्रभृति '*inde a*,' 'from a particular time,' 'beginning with,' with Abl.; प्राक् 'before,' with Abl., rarely with Gen. or Acc.; मध्ये 'in the middle,' with Gen.; बहिस् 'out,' 'outside of,' with Abl. or Gen.; यावत् 'up to,' 'as far as,' sometimes with Acc.; विना 'without,' with Inst. or Acc. or sometimes with Abl.; सकाशम् 'near,' with Gen.; सकाशात् 'from,' with Gen.; समक्षम् 'before the eyes,' 'in the presence of,' with Gen.; समम् 'together with,' with Inst.; समीपतस् or समीपम् 'near,' with Gen.; सह 'with,' 'along with,' with Inst.; साकम् 'with,' with Inst.; साक्षात् 'before the eyes,' 'in the presence of,' with Gen.; सार्धम् 'along with,' with Inst.; हेतोस् or हेतौ 'on account of,' 'for the sake of,' 'for,' with Gen.

Obs.—Many of the above, especially अर्थम्*, अर्थे, कारणात्, कृते, निमित्ते, हेतोस्, हेतौ, &c., are more usually found at the end of a compound, after a nominal stem.

a. The adverb अलम्, 'enough,' is used with the Inst. (see 918).

b. Some of the adverbs enumerated at 714, 715, may be used in government with the cases of nouns; e. g. दक्षिणेन, उत्तरेण above. व्यतिरेकेण, 'without,' is generally placed after the stem of a noun.

INTERJECTIONS.

732. भोस्, भो, हे are vocative; रे, अरे less respectfully vocative, or sometimes expressive of 'contempt.' धिक् expresses 'contempt,' 'abhorrence,' 'fie!' 'shame!' (with Accusative case); आस्, अहो, अहह, 'surprise,' 'alarm;' हा, हाहा, अहो, अहोवत, वत, 'grief;' साधु, सुष्ठु, 'approbation;' स्वस्ति, 'salutation.'

CHAPTER VIII.

COMPOUND WORDS.

733. Compounds abound in Sanskṛit to a degree wholly unequalled in any other language, and it becomes necessary to study the principles on which they are constructed, before the learner can hope to

---

* अर्थम् is generally found in composition with a nominal stem, and may be compounded adjectively to agree with another noun; as, द्विजार्थः सूपस् 'broth for the Bráhman;' द्विजार्थं पयस् 'milk for the Bráhman.' See 760. *d.*

understand the simplest sentence in the most elementary book. In the foregoing chapters we have treated of simple nouns, simple verbs, and simple adverbs. We have now to treat of compound nouns, compound verbs, and compound adverbs.

a. Observe, that in this chapter the nom. case, and not the stem, of a substantive terminating a compound will be given; and in the instance of an adjective forming the last member of a compound, the nom. case masc., fem., and neut. The examples are chiefly taken from the Hitopadeśa, and sometimes the oblique cases in which they are there found have been retained.

SECTION I.

COMPOUND NOUNS.

734. The student has now arrived at that portion of the grammar in which the use of the stem of the noun becomes most strikingly apparent. This use has been already noticed at 77; and its formation explained at 80–87.

a. In almost all compound nouns the last word alone admits of inflexion, and the preceding word or words require to be placed in the stem, to which a plural as well as singular signification may be attributed. Instances, however, will be given in which the characteristic signs of case and number are retained in the first member of the compound, but these are exceptional.

b. It may here be noted, that while Sanskṛit generally exhibits the first member or members of a compound in the stem with the final letter unchanged, except by the usual euphonic laws, Latin frequently and Greek less frequently change the final vowel of the stem into the light vowel *i*; and both Greek and Latin often make use of a vowel of conjunction, which in Greek is generally *o*, but occasionally *ι*; thus, *cœli-cola* for *cœlu-cola* or *cœlo-cola*; *lani-ger* for *lana-ger*; *χαλκί-ναος*, *ἰχθυ-ο-φάγος*, *fœder-i-fragus*. Both Greek and Latin, however, possess many compounds which are completely analogous to Sanskṛit formations. In English we have occasional examples of the use of a conjunctive vowel, as in 'handicraft' for 'hand-craft.'

Obs.—A dot placed underneath words in Nágarí type marks the division of the different members of a compound.

735. Native grammarians class compound nouns under six heads:

I. Dvandva, or those formed by the aggregation into one compound of two or more nouns (the last word being, according to circumstances, either in the dual, plural, or neuter singular, and the preceding word or words being in the stem), when, if uncompounded, they would all be in the same case, connected by a copulative conjunction; as, गुरुशिष्यौ 'master and pupil' (for गुरुः शिष्यश्च); मरणव्याधिशोकाः 'death, sickness, and sorrow' (for मरणं व्याधिः शोकश्च); पाणिपादम् 'hand and foot' (for पाणिः पादश्च).

II. TAT-PURUSHA, or those composed of two nouns, the first of which (being in the stem) would be, if uncompounded, in a case different from, or dependent on, the last; as, चन्द्रप्रभा 'moon-light' (for चन्द्रस्य प्रभा 'the light of the moon'); शस्त्रकुशलः, -ला, -लम्, 'skilled in arms' (for शस्त्रेषु कुशलः); मणिभूषितः, -ता, -तम्, 'adorned with gems' (for मणिभिर् भूषितः).

III. KARMA-DHÁRAYA, or those composed of an adjective or participle and substantive, the adjective or participle being placed first in its stem, when, if uncompounded, it would be in grammatical concord with the substantive; as, साधुजनः 'a good person' (for साधुर् जनः); सर्वद्रव्याणि 'all things' (for सर्वाणि द्रव्याणि).

IV. DVIGU, or those in which the stem of a numeral is compounded with a noun, either so as to form a singular collective noun, or an adjective; as, त्रिगुणम् 'three qualities' (for त्रयो गुणाः); त्रिगुणः, -णा, -णम्, 'possessing the three qualities.'

V. BAHU-VRÍHI, or attributive compounds, generally epithets of other nouns. These, according to Páṇini (II. 2, 24), are formed by compounding two or more words to qualify the sense of another word; thus, प्राप्तोदको ग्रामः for प्राप्तम् उदकं यं ग्रामम् 'a village to which the water has come.'

VI. AVYAYÍ-BHÁVA, or those resulting from the combination of a preposition or adverbial prefix with a noun. The latter, whatever may be its gender, always takes the form of an accusative neuter and becomes indeclinable.

a. Observe—These names either furnish examples of the several kinds of compounds, or give some sort of definition of them; thus, द्वन्द्वः (scil. समासः) is a definition of the 1st kind, meaning 'conjunction;' तत्पुरुषः, 'his servant,' is an example of the 2nd kind (for तस्य पुरुषः); कर्मधारयः is a somewhat obscure definition of the 3rd kind, i.e. 'that which contains or comprehends (धारयति) the object' (कर्म); द्विगुः is an example of the 4th kind, meaning 'anything to the value of two cows;' बहुव्रीहिः is an example of the 5th kind, meaning 'possessed of much rice.' The 6th class, अव्ययीभावः *avyayí-bhávaḥ*, means 'the indeclinable state' ('that which does not change,' *na vyeti*).

736. It should be stated, however, that the above six kinds of compounds really form, according to the native theory, only four

classes, as the 3rd and 4th (i. e. the Karma-dháraya and Dvigu) are regarded as subdivisions of the Tat-purusha class.

Obs.—Páṇini (1. 2, 42) calls a *Karma-dhárayaḥ* a *Tatpurushaḥ samánádhikaraṇaḥ*.

As such a classification appears to lead to some confusion from the absence of sufficient distinctness and opposition between the several parts or members of the division, the subject will be discussed according to a different method, although it has been thought desirable to preserve the Indian names and to keep the native arrangement in view.

737. Compound nouns may be regarded either as *simply* or *complexly* compounded. The latter have reference to a class of compounds within compounds, very prevalent in poetry, involving two or three species of simple compounds under one head.

SIMPLY COMPOUNDED NOUNS.

738. These we will divide into, 1st, Dependent compounds or compounds dependent in case (corresponding to *Tat-purusha*); 2nd, Copulative (or Aggregative, *Dvandva*); 3rd, Descriptive* (or Determinative, *Karma-dháraya*); 4th, Numeral (or Collective, *Dvigu*); 5th, Adverbial (or Indeclinable, *Avyayí-bháva*); 6th, Relative (*Bahu-vríhi*). This last consists of, *a.* Relative form of absolute Dependent compounds, terminated by substantives; *b.* Relative form of Copulative or Aggregative compounds; *c.* Relative form of Descriptive or Determinative compounds; *d.* Relative form of Numeral or Collective compounds; *e.* Relative form of Adverbial compounds.

a. Observe—A list of the substitutions which take place in the final syllables of certain words in compounds is given at 778.

DEPENDENT COMPOUNDS (TAT-PURUSHA).

Accusatively Dependent.

739. These comprehend all those compounds in which the relation of the first word (being in the stem) to the last is equivalent to that of an accusative case. They are generally composed of a noun in the first member, and a participle (but not a present or indeclinable

---

* As being composed of an adjective or participle preceding a substantive, and always descriptive of the substantive. Bopp calls them 'Determinativa,' a word of similar import.

participle), root, or noun of agency in the last; as, स्वर्ग-प्राप्तः, -प्ता, -प्तम्, 'one who has obtained heaven' (equivalent to स्वर्गं प्राप्तः); प्रिय-वादी 'one who speaks kind words;' बहु-दः 'one who gives much;' देवस्तुत् 'god-praising;' शस्त्र-भृत् 'one who bears arms;' पत्र-गतः, -ता, -तम्, 'committed to a leaf,' 'committed to paper' (as 'writing'); चित्र-गतः, -ता, -तम्, 'committed to painting;' दर्शनीय-मानी, -मिनी, -मि, 'thinking one's self handsome.'

a. गत 'gone' (past pass. part. of गम् 'to go') is used loosely at the end of compounds of this description to express relationship and connexion, without any necessary implication of motion. In पत्रगत, चित्रगत above, and in others (such as शिला-भेद-गतो मणिः 'a jewel lying in the cleft of a rock;' हस्त-तल-गतः, -ता, -तम्, 'lying in the palm of the hand'), it has the sense of स्थ 'staying:' but it may often have other senses; as, गोष्ठी-गतः, -ता, -तम्, 'engaged in conversation;' सखी-गतं किंचित् 'something relating to a friend.'

b. In theatrical language आत्म-गतम् and स्वगतम् (lit. 'gone to one's self') mean 'spoken to one's self,' 'aside.'

c. Before nouns of agency and similar forms the accusative case is often retained, especially in poetry; as, अरिन्दमः, -मा, -मम्, 'enemy-subduing;' हृदयङ्गमः, -मा, -मम् 'heart-touching;' भयङ्करः, -री, -रम्, 'fear-inspiring' (see 580. *a*); सागरङ्गमः, -मा, -मम्, 'going to the ocean;' पण्डितम्मन्यः, -न्या, -न्यम्, 'one who thinks himself learned;' रात्रिम्मन्यः 'one who thinks it night.'

Instrumentally Dependent,

740. Or those in which the relation of the first word (being in the stem) to the last is equivalent to that of an instrumental case. These are very common, and are, for the most part, composed of a substantive in the first member, and a past passive participle in the last; as, लोभ-मोहितः, -ता, -तम्, 'beguiled by avarice' (for लोभेन मोहितः); वस्त्र-वेष्टितः, -ता, -तम्, 'covered with clothes;' राज-पूजितः, -ता, -तम्, 'honoured by kings;' विद्या-हीनः, -ना, -नम्, 'deserted by (i.e. destitute of) learning;' बुद्धि-रहितः, -ता, -तम्, 'destitute of intelligence;' दुःखार्तः, -र्ता, -र्तम्, 'pained with grief;' आत्म-कृतः, -ता, -तम्, 'done by one's self;' आदित्य-सदृशः, -शी, -शम्, 'like the sun' (for आदित्येन सदृशः, see 826); अस्मदुपार्जितः, -ता, -तम्, 'acquired by us.'

a. Sometimes this kind of compound contains a substantive or noun of agency in the last member; as, विद्या-धनम् 'money acquired by science;' शस्त्रोपजीवी 'one who lives by arms.'

Datively Dependent,

741. Or those in which the relation of the first word to the last is equivalent to that of a dative; as, परिधान-वल्कलम् 'bark for clothing;'

पादोदकम् 'water for the feet;' यूपदारु 'wood for a sacrificial post;' शरणागतः, -ता, -तम्, 'come for protection' (for शरणाय आगतः). This kind of compound is not very commou, and is generally supplied by the use of अर्थम् (731); as, शरणार्थम् आगतः.

a. *Parasmai-pada* and *Átmane-pada* (see 243) are instances of compounds in which the sign of the dative case is retained.

Ablatively Dependent,

742. Or those in which the relation of the first word to the last is equivalent to that of an ablative; as, पितृप्राप्तः, -प्ता, -प्तम्, 'received from a father;' राज्यभ्रष्टः, -ष्टा, -ष्टम्, 'fallen from the kingdom' (for राज्याद् भ्रष्टः); तरङ्गचञ्चलतरः, -रा, -रम्, 'more changeable than a wave;' भवदन्यः 'other than you' (for भवतोऽन्यः); भवद्भयम् 'fear of you' (814. *e*); कुक्कुरभयम् 'fear of a dog;' शास्त्रपराङ्मुखः, -खी, -खम्, 'turning the face from books,' 'averse from study.'

Genitively Dependent,

743. Or those in which the relation of the first word to the last is equivalent to that of a genitive. These are the most common of all dependent compounds, and may generally be expressed by a similar compound in English. They are for the most part composed of two substantives; as, समुद्रतीरम् 'sea-shore' (for समुद्रस्य तीरम् 'shore of the sea').

a. Other examples are, अश्वपृष्ठम् 'horse-back;' धनुर्गुणः 'bow-string;' इष्टिकागृहम् 'brick-house;' गिरिनदी 'mountain-torrent;' जलतीरम् 'water's edge;' अर्थागमः or अर्थोपार्जना 'acquisition of wealth;' विपद्दशा 'state of misfortune;' सुहृद्भेदः 'separation of friends;' यन्मूर्ध्नि 'on whose brow' (locative); तद्वचः 'his words;' जन्मस्थानम् or जन्मभूमिः 'birth-place;' मूर्खशतैः 'with hundreds of fools' (inst. pl.); श्लोकद्वयम् 'a couple of S'lokas;' भूतलम् 'the surface of the earth;' पृथिवीपतिः 'lord of the earth;' तज्जीवनाय 'for his support' (dative); ब्राह्मणपुत्राः 'the sons of a Bráhman;' अस्मत्पुत्राः 'our sons;' त्वत्कर्म 'thy deed;' पितृवचनम् 'a father's speech;' मृत्युद्वारम् 'the gate of death;' इच्छासम्पत् 'fulfilment of wishes;' मात्रानन्दः 'a mother's joy;' जलाशयः 'a water-receptacle,' 'lake;' विद्यार्थी 'knowledge-seeker,' 'a scholar;' कुक्कुटाण्डम् (for कुक्कुट्यण्डम्) 'a hen's egg.'

b. Sometimes an adjective in the superlative degree, used substantively, occupies the last place in the compound; as, नरश्रेष्ठः or पुरुषोत्तमः 'the best of men.'

c. In occasional instances the genitive case is retained; as, विशाम्पतिः 'lord of men;' दिवस्पतिः 'lord of the sky.'

d. Especially in terms of reproach; as, दास्याःपुत्रः (or दासीपुत्रः) 'son of a slave girl.'

Locatively Dependent,

744. Or those in which the relation of the first word to the last is equivalent to that of a locative case; as, पङ्कमग्नः, -ग्ना, -ग्नम्, 'sunk in the mud' (for पङ्के मग्नः); गगनविहारी 'sporting in the sky;' जलक्रीडा 'sport in the water;' ग्रामवासी 'a dweller in a village;' जलचरः 'going in the water;' जलजः 'born in the water;' शिरोरत्नम् 'gem on the head.'

a. The sign of the locative case is retained in some cases, especially before nouns of agency; as, ग्रामेवासी 'a villager;' जलेचरः 'going in the water;' उरसिभूषितः, -ता, -तम्, 'ornamented on the breast;' अग्रेगः or अग्रेसरः 'going in front;' दिविषत् (rt. सद्) 'abiding in the sky;' दिविस्पृक् (rt. स्पृश्) 'touching the sky;' युधिष्ठिरः 'firm in war.'

Dependent in more than one Case.

745. Dependent compounds do not always consist of two words. They may be composed of almost any number of nouns, all depending upon each other, in the manner that one case depends upon another in a sentence; thus, चक्षुर्विषयातिक्रान्तः, -न्ता, -न्तम्, 'passed beyond the range of the eye' (for चक्षुषो विषयम् अतिक्रान्तः); रथमध्यस्थः 'standing in the middle of the chariot;' भीतपरित्राणवस्तूपालम्भपण्डितः 'skilful in censuring the means of rescuing those in danger.'

a. There is an anomalous form of Tat-purusha, which is really the result of the elision of the second or middle member (*uttara-pada-lopa, madhyama-pada-lopa*) of a complex compound; e.g. शाकपार्थिवः for शाकप्रियपार्थिवः (see 775).

b. Dependent compounds abound in all the cognate languages. The following are examples from Greek and Latin; *οἰνο-θήκη, οἰκο-φύλαξ, λιθό-στρωτος, γυναικο-κήρυκτος, ἀνθρωπο-δίδακτος, θεό-δοτος, θεό-τρεπτος, χειρο-ποίητος, auri-fodina, manu-pretium, parri-cida* for *patri-cida, parri-cidium, matri-cidium, marti-cultor, mus-cerda.* English furnishes innumerable examples of dependent compounds; e.g. 'ink-stand,' 'snow-drift,' 'moth-eaten,' 'priest-ridden,' 'door-mat,' 'writing-master,' &c.

COPULATIVE (OR AGGREGATIVE) COMPOUNDS (DVANDVA).

746. This class has no exact parallel in other languages.

When two or more persons or things are enumerated together, it is usual in Sanskṛit, instead of connecting them by a copulative, to aggregate them into one compound word. No syntactical dependence of one case upon another subsists between the members of Dvandva compounds, since they must always consist of words which, if uncompounded, would be in the *same* case. The only grammatical connexion between the members is that which would be expressed by the copulative conjunction *and* in English, or च in Sanskrit. In fact, the difference between this class and the last turns upon this dependence *in case* of the words compounded on each other; insomuch that the existence or absence of such dependence, as deducible from the context, is, in some cases, the only guide by which the student is enabled to refer the compound to the one head or to the other; thus, गुरु-शिष्य-सेवकाः may either be a Dependent compound, and mean 'the servants of the pupils of the Guru,' or a Copulative, 'the Guru, and the pupil, and the servant.' And मांस-शोणितम् may either be Dependent, 'the blood of the flesh,' or Copulative, 'flesh and blood.' This ambiguity, however, can never occur in Dvandvas inflected in the dual, and rarely occasions any practical difficulty.

747. There are three kinds of Copulative compounds: 1st, inflected in the plural; 2nd, inflected in the dual; 3rd, inflected in the singular. In the first two cases the final letter of the stem of the word terminating the compound determines the declension, and its gender the particular form of declension; in the third case it seems to be a law that this kind of compound cannot be formed unless the last word ends in अ *a*, or in a vowel changeable to अ *a*, or in a consonant to which अ *a* may be subjoined; and the gender is invariably neuter, whatever may be the gender of the final word.

Inflected in the Plural.

748. When *more than two* animate objects are enumerated, the last is inflected in the plural, the declension following the gender of the last member of the compound; as, इन्द्रानिल-यमार्काः 'Indra, Anila, Yama, and Arka' (for इन्द्रोऽनिलो यमोऽर्कश्च); राम-लक्ष्मण-भरताः 'Ráma, Lakshmaṇa, and Bharata;' मृग-व्याध-सर्प-शूकराः 'the deer, the hunter, the serpent, and the hog.' The learner will observe, that although the last member of the compound is inflected in the plural, each of the members has here a singular acceptation. But a plural signification may often be inherent in some or all of the words constituting the compound; thus, ब्राह्मण-क्षत्रिय-वैश्य-शूद्राः 'Bráhmans, Kshatriyas, Vaiśyas, and Śúdras;' मित्रोदासीन-शत्रवः 'friends, neutrals, and foes' (for मित्राणि उदासीनाः शत्रवश्च); ऋषि-देव-पित्रतिथि-भूतानि 'sages, gods, ancestors, guests, and spirits' (for ऋषयो देवाः पितरोऽतिथयो भूतानि च); सिंह-व्याघ्र-महोरगाः 'lions, tigers, and immense serpents;' श्व-गृध्र-कङ्क-काको-

ल-भास-गोमायु-वायसाः 'dogs, vultures, herons, ravens, kites, jackals, and crows.'

749. So also when *more than two* inanimate objects are enumerated, the last may be inflected in the plural; as, धर्मार्थ-काम-मोक्षास् 'virtue, wealth, enjoyment, and beatitude' (for धर्मोऽर्थः कामो मोक्षश्च); इज्याध्ययन-दानानि 'sacrifice, study, and liberality' (for इज्या अध्ययनं दानं च). In some of the following a plural signification is inherent; as, पुष्प-मूल-फलानि 'flowers, roots, and fruits;' अजात-मृत-मूर्खाणाम् 'of the unborn, the dead, and the foolish' (for अजातानां मृतानां मूर्खाणां च); नेत्र-मनः-स्वभावाः 'eyes, mind, and disposition;' रोग-शोक-परिताप-बन्धन-व्यसनानि 'sickness, sorrow, anguish, bonds, and afflictions;' काष्ठ-जल-फल-मूल-मधूनि 'wood, water, fruit, roots, and honey.'

750. So also when *only two* animate or inanimate objects are enumerated, in which a *plural* signification is inherent, the last is inflected in the plural; as, देव-मनुष्याः 'gods and men;' पुत्र-पौत्राः 'sons and grandsons;' पातोत्पाताः 'falls and rises;' प्राकार-परिखाः 'ramparts and trenches;' सुख-दुःखेषु 'in pleasures and pains' (for सुखेषु दुःखेषु च); पाप-पुण्यानि 'sins and virtues.'

Inflected in the Dual.

751. When *only two* animate objects are enumerated, in each of which a *singular* signification is inherent, the last is inflected in the dual, the declension following the gender of the last member; as, राम-लक्ष्मणौ 'Ráma and Lakshmaṇa' (for रामो लक्ष्मणश्च); चन्द्र-सूर्यौ 'moon and sun;' मृग-काकौ 'a deer and a crow;' भार्या-पती 'wife and husband;' मयूरीकुक्कुटौ 'pea-hen and cock;' कुक्कुटमयूर्यौ 'cock and pea-hen.'

752. So also when *only two* inanimate objects are enumerated, in each of which a *singular* signification is inherent, the last is inflected in the dual; as, आरम्भावसाने 'beginning and end' (for आरम्भोऽवसानं च); अनुरागापरागौ 'affection and enmity' (for अनुरागोऽपरागश्च); हर्ष-विषादौ 'joy and sorrow;' क्षुत्पिपासे 'hunger and thirst' (for क्षुत् पिपासा च); क्षुद्व्याधी 'hunger and sickness;' स्थानासनाभ्याम् 'by standing and sitting' (for स्थानेन आसनेन च); मधु-सर्पिषी 'honey and ghee;' सुख-दुःखे 'pleasure and pain;' उलूखल-मुसले 'mortar and pestle;' प्रत्युत्थानाभिवादाभ्याम् 'by rising and saluting;' मृद्वारिभ्याम् 'by earth and water.'

Inflected in the Singular Neuter.

753. When two or more *inanimate* objects are enumerated, whether

singular or plural in their signification, the last may either be inflected as above (748, 749, 750, 751), or in the singular number, neut. gender; as, पुष्प-मूल-फलम् 'flowers, roots, and fruits' (for पुष्पाणि मूलानि फलानि च); यवसान्नोदकेन्धनम् 'grass, food, water, and fuel' (for यवसोऽन्नम् उदकम् इन्धनं च); अहोरात्रम् 'a day and night' (for अहो रात्रिश्च. A form अहोरात्रः masc. sing. also occurs); दिग्देशम् 'quarters and countries' (for दिशो देशाश्च); द्युनिशम् or दिवानिशम् 'day and night;' शिरोग्रीवम् 'head and neck;' चर्ममांसरुधिरम् 'skin, flesh, and blood.'

a. Sometimes two or more animate objects are thus compounded; as, पुत्रपौत्रम् 'sons and grandsons;' हस्त्यश्वम् 'elephants and horses:' especially inferior objects; as, श्वचाण्डालम् 'a dog and an outcast.'

754. In enumerating two qualities the opposite of each other, it is common to form a Dvandva compound of this kind, by doubling an adjective or participle, and interposing the negative अ *a;* as, चराचरम् 'moveable and immoveable' (for चरम् अचरं च); शुभाशुभम् 'good and evil;' प्रियाप्रिये 'in agreeable and disagreeable' (for प्रिये अप्रिये च); दृष्टादृष्टम् 'seen and not seen;' कृताकृतम् 'done and not done;' मृदुक्रूरम् 'gentle and cruel.'

a. In the Dvandvas which occur in the Vedas the first member of the compound, as well as the last, may sometimes take a dual termination; thus, मित्रावरुणौ (see 97. *a*), इन्द्राविष्णू, पितरामातरौ: and some of the anomalous Dvandvas used in more modern Sanskṛit are probably Vedic in their character; thus, द्यावापृथिवी 'heaven and earth;' मातापितरौ 'mother and father,' &c.

b. It is a general rule, however, that if a compound consists of two stems in *ṛi*, the final of the first becomes आ, as in मातापितरौ above. This also happens if the last member of the compound be पुत्र, as पितापुत्रौ 'father and son.'

c. Greek and Latin furnish examples of complex compounds involving Dvandvas; thus, βατραχο-μυο-μαχία, 'frog-mouse war;' *su-ovi-taurilia*, 'pig-sheep-bull sacrifice;' ζωό-φυτον, 'animal-plant.' *Zoophyte* is thus a kind of Dvandva. In English, compounds like 'plano-convex,' 'convexo-concave' are examples of the relative form of Dvandva explained at 765.

DESCRIPTIVE (OR DETERMINATIVE) COMPOUNDS (KARMA-DHÁRAYA).

755. In describing, qualifying, or defining a substantive by means of an adjective or participle, it is common in Sanskṛit to compound the two words together, placing the adjective or participle in the first member of the compound in its stem; as, साधुजनः 'a good man' (for साधुर् जनः); चिरमित्रम् 'an old friend' (for चिरं मित्रम्); क्षुब्धार्णवः 'a troubled ocean;' पुण्यकर्म 'a holy act;' अनन्तात्मा 'the infinite soul;' संस्कृतोक्तिः 'polished speech;' पुण्यकर्माणि 'holy acts' (for पुण्यानि कर्माणि); उत्तमनराणाम् 'of the best men' (for उत्तमानां नराणाम्); महापातकम् 'a great

crime' (see 778); महा॰राज: 'a great king' (see 778); प्रिय॰सख: 'a dear friend' (778); दीर्घ॰रात्रम् 'a long night' (778).

a. The feminine stems of adjectives do not generally appear in compounds; thus, प्रिय॰भार्या 'a dear wife' (for प्रिया भार्या); महा॰भार्या 'a great wife' (for महती भार्या, see 778); रूपवद्भार्या 'a beautiful wife' (for रूपवती भार्या); पाचक॰स्त्री 'a female cook' (for पाचिका स्त्री).

b. There are, however, a few examples of feminine adjective stems in compounds; e.g. वामोरूभार्या 'a wife with beautiful thighs;' कामिनी॰जन: 'an impassioned woman,' where कामिनी may be used substantively (cf. 766. *b*).

756. An indeclinable word or prefix may take the place of an adjective in this kind of compound; thus, सु॰पथ: 'a good road;' सु॰दिनम् 'a fine day;' सु॰भाषितम् 'good speech;' दुश्चरितम् 'bad conduct;' अभयम् 'not fear,' 'absence of danger;' वहि:॰शौचम् 'external cleanliness' (from *vahis*, 'externally,' and *śauća*, 'purity'); अन्त:॰शौचम् 'internal purity;' ईषद्दर्शनम् 'a slight inspection;' कु॰पुरुष: 'a bad man.'

757. Adjectives used as substantives sometimes occupy the last place in Descriptive compounds; as, परम॰धार्मिक: 'a very just man;' परमाद्भुतम् 'a very wonderful thing.'

a. In the same manner, substantives, used adjectively, may occupy the first place; as, मल॰द्रव्याणि 'impure substances;' राजर्षि: 'a royal sage.'

758. Descriptive compounds expressing 'excellence' or 'eminence' fall under this class, and are composed of two substantives, one of which is used as an adjective to describe or define the other, and is placed last, being generally the name of an animal denoting 'superiority;' as, पुरुष॰व्याघ्र: 'man-tiger,' पुरुष॰पुङ्गव: 'man-bull,' पुरुष॰सिंह: 'man-lion,' पुरुष॰र्षभ: 'man-bull,' i. e. 'an illustrious man.'

Similarly, स्त्री॰रत्नम् 'an excellent woman' (gem of a woman); वदना॰ब्जम् 'face-lotus,' i. e. 'lotus-like face.'

a. So other compounds expressive of 'comparison' or 'resemblance' are usually included in native grammars under the Karma-dháraya class. In these the adjective is placed last; as, छाया॰चञ्चल:, -ला, -लम्, 'fickle as a shadow;' अम्बुद॰श्याम:, -मा, -मम्, 'dark as a cloud;' भूधर॰विस्तीर्ण:, -र्णा, -र्णम्, 'spread out like a mountain.'

b. The following are examples of Greek and Latin compounds falling under this class; *μεγαλο-μήτηρ*, *ἰσό-πεδον*, *μεγαλό-νοια*, *ἡμι-κύων*, *sacri-portus*, *meri-dies* (for *medi-dies*), *decem-viri*, *semi-deus*. Parallel compounds in English are, 'good-will,' 'good-sense,' 'ill-nature,' 'holiday,' 'blackguard,' &c.

NUMERAL (OR COLLECTIVE) COMPOUNDS (DVIGU).

759. A numeral is often compounded with a substantive to form a collective noun, but the last member of the compound is generally in the neuter singular; thus, चतुर्युगम् 'the four ages' (for चत्वारि युगानि);

चतुर्दिशम् 'the four quarters;' त्रिदिनम् 'three days' (*triduum*); त्रिरात्रम् 'three nights' (रात्र being substituted for रात्रि, see 778); त्र्यब्दम् 'three years' (*triennium*); पञ्चाग्नि 'the five fires.'

a. Rarely the stems of numerals are compounded with plural substantives; as, चतुर्वर्णाः 'the four castes;' पञ्चबाणाः 'five arrows;' सप्तर्षयः 'the seven stars of Ursa Major.'

b. Sometimes the last member of the compound is in the feminine singular, with the termination ई; as, त्रिलोकी 'the three worlds.'

c. Compare Greek and Latin compounds like τετραόδιον, τριvύκτιον, τέθριππον, *triduum, triennium, trinoctium, quadrivium, quinquertium.*

ADVERBIAL OR INDECLINABLE COMPOUNDS (AVYAYÍ-BHÁVA).

760. In this class of indeclinable (*avyaya*, i. e. *na vyeti*, 'what does not change') compounds the first member must be either a preposition (such as अति, अधि, अनु, प्रति, &c., at 783) or an adverbial prefix (such as यथा 'as,' यावत् 'as far as,' अ or अन् 'not,' सह 'with,' &c.) The last member is a substantive which takes the form of an accusative case neuter, whatever may be the termination of its stem; thus, यथाश्रद्धम् 'according to faith' (from यथा and श्रद्धा); प्रतिनिशम् 'every night' (from प्रति and निशा); प्रतिदिशम् 'in every quarter' (from प्रति and दिश्); अतिनु 'beyond the ship' (from अति and नौ).

a. Many of these compounds are formed with the adverbial preposition सह, generally contracted into स; thus, सकोपम् 'with anger' (from स and कोप); सादरम् 'with respect' (स आदरम्); साष्टाङ्गपातम् 'with prostration of eight parts of the body;' सोपधि (i. e. *sa-upadhi*) 'fraudulently;' साग्नि 'with fire.' Páṇini (II. 1, 9, &c.) gives some unusual forms with postpositions; as, सूपप्रति 'a little sauce.'

b. The following are examples of indeclinable compounds with other prefixes; अनुज्येष्ठम् 'according to seniority;' प्रत्यङ्गम् 'over every limb;' प्रतिमासम् 'every month' (730. *e*); यथाविधि 'according to rule;' यथाशक्ति or यावच्छक्यम् (49) 'according to one's ability;' यथासुखम् 'happily;' यथार्हम् 'suitably,' 'worthily;' यथोक्तम् 'as described;' अनुक्षणम् 'every moment;' समक्षम् 'before the eyes' (778); प्रतिस्कन्धम् 'upon the shoulders;' अधिवृक्षम् 'upon the tree;' उपमालिनीतीरम् 'near the banks of the Máliní;' असंशयम् 'without doubt;' निर्विशेषम् 'without distinction;' मध्येगङ्गम् 'in the middle of the Ganges.'

c. Analogous indeclinable compounds are found in Latin and Greek, such as *admodum, obviam, affatim,* ἀντιβίην, ἀντίβιον, ὑπέρμορον, παράχρημα. In these, however, the original gender is retained, whereas, according to the Sanskṛit rule, *obvium* would be written for *obviam*, and *affate* for *affatim*. In Greek compounds like σήμερον, the feminine ἡμέρα appends a neuter form, as in Sanskṛit. In English 'uphill.'

d. The neuter word अर्थम् 'for the sake of,' 'on account of' (see 731. Obs.), is often used at the end of compounds; thus, स्वप्नार्थम् 'for the sake of sleep;' कर्मानुष्ठानार्थम् 'for the sake of the performance of business.' See, however, 731, note.

e. There is a peculiar adverbial compound formed by doubling a nominal stem, the final of the first member of the compound being lengthened, and the final of the last changed to इ *i*. It generally denotes mutual contact, reciprocity, or opposition; thus, मुष्टीमुष्टि 'fist to fist;' दण्डादण्डि 'stick to stick' (fighting); अंशांशि 'share by share;' केशाकेशि 'pulling each other's hair;' अङ्गाङ्गि 'body to body;' बाहूबाहवि 'arm to arm;' नखानखि 'scratching each other.'

f. Something in the same manner, अन्य and पर, 'another,' are doubled; thus, अन्योन्यम्, परस्परम्, 'one another,' 'mutually,' 'together.'

RELATIVE COMPOUNDS (MOSTLY EQUIVALENT TO BAHU-VRÍHI).

761. The compounds in the preceding four divisions are generally terminated by substantives, the sense of each being in that case absolute and complete in itself. Most of such compounds may be used *relatively*, that is, as epithets of other words, the final substantive becoming susceptible of three genders, like an adjective (see 108, 119, 130, 134. *a*). We have given the name *relative* to compounds when thus used, not only for the obvious reason of their being relatively and not absolutely employed, but also because they usually involve a relative pronoun, and are sometimes translated into English by the aid of this pronoun, and are, moreover, resolved by native commentators into their equivalent uncompounded words by the aid of the genitive case of the relative (यस्य). Thus, महाधनम् is a Descriptive compound, meaning 'great wealth,' and may be used adjectively in relation to पुरुषः, thus महाधनः पुरुषः 'a man *who* has great wealth;' or to स्त्री, thus महाधना स्त्री 'a woman *who* has great wealth;' and would be resolved by native commentators into यस्य or यस्या महद् धनम्. In English we have similar compounds, as 'high-minded,' 'left-handed,' and the like, where the substantive terminating the compound is converted into an adjective.

Relative form of Tat-purusha or Dependent Compounds.

762. Many Dependent compounds (especially those that are instrumentally dependent at 740) are already *in their own nature* relative, and cannot be used except in connexion with some other word in the sentence. But, on the other hand, many others, and especially

those which are genitively dependent, constituting by far the largest number of this class of compounds, are in their nature absolute, and yield a sense complete in itself. These may be made relative by declining the final word after the manner of an adjective; thus, चन्द्राकृतिः, -तिः, -ति, 'moon-shaped' (see 119), from the absolute compound चन्द्राकृतिः 'the shape of the moon.'

a. Other examples are, देवरूपः, -पा, -पम्, 'whose form is godlike' (see 108); सूर्यप्रभावः, -वा, -वम्, 'splendid as the sun' (108); हस्तिपादः, -दा, -दम्*, 'elephant-footed' (see 57); सागरान्तः, -न्ता, -न्तम्, 'ending at the sea;' मरणान्तः, -न्ता, -न्तम्, 'terminated by death;' कर्णपुरोगमः, -मा, -मम्, or कर्णमुखः, -खा, -खम्, 'headed by Karṇa;' विष्णुशर्मनामा, -मा, -म, 'named Vishṇuśarman' (see 154); पुण्डरीकाक्षः, -क्षी, -क्षम्, 'lotus-eyed' (see 778); नारायणाख्यः, -ख्या, -ख्यम्, 'called Náráyaṇa;' धनमूलः, -ला, -लम्, 'founded on wealth;' लक्षसंख्यानि (agreeing with धनानि), 'money to the amount of a lac;' गदाहस्तः, -स्ता, -स्तम्, 'having a club in the hand,' or 'club-in-hand;' शस्त्रपाणिः, -णिः, -णि, 'arms-in-hand;' जालहस्तः, -स्ता, -स्तम्, 'net-in-hand;' पुष्पविषयः, -या, -यम्, 'on the subject of flowers,' 'relating to flowers;' ध्यानपरः, -रा, -रम्, 'having meditation for one's chief occupation;' तद्विद्यः, -द्या, -द्यम्, 'having his knowledge.' These examples are not distinguishable from absolute dependent compounds, except by declension in three genders.

b. Similar compounds are found in Greek; e.g. ἱππό-γλωσσος, 'horse-tongued.'

763. Many of them, however, are not found, except as relatives; and if used absolutely would yield a different sense; thus, कर्णमुखम् means 'the face of Karṇa,' but when used relatively, as कर्णमुखा राजानः, 'the kings headed by Karṇa.' So also चारचक्षुः signifies 'the eye of the spy,' but when used relatively, as चारचक्षू राजा, 'a king who sees by means of his spies.' See 166. *c.*

764. The substantive आदि, 'a beginning,' when it occurs in the last member of a compound of this nature, is used relatively to some word expressed or understood, and yields a sense equivalent to *et cetera.* It is generally found either in the plural or neuter singular; as, इन्द्रादयः 'Indra and the others' (agreeing with the nom. case सुराः expressed or understood, 'the gods commencing with Indra'); अग्न्यादीनाम् 'of Agni and the others' (agreeing with पूर्वोक्तानाम् understood, 'of those above-named things of which Agni was the first'); चक्षुरादीनि 'the eyes, &c.' (agreeing with इन्द्रियाणि 'the senses commencing with the eyes'). When used in the neut. sing. it either agrees with पूर्वोक्तम्, 'the aforesaid,' understood, or

* पाद् may be substituted for पाद in compounds of this kind, but not after हस्तिन्. See 778.

with a number of things taken collectively, and the adverb *iti* * may be prefixed; as, देवानित्यादि 'the word *deván*, &c.' (agreeing with पूर्वोक्तम् understood, 'the aforesaid sentence of which *deván* is the first word'); दानादिना 'by liberality, &c.' (agreeing with some class of things understood, 'by that class of things of which liberality is the first'). See also 772.

a. It may occasionally be used in the masc. sing.; as, मार्जन्यादिः 'brooms, &c.' (agreeing with उपस्करः 'furniture').

b. Sometimes आदिक is used for आदि; as, दानादिकम् 'gifts, &c.:' and sometimes आद्य; as, इन्द्राद्याः सुराः 'the gods of whom Indra is the first.'

c. The feminine substantive प्रभृति, 'beginning,' may be used in the same way; thus, इन्द्रप्रभृतयः सुराः 'the gods, beginning with Indra;' तेषां ग्रामनिवासिप्रभृतीनाम् 'of those villagers, &c.'

d. Observe—The neuter of आदि may optionally take the terminations of the masculine in all but the nom. and acc. cases; thus, हस्त्यश्वादेः 'of elephants, horses, &c.' (agreeing with बलस्य gen. neut. of बल 'an army').

Relative form of Dvandva or Copulative Compounds.

765. Copulative (or Aggregative) compounds are sometimes used relatively; especially in the case of adjectives or participles; as, कृष्णशुक्लः, -क्ला, -क्लम्, 'black and white' (cf. λευκο-μέλας); स्नातानुलिप्तः, -प्ता, -प्तम्, 'bathed and anointed;' पौरजानपदः, -दा, -दम्, 'belonging to town and country;' कृतापकृतः, -ता, -तम्, 'done and done badly;' शुभाशुभः, -भा, -भम्, 'good and evil' (754); सान्द्रस्निग्धः, -ग्धा, -ग्धम्, 'thick and unctuous;' निःशब्दस्तिमितः, -ता, -तम्, 'noiseless and motionless' (night); गृहीतप्रतिमुक्तस्य 'of him taken and let loose.' See other examples under Complex Compounds.

Obs.—Many compounds of this kind are classed by native grammarians under the head of Tat-purusha (Páṇ. II. 1, 69), though the accent in many conforms to the rule for Bahu-vríhi (VI. 2, 3).

Relative form of Karma-dháraya or Descriptive Compounds.

766. A greater number of compound words may be referred to this head than to any other. Every style of writing abounds with them; thus, अल्पशक्तिः, -क्तिः, -क्ति, 'whose strength is small' (119).

a. Other examples are, महाबलः, -ला, -लम्, 'whose strength is great' (108, see also 778); महातेजाः, -जाः, -जः, 'whose glory is great' (164. *a*); अल्पधनः, -ना, -नम्, 'whose wealth is small;' महात्मा, -त्मा, -त्म, 'high-minded' (151); उदारचरितः, -ता, -तम्, 'of noble demeanour;' बहुमत्स्यः, -त्स्या, -त्स्यम्, 'having

---

* Sometimes *evam* is prefixed; as, एवमादीनि प्रलापानि 'lamentations beginning thus.'

many fish;' स्वल्पसलिलः, -ला, -लम्, 'having very little water;' पण्डितबुद्धिः, -द्धिः, -द्धि, 'of wise intellect' (119); प्रियभार्यः, -र्या, -र्यम्, 'having a dear wife;' अशक्यसन्धानः, -ना, -नम्, 'not to be reconciled;' संवृतसंवार्यः, agreeing with राजा, 'a king who conceals what ought to be concealed.'

b. Occasionally the feminine of the adjective appears in the compound; as, षष्ठीभार्यः 'having a sixth wife.' Compare 755. *b.*

767. Although a passive participle is not often prefixed to a noun in an absolute sense, this kind of combination prevails most extensively in the formation of relative compounds; as, प्राप्तकालः, -ला, -लम्, 'whose time has arrived.'

a. Other examples are, जितेन्द्रियः, -या, -यम्, 'whose passions are subdued;' शान्तचेताः, -ताः, -तः, 'whose mind is composed;' संहृष्टमनाः, -नाः, -नः, 'whose mind is rejoiced' (see 164); भग्नाशः, -शा, -शम्, 'whose hopes are broken;' हृतराज्यः, -ज्या, -ज्यम्, 'whose kingdom is taken away;' अमिततेजाः, -जाः, -जः, 'whose glory is boundless;' आसन्नमृत्युः, -त्युः, -त्यु, 'whose death is near;' कृतकामः, -मा, -मम्, 'whose desire is accomplished,' i.e. 'successful;' कृतभोजनः, -ना, -नम्, 'one who has finished eating;' अनधिगतशास्त्रः, -स्त्रा, -स्त्रम्, 'one by whom the Śástras have not been read;' भिन्नहृदयः, -या, -यम्, or दलहृदयः, 'whose heart is pierced;' जितशत्रुः, -त्रुः, -त्रु, 'who has conquered his enemies;' छिन्नकेशः, -शा, -शम्, 'having the hair cut;' मिताशनः, -ना, -नम्, 'eating sparingly;' पूतपापः, -पा, -पम्, 'purified from sin.'

b. The suffix क *ka* is often added; as, हतश्रीकः, -का, -कम्, 'reft of fortune;' हतत्विट्कः, -ट्का, -ट्कम्, 'shorn of (his) beams.' Cf. 769. *a.*

c. Examples of Greek and Latin compounds of this kind are, μεγαλο-κέφαλος, μεγαλό-μητις, λευκό-πτερος, πολύ-χρυσος, χρυσεο-στέφανος, ἡδύ-γλωσσος, ἐρημό-πολις, *magn-animus, longi-manus, multi-comus, albi-comus, multi-vius, atri-color.* In English compounds of this kind abound; e.g. 'blue-eyed,' 'narrow-minded,' 'good-tempered,' 'pale-faced,' &c.

Relative form of Dvigu or Numeral Compounds.

768. Numeral or Dvigu compounds may be used relatively; as, द्विपर्णः, -र्णी, -र्णम्, 'two-leaved;' त्रिलोचनः, -ना or -नी, -नम्, 'tri-ocular.'

a. Other examples are, त्रिमूर्धः, -र्धा, -र्धम्, 'three-headed' (मूर्ध being substituted for मूर्धन्, see 778); चतुर्मुखः, -खी, -खम्, 'four-faced;' चतुष्कोणः, -णा, -णम्, 'quadrangular;' शतद्वारः, -रा, -रम्, 'hundred-gated;' चतुर्विद्यः, -द्या, -द्यम्, 'possessed of the four sciences' (108); सहस्राक्षः, -क्षी, -क्षम्, 'thousand-eyed' (see 778); पञ्चगवधनः, -ना, -नम्, 'having the wealth of five bullocks.'

Relative form of Compounds with Adverbial Prefixes.

769. The adverbial compounds most frequently employed relatively as adjectives are those formed with the adverbial preposition

सह 'with,' contracted into स; thus, स-क्रोधः, -धा, -धम्, 'angry' (lit. 'with-anger,' 'having anger'); स-फलः, -ला, -लम्, 'fruitful' (108); स-बन्धुः, -न्धुः, -न्धु, 'possessed of kindred' (119); स-यत्नः, -त्ना, -त्नम्, 'energetic;' स-जीवः, -वा, -वम्, 'possessed of life,' 'living;' सानन्दः, -न्दा, -न्दम्, 'joyful;' स-सचिवः, -वा, -वम्, 'accompanied by ministers;' स-भार्यः 'accompanied by a wife,' 'having a wife;' स-ज्यः, -ज्या, -ज्यम्, 'strung' (as a bow, lit. 'with-bowstring').

Obs.—When adverbial compounds like यथोक्तम् (760. *b*) are used at the beginning of relative compounds, the final म् is dropped; e.g. यथोक्त-व्यापारः, -रा, -रम्, 'employed in the manner described.'

a. The suffix क *ka* (80. LVI) is often added to this kind of compound; as, स-श्रीकः, -का, -कम्, 'possessed of fortune;' स-स्त्रीकः, -का, -कम्, 'accompanied by women.'

b. In some compounds सह remains; as, सह-वाहनः 'with his army;' सह-पुत्रः 'along with his son.'

c. स is also used for समान 'same;' as, स-गोत्रः, -त्रा, -त्रम्, 'of the same family.'

d. There are of course many examples of nouns combined with adverbial prefixes, so as to form relative compounds, which cannot be regarded as relative forms of Avyayí-bháva; thus, उद्-आयुधः, -धा, -धम्, 'with uplifted weapon;' नाना-प्रकारः, -रा, -रम्, 'of various shapes;' क्व-निवासः, -सा, -सम्, 'where dwelling?' क्व-जन्मा, -न्मा, -न्म, 'where born?' निरपराधः, -धा, -धम्, 'without fault;' निराहारः, -रा, -रम्, 'having no food;' अप-भीः, -भीः, -भि, 'fearless' (123. *b*); तथा-विधः, -धा, -धम्, 'of that kind,' 'in such a state;' दुर्बुद्धिः, -द्धिः, -द्धि, 'weak-minded;' दुष्प्रकृतिः, -तिः, -ति, 'ill-natured;' सुमुखः, -खा or -खी, -खम्, 'handsome-faced;' सुबुद्धिः, -द्धिः, -द्धि, 'of good understanding.' Some of the above may be regarded as relative forms of Descriptive compounds, formed with indeclinable prefixes; see 756. Similar compounds in Greek and Latin are, *ἀν-ήμερος, εὔ-δηλος, in-imicus, in-felix, dis-similis, semi-plenus.*

e. Observe—The adverbial prefixes दुस् and सु (726. *d. f*) impart a passive sense to participial nouns of agency, just as δυσ and εὖ in Greek; thus, दुष्कर 'difficult to be done,' सुकर 'easy to be done;' दुर्लभ 'difficult to be obtained,' सुलभ 'easy to be attained;' दुस्तर 'difficult to be crossed.' Cf. *εὔφορος*, 'easy to be borne;' *δύσπορος*, 'difficult to be passed,' &c.

f. स-नाथः, -था, -थम्, 'possessed of a master,' is used at the end of compounds to denote simply 'possessed of,' 'furnished with;' thus, वितान-सनाथं शिलातलम् 'a stone-seat furnished with a canopy;' शिलापट्ट-सनाथो मण्डपः 'an arbour having a marble-slab as its master,' i. e. 'furnished with,' 'provided with,' &c. Similarly, बहु-बक-सनाथो वट-पादपः 'a fig-tree occupied by a number of cranes.'

g. Observe—The relative form of a compound would be marked in Vedic Sanskrit by the accent. In the Karma-dháraya compound *mahá-báhu*, 'great arm,' the accent would be on the last syllable, thus महाबाहु; but in the Relative *mahá-báhu*, 'great-armed,' on the ante-penultimate, thus, महाबाहु. So, native commentators often quote as an example of the importance of right accentuation, the word *Indra-śatru*, which, accented on the first syllable, would be Bahu-vrīhi (see Páṇ. VI. 2, 1, by which the first member retains its original accent); but accented on the penultimate would be Tat-purusha. The sense in the first case is 'having Indra for a conqueror or destroyer;' in the second, 'the destroyer of Indra.'

h. Note, that आत्मक and रूप (80. LXXIX) are used at the end of relative compounds to denote 'composed of,' 'consisting of;' but are more frequently found at the end of complex relatives; see 774.

COMPLEX COMPOUND NOUNS.

770. We have now to speak of complex compound words, or compounds within compounds, which form a most remarkable feature in Sanskṛit composition. Instances might be given of twenty or thirty words thus compounded together; but these are the productions of the vitiated taste of more modern times, and are only curious as shewing that the power of compounding words may often be extravagantly abused. But even in the best specimens of Sanskṛit composition, and in the simplest prose writings, four, five, or even six words are commonly compounded together, involving two or three forms under one head. It will be easy, however, to determine the character of the forms involved, by the rules propounded in the preceding pages.

Instances of absolute complex compounds, whose sense is complete and unconnected, are not rare.

a. The following are examples: कालान्तरावृत्तिशुभाशुभानि 'good and evil (occurring) in the revolutions of the interval of time,' the whole being a dependent, involving a dependent and a copulative; सेनापतिबलाध्यक्षौ 'the general of the army and the overseer of the forces,' the whole being a copulative, involving two dependents; शोकारातिभयत्राणम् 'the protection from sorrow, enemies, and perils,' the whole being a dependent, involving an aggregative; अवधीरितसुहृद्वाक्यम् 'the disregarded words of a friend,' the whole being a descriptive, involving a dependent; शुक्लाम्बरमाल्यदाम 'a white robe and a string of garlands,' the whole being a copulative, involving a descriptive and dependent; सर्वशास्त्रपारगः 'one who has gone to the opposite bank (*pára*) of all the Śástras,' i. e. 'one who has read them through;' मृतसिंहास्थीनि 'the bones of a dead lion.'

771. Complex compounds are generally used as adjectives, or relatively, as epithets of some other word in the sentence; thus, गलितनखनयनः, -नी, -नम्, 'whose nails and eyes were decayed,' the whole being the relative form of descriptive, involving a copulative; क्षुत्क्षामकण्ठः 'having a throat emaciated with hunger,' the whole being the relative form of descriptive, involving a dependent.

a. Other examples are, शुक्ल-माल्यानुलेपनः, -ना, -नम्, 'having a white garland and unguents,' the whole being the relative form of copulative, involving a descriptive; पीन-स्कन्धोरु-बाहुः 'broad-shouldered and strong-armed,' the whole being a copulative, involving two descriptives; पूर्व-जन्म-कृतः, -ता, -तम्, 'done in a former birth,' the whole being a dependent, involving a descriptive; विद्या-वयो-वृद्धः, -द्धा, -द्धम्, 'advanced in learning and age,' the whole being a dependent, involving a copulative; हृषित-स्रग्-रजो-हीनः, -ना, -नम्, 'having fresh garlands, and being free from dust,' the whole being the relative form of copulative, involving a descriptive and dependent; अभिषेकार्द्र-शिराः, -राः, -रः, 'whose head was moist with unction;' यथेप्सित-मुखः, -खा or -खी, -खम्, 'having the face turned in any direction one likes;' शूल-मुद्गर-हस्तः, -स्ता, -स्तम्, 'spear and club in hand;' एक-रात्र-निर्वाहोचितः, -ता, -तम्, 'sufficient for support during one night' (see 778); ऋग्-यजुः-सामाख्य-त्रय-ग्रन्थार्थाभिज्ञाः 'those who are acquainted with the meaning of the three Vedas, called Ṛig, Yajur, and Sáma;' सन्दष्ट-दन्तच्छद-ताम्र-नेत्राः 'biting their lips and having red eyes' (agreeing with राजानः); पर-द्रोह-कर्म-धीः 'injuring another by action or by intention.'

772. The substantive आदि, 'a beginning,' often occurs in complex relative compounds, with the force of *et cetera*, as in simple relatives at 764; thus, शुक-सारिकादयः 'parrots, starlings, &c.' (agreeing with पक्षिणः 'birds beginning with parrots and starlings'), the whole being the relative form of dependent, involving an aggregative; सन्धि-विग्रहादि 'peace, war, &c.' (agreeing with पूर्वोक्तम् understood); गृह-देवागारादि-युक्तः, -क्ता, -क्तम्, 'possessed of houses, temples, &c.;' करि-तुरग-कोषादि-परिच्छद-युक्तः, -क्ता, -क्तम्, 'possessed of property such as elephants, horses, treasure, &c.'

a. Similarly, आद्य in the example उत्तम-गन्धाद्याः (agreeing with स्रजः 'garlands possessing the best odour and other qualities').

773. Long complex compounds may be generally translated by beginning at the last word and proceeding regularly backwards, as in the following: मत्त-मधुकर-निकर-मुक्त-झङ्कार-मिलित-कोकिलालाप-सङ्गीतक-सुखावहः, -हा, -हम्, 'causing pleasure by the music of the voice of the cuckoo, blended with the hum emitted by the swarms of joyous bees.'

774. आत्मक or रूप, at the end of a complex relative, denotes 'composed of;' thus, हस्त्यश्व-रथ-पदाति-कर्मकरात्मकं बलम् 'a force consisting of elephants, horses, chariots, infantry, and servants;' प्राग्-जन्म-सुकृत-दुष्कृत-रूपे कर्मणी 'the two actions consisting of the good and evil done in a former birth.'

775. Complex compounds may sometimes have their second or middle member omitted; thus, अभिज्ञान-शकुन्तलम् is really a complex compound, the whole being a descriptive, involving a dependent; but the middle member स्मृत is elided. Similarly, शाक-पार्थिवः 'the era-king' is for शाक-प्रिय-पार्थिवः 'the king (beloved) by the era;' विक्रमोर्वशी for विक्रमप्राप्तोर्वशी 'Urvaśí gained by valour.'

a. Complex compounds expressive of comparison are not uncommon; as, जल-बिन्दु-लोल-चपलः, -ला, -लम्, 'unsteady and trembling as a drop of water;'

नलिनी-दल-तोय-तरलः, -ला, -लम्, 'tremulous as water on the leaf of a lotus;' the last two examples are complex. Compare 758. *a*.

b. A peculiar compound of this kind is formed from Dvandvas by adding the suffix *íya;* thus, काक-तालीयः, -या, -यम्, 'like the story of the crow and the palm-tree;' श्येन-कपोतीयः, -या, -यम्, 'like the story of the hawk and the pigeon.'

c. The substantive verb must often be supplied in connexion with a relative compound; as, प्रारम्भ-सदृशोदयः 'his success was proportionate to his undertakings;' पीताम्भसि 'on his drinking water,' for तेन अम्भसि पीते सति.

776. Complex compound adverbs, or indeclinable compounds, involving other compounds, are sometimes found; as, स्व-गृह-निर्विशेषेण 'not differently from one's own house;' शब्दोच्चारणानन्तरम् 'after uttering a sound;' स्तन-भर-विनमन्मध्य-भङ्गानपेक्षम् 'regardlessly of the curving of her waist bending under the weight of her bosom;' यथा-दृष्ट-श्रुतम् 'as seen and heard.'

ANOMALOUS COMPOUNDS.

777. There are certain compounds which are too anomalous in their formation to admit of ready classification under any one of the preceding heads.

a. कल्प, देशीय, दघ्न, द्वयस, मात्र, affixed to stems, form anomalous compounds; see 80. LVII, LXX—LXXII, LXXVI.

b. There is a common compound formed by placing अन्तर after a nominal stem, to express 'another,' 'other;' as, स्थानान्तरम् or देशान्तरम् 'another place;' राजान्तरेण सह 'along with another king;' जन्मान्तराणि 'other births.'

c. Similarly, मात्र is added to express 'mere;' see 919.

d. पूर्व or पूर्वक or पुरःसर (meaning literally 'preceded by') may be added to nominal stems to denote the manner in which anything is done; as, क्रोध-पूर्वम् 'with anger;' पूजा-पूर्वकम् अन्नं ददौ 'he gave food with reverence.'

e. A peculiar compound is formed by the use of an ordinal number as the last member; thus, सारस-द्वितीयः 'accompanied by the Sárasa;' सीता-तृतीयः (agreeing with रामः) 'having Sítá for his third (companion),' i. e. including Lakshmaṇa; छाया-द्वितीयः (नलः) 'Nala made double by his shadow;' मातृ-षष्ठाः (पाण्डवाः) 'the Páṇḍavas with their mother as the sixth;' वेदा आख्यान-पञ्चमाः 'the Vedas with the Ákhyánas as a fifth;' वृषभैकादशा गावः 'ten cows and one bull' (Manu XI. 129).

f. The following are peculiar: त्यक्त-जीवित-योधी 'a fighter who abandons life;' अकुतोभयः, -या, -यम्, 'having no fear from any quarter;' अदृष्ट-पूर्वः, -र्वा, -र्वम्, 'never before seen;' सप्त-रात्रोषितः 'one who has lodged seven nights.'

g. With regard to compounds like गन्तु-काम 'desirous of going,' see 871.

h. The Veda has some peculiar compounds; e. g. *vidad-vasu*, 'granting wealth;' *yávayad-dveshas*, 'defending from enemies;' *kshayad-víra*, 'ruling over men.' These are a kind of inverted Tat-purusha.

CHANGES OF CERTAIN WORDS IN CERTAIN COMPOUNDS.

778. The following is an alphabetical list of the substitutions and changes which take place in the final syllables of certain words when used in certain compounds. They are called by native grammarians Samásánta suffixes. They are properly only added to Tat-purusha compounds (which include Karma-dháraya).

अक्ष at end of various compounds for अक्षि n. 'the eye;' e.g. गवाक्षः 'a bull's eye (window);' लोहिताक्षः, -क्षी, -क्षम्, 'red-eyed.'—अङ्गुल for अङ्गुलि f. 'the finger;' e.g. द्व्यङ्गुलः, -ला, -लम्, 'measuring two fingers.'—अञ्जल for अञ्जलि m. 'joining the hands in reverence.'—अध्व for अध्वन् m. 'a road;' e.g. प्राध्वः, -ध्वा, -ध्वम्, 'distant (as a road).'—अनडुह in Dvandvas for अनडुह् m. 'a bull;' e.g. धेन्वनडुहम् or -हौ 'cow and bull.'—अनस in Karma-dhárayas for अनस् n. 'a cart,' 'a carriage;' e.g. महानसम् 'a large cart' (Páṇ. v. 4, 94).—अयस in Karma-dhárayas for अयस् n. 'iron.'—अश्म in Karma-dhárayas for अश्मन् m. 'a stone.'—अश्र for अश्रि f. 'an angle;' e.g. चतुरश्रः, -श्रा, -श्रम्, 'quadrangular.'—अष्टा in Dvigus and relative compounds for अष्टन्; e.g. अष्टागवम् 'a car drawn by eight oxen;' अष्टाकपालः, -ला, -लम्, 'having eight receptacles.'—अष्ठीव in Dvandvas for अष्ठीवत् m. n. 'the knee;' e.g. ऊर्वष्ठीवम् 'thigh and knee.'—अस्थ for अस्थि 'a bone.'—अह or अहर् for अहन् n. 'a day;' e.g. एकाहः 'the period of one day;' पुण्याहम् 'a holy-day;' अहर्पतिः 'the lord of day.'—अह्न for अहन् n. 'a day;' e.g. पूर्वाह्णः 'the forenoon.'—ईप for अप् f. 'water;' e.g. द्वीपम् 'an island;' अन्तरीपम् 'an island.'—ईर्मन् for ईर्म 'a wound' (Páṇ. v. 4, 126).—उक्ष in Karma-dhárayas for उक्षन् m. 'an ox;' e.g. महोक्षः 'a large ox.'—उद for उदक n. 'water;' e.g. उदकुम्भः 'a water-jar;' क्षीरोदः 'the sea of milk.'—उरस in Karma-dhárayas for उरस् n. 'the breast;' e.g. अश्वोरसः, -सी, -सम्, 'broad-chested as a horse.'—उषासा an old dual form in Dvandvas for उषस् f. n. 'the dawn;' e.g. उषासासूर्यम् 'dawn and sun' (Páṇ. VI. 3, 31).—ऊधन् (f. ऊध्नी) for ऊधस् n. 'an udder,' at end of Bahu-vríhis (Páṇ. IV. 1, 25); e.g. पीनोध्नी 'having a full udder;' द्व्यूध्नी 'having two udders;' अत्यूध्नी 'having an exceedingly large udder.'—ऊप for अप् f. 'water;' e.g. अनूपः, -पा, -पम्, 'near water,' 'watery.'—ऋच for ऋच्; see 779.—ककुद् for ककुद m. 'the top,' 'head;' e.g. त्रिककुत् 'three-peaked (mountain).'—कद् or का or कव for कु expressing *inferiority* or *diminution;* e.g. कदुष्ण or कोष्ण or कवोष्ण 'slightly warm;' कदक्षरम् 'a bad letter;' कापुरुषः 'a coward.'—काकुद् at end of Bahu-vríhis for काकुद m. 'the palate;' e.g. विकाकुत् 'having no palate.'—कुक्ष for कुक्षि m. 'the belly.'—खार for खारी; e.g. अर्धखारम् 'half a khárí' (a measure).—गन्धि for गन्ध m. 'smell;' e.g. पूतिगन्धिः, -न्धिः, -न्धि, 'fetid.'—गव in Dvigus for गो m. f. 'an ox;' e.g. पञ्चगवम् 'a collection of five cows.'—चतुर for चतुर् 'four;' see 779.—जम् for जाया 'a wife;' e.g. जम्पती du. 'husband and wife.'—जम्भन् for जम्भ 'a tooth;' e.g. तृणजम्भा, -म्भा, -म्भ, 'grass-toothed,' 'graminivorous.'—जानि for जाया f. 'a wife;' e.g. युवजानिः 'having a young wife.'—ज्ञ and ज्ञु in Bahu-vríhis for जानु n. 'the knee;' e.g. प्रज्ञुः, -ज्ञुः, -ज्ञु, or प्रज्ञः, -ज्ञा, -ज्ञम्, 'bandy-kneed.'—तक्ष for तक्षन् m. 'a carpenter;' e.g. कौटतक्षः 'a carpenter who works on his own account;' ग्रामतक्षः 'the village carpenter.'—तमस in Karma-dhárayas (preceded by सम्, अव, or अन्ध) for तमस् n. 'darkness;' e.g. अवतमसम् 'slight darkness.'—त्वच for त्वच्, see 779.—दत् (f. दती) for दन्त m. 'a tooth;' e.g. सुदन्, -दती, -दत्, 'having beautiful teeth.'—दम् for जाया 'a wife;' e.g. दम्पती 'husband and wife' (according to some, 'the two lords of the *dama* or house').—दिव at end and दिवा at beginning for दिवन् m. 'the day;' e.g. नक्तंदिवम् 'night and day;' दिवानिशम् 'day and night.'—दिश at end for दिश्, see Gaṇa *S'arad-ádi* to Páṇ. v. 4, 107.—दुघ at end for दुह् 'yielding milk;' e.g. कामदुघा 'the cow of plenty.'—द्यावा an old dual form for दिव् f. 'heaven;' द्यावापृथिव्यौ du. 'heaven and earth.'—धन्वन् at end of Bahu-vríhis for धनुस् n. 'a bow;' e.g. दृढधन्वा, -न्वा, -न्व, 'a strong archer.'—धर्मन् at end for धर्म m. 'virtue,' 'duty;' e.g. कल्याणधर्मा, -र्मा, -र्म, 'virtuous.'—धुर for धुर् f. 'a load;' e.g. राजधुरः 'a royal load.'—न at the beginning of a few compounds for अ 'not;' e.g. नपुंसकः 'a eunuch.'—नद for नदी 'a river;' e.g. पञ्चनदम् 'the Pañjáb.'—नस or नस् for नासिका 'nose;' e.g. खरणाः, -णाः, -णः, or खरणसः, -सा, -सम्, 'sharp-nosed.'—नाभ for नाभि f. 'the navel;' e.g. पद्मनाभः 'lotus-naveled,' a name of Vishṇu.—नाव for नौ f. 'a ship;' but only in Dvigu compounds and after *ardha* (Páṇ. v. 4, 99, 100); e.g. द्विनावम् 'two boats;' अर्धनावम् 'half of a boat.'—पथ for पथिन् m. 'a road;' e.g. सुपथः 'a good road.'—पद् and पाद् (fem. पदी) for पाद m. 'the foot;' e.g. पद्धिमम् 'coldness of the feet;' द्विपात्, -पदी, -पत्, 'a biped;' चतुष्पात् 'a quadruped.'—पद for पाद m. 'the foot;' e.g. पदगः, -गा, -गम्, 'going on foot.'—पुंस in Dvandvas for पुंस् m. 'a male;' e.g. स्त्रीपुंसौ nom. du. 'man and woman.'—पृत् for पृतना f. 'an army.'—प्रजस् at end of Bahu-vríhis (preceded by अ, सु, or दुस्) for प्रजा f. 'people,' 'progeny;' e.g. बहुप्रजाः, -जाः, -जः, 'having a numerous progeny.'—ब्रह्म for ब्रह्मन् m. 'a Bráhman;' e.g. कुब्रह्मः 'a contemptible Bráhman.'—भूम for भूमि f. 'the earth;' e.g. उदग्भूमः 'land towards the north.'—भ्रुव in Dvandvas for भ्रू f. 'the eye-brow;' e.g. अक्षिभ्रुवम् 'eye and brow.'—मनस in Dvandvas for मनस् n. 'the mind;' e.g. वाङ्मनसे nom. du. n. 'speech and heart.'—मह and मही (preceded by पिता, माता, &c., 754. *a*) for महत् 'great;' e.g. पितामहः 'grandfather.'—महा at beginning of Karma-dhárayas and Bahu-vríhis for महत् m. f. n. 'great;' but in Tat-purusha or dependent compounds महत् is retained, as in महदाश्रयः 'recourse to the great;' also before भूत 'become,' and words of a similar import, as महद्भूतः 'one who has become great;' but महाभूतम् 'an element.'—मूर्ध at end of Bahu-vríhis (preceded by द्वि, त्रि, &c.) for मूर्धन् m. 'the head;' e.g. द्विमूर्धः, -र्धा, -र्धम् (see Páṇ. v. 4, 115; VI. 2, 197).—मेधस् at end of Bahu-vríhis (preceded by अ, सु, दुस्, अल्प, मन्द) for मेधा f. 'intellect;' e.g. अल्पमेधाः, -धाः, -धः.—रहस for रहस्, after अनु, अव, and तप्त; e.g. अनुरहसः 'solitary.'—राज at end of Karma-dhárayas and Tat-purushas for राजन् m. 'a king' (see 151. *a*); e.g. परमराजः 'a supreme monarch;' देवराजः 'the king of the gods.' But occasional instances occur of राजन् at the end of Tat-purushas; e.g. विदर्भराजः

gen. 'of the king of Vidarbha' (Nala XI. 21).—रात्र at end of Dvigus, Karma-dhárayas, and Dvandvas, for रात्रि f. 'night;' e.g. अहोरात्रम् 'day and night;' द्विरात्रम् 'a period of two nights;' मध्यरात्रः 'midnight.'—लोम (after अनु, अव, and प्रति) for लोमन् n. 'hair;' e.g. अनुलोमः, -मा, -मम्, 'with the hair.'—वर्चस in Tat-purushas for वर्चस् n. 'splendour;' e.g. ब्रह्म-वर्चसम् 'the power of a Bráhman.'—श्रेयस in Karma-dhárayas and Bahu-vríhis for श्रेयस् n. 'virtue,' 'felicity;' e.g. निःश्रेयसः, -सी, -सम्, 'destitute of excellence or happiness.'—श्व or श्वा for श्वन् m. 'a dog;' e.g. अतिश्वः, -श्वी, -श्वम्, 'worse than a dog;' श्वापदः 'a beast of prey;' श्वादन्तः 'a dog's tooth.'—स at beginning of Avyayí-bhávas and Bahu-vríhis for सह 'with;' e.g. सकोपम् 'with anger;' सपुत्रः 'accompanied by a son' (सहपुत्रः would be equally correct).—स for समान 'same;' e.g. सपिण्डः 'one who eats the same cake.'—सक्थ in Karma-dhárayas and Bahu-vríhis for सक्थि n. 'the thigh;' e.g. असक्थः, -क्था, -क्थम्, 'having no thighs.'—सख in Tat-purushas and Dvigus for सखि m. 'a friend;' e.g. मरुत्सखः 'the friend of the winds' (Indra).—सरस in Karma-dhárayas for सरस् n. 'a lake;' e.g. महासरसम् 'a great lake.'—साम (after अनु, अव, प्रति) for सामन् n. 'conciliation;' e.g. अनुसामः, -मा, -मम्, 'friendly.'—हल for हलि m. 'a furrow;' e.g. अहलः, -ला, -लम्, 'unploughed.'—हृद् for हृदय n. 'the heart;' e.g. हृच्छयः 'sleeping in the heart;' सुहृत् m. 'a friend.'

779. It is evident from the above list that the most common substitution is that of अ *a* for the final vowel or final vowel and consonant of a word. Other stems ending in च्, श्, ज्, ष्, द्, प्, स्, ह् may add *a;* as, त्वच for त्वच् in वाक्त्वचम् 'voice and skin;' यजुष for यजुस् in ऋग्यजुषम् 'the Ṛig and Yajur-veda.' Also रजस for रजस्, आयुष for आयुस्, शरद for शरद्, &c. Also ऋच for ऋच् in अर्धर्चः, -र्चम्, 'half a verse of the Veda;' and बह्वृचः 'one conversant with the Ṛig-veda.'

a. Some words as the first member of a compound lengthen their finals (see Páṇ. VI. 3, 117; VIII. 4, 4); e.g. कोटर before वन (कोटरा-वणम् 'a wood full of hollow trees'); अञ्जन before गिरि (अञ्जनागिरिः 'name of a mountain'); विश्व before राज् and मित्र (विश्वा-राट् 'a universal sovereign;' विश्वामित्रः 'Viśvámitra'). This is more common in the Veda.

b. Some few shorten their finals, when they stand as the first member, especially nouns terminating in ऊ *ú* or ई *í;* e.g. भ्रु for भ्रू in भ्रुकुटिः f. 'a frown;' ग्रामणि for ग्रामणी in ग्रामणिपुत्रः 'the son of a harlot' (Páṇ. VI. 3, 61): so लक्ष्मि-सम्पन्नः for लक्ष्मीसम्पन्नः 'endowed with good fortune' (Rámáy. I. 19, 21).

c. A few feminine words in आ *á* (such as छाया, सभा, निशा, शाला, कन्या) may be made neuter at the end of certain compounds; e.g. इक्षु-च्छायम् 'the shade of sugar-canes' (Páṇ. II. 4, 22); प्रच्छायम् 'a shady place;' ईश्वर-सभम् 'an assembly of princes;' स्त्रीसभम् 'an assembly of women;' श्व-निशम् (or -शा) 'a night when dogs howl.'

d. A sibilant is sometimes inserted between two members of a compound; as, प्रायश्चित्तम् (for प्राय-चित्तम्) 'expiation of sin;' परस्परम् 'mutually:' cf. आस्पदम् 'place.'

780. Numerals, when preceded by particles, prepositions, or other numerals,

may change their finals to अ *a;* or if their final letter be a consonant, may either drop that consonant or add अ *a* to it; thus, द्वित्र (nom. -त्रास्, -त्रास्, -त्राणि) 'two or three;' पञ्चष (nom. -षास्, -षास्, -षाणि), 'five or six;' उपचतुर (nom. -रास्) 'nearly four.'

781. अहम् is found in the beginning of certain anomalous compounds (such as अहङ्कार, अहम्पूर्विका, &c.) for मद् 'I.'

SECTION II.

COMPOUND VERBS.

782. It might be supposed that 2000 simple roots (74. *b*) would convey every possible variety of idea, and that the aid of prepositions and adverbial prefixes to expand and modify the sense of each root would be unnecessary. But in real fact there are comparatively few Sanskṛit roots in common use; and whilst those that are so appear in a multitude of different forms by the prefixing of one or two or even three prepositions, the remainder are almost useless for any practical purposes, except the formation of nouns. Hence it is that compound verbs are of more frequent occurrence than simple ones.

They are formed in two ways: 1st, by combining roots with prepositions or prefixes; 2ndly, by combining the auxiliaries कृ 'to do' and भू 'to be' with adverbs, or nouns converted into adverbs.

Compound Verbs formed by combining Prepositions and Prefixes with roots.

783. The following list exhibits the prepositions chiefly used in combination with roots:

a. अति *ati*, 'across,' 'beyond,' 'over;' as, अतिया, अती (pres. अत्येमि, &c.), अतिक्रम्, 'to pass by,' 'to pass along,' 'to transgress.'

b. अधि *adhi*, 'above,' 'upon,' 'over;' as, अधिष्ठा 'to stand over,' 'to preside' (pres. अधितिष्ठामि); अधिरुह् 'to climb upon;' अधिशी 'to lie upon;' अधिगम् 'to go over towards;' अधी 'to go over,' in the sense of 'reading.' The initial अ *a* is rarely rejected in Epic poetry; as, धिष्ठित for अधिष्ठित.

c. अनु *anu*, 'after;' as, अनुचर् 'to follow;' अनुष्ठा 'to stand by,' 'to perform;' अनुकृ 'to imitate;' अनुमन् 'to assent;' अनुभू 'to experience,' 'to enjoy.'

d. अन्तर् *antar*, 'between,' 'within' (Gr. ἐν-τός; Lat. *in-tus, inter*); as, अन्तर्धा 'to place within,' 'to conceal,' in pass. 'to vanish;' अन्तर्भू 'to be within;' अन्तश्चर् 'to walk in the midst.'

e. अप *apa*, 'off,' 'away,' 'from' (ἀπό); as, अपगम्, अपसृ, अपे (from अप and इ), 'to go away;' अपनी 'to lead away;' अपकृष् 'to abstract;' अपवह् 'to bear away.' It also implies 'detraction;' as, अपवद् 'to defame.'

f. अपि *api*, 'on,' 'over' (ἐπί), only used with धा and नह्; as, अपिधा 'to cover over;' अपिनह् 'to bind on.' The initial अ *a* is often rejected, leaving पिधा, पिनह्.

g. अभि *abhi*, 'to,' 'unto,' 'towards;' as, अभिया, अभी, 'to go towards;' अभि-धाव् 'to run towards;' अभिदृश् 'to behold;' अभिवद् or अभिधा (see धा at 664) 'to address,' 'to accost,' 'to speak to,' 'to salute.'

h. अव *ava*, 'down,' 'off;' as, अवरुह्, अवतृ, 'to descend;' अवेक्ष् 'to look down;' अवकृ 'to throw down,' 'to scatter;' अवकृत् 'to cut off.' It also implies 'disparagement;' as, अवज्ञा 'to despise;' अवक्षिप् 'to insult.' With धा, 'to attend.' The initial अ *a* may be optionally rejected from अवगाह 'bathing.'

i. आ *á*, 'to,' 'towards,' 'near to' (Latin *ad*); as, आविश् 'to enter;' आक्रम् 'to go towards;' आरुह् 'to mount up.' When prefixed to गम्, या, and इ, 'to go,' and दा 'to give,' it reverses the action; thus, आगम्, आया, ए, 'to come;' आदा 'to take.' With चर्, 'to practise.'

j. उद् *ud*, 'up,' 'upwards,' 'out' (opposed to नि); as, उच्चर् (48), उदि, 'to go up,' 'to rise;' उड्डी 'to fly up;' उद्धन् 'to strike up' (उद् and हन्, 50); उद्धृ (उद् and हृ, 50) 'to extract;' उन्मिष् and उन्मील् (47) 'to open the eyes;' उत्कृत्, उच्छिद्, 'to cut up;' उन्मूल् 'to root up;' उच्छ्रि 'to lift up' (उद् and श्रि, 49).

When prefixed *immediately* to स्था and स्तम्भ् it causes the elision of *s;* as, उत्था 'to stand up;' उत्तम्भ् 'to prop up.' In some cases it reverses the action; as, from नम् 'to bend down,' उन्नम् (47) 'to raise up;' from यम् 'to keep down,' उद्यम् 'to lift up.'

k. उप *upa* (opposed to *apa*), 'to,' 'towards' (ὑπό), 'near,' 'down,' 'under,' joined like आ and अभि to roots of motion; as, उपया 'to approach;' उपचर् 'to wait upon;' उपस्था 'to stay near,' 'to be present,' 'to arrive.' With विश् (cl. 6, उपविशति), 'to sit down;' with आस्, 'to sit near.'

Obs.—उप with ओषति (from उष्) = उपोषति 'he burns;' see 784. *a*.

l. नि *ni* (thought to be for primitive *ani;* cf. Lat. *in*, Gr. ἐνί, ἐν, εἰν), 'in,' 'on,' 'down,' 'downwards,' 'under' (opposed to उद्); as, निपत् 'to fall down;' नियम् 'to suppress;' निमिष् and निमील् 'to close the eyes;' निक्षिप्, निधा, न्यस्, 'to lay down,' 'to deposit;' निविश् 'to go within,' 'to encamp.' With वृत्, 'to return,' 'to desist;' with शम्, 'to hear.' In some cases it does not alter, or simply intensifies the sense; as, निहन् 'to kill outright.'

m. निस् *nis*, 'out;' as, निष्क्रम् (69. *a*), निर्गम्, निःसृ, 'to go out,' 'to come out;' निष्कृत् 'to cut up;' निर्वृत् 'to come to an end,' 'to cease;' निश्चि 'to determine.'

n. परा *pará*, 'back,' 'backwards' (παρά), combined with जि and भू in the sense of 'defeat;' as, पराजि 'to overcome' (cf. παρανικάω); पराभू 'to be defeated.' With इ, cl. 2, it signifies 'to retreat' (pres. परैमि); with इ or अय्, cl. 1, Átm., 'to run away,' *pará* being changed to *palá* (pres. पलाये).

o. परि *pari*, 'around,' 'about' (περί, *per*); as, परिवेष्ट्, परिवृ, 'to surround;' परिचर्, परिगम्, 'to go round;' परीक्ष् 'to look round,' 'to examine;' परिवृत् 'to turn round;' परिधाव् 'to run round.' When prefixed to कृ it signifies 'to adorn,' and स् is inserted, परिष्कृ. With भू, 'to despise,' and with हृ, 'to avoid.' It sometimes merely gives intensity or completeness to the action; as, परित्यज् 'to abandon altogether;' परिज्ञा 'to ascertain completely.'

p. प्र *pra*, 'before,' 'forward' (πρό, *pro*, *præ*); as, प्रगम्, प्रसृप्, 'to proceed;' प्रयम् 'to set before,' 'to present;' प्रक्रम् 'to begin;' प्रवृत् 'to proceed,' 'to begin;' प्रधाव् 'to run forward;' प्रस्था 'to set out,' 'to advance;' प्रभू 'to be superior,' 'to prevail;' प्रदृश् 'to foresee.' With लभ्, 'to deceive.'

Obs.—प्र with ऋच्छति 'he goes,' makes प्रार्च्छति (or प्रार्छति) 'he goes on quickly' (38. *f*); प्र with एषय, causal stem of इष् 'to go,' makes प्रेषयामि 'I send.' Similarly, प्र + एजते = प्रेजते 'he trembles;' and प्र + ओषति (from उष्) = प्रोषति 'he burns.' See 784. *a.*

The *r* of *pra* influences a following *n* by 58; as, प्रणम् 'to bend before,' 'to salute.' Sometimes प्र does not alter the sense of a root, as in प्राप् 'to obtain' (see 681).

q. प्रति *prati*, 'against,' 'to,' 'towards,' 'near,' 'at,' 'back again' (πρός); as, प्रतियुध् 'to fight against;' प्रती 'to go towards' (pres. प्रत्येमि); प्रतिगम् 'to go towards,' 'to return;' प्रतिवस् 'to dwell near or at;' प्रतिकृ 'to counteract;' प्रतिहन् 'to beat back,' 'to repel;' प्रतिवच् 'to answer;' प्रतिलभ् 'to recover;' प्रतिनी 'to lead back;' प्रतिनन्द् 'to re-salute.' With श्रु, 'to promise;' with पद्, 'to arrive at,' 'to obtain;' with ईक्ष्, 'to wait for,' 'to expect.'

r. वि *vi*, 'apart,' 'asunder,' implying 'separation,' 'distinction,' 'distribution,' 'dispersion' (Latin *dis-*); as, विचर् 'to wander about;' विचल् 'to vacillate;' विहृ 'to roam for pleasure;' विकॄ 'to dissipate;' विदॄ 'to tear asunder;' विभज् 'to divide;' विविच् 'to distinguish.' Sometimes it gives a privative signification; as, वियुज् 'to disunite;' विस्मृ 'to forget;' विक्री 'to sell.' With कृ, 'to change for the worse.' Sometimes it has little apparent influence on the root; as, विनश् 'to perish,' or 'to perish entirely;' विचिन्त् 'to think.'

s. सम् *sam*, 'with,' 'together with' (σύν, *con*); as, सञ्चि, सङ्गृह्, 'to collect;' संयुज् 'to join together;' सङ्क्रम् 'to meet together;' सम्पद् 'to happen;' सङ्क्षिप् 'to contract.' With कृ it signifies 'to perfect,' and स् is inserted, संस्कृ. It is often prefixed without altering the sense; as, सञ्जन् 'to be produced.'

t. दुस् *dus*, 'badly,' and सु *su*, 'well,' are also prefixed to verbs or verbal derivatives; see 726. *d. f.*

u. Also other indeclinable prefixes; thus, अस्तम् 'decline' is compounded with इ in the sense of 'to go down,' 'to set;' तिरस् 'across,' with धा in the sense of 'to conceal,' with गम् 'to disappear,' with कृ 'to revile;' श्रत् with धा 'to believe.'

784. Two prepositions are often combined with a root; as, व्यादा (वि + आ) 'to open;' व्यापद् (cl. 10) 'to kill;' उपागम् (उप + आ) 'to go under,' 'to undergo,' 'to arrive at;' समे (सम् + आ + rt. इ) 'to assemble;' प्रणिपत् (प्र + नि, 58) 'to prostrate one's self;' प्रोद्ध (प्र + उद् + rt. हृ) 'to raise up:' and occasionally three; as, प्रव्याहृ (प्र + वि + आ) 'to predict;' प्रत्युदाहृ (प्रति + उद् + आ) 'to answer.' Other combinations of three prepositions, occasionally prefixed to roots, are सं + उप + आ; अभि + वि + आ; सं + अभि + प्र; उप + सं + प्र; अनु + सं + वि.

a. Observe—Final अ *a* and आ *á* of a preposition combine with the initial ऋ *ṛi* of a root into *ár*, and are rejected before initial ए *e* and ओ *o* (except in forms from the roots इ *i*, 'to go,' and एध् 'to increase), see 38. *f. g*: and see प्र and उप above: but in other cases prepositions ending in vowels combine with roots beginning with vowels according to the rules of Sandhi; thus, आ with इ 'to go' becomes ए (32), and in pres. ऐमि (आ + एमि 33), &c.; in impf. आयम्, ऐस् (645, 33), &c.; in pot. एयाम् (आ + इयाम्), &c.; in impv. आयानि (आ + यानि), &c. Similarly, अप with एमि becomes अपैमि by 33.

b. Observe also, a sibilant is generally inserted between the prepositions अप, उप, परि, प्रति, सम्, and the roots कृ 'to do' and कॄ 'to scatter;' see above under परि and सम्. Similarly, from अव and कृ is formed अवस्कर 'excrement.'

c. The final *i* of अति, प्रति, परि, नि, is optionally lengthened in forming certain nouns from compound verbs; as, अतीसार, प्रतीकार, परीहास, नीकार.

785. In conjugating compound verbs formed with prepositions, neither the augment nor the reduplication change their position, but remain attached to the root*; as, पर्यणयम्, impf. of नी, with परि; उपाविशम्, impf. of विश्, with उप; अन्वतिष्ठम्, impf. of स्था, with अनु; प्रतिजघान, perf. of हन्, with प्रति; प्रोज्जहार, perf. of हृ, with प्र and उद्.

a. In the Veda, as in Homer, prepositions may be separated from the root by other words; as, आ त्वा विशन्तु 'let them enter thee.'

786. Grammarians restrict certain roots to either Parasmai-pada or Átmane-pada when in combination with particular prepositions or when peculiar meanings are involved †. Most of the examples specified by Pāṇini (I. 3, 1–93) are here added. The 3rd sing. present will be given, the termination either in *ti* or *te* marking the Pada to which in each case the root is supposed to be limited.

अस् 'to throw' is generally Parasmai, and ऊह् 'to reason' is generally Átmane, but combined with any preposition may take either Pada.—कृ 'to do;' *anu-karoti*, 'he imitates;' *adhi-kurute*, 'he overcomes;' *ut-kurute*, 'he informs against,' 'reviles;' *ud-á-kurute*, 'he reviles;' *upa-kurute*, 'he worships;' *upa-s-kurute* (784. *b*), 'he prepares;' *upa-s-karoti*, 'he polishes;' *pará-karoti*, 'he rejects;' *pra-kurute*, 'he offers violence,' 'he recites (stories).'—कॄ 'to scatter;' *apa-s-kirate* (784. *b*), 'he (the cock) throws up earth;' but *apa-kirati*, 'he scatters (as flowers).'—क्रम् 'to go;' *á-kramate*, 'he (the sun) ascends;' but *á-krámati* when not in the

* There are a few exceptions to this rule in the Mahá-bhárata; as in अन्वसञ्चरत् (Johnson's Selections, p. 33, l. 14).

† In Epic poetry, however, there is much laxity; e.g. यत् and प्रार्थ्, which are properly Átmane-pada verbs, are found in Parasmai. Instances of passive verbs taking Parasmai terminations have been given at 461. *c*. On the other hand, नन्द् 'to rejoice,' which is properly Parasmai, is found in Átmane.

sense of 'the rising of a luminary, &c.;' *vi-kramate*, 'he (the horse) steps out;' but *vi-krámati*, 'it (the joint) splits in two;' *upa-kramate* or *pra-kramate*, 'he is valiant;' but *upa-krámati*, 'he approaches;' and *pra-krámati*, 'he departs.'—क्री 'to buy;' *ava-kríṇíte, pari-kríṇíte*, 'he buys;' *vi-kríṇíte*, 'he sells;' but *krí* alone takes either Pada.—क्रीड् 'to play;' *á-kríḍate* or *anu-kríḍate*, 'he sports;' *pari-kríḍate*, 'he plays about;' *san-kríḍate*, 'he plays;' but *san-kríḍati*, 'it (the wheel) creaks.'—क्षिप् 'to throw;' *ati-kshipati*, 'he throws beyond;' *abhi-kshipati*, 'he throws on;' *prati-kshipati*, 'he throws back or towards.'—क्ष्णु 'to sharpen;' *san-kshṇute*, 'he sharpens.'—गम् 'to go;' *á-gamayate*, 'he delays or waits patiently;' *vy-ati-gaććhanti*, 'they go against each other;' *san-gaććhati* when motion towards anything is implied, as 'he goes towards (the village);' but Átm. in the sense of 'he goes with' or 'agrees with.'—गॄ 'to swallow;' *san-girate*, 'he promises,' 'he proclaims;' but *san-girati*, 'he swallows;' *ava-girate*, 'he swallows.'—चर् 'to go;' *uć*(for *ud*)-*ćarate*, 'he goes astray;' *uć-ćarati*, 'it (the tear) overflows;' *san-ćarate* or *sam-ud-á-ćarate*, 'he goes in a chariot.'—जि 'to conquer;' *vi-jayate, pará-jayate*, 'he conquers;' with other prepositions *ji* is generally Parasmai.—ज्ञा 'to know;' *apa-jáníte*, 'he denies (the debt);' *prati-jáníte* or *saṅ-jáníte*, 'he acknowledges.' Without a prep. this root is restricted to either Pada if certain meanings are involved; as, *sarpisho* (for *sarpishá*) *jáníte*, 'he engages (in sacrifice) by means of ghee;' *gáṃ jáníte*, 'he knows (his own) cow;' *sváṃ gáṃ jánáti* or *jáníte*, 'he knows his own cow.'—नी 'to lead;' *un*(for *ud*)-*nayate*, 'he lifts up;' *upa-nayate*, 'he invests (with the sacred thread);' *vi-nayate*, 'he pays,' or 'he grants,' or 'he restrains;' *vi-nayati*, 'he takes away' (the anger of his master); *vi-nayati*, 'he turns away (his cheek).' Without a prep. this root is Átm. if it means 'to excel,' or 'to ascertain.'—नु 'to praise;' *á-nute*, 'he praises.'—तप् 'to burn;' *ut-tapati* or *vi-tapati*, 'he warms;' *ut-tapate* or *vi-tapate*, 'it shines,' 'he warms (his own hand).' Without a prep. this root is Átm., cl. 4, if it means 'to perform penance.'—दा 'to give;' *á-datte*, 'he receives;' *vy-á-dadáti*, 'he opens (his mouth);' *vy-á-datte*, 'he opens (the mouth of another);' *saṃ-yaććhate*, 'he gives' (as *dásyá*, 'to the female slave,' the instr. being used for the dative).—दृश् 'to see;' *sam-paśyate*, 'he considers thoroughly.'—नाथ् 'to ask for;' always Átm. if used with gen., as *madhuno náthate*, 'he asks for honey.'—प्रछ् 'to ask;' *á-pṛiććhate*, 'he bids adieu to;' *sam-pṛiććhate*, 'he interrogates.'—भुज् 'to eat' is Átm. if it means 'to eat,' 'to possess,' or 'to suffer;' but Par. if it means 'to protect.'—मृष् 'to bear;' *pari-mṛishyati*, 'he endures or forgives.'—यम् 'to restrain;' *á-yaććhate*, '(the tree) spreads;' *á-yaććhate*, 'he stretches out (his hand);' but *á-yaććhati*, 'he draws up' (as a rope from a well); *upa-yaććhate*, 'he takes (a woman) to wife;' but *upa-yaććhati*, 'he takes the wife (of another);' *á-yaććhate*, 'he puts on (clothes);' *ud-yaććhate*, 'he takes up (a load);' but *ud-yaććhati*, 'he studies vigorously (the Veda, &c.);' *saṃ-yaććhate*, 'he collects' (or stacks as rice, &c.)—युज् 'to join;' *ud-yunkte*, 'he makes effort;' *anu-yunkte*, 'he examines;' *ni-yunkte*, 'he appoints;' *pra-yunkte*, 'he applies;' but *pra-yunakti*, 'he sets in order (sacrificial vessels).'—रम् 'to sport;' *upa-ramati*, 'he causes to refrain *;' *á-ramati*, 'he rests;' *vi-ramati*, 'he ceases.'—लू 'to cut;' *vy-ati-*

* This is an instance of a simple verb involving the sense of a causal.

lunîte, 'he performs cutting (of wood) which was the office of another.'—वद् 'to speak;' *anu-vadate*, 'he speaks after or like' (with gen.); but *anu-vadati*, 'he imitates' (as *giram*, 'a voice,' acc.); *upa-vadate*, 'he coaxes,' 'he advises;' *vi-pra-vadante* or *vi-pra-vadanti*, 'they dispute;' *sam-pra-vadante*, 'they speak together;' but *sam-pra-vadanti*, 'they (the birds) sing together;' *apa-vadate*, 'he reviles improperly;' but *apa-vadati*, 'he speaks against.' Without prep. *vad* is Átm., 'to be learned in interpreting' (the S'ástras), or 'to be earnest in the study of anything' (as agriculture, &c.)—वह् 'to carry;' *pra-vahati*, 'it (the river) flows along.'—विद् 'to know;' *saṃ-vitte*, 'he is conscious;' *saṃ-vidate* or *saṃ-vidrate*, 'they are conscious' (308).—विश् 'to enter;' *ni-viśate*, 'he enters.'—शप् 'to swear;' *śapate*, 'he swears at' (with dat.)—श्रु 'to hear;' *saṃ-śriṇoti*, 'he hears (the speech);' but *saṃ-śriṇute*, 'he hears well' (intransitively).—स्था 'to stand;' *ava-tishṭhate*, 'he waits patiently;' *pra-tishṭhate*, 'he sets out;' *vi-tishṭhate*, 'he stands apart;' *san-tishṭhate*, 'he stays with;' *upa-tishṭhate*, 'he worships,' 'he attends on.' Without prep. *sthá* takes the Átmane when it denotes 'adhering to,' 'giving one's self up to shewing amatory feelings' (Páṇ. I. 3. 23), as *tishṭhate gopí Kṛishṇáya*, 'the shepherdess gives herself up to Kṛishṇa;' but *upa-tishṭhati*, 'he waits on' (not in a religious sense, and governing an acc.); *ut-tishṭhate*, 'he aspires' (to salvation); but *ut-tishṭhati*, 'he rises' (from a seat).—हन् 'to strike;' *á-hate* (see 654), 'he or it strikes' ('himself or itself,' the object being omitted); but *á-hanti vṛishabham*, 'he strikes the bull.'—स्वृ 'to sound;' *saṃ-svarate*, 'it sounds clearly.'—हृ 'to seize;' *anu-harate*, 'he takes after' (the disposition of his father or mother), otherwise *anu-harati*.—ह्वे 'to call;' *upa-hvayate* or *ni-hvayate* or *vi-hvayate* or *saṃ-hvayate*, 'he calls,' 'he invokes;' *á-hvayate*, 'he challenges' (an enemy); but *á-hvayati*, 'he calls' (his son).

a. Some causals are also restricted to either Parasmai or Átmane, according to the preposition prefixed or the meaning involved; thus the causal of मुह् with परि, meaning 'to bewitch,' is limited to Átm. So also, गृध् 'to be greedy,' when its causal means 'to deceive,' is restricted to Átm.: and the causal of वञ्च्, meaning 'to deceive,' takes Átm.; meaning 'to avoid,' Par. Again, कृ in the causal, when joined with *mithyá*, and signifying 'to pronounce badly,' takes Par.; but only in the sense of doing so *once*. In the sense of 'causing a false alarm' it requires Átm.; but the above specimens will suffice to shew the little profit likely to be derived from pursuing this part of the subject farther.

Compound Verbs formed by combining Adverbs with कृ *and* भू.

787. These are of two kinds: 1st, those formed by combining adverbs with कृ 'to make' and भू 'to become;' 2ndly, those formed by combining nouns used adverbially with these roots.

a. Examples of the first kind are, अलंकृ 'to adorn;' आविष्कृ 'to make manifest' (see 72); बहिष्कृ 'to eject;' पुरस्कृ 'to place in front,' 'to follow;' विनाकृ 'to deprive;' सत्कृ 'to entertain as a guest;' नमस्कृ 'to revere;' साक्षाद्भू, प्रादुर्भू, 'to become manifest,' &c.

788. In forming the second kind, the final of a stem, being *a* or *á*, is changed to *í*; as, from सज्ज, सज्जीकृ 'to make ready,' सज्जीभू 'to become ready;' from कृष्ण, कृष्णीकृ 'to blacken;' from परिखा 'a ditch,' परिखीकृ 'to convert into a ditch:' and sometimes *a* becomes *á*; as, प्रियाकृ 'to please,' from प्रिय. A final *i* or *u* is lengthened; as, from शुचि, शुचीभू 'to become pure;' from लघु, लघूकृ 'to lighten.' A final *ṛi* is changed to री *rí*; as, from मातृ, मात्रीभू 'to become a mother.' A final *as* and *an* become *í*; as, from सुमनस्, सुमनीभू 'to be of good mind;' from राजन्, राजीभू 'to be a king.'

a. But the greater number of compounds of this kind are formed from nominal stems in *a*. The following are other examples: तृणीकृ 'to esteem as a straw;' स्तम्भीकृ 'to stiffen;' एकचित्तीभू 'to fix the mind on one object;' स्वीकृ 'to make or claim as one's own;' मैत्रीभू 'to become friendly.' Substantives are sometimes formed from these; as, मैत्रीभाव 'the state of being friendly,' 'friendship.'

Obs.—This change of a final to *í* before *kṛi* and *bhú* is technically said to be caused by the suffix *ćvi*, and the change to *á* by *ḍáć*.

b. These compounds often occur as passive participles; thus, अलङ्कृत 'adorned;' प्रादुर्भूत 'become manifest;' सज्जीभूत 'made ready;' लघूकृत 'lightened;' स्वीकरणीय 'to be agreed to.'

789. Sometimes सात्, placed after a nominal stem, is used to form a compound verb of this kind; as, from जल 'water,' जलसात्कृ 'to reduce to liquid;' from भस्मन् 'ashes,' भस्मसात्कृ (57) 'to reduce to ashes.' *Cf.* 725. *a*.

SECTION III.

COMPOUND ADVERBS.

790. Compound adverbs are formed, 1st, by combining adverbs, prepositions, and adverbial prefixes, with nouns in the acc. singular neuter; 2ndly, by placing adverbs, or adjectives used as adverbs, after nominal stems.

a. The first kind are identical with indeclinable compounds (760).

791. Most of the adverbs at 731 may be placed after the stems of nouns; thus, बालकसमीपम् 'near the child;' रक्षार्थम् 'for the sake of protection;' प्रजार्थे 'for the sake of offspring;' किमर्थम् 'on what account?' शब्दोच्चारणानन्तरम् 'after uttering a sound.' See also 777. *d*.

792. The indeclinable participle आरभ्य, 'having begun,' is joined with अद्य, 'to-day' (अद्यारभ्य), in the sense of 'from this time forward;' and with the stems of words to express 'beginning from;' see 925. प्रभृति is used adverbially in the same sense; as, जन्मप्रभृति 'from birth upwards;' तदाप्रभृति 'from that time forward' (see 917).

CHAPTER IX.

SYNTAX.

793. Sanskṛit syntax, unlike that of Greek and Latin, offers fewer difficulties than the other portions of the Grammar. In fact, the writer who has fully explained the formation of compounds has already more than half completed his exposition of the laws which regulate the order, arrangement, and collocation of the words in a sentence (*vákya-vinyása, vákya-viveka, padánvaya*).

794. Observe—In the present chapter on Syntax, that the subject may be made as clear as possible, each word will be separated from the next, and vowels will not be allowed to coalesce, although such coalition be required by the laws of combination. When compounds are introduced, a dot will generally be placed underneath, to mark the division of the different members. Much vagueness and uncertainty, however, may be expected to attach to the rules propounded, when it is remembered that Sanskṛit literature consists almost entirely of poetry, and that the laws of syntax are ever prone to yield to the necessities of metrical composition.

THE ARTICLE.

795. There is no indefinite article in classical Sanskṛit; but कश्चिद् (228) and in modern Sanskṛit एक (200) are sometimes used to supply the place of such an article; thus, एकस्मिन् प्रदेशे 'in a certain country;' कश्चित् शृगालः 'a certain jackal.' The definite article may not unfrequently be expressed by the pronoun तद् (220); thus, स पुरुषः may mean simply 'the man,' not necessarily 'that man.' It is, however, more commonly omitted, and तद् when joined to a noun must generally be translated by 'that.'

CONCORD OF THE VERB WITH THE NOMINATIVE CASE.

796. The verb must agree with the nominative case in number and person; as, अहं करवाणि 'I must perform.'

a. Other examples are, त्वम् अवधेहि 'do thou attend;' स ददाति 'he gives;' आवां ब्रूवः 'we two say;' कपोता ऊचुः 'the pigeons said;' युवां चिन्तयतम् 'do you two reflect;' यूयम् आयात 'do ye come;' सज्जनाः पूज्यन्ते 'good men are honoured;' वाति पवनः 'the wind blows;' उदेति शशाङ्कः 'the moon rises;' स्फुटति पुष्पम् 'the flower blossoms.'

Obs.—Of course, therefore, two nouns in the singular connected by च require the verb in the dual; as, राजा मन्त्री च जग्मतुः 'the king and minister went;' यावच् चन्द्रार्कौ तिष्ठतः 'as long as the moon and sun remain.'

b. The position of the verb is not always the same as in English. It may sometimes come last in the sentence.

797. When a participle takes the place of a finite verb, it must agree with the nominative in number and *gender;* as, स गतः 'he went;' सा गता 'she went;' नार्यौ उक्तवत्यौ 'the two women spoke;' राजा हतः 'the king was killed;' बन्धनानि छिन्नानि 'the bonds were cut.'

a. Sometimes, when it is placed between two or more nominative cases, it agrees with one only; as, स्त्र्‌ वधूः प्रबोधिता पुत्रश्च 'his wife and son were awakened.'

b. The following is noticeable: राज्यम् आत्मा वयं वधूर् नीतानि पणताम् 'kingdom, self, we, and wife were brought (neut. pl.) to the state of a stake (to be played for),' Kirát. XI. 47. See also 906.

c. Very often the copula, or verb which connects the subject with the predicate, is omitted; when, if an adjective stand in the place of the verb, it will follow the rules of concord in gender and number; as, धनं दुर्लभम् 'wealth is difficult of attainment;' आवां कृताहारौ 'we two have finished eating.' But if a substantive stand in the place of the verb, no concord of gender or number need take place; as, सम्पदः पदम् आपदाम् 'successes are the road to misfortune.'

CONCORD OF THE ADJECTIVE WITH THE SUBSTANTIVE.

798. An adjective, participle, or adjective pronoun, qualifying a substantive, when not compounded with it, must agree with the substantive in gender, number, and case; as, साधुः पुरुषः 'a good man;' महद् दुःखम् 'great pain;' एतेषु पूर्वोक्तेषु राष्ट्रेषु 'in these before-mentioned countries;' त्रीणि मित्राणि 'three friends.'

CONCORD OF THE RELATIVE WITH THE ANTECEDENT.

799. The relative must agree with the antecedent noun in gender, number, and person; but in Sanskṛit the relative pronoun generally precedes the noun to which it refers, this noun being put in the same case with the relative, and the pronoun तद् follows in the latter clause; as, यस्य नरस्य बुद्धिः स बलवान् 'the man who has intellect is strong' (lit. 'of whatever man there is intellect, he is strong').

a. The noun referred to by the relative may also be joined with तद्, as यस्य बुद्धिः स नरो बलवान्; or may be omitted altogether, as यत् प्रतिज्ञातं तत् पालय 'what you have promised, that abide by;' येषाम् अपत्यानि खादितानि तैः (पक्षिभिः understood) जिज्ञासा समारब्धा 'by those (birds) whose young ones were devoured an inquiry was set on foot;' यः सर्वान् विषयान् प्राप्नुयाद् यश्च एतान् उपेक्षते तयोर् विषयापेक्षकः श्रेयान् 'he who would obtain all objects of sense, and he who despises them, of the two the despiser is the best.'

800. The relative sometimes stands alone, an antecedent noun or pronoun being

understood, from which it takes its gender and number; as, श्रुतेन किं यो न धर्मम् आचरेत् 'Of what use is scriptural knowledge (to one) who does not practice virtue?' धनेन किं यो न ददाति 'What is the use of wealth (to him) who does not give?'

a. Sometimes, though rarely, the antecedent noun precedes the relative in the natural order; as, न सा भार्या यस्यां भर्ता न तुष्यति 'she is not a wife in whom the husband does not take pleasure.'

801. तावत् and यावत् stand to each other in the relation of demonstrative and relative; as, यावन्ति तस्य द्वीपस्य वस्तूनि तावन्ति अस्माकम् उपनेतव्यानि 'as many products as belong to that island, so many are to be brought to us.' See also 876.

a. Similarly, तादृश and यादृश; as, यादृशं वृत्तं तादृशं तस्मै कथितवन्तः 'as the event occurred, so they related it to him.' Cf. 920. *a.*

SYNTAX OF SUBSTANTIVES.

802. Under this head it is proposed to explain the construction of substantives, without special reference to the verbs which govern them; and for this purpose it will be desirable to exhibit examples beginning with the nominative case.

Nominative Case.

803. A substantive simply and absolutely expressed must be placed in the nominative case; as, हितोपदेशः 'the Hitopadeśa;' भट्टि-काव्यम् 'the poem of Bhaṭṭi.'

a. Two nominative cases in different numbers may be placed in apposition to each other; as, तृणानि शय्या 'grass as a bed.'

Accusative Case.

804. Substantives are not found in the accusative, unconnected with verbs or participles, except as expressing '*duration of time*' or '*space.*' See 821.

Instrumental Case.

805. This case yields a variety of senses. The most usual is that of '*the agent*' and '*the instrument*' or '*means*' by which anything is done; as, मया (उक्तम्) 'by me it was said;' व्याधेन (पाशो योजितः) 'by the fowler a snare was laid;' वेदाध्ययनेन 'by the study of the Vedas;' स्व-चक्षुषा 'with one's own eye.'

806. It also has the force of '*with*' in expressing other collateral ideas; as, बलीयसा स्पर्धा 'vying with the strong;' मित्रेण सम्भाषः 'conversation with a friend;' पशुभिः सामान्यम् 'equality with beasts;' पितुर्

गोचरेण 'with the knowledge of (his) father:' especially when '*accompaniment*' is intended; as, शिष्येण गुरुः 'the master with his pupil;' आत्मनापञ्चमः 'the fifth with myself,' i. e. 'myself and four others.'

807. The other senses yielded by this case are, '*through*,' '*by reason of*,' '*on account of*;' as, कृपया 'through compassion;' तेन अपराधेन 'on account of that transgression:' especially in the case of abstract nouns formed with ता (80. LXII); as, मूढतया 'through infatuation.'

a. '*According to*,' '*by*;' as, विधिना 'according to rule;' मम सम्मतेन 'according to my opinion;' जात्या 'by birth.'

b. '*The manner*' in which anything is done, as denoted in English by the adverbial affix 'ly,' or by the prepositions 'in,' 'at;' as, बाहुल्येन 'in abundance;' धर्मेण 'virtuously;' यथेच्छया or स्वेच्छया 'at pleasure;' सुखेन 'at ease;' अनेन विधिना 'in this way;' महता स्नेहेन (निवसतः) 'they both dwell together in great intimacy;' (नृपः सर्वभूतानि अभिभवति) तेजसा 'a king surpasses all beings in glory;' मनसा (न कर्तव्यम्) 'such a deed must not even be imagined in the mind;' मानुषरूपेण 'in human form;' प्रतिबन्धेन 'for a hindrance.'

808. Substantives expressive of '*want*,' '*need*,' may be joined with the instrumental of the thing wanted; as, अर्थेन न प्रयोजनम् 'there is no occasion for inquiry;' मया सेवकेन न प्रयोजनम् 'there is no need of me as a servant;' तृणेन कार्यम् 'there is use for a straw.'

809. '*The price*' for which anything is done may be in the instrumental; as, पञ्चभिः पुराणैर् (याति दासत्वम्) 'for five Puráṇas he becomes a slave;' बहुभिर् दत्तैर् (युध्यन्ते) 'they fight for great rewards.' Similarly, प्राणपरित्यागमूल्येन (श्रीर् न लभ्यते) 'fortune is not obtained at the price of the sacrifice of life.'

a. So also '*difference between*' two things; as, त्वया समुद्रेण च महद् अन्तरम् 'there is great difference between you and the ocean.'

b. '*Separation from*,' either with or without सह; as, भर्त्रा वियोगः 'separation from a husband' (or भर्त्रा सह वियोगः). Similarly, विच्छेदो हरिणा सह 'separation from Hari.'

c. The English expression '*under the idea that*' is expressed by the instrumental case of the substantive बुद्धि; as, व्याघ्रबुद्ध्या 'under the idea that he was a tiger.'

Double Instrumental.

810. Sometimes when two substantives come together, expressing '*parts*' of a common idea, they are both placed in the instrumental, instead of one in the genitive; as, बकुलैः पुष्पैर् वास्यते 'an odour is emitted by the Vakula-plants by their flowers' (for बकुलानां पुष्पैः). Similarly, ताम् आश्वासयामास प्रेष्याभिश् चन्दनोदकैः 'he caused her to revive by her attendants by sandal-water.'

Dative Case.

811. This case is of very limited applicability, and its functions, irrespectively of the influence of verbs, are restricted to the expression

of '*the object*,' '*motive*,' or '*cause*' for which anything is done, or '*the result*' to which any act tends; as, आत्मविवृद्धये 'for self-aggrandizement;' आपत्प्रतीकाराय 'for the counteraction of calamity;' शस्त्रं च शास्त्रं च प्रतिपत्तये 'arms and books (lead) to renown.'

a. When, as in the last example, '*the result*' or '*end*' to which anything leads is denoted by this case, the verb is seldom expressed, but appears to be involved in the case itself. The following are other examples: यत्र आस्ते विषसंसर्गोऽमृतं तदपि मृत्यवे 'where there is admixture of poison, then even nectar (leads) to death;' उपदेशो मूर्खाणां प्रकोपाय न शान्तये 'advice to fools (leads) to irritation, not to conciliation;' स वृद्धपतिस् तस्याः सन्तोषाय न अभवत् 'that old husband was not to her liking;' स राजा तस्या रुचये न बभूव 'that king was not to her liking;' सिद्ध्यै गच्छ 'go for the accomplishment' (of this matter).

b. It will be seen hereafter that certain verbs of *giving* and *relating* govern the dative. Substantives derived from such verbs exercise a similar influence; as, अन्यस्मै दानम् 'the *giving* to another;' अन्यस्मै कथनम् 'the *telling* to another.'

c. Words expressive of '*salutation*' or '*reverence*' are joined with the dative; as, गणेशाय नमः 'reverence to Gaṇeśa;' कुशलं ते 'health to thee.'

Ablative Case.

812. The proper force of the ablative case is expressed by '*from;*' as, लोभात् (क्रोधः प्रभवति) 'from avarice anger arises;' गिरेः पतनम् 'falling from a mountain;' चाराणां मुखात् 'from the mouth of the spies.'

813. Hence this case passes to the expression of various correlative ideas; as, आहारात् किञ्चित् 'a portion of (from) their food:' and like the instrumental it very commonly signifies '*because*,' '*by reason of*,' '*in consequence of;*' as, गोमनुष्याणां वधात् 'on account of the slaughter of cows and men;' अनवसरप्रवेशात् (पुत्रं निन्दति) 'he blames his son for entering inopportunely;' दण्डभयात् 'through fear of punishment;' अस्मत्पुण्योदयात् 'by reason of my good fortune;' फलतोऽविशेषात् 'because (there is) no difference as to the result.'

a. '*According to;*' as, मन्त्रिवचनात् 'according to the advice of the minister.' Abstract nouns in त्व are often found in this case to express some of these ideas; as, अनवस्थितचित्तत्वात् 'by reason of the unsteadiness of his mind:' especially in the writings of commentators; as, वक्ष्यमाणत्वात् 'according to what will be said hereafter;' स्पृष्टेषत्स्पृष्टेषद्विवृतविवृतसंवृतभेदात् 'according to the division of touched, slightly touched, slightly open, open and contracted.'

814. It also expresses '*through the means*' or '*instrumentality of;*' as, शृगालात् पाशबद्धः 'caught in the toils through the instrumentality of the jackal;' न औषधपरिज्ञानाद् (व्याधेः शान्तिर् भवेत्) 'the alleviation of disease is not effected by the mere knowledge of the medicine.'

a. '*The manner*' in which anything is done is often expressed by the ablative; it is then used adverbially (compare 715); as, यत्नात् 'with diligence,' or 'diligently;' बलात् 'forcibly;' कुतूहलात् 'with wonder;' उपचारात् 'figuratively;' मूलाद् उद्धरणम् 'tearing up by the roots:' or by the ablative suffix तस्; as, स्वेच्छातः 'at one's own pleasure' (see 719. *a. b*).

b. This case also denotes '*after*;' as, शरीरविगमात् 'after separation from the body;' मुख्यप्रतिबन्धनात् 'after the imprisonment of the chief;' तस्य आगमनात् 'since his arrival.'

c. So also, in native grammars the ablative case is used to express '*after*;' thus, रहाभ्याम् 'after the letters *ra* and *ha*;' शात् 'after the letter *śa*;' ऋवर्णाद् नस्य णत्वं वाच्यम् 'it should be stated that after the letters *ṛi* and *ṛī* the cerebral ण *ṇ* is substituted in place of the dental न् *n*.'

d. In reference to *time*, '*within*;' as, त्रिपक्षात् 'within three fortnights.'

e. Nouns expressive of '*fear*' are joined with the ablative of the thing feared; as, मृत्योर् भयम् 'fear of death;' चौरतो भयम् 'fear of robbers.'

Genitive Case.

815. This and the locative case are of the most extensive application, and are often employed, in a vague and indeterminate manner, to express relations properly belonging to the other cases.

a. The true force of the genitive is equivalent to '*of*,' and this case appears most frequently when two substantives are to be connected, so as to present one idea; as, मित्रस्य वचनम् 'the speech of a friend;' भर्ता नार्याः परमं भूषणम् 'the best ornament of a woman is her husband;' न नरस्य नरो दासो दासस् तु अर्थस्य 'man is not the slave of man, but the slave of wealth.'

816. '*Possession*' is frequently expressed by the genitive case alone, without a verb; as, सर्वाः सम्पत्तयस् तस्य सन्तुष्टं यस्य मानसम् 'all riches belong to him who has a contented mind;' धन्योऽहं यस्य ईदृशी भार्या 'happy am I in possessing such a wife.'

a. It often, however, has the force of '*to*,' and is very generally used to supply *the place of the dative*; as, प्राणा आत्मनोऽभीष्टाः 'one's own life is dear to one's self;' न योजनशतं दूरं वाह्यमानस्य तृष्णया 'a hundred Yojanas is not far to one borne away by thirst (of gain);' किं प्रज्ञावताम् अविदितम् 'What is unknown to the wise?' किम् अन्धस्य (प्रकाशयति) प्रदीपः 'What does a lamp (shew) to a blind man?' किं मया अपकृतं राज्ञः 'What offence have I committed towards the king;' किम् अयम् अस्माकं (कर्तुं समर्थः) 'What can this man do to us?'

b. And not unfrequently of '*in*' or '*on*;' as, स्त्रीणां विश्वासः 'confidence in women;' मम आयत्तत्वम् 'dependence on me.'

c. It is even equivalent occasionally to '*from*' or '*by*,' as usually expressed by the ablative or instrumental; as, न कस्यापि (उपायनं गृह्णीयात्) 'one ought not to accept a present from any one;' अस्माकं (वनं त्याज्यम्) 'the wood is to be abandoned by us;' स धन्यो यस्य अर्थिनो न प्रयान्ति विमुखाः 'he is blessed from whom suppliants do not depart in disappointment;' नलस्य उपसंस्कृतं मांसम् 'meat cooked by Nala.'

d. '*Difference between two things*' is expressed by the genitive; as, सेव्यसेवकयोर् महद् अन्तरम् 'there is great difference between the master and the servant' (cf. 809. *a*).

e. In native grammars it expresses '*in place of*;' as, उरण् रपरः '*aṇ* in place of *ṛi* is followed by *ra*.'

Locative Case.

817. The locative, like the genitive, expresses the most diversified relations, and frequently usurps the functions of the other cases. Properly it has the force of '*in*,' '*on*,' or '*at*,' as expressive of many collateral and analogous ideas; thus, रात्रौ 'in the night;' ग्रामे 'in the village;' पृष्ठे 'on the back;' त्वयि विश्वासः 'confidence in you;' मरुस्थल्यां वृष्टिः 'rain on desert ground;' प्रथमक्षुधायाम् 'at the first desire of eating;' पृथिव्यां रोपितो वृक्षः 'a tree planted in the earth.'

818. Hence it passes into the sense '*towards*;' as, क्षमा शत्रौ च मित्रे च 'leniency towards an enemy as well as a friend;' सर्वभूतेषु दया 'compassion towards all creatures;' सुहृत्सु अजिह्मः 'upright towards friends;' सुकृतशतम् असत्सु नष्टम् 'a hundred good offices are thrown away upon the wicked;' नलेऽनुरागः 'love for Nala;' तस्याम् अनुरागः 'affection for her.'

819. Words signifying '*cause*,' '*motive*,' or '*need*' are joined with the locative; as, सत्रपत्वे हेतुः 'the cause of his modesty;' भूपालयोर् विग्रहे भवद्वचनं निदानम् 'your speech was the cause of the war between the two princes;' प्रार्थकाभावः सतीत्वे कारणं स्त्रियाः 'the absence of a suitor is the cause of a woman's chastity;' नौकायां किं प्रयोजनम् 'What need of a boat?' Also words signifying '*employment*' or '*occupation*;' as, अर्थार्जने प्रवृत्तिः 'engaging in the acquisition of wealth.'

a. So words derived from the root *yuj* usually require the locative; as, मम राज्यरक्षायाम् उपयोगः 'I am of service in preserving the kingdom.'

b. This case may yield other senses equivalent to '*by reason of*,' '*for*,' &c.; as, मे छिद्रेषु 'through my faults;' चारः परराष्ट्राणाम् अवलोकने 'a spy is *for the sake* of examining the territory of one's enemies;' युद्धे कालोऽयम् 'this is the time *for* battle;' उपदेशेऽनादरः 'disregard for advice;' का चिन्ता मरणे रणे 'What anxiety *about* dying in battle!' कालं मन्ये पलायने 'I think the time has come for escaping;' पुत्रस्य अनुमते 'with the consent of a son.'

c. It is also used in giving the meaning of a root; as, ग्रह् उपादाने 'the root *grah* is in *taking*,' i. e. conveys the idea of 'taking.'

d. In native grammars it expresses '*followed by*;' thus ङिति means 'when anything having an indicatory *n* follows.' So again, मान्तस्य पदस्य अनुस्वारो हलि 'in the room of *m* final in a word followed by any consonant (*hal*) there is Anusvára.'

e. The locative case is often used absolutely; see 840.

SYNTAX OF NOUNS OF TIME.

820. When reference is made to *any particular division* of time, the instrumental case is usually required; as, त्रिभिर् वर्षैः 'in three years;' द्वादशभिर् मासैः 'in twelve months;' क्षणेन 'in an instant;' कियता कालेन 'In how long time?' वर्षशतैः 'in hundreds of years;' कालपर्यायेण (or simply कालेन) 'in process of time;' मासेन 'in a month;' मासमात्रेण 'in the space of a month;' एतावता कालेन 'in so much time.'

821. When *duration of time* is implied, the accusative case is generally used; as, क्षणम् 'for a moment;' अनेककालम् 'for a long time;' कियन्तं कालम् 'for some time;' एकं मासम् 'for one month;' विंशतिं मासान् 'for twenty months;' द्वौ मासौ 'for two months;' वर्षशतम् 'for a hundred years;' शाश्वतीः समाः 'to all eternity;' शतं वर्षाणि 'for a hundred years;' बहूनि अहानि 'for many days.' The instrumental, however, is sometimes used in this sense, and to express other relations of time; as, द्वादशभिर् वर्षैर् वाणिज्यं कृत्वा 'having traded for twelve years;' कतिपयदिवसैः 'for a few days:' and even the genitive; as, चिरस्य कालस्य (or simply चिरस्य) 'for a long time;' कतिपयाहस्य 'after a few days.'

822. When any *particular day* or *epoch* is referred to, as the date on which any action has taken place or will take place, the locative may be employed; as, कस्मिंश्चिद् दिवसे 'on a certain day;' तृतीये दिवसे 'on the third day;' द्वादशेऽह्नि 'on the twelfth day;' इतः सप्तदशेऽहनि 'seventeen days from this time.' Or sometimes the accusative; as, यां रात्रिं ते दूताः प्रविशन्ति स्म पुरीं तां रात्रिं भरतेन स्वप्नो दृष्टः 'on the night when the ambassadors entered the city, on that night a dream was seen by Bharata.'

a. The adverbs at 731 may often be found expressing *relations of time;* as, षण्मासाद् ऊर्ध्वम् or परम् 'after six months;' षण्मासेन or षण्मासाभ्यन्तरेण पूर्वम् 'six months ago;' or (employing the locative absolute) पूर्णे वर्षसहस्रे 'after a thousand years.'

NOUNS OF PLACE AND DISTANCE.

823. Nouns expressive of '*distance or space between two places*' (according to Carey) may be in the nominative; as, शतं क्रोशाः सोमनाथात् 'a hundred Kos from Somanáth:' but they are more properly in the accusative; as, योजनम् 'for a Yojana;' क्रोशम् 'for a Kos:' or

in the instrumental; as, क्रोशेन गत्वा 'having gone for a Kos.' '*The place*' in which anything is done is expressed by the locative; as, विदर्भेषु 'in Vidarbha.'

SYNTAX OF ADJECTIVES.

Accusative after the Adjective.

824. Adjectives formed from *desiderative* stems will often be found governing an accusative in the same way as the verbs from which they are derived; as, स्वगृहं जिगमिषुः 'desirous of going home;' पुत्रम् अभीप्सुः 'desirous of obtaining a son;' राजानं दिदृक्षुः 'desirous of seeing the king.'

Instrumental after the Adjective.

825. Adjectives, or participles used adjectively, expressive of '*want*' or '*possession*,' require the instrumental case; as, अर्थेन हीनः 'destitute of wealth;' अर्थैः समायुक्तः 'possessed of riches;' वारिणा पूर्णो घटः 'a jar full of water.'

826. So also of '*likeness*,' '*comparison*,' or '*equality*;' as, अनेन सदृशो लोके न भूतो न भविष्यति 'there never has been, nor will there ever be, any one like him in this world;' ब्राह्मणेन तुल्यम् अधीते 'he reads like a Bráhman;' प्रारम्भैः सदृश उदयः 'his success was equal to his undertakings;' प्राणैः समा पत्नी 'a wife as dear as life;' दाता अभ्यधिको नृपैः 'more liberal than (other) kings;' आदित्येन तुल्यः 'equal to the sun.' These are sometimes joined with a genitive; see 827. *b*.

Genitive after the Adjective.

827. Adjectives signifying '*dear to*,' or *the reverse*, are joined with the genitive; as, राज्ञां प्रियः 'dear to kings;' भर्तारः स्त्रीणां प्रियाः 'husbands are dear to women;' न कश्चित् स्त्रीणाम् अप्रियः 'women dislike nobody;' द्वेष्यो भवति मन्त्रिणाम् 'he is detestable to his ministers.'

a. Adjectives expressive of '*fear*' may govern the genitive or ablative; as, मुनेर् भीतः 'afraid of the sage.'

b. Adjectives expressive of '*equality*,' '*resemblance*,' '*similitude*,' sometimes require the genitive as well as the instrumental (826); thus, सर्वस्य समः 'equal to all;' तस्य अनुरूपः 'like him;' चन्द्रस्य कल्पः 'rather like the moon;' न तस्य तुल्यः कश्चन 'nobody is equal to him.'

c. So also other adjectives; as, परोपदेशः सर्वेषां सुकरः नृणाम् 'giving advice to others is *easy* to all men;' सुखानाम् उचितः '*worthy* of happiness;' उचितः क्लेशानाम् '*capable* of toil;' अज्ञातं धृतराष्ट्रस्य '*unknown* to Dhṛita-ráshṭra;' धर्मस्य कल्पः 'competent for duty.'

Locative after the Adjective.

828. Adjectives, or participles used adjectively, expressive of '*power*' or '*ability*,' are joined with a locative; as, अध्वनि क्षमा अश्वाः 'horses able for the journey;' महति शत्रौ क्षमो राजा 'a king who is a match for a great enemy;' अशक्ता गृह-करणे शक्ता गृह-भञ्जने 'unable to build a house, but able to demolish one.'

a. So also other adjectives; as, शस्त्रेषु कुशलः '*skilled* in arms;' अल्पेषु प्राज्ञः '*wise* in trifles;' त्वयि अनुरक्तो विरक्तो वा स्वामी 'Is your master *attached* or *adverse* to you?' अनुजीविषु मन्दादरः '*neglectful* of his dependants.'

SYNTAX OF THE COMPARATIVE AND SUPERLATIVE DEGREE.

829. Adjectives in the comparative degree require the ablative case; as, पत्नी प्राणेभ्योऽपि गरीयसी 'a wife *dearer even than* one's life;' पुत्र-स्पर्शात् सुखतरः स्पर्शो लोके न विद्यते 'there is no pleasanter touch in this world than the touch of a son;' वर्धनात् प्रजा-रक्षणं श्रेयः 'the protection of one's subjects is *better than* aggrandizement;' न मत्तो (719. *a*) दुःखिततरः पुमान् अस्ति 'there is not a more wretched man than I;' मतिर् बलाद् बलीयसी 'mind is more powerful than strength.'

830. Sometimes they govern the instrumental; as, प्राणैः प्रियतरः 'dearer than life;' न अस्ति मया कश्चिद् अल्प-भाग्यतरो भुवि 'there is nobody upon earth more unfortunate than I.'

a. When it is intended to express '*the better of two things*' the genitive may be used; as, अनयोर् देशयोः को देशो भद्रतरः 'Of these two countries which is the better?'

831. The comparative in Sanskṛit is often expressed by '*better and not*' or '*but not;*' as, वरं प्राण-परित्यागो न पुनर् ईदृशे कर्मणि प्रवृत्तिः 'better abandon life than (but not) engage in such an action;' वरं मौनं कार्यं न च वचनम् उक्तं यद् अनृतम् 'it is better that silence should be kept than a speech uttered which is untrue;' विद्यया सह वेदा-ध्यापकेन वरं मर्तव्यं न तु अध्यापन-योग्य-शिष्या-भावे अपात्राय एतां प्रतिपादयेत् 'a teacher of the Veda should rather die with his learning than commit it to an unworthy object, in the absence of a pupil worthy to be instructed in it.'

832. The superlative degree is usually joined with the genitive; as, ब्राह्मणो द्विपदां श्रेष्ठो गौर् वरिष्ठा चतुष्पदाम्। गुरुर् गरीयसां श्रेष्ठः पुत्रः स्पर्शवतां वरः 'a Bráhman is the best of all bipeds, a cow of quadrupeds, a Guru of venerable things, a son of things possessed of touch:' but

sometimes with the locative; as, नरेषु बलवत्तमः 'the most powerful of men:' and even with an ablative; as, धान्यानां सङ्ग्रह उत्तमः सर्वसङ्ग्रहात् 'a store of grain is the best of all stores.'

a. Rarely with an instrumental; as, नृवीरः कुन्त्याः प्राणैर् इष्टतमः 'a hero dearer than the life of Kuntí.' Hence it appears that comparison may sometimes be expressed by a superlative suffix. Another example is अज्ञेभ्यो ग्रन्थिनः श्रेष्ठाः 'people well-read in books are better than ignorant people.'

b. A superlative degree may even take a comparative suffix, and govern the genitive; as, तेषां ज्येष्ठतरः 'the eldest of them.' See 197. *a.*

c. A comparative word may have a superlative sense; as, दृढतरः 'very firm.'

833. '*Comparison*' is often expressed by an adjective in the *positive* degree, joined with a noun in the ablative or instrumental case; as, नास्ति तस्मात् पुण्यवान् 'there is not a happier than he;' स मत्तो (719. *a*) महान् 'he is greater than I.' Similarly, अन्यैर् विशेषतः 'more excellently than all.'

a. In more modern Sanskṛit 'comparison' is sometimes expressed by the use of अपेक्ष्य 'regarding,' 'with reference to' (indecl. part. of root ईक्ष् with अप), which may take the place of 'than' in English; thus, दशोपाध्यायान् अपेक्ष्य आचार्य आचार्यशतम् अपेक्ष्य पिता गौरवेण अतिरिक्तो भवति 'an Áćárya ought to be higher in estimation than ten Upádhyáyas, a father than a hundred Áćáryas.'

834. Many words have a kind of comparative influence, and require an ablative case, especially वरम्, अवरम्, अन्य, अन्यदा, अन्यत्र, इतर, पर, पूर्व, अधिक, ऊन, अवशिष्ट, गुण; as, प्रक्षालनात् पङ्कस्य अस्पर्शनं वरम् 'it is better not to touch mud than to wash it off;' दारिद्र्यम् अवरं मरणात् 'poverty is less desirable than death;' को मां मित्राद् अन्यस् त्रातुं समर्थः 'Who is able to rescue me, other than a friend?' किन्नु दुःखम् अतः परम् 'What grief is greater than this?' न श्रुताद् अन्यद् विब्रूयात् 'one ought not to speak differently from what one has heard;' तत्कालाद् अन्यदा 'at another time than the present;' नरस्य न अन्यत्र मरणाद् भयम् 'there is no cause of fear to man from any other quarter than from death;' श्राद्धाहात् (731; 778) पूर्वदिने 'on the day before that of the S'ráddha;' योजनशताद् अधिकम् 'more than a hundred Yojanas;' कान्तोदन्तः सङ्गमात् किञ्चिद् ऊनः 'intelligence of a lover is something less than a meeting;' अन्नाद् अवशिष्टम् 'the remainder of the food;' मूल्यात् पञ्चगुणम् 'five times more than the value.'

NUMERALS.

835. The syntax of numerals is explained at 206, 207. The following examples may be added: नवतेर् नराणाम् 'of ninety men;' षष्टेर् नराणाम् 'of sixty men;' सहस्रस्य नराणाम् 'of a thousand men;' सहस्रं पितरः 'a thousand ancestors;' त्रिभिर् गुणितं शतम् 'one hundred multiplied by three;' फलसहस्रे द्वे 'two thousand fruits;' एषां त्रयाणां मध्याद् अन्यतमः 'one of these three;' अयुतं गा ददौ 'he gave ten thousand cows;' पञ्चशतं मृगान् जघान 'he killed five hundred deer.'

a. Sometimes the plural of the numerals from ऊनविंशति upwards may be used; as, पञ्चाशद्भिर् बाणैः 'with fifty arrows.'

b. The aggregative numerals may be employed at the end of compounds for the cardinals; thus, सैन्य-द्वयम् 'two armies;' विवाह-चतुष्टयम् 'four marriages.' See 214.

c. Numerals from nineteen (*úna-vinśati*) upwards may take the genitive after them of the things numbered; as, अश्वानां शतसहस्राणि 'a hundred thousand of horses;' पत्तीनां सप्तशतानि 'seven hundred foot-soldiers;' शतम् आचार्याणाम् 'a hundred preceptors;' गवां पञ्चशतानि षष्टिश्च 'five hundred and sixty cows;' सर्गाणां षट् शतानि विंशतिश्च 'six hundred and twenty chapters;' नराणां त्रिंशदधिकशतं द्वे सहस्रे च 'two thousand one hundred and thirty men;' पञ्च रथसहस्राणि 'five thousand chariots;' एकशतं गवाम् 'a hundred and one cows' (Manu XI. 129). They may be used at the end of genitively dependent compounds; as, तृचाशीति 'eighty Tṛićas,' i. e. eighty of Tṛićas.

Obs.—But the genitive is not admissible after numerals below nineteen; e. g. दश नराः 'ten men' (not दश नराणाम्).

d. When numerals are used comparatively they may take an ablative; as, विवादाद् द्विगुणो दमः 'a fine the double of that in dispute.'

SYNTAX OF PRONOUNS.

836. The chief peculiarities in the syntax of pronouns have already been noticed at 216–240, and at 799–801.

With regard to the alternative of एनम्, &c. (see 223), it is properly only allowed in case of the re-employment (*anvádeśa*) of this pronoun in the subsequent part of a sentence in which इदम् or एतद् has already been used; thus, अनेन व्याकरणम् अधीतम् एनं छन्दोऽध्यापय 'the grammar has been studied by him, now set him to study the Veda' (cf. Nala XII. 31, 32). It is an enclitic, and ought not to begin a sentence.

a. In the use of the relative and interrogative pronouns a very peculiar *attraction* is often to be observed; that is, when either a relative or interrogative pronoun has been used, and an indefinite pronoun would naturally be expected to follow, the relative or interrogative is repeated, as in the following examples: यो यस्य (for कस्यचिद्) भावः स्यात् 'whatever may be the disposition of whom (i. e. any one);' यद् रोचते यस्मै 'whatever is pleasing to any one;' यो यस्य मांसम् अश्नाति 'whoever eats the flesh of any animal;' यस्य ये गुणाः सन्ति 'whatever excellences belong to any one;' यद् येन युज्यते 'whatever corresponds with anything;' केषां किं शास्त्रम् अध्ययनीयम् 'What book is to be read by whom?'

837. The relative and interrogative are sometimes used together, in an indefinite distributive sense; as, यानि कानि मित्राणि 'any friends whatever:' or more usually with चिद् affixed to the interrogative; as, यस्मै कस्मैचित् 'to any one whatever.'

a. The neuter of the interrogative (किम्) is often joined with the instrumental to signify 'What is the use of?' 'there is no need of;' as, श्रुतेन किं यो न धर्मम् आचरेत् । किम् आत्मना यो न जितेन्द्रियो भवेत् 'Of what use is scriptural knowledge (to one) who does not practice virtue? Of what use is a soul (to one) whose passions are not kept in subjection?' किं ते अनेन प्रश्नेन 'What business have you to make this inquiry?' किं बहुना 'What need of more!' 'in short.'

b. As already shewn at 761, a relative pronoun is sometimes rendered unnecessary by the use of the relative compound; thus, नगरी चन्द्रिकाधौतहर्म्या is equivalent to नगरी यस्याश् चन्द्रिकाधौतानि हर्म्याणि 'a city whose palaces were silvered by the moon-beams.'

c. The relative, when followed by a pluperfect tense in English, may be expressed in Sanskṛit by the indeclinable participle; thus, सिंहो व्याधं हत्वा 'a lion having killed a hunter,' or 'a lion who had killed a hunter.'

838. The following examples will illustrate the use of pronouns of quantity and pronominals: यावतः (or यत्संख्यकान्) ग्रासान् भुंक्ते तावतः (or तत्संख्यकान्) ददाति 'as many mouthfuls as he eats, so many he gives away;' यदि एतावन् मह्यं दीयते तदा एतावद् अध्यापयामि 'if so much is given to me, then I will give so much instruction;' तेषां सर्वेषां मध्याद् एकतमः 'one out of all those.' See also 801.

SYNTAX OF VERBS.

839. Nothing is more common in Sanskṛit syntax than for the verb to be omitted altogether, or supplied from the context.

a. This is more especially the case with the copula, or substantive verb; thus, यावन् मेरुस्थिता देवा यावद् गङ्गा महीतले । चन्द्रार्कौ गगने यावत् तावद् विप्रकुले वयम् 'as long as the gods have existed in Meru, as long as the Ganges upon earth, as long as the sun and moon in the sky, so long have we (existed) in the family of Bráhmans;' परिच्छेदः पाण्डित्यम् 'discrimination (is) wisdom.'

Locative and Genitive absolute.

840. The locative case is very commonly used absolutely with participles; as, तस्मिन् जीवति जीवामि मृते तस्मिन् म्रिये पुनः 'he living I live, he dying I die;' अवसन्नायां रात्रौ 'the night being ended;' ज्येष्ठे भ्रातरि अनूढे 'the elder brother being unmarried;' असति उपायान्तरे 'there being no other expedient;' तथा सति 'it being so.' Sometimes the participle is omitted; as, दूरे भये 'the danger (being) distant.' When the past passive participle is thus used absolutely with a noun in the locative, the present participle of अस्, 'to be,' is often redundantly added; as, तथा कृते सति or तथा अनुष्ठिते 'it being so done*.'

* Possibly the object of adding the word *sati* may be to shew that the passive participle is here used as a participle, and not as a past tense. So also in commentaries सति is placed after a word like आगच्छति, to indicate the loc. sing. of the pres. part., as distinguished from the 3rd sing. of the pres. tense.

a. The genitive is less commonly used absolutely; as, आपदाम् आपतन्तीनाम् 'calamities impending;' पश्यतां नराणाम् 'the men looking on.'

b. When the nominative appears to be thus used there are really two sentences; as, सुहृन् मे समायातः पुण्यवान् अस्मि 'my friend having arrived, I am happy.'

c. It is evident that the locative and genitive absolute may often take the place of the English particles 'when,' 'while,' 'since,' 'although;' and may supply the place of a *pluperfect tense;* thus, तस्मिन् अपक्रान्ते 'when he had departed.'

Nominative Case after the Verb.

841. Verbs signifying 'to be,' 'to become,' 'to appear,' 'to be called,' or 'to be esteemed,' and other passive verbs similarly used, may take a nominative after them; as, राजा प्रजा-पालकः स्यात् 'let a king be the protector of his subjects;' सा निरानन्दा प्रतिभाति 'she appears sorrowful;' ग्रामोऽरण्यं प्रतिभाति 'the village appears like a desert;' राजा धर्म अभिधीयते 'a king is called Justice.'

Accusative Case after the Verb.

842. Transitive verbs generally govern an accusative; as, विश्वं ससर्ज वेधाः 'Brahmá *created* the universe;' पुष्पाणि चिनोति नारी 'the woman *gathers* flowers;' प्राणान् जहौ मुमूर्षुः 'the dying man *gave up* the ghost;' मधु वर्जयेत् 'one should *avoid* wine;' तत्त्वं ब्रूहि '*speak* the truth.'

a. Verbs of *speaking to* or *addressing* take an accusative; as, तम् अब्रवीत् 'he said to him;' इति उवाच फाल्गुनम् 'he thus addressed Arjuna.'

843. So also verbs of *motion;* as, सरति तीर्थं मुनिः 'the holy man *goes* to the place of pilgrimage;' नद्यः समुद्रं द्रवन्ति 'rivers *run* into the ocean;' भ्रमति महीम् 'he *wanders* over the earth.'

844. Verbs of *motion* are not unfrequently used with substantives, to supply the place of other verbs; as, ख्यातिं याति 'he goes to fame,' for 'he becomes famous;' समताम् एति 'he goes to equality,' for 'he becomes equal;' तयोर् मित्रताम् आजगाम 'he came to the friendship of those two,' for 'he became a friend of those two;' पञ्चत्वं गतः 'he went to death,' for 'he died;' नृपतिं तुष्टिं नयति 'he leads the king to satisfaction,' for 'he satisfies,' &c.

a. The following are other examples: अन्येषां पीडां परिहरति 'he *avoids* paining others;' अप्राप्यम् इच्छति 'he *desires* what is unattainable;' विद्यां चिन्तयेत् 'he should *think on* wisdom;' अश्वम् आरोहति 'he *mounts* his horse;' कर्माणि आरेभिरे 'they *began* the business;' गतान् मा शुचः '*grieve not for* the departed;' सर्व-लोकाधिपत्यम् अर्हति 'he *deserves* the sovereignty of the universe;' पर्वत-कन्दरम् अधिशेते 'he *lies down* in a cave of the mountain;' गां क्षीरं पिबन्तीं न निवारयेत् 'one ought not to *prevent* a cow from drinking milk.'

845. There are certain verbs which take a redundant accusative case after them of a substantive derived from the same root; as, शपथं शेपे 'he swore an oath;' वसति वासम् 'he dwells;' वर्तते वृत्तिम् 'he conducts himself;' वाक्यं वदति 'he speaks a speech;' जीविकां जीवति 'he lives a life;' नदति नादम् 'he raises a cry' (cf. the Greek expressions λέγω λόγον, χαίρω χαράν, &c.)

Double Accusative after the Verb.

846. Verbs of *asking* govern a double accusative; as, देवं वरं याचते 'he seeks a boon of the god;' धनं राजानं प्रार्थयते 'he begs money from the king;' तं सुस्नातं पृच्छति 'he asks whether he has had a good ablution.' Of *speaking;* as, राजानं वचनम् अब्रवीत् 'he addressed a speech to the king.' Of *leading;* as, तं गृहं नयति 'he leads him home;' राज-सुतां राजान्तरं निनाय 'he led the princess to another king.'

a. Other examples of the use of verbs of this kind are, गां दोग्धि पयः 'he *milks* milk from the cow;' दुदुहुर् धरित्रीं रत्नानि 'they *milked* jewels out of the earth' (cf. 895. *b*); जित्वा नलं राज्यम् 'having *won* his kingdom from Nala,' i. e. 'having by play deprived Nala of his kingdom' (cf. 895. *b*); अवचिनोति कुसुमानि वृक्षान् 'she *gathers* blossoms from the trees;' तान् प्राहिणोद् यम-सादनम् 'he *sent* them to the abode of Yama;' स्व-चेष्टितानि नरं गुरुत्वं विपरीततां वा नयन्ति 'his own acts *lead* a man to eminence or the reverse;' शिक्षयामास तान् अस्त्राणि 'he *taught* them the use of arms;' तं सेनापतिम् अभिषिषिचुः 'they *inaugurated* him general,' more usually joined with an acc. and loc.; देवं पतिं वरयति 'she *chooses* a god for her husband.'

Obs.—When verbs which govern a double accusative are used in the passive, one accusative will remain (cf. 895. *b*); as, अम्बु-निधिर् अमृतंममन्थे 'the ocean was churned for nectar' (Kirát. v. 30).

847. Causal verbs; as, अतिथिं भोजयति अन्नम् 'he causes the guest to eat food' (see Páṇ. I. 4, 52); त्वां बोधयामि यत् ते हितम् 'I cause you to know what is for your interest;' शिष्यं वेदान् अध्यापयति गुरुः 'the Guru teaches his pupil the Vedas;' तां गृहं प्रवेशयति 'he causes her to enter the house;' फल-पुष्पोदकं ग्राहयामास नृपात्मजम् 'he presented the king's son with fruits, flowers, and water;' पुत्रम् अङ्कम् आरोपयति 'she causes her son to sit on her lap' (literally, 'her hip'); विद्या नरं नृपं सङ्गमयति 'learning causes a man to have access to a king.'

Instrumental Case after the Verb.

848. Any verb may be joined with the instrumental, to express '*the agent*,' '*instrument*,' or '*cause*,' or '*manner*' of the action; as, पुष्पं वातेन म्लायति 'the flower fades by reason of the wind;' अक्षैः क्रीडति 'he plays with dice;' मेघोऽग्निं वर्षैर् निर्वापयति 'the cloud puts out the fire with its rain;' सुखेन जीवति 'he lives happily.' See 865.

a. In this sense many causals take an instrumental; as, तां मिष्टान्नैर् भोजयामास

'he caused her to eat sweetmeats;' पक्षिभिः पिण्डान् खादयति 'he causes the pieces to be eaten by the birds.' Cf. 847.

849. After verbs of *motion* this case is used in reference either to *the vehicle by which*, or *the place on which*, the motion takes place; as, रथेन प्रयाति 'he goes *in a chariot;*' अश्वेन सञ्चरति 'he goes *on horseback;*' मार्गेण गच्छति 'he goes *on the road;*' शस्यक्षेत्रेण गच्छति 'he goes *through a field of corn;*' पुप्लुवे सागरं नौकया 'he navigated the ocean *in a boat.*' Similarly, सुस्राव नयनैः सलिलम् 'tears flowed *through the eyes.*'

a. After verbs of *carrying, placing*, &c., it is used in reference to 'the place' on which anything is carried; as, वहति मूर्ध्ना इन्धनम् 'he bears fuel *on his head;*' कुक्कुरः स्कन्धेन उह्यते 'the dog is borne *on the shoulders.*' कृ is found with this case in the sense of *placing;* as, शिरसा पुत्रम् अकरोत् 'he *placed* his son on his head.'

The following are other examples: शिष्येण गच्छति गुरुः 'the master *goes in company with* the pupil;' मन्त्रयामास मन्त्रिभिः 'he *consulted with* his ministers;' but in this sense सह is usually placed after it. भर्ता भार्यया सङ्गच्छति 'the husband *meets* the wife;' संयोजयति रथं हयैः 'he *harnesses* the horses to the chariot;' युध्यते शत्रुभिः 'he *fights* his enemies,' or शत्रुभिः सह, &c.; वैरं न केनचित् सह कुर्यात् 'one ought not to be at *enmity* with any one;' मां दोषेण परिशङ्कते 'he *suspects* me of a crime.'

850. Verbs of *boasting*, &c.; as, विद्यया विकत्थसे 'you *boast* of your learning;' परेषां यशसा श्लाघसे 'you *glory* in the fame of others.'

a. Of *swearing;* as, धनुषा शेपे 'he *swore* by his bow.'

b. Of *thinking, reflecting;* as, मनसा विचिन्त्य '*thinking* in his mind.'

c. Of *comparing;* as, जलौकया उपमीयते प्रमदा 'a beautiful woman is *compared* to a leech.'

851. Verbs denoting *liberation, freedom from*, sometimes take an instrumental after them; as, सर्वैः पापैः प्रमुच्यते 'he *is released from* all sins;' देहेन वियुज्यते 'he *is separated from* the body' (more usually with ablative).

852. Verbs of *buying* and *selling* take the instrumental of the price; as, सहस्रैर् अपि मूर्खाणाम् एकं क्रीणीष्व पण्डितम् '*buy* one wise man even for thousands of fools;' गवां सहस्रेण गृहं विक्रीणीते 'he *sells* his house for a thousand cows;' क्रीणीष्व तद् दशभिः सुवर्णैः '*buy* that for ten Suvarṇas.'

Dative after the Verb.

853. All verbs in which a sense of *imparting* or *communicating* anything is inherent, may take an accusative of the thing imparted, and a dative of the person to whom it is imparted. (Frequently, however, they take a genitive or even a locative of the recipient; see 857.) पुत्राय मोदकान् ददाति 'he *gives* sweetmeats to his son;' विप्राय गां प्रतिशृणोति 'he *promises* a cow to the Bráhman;' देवदत्ताय धनं धारयति 'he *owes* money to Devadatta;' कन्यां तस्मै प्रतिपादय '*consign* the maiden to him,' more usually with the locative; see 861.

a. Other examples of the dative are, तेषां विनाशाय प्रकुरुते मनः 'he *sets his mind on* their destruction;' गमनाय मतिं दधौ 'he *set his mind on* departure,' or with the locative. तन् मह्यं रोचते 'that *is pleasing to* me;' शिष्येभ्यः प्रवक्ष्यामि तत् 'I will *declare* this to my pupils;' सर्वं राज्ञे विज्ञापयति 'he *makes known* all to the king,' these are also joined with the genitive of the person. अमृतत्वाय कल्पते 'he is *rendered fit for* immortality;' प्रभवति मम वधाय 'he *has the power* to kill me;' तान् मातुर् वधाय अचोदयत् 'he *incited* them to the murder of their mother;' पुत्राय क्रुध्यति 'he is *angry* with his son;' इयं मांस-पेशी जाता पुत्र-शताय 'this lump of flesh *is produced for* a hundred sons;' नाशंसे विजयाय 'I had *no hopes of* success.'

Ablative after the Verb.

854. All verbs may take an ablative of the object from which anything proceeds, or arises, or is produced; as, भ्रश्यति वृक्षात् पत्त्रम् 'the leaf *falls* from the tree;' रुधिरं स्रवति गात्रात् 'blood *flows* from the body;' आसनाद् उत्तिष्ठति 'he *rises* from his seat;' मृत्-पिण्डतः (719) कर्ता कुरुते यद्यद् इच्छति 'from the lump of clay the artist *makes* whatever he wishes;' विनयाद् याति पात्रताम् 'from education a person *attains* capacity;' निर्जगाम नगरात् 'he *went* out from the city.'

855. Verbs of *fearing* are joined with the ablative, and sometimes with the genitive; as, साधुर् न तथा मृत्योर् बिभेति यथा अनृतात् 'a good man does not *fear* death so much as falsehood;' मा शब्दाद् बिभीत 'be not *afraid* of a noise;' दण्डाद् उद्विजते जगत् 'the whole world *stands in awe* of punishment;' दक्षिणस्य ते कृत-पश्चात्तापस्य बिभेमि 'I fear thee, a cunning penitent;' see 859.

856. Verbs which express *superiority* or *comparison* govern an ablative; as, प्रापणात् कामानां परित्यागो विशिष्यते 'the abandonment of pleasure is *superior* to (better than) the possession.'

a. Other examples of verbs followed by ablative cases are, प्रासादाद् अवरोहति 'he *descends from* the palace;' विष्णुः स्वर्गाद् अवततार 'Vishṇu *descended from* heaven;' कनक-सूत्रम् अङ्गाद् अवतारयति 'he *takes off* (causes to descend) the golden bracelet from his body;' निवर्तते पापात् 'he *ceases from* wickedness;' वचनाद् विरराम 'he *left off* speaking;' नरकात् पितरं त्रायते पुत्रो धार्मिकः 'a virtuous son *saves* his father from hell;' अश्वमेध-सहस्रात् सत्यम् अतिरिच्यते 'truth *is superior to* a thousand sacrifices;' स्व-हितात् प्रमाद्यति 'he *neglects* his own interest;' मित्रम् अकुशलाद् निवारयति 'a friend *guards* one from evil.'

Genitive after the Verb.

857. The genitive in Sanskrit is constantly interchangeable with the dative, locative, or even instrumental and accusative *. It is

* This vague use of the genitive to express 'various relations' prevails also in early Greek.

more especially, however, used to supply the place of the first of these cases, so that almost all verbs may take a genitive as well as dative of 'the recipient;' e.g. दरिद्रस्य धनं ददाति 'he *gives* money to the poor;' उपकुरुते परेषाम् 'he *benefits* others.'

858. It may be used for the locative after verbs of *consigning*, as निक्षेपं मम समर्पयति 'he *deposits* a pledge with me;' or of *trusting*, as न कश्चित् स्त्रीणां श्रद्दधाति 'nobody puts *trust* in women:' and for the accusative in examples such as अचिन्तितानि दुःखानि आयान्ति देहिनाम् 'unexpected ills *come* upon corporeal beings.'

859. It is sometimes used after verbs of *fearing;* as, तस्य किं न भेष्यसि 'Why wilt thou not be *afraid* of him?' see 855. Also after verbs of *longing for, desiring, envying;* as, अवमानस्य आकांक्षेत् 'he should *desire* contempt;' स्पृहयामि पुरुषाणां सचक्षुषाम् 'I *envy* men who possess eyes.' After verbs of *remembering;* as, दिवो न स्मरन्ति 'they do not remember heaven' (Kirát. v. 28).

a. Other examples of verbs followed by genitive cases are, अजानताम् अस्माकं ख्यापय कस्य असि भार्या '*tell* us, who are ignorant of it, whose wife you are;' कस्य (for कस्मात्) बिभ्यति धार्मिकाः 'Of whom are the righteous *afraid?*' यद् अन्यस्य प्रतिजानीते न तद् अन्यस्य दद्यात् 'one should not *give* to one what one *promises* to another;' मम न शृणोति 'he does not *hear* me' (cf. the Greek usage); मम स्मरेः '*remember* me,' or with an accusative. अस्माकं मृत्युः प्रभवति 'death *overcomes* us;' अग्निर् न तृप्यति काष्ठानाम् 'fire is not *satisfied with* fuel;' तेषां क्षमेथाः '*forgive* them;' किं मया तस्य अपराद्धम् 'What *offence have I given him?*'

Locative after the Verb.

860. This case is very widely applicable, but, as elsewhere remarked, is frequently interchangeable with the dative and genitive. The first sense of the locative requires that it should be united with verbs in reference only to 'the place' or 'time' in which anything is done; as, पङ्के मज्जति 'he *sinks* in the mud;' पुरे वसति 'he *dwells* in the city;' रणभूमौ तिष्ठति 'he *stands* in the front of the fight;' सूर्योदये प्रबुध्यते 'at sunrise he *awakes.*'

861. The transition from 'the place' to 'the object' or 'recipient' of any action is natural; and hence it is that verbs are found with the locative of 'the object' to which anything is imparted or communicated, as in the following examples: मा प्रयच्छ ईश्वरे धनम् '*bestow* not money on the mighty;' तस्मिन् कार्याणि निक्षिपामि 'I *entrust* my affairs to him;' पुत्रे अङ्गुरीयकं समर्पयति 'he *consigns* a ring to his son;' योग्ये सचिवे न्यस्यति राज्यभारम् 'he *entrusts* the burden of the kingdom to a capable minister;' राज्ञि or राजकुले निवेदयति 'he *informs* the king;' नले वद '*say to* Nala.'

a. प्रेतं भूमौ निदध्यात् 'one should *place* (bury) a dead man in the ground;' धर्मे मनो दधाति 'he *applies* his mind to virtue.' In this sense कृ may be used; as,

पृष्ठे इन्धनम् अकरोत् 'he *placed* the wood on his back;' मतिं पापे करोति 'he *applies* his mind to sin.'

862. When दा, 'to give,' is used for 'to put,' it follows the same analogy; as, तस्य पुच्छाग्रे हस्तं देहि '*put* your hand on the end of its tail;' भस्मचये पदं ददौ 'he *placed* his foot on a heap of ashes.' Similarly, वस्त्राञ्चले धृतोऽस्ति 'he was *held* by the skirt of his garment.' So also verbs of *seizing, striking;* as, केशेषु गृह्णाति or आकृषति 'he *seizes* or *drags* him by the hair;' सुप्ते प्रहरति 'he *strikes* a sleeping man;' गृहीत्वा तं दक्षिणे पाणौ 'having *taken* hold of him by the right hand.'

863. The locative is often put for the dative in sentences where the latter case stands for the infinitive; thus, भर्तुर् अन्वेषणे त्वरस्व '*hasten* to seek thy spouse;' नलस्य आनयने यतस्व '*strive* to bring Nala hither;' न शेकुस् तस्य धनुषो ग्रहणे 'they could not *hold* that bow;' न शक्तोऽभवन् निवारणे 'he *was not able to* prevent it.'

a. Other examples are, उग्रे तपसि वर्तते 'he is *engaged in* a very severe penance;' परकार्येषु मा व्यापृतो भूः 'do not *busy yourself* about other people's affairs;' विषयेषु सज्जते 'he is *addicted to* objects of sense;' सर्वलोकहिते रमते 'he *delights in* the good of all the world;' दुर्गाधिकारे नियुज्यते 'he is *appointed to* the command of the fort;' द्वौ वृषभौ धुरि नियोजयति 'he *yokes* two bulls to the pole;' सैनापत्ये अभिषिञ्च माम् '*anoint* me to the generalship;' यतते पापनिग्रहे 'he *strives to* suppress evil-doers;' कोपस् तेषाम् आसीन् नृपे 'they had *anger against* the king;' परीक्षां कुरु वाहुके '*make trial of* Váhuka;' आधास्ये त्वयि दोषम् '*I will lay the blame* on you;' वरयस्व तं पतित्वे '*choose him for* thy husband;' देवा अमृते यत्नवन्तो बभूवुः 'the gods *exerted themselves* for the nectar.'

b. न मद्विधे युज्यते वाक्यम् ईदृशम् 'such language is not *suited* to a person like me;' प्रभुत्वं त्वयि प्रयुज्यते 'sovereignty is *suited* to you;' आसने उपाविशत् 'he *reclined* on a seat;' वृष्याम् आसस्व * '*sit* thou on a cushion;' शत्रुषु विश्वसिति 'he *confides* in his enemies;' चरणयोः पतति 'it *falls* at his feet;' लुठति पादेषु 'it *rolls* at the feet.'

Change of Case after the same Verb.

864. This sometimes occurs; as, विधुरो धृतराष्ट्राय कुन्ती च गान्धार्याः सर्वं न्यवेदयेताम् 'Vidhura and Kuntí *announced* everything, the one to Dhṛita-ráshṭra, the other to Gándhárí' (Astraśikshá 34), where the same verb governs a dative and genitive. Similarly, in the Hitopadeśa, शृङ्गिणां विश्वासो न कर्तव्यः स्त्रीषु च 'confidence is not to be *placed* in horned animals or women.'

INSTRUMENTAL CASE AFTER PASSIVE VERBS.

865. The prevalence of a passive construction is the most remarkable feature in the syntax of this language. Passive verbs are joined

---

* आसस्व Epic form for आस्स्व or आस्व.

with 'the agent, instrument, or cause,' in the instrumental case *, and agree with 'the object' in number and person; as, वातेन रज उद्धूयते 'the dust is raised by the wind;' तेन सर्वं द्रव्याणि सज्जीक्रियन्ताम् 'let all things be prepared by him;' इषुभिर् आदित्योऽन्तरधीयत 'the sun was concealed by arrows.'

866. But the past passive participle usually takes the place of the *past tenses* of the passive verb, and agrees with 'the object' in *gender* and *case* as well as number; as, नेत्राणि समाप्लुतानि वारिणा '(their) eyes were suffused with tears;' तेन उक्तम् (इदम् being understood) 'it was said by him.' Cf. 895.

a. This instrumental construction after passive verbs is a favourite idiom in Sanskṛit prose composition, and the love for it is remarkably displayed in such phrases as the following: दुःखेन गम्यते, 'he is gone to by misery,' for दुःखं गच्छति; and आगम्यतां देवेन, 'let it be come by your majesty,' for आगच्छतु देवः; and again, अस्माभिर् एकत्र स्थीयताम्, 'let it be remained by us in one spot,' for 'let us remain in one spot;' येन मार्गेण इष्टं तेन गम्यताम् 'by whatever road it is desired, by that let it be gone.'

b. Active or causal verbs, which take a double accusative, will retain one accusative when constructed passively; but the other accusative passes into a nominative case; thus, instead of स मां परुषाणि उवाच, 'he addressed me in harsh words,' may be written तेन अहं परुषाणि उक्तः, 'by him I was addressed in harsh words.'

SYNTAX OF THE INFINITIVE.

867. The infinitive (formed with तुम् *tum*) in Sanskṛit cannot be employed with the same latitude as in other languages. Its use is very limited, corresponding to that of the Latin Supines, as its termination *tum* indicates.

a. Let the student, therefore, distinguish between the infinitive of Sanskṛit and that of Latin and Greek. In these latter languages we have the infinitive made the subject of a proposition; or, in other words, standing in the place of a nominative, and an accusative case often admissible before it. We have it also assuming different forms, to express present, past, or future time, and completeness or incompleteness in the progress of the action. The Sanskṛit infinitive, on the other hand, can never be made the subject of a verb, admits of no accusative before it, and can only express indeterminate time and incomplete action. Wherever it occurs it must be considered as the object, and never the subject, of some verb expressed or understood. As the object of the verb, it may be regarded as equivalent to a verbal substantive, in which the force of two cases, an accusative and dative, is inherent, and which differs from other substantives in its power of

---

* There are a few instances of the agent in the genitive case; as, मम कृतं पापम्, 'a crime committed by me,' for मया.

governing a case. Its use as a substantive, with the force of the *accusative* case, corresponds to one use of the Latin infinitive; thus, तत् सर्वं श्रोतुम् इच्छामि 'I desire to hear all that,' '*id audire cupio,*' where श्रोतुम् and *audire* are both equivalent to accusative cases, themselves also governing an accusative. Similarly, रोदितुं प्रवृत्ता 'she began to weep;' and महीं जेतुम् आरेभे 'he began to conquer the earth,' where महीजयम् आरेभे, 'he began the conquest of the earth,' would be equally correct.

b. Bopp considers the termination of the infinitive to be the accusative of the suffix *tu* (458. Obs.), and it is certain that in the Veda other cases of nouns formed with this suffix in the sense of infinitives occur; e.g. a dative in *tave* or *tavai*, as from *han* comes *hantave*, 'to kill;' fr. *anu-i*, *anvetave*, 'to follow;' fr. *man*, *mantavai*, 'to think:' there is also a form in *tos*, generally in the sense of an ablative; e.g. fr. *i* comes *etos*, 'from going;' fr. *han*, *hantos*, as in *purá hantos*, 'before killing:' and a form in *tví* corresponding to the indeclinable participle in *tvá* of the classical language; e.g. fr. *han*, *hatví*, 'killing;' fr. *bhú*, *bhútví*, 'being.' Infinitives may also be formed in the Veda by simply adding the usual case-terminations to the root; e.g. in the sense of an accusative, fr. *á-ruh* may come *áruham*, 'to ascend;' fr. *á-sad*, *ásadam*, 'to sit down:' of a dative, fr. *á-dhṛish*, *ádhṛishe*, 'to get at,' 'subdue;' fr. *saṅ-ćaksh*, *saṅćakshe*, 'to survey:' of an ablative, fr. *ava-pad*, *avapadas*, 'from falling down.' Infinitives are also formed by changing the final *á* of roots ending in this letter to *ai*; e.g. fr. *pra-yá*, *prayai*, 'to approach:' or by adding *se* (liable to be changed to *she*) to a root, as fr. *ji* comes *jishe*, 'to conquer:' or by adding *ase*; e.g. fr. *jív*, *jívase*, 'to live:' or *adhyai*; e.g. fr. *bhṛi*, *bharadhyai*, 'to bear;' fr. *yaj*, *yajadhyai*, 'to sacrifice,' &c.

868. But the Sanskṛit infinitive most commonly involves a sense which belongs especially to the Sanskṛit dative, viz. that of 'the end' or 'purpose' for which anything is done; thus, शावकान् भक्षितुम् आगच्छति 'he comes to devour the young ones;' शत्रून् योद्धुं सैन्यं प्राहिणोत् 'he sent an army to fight the enemy.'

a. In these cases it would be equally correct in Sanskṛit to substitute for the infinitive the dative of the verbal noun, formed with the suffix *ana*; thus, भक्षणाय, 'for the eating,' for भक्षितुम्; योधनाय, 'for the fighting,' for योद्धुम्; and in Latin the infinitive could not be used at all, but either the supine, *devoratum*, *pugnatum*, or, still more properly, the conjunction *ut* with the subjunctive mood, '*ut devoret*,' '*ut pugnarent*.' The following are other examples in which the infinitive has a dative force in expressing '*the purpose*' of the action: पानीयं पातुं नदीम् अगमत् 'he went to the river to drink water;' मम बन्धनं छेत्तुम् उपसर्पति 'he comes to cut asunder my bonds;' मां त्रातुं समर्थः 'he is able to rescue me;' पाशान् संवरितुं प्रयत्नो बभूव 'he busied himself about collecting together the snares.'

b. The best Paṇḍits think that the infinitive ought not to be used when the verb which is connected with it refers to a different person, or is not समानाधिकरणे; thus तं गन्तुम् आज्ञापय, 'command him to go,' would be better expressed by तं गमनाय आज्ञापय.

c. The infinitive cannot be used after an accusative to express '*that,*' as in Latin; thus, 'having heard that Duryodhana was killed' would be expressed by हतं दुर्योधनं श्रुत्वा.

869. The Sanskṛit infinitive, therefore, has the character of a Supine, and in this character is susceptible of either an active or passive signification. In its passive character, however, like the Latin Supine in *u*, it is joined with certain words only, the most usual being the passive verbs शक् 'to be able' and युज् 'to be fitting,' and their derivatives; thus, त्यक्तुं न शक्यते 'it cannot be abandoned;' पाशो न छेत्तुं शक्यते 'the snare cannot be cut;' न शक्याः समाधातुं ते दोषाः 'those evils cannot be remedied;' श्रोतुं न युज्यते 'it is not fitting to be heard;' छेत्तुम् अयोग्यः 'unfit to be cut;' त्वया न युक्तम् अवमानम् अस्य कर्तुम् 'contempt is not proper to be shewn by thee for him;' कीर्तयितुम् योग्यः 'worthy to be celebrated.'

a. The following are other instances: मण्डपः कारयितुम् आरब्धः 'the shed was begun to be built;' राज्ये अभिषेक्तुं भवान् निरूपितः 'your Honour has been selected to be inaugurated to the kingdom;' अर्हति कर्तुम् 'it deserves to be done;' कर्तुम् अनुचितम् 'improper to be done' (cf. *factu indignum* and *ποιεῖν αἰσχρόν*); सा मोचयितुं न्याय्या 'she ought to be released;' किम् इदं प्रार्थितं कर्तुम् 'what is sought to be done.' The infinitive of neuter verbs, which have a passive sense, will of course be passive; as, क्रोद्धुं न अर्हसि 'deign not to be angry.'

870. The root अर्ह् 'to deserve,' when used in combination with an infinitive, is usually equivalent to 'an entreaty' or 'respectful imperative;' as, धर्मान् नो वक्तुम् अर्हसि 'deign (or simply 'be pleased') to tell us our duties.' It sometimes has the force of the Latin *debet;* as, न मादृशी त्वाम् अभिभाषितुम् अर्हति 'such a person as I ought not to address you;' न तं शोचितुम् अर्हसि 'you ought not to bewail him.'

871. The infinitive is sometimes joined with the noun काम, 'desire,' to form a kind of compound adjective, expressive of wishing to do anything, but the final *m* is then rejected; thus, द्रष्टुकामः, -मा, -मम्, 'desirous of seeing;' जेतुकामः, -मा, -मम्, 'wishing to conquer.'

a. Sometimes the infinitive is joined in the same way with मनस्; thus, स द्रष्टुमनाः 'he has a mind to see.'

872. When *kim* follows the infinitive a peculiar transposition sometimes takes place, of which the 1st Act of S'akuntalá furnishes an example; thus, सखीं ते ज्ञातुम् इच्छामि किम् अनया वैखानसं व्रतं निषेवितव्यम्, 'I wish to know thy friend, whether this monastic vow is to be observed by her,' for ज्ञातुम् इच्छामि किं सख्या ते &c. 'I wish to know whether this vow is to be observed by thy friend.'

USE AND CONNEXION OF THE TENSES.

873. Present Tense.—This tense, besides its proper use, is often used for the future; as, क्व गच्छामि 'Whither shall I go?' कदा त्वां

पश्यामि 'When shall I see thee?' किं करोमि 'What shall I do?' and sometimes for the imperative; as, तत् कुर्मः 'let us do that.'

874. In *narration* it is commonly used for the past tense; as, स भूमिं स्पृष्ट्वा कर्णौ स्पृशति ब्रूते च 'he, having touched the ground, touches his ears, and says.'

875. It may denote '*habitual*' or '*repeated*' action; as, मृगः प्रत्यहं तत्र गत्वा शस्यं खादति 'the deer going there every day was in the habit of eating the corn;' यदा स मूषिकशब्दं शृणोति तदा विडालं संवर्धयति 'whenever he heard the noise of the mouse, then he would feed the cat.'

876. It is usually found after यावत् and तावत्; as, यावन् मे दन्ता न त्रुट्यन्ति तावत् तव पाशं छिनद्मि 'as long as my teeth do not break, so long will I gnaw asunder your fetters.' (Compare the use of the Latin *dum.*)

877. The present tense of the root आस्, 'to sit,' 'to remain,' is used with the present participle of another verb, to denote '*continuous*' or '*simultaneous*' action; as, पशूनां वधं कुर्वन् आस्ते 'he keeps making a slaughter of the beasts;' मम पश्चाद् आगच्छन् आस्ते 'he is in the act of coming after me.'

878. The particle स्म, when used with the present, gives it the force of a perfect; as, प्रविशन्ति स्म पुरीम् 'they entered the city;' निवसन्ति स्म 'they dwelt.' See 251. Obs.

879. POTENTIAL.—The name of this tense is no guide to its numerous uses. Perhaps its most common force is that of '*fitness*' in phrases, where in Latin we should expect to find *oportet* with the infinitive; as, आगतं भयं वीक्ष्य नरः कुर्याद् यथोचितम् 'having beheld danger actually present, a man should act in a becoming manner.'

880. It is also employed, as might be expected, in *indefinite general expressions;* as, यस्य यो भावः स्यात् 'whatever may be the disposition of any one;' यदा राजा स्वयं न कुर्यात् कार्यदर्शनम् 'when the king may not himself make investigation of the case;' अप्राप्तकालवचनं ब्रुवन् प्राप्नुयाद् अपमानम् 'by uttering unseasonable words one may meet with dishonour.'

a. Especially in *conditional* sentences and suppositions; as, यदि राजा दण्डं न प्रणयेत् स्वाम्यं कस्मिंश्चिन् न स्यात् सर्वसेतवश्च भिद्येरन् 'if the king were not to inflict punishment, ownership would remain with nobody, and all barriers would be broken down.' Sometimes the conjunction is omitted; as, न भवेत् 'should it not be so;' न स्यात् पराधीनः 'were he not subject to another.'

881. The potential often occurs as a *softened imperative,* the Sanskṛit language, in common with others in the East, being averse to the more abrupt form; thus, गच्छेः, 'do thou go,' for गच्छ; and अद्यात् फलानि, 'let him eat fruits,' for अत्तु; स्यात्, 'let there be,' for 'there must be' (in comment. to Páṇ.)

882. IMPERATIVE.—This tense yields the usual force of '*command*' or '*entreaty;*' as, आश्वसिहि 'take courage;' माम् अनुस्मर 'remember me.'

मा, *and not* न, *must be used in prohibition;* as, अनृतं मा ब्रूहि 'do not tell a falsehood;' मा लज्जस्व 'be not ashamed;' see 889. The first person is used to express '*necessity*,' see example at 796.

a. The 3rd pers. singular is sometimes used interjectionally; thus, भवतु 'Be it so!' 'Well!' यातु 'Let it go!' 'Come along!' 'Come!'

883. The imperative is sometimes used in conditional phrases to express '*contingency*;' as, अनुजानीहि मां गच्छामि 'permit me, (and) I will go,' i. e. 'if you will permit me, I will go;' आज्ञापय हन्मि दुष्टजनम् 'if you command me, I will kill the villain;' अभयवाचं मे यच्छ गच्छामि 'if you give me a promise of security, I will go.'

884. Imperfect.—Although this tense (see 242) properly has reference to '*past incomplete action*,' and has been so rendered in the paradigms of verbs, yet it is commonly used to denote '*indefinite past time*,' without any necessary connexion with another action; as, अर्थं ग्रहीतुं यत्नम् अकरवम् 'I made an effort to collect wealth,' not necessarily 'I was making.'

Obs.—The augment may be cut off after मा, as in the aorist; thus, मा स्म भवत् 'May he not become?' See 242. Obs.; Páṇ. vi. 4, 74.

885. Perfect.—As explained at 242, this tense is properly used to express '*an action done at some definite period of past time*;' as, कौशल्यादयो नृपतिं दशरथं चक्रन्दुः 'Kauśalyá and the others bewailed king Daśaratha.' It is frequently, however, employed indeterminately.

886. First Future.—This tense (see 242) expresses '*definite* but *not immediate* futurity;' as, तासु दिक्षु कामस्य फलं लब्धासि 'in those regions thou shalt (one day) obtain the fruit of thy desire.'

887. Second Future.—This tense, although properly indefinite, is employed to express '*all degrees and kinds of futurity*,' immediate or remote, definite or indefinite; as, स्वादु पयः पास्यसि 'thou shalt drink sweet water;' तत्र अवश्यं पत्नीं द्रक्ष्यति 'there certainly he will see his wife;' अद्य गमिष्यसि 'this very day thou shalt go.'

a. It is sometimes used for the imperative; as, यद् देयं तद् दास्यसि 'whatever is to be given, that you will give,' (do thou give.)

888. Aorist.—This tense (see 242) properly expresses '*time indefinitely past*;' as, अभूत् नृपः 'there lived (in former times) a king.'

889. It is also employed to supply the place of the imperative, after the prohibitive particle मा or मा स्म, the augment being omitted (see 242. Obs.); as, मा कृथाः 'do not make;' मा त्याक्षीः समयम् 'do not lose the opportunity;' मा स्म अनृतं वादीः 'do not tell an untruth;' मा क्रुधः 'do not be angry;' मा शुचः 'do not grieve;' मा हिंसीः 'do not injure;' मा नीनशः 'do not destroy;' मैवं वोचः 'do not speak so;' मा भैषीः 'be not afraid' (contracted into मा भैः in Nala xiv. 3).

890. PRECATIVE.—Only one example of this tense occurs in the Hitopadeśa: नित्यं भूयात् सकल-सुख-वसतिः 'May he constantly be the abode of all happiness!' It is chiefly used in pronouncing benedictions. Also in imprecations.

a. In the latter case a noun formed with a suffix *ani* is frequently used; thus, अजीवनिस् ते भूयात् 'May there be loss of life to thee!' 'Mayst thou perish!'

891. CONDITIONAL.—This tense (see 242) is even less frequent than the last. The following are examples: यदि राजा दण्डं न प्रणयेत् तदा शूले मत्स्यान् इव अपक्ष्यन् दुर्बलान् बलवत्तराः 'if the king were not to inflict punishment, then the stronger would roast the weak like fish on a spit;' or, according to the Scholiast, हिंसाम् अकरिष्यन् 'would cause injury;' सुवृष्टिश् चेद् अभविष्यत् तदा सुभिक्षम् अभविष्यत् 'if there should be abundant rain, then there would be abundance of food.' According to Páṇini (III. 3, 139) it is used क्रियातिपत्तौ 'when the action is supposed to pass by unaccomplished' (क्रियाया अनिष्पत्तौ Schol.)

a. LEṬ.—The Vedic mood, called *Leṭ* by native grammarians, corresponds to the subjunctive of the Greek language. In forming it a short *a* is inserted between the conjugational stem and the termination, or if the conjugational stem ends in *a*, this letter is lengthened; at the same time the augment of the imperfect and aorist is dropped, e.g. from *han* comes pres. ind. *han-ti;* but subj. *han-a-ti:* from *pat*, pres. ind. *pata-ti;* subj. *patá-ti:* from *aś*, impf. ind. *áśno-t;* subj. *aśnava-t*, i.e. *aśno+a+t*. So also, from *pat*, impf. ind. *apata-t;* subj. *patá-t:* from *tṛí*, aor. ind. *atárít* (for *atárish-t*, cf. du. *atárish-va*, &c.); subj. *tárish-a-t*. It may also be mentioned that in the Átmane the final *e* may optionally be changed to *ai*, e.g. *mádayádhvai;* and that the subjunctive of the aorist sometimes takes the terminations of the present tense without lengthening *a*, e.g. from *vać* comes aor. ind. *avoćat*, subj. *voćati*.

Observe—The characteristic of *Leṭ* is the insertion of *a*.

SYNTAX OF PARTICIPLES.

892. Participles in Sanskṛit often discharge the functions of the tenses of verbs. They are constantly found occupying the place of past and future tenses, and more especially of passive verbs.

893. Participles govern the cases of the verbs whence they are derived; as, व्याधं पश्यन् 'seeing the fowler;' अरण्ये चरन् 'walking in the forest;' तत् कृतवान् 'he did that;' शब्दम् आकर्ण्य 'having heard a noise;' पानीयम् अपीत्वा गतः 'he went away without drinking water.'

a. In the case of passive participles, as will presently appear, the agent is put in the instrumental case; and the participle agrees with the object, like an adjective.

Present Participles.

894. These are not so commonly used in Sanskṛit composition as past and future participles, but they are often idiomatically employed,

especially where in English the word 'while' or 'whilst' is introduced; thus, अहं दक्षिणारण्ये चरन् अपश्यम् 'whilst walking in the southern forest, I beheld,' &c.

Past Passive Participle.

895. This most useful participle is constantly used to supply the place of a *perfect tense passive*, sometimes in conjunction with the auxiliary verbs *as* and *bhú*, 'to be;' thus, आदिष्टोऽस्मि 'I have been commanded;' वयं विस्मिताः स्मः 'we were astonished;' उषितोऽस्मि 'I have dwelt' (cf. 866). Of course the participle is made to agree adjectively with the object in gender, number, and case, as in Latin; and the agent, which in English would probably be in the nominative, and in Latin in the ablative, becomes in Sanskṛit instrumental. Thus, in Sanskṛit, the phrase 'I wrote a letter' would not be so idiomatically expressed by अहं पत्रं लिलेख, as by मया पत्रं लिखितम् 'by me a letter was written,' '*a me epistola scripta.*' So again, तेन बन्धनानि छिन्नानि 'by him the bonds were cut' is more idiomatic than स बन्धनानि चिच्छेद 'he cut the bonds;' and तेन उक्तम् 'by him it was said' is more usual than स उवाच 'he said *.'

a. This participle may often be used impersonally, when, if the verb belong to the first group of classes, it may optionally be gunated; as, द्युतितम् or द्योतितं सूर्येण 'it is shone by the sun.' The same holds good if the beginning of an action is denoted; as, सूर्यः प्रद्युतितः or प्रद्योतितः 'the sun has begun to shine.'

b. When a verb governs a double accusative case (see 846), one accusative will be preserved after the past passive participle; as, विश्वामित्रेण दशरथो रामं याचितः 'Daśaratha was asked for Ráma by Viśvámitra;' मनीषितं द्यौर् दुग्धा 'the sky has been milked of your wish,' i. e. 'your wish has been milked out of the sky;' जितो राज्यं वसूनि च 'deprived by defeat in play of his kingdom and property' (cf. 846. Obs.)

896. But frequently the past passive participle is used for the active past participle; in which case it may sometimes govern the accusative case, like a perfect tense active; thus, स वृक्षम् आरूढः 'he ascended the tree;' स गृहं गतः or आगतः 'he went home;' वर्त्म तीर्णः 'having crossed the road;' अहं पदवीम्

---

* This instrumental or passive construction, which is so prevalent in Sanskṛit, has been transferred from it to Hindí, Maráthí, Gujaráthí, and other dialects of India. The particle *ne* in Hindí and Hindústání corresponds to the Sanskṛit न *na*, the final letter of the commonest termination for the instrumental case, and can never occasion any difficulty if so regarded.

अवतीर्णोऽस्मि 'I have descended to the road;' अहं नगरीम् अनुप्राप्तः 'I reached the city;' आवाम् आश्रमं प्रविष्टौ स्वः 'we two have entered the hermitage.' But observe, that its use for the active participle is generally, though not invariably, restricted to intransitive verbs which involve the idea of '*motion*,' and to a few other neuter verbs. The following are other examples: पक्षिण उत्पतिताः 'the birds flew away;' स मृतः 'he died;' व्याधो निवृत्तः 'the fowler returned;' स भक्षयितुं प्रवृत्तः 'he proceeded to eat;' स आश्रितः 'he had recourse to;' स प्रसुप्तः 'he fell asleep;' ते स्थिताः 'they stood;' उषितः 'he lodged.'

a. This participle has sometimes a *present signification;* thus, स्थित 'stood' may occasionally be translated 'standing,' भीत 'fearing,' स्मित 'smiling,' आश्लिष्ट 'embracing;' and all verbs characterized by the Anubandha ञि may optionally use this participle in the sense of the present. See 75. *e*.

b. The neuter of the passive participle is sometimes used as a substantive; thus, दत्तम् 'a gift;' खातम् 'an excavation;' अन्नम् 'food;' दुग्धम् 'milk.'

Active Past Participle.

897. This participle is much used (especially in modern Sanskṛit and the writings of commentators) to supply the place of a *perfect tense active.* It may govern the case of the verb; as, सर्वं श्रुतवान् 'he heard everything;' पत्नी पतिम् आलिङ्गितवती 'the wife embraced her husband;' राज्ञो हस्ते फलं दत्तवान् 'he gave the fruit into the hand of the king;' तत् कृतवती 'she did that.' This participle may also be used with the auxiliaries *as* and *bhú*, 'to be,' to form a compound perfect tense; thus, तत् कृतवान् अस्ति 'he has done that;' तत् कृतवान् भविष्यति 'he will have done that.'

Indeclinable Past Participles.

898. The sparing use made in Sanskṛit composition of relative pronouns, conjunctions, and connective particles, is mainly to be attributed to these participles or gerunds, by means of which the action of the verb is carried on, and sentence after sentence strung together without the aid of a single copulative. They occur in narration more commonly than any other kind of participle; and some of the chief peculiarities of Sanskṛit syntax are to be traced to the frequency of their occurrence.

899. They are generally used for the *past tense*, as united with a copulative conjunction, and are usually translatable by the English 'having,' 'when,' 'after,' 'by,' see 555; thus, तद् आकर्ण्य निश्चितम् एव अयं कुक्कुर इति मत्वा छागं त्यक्त्वा स्नात्वा स्वगृहं ययौ 'having heard this, having thought to himself "this is certainly a dog," having left the goat,

having bathed, he went to his own house.' In all these cases we should use in English the past tense with a conjunction; thus, 'When he had heard this, he thought to himself that it must certainly be a dog. He then left the goat, and, when he had bathed, went to his own house.'

a. It is evident from the above example that the indeclinable participles often stand in the place of a *pluperfect* tense, a tense which does not really exist in Sanskṛit.

b. But although they always refer to something past, it should be observed that they are frequently rendered in English by the present participle, as in the fifth sentence of the story at 930.

900. Another, though less frequent use of them is as *gerunds* in *do;* thus, नराः शास्त्राण्य् अधीत्य* भवन्ति पण्डिताः 'men become wise *by* reading the S'ástras;' भार्या अपि अकार्यशतं कृत्वा भर्तव्या 'a wife is to be supported even *by* [or *in*] doing a hundred wrong things;' किं पौरुषं हत्वा सुप्तम् 'What bravery is there *in* killing a sleeping man?'

Observe—This participle is occasionally capable of a passive sense.

901. Note—The termination त्वा *tvá* is probably an instrumental case, and bears much of the character of an instrumental, as it is constantly found in grammatical connexion with the agent in this case; thus, सर्वैः पशुभिर् मिलित्वा सिंहो विज्ञप्तः 'by all the beasts having met together the lion was informed;' सर्वैर् जालम् आदाय उड्डीयताम् 'by all having taken up the net let it be flown away.'

a. Another and stronger proof of its instrumental character is, that the particle अलम्, which governs an instrumental, is not unfrequently joined with the indeclinable participle; thus, अलं भोजनेन, 'enough of eating,' is with equal correctness of idiom expressed by अलं भुक्त्वा; see 918. *a.*

Future Passive Participles.

902. The usual sense yielded by this gerundive participle is that of '*fitness,*' '*obligation,*' '*necessity*' (see 568); and the usual construction required is, that the agent on whom the duty or necessity rests be in the instrumental, and the participle agree with the object; as, त्वया प्रवृत्तिर् न विधेया 'by you the attempt is not to be made.'

a. Sometimes, however, the agent is in the genitive case; thus, द्विजातीनां भक्ष्यम् अन्नम् 'boiled rice is to be eaten by Bráhmans.' Compare 865, note.

903. Occasionally the future passive participle may yield a sense equivalent to '*worthy of,*' '*deserving;*' as, कशय 'deserving a whipping;' ताडनीय 'worthy of being beaten;' मुसल्य 'deserving death by pounding;' वध्य 'worthy of death.'

904. If the verb govern two accusatives, one may be retained after the future

---

* As the Latin gerund is connected with the future part. in *dus*, so the Sanskṛit indeclinable part. in *ya* is probably connected with the future passive part. in *ya*.

passive participle; as, नयनसलिलं त्वया शान्तिं नेयम् 'the tear of the eye is to be brought to assuagement by thee.'

905. Occasionally the neuter of this participle is used impersonally; in which case it does not agree with the object, but may govern it in the manner of the verb; thus, मया ग्रामं गन्तव्यम्, 'it is to be gone by me to the village,' for मया ग्रामो गन्तव्यः. So also, त्वया सभां प्रवेष्टव्यम् 'by you it is to be entered into the assembly.'

a. The neuter भवितव्यम् (from भू) is thus used, and, in accordance with 841, requires the instrumental after it, as well as before; thus, केनापि कारणेन भवितव्यम् 'by something it must become the cause,' i.e. 'there must be some cause;' स्वामिना सविशेषेण भवितव्यम् 'a ruler ought to be possessed of discrimination;' मया तव अनुचरेण भवितव्यम् 'I must become your companion;' आर्यया प्रवहणारूढया भवितव्यम् 'the lady must be seated in the carriage.'

906. Similarly, the neuter of शक्य may be adverbially used, and impart at the same time a passive sense to the infinitive; thus, पवनः शक्यम् आलिङ्गितुम् अङ्गैः for पवनः शक्यः &c. 'the breeze is able to be embraced by the limbs' (Śakuntalá, verse 60). Again, शक्यम् अञ्जलिभिः पातुं वाताः 'the breezes are able to be drunk by the hollowed palms;' विभूतयः शक्यम् अवाप्तुम् 'great successes are able to be obtained.' Observe a similar use of युक्तम् in न युक्तं भवान् वक्तुम् 'his Highness is not proper to be addressed' (Mahá-bh. Ádi-p. 27).

907. It is not uncommon to find this participle standing merely in the place of a future tense, no propriety or obligation being implied, just as the past passive participle stands in the place of a past tense; thus, नूनम् अनेन लुब्धकेन मृगमांसार्थिना गन्तव्यम् 'in all probability this hunter will go in quest of the deer's flesh,' where गन्तव्यम् is used impersonally; त्वां दृष्ट्वा लोकैः किञ्चिद् वक्तव्यम् 'when the people see you, they will utter some exclamation;' यदि पक्षी पतति तदा मया खादितव्यः 'if the bird falls, then it shall be eaten by me.' See 930. xi.

908. The neuter of this participle is sometimes used infinitively or substantively, as expressive merely of 'the indeterminate action' of the verb, without implying 'necessity' or 'fitness.' In such cases इति may be added; thus, वञ्चयितव्यम् इति 'the being about to deceive,' 'deception' (Hitop. line 416); मर्तव्यम् इति 'the being about to die,' 'dying:' but not always; as, जीवितव्यम् 'life.'

Participial Nouns of Agency.

909. The first of these nouns of agency (580) is constantly used in poetry as a substitute for the present participle; implying, however, 'habitual action,' and therefore something more than present time. It is sometimes found governing the same case as the present participle, but united with the word which it governs in one compound; thus, पुरञ्जय 'city-conquering;' प्रियंवद 'speaking kind words;' जलेचर 'going in the water;' सरसिज 'lake-born.' But the word governed is often in the stem; thus, तेजस्कर, 'light-making' (see 69), from *tejas* and *kṛi*; मनोहर, 'mind-captivating,' from *manas* and *hṛi* (64); बहुद, 'giving much,' from *bahu* and *dá*; आत्मज्ञ, 'self-knowing,' from *átman* and *jñá* (57. *b*).

910. The second (581) is sometimes, but rarely, found as a participle governing the case of the verb; thus, वाक्यं वक्ता 'speaking a speech;' गङ्गां वोढा 'bearing the Ganges.'

911. The first and second species of the third (582. *a*. *b*), like the first, have often the sense of present participles, and are then always united with the stem of the word which they govern in one compound; thus, मनोहारिन्, 'mind-captivating,' from *manas* and *hṛi*; कार्यसाधक, 'effective of the business,' from *kárya* and *sidh*. They may sometimes govern the case of the verb whence they are derived, and may then be compounded, or not, with the word which they govern; thus, ग्रामेवासिन् or ग्रामे वासिन् 'dwelling in a village;' मुकुलानि चुम्बकः 'kisser of the buds' (Ratnávalí, p. 7).

SYNTAX OF CONJUNCTIONS, PREPOSITIONS, ADVERBS, &c.

Conjunctions.

912. च 'and' (727) is always placed after the word which it connects with another, like *que* in Latin, and can never stand first in a sentence, or in the same place as 'and' in English; thus, परिक्रम्य अवलोक्य च 'walking round and looking.' Unlike *que*, however, which must always follow the word of which it is the copulative, it may be admitted to any other part of the sentence, being only excluded from the first place; thus, तनयम् अचिरात् प्राची इव अर्कं प्रसूय च पावनम् 'and having after a short time given birth to a pure son, as the eastern quarter (gives birth to) the sun.'

a. Sometimes two *ća*'s are used, when one may be redundant or equivalent to the English 'both;' or the two *ća*'s may be employed antithetically or disjunctively, or to express the contemporaneousness of two events; thus, अहश्च रात्रिश्च 'both day and night;' क्व हरिणकानां जीवितं च अतिलोलं क्व च शरास् ते 'Where on the one hand is the frail existence of fawns? Where on the other are thy arrows?' क्रन्दितुं च प्रवृत्ता स्त्रीसंस्थानं च ज्योतिर् उत्क्षिप्य एनां जगाम 'no sooner had she began to weep, than a shining apparition in female shape, having snatched her up, departed' (S'akuntalá, verse 131); ते च प्रापुर् उदन्वन्तं बुबुधे च आदिपुरुषः 'they reached the ocean and the Supreme Being awoke' (from his sleep), Raghu-v. x. 6.

b. Observe—When क्व, 'where?' is used as in the above example, it implies '*excessive incompatibility*,' or '*incongruity*.'

c. Sometimes च is used as an emphatic particle, and not as a copulative; thus, किं च मया परिणीतपूर्वा 'Was she indeed married by me formerly?'

913. तथा 'so,' 'likewise' (727. *b*), frequently supplies the place of च; thus, अनागतविधाता च प्रत्युत्पन्नमतिस् तथा 'both Anágata-vidhátṛi and Pratyutpanna-mati' (names of the two fish in Hitop. Book IV).

914. हि 'for,' तु 'but,' वा 'or' (727. *d*, 728. *a*), like च, are excluded from the first place in a sentence; thus, पूर्वावधीरितं श्रेयो दुःखं हि परिवर्तते 'for happiness formerly scorned turns to misery;' विपर्यये तु 'but on the contrary;' एनां त्यज वा गृहाण वा 'either abandon her or take her.'

915. यदि 'if' and चेद् 'if' (727. *e*) may govern the potential or conditional (see

891), but are also used with the indicative; thus, यदि जीवति भद्राणि पश्यति 'if he live, he will behold prosperity;' यदि मया प्रयोजनम् अस्ति 'if there is need of me;' तृष्णा चेत् परित्यक्ता को दरिद्रः 'If avarice were abandoned, who would be poor?'

Prepositions and Adverbs.

916. Prepositions often govern cases of nouns. See 729, 730.

917. The following examples illustrate the use of adverbs in construction with cases of nouns, as explained at 731.

मांसं शुनोऽग्रे निक्षिप्तम् 'flesh thrown *before* the dog;' तरूणाम् अधः '*under* the trees;' नाभेर् अधस्तात् '*below* the navel;' वृक्षस्य अधस्तात् '*beneath* the tree;' भोजनानन्तरम् '*after* eating;' फलम् अन्तरेण '*without* fruit;' भर्तुर् अनुमतिम् अन्तरेण '*without* the consent of her husband;' धनस्य अर्थम्, or more usually धनार्थम्, '*for the sake of* wealth;' विवाहाद् अर्वाक् '*after* marriage;' अर्वाक् सञ्चयनाद् अस्थ्नाम् '*after* collecting the bones:' उपरि, with genitive, occurs rather frequently, and with some latitude of meaning; thus, नाभेर् उपरि '*above* the navel;' सिंहस् तस्य उपरि पपात 'the lion fell *upon* him;' मम उपरि विकारितः 'changed in his feelings *towards* me;' तव उपरि असदृश-व्यवहारी 'not behaving properly *towards* thee;' पुत्रस्य उपरि क्रुद्धः 'angry *with* his son;' नाभेर् ऊर्ध्वम् '*above* the navel;' तदवधेर् ऊर्ध्वम् '*after* that period;' संवत्सराद् ऊर्ध्वम् '*after* a year,' i.e. 'above a year having expired;' न दण्डाद् ऋते शक्यः कर्तुं पाप-विनिग्रहः 'the restraint of crime cannot be made *without* punishment;' तव कारणात् '*on* thy *account*;' तस्याः कृते or तत्कृते '*for* her *sake*;' वाटिकाया दक्षिणेन '*to the right of* the garden;' तन्निमित्ते '*on that account*;' अभिवादनात् परम् '*after* saluting;' अस्माकं पश्चात् '*after* us;' स्नानात् पूर्वम् '*before* bathing;' विवाहात् पूर्वम् '*before* marriage;' अवलोकन-क्षणात् प्रभृति '*from* the moment of seeing (him);' जन्मप्रभृति '*from* birth;' ततः प्रभृति '*from* that time forward;' उपनयनात् प्रभृति '*from the time of* investiture;' प्राङ् निवेदनात् '*before* telling;' प्राग् उपनयनात् '*before* investiture;' भोजनात् प्राक् '*before* eating:' प्राक् may take an accusative; as, प्राग् द्वादश-समाः '*before* twelve years are over;' शतं जन्मानि यावत् '*for* a hundred births;' सर्प-विवरं यावत् '*up to* the serpent's hole;' विवराद् बहिर् निःसृत्य 'creeping *out of* the hole;' हेतुं विना '*without* cause;' अपराधेन विना '*without* fault;' प्राणि-हिंसा-व्यतिरेकेण '*without* injury to living beings;' पितुः सकाशाद् धनम् आदत्ते 'he receives money *from* his father;' मम समक्षम् '*in* my *presence*;' राज्ञः समीपम् '*near* the king;' पुत्रेण सह '*along with* his son:' साक्षात् may take an instrumental; as, अन्यैः साक्षात् '*before* others;' पुत्र-हेतोः '*for the sake of* a son.'

918. अलम्, 'enough,' is used with the instrumental, with the force of a prohibitive particle; as, अलं शङ्कया 'away with fear,' 'do not fear.'

a. It is also used with the indeclinable participle; as, अलं रुदित्वा 'enough of weeping!' अलं विचार्य 'enough of consideration!' see also 901. *a.*

Obs.—खलु is used in the same way; e.g. खलु कृत्वा = अलं कृत्वा (Páṇ. III. 4, 18).

b. It is sometimes followed by an infinitive; as, न अलम् अस्मि हृदयं निवर्तयितुम् 'I am not able to turn back my heart.'

919. मात्रम् 'even,' 'merely,' at the end of a compound is declinable; as, उत्तर-मात्रं न ददाति 'he does not even give an answer;' न शब्द-मात्राद् भेतव्यम् 'one ought not to be afraid of mere noise;' शब्द-मात्रेण 'by mere sound;' वचन-मात्रेण 'by mere words;' उक्त-मात्रे वचने 'immediately on the mere utterance of the speech.'

920. तथा and यथा, when used as correlatives, are equivalent to the English 'so that,' and the Latin *ita ut*: thus, यथा स्वामी जागर्ति तथा मया कर्तव्यम् 'I must so act that my master awake,' i. e. 'I must do something to make my master awake.'

So also, त्वं न जानासि यथा गृह-रक्षां करोमि 'Do not you know that I keep watch in the house?'

a. ईदृशम्, तादृशम्, and यादृशम् may be used in the same way; thus, तादृशम् अनायुष्यं न किञ्चिद् विद्यते यादृशं पर-दार-गमनम् 'nothing is so opposed to length of life as intercourse with the wife of another.'

b. यत्, as well as यथा, is used for 'that;' thus, अयं नूतनो न्यायो यद् अरातिं हत्वा सन्तापः क्रियते 'this is a new doctrine, that having killed an enemy remorse should be felt.'

921. किम्, 'why?' may often be regarded as a mark of interrogation which is not to be translated, but affects only the tone of voice in which a sentence is uttered; as, जाति-मात्रेण किं कश्चित् पूज्यते 'Is any one honoured for mere birth?' (Cf. 837. *a.*)

a. It sometimes has the force of 'whether;' as, ज्ञायतां किम् उपयुक्त एतावद् वर्तनं गृह्णाति अनुपयुक्तो वा 'let it be ascertained whether he is worthy to receive so large a salary, or whether he is unworthy;' मन्त्री वेत्ति किं गुण-युक्तो राजा न वा 'the minister knows whether the king is meritorious or not.'

922. वत् (technically *vati*) as a suffix of comparison or similitude (724) may be compounded with a nominal stem, which if uncompounded would be in the accusative case; thus, आत्मानं मृतवत् सन्दर्श्य 'shewing himself as if dead;' आश्चर्यवद् इदं पश्यति 'he regards it as a wonder.' Also in the locative or genitive case; thus, मथुरावत् स्रुघ्ने प्राकारः 'a wall in Srughna like that in Mathurá.' According to Páṇini v. 1, 115, it is used for the instrumental after adjectives of comparison, when some action is expressed; thus, ब्राह्मणेन तुल्यम् अधीते (see 826) may be rendered ब्राह्मणवद् अधीते, but it would not be correct to say पुत्रवत् स्थूलः for पुत्रेण तुल्यः स्थूलः.

923. The negative न is sometimes repeated to give intensity to an affirmation; thus, न न वक्ष्यति 'he will not not say'=वक्ष्यति एव 'he will certainly say.'

924. The indeclinable participle उद्दिश्य, 'having pointed out,' is sometimes used adverbially to express 'on account of,' 'with reference to,' 'towards,' and governs an accusative; thus, किम् उद्दिश्य 'On account of what?' तम् उद्दिश्य 'with reference to him.'

925. The indeclinable participle आरभ्य, 'having begun,' is used adverbially to express 'from,' 'beginning with,' and may either govern an ablative or be placed

after a nominal stem; thus, निमन्त्रणाद् आरभ्य श्राद्धं यावत् 'from the time of invitation to the time of the S'ráddha.' निमन्त्रणारभ्य would be equally correct.

926. The interjections धिक् and हा require the accusative; as, धिक् पापिष्ठम् 'Woe to the wretch!' and the vocative interjections the vocative case; as, भोः पान्थ 'O traveller!'

a. Adverbs are sometimes used for adjectives in connexion with substantives; as, तत्र शालायाम् for तस्यां शालायाम् 'in that hall;' अमात्येषु मुख्यशः for अमात्येषु मुख्येषु 'among the principal ministers.'

ON THE USE OF THE PARTICLE इति.

927. In Sanskṛit the *obliqua oratio* is rarely admitted; and when any one relates the words or describes the sentiments or thoughts of another, the relator generally represents him as speaking the actual words, or thinking the thoughts, in his own person.

a. In such cases the particle इति (properly meaning 'so,' 'thus') is often placed after the words quoted, and may be regarded as serving the purpose of inverted commas; thus, शिष्या ऊचुः कृतकृत्या वयम् इति 'the pupils said, "We have accomplished our object;"' not, according to the English or Latin idiom, 'the pupils said *that they had* accomplished their object.' So also, कलहकारी इति ब्रूते भर्ता 'your husband calls you "quarrelsome,"' where कलहकारी is in the nominative case, as being the actual word supposed to be spoken by the husband himself in his own person. So again, युष्मान् विश्वासभूमय इति सर्वे पक्षिणो मम अग्रे प्रस्तुवन्ति 'all the birds praise you in my presence, saying, "He is an object of confidence,"' where the particle इति is equivalent to 'saying,' and the word विश्वासभूमयः is not in the accusative, to agree with युष्मान्, as might be expected, but in the nominative, as being the actual word supposed to be uttered by the birds in their own persons. In some cases, however, the accusative is retained before इति, as in the following example (Manu II. 153): अज्ञं बालम् इति आहुः 'they call an ignorant man "child."' But in the latter part of the same line it passes into a nominative; as, पिता इति एव तु मन्त्रदम् 'but (they call) a teacher of scripture "father."'

928. In narratives and dialogues इति is often placed redundantly at the end of a speech. Again, it may have reference merely to what is passing in the mind either of another person or of one's self. When so employed, it is usually joined with the indeclinable participle, or of some other part of a verb signifying 'to think,' 'to suppose,' &c., and may be translated by the English conjunction 'that,' to which, in fact, it may be regarded as equivalent; thus, मर्कटो घण्टां वादयति इति परिज्ञाय 'having ascertained *that* it is a monkey who rings the bell;' पुनर् अर्थवृद्धिः करणीया इति मतिर् बभूव 'his idea was *that* an increase of wealth ought again to be made;' धन्योऽहं यस्य एतादृशी भार्या इति मनसि निधाय 'reflecting in his mind *that* I am happy in possessing such a wife.' The accusative is also

retained before इति in this sense; as, मृतम् इति मत्वा 'thinking that he was dead.' In all these examples the use of इति indicates that a quotation is made of the thoughts of the person at the time when the event took place.

929. Not unfrequently the participle 'saying,' 'thinking,' 'supposing,' &c., is omitted altogether, and इति itself involves the sense of such a participle; as, बालोऽपि न अवमन्तव्यो मनुष्य इति भूमिपः 'a king, even though a child, is not to be despised, *saying to one's self*, "He is a mortal;"' सौहार्दाद् वा विधुर इति वा मयि अनुक्रोशात् 'either through affection or through compassion towards me, *saying to yourself*, "What a wretched man he is!"' अयं वराहः । अयं शार्दूल इति वन.राजिषु आहिण्ड्यते 'There's a boar! Yonder's a tiger! *so crying out*, it is wandered about (by us) in the paths of the woods.'

CHAPTER X.

EXERCISES IN TRANSLATION AND PARSING.

930. STORY OF THE SAGE AND THE MOUSE, FROM THE HITOPADEŚA, TRANSLATED AND PARSED.

i. अस्ति गौतमस्य मुनेस् तपो.वने महा.तपा नाम मुनिः। 'There is in the sacred grove of the sage Gautama a sage named Mahátapas (Great-devotion).'

ii. तेनाश्रम.सन्निधाने मूषिक.शावकः काक.मुखाद् भ्रष्टो दृष्टः। 'By him, in the neighbourhood of his hermitage, a young mouse, fallen from the beak of a crow, was seen.'

iii. ततो दया.युक्तेन तेन मुनिना नीवार.कणैः संवर्धितः। 'Then by that sage, touched with compassion, with grains of wild rice it was reared.'

iv. तद.नन्तरं मूषिकं खादितुम् अनुधावन् विडालो मुनिना दृष्टः। 'Soon after this, a cat was observed by the sage running after the mouse to devour it.'

v. तं मूषिकं भीतम् आलोक्य तपःप्रभावात् तेन मुनिना मूषिको बलिष्ठो विडालः कृतः। 'Perceiving the mouse terrified, by that sage, through the efficacy of his devotion, the mouse was changed into a very strong cat.'

vi. स विडालः कुक्कुराद् बिभेति । ततः कुक्कुरः कृतः । कुक्कुरस्य व्याघ्रान् महद् भयम् । तदनन्तरं स व्याघ्रः कृतः । 'The cat fears the dog: upon that it was changed into a dog. Great is the dread of the dog for a tiger: then it was changed into a tiger.'

vii. अथ व्याघ्रम् अपि मूषिकनिर्विशेषं पश्यति मुनिः । 'Now the sage regards even the tiger as not differing at all from the mouse.'

viii. अतः सर्वे तत्रस्था जनास् तं व्याघ्रं दृष्ट्वा वदन्ति । 'Then all the persons residing in the neighbourhood, seeing the tiger, say.'

ix. अनेन मुनिना मूषिकोऽयं व्याघ्रतां नीतः । 'By this sage this mouse has been brought to the condition of a tiger.'

x. एतच् छ्रुत्वा स व्याघ्रः सव्यथोऽचिन्तयत् । 'The tiger overhearing this, being uneasy, reflected.'

xi. यावद् अनेन मुनिना जीवितव्यं तावद् इदं मम स्वरूपाख्यानम् अकीर्त्तिकरं न पलायिष्यते । 'As long as it shall be lived by this sage, so long this disgraceful story of my original condition will not die away.'

xii. इति समालोच्य मुनिं हन्तुं समुद्यतः । 'Thus reflecting, he prepared (was about) to kill the sage.'

xiii. मुनिस् तस्य चिकीर्षितं ज्ञात्वा पुनर् मूषिको भव इत्य् उक्त्वा मूषिक एव कृतः । 'The sage discovering his intention, saying, "Again become a mouse," he was reduced to (his former state of) a mouse.'

931. Observe in this story: 1st, the simplicity of the style; 2ndly, the prevalence of compound words; 3rdly, the scarcity of verbs; 4thly, the prevalence of the past passive participle with the agent in the instrumental case for expressing indefinite past time, in lieu of the past tense active with the nominative: see 895, with note.

932. i.—*Asti*, 'there is,' 3rd sing. pres. of rt. *as*, cl. 2 (584). *Gautamasya*, 'of Gautama,' gen. m. (103). *Munes*, 'of the sage,' gen. m. (110): final *s* remains by

62. *Tapo-vane*, 'in the sacred grove' (lit. 'in the penance-grove'), genitively dependent comp. (743); the first member formed by the stem *tapas*, 'penance,' *as* becoming *o* by 64; the last member, by the loc. case of *vana*, 'grove,' neut. (104). *Mahá-tapá*, 'having great devotion' (164. *a*), relative form of descriptive comp. (766); the first member formed by *mahá* (substituted for *mahat*, 778), 'great;' the last member, by the nom. case masc. of the neuter noun *tapas*, 'devotion' (164. *a*): final *s* dropped by 66. *a*. *Náma*, 'by name,' an adverb (713. *b*). *Muniḥ*, 'a sage,' nom. masc. (110): final *s* passes into Visarga by 63. *a*.

ii.—*Tena*, 'by him,' instr. of pron. *tad* (220). *Áśrama-sannidháne*, 'in the neighbourhood of his hermitage,' genitively dependent comp. (743); the first member formed by the nominal stem *áśrama*, 'hermitage;' the last member, by the loc. case of *sannidhána*, 'neighbourhood,' neut. (104). The final *a* of *tena* blends with the initial *á* of *áśrama* by 31. *Múshika-śávakaḥ*, 'a young mouse,' or 'the young of a mouse,' genitively dependent comp. (743); formed from the nominal stem *múshika*, 'a mouse,' and the nom. of *śávaka*, 'the young of any animal' (103): final *s* becomes Visarga by 63. *Káka-mukhád*, 'from the beak (or mouth) of a crow,' genitively dependent comp.; formed from the nominal stem *káka*, 'a crow,' and the abl. of *mukha*, 'mouth,' neut. (104); *t* being changed to *d* by 45. *Bhrashṭo*, 'fallen,' nom. sing. masc. of the past pass. part. of rt. *bhranś* (544. *a*): *as* changed to *o* by 64. *Dṛishṭaḥ*, 'seen,' nom. sing. masc. of the past pass. part. of rt. *dṛiś*: final *s* becomes Visarga by 63. *a*.

iii.—*Tato*, 'then,' adv. (719): *as* changed to *o* by 64. *Dayá-yuktena*, 'touched with compassion,' instrumentally dependent comp. (740); formed from the nominal stem *dayá*, 'compassion,' and the instr. of *yukta*, 'endowed with,' past pass. part. of rt. *yuj* (670). *Tena*, see ii. above. *Muniná*, 'by the sage,' instr. m. (110). *Nívára-kaṇaiḥ*, 'with grains of wild rice,' genitively dependent comp. (743); formed from the nominal stem *nívára*, 'wild rice,' and the instr. pl. of *kaṇa*: final *s* becomes Visarga by 63. *Saṃvardhitaḥ*, 'reared,' nom. sing. of past pass. part. of causal of *vṛidh* with *sam* (549): final *s* becomes Visarga by 63. *a*.

iv.—*Tad-anantaraṃ*, 'soon after this,' compound adverb; formed with the pronominal stem *tad*, 'this' (220), and the adverb *anantaram*, 'after' (731, 917). *Múshikaṃ*, acc. m. (103). *Kháditum*, 'to eat,' infinitive of rt. *khád* (458, 868). *Anudhávan*, 'pursuing after,' 'running after,' nom. sing. masc. of the pres. part. Par. of rt. *dháv*, 'to run,' with *anu*, 'after' (524). *Viḍálo*, 'a cat,' nom. case masc. (103): *as* changed to *o* by 64. *Muniná*, see iii. above. *Dṛishṭaḥ*, see ii.

v.—*Taṃ*, acc. case masc. of pron. *tad* (220), used as a definite article, see 795. *Múshikaṃ*, see iv. *Bhítam*, 'terrified,' acc. sing. masc. of the past pass. part. of rt. *bhí* (532). *Álokya*, 'perceiving,' indec. part. of rt. *lok*, with prep. *á* (559). *Tapaḥ-prabhávát*, 'through the efficacy of his devotion' (814), genitively dependent comp. (743); formed by the nominal stem *tapas*, 'devotion,' *s* being changed to Visarga by 63, and the abl. case of *prabháva*, noun of the first class, masc. (103). *Tena*, see ii. *Muniná*, see iii. *Múshiko*, nom. m. (103): *as* changed to *o* by 64. *Balishṭho*, 'very strong,' nom. masc. of the superlative of *balin*, 'strong' (see 193): *as* changed to *o* by 64. *Viḍálaḥ*, see iv: final *s* becomes Visarga by 63. *Kṛitaḥ*, 'changed,' 'made,' nom. sing. masc. of past pass. part. of rt. *kṛi* (682): final *s* becomes Visarga by 63. *a*.

vi.—*Sa*, nom. case of *tad* (220), used as a definite article (795): final *s* dropped by 67. *Viḍálaḥ*, see iv. *Kukkurád*, 'the dog' (103), abl. after a verb of 'fearing' (855): *t* changed to *d* by 45. *Bibheti*, 'fears,' 3rd sing. pres. of rt. *bhí*, cl. 3 (666). *Tataḥ*, 'upon that,' adv. (719): *as* changed to *aḥ* by 63. *Kukkuraḥ*, 'the dog,' nom. m. (103): final *s* becomes Visarga by 63. *Kṛitaḥ*, see v. *Kukkurasya*, 'of the dog,' gen. masc. (103). *Vyághrán*, 'for the tiger' (103), abl. after a noun of 'fear' (814. *e*): *t* changed to *n* by 47. *Mahad*, 'great' (142), nom. case, sing. neut.: *t* changed to *d* by 45. *Bhayam*, 'fear,' nom. neut. (104). *Tad-anantaram*, see iv. *Vyághraḥ*, nom. case: final *s* becomes Visarga by 63. *Kṛitaḥ*, see v.

vii.—*Atha*, 'now,' inceptive particle (727. *c*). *Vyághram*, acc. case. *Api*, 'even,' adv. *Múshika-nirviśesham*, 'as not differing at all from the mouse,' relative form of dependent comp. (762); formed from the nominal stem *múshika*, and the acc. of *viśesha*, 'difference,' with *nir* prefixed: or it may be here taken adverbially, see 776. *Paśyati*, 3rd sing. pres. of rt. *dṛiś*, cl. 1 (604). *Muniḥ*, see i.

viii.—*Ataḥ*, 'then,' adv. (719). *Sarve*, 'all,' pronominal adj., nom. plur. masc. (237). *Tatra-sthá*, 'residing in the neighbourhood,' comp. resembling a locatively dependent; formed from the adverb *tatra* (720), 'there,' 'in that place,' and the nom. plur. masc. of the participial noun of agency of rt. *sthá*, 'to remain' (587): final *s* dropped by 66. *a*. *Janás*, 'persons,' nom. pl. masc. (103): final *s* remains by 62. *Tam*, acc. of pron. *tad* (220), used as a definite article (795). *Vyághram*, 'tiger,' acc. masc. (103). *Dṛishṭvá*, 'having seen,' indec. past part. of rt. *dṛiś* (556). *Vadanti*, 'they say,' 3rd pl. pres. of rt. *vad*, cl. 1 (599).

ix.—*Anena*, 'by this,' instr. of pron. *idam* (224). *Muniná*, see iii. *Múshiko*, nom. masc.: *as* changed to *o* by 64. *a*. *Ayam*, 'this,' nom. masc. (224): the initial *a* cut off by 64. *a*. *Vyághratám*, 'the condition of a tiger,' fem. abstract noun (105), acc. case, formed from *vyághra*, 'a tiger,' by the suffix *tá* (80. LXII). *Nítaḥ*, 'brought,' nom. sing. masc. of past pass. part. of rt. *ní* (532).

x.—*Etać*, 'this,' acc. neut. of *etad* (223): *t* changed to *ć* by 49. *Ćhrutvá*, 'overhearing,' indec. part. of rt. *śru* (676, 556); see 49. *Vyághraḥ*, nom. case: final *s* becomes Visarga by 63. *Sa-vyatho*, 'uneasy,' relative form of indeclinable comp., formed by prefixing *sa* to the fem. substantive *vyathá* (769): *as* changed to *o* by 64. *a*. *Aćintayat*, 'reflected,' 3rd sing. impf. of *ćint*, cl. 10 (641): the initial *a* cut off by 64. *a*.

xi.—*Yávad*, 'as long as,' adv. (713. *a*): *t* changed to *d* by 45. *Anena*, see ix. *Jívitavyam*, 'to be lived,' nom. neut. of the fut. pass. part. of rt. *jív* (569, 905. *a*, 907). *Távad*, 'so long,' adv. correlative to *yávat* (713. *a*). *Idam*, 'this,' nom. neut. of the demonstrative pron. at 224. *Mama*, 'of me,' gen. of pron. *aham*, 'I' (218). *Svarúpákhyánam*, 'story of my original condition,' genitively dependent comp. (743); formed from the nominal stem *svarúpa*, 'natural form' (see 232. *b*), and the nom. of *ákhyána*, neut. (104): *m* retained by 60. *Akírtti-karam*, 'disgraceful,' accusatively dependent comp. (739); formed from the nominal stem *akírtti*, 'disgrace,' and the nom. neut. of the participial noun of agency *kara*, 'causing,' from *kṛi*, 'to do' (580). *Na*, 'not,' adv. (717. *a*). *Paláyishyate*, 'will die away,' 3rd sing. 2nd fut. Átm. of the compound verb *paláy*, formed by combining rt. *i* or *ay* with prep. *pará* (783. *n*).

xii.—*Iti*, 'thus,' adv. (717. *e*; see also 928). *Samálośya*, 'reflecting,' indec. part. of the verb *sam-á-loś* (559), formed by combining rt. *loś* with the preps. *sam* and *á* (784). *Muniṃ*, acc. case. *Hantuṃ*, 'to kill,' infinitive of rt. *han* (458, 868, 654). *Samudyataḥ*, 'prepared,' nom. sing. masc. of past pass. part. of *sam-ud-yam*, formed by combining rt. *yam* with the preps. *sam* and *ud* (545).

xiii.—*Munis*, nom. case: final *s* remains by 62. *Tasya*, 'of him,' gen. of *tad* (220). *Ćikírshitaṃ*, 'intention,' acc. neut. of past pass. part. of desid. of rt. *kṛi*, 'to do' (550, 502), used as a substantive (896. *b*). *Jńátvá*, 'discovering,' indec. part. of rt. *jńá* (556, 688). *Punar*, 'again,' adv. (717. *e*): *r* remains by 71. *d*. *Múshiko*, nom. case: *as* changed to *o* by 64. *Bhava*, 'become,' 2nd sing. impv. of rt. *bhú* (585). *Ity* answers to inverted commas, see 927. *a*: the final *i* changed to *y* by 34. *Uktvá*, 'saying,' indec. part. of rt. *vać* (556, 650). *Múshika*, nom. case: final *s* dropped by 66. *Eva*, 'indeed,' adv. (717).

SENTENCES TO BE TRANSLATED AND PARSED.

933. Note—The numbers over the words in the following sentences refer to the rules of the foregoing grammar.

[220] स [783. i, 602] आगच्छतु। [220] तौ आगच्छताम्। [218] आवाम् आगच्छाव। [220] ते [783. k] उपविशन्तु। तौ [676] शृणुताम्। ते [676] शृण्वन्तु। [218] अहं [587] तिष्ठानि। [219] युवां [587] तिष्ठतम्। [218] वयम् [783. j, 587] उत्तिष्ठाम। [220] स करोतु। [219] त्वं कुरु। वयं करवामहै। स चिन्तयतु। त्वम् [783. h, 661] अवधेहि। ते [663] ददतु। [219] यूयं [663] दत्त। [233] भवान् एतु। कुत्र [233] भवान् [607] वसति। [219] यूयं कुत्र [607] वसथ। भवान् [646] शेताम्। ते [646] शेरताम्। नरः [655] स्वपितु। ते सर्वे [655] सुषुपुः। नरो गृहं [644] याति। [219] युष्माभिः [228] किञ्चिद् [868. a] भोक्तव्यम्। वयं शास्त्रम् [311] अध्ययामहै। [218] अस्माभिः [311, 569] शास्त्राण्यध्येतव्यानि। त्वम् [898. b] अन्नं [668. a] भुङ्क्ष्व। [218, 896. b] मयान्नं [668. a] भुज्यताम्। [219] त्वया [896. b] दुग्धं [589] पीयताम्। [219] यूयं जलं [589] पिबत। यद् अहं [688] जानामि तद् [219] युष्मान् [485] अध्यापयिष्यामि। [889] मा [714] दिवा [655] स्वाप्सीः। [108] नदीं [889] मा [438. e] गाः। [882] मा [655] शब्दाद् [668] बिभीत। [882] मा मां [769. b] निरपराधं [692] बधान ॥

रात्रि.शेषे विद्यार्थी[743.a] शयनाद् उत्तिष्ठेत्[783.j] ॥

माता.पित्रोस्[754.a] तुष्ट्या सर्वस्य[237] तपसः फलं प्राप्यते[783.p] ॥

ईरिणे बीजम् उप्त्वा कर्षकः फलं न प्राप्नोति[783.p] ॥

रात्रिर् भूतानां स्वप्नार्थं भवति[685] दिनं च कर्मानुष्ठानार्थम् ॥

बहिः.शौचं[756] मृद्वारिभ्याम्[752] अन्तः.शौचं[756] राग.द्वेषादि.त्यागेन क्रियते[701] ॥

न जातु[717.f] कामः कामानाम् उपभोगेन शाम्यति[619] ॥

व्यसनस्य च मृत्योश्च व्यसनं कष्टम् उच्यते[471, 650] ॥

आ[730] मृत्योः श्री.सिद्ध्यर्थम् उद्यमं कुर्यात्[682] ॥

अद्भिर्[178.b] गात्राणि शुध्यन्ति मनस्[164] तु[728.a] निषिद्ध.चिन्तादिना दूषितं सत्याभिधानेन ॥

SCHEME OF THE MORE COMMON SANSKṚIT METRES.

934. Metres are divided into two grand classes: 1. *Varṇa-vṛitta*, 2. *Mátrá-vṛitta.* The first has two subdivisions, A and B.

Class I.—*Varṇa-vṛitta.*

A. *Metres, consisting of two half-verses, determined by the number of* SYLLABLES *in the Páda or quarter-verse.*

Note—It may be useful to prefix to the following schemes of metres a list of technical prosodial terms: पाद = the fourth part of a verse; मात्रा = an instant or prosodial unit = a short syllable; गण = four Mátrás; यति = a pause; गुरु or ग = a long syllable (–); लघु or ल = a short syllable (⏑); गग = a spondee (– –); लल = a pyrrhic (⏑ ⏑); गल = a trochee (– ⏑); लग = an iambus (⏑ –); म = a molossus (– – –); भ = a dactyl (– ⏑ ⏑); न = a tribrach (⏑ ⏑ ⏑); य = a bacchic (⏑ – –); र = a cretic (– ⏑ –); स = an anapæst (⏑ ⏑ –); त = an anti-bacchic (– – ⏑); ज = an amphibrach (⏑ – ⏑).

Śloka or *Anushṭubh* (8 syllables to the Páda or quarter-verse).

935. The commonest of all the infinite variety of Sanskṛit metres is the Śloka or Anushṭubh. This is the metre which chiefly prevails in the great epic poems.

It consists of four quarter-verses of 8 syllables each or two lines of 16 syllables, but the rules which regulate one line apply equally to the other; so that it is only necessary to give the scheme of one line, as follows :—

1	2	3	4	5	6	7	8	‖	9	10	11	12	13	14	15	16	‖
•	•	•	•	◡	⏒	⏒	•	‖	•	•	•	•	◡	—	◡	•	‖

Note—The mark • denotes either long or short.

The 1st, 2nd, 3rd, 4th, 9th, 10th, 11th, and 12th syllables may be either long or short. The 8th, as ending the Páda, and the 16th, as ending the half-verse, are also common. Since the half-verse is considered as divided into two parts at the 8th syllable, it is an almost universal rule that this syllable must end a word, *whether simple or compound* *.

The 5th syllable ought always to be short. The 6th and 7th should be long; but instances are not unusual in the Mahá-bhárata of the 6th being short, in which case the 7th should be short also. But occasional variations from these last rules occur.

The last 4 syllables form two iambics; the 13th being always short, the 14th always long, and the 15th always short.

Every S'loka, or couplet of two lines, ought to form a complete sentence in itself, and contain both subject and predicate. Not unfrequently, however, in the Rámáyaṇa and Mahá-bhárata, three lines are united to form a triplet.

936. In the remaining metres determined by the number of *syllables* in the Páda, each Páda is exactly alike (*sama*); so that it is only necessary to give the scheme of one Páda or quarter-verse.

In printed books each Páda, if it consist of more than 8 syllables, is often made to occupy a line.

937. *Trishṭubh* (11 syllables to the Páda or quarter-verse).

Of this there are 22 varieties. The commonest are—

	1	2	3	4	5	6	7	8	9	10	11	‖
938. *Indra-vajrá*,	—	—	◡	—	—	◡	◡	—	◡	—	•	‖
939. *Upendra-vajrá*,	◡	—	◡	—	—	◡	◡	—	◡	—	•	‖

There is generally a cæsura at the 5th syllable.

Note—The above 2 varieties are sometimes mixed in the same stanza; in which case the metre is called *Upajáti* or *Ákhyánakí*.

	1	2	3	4	5	6	7	8	9	10	11	‖
940. *Rathoddhatá*,	—	◡	—	◡	◡	◡	—	◡	—	◡	—	‖

941. *Jagatí* (12 syllables to the Páda or quarter-verse).

Of this there are 30 varieties. The commonest are—

* There are, however, rare examples of compound words running through a whole line.

	1	2	3	4	5	6	7	8	9	10	11	12
942. *Vaṇśa-sthavila*,	⏑	—	⏑	—	—	⏑	⏑	—	⏑	—	⏑	⏓*
943. *Druta-vilambita*,	⏑	⏑	⏑	—	⏑	⏑	—	⏑	⏑	—	⏑	⏓

944. *Atijagatí* (13 syllables to the Páda or quarter-verse).

Of this there are 16 varieties. The commonest are—

	1	2	3	4	5	6	7	8	9	10	11	12	13
945. *Mañju-bháshiṇí*,	⏑	⏑	—	⏑	—	⏑	⏑	⏑	—	⏑	—	⏑	⏓
946. *Praharshiṇí*,	—	—	—	⏑	⏑	⏑	⏑	—	⏑	—	⏑	—	⏓
947. *Rućirá* or *Prabhávatí*,	⏑	—	⏑	—	⏑	⏑	⏑	⏑	—	⏑	—	⏑	⏓

948. *Śakvarí* or *Śakkarí* or *Śarkarí* (14 syllables to the Páda).

Of this there are 20 varieties. The commonest is—

	1	2	3	4	5	6	7	8	9	10	11	12	13	14
949. *Vasanta-tilaká*,	—	—	⏑	—	⏑	⏑	⏑	—	⏑	⏑	—	⏑	—	⏓

950. *Atiśakvarí* or *Atiśakkarí* (15 syllables to the Páda).

Of this there are 18 varieties. The commonest is—

	1	2	3	4	5	6	7	8	9	10	11	12	13	14	15
951. *Málìní* or *Mániní*,	⏑	⏑	⏑	⏑	⏑	⏑	—	—	—	⏑	—	—	⏑	—	⏓

There is a cæsura at the 8th syllable.

952. *Ashṭi* (16 syllables to the Páda or quarter-verse).

Of this there are 12 varieties; none of which are common.

953. *Atyashṭi* (17 syllables to the Páda or quarter-verse).

Of this there are 17 varieties. The commonest are—

	1	2	3	4	5	6	7	8	9	10	11	12	13	14	15	16	17
954. *S'ikhariṇí*,	⏑	—	—	—	—	—	⏑	⏑	⏑	⏑	⏑	—	—	⏑	⏑	⏑	⏓

Cæsura at the 6th syllable.

	1	2	3	4	5	6	7	8	9	10	11	12	13	14	15	16	17
955. *Mandákrántá*,	—	—	—	—	⏑	⏑	⏑	⏑	⏑	—	—	⏑	—	—	⏑	—	⏓

Cæsura at the 4th and 10th syllables.

	1	2	3	4	5	6	7	8	9	10	11	12	13	14	15	16	17
956. *Hariṇí*,	⏑	⏑	⏑	⏑	⏑	—	—	—	—	—	⏑	—	⏑	⏑	—	⏑	⏓

Cæsura at the 6th and 10th syllables.

957. *Dhṛiti* (18 syllables to the Páda or quarter-verse).

Of this there are 17 varieties, one of which is found in the Raghu-vaṇśa—

	1	2	3	4	5	6	7	8	9	10	11	12	13	14	15	16	17	18
958. *Mahá-máliká*,	⏑	⏑	⏑	⏑	⏑	⏑	—	⏑	—	—	⏑	—	—	⏑	—	—	⏑	⏓

* The mark ⏓ is meant to shew that the last syllable is long at the end of the Páda or quarter-verse, but long or short at the end of the half-verse.

959. *Atidhṛiti* (19 syllables to the Páda or quarter-verse).

Of this there are 13 varieties. The commonest is—

	1 2 3 4 5 6 7 8 9 10 11 12	13 14 15 16 17 18 19
960. *S'árdúla-vikríḍita*,	— — — ᴗ ᴗ — ᴗ — ᴗ ᴗ ᴗ —	— — ᴗ — — ᴗ —̣ ‖

Cæsura at the 12th syllable.

961. *Kṛiti* (20 syllables to the Páda or quarter-verse).

Of these there are 4 varieties; none of which are common.

962. *Prakṛiti* (21 syllables to the Páda or quarter-verse).

	1 2 3 4 5 6 7	8 9 10 11 12 13 14	15 16 17 18 19 20 21
963. *Sragdhará*,	— — — — ᴗ — —	ᴗ ᴗ ᴗ ᴗ ᴗ ᴗ —	— ᴗ — — ᴗ — —̣ ‖

Cæsura at the 7th and 14th syllables.

964. Of the remaining metres determined by the number of syllables in the Páda, *Ákṛiti* has 22 syllables, and includes 3 varieties; *Vikṛiti* 23 syllables, 6 varieties; *Sankṛiti* 24 syllables, 5 varieties; *Atikṛiti* 25 syllables, 2 varieties; *Utkṛiti* 26 syllables, 3 varieties; and *Daṇḍaka* is the name given to all metres which exceed *Utkṛiti* in the number of syllables.

965. There are two metres, called *Gáyatrí* and *Ushṇih*, of which the first has only 6 syllables to the quarter-verse, and includes 11 varieties; the second has 7 syllables to the quarter-verse, and includes 8 varieties.

a. When the Páda is so short, the whole verse is sometimes written in one line.

b. Observe, that great license is allowed in metres peculiar to the Vedas; thus in the

966. *Gáyatrí*,

which may be regarded as consisting of a triplet of 3 divisions of 8 syllables each, or of 6 feet of 4 syllables each, generally printed in one line, the quantity of each syllable is very irregular. The following verse exhibits the most usual quantities:

1		2		3	
a	*b*	*a*	*b*	*a*	*b*
• • • •	ᴗ — ᴗ • ‖	• • • •	ᴗ — ᴗ • ‖	• • • •	ᴗ — ᴗ • ‖

but even in the *b* verse of each division the quantity may vary.

B. *Metres, consisting of two half-verses, determined by the number of* SYLLABLES* *in the* HALF-VERSE (*each half-verse being alike, ardha-sama*).

967. This class contains 7 genera, but no varieties under each genus. Of these the commonest are—

* This class of metres is said to be regulated by the number of feet or Mátrás in the half-verse, in the same way as class II. But as each half-verse is generally distributed into fixed long or short syllables, and no option is allowed for each foot between a spondee, anapæst, dactyl, proceleusmaticus, and amphibrach, it will obviate confusion to regard this class as determined by syllables, like class I. A.

968. *Vaitálíya* (21 syllables to the half-verse).

1	2	3	4	5	6	7	8	9	10		11	12	13	14	15	16	17	18	19	20	21
⏑	⏑	—	⏑	⏑	—	⏑	—	⏑	—	|	⏑	⏑	—	—	⏑	⏑	—	⏑	—	⏑	•

There is a cæsura at the 10th syllable.

969. *Aupaććhandasika* (23 syllables to the half-verse).

The scheme of this metre is the same as the last, with a long syllable added after the 10th and last syllable in the line; the cæsura being at the 11th syllable.

970. *Pushpitágrá* (25 syllables to the half-verse).

1	2	3	4	5	6	7	8	9	10	11	12		13	14	15	16	17	18	19	20	21	22	23	24	25
⏑	⏑	⏑	⏑	⏑	⏑	—	⏑	—	⏑	—	—	|	⏑	⏑	⏑	⏑	—	⏑	⏑	—	⏑	—	⏑	—	•

There is a cæsura at the 12th syllable.

Class II.—*Mátrá-vṛitta, consisting of two half-verses, determined by the number of* FEET *in the whole verse (each foot containing generally four Mátrás).*

971. Note—Each foot is supposed to consist of four Mátrás or instants, and a short syllable is equivalent to one instant, a long syllable to two. Hence only such feet can be used as are equivalent to four Mátrás; and of this kind are the dactyl (— ⏑ ⏑), the spondee (— —), the anapæst (⏑ ⏑ —), the amphibrach (⏑ — ⏑), and the proceleusmaticus (⏑ ⏑ ⏑ ⏑); any one of which may be employed.

Of this class of metres the commonest is the

972. *Áryá* or *Gáthá*.

Each half-verse consists of seven and a half feet; and each foot contains four Mátrás, excepting the 6th of the second half-verse, which contains only one, and is therefore a single short syllable. Hence there are 30 Mátrás in the first half-verse, and 27 in the second. The half-foot at the end of each half-verse is generally, but not always, a long syllable; the 6th foot of the first half-verse must be either an amphibrach or proceleusmaticus; and the 1st, 3rd, 5th, and 7th feet must not be amphibrachs. The cæsura commonly takes place at the end of the 3rd foot in each half-verse, and the measure is then sometimes called *Paṭhyá*. The following are a few examples:

1	2	3	4	5	6	7	
`— —`	`⏑ — ⏑`	`⏑ ⏑ —`	`— ⏑ ⏑`	`— ⏑ ⏑`	`⏑ — ⏑`	`— —`	`—`
`⏑ ⏑ —`	`⏑ — ⏑`	`⏑ ⏑ —`	`— —`	`⏑ ⏑ —`	`⏑`	`— —`	`⏑`

1	2	3	4	5	6	7	
`— —`	`⏑ ⏑ —`	`— —`	`— —`	`— ⏑ ⏑`	`⏑ — ⏑`	`— ⏑ ⏑`	`—`
`⏑ ⏑ —`	`— ⏑ ⏑`	`⏑ ⏑ —`	`⏑ — ⏑`	`— —`	`⏑`	`— ⏑ ⏑`	`—`

1	2	3	4	5	6	7	
`⏑ ⏑ —`	`— ⏑ ⏑`	`— —`	`⏑ ⏑ —`	`— ⏑ ⏑`	`⏑ — ⏑`	`— —`	`⏑`
`⏑ ⏑ —`	`⏑ ⏑ ⏑ ⏑`	`— ⏑ ⏑`	`— —`	`⏑ ⏑ —`	`⏑`	`— —`	`—`

1	2	3	4	5	6	7	
– ⏑ ⏑	⏑ – ⏑	⏑ ⏑ – ‖	– ⏑ ⏑	– ⏑ ⏑	⏑ – ⏑	– –	–
– –	⏑ – ⏑	– – ‖	⏑ ⏑ ⏑ ⏑	⏑ ⏑ –	⏑	– –	–

1	2	3	4	5	6	7	
– ⏑ ⏑	– –	– ⏑ ⏑ ‖	– –	– –	⏑ ⏑ ⏑ ⏑	⏑ ⏑ –	–
⏑ ⏑ ⏑ ⏑	⏑ ⏑ ⏑ ⏑	– – ‖	– –	⏑ ⏑ –	⏑	– –	⏑

973. The *Udgíti* metre only differs from the *Áryá* in inverting the half-verses, and placing the short half-verse, with 27 Mátrás, first in order.

974. There are three other varieties:—In the *Upagíti*, both half-verses consist of 27 Mátrás; in the *Gíti*, both consist of 30 Mátrás; and in the *Áryágíti*, of 32.

ACCENTUATION.

975. Accentuation (*svara*, 'tone') in Sanskṛit is only marked in the Vedas. Probably the original object of the marks used was to denote that peculiar change in the ordinary intonation practised in reciting the hymns, which consisted in the occasional raising of the voice to a higher pitch than the usual monotone. Only three names for different kinds of accent or tone are generally recognized by grammarians; viz. 1. *Udátta*, 'raised,' i. e. the elevated tone or high pitch, marked in Roman writing by the acute accent; 2. *An-udátta*, 'not raised,' i. e. the accentless tone; 3. *Svarita*, 'sounded,' i. e. the moderate tone, neither high nor low, but a combination of the two (*samáhára*, Páṇ. 1. 2, 32), which is produced in the following manner: In pronouncing the syllable immediately following the high-toned syllable, the voice unable to lower itself abruptly to the level of the low intonation, is sustained in a tone not as high as the *udátta*, and yet not so low as the *an-udátta*. A syllable uttered with this mixed intonation is said to be *svarita*, 'sounded.' These three accents, according to native grammarians, are severally produced, through intensifying (*áyáma*), relaxing (*viśrambha*), and throwing out the voice (*ákshepa*); and these operations are said to be connected with an upward, downward, and horizontal motion (*tiryag-gamana*) of the organs of utterance, which may be illustrated by the movements of the hand in conducting a musical performance *.

976. But although there are only three general names for the accents, it is clear that there are only two positive tones, viz. the *udátta* or high tone, and *svarita* or mixed tone, the *an-udátta* representing the neutral, monotonous, accentless sound, which lies like a flat horizontal line below the two positive sounds. There remains

* In native grammars the *udátta* sound of a vowel is said to result from employing the upper half of the organs of utterance, and the *an-udátta* from employing the lower half. In my recent travels in India I frequently heard the Vedas recited and intoned by Paṇḍits at Benares, Calcutta, Bombay, Poona, &c., and found to my surprise that the voice is not now raised in pronouncing the *udátta* syllable. Great stress is laid on the *an-udátta* and *svarita*, but none upon the *udátta*; and I was told that the absence of all mark on this latter syllable is an indication of the absence of accent in intoning.

no designation for the low tone, properly so called, i. e. the tone which immediately precedes the high and is lower than the flat horizontal line taken to represent the general accentless sound. The fact is that the exertion required to produce the high tone (*udátta*) is so great that in order to obtain the proper pitch, the voice is obliged to lower the tone of the preceding syllable as much below this flat line as the syllable that bears the *udátta* is raised above it; and Páṇini himself explains this lower tone by the term *sannatara* (compar. of *sanna*, 'sunk,' for which the commentators have substituted the expression *anudáttatara*), while he explains the neutral, accentless tone by the term *eka-śruti*, i. e. the one accentless sound in which the ear can perceive no variation.

977. The expression *anudáttatara*, then, is now adopted to designate the lowest sound of all, or that immediately preceding the *udátta* or high tone. But no special mark distinguishes this sound from the *an-udátta*. It must be borne in mind that no simple uncompounded word, whatever the number of its syllables, has properly more than one syllable accented. This syllable is called either *udátta* or *svarita*, according as it is pronounced with a high or mixed tone. But if a word have only a *svarita* accent, then this *svarita* must be of the kind called independent, although it may have arisen from the blending of two syllables, one of which was originally *udátta*, as in त॒न्वा॑ (for *tanu-á*, where the middle syllable was *udátta*). A word having either the *udátta* or the *svarita* accent on the first syllable is called in the one case *ády-udátta*, in the other *ádi-svarita*; having either the one or other accent on the middle is in the one case *madhyodátta*, in the other *madhya-svarita*; having either the one or other accent at the end is in the one case *antodátta*, in the other *anta-svarita*. All the syllables of a word except the one which is either an *udátta* or independent *svarita* are *an-udátta*. Although, however, no one word can have both an *udátta* and an independent *svarita*, yet, if a word having an *udátta* is followed by an *an-udátta*, this *an-udátta* becomes a dependent *svarita*, which is really the commonest form of *svarita* accent.

978. As to the method of marking the tones, the *udátta* or high tone is never marked at all, so that if a word of one syllable is *udátta* it remains simply unmarked, as पूः; if a monosyllable is *an-udátta* it has a horizontal stroke underneath, as नो॒; if *svarita*, it has an upright mark above, as क्व॑. A word of two syllables, both of which are *an-udátta*, has two horizontal marks below, thus स॒म॒ः; and if the first syllable is *udátta* it is marked thus, इन्द्र॑ः; if the last is *udátta*, thus अ॒ग्नि. A word of more than two syllables being entirely *an-udátta* (*sarvánudátta*) has horizontal marks under all the syllables, thus अ॒व॒र्ध॒न्त॒; but if one of the syllables is *udátta*, the horizontal stroke immediately preceding it marks the *anudáttatara*, as in आ॒मु॒षा॒नः, where the first and second syllables are *an-udátta* and the third *anudáttatara*, the fourth being *udátta*; and if the *udátta* syllable is followed by another *an-udátta*, this becomes a dependent *svarita*, and is marked by an upright stroke, as in वै॒श्वा॒न॒राय॑ (Ṛig-veda III. 3, 1). Similarly, in a word of three syllables like च॒कार॑, the syllable च is *anudáttatara*, का is *udátta*, and र is *svarita*.

It should be noted that in Romanized Sanskṛit printing and writing it is usual instead of leaving the *udátta* unmarked to treat that as the only accent to be marked, and to treat both *anudáttatara* and dependent *svarita* as *an-udátta* or without any accent at all.

979. The foregoing explanations will make clear how it is that in the Saṃhitá of the Ṛig-veda an *anudáttatara* mark is generally the beginning of a series of three accents, of which the dependent *svarita* is the end; the appearance of this *anudáttatara* mark preparing the reader for an *udátta* immediately following, as well as for a dependent *svarita*. This last, however, may sometimes be retarded by a new *udátta* syllable, as in दिवा पतयन्तम्, where the syllable प, which would otherwise be a dependent *svarita*, becomes changed to an *anudáttatara* because of the *udátta* syllable त following.

980. But if an independent *svarita* is immediately followed by an *udátta* or by another independent *svarita*, a curious contrivance is adopted. Should the syllable bearing the independent *svarita* end in a short vowel, the numeral १ is used to carry the *svarita* with an *anudáttatara* under it, e.g. अपस्व१न (Ṛig-veda x. 89, 2), सुम्न्व१: पर्वतास (iv. 17, 2); and should the syllable end in a long vowel, the numeral ३ is employed in the same way, but the *anudáttatara* mark is placed both under the long vowel and the numeral, e.g. विभ्वो३विभूतयो (i. 166, 11), नद्यो३चपं (iv. 55, 6), क्षा३पि: (vi. 21, 8).

981. It should also be pointed out that the absence of mark is employed in a sentence to denote *an-udátta* as well as *udátta*; thus, in the Saṃhitá of the Veda, at the commencement of a sentence a horizontal stroke underneath marks the first *anudáttatara* syllable of the sentence as well as all such *an-udátta* syllables as precede; the next syllable, if without mark, is *udátta*; and the next, if it has an upright mark, is *svarita*; but the next, if it has no mark, is *an-udátta*; and the absence of all mark after the upright mark, continues to denote *an-udátta* until the appearance of the next horizontal mark, which is *anudáttatara*. In fact, all the syllables, both in words and sentences, which follow the *svarita* are supposed to be pronounced in the accentless tone until the voice has to be depressed for the utterance of another *udátta* syllable.

With regard to the absence of accentuation, we may note that in direct sentences a verb (unless it is the first word) is regarded as an enclitic and loses its accent. The same rule applies to Vocative cases, which are accented only when they begin a sentence, and then on the first syllable. Verbs preserve their accent in conditional sentences and in a few exceptional cases.

982. The system of accentuation in the Prátiśákhyas often differs from that of Páṇini. The rules given by these treatises for determining the accent when two vowels (each bearing an accent) blend into one are very precise, but are liable to exceptions. The following are some of those most usually given: *udátta+udátta =udátta; udátta+anudátta=udátta; anudátta+anudátta=anudátta; anudátta+udátta=udátta; svarita+udátta=udátta; svarita+anudátta=svarita.*

When *anudátta* vowels are pronounced with the *udátta* tone, this is called in the

Prátiśákhyas *praćaya.* When the accent of two vowels is blended into one, this is called *praślishṭa, samáveśa, ekíbháva.* The expressions *tairovyañjana* and *vaivṛitta* are used to denote forms of the dependent *svarita;* while *kshaipra* and *játya* apply to the independent *svaritas* caused by the blending of the accents of two vowels, the first of which has passed into the semivowel *y* or *v.*

983. A few compound words (generally names of Vedic deities) have two accents, and are therefore called *dvir-udátta,* e.g. बृहस्पतिः, तनूनपात्, where the first syllable being *udátta* remains unmarked, and the second being *an-udátta* ought to become a dependent *svarita,* but the third being *udátta* again the second becomes *anudáttatara* and is so marked. In मित्रावरुणौ both the second and third syllables are *udátta.* A compound (called *trir-udátta*) may even have three *udátta* syllables, as in इन्द्राबृहस्पती.

984. In the Pada text where compounds are divided, if the first half of the compound ends in a *svarita* coming after an *udátta,* and the second begins with an *udátta,* the *svarita* accent at the end of the first member of the compound is called *táthábhávya.*

985. Observe—The accent in Sanskṛit is not confined to the last three syllables of a word, as in Greek and Latin.

Observe also—Although the Sanskṛit independent *svarita* is in some respects similar to the Greek circumflex, it should be borne in mind, that the latter is confined to long, whereas the *svarita* may also be applied to short syllables *.

---

* See on the subject of Vedic accentuation, Roth's preface to the Nirukta: two treatises by Whitney in the Journal of the American Oriental Society, vol. IV. p. 195 &c., and vol. V. p. 387 &c.: *Aufrecht,* de accentu compositorum Sanscriticorum, Bonnae, 1847; reviewed by *Benfey,* Göttinger Gelehrte Anzeigen, 1848, pp. 1995–2010.

INDEX I.

ENGLISH.

(The numbers refer to the paragraphs, except where the page is specified.)

frequentatives, 514; nouns, 80. i.
Future, first and second, 386; formation of stem, 388; syntax of, 886, 887.
Genders of nouns, 89.
General tenses, 248, 363-456.
Hard consonants, 18. *a*. *b*, 20. *b*, 39.
Imperative, 241; terminations of, 245, 246; formation of stem, 261, 272, 278, 283, 307, 330, 342, 349, 353, 356; syntax of, 882.
Imperfect tense, 242; formation of stem, 261, 264, 272, 278, 283, 307, 330, 342, 349, 353, 356; syntax of, 884.
Indeclinable words, 712; syntax of, 912.
Indefinite pronouns, 228, 229.
Indicative mood, 241.
Infinitive, 458, 459; syntax of, 867; Vedic, 459. *a*, 867. *b*.
Intensive verb, see Frequentative.
Interjections, 732; syntax of, 926.
Interrogative pronouns, 227.
Letters, 1; classification of, 18; interchange of letters in cognate languages, 25; euphonic combination of, 27.
Metre, schemes of, 935-974.
Moods, 241, 242. *a*.
Nominal verbs, 518-523.
Nouns, formation of stem, 74, 80-87; declension of, 103-183; defective, 184; syntax of, 802-823.
Numbers, 91, 243.
Numerals, 198-215; syntax of, 206, 835; compounded, 759.
Numerical figures, page 3.
Ordinals, 208.
Participial nouns of agency, 579-582.
Participles, present, 524-529; past passive, 530-552; past active, 553; of the perfect, 554; past indeclinable, 555-566; adverbial indeclinable, 567; future passive, 568-577; of the 2nd future, 578; syntax of, 892.
Particles, 717.
Passive verbs, 243. *a*, 461; terminations of, 462; formation of stem, 463; examples, 700-702.
Patronymics, 80. xxxv, 81. viii-x, &c.
Perfect (reduplicated), 364-384; (periphrastic), 385; syntax of, 885.
Persons of the tenses, 244.
Possessive adjectives, 84. vi, vii, 85. vi, viii; pronouns, 231.
Potential, 241; terminations of, 245, 246; formation of stem, 261, 272, 278, 283, 307, 330, 342, 349, 353, 356; syntax of, 879.
Precative, 242, 442; formation of stem, 443-454; syntax of, 890.
Prefixes, adverbial, 726.
Prepositions, 729, 783; syntax of, 916.
Present, 241; terminations of, 246, 247; formation of stem, 261, 272, 278, 283, 307, 330, 342, 349, 353, 356; syntax of, 873.
Pronominals, 235-240.
Pronouns, 216-234; syntax of, 836.
Pronunciation, of vowels, 11; of consonants, 12.
Prosody, 935-974.
Reduplication, 252, 367.
Relative pronouns, 226.
Root, 74, 75.
Sandhi, rules of, 27-71, 296-306.
Soft or sonant letters, 18. *a*. *b*, 20. *b*, 39.
Special tenses, 241, 248, 249.
Stem, nominal, 74, 77; formation of nominal, 79, 80-87; inflexion of, 88-183; verbal, 244; formation of verbal, 249-517.
Strong cases, 135. *a*.
Strong forms in verbal terminations, 246. *c*.
Suffixes, forming substantives, adjectives, &c., 80-87; adverbial, 718-725.
Superlative degree, 191, 192.
Surd consonants, 18. *a*. *b*, 20. *b*, 39.
Symbols, 6-10.
Syntax, 793-929.
Tables of verbs, 583.
Tenses, 241, 248.
Terminations, of nouns, 91, 96; of verbs, 244-248.
Verb, 241; syntax of, 839.
Voices, 243; roots restricted to, 786.
Vowels, 1; method of writing, 2, 3; pronunciation of, 11; combination of, 27.
Weak cases, 135. *a*.
Writing, method of, 26.

INDEX II.

SANSKRIT.

अ or अन् prefix, 726.
अ augment, 251.
अक्षि 'eye,' 122.
अग्नि 'fire,' 110.
अग्रे 'before,' 731, 917.
अञ्ज् 'to anoint,' 347, 668.
अति prefix, 726. *a*; prep., 783. *a*.
अतिचमू 126. *i*.
अतिलक्ष्मी 126. *i*.
अथ 'then,' 727. *c*.
अथवा 'yet,' 728. *b*. *c*.
अथो 'then,' 727. *c*.
अद् 'to eat,' 317, 652.
अदत् 'eating,' 141. *c*.
अदस् 'this,' 'that,' 225.
अधरेण 'under,' 731.
अधस् 'under,' 731.
अधि prep., 783. *b*.
अधी 'to read,' 311, 367. *a*.
अध्वन् 'a road,' 147.
अन् 'to breathe,' 322. *a*.
अनडुह् 'an ox,' 182. *f*.
अनन्तरम् 'after,' 731, 917.
अनु prep., 730. *d*. *e*, 783. *c*.
अनेहस् 'time,' 170.
अन्तर् 'within,' 731, 783. *d*.
अन्तर 'another,' 777. *b*.
अन्तरेण 'without,' 731, 917.
अन्तिकम् 'near,' 731.
अन्य 'other,' 236; °तम 238; °तर 236.
अन्योन्यम् 'mutually,' 760. *f*.
अप् 'water,' 178. *b*.
अप prep., 783. *e*.
अपि prep., 783. *f*; adv., 717. *i*.
अपेक्ष्य 833. *a*.
अप्सरस् 'a nymph,' 163. *a*.
अभि prep., 730. *f*, 783. *g*.
अभितस् 'on both sides,' 731.
अभिमुखम् 'in front of,' 731.
अभ्यासे 'near,' 731.
अम्बा 'a mother,' 108. *d*.
अय् 'to go,' 385. *e*.
अर्च् 'to worship,' 367. *b*.
अर्थ् 'to ask,' 642.
अर्थम् 'on account of,' 731, 760. *d*, 917.
अर्थे or अर्थाय 'on account of,' 731.
अर्यमन् 'the sun,' 157.
अर्वन् 'a horse,' 158.
अर्वाक् 'after,' 731, 917.
अर्ह् 'to deserve,' 608.
अलम् 'enough,' 901. *a*, 918.
अल्प 'a few,' 240.
अल्पमति 119.
अल्पविद्य 108.
अव prep., 783. *h*.
अवधीर् 'to despise,' 75. *a*.
अवयाज् 'a priest,' 176. *f*.
अवाच् 'southern,' 176. *b*.
अश् 'to eat,' 357. *a*, 696.
अश् 'to obtain,' 'to pervade,' 367. *c*, 681. *a*.
अश्मन् 'a stone,' 147.
अस् 'to be,' 327, 364. *a*, 584.
अस् 'to throw,' 622.
असृज् 'blood,' 176. *d*.
अस्तम् 'setting,' 712.
अस्ति 'existence,' 712.
अस्थि 'a bone,' 122.
अस्मद् 'we,' 218.
अह् 'to say,' 384. *b*.
अहन् 'a day,' 156.
आ prefix, 726. *b*; prep., 730, 730. *a*. *b*, 783. *i*.
आञ्छ् 'to stretch,' 385.
आत्तलक्ष्मी 126. *i*.
आत्मक 'consisting of,' 769. *h*, 774.
आत्मन् 'soul,' 'self,' 147, 232.
आदि 'beginning with,' 'et cetera,' 764, 772.
आदिक or आद्य (= आदि) 764. *b*.
आप् 'to obtain,' 351, 364. *a*, 681.

आरभ्य 'beginning from,' 792, 925.
आरु 'tawny,' 126. *f.*
आशिस् 'a blessing,' 166.
आस् 'to sit,' 317; with pres. part., 877.
इ 'to go,' 310, 367. *a*, 645.
इ inserted, 391–415.
इतर 'other,' 236.
इति 'so,' 927–929.
इदम् 'this,' 224.
इन्ध् 'to kindle,' 347.
इयत् 'so much,' 234. *b.*
इष् 'to wish,' 282, 367, 637.
ईक्ष् 'to see,' 605.
ईड् 'to praise,' 325.
ईदृश 'so like,' 234.
ईश् 'to rule,' 325. *a*, 385. *a.*
ईषत् 'a little,' 717. *d*, 726. *b.*
उख् 'to move,' 367.
उत 'also,' 717. *h*, 727. *a.*
उत्तम, उत्तर 195.
उत्तरात् or उत्तरेण 731.
उत्पलचक्षुस् 166. *c.*
उद् prep., 783. *j.*
उदञ्च् 'northern,' 176. *b.*
उद्दिश्य 'with reference to,' 924.
उन्द् 'to moisten,' 347.
उप prep., 783. *k.*
उपरि 'above,' 731, 917.
उपानह् 'a shoe,' 183.
उभ, उभय 'both,' 238.
उशनस् 'Venus,' 170.
उष् 'to burn,' 385. *e.*
उष्णिह् a metre, 182. *b.*
ऊष्मन् 'the hot season,' 147.
ऊर्ज् 'strength,' 176. *h.*
ऊर्णु 'to cover,' 316, 374. *j.*
ऊर्ध्वम् 'above,' 731, 917.
ऋ 'to go,' 334, 374. *n.*
ऋच्छ् 'to go,' 381. *a.*
ऋण् 'to go,' 684.
ऋते 'except,' 731.
ऋत्विज् 'a priest,' 176. *e.*
ऋध् 'to flourish,' 367. *b*, 680.
ऋभुक्षिन् 'Indra,' 162.
ॠ 'to go,' 358.
एक 'one,' 200; °तम 236; °तर 238.
एतद् 'this,' 223.
एध् 'to increase,' 600.
ओम् 'the syllable Om,' 712.
कतिचिद् 'a few,' 230.
कथ् 'to say,' 286. *a*, 643.
कनीयस्, कनिष्ठ 194.
कम् 'to love,' 440. *a.*
कर्मन् 'an action,' 152.
कश्चिद् 'any one,' 228.
का prefix, 726. *c.*
काम 'desirous,' with inf., 871.
कारणात् 'on account of,' 731.
कारिन् 'doer,' 159. Obs.
कास् 'to shine,' 385. *e.*
किन्तु 'but,' 728. *a.*
किम् 'who?' 'what?' 227.
किम् 'why?' 921.
कियत् 'how many,' 234. *b.*
कु prefix, 726. *c.*
कुन्थ् 'to pain,' 360.
कुमार् 'to play,' 75. *a.*
कुमारी 'a girl,' 107.
कुमुद् n. 'a lotus,' 137.
कुर्द् 'to play,' 271. *a.*
कू 'to sound,' 358. *a.*
कृ 'to do,' 355, 366, 369, 682, 683, 701.
कृत् 'to cut,' 281.
कृतवत् 'who made,' 140. *a. b.*
कृते 'on account of,' 731.
कृत्वस् 'times,' 723. *a.*
कृष् 'to draw,' 606.
कॄ 'to scatter,' 280, 627.
कॄ 'to hurt,' 358.
कॄत् 'to celebrate,' 287.
कॢप् 'to make,' 263.
कोऽपि 'any one,' 229.
क्री 'to buy,' 374. *e*, 689.
क्रुञ्च् 'a curlew,' 176. *c.*
क्रोष्टु 'a jackal,' 128. *c*, 185.
क्लिश् 'to harass,' 697.
क्षण् 'to kill,' 684, 685.
क्षत्तृ 'a charioteer,' 128. *d.*
क्षिण् 'to kill,' 684.
क्षिप् 'to throw,' 274, 279, 635; freq., 710.
क्षु 'to sneeze,' 392. *a.*
क्षुभ् 'to agitate,' 694.
क्ष्णु 'to sharpen,' 392. *a.*
खन् 'to dig,' 376.
खलपू 'a sweeper,' 126. *b*, 190.
खिद् 'to vex,' 281.
ख्या 'to tell,' 437. *b.*
गत 'gone,' at end of comps., 739. *a. b.*
गतभी 'fearless,' 126. *h.*
गम् 'to go,' 270, 376, 602; freq., 709.
गरीयस् 'heavier,' 194.
गिर् 'speech,' 180.
गुप् 'to protect,' 271.
गुह् 'to conceal,' 270. *b*, 609.
गॄ 'to evacuate,' 430.

गॄ 'to sound,' 358.
गै 'to sing,' 268, 373. *d*, 595. *a*.
गो 'a cow,' 133.
गोरक्ष् 'cow-keeper,' 181. *c*.
गौरी 'the goddess,' 124.
ग्रन्थ् 'to tie,' 360, 375. *h*, 693.
ग्रस् 'to swallow,' 286.
ग्रह् 'to take,' 359, 699; freq., 711.
ग्रामणी 126. *d*.
ग्लै 'to be weary,' 268, 595. *b*.
घस् 'to eat,' 377.
घुष् 'to proclaim,' 643. *a*.
घृण् 'to shine,' 684.
घ्रा 'to smell,' 269, 588.
च 'and,' 727, 912.
चकास् 'to shine,' 75. *a*, 329.
चकास् 'brilliant,' 164. *b*.
चक्ष् 'to speak,' 326.
चक्षुस् 'eye,' 165. *a*.
चतुर् 'four,' 203.
चनस् 'food,' 712.
चन्द्रमस् 'the moon,' 163.
चमू 'a host,' 125.
चर् 'one who goes,' 180.
चर्मन् 'leather,' 153.
चल् 'to move,' 602. *b*.
चि 'to gather,' 350, 374, 583.
चिकीर्ष् 'desirous of doing,' 166. *a*.
चित्रलिख् 'a painter,' 175. *a*.
चिन्त् 'to think,' 641.
चुर् 'to steal,' 284, 638, 639.
चेद् 'if,' 727. *e*, 915.
छद्मन् 'a pretext,' 153.
छिद् 'to cut,' 667.
छुर् 'to cut,' 390. *a*.
जक्ष् 'to eat,' 310. Obs., 322. *a*.
जगत् 'the world,' 142. *a*.
जन् 'to be born,' 276, 376, 424. *a*, 617. *a*.
जन् 'to produce,' 339, 666. *b*.
जन्मन् 'birth,' 153.
जरस् 'decay,' 171, 185.
जलपी 126. *b*.
जागृ 'to be awake,' 75. *a*, 310. *a*, 374. *p*, 392. *d*.
जाग्रत् 'watching,' 141. *a*.
जि 'to conquer,' 263, 374. *b*, 590.
जिगदिस् 166. *a*.
जीव् 'to live,' 267, 603.
जुह्वत् 'sacrificing,' 141. *c*.
जॄ 'to grow old,' 277, 358, 375. *k*, 437. *b*.
ज्ञा 'to know,' 361, 688.
ज्या 'to grow old,' 359. *a*.
डी 'to fly,' 274, 392.
तक्षन् 'a carpenter,' 148.
ततस् 'then,' 719, 727. *f*.
तथा 'thus,' 727. *b*.
तद् 'he,' 'that,' 220, 221.
तन् 'to stretch,' 354, 583, 684.
तनु 'thin,' 118, 119. *a*.
तन्त्री 'a lute-string,' 124.
तप् 'to burn,' 600. *a*.
तरी 'a boat,' 124.
तादृश 'such like,' 234.
तादृशम् 'so,' 801. *a*, 920. *a*.
तावत् 'so many,' 234, 801, 838, 876.
तिर्यञ्च् 176. *b*.
तु 'but,' 728. *a*, 914.
तुद् 'to strike,' 279, 634.
तुरासाह् 'Indra,' 182. *e*.
तृण् 'to eat grass,' 684.
तृप् 'to be satisfied,' 618.
तृह् 'to kill,' 348, 674.
तॄ 'to cross,' 364, 374. *r*.
त्यज् 'to abandon,' 596.
त्यद् 'he,' 'that,' 222.
त्रि 'three,' 202.
त्रुट् 'to break,' 390. *a*.
त्रै 'to preserve,' 268.
त्वद् 'thou,' 219.
त्वदीय 'thine,' 231.
त्वष्टृ 'a carpenter,' 128. *d*.
दंश् 'to bite,' 270. *d*.
दक्षिणात् or दक्षिणेन 'to the south,' 731, 917.
दण्डादण्डि 760. *e*.
ददत् 'giving,' 141. *a*.
दधि 'ghee,' 122.
दधृष् 'impudent,' 181.
दम् 'to be tamed,' 275.
दय् 'to pity,' 385. *e*.
दरिद्रा 'to be poor,' 75. *a*, 318, 385.
दह् 'to burn,' 610.
दा 'to give,' 335, 663, 700.
दातृ 'a giver,' 127, 129. *b*.
दामन् 'a string,' 153.
दिव् 'to play,' 275.
दिव् 'sky,' 180. *b*.
दिवन् 'a day,' 156. *a*.
दिश् 'to point out,' 279, 439. *a*, 583.
दिश् 'a quarter of the sky,' 181.
दिह् 'to anoint,' 659.
दीधी 'to shine,' 319.
दुर्मनस् 'evil-minded,' 164. *a*.
दुस् prefix, 726. *d*, 783. *t*.
दुह् 'to milk,' 330, 660.

दुह् 'a milker,' 182.
दृन्भू 'a thunderbolt,' 126. *c.*
दृश् 'to see,' 181, 270, 604.
दृश्वन् 'a looker,' 147, 149.
दॄ 'to split,' 358, 374. *m.*
दे 'to pity,' 373. *f.*
देवेज् 176. *e.*
दोस् 'an arm,' 166. *d.*
द्युत् 'to shine,' 597. *b.*
द्रु 'to run,' 369, 592.
द्रुह् 'to injure,' 623.
द्रुह् 'one who injures,' 182.
द्वार् 'a door,' 180.
द्वि 'two,' 201.
द्विमातृ 'having two mothers,' 130.
द्विष् 'to hate,' 309, 657.
द्विष् 'one who hates,' 181.
धनवत् 'rich,' 140.
धनिन् 'rich,' 159, 160, 161.
धर्मविद् 'knowing one's duty,' 137.
धा 'to place,' 336, 664.
धामन् 'a house,' 153.
धाव् 'to run,' 'to wash,' 603. *a.*
धी 'understanding,' 123. *a.*
धीमत् 'wise,' 140.
धू 'to agitate,' 280, 358, 374. *g*, 677.
धृ 'to hold,' 285.
धे 'to drink,' 438. *c*, 440. *a.*
धेनु 'a cow,' 112.
ध्मा 'to blow,' 269.
ध्यै 'to meditate,' 268, 595. *b.*
ध्रु 'to be firm,' 421. *f.*
नदी 'a river,' 105.
नप्तृ 'a grandson,' 128. *a.*
नम् 'to bend,' 433, 602. *a.*
नमस् 'reverence,' 712.
नश् 'to perish,' 181, 620.
नह् 'to bind,' 624.
नह् 'one who binds,' 183.
नामन् 'a name,' 152.
नास्ति 'non-existence,' 712.
नि prep., 783. *l.*
निज् 'to purify,' 341.
निमित्ते 'for the sake of,' 731.
निस् prefix, 726. *e*, 783. *m.*
नी 'to lead,' 374. *a*, 590. *a.*
नु 'to praise,' 280, 313, 392. *a.*
नृ 'a man,' 128. *b.*
नृत् 'to dance,' 274, 364, 583.
नॄ 'to lead,' 358.
नेदीयस्, नेदिष्ठ 194.
नौ 'a ship,' 94.
पच् 'to cook,' 267, 595. *c.*
पचत् 'cooking,' 141.
पञ्चन् 'five,' 204.
पत् 'to fall,' 441, 597. *c.*
पति 'a lord,' 121.
पथिन् 'a road,' 162.
पद् 'to go,' 424. *a.*
पपी 'the sun,' 126. *f.*
परतस् 'behind,' 731.
परम् 'after,' 731.
परमक्री 126. *a.*
परस्परम् 'mutually,' 760. *f.*
परा prep., 783. *n.*
परि prep., 783. *o.*
परिमृज् 'a cleanser,' 176. *e.*
परिव्राज् 176. *e.*
परेण 'after,' 731.
पश्चात् 'after,' 731.
पा 'to drink,' 269, 589.
पा 'to protect,' 317.
पाण्डु 'pale,' 187.
पाद् 'a foot,' 145.
पाप्मन् 'sin,' 147.
पारे 'on the further side,' 731.
पिण्डग्रस् 164. *b.*
पितृ 'a father,' 127, 128.
पिपक्ष् 'desirous of cooking,' 181. *d.*
पिपासु 'thirsty,' 118.
पिश् 'to form,' 281.
पीवन् 'fat,' 147, 149.
पुंस् 'a male,' 169.
पुट् 'to embrace,' 390. *a.*
पुण्य 'holy,' 191.
पुनर्भू 'born again,' 126. *c.*
पुरःसर 'preceded by,' 777. *d.*
पुरतस् or पुरस् 'before,' 731.
पुरुष 'a man,' 107.
पुरोडाश् 'a priest,' 181. *a.*
पुष् 'to nourish,' 357. *a*, 698; 'to be nourished,' 621.
पू 'to purify,' 358, 364, 583.
पूर्व or पूर्वक 'preceded by,' 'with,' 777. *d.*
पूर्वम् 'before,' 731.
पूषन् 'the sun,' 157.
पृषत् 'a deer,' 142. *a.*
पॄ or पूर् 'to fill,' 358, 374. *m*, 640.
प्यै 'to grow fat,' 373. *i*, 395. *b.*
प्र prep., 783. *p.*
प्रछ् 'to ask,' 282, 381, 631.
प्रति prep., 730. *c*, 783. *q.*
प्रत्यच् 'western,' 176. *b.*
प्रधी 'superior understanding,' 126. *g.*
प्रभृति 731, 764. *c*, 792.
प्रशाम् 'quiet,' 179. *a.*
प्रष्ठवाह् 'a steer,' 182. *c.*

प्राक् 'before,' 717. *f*, 731, 917.
प्राछ् 'an asker,' 176.
प्राञ्च् 'eastern,' 176. *b*.
प्राञ्च् 'worshipping,' 176. *c*.
प्रिय 'dear,' 187.
प्री 'to please,' 285, 358. *a*, 690.
प्रेमन् 'love,' 153.
बन्ध् 'to bind,' 360, 692.
बलिष्ठ 'strongest,' 193.
बलीयस् 'stronger,' 167, 193.
बहुनौ 134. *a*, 190.
बहुरै 'rich,' 134. *a*, 190.
बहुश्रेयसी 126. *i*.
बुध् 'to know,' 262, 364; cl. 1. 583; cl. 4. 614.
बुध् 'one who knows,' 177.
बुद्ध्या 'under the idea,' 809. *b*.
ब्रह्महन् 157.
ब्रू 'to speak,' 314, 649.
भक्ष् 'to eat,' 643. *b*.
भञ्ज् 'to break,' 347, 669.
भवत् 'your Honour,' 143, 233.
भवदीय 'yours,' 231.
भस् 'to shine,' 340.
भानु 'the sun,' 110.
भारवाह् 182. *c*.
भार्या 'a wife,' 107.
भाष् 'to speak,' 606. *a*.
भिक्ष् 'to beg,' 267.
भिद् 'to break,' 298. *c*, 343, 583.
भी 'to fear,' 333, 666.
भी 'fear,' 123. *a*.
भीरु 'timid,' 118. *a*, 187.
भुज् 'to eat,' 346, 668. *a*.
भुवर् 'sky,' 712.
भू 'to be,' 263, 374. *i*, 585, 586; caus., 703; desid., 705; freq., 706, 707.
भू 'the earth,' 125. *a*.
भूपति 'a king,' 121.
भूर् 'earth,' 712.
भृ 'to bear,' 332, 369, 583.
भृ 'to bear,' 'to blame,' 358.
भ्रंश् 'to fall,' 276.
भ्रज्ज् 'to fry,' 282, 381, 632.
भ्रज्ज् 'one who fries,' 176. *g*.
भ्रम् 'to wander,' 275, 375. *g*.
भ्राज् 'to shine,' 375. *i*.
भ्राश् 'to shine,' 375. *i*.
भ्री 'to fear,' 358.
मघवन् 'Indra,' 155. *c*.
मज्ज् 'to be immersed,' 633.
मति 'the mind,' 112.
मथिन् 'a churning-stick,' 162.
मद् 'to be mad,' 275.
मद् 'I,' 218.
मदीय 'mine,' 231.
मधु 'honey,' 114.
मध्ये 'in the middle,' 731.
मन् 'to imagine,' 617, 684.
मनस् 'the mind,' 164.
मन्थ् 'to churn,' 360, 693. *a*.
महत् 'great,' 142.
महामनस् 'magnanimous,' 164. *a*.
महाराज 'a great king,' 151. *a*.
मा 'to measure,' 274, 338, 664. *a*.
मा 'not,' in prohibition, 882, 889.
मा स्म 242. *a*.
मांसभुज् 'flesh-eater,' 176.
मात्र 'merely,' 'even,' 919.
मामक 'my,' 231. *a*.
मामकीन 'mine,' 231. *a*.
मिद् 'to be viscid,' 277.
मुच् 'to let go,' 281, 628.
मुह् 'to be troubled,' 612.
मुह् 'foolish,' 182.
मूर्धन् 'the head,' 147.
मृ 'to die,' 280, 626.
मृग 'a deer,' 107.
मृज् 'to cleanse,' 321, 651.
मृदु 'tender,' 118. *a*, 187.
मृश् 'one who touches,' 181.
मृष् 'one who endures,' 181.
मेधाविन् 'intellectual,' 159.
म्ना 'to repeat over,' 269.
म्लै 'to fade,' 268, 374, 595. *b*.
यकृत् 'the liver,' 144.
यज् 'to sacrifice,' 375. *e*, 597.
यज्वन् 'a sacrificer,' 149.
यथा 'as,' 721; at beginning of comps., 760, 760. *b*.
यद् 'who,' 226.
यदि 'if,' 727. *e*, 880. *a*, 915.
यम् 'to restrain,' 270, 433.
यवक्री 126. *b*.
या 'to go,' 317, 644.
याच् 'to ask,' 364, 392, 595. *d*.
यावत् 'as many,' 234, 801, 838, 876; 'up to,' 731, 917.
यु 'to mix,' 313, 357, 391. *a*, 583, 686, 687.
युज् 'to join,' 346, 670; pass., 702.
युवन् 'a youth,' 155. *b*.
युष्मद् 'you,' 219.
रक्ष् 'to preserve,' 606. *b*.
रभ् (with आ) 'to begin,' 601. *a*.
रम् 'to sport,' 433.
राज् 'to shine,' 375. *i*.
राज् 'a ruler,' 176. *e*.

राजन् 'a king,' 148, 151.
राज्ञी 'a queen,' 150.
रि 'to go,' 280.
री 'to go,' 358.
रु 'to sound,' 313, 392. *a.*
रुद् 'to weep,' 322, 653.
रुध् 'to hinder,' 344, 671.
रुन्धत् 'hindering,' 141. *c.*
रूप 'consisting of,' 769. *h*, 774.
रै 'wealth,' 132.
रोमन् 'hair,' 153.
लक्ष्मी 'fortune,' 124.
लघिमन् 'lightness,' 147.
लघिष्ठ 'lightest,' 193.
लघीयस् 'lighter,' 193.
लभ् 'to take,' 601.
लभ् 'one who obtains,' 178.
लिख् 'one who paints,' 175. *a.*
लिप् 'to anoint,' 281, 436.
लिह् 'to lick,' 330, 661.
लिह् 'one who licks,' 182.
ली 'to adhere,' 358, 373. *c.*
लुप् 'to break,' 281.
लू 'to cut,' 358, 691.
वच् 'to speak,' 320, 375. *c*, 650.
वद् 'to speak,' 375. *c*, 599.
वदि 'the fortnight of the month's wane,' 712.
वधू 'a wife,' 125.
वन् 'to ask,' 684.
वप् 'to sow,' 375. *c.*
वम् 'to vomit,' 375. *d.* Obs.
वर्त्मन् 'a road,' 153.
वर्मन् 'armour,' 153.
वर्षाभू 'a frog,' 126. *c.*
वश् 'to wish,' 324, 375. *c*, 656.
वस् 'to dwell,' 375. *c*, 607; 'to wear,' 657. *a.*
वह् 'to carry,' 375. *c*, 611.
वहिस् 'out,' 731.
वा 'or,' 728, 914.
वाच् 'speech,' 176.
वातप्रमी 'an antelope,' 126. *f.*
वार् 'water,' 180.
वारि 'water,' 114.
वाह् 'bearing,' 182. *c.*
वि prep., 783. *r.*
विच् 'to distinguish,' 341, 346.
विज् 'to shake,' 341, 390. *a.*
विद् 'to know,' 308, 583; 'to find,' 281.
विद्वस् 'wise,' 168. *e.*
विना 'without,' 731.
विभ्राज् 'splendid,' 176. *e.*
विवक्षु 'desirous of saying,' 181. *d.*
विश् 'to enter,' 635. *a.*
विश् 'one who enters,' 181.
विश्ववाह् 182. *c.*
विश्वसृज् 176. *e.*
विष् 'to pervade,' 341.
वी 'to go,' 312.
वृ 'to cover,' 'to choose,' 369, 675.
वृत् 'to be,' 598.
वृध् 'to increase,' 599. *b.*
वृहत् 'great,' 142. *a.*
वॄ 'to choose,' 358. See वृ.
वे 'to weave,' 373. *h.*
वेमन् 'a loom,' 147.
वेवी 'to go,' 75. *a*, 319.
वेश्मन् 'a house,' 153.
व्यच् 'to deceive,' 282, 383, 629.
व्यतिरेकेण 'without,' 731. *b.*
व्यथ् 'to be pained,' 383.
व्यध् 'to pierce,' 277, 383, 615.
व्ये 'to cover,' 373. *g.*
व्योमन् 'sky,' 153.
व्रश्च् 'to cut,' 282, 630.
व्रश्च् 'one who cuts,' 176. *g.*
व्री 'to choose,' 358.
व्ली 'to go,' 358.
शक् 'to be able,' 400, 679.
शकृत् 'ordure,' 144.
शद् 'to fall,' 270.
शम् 'to be appeased,' 275, 619.
शम् 'ease,' 712.
शालिवाह् 'bearing rice,' 182. *c.*
शास् 'to rule,' 310. Obs., 328, 658.
शासत् 'ruling,' 141. *a.*
शिव 'Śiva,' 'prosperous,' 103, 104, 105.
शिष् 'to distinguish,' 672.
शी 'to lie down,' 315, 646.
शुच् 'to grieve,' 595. *e.*
शुचि 'pure,' 117, 119. *a*, 187.
शुचिरोचिस् 166. *c.*
शुद्धधी 126. *h.*
शुभ 'fortunate,' 187.
शुष्मन् 'fire,' 147.
शॄ 'to hurt,' 358, 374. *m.*
शो 'to sharpen,' 373. *d.*
श्रन्थ् 'to loose,' 360, 375. *h*, 693. *a.*
श्रि 'to resort to,' 374. *e*, 392, 440. *a.*
श्री 'prosperity,' 123.
श्रु 'to hear,' 352, 369, 374. *h*, 676.
श्वन् 'a dog,' 155.

श्वश्रू 'a mother-in-law,' 125.
श्वस् 'to breathe,' 322. *a.*
श्वि 'to swell,' 374. *f*, 392, 437. *b.*
श्वेतवाह् 'Indra,' 182. *d.*
स (= सह) 'with,' 760. *a*, 769; (= समान) 769. *c.*
संवत् 'a year,' 712.
सकाशम् 'near,' 731.
सकाशात् 'from,' 731.
सकृत् 'once,' 717. *f.*
सक्थि 'a thigh,' 122.
सखि 'a friend,' 120.
सङ्ग्राम् 'to fight,' 75. *a.*
सजुस् 'an associate,' 166.
सञ्ज् 'to adhere,' 270. *d*, 422, 597. *a.*
सद् 'to sink,' 270, 599. *a.*
सन् 'to give,' 354, 424. *e*, 684.
सनाथ 'possessed of,' 769. *f.*
सम् prep., 783. *s.*
समक्षम् 'before the eyes,' 731.
समम् 'with,' 731.
समीपतस् or समीपम् 'near,' 731.
सम्यच् 'fit,' 176. *b.*
सरित् 'a river,' 136.
सर्पिष्टर 195.
सर्व 'all,' 237.
सर्वशक् 'omnipotent,' 175.
सव्येष्ठृ 'a charioteer,' 128. *d.*
सह् 'to bear,' 611. *a.*
सह 'with,' 731, 769. *b.*
साकम् 'with,' 731.
साक्षात् 'before,' 731.
साधु 'good,' 187.
सामन् 'conciliation,' 153.
सार्धम् 'along with,' 731.
सिच् 'to sprinkle,' 281.
सिध् 'to succeed,' 273, 364, 616.
सीमन् 'a border,' 146.
सु prefix, 726. *f*, 783. *t.*
सु 'to bring forth,' 647.
सु 'to press out juice,' 677. *a.*
सुखी 126. *g.*
सुती 126. *g.*
सुतुस् 'well-sounding,' 166. *b.*
सुदि 'the fortnight of the moon's increase,' 712.
सुधी 'intelligent,' 126. *h.*
सुन्दर 'beautiful,' 187.
सुपथिन् 162. *a.*
सुपाद् 145.
सुभ्रू 126. *h.*
सुमनस् 'well-intentioned,' 164. *a.*
सुवल्ग् 'jumping well,' 175. *c.*
सुहिंस् 'very injurious,' 181. *b.*
सू 'to bring forth,' 312, 647.
सृ 'to go,' 369, 437. *b.*
सृज् 'to create,' 625.
सृप् 'to creep,' 263.
सेनानी 'a general,' 126. *d.*
सेव् 'to serve,' 364.
सो 'to destroy,' 276. *a*, 613.
सोमपा 'a Soma-drinker,' 108. *a.*
स्तम्भ् 'to stop,' 695.
स्तु 'to praise,' 313, 369, 648.
स्तॄ or स्तृ 'to spread,' 358, 678.
स्त्री 'a woman,' 123. *b.*
स्था 'to stand,' 269, 587.
स्नु 'to drip,' 392. *a.*
स्पृश् 'to touch,' 636.
स्पृह् 'to desire,' 288.
स्फुट् 'to expand,' 390. *a.*
स्फुर् 'to vibrate,' 390. *a.*
स्म particle, 251. *b.* Obs., 717. *f.* Obs., 878.
स्मि 'to smile,' 591.
स्मृ 'to remember,' 374. *k*, 594.
स्रु 'to flow,' 369, 592. *a.*
स्व 'own,' 232. *b.*
स्वक, स्वकीय 'own,' 232. *c.*
स्वधा 'Svadhá,' 312.
स्वन् 'to sound,' 375. *f.*
स्वप् 'to sleep,' 322. *a*, 382, 655.
स्वयम् 'self,' 232. *a.*
स्वयम्भू or स्वभू 'self-existent,' 126. *e.*
स्वर् 'heaven,' 712.
स्वसृ 'a sister,' 129. *a.*
स्वस्ति salutation, 712.
स्वीय 'own,' 232. *c.*
हन् 'to kill,' 323, 654; freq., 708.
हरित् 'green,' 95, 136, 137.
हविस् 'ghee,' 165.
हा 'to abandon,' 337, 665.
हाहा 'a Gandharva,' 108. *c.*
हि 'to send,' 374. *c.*
हि 'for,' 727. *d*, 914.
हिंस् 'to injure,' 673.
हु 'to sacrifice,' 333, 662.
हूहू 'a Gandharva,' 126. *f.*
हृ 'to seize,' 593.
हृद् 'the heart,' 139, 184.
हेतोस् or हेतौ 'for the sake of,' 731.
ह्री 'to be ashamed,' 333. *a*, 666. *a.*
ह्री 'shame,' 123. *a.*
ह्वे 'to call,' 373. *e*, 595.

INDEX III.

GRAMMATICAL TERMS, AND NAMES OF METRES.

Ak, the simple vowels, 18, note *, *b*.
A-ghosha, 8, 20. *b*.
Anga, 74, 135. *c*.
Ać, the vowels, 18, note *, *b*.
Aṇ, a Pratyáhára, 18, note *, *b*.
Atikṛiti, a metre, 964.
Atijagatí, a metre, 944.
Atidhṛiti, a metre, 959.
Atiśakvarí, a metre, 950.
Atyashṭi, a metre, 953.
Adádi, 249. Obs.
Anudátta, 75. *c*; accent, 975.
Anudáttet, 75. *c*.
Anunásika, 7, 7. *a*.
Anubandha, 75. *c*.
Anushṭubh, a metre, 935.
Anusvára, 6, 7.
Antaḥ-stha, semivowel, 22.
Abhinidhána, suppression, 10.
Abhyása, reduplication, 252.
Ardha-visarga, 8. *a*, 23. *b*.
Ardhákára, 10.
Al, the alphabet, 18, note *, *b*.
Alpa-práṇa, 11, 14. *a*.
Avagraha, 10.
Avyaya, 760.
Avyayí-bháva compounds, 760.
Ashṭi, a metre, 952.
Ákṛiti, a metre, 964.
Ákhyáta, a verb, 241.
Ákhyánakí, a metre, 939.
Ágama, augment, 251.
Átmane-pada, 243, 786.
Árdhadhátuka, 247. c.
Áryá, a metre, 972.
Áryágíti, a metre, 974.
Áśir liṅ, Precative, 241.
I, rejected from *itha* in 2nd sing. Perf., 370; rules for insertion or rejection of *i*, 391–415.
Iṭ, an Ágama, 250. *b*, 391. *a*.
It, 75. *c*.
Indra-vajrá, a metre, 938.
Íshat-spṛishṭa, 20.
U, a Vikaraṇa, 250. *b*.
Uṇádi, 79, note *.
Utkṛiti, a metre, 964.
Uttara-pada-lopa, 745. *a*.
Udátta, 75. *c*; accent, 975.
Udáttet, 75. *c*.
Udgíti, a metre, 973.
Upagíti, a metre, 974.
Upajáti, a metre, 939.
Upadhmáníya, 8. *a*, 14. *a*, 23. *b*.
Upasarga, 729.
Upendra-vajrá, a metre, 939.
Ushṇih, a metre, 965.
Úshman, a sibilant, 23, 23. *a*, *b*.
Eka-vaćana, singular, 91.
Eka-śruti, 976.
Ekíbháva, 982.
Eć, the diphthongs, 18, note *, *b*.
Oshṭhya, labial, 18.
Aupaććhandasika, a metre, 969.
Kaṇṭhya, guttural, 18.
Karma-kartṛi, 461. *d*.
Karma-dháraya compounds, 755-758.
Karman, 90, 461. *d*.
Karma-pravaćaníya, 729.
Ka-varga, the gutturals, 18, note *, *a*.
Kála, tense, 241.
Kṛit suffixes, 79.
Kṛiti, a metre, 961.
Kṛitya, 79.
Kṛid-anta, 79.
Kriyá, verb, 241.
Kryádi, 249. Obs.
Klíva, neuter, 91.
Kvip, 87.
Ga, a long syllable, 934.
Gaga, a spondee, 934.
Gaṇa, four short syllables, 934.
Gati, 729.
Gala, a trochee, 934.
Gáthá, a metre, 972.
Gáyatrí, a metre, 965, 966.
Gíti, a metre, 974.
Guṇa change of vowels, 27-29; roots forbidding Guṇa, 390.
Guru, a long syllable, 934.
Ghoshavat, 20. *b*.
Ṅit, a Pratyáhára, 91, note *.

Ćaturthí, Dative, 90.
Ćandra-vindu, 7.
Ća-varga, the palatals, 18, note *, *a*.
Ćuráḍi, 249. Obs.
Ćli, 250. *b*.
Ćvi, 788. *a*. Obs.
Ja, an amphibrach, 934.
Jagatí, a metre, 941.
Jaś, a Pratyáhára, 18, note *, *b*.
Játya, 982.
Jihvámúlíya, 8. *a*, 14. *a*, 23. *b*.
Juhotyádi, 249. Obs.
Jhar, a Pratyáhára, 18, note *, *b*.
Jhal, a Pratyáhára, 18, note *, *b*.
Jhaś, a Pratyáhára, 18, note *, *b*.
Jhash, a Pratyáhára, 18, note *, *b*.
Ṭa-varga, the cerebrals, 18, note *, *a*.
Ṇal, 247. Obs.
Ṇić, 250. *b*.
Ta, an antibacchic, 934.
Tat-purusha compounds, 739-745.
Taddhita suffixes, 79.
Tanádi, 249. Obs.
Ta-varga, the dentals, 18, note *, *a*.
Táthábhávya, 984.
Tálavya, palatal, 18.
Tási, 250. *b*.
Tudádi, 249. Obs.
Tṛitíyá, Instrumental, 90.
Tairovyañjana, 982.
Trishṭubh, a metre, 937.
Daṇḍaka, a metre, 964.
Dantya, dental, 18.
Divádi, 249. Obs.
Dírgha, 11. *f*.
Deva-nágarí, 1.
Druta-vilambita, a metre, 943.
Dvandva compounds, 746.
Dvigu compounds, 759.
Dvitíyá, Accusative, 90.
Dvi-vaćana, dual, 91.
Dhátu, 74.
Dhṛiti, a metre, 957.
Na, a tribrach, 934.
Nati, 57. Obs. 3.
Napuṇsaka, neuter, 91.
Nipáta, adverb, 712. *a*.
Pañćamí, Ablative, 90.
Pada, 135. *c*; a complete word, 74; voice, 243; restriction of, 786.
Parasmai-pada, 243, 786.
Pa-varga, the labials, 18, note *, *a*.
Páda, a quarter-verse, 934.
Pit, 247.
Puṃ-linga, masculine, 91.
Pushpitágrá, a metre, 970.
Prakṛiti, a metre, 962.
Pragṛihya exceptions, 38.
Pratyaya, a suffix, 74.
Pratyáhára, 91.
Prathamá, Nominative, 90.
Prabhávatí, a metre, 947.
Praślishṭa, 982.
Praharshiṇí, a metre, 946.
Prátipadika, a stem, 74, 79, 135. *c*.
Pluta, 11. *f*.
Bahu-vaćana, plural, 91.
Bahu-vríhi compounds, 761-769.
Bha stem, 135. *c*.
Bha, a dactyl, 934.
Bháva, Passive, 461. *d*.
Bhvádi, 249. Obs.
Ma, a molossus, 934.
Mañju-bháshiṇí, a metre, 945.
Madhyama-pada-lopa, 745. *a*.
Mandákrántá, a metre, 955.
Mahá-práṇa, 14. *a*.
Mahá-máliká, a metre, 958.
Mátrá, 11. *f*, 934.
Mátrá-vṛitta, 934.
Máninî or *Máliní*, a metre, 951.
Múrdhanya, cerebral, 18.
Ya, a bacchic, 934.
Yak, 250. *b*.
Yaṇ, a Pratyáhára, 18, note *, *b*.
Yati, a pause, 934.
Yama, 73. *b*.
Yar, a Pratyáhára, 18, note *, *b*.
Ya-varga, the semivowels, 18, note *, *a*.
Yásuṭ, 250. *b*.
Ra, a cretic, 934.
Rathoddhatá, a metre, 940.
Rućirá, a metre, 947.
Rudhádi, 249. Obs.
Repha, the letter र, 1.
La or *laghu*, a short syllable, 934.
Laga, an iambus, 934.
Lan, Imperfect, 241.
Laṭ, Present tense, 241.
Lala, a pyrrhic, 934.
Lin, Potential, 241.
Liṭ, Perfect, 241.
Luk, 135. *b*.
Lun, Aorist, 241.
Luṭ, First Future, 241.
Lṛin, Conditional, 241.
Lṛiṭ, Second Future, 241.
Leṭ, the Vedic mood, 241. *a*, 891. *a*.
Loṭ, Imperative, 241.
Lopa, elision, 10, 135. *b*.
Vaṇśa-sthavila, a metre, 942.

Varga, class of letters, 18, note *, *a*.
Varṇa-vṛitta, 934.
Vasanta-tilaká, a metre, 949.
Váhya-prayatna, 8.
Vikaraṇa, 250. *b*.
Vikṛiti, a metre, 964.
Vibhakti, a case-ending, 74, 90; a verbal termination, 244.
Virâma, 9.
Vivára, expansion, 18. *a*.
Visarga, 8, 61.
Vṛiddhi change of vowels, 27, 28, 29. *a*.
Vaitálíya, a metre, 968.
Vaivṛitta, 982.
Vyañjana, consonant, 20.
Śa, a Vikaraṇa, 250. *b*.
Śakvarí, a metre, 948.
Śap, a Vikaraṇa, 250. *b*.
Śapo luk, a Vikaraṇa, 250. *b*.
Śa-varga, the sibilants and *h*, 18, note *, *a*.
Śárdúla-vikríḍita, a metre, 960.
Śikhariṇí, a metre, 954.
Śiva-sútra, 18, note *, *b*.
Śnam, a Vikaraṇa, 250. *b*.
Śná, a Vikaraṇa, 250. *b*.
Śnu, a Vikaraṇa, 250. *b*.
Śyan, a Vikaraṇa, 250. *b*.
Ślu, a Vikaraṇa, 250. *b*.
Śloka, a metre, 935.
Shashṭhí, Genitive, 90.
Sa, an anapæst, 934.
Saṃvára, contraction, 18. *a*.
Sankṛiti, a metre, 964.
Sandhi, pages 23-49.
Sandhy-akshara, 18. *c*.
Sannatara, 976.
Saptamí, Locative, 90.
Samáveśa, 982.
Samásánta, 778.
Samprasáraṇa, 30, 471. Obs., 543. Obs.
Sambuddhi or *sambodhana*, Vocative case, 90.
Sarvanáman, a pronoun, 216.
Sarvanáma-sthána cases, 135. *c*.
Sárvadhátuka, 247. *c*.
Sip, 250. *b*.
Síyuṭ, 250. *b*.
Suṭ, a Pratyáhára, 91, note *.
Sup, 91, note *.
Strí-linga, feminine, 91.
Sparśa, 20.
Spṛishṭa, 20.
Sya, 250. *b*.
Sragdhará, a metre, 963.
Svara, vowel, 20; accentuation, 975.
Svarita, 75. *c*; accent, 975.
Svaritet, 75. *c*.
Sváđi, 249. Obs.
Hariṇí, a metre, 956.
Hal, the consonants, 18, note *, *b*.
Hrasva, 11. *f*.

INDEX IV.

SUFFIXES.

Obs.—K. = *Kṛit* or Primary (including *Kṛitya* and *Uṇádi*); T. = *Taddhita* or Secondary; adv. = adverbial suffix. For distinction between Kṛit, Kṛitya, Uṇádi, and Taddhita suffixes, see 79.

a, K. 80. i; T. 80. xxxv.
aka, K. 80. ii, 582. *b*; T. 80. xxxvi.
aki, T. 81. viii.
anga, K. 80. xxxiv.
aṇḍa, K. 80. xxxiv.
at, K. 84. i, 524, 525, 578.
ata, K. 80. xxxiv.
atra, K. 80. iii.
athu, K. 82. i.
an, K. 85. i.
ana, K. 80. iv, 582. *c*.
aníya, K. 80. v, 570.
anta, K. 80. xxxiv.
anya, K. 80. xxxiv.
apa, K. 80. xxxiv.
api, adv., 228-230, 718.
abha, K. 80. xxxiv.
am, adv. ind. part., 567.
ama, K. 80. xxxiv.
amba, K. 80. xxxiv.
ara, K. 80. xxix.
ala, K. 80. xxx.
as, K. 86. i.
asa, K. 80. xxxiv.
asána, K. 80. xxxiv.
á, K. 80. i.
áka, K. 80. vii.
áṭa, T. 80. xxxvii.
áṇaka, K. 80. xxxiv.
átu, K. 82. ii.
ána, K. 80. viii, 526. *a*. Obs., 527, 528.
ánaka, K. 80. xxxiv.
ání, T. 80. xxxviii.
áyana, T. 80. xxxix.
áyani, T. 81. ix.
áyya, K. 80. xxxiv.
ára, K. 80. xxxiv.
áru, K. 82. iii.
ála, K. 80. xxxiv; T. 80. xl.
álu, K. 82. iv.
i, K. 81. i; T. 81. x.
ika, K. 80. xxxiv; T. 80. xli.
it, K. 84. ii.
ita, K. 80. ix; T. 80. xlii.
itnu, K. 82. v.
in, K. 85. ii, 582. *a*; T. 85. vi.
ina, T. 80. xliii.
ineya, T. 80. xliv.
iman, K. 85. iv; T. 85. vii.
iya, T. 80. xlv.
ira, K. 80. x; T. 80. xlvi.
ila, K. 80. x; T. 80. xlvii.
ivas, K. 86. iv.
isha, K. 80. xxxiv.
ishṭha, 80. xlviii, 192.
ishṇu, K. 82. vi.
is, K. 86. ii.
í, K. 80. i, 82. xv.
íka, K. 80. xxxiv.
íṭa, K. 80. xxxiv.
ína, T. 80. xlix.
íya, T. 80. l, 775. *b*.
íyas, 86. v, 192.
íra, K. 80. xxxiv; T. 80. li.
íla, T. 80. li.
ísha, K. 80. xxxiv.
u, K. 82. vii.
uka, K. 80. xii.
utra, K. 80. xxxiv.
una, K. 80. xxxiv.
ura, K. 80. xxix; T. 80. lii.
ula, K. 80. xxx; T. 80. liii.
usha, K. 80. xxxiv.
us, K. 86. iii.
ú, K. 82. xvi.
úka, K. 80. xiii.
úkha, K. 80. xxxiv.
útha, K. 80. xxxiv.
úra, K. 80. xxxiv.
úla, K. 80. xxxiv; T. 80. liv.
enya, K. 80. xiv.
eya, T. 80. lv.
era, K. 80. xv.
elima, K. 80. xxxiv, 576. *b*.
ora, K. 80. xxxiv.
ka, K. 80. xvi; T. 80. lvi; 761. *a*.

kara, K. 80. xxxiv.
kalpa, T. 80. lvii, 777. *a*.
kṛitvas, adv., 723. *a*.
ćana, adv., 228-230, 718.
ćid, adv., 228-230, 718.
t, K. 84. iii.
ta, K. 80. xvii, 530.
tana, T. 80. lviii.
tama, T. 80. lix, 191, 211-213.
tamám, adv., 80. lix.
taya, T. 80. lx.
tara, T. 80. lxi, 191.
tarám, adv., 80. lxi, 197.
tavya, K. 80. xviii, 569.
tas, adv., 719.
tá, T. 80. lxii.
tát, K. 84. v; adv., 719. *c*.
táti, T. 81. xi.
ti, K. 81. ii; T. 81. xii; adv., 227. *a*.
titha, T. 80. lxiii, 234. *c*.
tíya, T. 80. lxiv, 208.
tu, K. 82. viii.
tṛi, K. 83.
tna, T. 80. lxv.
tya, K. 80. xix; T. 80. lxvi.
tra, K. 80. xx; adv., 721.
trá, K. 80. xx; T. 80. lxvii; adv., 720. *a*.
trima, K. 80. xxxiv.
tva, K. 80. xxi; T. 80. lxviii.
tvan, K. 85. iii.
tvana, T. 80. lxix.
tvá, ind. part., 80. xxi, 555.
tví, ind. part., 80. xxi, 555. Obs.
tvya, K. 80. xxii.
tha, K. 80. xxiii, 234. *c*.
thaka, K. 80. xxxiv.
tham, adv., 721.
thá, adv., 721.
daghna, T. 80. lxx, 777. *a*.
dá, adv., 722.
dáním, adv., 722.
deśíya, T. 80. lxxi.
dvayasa, T. 80. lxxii.
dhá, adv., 723.
na, K. 80. xxiv; T. 80. lxxiii.
ná, K. 80. xxiv.
ni, K. 81. iii.
ním, adv., 722.
nu, K. 82. ix.
ma, K. 80. xxv; T. 80. lxxiv.
mat, T. 84. vi.
man, K. 85. iv.
maya, T. 80. lxxv.
mara, K. 80. xxvi.
mátra, T. 80. lxxvi.
mána, K. 80. xxvii, 526, 527, 578.
mi, K. 81. iv.
min, T. 85. viii.
ya, K. 80. xxviii, 571-576; T. 80. lxxvii; ind. part., 555.
yas, 86. vi.
yá, K. 80. xxviii.
yu, K. 82. x; T. 82. xiii.
ra, K. 80. xxix; T. 80. lxxviii.
ri, K. 81. v.
ru, K. 82. xi.
rúpa, T. 80. lxxix.
rhi, adv., 722.
la, K. 80. xxx; T. 80. lxxx.
lu, T. 82. xiv.
va, K. 80. xxxi; T. 80. lxxxi.
vat, T. 84. vii, 234, 553; adv., 724, 922.
van, K. 85. v.
vara, K. 80. xxxii.
vala, T. 80. lxxxii.
vas, K. 86. iv.
vi, K. 81. vi.
vin, T. 85. ix.
vya, T. 80. lxxxiii.
śa, T. 80. lxxxiv.
śas, adv., 725.
sa, K. 80. xxxiv; T. 80. lxxxv.
sát, 725. *a*, 789.
si, K. 81. vii.
sna (*shṇa*), K. 80. xxxiii.
snu (*shṇu*), K. 82. xii.

LIST OF CONJUNCT CONSONANTS.

CONJUNCTIONS OF TWO CONSONANTS.

क्क *kka*, क्ख *kkha*, क्ण *kṇa*, क्त *kta*, क्थ *ktha*, क्न *kna*, क्म *kma*, क्य *kya*, क्र or क्र *kra*, क्ल *kla*, क्व *kva*, क्ष *ksha*. ख्य *khya*, ख्व *khva*. ग्घ *ggha*, ग्ध *gdha*, ग्न *gna*, ग्भ *gbha*, ग्म *gma*, ग्य *gya*, ग्र *gra*, ग्ल *gla*, ग्व *gva*. घ्न *ghna*, घ्य *ghya*, घ्र *ghra*, घ्व *ghva*. ङ्क *ṅka*, ङ्ख *ṅkha*, ङ्ग *ṅga*, ङ्घ *ṅgha*, ङ्भ *ṅbha*, ङ्म *ṅma*.

च्च *ćća*, च्छ *ććha*, च्न *ćna*, च्म *ćma*, च्य *ćya*. छ्य *ćhya*, छ्र *ćhra*. ज्ज *jja*, ज्झ *jjha*, ज्ञ *jña*, ज्म *jma*, ज्य *jya*, ज्र *jra*, ज्व *jva*. ञ्च *ńća*, ञ्छ *ńćha*, ञ्ज *ńja*.

ट्ट *ṭṭa*, ट्ठ *ṭṭha*. ट्य *ṭya*, ठ्य *ṭhya*. ड्ग *ḍga*, ड्ड *ḍḍa*, ड्ण *ḍṇa*, ड्ढ *ḍḍha*, ड्भ *ḍbha*, ड्य *ḍya*, ड्र *ḍra*. ढ्य *ḍhya*, ढ्र *ḍhra*. ण्ट *ṇṭa*, ण्ठ *ṇṭha*, ण्ड *ṇḍa*, ण्ढ *ṇḍha*, ण्ण *ṇṇa*, ण्म *ṇma*, ण्य *ṇya*, ण्व *ṇva*.

त्क *tka*, त्त *tta*, त्थ *ttha*, त्न *tna*, त्म *tma*, त्य *tya*, त्र *tra*, त्व *tva*, त्स *tsa*. थ्न *thna*, थ्य *thya*, थ्व *thva*. द्ग *dga*, द्घ *dgha*, द्द *dda*, द्ध *ddha*, द्न *dna*, द्ब *dba*, द्भ *dbha*, द्म *dma*, द्य *dya*, द्र *dra*, द्व *dva*. ध्न *dhna*, ध्म *dhma*, ध्य *dhya*, ध्र *dhra*, ध्व *dhva*. न्त *nta*, न्थ *ntha*, न्द *nda*, न्ध *ndha*, न्न *nna*, न्म *nma*, न्य *nya*, न्र *nra*, न्व *nva*, न्स *nsa*.

प्त *pta*, प्थ *ptha*, प्न *pna*, प्प *ppa*, प्फ *ppha*, प्म *pma*, प्य *pya*, प्र *pra*, प्ल *pla*, प्व *pva*, प्स *psa*. ब्ज *bja*, ब्द *bda*, ब्ध *bdha*, ब्ब *bba*, ब्भ *bbha*, ब्य *bya*, ब्र *bra*. भ्य *bhya*, भ्र *bhra*, भ्व *bhva*. म्ण *mṇa*, म्न *mna*, म्प *mpa*, म्फ *mpha*, म्ब *mba*, म्भ *mbha*, म्म *mma*, म्य *mya*, म्र *mra*, म्ल *mla*.

य्य *yya*, य्र *yra*, य्व *yva*.

र्क *rka*, र्ख *rkha*, र्ग *rga*, र्घ *rgha*, र्च *rća*, र्छ *rćha*, र्ज *rja*, र्ण *rṇa*, र्त *rta*, र्थ *rtha*, र्द *rda*, र्ध *rdha*, र्प *rpa*, र्ब *rba*, र्भ *rbha*, र्म *rma*, र्य *rya*, र्व *rva*, र्श *rśa*, र्ष *rsha*, र्ह *rha*.

ADDITIONS AND CORRECTIONS.

Page 29, line 27, for '260. *a*' read '251. *a*'
,, 40, last line, dele note †
,, 43, line 19, for '304. *a*' read '304. *b*'
,, 81, ,, 15, for '257. *a*' read '257'
,, 118, ,, 4, for उत् read उद्
,, 151, ,, 33, for 'bases' read 'stems'
,, 158, ,, 27, for 'by 51' read 'by 50. *a*'
,, 177, ,, 5, for 'bases' read 'stems'
,, 268, ,, 2 from below, for '667' read '666. *b*'

www.ingramcontent.com/pod-product-compliance
Lightning Source LLC
Chambersburg PA
CBHW030547300426
44111CB00009B/881
9783337809836